Contemporary Leadership Behavior

SELECTED READINGS

FIFTH EDITION

Contemporary Leadership Behavior

SELECTED READINGS

FIFTH EDITION

EDITED BY

ELEANOR C. HEIN, R.N., ED.D.
Professor Emerita
University of San Francisco School of Nursing
San Francisco

Lippincott
Philadelphia • New York

Sponsoring Editor: Jennifer E. Brogan
Coordinating Editorial Assistant: Susan V. Barta
Project Editor: Erika Kors
Production Manager: Helen Ewan
Production Coordinator: Patricia McCloskey
Design Coordinator: Doug Smock

5th Edition

9 8 7 6 5 4 3 2 1

Library of Congress Cataloging in Publication Data

Contemporary leadership behavior : selected readings / edited by
    Eleanor C. Hein. — 5th ed.
        p.   cm.
    Includes bibliographical references and index.
    ISBN 0-397-55458-3 (alk. paper)
        1. Nursing services—Administration.   2. Leadership.   I. Hein,
    Eleanor C.
RT89.C67   1998
362.1'73'068—dc21   97-21812
                                                                            CIP

Care has been taken to confirm the accuracy of the information presented and to describe generally accepted practices. However, the authors, editors, and publishers are not re-sponsible for errors or omissions or for any consequences from application of the informa-tion in this book and make no warranty, express or implied, with respect to the contents of the publication.

The authors, editors and publisher have exerted every effort to ensure that drug sug-gestion and dosage set forth in this text are in accordance with current recommendations and practice at the time of publication. However, in view of ongoing research, changes in government regulations, and the constant flow of information relating to drug therapy and drug reactions, the reader is urged to check the package insert for each drug for any change in indications and dosage and for added warnings and precautions. This is particu-larly important when the recommended agent is a new or infrequently employed drug.

Some drugs and medical devices presented in this publication have Food and Drug Administration (FDA) clearance for limited use in restricted research settings. It is the re-sponsibility of the health care provider to ascertain the FDA status of each drug or device planned for use in their clinical practice.

PREFACE

This edition of *Contemporary Leadership Behavior: Selected Readings* has undergone several changes during the course of its development. Earlier editions focused on helping professional nurses develop their leadership behaviors in the practice setting. That particular focus is no longer realistic. This is a time in which health care organizations are busily engaged in reinventing themselves. As they do so, the goals they set and the decisions they make will have far greater consequences for nurses and patients than one can imagine. Because of this, it becomes *every* nurse's responsibility to keep informed about how organizations function and how organizational decision making impacts professional nursing and patient care. The goal of this edition, therefore, is to assist all nurses, whether in clinical practice or administrative settings, to become knowledgeable about developing the leadership behaviors they need to function in today's health care environment.

Although the selection of readings for this edition continues to be drawn exclusively from the nursing literature, they were selected for a wider audience of nurses than has been the case in previous editions. Baccalaureate and non-baccalaureate students, graduate students, nurses in clinical practice and nurses with administrative responsibilities will find the selected readings relevant to their professional development. Although the majority of readings were written by nurses, a conscious effort was made to include authors in other health care professions and, in some instances, authors who are not nurses. Their diverse points of view offer a wide range of information that can both invigorate and sharpen the needed dialogue between nurses on the issues before them today. When possible, the readings selected for this edition attempt to strike a balance between the theoretical and the practical. Some sections have a greater number of readings, to reflect the primary areas of concern nurses have about the issues that impact their lives and their work. In today's climate of rapid change, nurses' knowledge base must be as current as possible. Unlike previous editions, all the readings in this edition are new, with the majority published in 1995 and 1996. The readings selected for this edition reflect the recent trends and issues that have emerged in the professional literature since the last edition of this book. These trends include: the continued exploration of caring and transformational leadership; the increasing concern about the ethical dilemmas facing nurses that have arisen as the health care system changes; issues of gender socialization and reverse discrimination that can separate nurses rather than unite them; further insights on patients and collegial advocacy; more specificity in the dynamics of change and its effect on nurses and the health care system; and the situational and behavioral dynamics that occur within an organizational setting.

Some aspects of the outline and content of this edition have also been changed. The content focus in Part I, The Culture of Nursing, now includes selected issues and concepts that are, at present, of professional concern. Part II, Leadership: Theories and Attributes, has undergone no change of focus. The contemporary leadership behaviors cited in Part III remain the same, but some categories of behavior have been broadened in scope. The section on assertiveness, for example, now includes behaviors that deal with nurses' attempts to use their communication skills constructively and effectively. The section on Advocacy now includes collegial advocacy, ethical obligations, and legal concerns that nurses must be aware of as they attempt to be advocates for their patients, their colleagues, and themselves.

The Organizational Setting, Part IV, has been enlarged and categorized into three subsections that more accurately portray what is currently taking place in the health care environment. These subsections focus on organizational assessment, the organizational setting, and organizational behaviors. The reading in Part V, Leadership Imperatives: Shaping Nursing's Future, have been increased and reflect broad futuristic projections as well as specifically oriented issues that provide nurses with the information they need to plan for their futures.

The parts of this book are arranged in a certain sequence, but can be read in any order. As in previous editions, readings dealing with theoretical material generally precede those of a practical nature. Each part of this edition concludes with a series of discussion questions designed to stimulate thought, exchange viewpoints, and encourage dialogue.

One last word: my thanks and appreciation to Lippincott-Raven Publishers for their continued wholehearted support in the development of this edition. To Jennifer E. Brogan and Susan V. Barta of the nursing division, my thanks and appreciation for their helpful counsel and assistance. This edition would not be possible without the cooperation of various nursing journals and authors who granted me permission to use their material. My thanks to all of them. No writer can survive without feedback that is tempered with a critical eye, infused with honesty, and softened with humor. For the generosity and quality of their feedback, I wish to thank Sr. M. Ellene Egan, R.N., Ed.D, Assistant Professor, University of San Francisco School of Nursing, San Francisco, California; Pamela A. Bunnell, R.N., M.S.N., Assistant Professor and Chair, School of Nursing, Dominican College, San Rafael, California; and Christine Wachsmuth, R.N., M.S., Associate Administrator, Paramedic and Emergency Services, San Francisco General Hospital, San Francisco, California. In closing, I wish to recognize and pay tribute to all nurses, who, in the face of the changes and upheaval around them, still continue to believe that the practice of professional nursing makes a difference. It does. It always will.

Eleanor C. Hein, R. N., Ed.D.
Professor Emerita

CONTRIBUTING AUTHORS

Diane J. Angelini, EdD, CNM, CNA
Director, Nursing Research and Development, Women and Infants Hospital, Providence R.I., Adjunct Assistant Professor, University of Rhode Island College of Nursing; Editor, *Journal of Perinatal and Neonatal Nursing*

Anne M. Barker, EdD, RN
Associate Professor, Sacred Heart University, Fairfield, Connecticut

Barbara Stevens Barnum, PhD, RN, FAAN
Editor, *Nursing Leadership Forum,* Springer Publications, Editor/Consultant Presbyterian Hospital, Columbia Medical Center, New York, New York

Marjorie Barter, ED, RN
Associate Professor, School of Nursing, University of San Francisco, San Francisco, California

James W. Begun, PhD
Professor and Director, Doctoral Program in Health Services Organizations and Research, Department of Health Administration, Medical College of Virginia Campus, Virginia Commonwealth University, Richmond, Virginia

Judith A. Blakeley, BScN, MBA
Assistant Professor, Memorial University of Newfoundland, St. John's, Canada

John G. Bruhn, PhD
Provost and Dean, Penn State Harrisburg, Middletown, Pennsylvania

Peter I. Buerhaus, PhD, RN, FAAN
Director, Harvard Nursing Research Institute and Assistant Professor, Department of Health Policy and Management, Harvard School of Public Health, Boston, Massachusetts.

Barbara E. Calfee, JD, LSW
President, Calfee and Associates, Huntsburg, Ohio

Virginia R. Cassidy, EdD, RN,
Associate Professor, School of Nursing, Northern Illinois University, Dekalb, Illinois.

Alan P. Chesney, PhD
Director, Office of Human Resources Services; The University of Texas at El Paso, El Paso, Texas

Gail Marchigiano Churchill, MSN, RN
Assistant Professor of Nursing, St. Joseph College, Windham, Maine

Harriet Van Ess Coeling, PhD, RN
Assistant Professor, Kent State University, Ohio

Karen T. Corder, MSN, MBA, RN
Consultant, Arthur Anderson Co., San Francisco, California

Cady Crimson, RN, MSN, CNS
Past Director of Practice and Compliance, Board of Nursing Examiners, State of Texas, Austin, Texas; Consultant, Texas Department of Health, Bureau of Community Oriented Primary Care, Austin, Texas

Susan H. Cummings, MN, RN
President, Cummings Associates, San Diego, California

Leah L. Curtin, EdD, MS, MA, RN
Editor, *Nursing Management*

Ruth Davidhizar, RN, DNS, CS, FAAN
Dean, Division of Nursing, Bethel College, Mishawaka, Indiana

Patricia Gentry Droppleman, RN, PhD
Associate Professor and Coordinator, Graduate Program in Women's and Children's Health, College of Nursing, University of Tennessee, Knoxville, Tennessee

Jane Dyson, M.Ed., BA (hons), RGN, DipN, RNT
Head of Nursing, University of Derby, Derby, England

Judith A. Erlen, PhD, RN
Associate Professor, School of Nursing and Faculty at the Center for Medical Ethics, University of Pittsburgh, Pittsburgh, Pennsylvania

Beverly Ferreiro, PhD, RN
Clinical Associate Professor, School of Nursing, University of North Carolina, Chapel Hill, North Carolina

Oney Fitzpatrick, PhD
Assistant Professor, Psychology Department, Lamar University, Beaumont, Texas

Nan Gaylord, MSN, MA, PNP, RN, CS
Instructor, Nursing of Women and Children, Graduate
Program, College of Nursing, University of Tennessee,
Knoxville, Tennessee

Suzanne Gordon, BA
Author and journalist, Boston, Massachusetts

David R. Graber, MPH, PhD
Assistant Professor, Department of Health
Administration and Policy, Medical University of South
Carolina, Charleston, South Carolina

Pamela Grace, MSN, RN, CS, ANP, PhD, candidate
Instructor, and Family Nurse Practitioner, in the
Graduate program, College of Nursing, University of
Tennessee, Knoxville, Tennessee

WITHDRAWN

Alexia Green, RN, PhD
Chair and Associate Professor, Department of Nursing,
Lamar University, Beaumont, Texas

Donna Sullivan Havens, PhD, RN
Assistant Professor, School of Nursing, Duke University,
Durham, North Carolina

Barbara S. Heater, RN, PhD
Professor and Department Head, College of Nursing,
Graduate Program, South Dakota State University, South
Dakota

Eleanor C. Hein, EdD, RN
Professor Emerita, School of Nursing, University of San
Francisco, San Francisco, California

Robert G. Hess, Jr. PhD, RN, CCRN, CNAA
Editor, *The Nursing Spectrum*, Philadelphia/Tristate
Edition and Corporate Director of Continuing Education,
The Nursing Spectrum

James A. Johnson, PhD
Chairman and Professor, Department of Health
Administration and Policy, Medical University of South
Carolina, Charleston, South Carolina

David Keepnews, JD, MPH, RN
Director, Office of Policy, American Nurses Association,
Washington, D.C.

Brighid Kelly, RN-C, PhD
Associate Professor, The Nell Hodgeson Woodruff School
of Nursing, Atlanta, Georgia

Thomas Kent, PhD
Director of Consulting Services, Medical University of
South Carolina, Charleston, South Carolina

Cynthia J. Koroll, MS, RN
Graduate Research Assistant, School of Nursing,
Northern Illinois University, DeKalb, Illinois; Staff Nurse,
Emergency Department, Rockford Memorial Hospital,
Rockford, Illinois

Judith K. Leavitt, RN, MEd, FAAN
Director, Generations United, a State and National
Coalition for Intergenerational Programs and Advocacy,
Washington, D.C., and Senior Partner, Transformations
Consultants, Ithaca, New York

Heather K. Spence Laschinger, PhD, RN
Associate Professor, Associate Dean, Research, Faculty of
Nursing, the University of Western Ontario, London,
Ontario

Margaret M. Mahon, PhD, RN, CPNP
Assistant Professor, University of Pennsylvania School of
Nursing, Philadelphia, Pennsylvania

Claire Manfredi, EdD, RN
Associate Professor, Villanova University College of
Nursing, Villanova, Pennsylvania

Jo Manion, RN, MA, CNAA
Consultant, Patient-Focused Development Team,
Lakeland Regional Medical Center, Lakeland, Florida

Richard Marcantonio, PhD
Visiting Assistant Professor, College of Nursing,
University of Illinois at Chicago.

Geri Marullo, MSN, RN
Executive Director, American Nurses Association,
Washington, D.C.

Diana J. Mason, RN C, PhD, FAAN
Director, Beatrice Renfield Division of Nursing Education
and Research, Beth Israel Medical Center, New York City,
and, Senior Partner, Transformations Consultants, Ithaca,
New York

Timothy B. McCall, MD
Internist, Boston, Massachusetts

Charles R. McConnell
Director of Human Resources, Myers Community
Hospital, Sodus, New York

Patricia C. McMullen, JD, MS, RN-C, NP
Assistant Professor, Graduate School of Nursing,
Uniformed Services University of the Health Sciences,
Rockville, Maryland

Mary Pat Mellors, MS, RN
Doctoral student, University of Pittsburgh, Pittsburgh,
Pennsylvania

Anne F. Minnick, PhD, RN
Professor, College of Nursing, Rush University, Chicago,
Illinois

Wanda K. Mohr, PhD, RNC
Assistant Professor, University of Pennsylvania School of
Nursing, Philadelphia, Pennsylvania

Jane Neubauer, MS, RN
Consultant, King Edward's Hospital-Fund for London,
London, England

Nayna Philipsen-Campbell, , JD, PhD, RN, ACCE
Senior Compliance Analyst, Maryland Department of
Health and Mental Hygiene, Board of Physician Quality
Assurance, Baltimore, Maryland

Janet Phoon, MSN, RN
Graduate, University of San Francisco School of Nursing,
San Francisco, California

Tim Porter-O'Grady, PhD, EdD, RN, FAAN
Senior Partner, Tim Porter-O'Grady Associates, Inc.,
Senior Consultant, Affiliated Dynamics, Inc., and,
Assistant Professor, Emory University, Atlanta, Georgia

Sylvia A. Price, PhD, RN
Professor, University of Tennessee, Memphis, Tennessee

Adeline R. Falk Rafael, PhD, RN
Assistant Professor of Nursing, D'Youville College,
Buffalo, New York; Doctoral Candidate, University of
Colorado School of Nursing, Boulder, Colorado

Violeta E. Ribeiro, BNSc, DNSc
Associate Professor, Memorial University of
Newfoundland, St. John's, Canada

Ruth G. Rinard, PhD, RN
Staff Nurse, Home Health Department, Mary Lane
Hospital, Ware, Massachusetts

Christine M. Rodwell, BSc (Hons), DipNEd, Dip N, RGN
Lecturer in Coronary Care Nursing/Health Promotion,
Kingston and St. George's NHS, College of Health
Studies, London, England

Kathleen Smith, BS, RN, CNN
Director of Legislative Services for Nursing Economic$,
Washington, D.C., and Legislative Consultant, NAON

Gloria Steinem
Editor, *MS.* Magazine, International Author, Feminist and
Political Activist

Sandra Paul Thomas, RN, PhD
Professor and Director, Doctoral Program, College of Nursing, University of Tennessee, Knoxville Tennessee

Jean Phillips Truscott, MEd, RN
Vice President, Acute Care Services, Concord Hospital, Concord, New Hampshire

William Umiker, MD
Adjunct Professor of Pathology, Pennsylvania State University—Hershey Medical Center, Lancaster, Pennsylvania

Constance E. Young, EdD, RN
Associate Professor of Nursing, Sacred Heart University, Fairfield, Connecticut

Wendy B. Young, PhD, RN
Associate Professor, College of Nursing, University of Illinois at Chicago

Louise Waddell, PhD, RN
Executive Director, Board of Nursing Examiners, Austin, Texas

Christine Webb, BA, MSc, PhD, RN, RSCN, RNT
Professor, Health Studies, The University of Phymouth, Plymouth, United Kingdom

Sherry S. Webb, MSN, RN
Supervisor, Special Projects, Trinity Healthcare Services, Memphis, Tennessee

Kenneth R. White, MPH, PhD, RN, FACHE
Instructor and Assistant Director, Professional Graduate Programs, Department of Health Administration, Medical College of Virginia Campus, Virginia Commonwealth University, Richmond, Virginia

Barbara Wise, MSN, RN
Clinic Manager, Wake County Department of Health, Raleigh, North Carolina.

David C. Wyld, DBA
Assistant Professor of Management, Southeastern Louisiana University, Department of Management, Hammond, Louisana

CONTENTS

Section Four   POWER

Section Five   POLITICS

Contemporary Leadership Behavior

SELECTED READINGS

FIFTH EDITION

PART I

•••

The Culture of Nursing

At the core of nursing's culture are deeply held and time-honored values and beliefs. Past generations of nurses have given us a legacy of values and beliefs that are rich in example, honed through experience, and born out of the need to change and grow. From this legacy we have come to know what nursing is, what it does, why it exists, where it practices, and who its practitioners are. These are the values and beliefs that have guided both our philosophy of care and our nursing practice.

Today, nursing's values and beliefs are being challenged by changes that 10 years ago were unimaginable in their scope and unthinkable in their impact on professional nursing. Rapid and tumultuous change threatens to undermine our values and beliefs and tempts us to sacrifice or trivialize them in order to survive. But the reality of change can also stimulate and sharpen thoughtful dialogue about what we value and believe. As in the past, our present thrives on discussion, reexamination, and argument. Historically, nurses have responded to the challenges of change because they have consistently been able to reclarify and reaffirm their values and beliefs. Change can confuse, threaten, discourage or anger us, but it should not and cannot prevent us from making use of the values and beliefs with which we have become identified and which are fundamental to the practice of professional nursing.

The concept of caring has been a value since the inception of nursing. In today's corporate world, concrete and measurable outcomes prevail. The intangible values we hold are often viewed as idealistic notions—nice but not needed, and certainly not relevant to corporate goals. Caring is such an intangible notion. Its conceptual ambiguity, however, does not discourage nurses from recognizing its importance in professional practice. Instead, caring continues to generate exploration and specificity. Part I begins with the exploration of caring through clarification of and differentiation from like concepts, and continues with an examination of caring's relationship to a dissimilar concept, namely, power. The exploration of caring concludes with a study of how nurses perceive caring, what characteristics illuminate the concept, and what nurses perceive themselves to be doing as they enact caring behaviors.

1

The concluding chapters in this section reexamine the values and beliefs associated with nursing as a female-dominated profession. Women in nursing have long been the recipients of discriminatory practices stemming from long-held stereotypical notions, all of which have undermined their professional role behavior and undervalued their efforts. These are not unique to women, however; men experience the same stereotyping and discriminatory practices in nursing. Reverse discrimination is a reality in our profession. That it exists at all requires serious reflection. To that end the concluding chapter in this section sets the stage for the thoughtful reexamination of those values and beliefs.

CHAPTER 1

●●●

Caring, Curing, Coping: Towards an Integrated Model

CHRISTINE WEBB

Introduction

The care:cure dilemma has been much discussed in nursing literature, which usually considers whether it is doctors who do the curing and nurses who do the caring. The patient, however, is rarely mentioned. The plan for this paper, therefore, is to examine issues concerned with caring and curing from the perspectives of nurses, doctors, and patients themselves, which will include some mention of "lay" or "informal" carers, as families and friends are frequently termed. I shall conclude by suggesting that many arguments surrounding the care:cure dilemma could be resolved by recasting the debate within an integrated model of coping, and that such a model takes us forward from the somewhat sterile discussions in the care:cure literature. It enables us to study the associated problems more fruitfully and educate practitioners more appropriately to the benefit of all three groups involved.

Female Caring and Male Curing?

The nursing literature stretches as far back as Florence Nightingale herself, and her book *Nursing. What It Is and What It Is Not,* which was first published in 1860 and republished more recently. It is well-known that Nightingale took an essentialist position in relation to nurses and doctors, believing that "to be a good nurse is to be a good woman" and that the role of nurses was to be obedient to doctors in order not to hinder and "diminish" doctors' work (Nightingale 1980).

A number of much more recent writers adopt a similar stance in the care:cure debate (see, for example, Gilligan 1982). Sometimes this essentialism is linked with criticism of doctors and "the medical model" for their concentration on biomedical or technological approaches termed "cure" at the expense of what is seen to be the more "humanistic" or "holistic" approach adopted by nurses. The *Penguin International Thesaurus of Quotations* (Tripp 1970) contains evidence that this attitude has a long history. For example, Heracli-

© 1996 Blackwell Science Ltd. Reprinted with permission from the *Journal of Advanced Nursing,* Volume 23, 960–968, 1996.

tus observed that "doctors cut, burn, and torture the sick, and then demand of them an undeserved fee for such services" (Tripp 1970).

Benjamin Franklin noted similar medical motivations when he said that "God heals, and the doctor takes the fees" and Proust wrote of "medicine being a compendium of the successive and contradictory mistakes of medical practitioners"(Tripp 1970).

In this approach women are said inherently and instinctively to behave in certain ways and are more suited to particular activities than men, who generally are held to have opposing attributes and ways of behaving. The evidence to support such a standpoint is weak to say the least (Webb 1985), and this article is based on the assumption that women and men are equally capable of curing and caring behaviors.

Doctors and Curing

Despite the modernization of medical curricula and adoption of more integrated and problem-solving approaches, Norbert Elias, a sociologist writing in 1985, considers that "It is perhaps not yet quite superfluous to say that care for people sometimes lags behind the care for their organs"(Elias 1985).

Writing particularly about aging and dying, at a time when he was himself experiencing serious illness, Elias (1985) observes that "to concentrate on medically correcting single organs, or areas of organs that are functioning more and more badly, is really worth-while only for the sake of the person within whom all these part-processes are integrated."

A similar position is taken by the American surgeon Sherwin Nuland, writing autobiographically in 1993 about his professional life and the lessons he has tried, and sometimes failed, to learn from it. He reports the case history of "Miss Welch," an elderly patient with peritonitis who was living in a residential home before transfer to the hospital. Miss Welch did not wish to consent to surgery, but Nuland "played down what she could realistically be expected to experience." After the operation, Miss Welch "didn't hesitate to let me know I had betrayed her," and Nuland knows that "although my intentions were only to serve what I conceived to be her welfare, I was guilty of the worst sort of paternalism. I had withheld information because I was afraid the patient might use it to make what I thought of as a wrong decision" (Nuland 1993).

Miss Welch died 2 weeks later after a massive stroke, to which the stress of major surgery had probably contributed. On this occasion she received no medical intervention, having learned from her previous experience and given written instructions that she receive "nursing care only."

Discussing the case, Nuland (1993) believes that the decision to be taken was "strictly a clinical decision, and ethics should not have been a consideration." If he had not operated, subsequent peer review would have accused him of "poor judgment, if not downright negligence." Nevertheless, he remains disturbed by his actions and concludes that "the rescue credo of high-tech medicine wins out, as it almost always does."

Katz also attributes medical authoritarianism to a thwarted need for certainty: "Professional uncertainty is carefully camouflaged and substituted with an infallible air of professional certainty" (Katz 1986).

When treatment is unsuccessful, doctors feel anxiety and guilt, and this becomes expressed in authoritarianism, so that if control over disease is not achieved at least domination of the decision-making process is secured.

Nuland is also concerned about "abandonment" of those who are dying, and particularly abandonment by doctors. In a discussion which has parallels with Eliot Freidson's concept of "the clinical mind" (Freidson 1975), Nuland describes doctors as "people who succeed" as evidenced by their achievement of medical qualifications and posts obtained in strong competition. As a result, "to be unsuccessful is to endure a blow to self-image that is poorly tolerated by members of this most egocentric of professions" (Nuland 1993).

Referring back to the case of Miss Welch, Nuland (1993) recognizes that it is easy for doctors to convince themselves that they know better than their patients, to give only that amount of information which they think appropriate, and thus influence patients' decision making. Once this possibility of control is lost, as for example with patients who are dying of cancer, doctors tend to abandon them in an "abrogation of responsibility."

Modern medicine has become "an exercise in applied science" (Nuland 1993). To counteract these tendencies, Nuland emphasizes the importance of empathy:

> I say these things not to condemn high-tech doctors. I have been one of them, and I have shared the excitement of last-ditch fights for life and the supreme satisfaction that comes when they are won. But more than a few of my victories have been Pyrrhic . . . I also believe that had I been able to project myself into the place of the family and the patient, I would have been less often certain that the desperate struggle should be undertaken.
>
> *(Nuland 1993)*

The writers quoted so far seem to imply that cure is inadequate unless it is accompanied by care, although they do not explicitly use this terminology. As we go on to consider some of the literature on care, we shall rapidly realize the difficulties and dilemmas associated with this concept too.

Care: What Is It?

To say that there is lack of consensus about the definition of care is a major understatement. A selection of the defining characteristics of care found in the literature reviewed is listed (in random order) in Table 1-1. Thus, confusion and ambiguity permeate attempts to define care and caring.

Dunlop (1986) asks, "Is a science of caring possible?," and this question will be familiar to those who have studied "nursing theory." Dunlop first notes that there is a distinct and "emergent" sense of the word caring which has both linkages with and differences from historical uses of the term. According to Bevis (1981) it is possible to trace both common origins for the words "care" and "cure" and to find separate derivations, with "care" being an old English term and "cure" coming from Latin via French. She concludes that if there is to be a science of caring (she has no problem with the notion of science *for* caring), it cannot be a science in the traditional sense, for this involves concepts of control, domination and measurement that are in contradiction with the notion of care put forward by nurse theorists.

TABLE 1-1   **Some Characteristics of Care**

Honesty	Feeling	Actualizing	Reciprocity
Patience	Mattering	Involvement	Engrossment
Courage	Autonomy	Relationships	Respect
Sensitivity	Trust	Dignity	Spirituality
Dedication	Assistive	Being with	Supportive
Commitment	Facilitative	Love	Satisfaction
Knowledge	Tenderness	Compassion	Integrity
Skills	Growing	Empathy	Closeness

Another source of ambiguity is the definition of nursing itself. Dunlop (1986) states that

> *If nursing is caring then the term "nursing care" is tautologous. Caring is an interactive process which requires the carer to be responsive to the needs of the person cared for, the resources available and the context in which care occurs. This involves skilled assessment, planning, action and evaluation of the implications and nuances of all of these factors. Nurses already have a word for this process—it is called "nursing."*
>
> (Dunlop 1993)

Hill (1991) also claims that nursing has "something special" to offer and that the "something" is care. She reports superior outcomes in a group of patients treated by rheumatology nurse practitioners (RNPs) in comparison with a group treated by a physician. Among the outcome measures showing better performance were increased articular function, less pain, reduced anxiety and depression, and increased patient knowledge and satisfaction. Hill (1991) attributes the differences to "dissimilarities in nursing and medical attitudes to care, that is "care v cure," the RNPs offering more "holistic" care. Similar claims are made in North American literature on nurse practitioners (see for example Linn 1984). Holden (1991) challenges the distinction between caring and curing by asking whether this separation means that "caring is not curative or that curing is not carative? Does this mean that nurses do not cure and that doctors do not care? When confronted with the implications of this statement one begins to realize how ridiculous it actually is."

Engelhardt (1985) similarly can see "no essential or conceptually significant differences between the professions of nursing and medicine in their caring for patients."

Leininger (1977) also suggests that caring and curing are intimately related when she writes that "caring acts and decisions make the crucial difference in effective curing consequences. Therefore, it is caring that is the most essential and critical ingredient to any curative process."

What, if anything, then, is distinctive about the nursing–caring link which marks it off from the medicine–curing relationship? Despite the multiple definitions illustrated earlier, there is wide agreement that it is the interpersonal relationships aspect that is distinctive to nursing and caring. Not to acknowledge this element in nursing is to deny the patient's and nurse's subjectivity, according to Gadow (1985). Without this intersubjectivity, both patient and nurse are reduced to objects, their personal dignity is lost, and the "coherent wholeness from which parts of the self" are made up is thereby excluded. Further, in Fry's (1988) view nurses and patients need "ample time to connect" in order to achieve the "reciprocity and mutuality" that are essential to the ethic of caring.

Logocentric Caring?

Some writers believe that the interpersonal aspects of the nurse–patient relationship achieve spiritual dimensions. This approach, which could be termed the "Woody Allen" or logocentric (Dunlop 1986) version of the caring relationship, is as heavily attacked and defended among nursing theorists as is the psychotherapeutic perspective from which it derives. Some defend it with an almost religious fervor which matches its own terminology.

Watson's work is an example of the genre. She states that "nursing within a transpersonal caring perspective attends to the human center of both the one caring and the one being cared for; it embraces a spiritual, even metaphysical dimension of the caring process" (Watson 1988).

Krysl, a follower of Watson, writes in a way which might make one question whether it is really the nurse–patient relationship that is being described:

> *When two of us enter into each other in this way, willingly and receptively, transformation takes place. The gestalt of our separate beings loosens and vibrates . . . And we are filled with energy, a living material, palpable, substantial.*
>
> *(Krysl 1988, cited in Watson 1988)*

Writing of her work as a midwife and using a poetic format, Krysl says of the third stage of labor

> *And when it comes I examine the placenta*
> *I'm sorting the particles and waves in the spectrum of light*
> *And when my work is finished and I go from the place of birth*
> *I walk out across the fields of the planets into the spaces between the furthest stars.*
>
> *(Krysl 1988, cited in Watson 1988)*

Others, including Phillips (1993) and Dunlop (1986), criticize this "overpsychologization" of nursing. Dunlop is concerned that this "dematerializing tendency" towards "disembodied caring," which nurses are adopting in order to separate nursing from the "physicality" of medicine and establish it as an autonomous profession, militates against the very "holism" that nurses are seeking.

Salvage, too, is skeptical about what she calls "new nursing," with its emphasis on a "quasi-psychotherapeutic" relationship drawing on humanistic psychology and psychoanalysis. She believes that while:

> *psychotherapy aims to help the client solve emotional problems . . . general hospital patients are seeking help for physical disorders, albeit with an affective component. Their immediate concern is likely to be relief from pain and discomfort, rather than a meaningful relationship.*
>
> *(Salvage 1990)*

Different Care Settings

This leads us on to the idea that what constitutes care and cure and an appropriate balance between the two are likely to vary in different settings. Reed & Bond (1991), for example, report on a study comparing nursing practice in long-term and acute care wards for elderly patients. They found that in both settings the concept of cure was the "yardstick" by which nurses evaluated their work. For those on acute care wards:

> *cure and subsequent discharge was the raison d'etre . . . and their efforts were directed towards this . . . nurses revealed that they felt that they achieved this and derived satisfaction from this achievement. Scientific assessment in line with the policy and objectives for hospital geriatric care was therefore important as a basis for planning nursing care.*
>
> *(Reed & Bond 1991)*

The authors comment that "This kind of *care* was as effective in curing their elderly patients as those in any other type of general acute care ward" (Reed & Bond 1991) (My emphasis).

On the long-stay wards, cure was also a reference point, but its "seeming inappropriateness" led nurses to seek:

satisfaction primarily from giving "good geriatric care" which was achievable within their own terms of reference. This involved investment in the speedy and efficient completion of ward routines, which precluded assessment of individual patients' problems . . . this espoused professionalism precluded addressing the needs of individual patients.

(Reed & Bond 1991)

It seems that in this example, care which was strongly focused on cure matched more closely the characteristics of care discussed earlier than care which recognized that cure was unrealistic and that nursing was more appropriate.

Gates (1991) compared hospital and hospice settings as caring environments "grappling with care and cure phenomena." She found similarities in the two settings in terms of "caring as closeness," staff needing to care for each other, and "caring as solidarity" between staff, patients and families. However, there were differences too, in perhaps expected directions. In the hospital a cure orientation was more prevalent, whereas in the hospice "cure of symptoms" was seen as more important. The hospital was more hierarchically organized, and it was not easy to be flexible over rules. "Symbolism and ritual activities" associated with dying were more in evidence in the hospice.

These writers, as well as both Nuland (1993) and Salvage (1990), whose work has already been discussed, suggest that a different care:cure balance is appropriate in different settings, including surgical work, care of the dying and care of mentally ill people.

Lay and Professional Caring

A final issue in relation to nursing and caring is whether there is any difference between caring when it is performed by family and friends as lay carers or when it is carried out by professionally qualified nurses. Kitson (1987) addresses this question, and defines the lay caring relationship as one based on trust by the recipient of care, the commitment of the caregiver, the recipient's belief that this will promote her best interests and respect her integrity, and the carer having the necessary knowledge and skills. In summary, "The whole interaction is given shape and direction by the close personal relationship existing between the two" (Kitson 1987).

In a professional caring relationship, these elements should also be present but the contractual nature of the arrangement makes it more complex (Melia 1981). Patients and nurses come from different backgrounds, do not know each other personally, and may not share the same expectations. This can lead the nurse to fail to see the patient as an individual. Because of this complexity, for Kitson (1987) it is "of vital importance" that professional carers are able to "assess the effectiveness of the service they are providing" and:

Where lay caring and professional care differ is in the extent to which professional carers set themselves up as a specialist service meeting the care needs of those who are either unable to care for themselves or others in an acceptable manner.

(Kitson 1987)

Once again, then, there is an emphasis on the interpersonal aspects of care, whether it is given by lay or professional nursing carers.

Having reviewed a variety of contributions to the care:cure debate, one does not necessarily feel that the essence of caring has been defined. However, one crucial perspective, that of patients, has not so far been considered. It is to this that I shall now turn.

Patients, Care, and Cure

It is only relatively recently that patients' views have been sought using research methods that allow patients themselves to express what is important to them and to choose which topics they wish to comment upon. Previously work in this area tended to fall under the heading of "patient satisfaction" surveys and the most common research tool was a structured questionnaire in which patients were asked to respond to items considered important by nurses and/or managers. This has been dubbed the "charm school and better wallpaper" approach (Cooke 1994).

Limited though this approach is, in a number of instances researchers have identified disparate views between patients and nurses about what are the most important aspects of care or what are patients' greatest concerns (Allanach & Golden 1988). For example, Johnston (1982) found greater similarity between the views of fellow patients than between patients and nurses with regard to patients' worries. These findings should alert us to the possibility that what nurses consider to be the defining characteristics of care are not those which patients themselves would identify.

A more recent research approach has been the Q-sort. Q methodology was designed to allow study participants "opportunities to express their viewpoints or beliefs or 'versions of reality' by the way in which they sort a number of items" (Rogers 1991). The researcher supplies a set of statements, normally derived from the literature or preparatory research, and usually on cards, which "reflect the broad range of ideas, statements, and arguments about the topic in question" (Rogers 1991). Participants are asked to sort the cards into piles according to their degree of agreement or disagreement with the statements printed on them. They may also be asked to explain the reasoning behind the ways in which they arrange the cards or items.

One of the most common uses of Q methodology in the nursing literature is the CARE-Q, a 50-item instrument designed by Larson (1984). The tool has been used to compare patients' and nurses' views about caring behaviors in oncology and other settings.

In Larson's own study (Larson 1981) and a replication by Mayer (1987) comparing oncology nurses' and cancer patients' views, nurses more frequently judged expressive, ie, emotional, aspects of care as important, while patients ranked instrumental or physical and technical care as most important. In a further replication by Gooding *et al.* (1993), patients again focused on technical care as "most important in making them feel cared for." The five highest ranking items for patients were:

1. Knows how to give shots, IVs, etc.
2. Gives a quick response to patient's call.
3. Gives the patient's treatments and medications on time.
4. Knows when to call the doctor.
5. Is perceptive of patient's needs and plans and acts accordingly (eg, gives antinausea medication when patient is receiving medication that will probably induce nausea).

As in the original research, nurses "did not rank the clinical caring subscale highly" (Gooding et al. 1993). Their five highest ranked items were:

1. Listens to the patient.
2. Allows the patient to express his feelings and to discuss his/her disease and treatment fully and treats the information confidentially.

3. Realizes that the patient knows himself best and whenever possible includes the patient in planning and management of his/her disease.

4. Is perceptive of patient's needs and plans and acts accordingly.

5. Gets to know the patient as a person.

The authors suggest that nurses "took clinical competence for granted" and therefore did not rank it highly, while patients could not focus on other aspects of care until their physical needs had been met.

Similar findings emerged in a study by Brown (1986). Using a critical incident technique, 50 patients were asked to describe an experience during their hospitalization when they felt cared for by a nurse. Analysis of these tape-recorded interviews yielded a four-part process of care. These parts were: patient perception of a need or wish that the patient cannot satisfy; recognition and acknowledgement by the nurse of the patient's need; action taken to satisfy the need; and the way in which the nursing action is performed. Brown (1986) reports that:

Patients speak clearly to the importance of the nurse meeting their treatment needs (instrumental activities) and doing this in a way that protects and enhances the unique identity of the individual (expressive activities) . . . Fundamental to the experience of care is the patient's confidence in the ability of the nurse to provide the necessary physical care and treatment. As this professional competency is demonstrated, the more expressive activities become important.

Von Essen & Sjödén (1991) used a Swedish version of the CARE-Q and a questionnaire to tap patient and nurse perceptions of caring for medical and surgical patients in both a "community" and "university" hospital. "Knowing how to give shots" was again ranked highly (second) by patients.

Nurses in this study ranked listening to the patient, touching the patient, putting the patient first, talking in understandable language, and being calm as the five most important caring behaviors.

Von Essen & Sjödén (1991) note that their study "reconfirms evidence that patients and staff have different perceptions of the most important caring behaviors. The results should provide staff with a cautionary note not to assume that intended caring is always perceived as such by the patient."

Medical and surgical patients and staff, and those in the different locations studied, did not differ in their judgments of the relative importance of the caring behaviors. Remarking that staff tend to overestimate patients' emotional needs, the authors suggest that this implies that, "in their own judgment, staff can never provide enough support and encouragement to patients which may contribute to staff stress and burnout" (von Essen & Sjödén 1991).

UNCARING

Burnout has been much discussed in the nursing literature (see, for example, Llewelyn 1984). Noddings (1984) defines caring in terms of "engrossment" of the carer in the caring role and the relationship with the one cared for. When tasks are done in a perfunctory or grudging way, then this cannot be called "care," and this may arise as a result of burnout. Harrison (1990) is concerned that resource constraints may lead to burnout when nurses are not able to give care in the way they wish and therefore cannot receive the emotional rewards that are part of the reciprocity and mutuality of the caring relationship. "Uncaring" may then replace caring.

A CONSENSUS ABOUT CARE?

A consensus seems to emerge from the empirical studies discussed that patients are most concerned about the physical or technical aspects of care. They have presented for treatment in order to be treated for an illness or condition and it is only when they see this being efficiently and effectively dealt with that they begin to be concerned with more affective or expressive aspects. Nurses, probably influenced by recent theorists of nursing, may misjudge patients' priorities by placing too much emphasis on the psychological aspects of care. That these findings hold good for cancer patients, for whom a strong emotional component might be expected, as well as for medical and surgical patients, adds to their importance for nurses.

Caring, Curing, Coping

There appear to be many dilemmas associated with the issues of caring and curing. Doctors seem to concentrate on cure at the expense of care; nurses are perhaps erring too far towards the care extreme and could be neglecting physical or technical care and concentrating on emotional aspects. Patients are rarely consulted in a meaningful way, and when they are they do not always seem to realize or appreciate the full range of care that nurses could give because the emergent caring skills that nurses are developing are not valued highly.

How can we bring these issues together in order to understand what all three sets of actors have to offer to the care:cure process and move forward to a more balanced set of contributions?

The coping model developed by Lazarus and his colleagues seems to offer great potential (see Folkman & Lazarus 1980, Folkman et al. 1986). The model is based on the belief that how people cope with stress affects their physical, psychological and social well-being. Stress is viewed as a transaction between a person and the environment, and these two are in a dynamic, reciprocal, bidirectional relationship with each other. In a stressful encounter or process such as illness or health care work, people attempt to deal with their environment in order to cope with the situation. This in turn alters the environment and its effect on the person, who then continues responding to the new stage in the process.

The person appraises the stressor in two ways. In primary appraisal, the person assesses whether and to what extent there is stress involved. Personality characteristics come into play at this stage. Secondary appraisal then occurs, to judge what, if anything, the person can do to deal with the situation, prevent harm, and improve things. Secondary appraisal involves considering the options, constraints, and resources available, including social support. The resulting coping behavior to manage the demands of the stressful event or process has two functions, which are dealing with the problem (problem-focused coping) and regulating emotion (emotion-focused coping). Research has shown that people tend to use a mixture of both types of coping in any one situation.

Lazarus' integrated model of coping has several advantages over other approaches. Research has yielded little support for personality characteristics alone as a major influence in coping (Cohen & Lazarus 1973). Coping styles research is based on the assumption that people tend to cope with stressful events in a stable way. Focusing on the characteristics of stressful situations may tell us more about the cumulative effects of stress on individuals than about the effects of different stressors per se. Putting together work on personality characteristics and coping responses to assess psychological well-being (Pearlin & Schooler 1978) may help to show which personality characteristics are more helpful in different situations. Lazarus' model integrates all these approaches into a unified framework

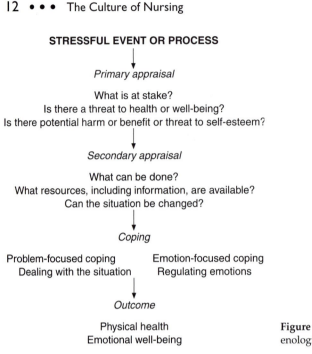

STRESSFUL EVENT OR PROCESS

Primary appraisal

What is at stake?
Is there a threat to health or well-being?
Is there potential harm or benefit or threat to self-esteem?

Secondary appraisal

What can be done?
What resources, including information, are available?
Can the situation be changed?

Coping

Problem-focused coping   Emotion-focused coping
Dealing with the situation   Regulating emotions

Outcome

Physical health
Emotional well-being

Figure 1–1   Lazarus' cognitive-phenomenological model of coping.

which is able to overcome or offset their individual limitations. The model is illustrated in Figure 1-1.

Research has discovered that various different types of coping behavior tend to be used in combination in the face of particular kinds of stressful situations (Folkman & Lazarus 1980). Some of these types of coping behavior are shown in Table 1-2. Threats to a loved one's well-being tend to be associated with confrontive or escape–avoidance coping and distancing is less used, while threats to one's own physical health are linked with seeking social support or escape–avoidance. Events causing high degrees of threat to self-esteem are associated with self-controlling or confrontive coping or accepting responsibility. On the other hand, where there is a low threat to self-esteem escape–avoidance is more common. Strain on financial resources is linked with seeking social support and confrontive coping.

Apparently negative forms of coping are not necessarily negative in terms of outcome. For example, in breast cancer research denial has been shown to be a more helpful

Table 1–2   Some Types of Coping Response

Confrontive
Escape–avoidance
Distancing
Self-controlling
Seeking social support
Accepting responsibility
Planful problem-solving
Positive re-appraisal
Self-blame

response than stoic acceptance (Greer et al. 1979). Studies with spinal injury patients demonstrate that self-blame may act as a motivator in rehabilitation (Folkman & Lazarus 1980).

Coping is context-related, and work problems tend to call forth problem-focused coping while health problems are associated with emotion-focused coping. Where a person judges that something can be done to alleviate the problem, then problem-focused coping tends to be used, whereas when there seems to be little that can be done emotion-focused coping predominates. Age does not appear to be related to coping strategy, and no gender differences are found in emotion-focused coping, perhaps contrary to expectations (Folkman & Lazarus 1980).

Using this approach instead of the care:cure approach can be illustrated by considering the example of a woman who is told that she has a malignant breast lump requiring mastectomy. The care:cure approach leads us to see the doctor as making the diagnosis, breaking the bad news, and then referring the woman to a breast care nurse specialist for counselling before carrying out the surgery. The nurse will be alert to the possibility of postoperative depression and will observe the woman's coping responses in an attempt to identify less constructive ones and counsel or refer her appropriately.

What of the woman herself? According to the care:cure literature she is likely to be concerned with technical care, that is, the successful removal of the cancer, before emotional aspects, but will value time spent with her by the nurse, information given in language that she can understand, and concern shown for her well-being. But what of the dynamics of the relationships among the three? The care:cure notion has little to offer in understanding these.

Using the coping model allows us to see the dynamics of the triadic relationship between doctor, nurse, and patient in a more integrated and sophisticated way. It can also incorporate families, friends and other health care workers. It allows us to consider the personality characteristics, personal beliefs, appraisals of threats, harm, and benefits that each individual brings to the encounter, including their assessments of what can be done separately and together, what resources and information are available to them, and whether and how they can act upon the situation. How they deal with events and regulate their emotions can be studied, as they lead towards possible physical health and emotional outcomes. The particular options and balance of coping strategies used individually and in interaction can be assessed.

No longer does the doctor appear as simply a technocrat implementing decisions without consideration of their wider effects on others and on himself as a professional and a person. The nurse can be seen as having a wide range of professional and personal strategies to draw upon to give high-quality care as part of a team which includes the patient. The patient's experiences can be understood in all their complexity and interrelatedness as she struggles with issues of self-concept, body image, relationships, and sexuality on the long path to coping and adjustment.

Analyzing and understanding the process becomes much more complex when it is seen as a multiperson transaction involving a number of options for all three participants—patient, nurse and doctor—at various stages, and leading to a variety of possible outcomes for each and all of them. Using the model also opens up many potential areas of further research, such as comparing different responses and interactions, trying to identify which is more effective in which circumstances, and whether interventions can facilitate coping and promote more favorable outcomes for all concerned. The implications for professional education and team working seem similarly fruitful in terms of a deeper mutual understanding of each others' roles, and improved reciprocal support.

The concept of "coping" is sometimes criticized as implying that some people cope, that is, they deal successfully with a stressor or challenge, while others do not cope and are seen to fail. This is a misinterpretation of the model, in which *all* reactions are seen as a form of coping. Everyone copes with life situations, but they do this in a whole variety of different ways. The coping model is not judgmental, but can be used to study different ways of coping, to try to detect which are more or less effective in particular circumstances, and to help people to adapt their responses to more productive ones if they wish.

McCorkle (1984) has written:

> *I am not convinced that it is as important to distinguish between the care given by specific professional groups as it is to be clear about the goals of care, and to share these goals with patients and other providers so that a common and unified approach is used.*
>
> (McCorkle 1984)

Lazarus' model of coping offers this possibility. It is also able to take into account the issues discussed under the care:cure heading, including the influence of different care settings, differing needs at various stages of the illness trajectory, and both lay and professional caring. In contrast with Bishop & Scudder's book entitled *Caring, Curing, Coping,* which considers nurses as caring, doctors as curing and patients as coping (Bishop & Scudder 1985), the model reconceptualizes the debate in a more comprehensive and integrated way. The time has come to reject overly simplistic notions of care and cure in the interests of patients and their families and friends, professional maturity, and our own personal well-being.

REFERENCES

Allanach E.J. & Golden B.M. (1988) Patients' expectation and values clarification: a service audit. *Nursing Administration Quarterly* **1**(3), 17–22.

Bevis E.O. (1981) Caring: a life force. In Caring: *An Essential Human Need* (Leininger M. ed.), Charles B. Slack, Thorofare, New Jersey, pp. 49–59.

Brown L. (1986) The experience of care: patient perspectives. *Topics in Clinical Nursing* **8**(2), 56–62.

Cohen F. & Lazarus R. (1973) Active coping process, coping dispositions, and recovery from surgery. *Psychosomatic Medicine* **35**, 375–389.

Cooke H. (1994) The role of the patient in standard setting and audit. *British Journal of Nursing* **3**(22), 1182–1188.

Dunlop M.J. (1986) Is a science of caring possible? *Journal of Advanced Nursing* **11**, 661–670.

Engelhardt H.T. (1985) Physicians. patients, health care institutions—and the people in between: nurses. In *Caring, Curing, Coping* (Bishop A.H. & Scudder J.R. eds), University of Alabama Press, Alabama, pp. 142–159.

Elias N. (1985) *The Loneliness of the Dying.* Basil Blackwell, Oxford.

Folkman S. & Lazarus R.D. (1980) An analysis of coping in a middle—aged community sample. *Journal of Health and Social Behaviour* **211**, 219–239.

Folkman S., Lazarus R., Dunkel-Schetter C., DeLongis A. & Gruen R. (1986) Dynamics of a stressful encounter: cognitive appraisal coping, and encounter, outcomes. *Journal of Personality and Social Psychology* **50**(5), 992–1003.

Freidson E. (1975) *Profession of Medicine.* Dodd, Mead, New York.

Fry S.T. (1988) The ethic of caring: can it survive in nursing? *Nursing Outlook* **36**(1), 48.

Gadow S. (1985) Nurse and patient: the caring relationship. In *Caring, Curing, Coping* (Bishop A.H. & Scudder J.R. eds), University of Alabama Press. Alabama, pp. 31–43.

Gates M.F. (1991) Transcultural comparison of hospital and hospice as caring environments for dying patients. *Journal of Transcultural Nursing* **2**(2), 3–15.

Gilligan C. (1982) In a different voice. Women's conceptions of self and of morality. *Harvard Educational Review* **47**(4), 481–517.

Gooding B.A., Sloan M. & Gagnon L. (1993) Important nurse caring behaviours: perceptions of oncology patients and nurses. *Canadian Journal of Nursing Research* **25**(3), 65–76.

Greer S., Morris T. & Pettingale K.W. (1979) Psychological responses to breast cancer: effect on outcome. *Lancet* **ii**, 785–787.

Harrison L.L. (1990) Maintaining the ethic of caring in nursing. Guest editorial. *Journal of Advanced Nursing* **15**, 125–127.

Hill J. (1991) In defence of Cartesian dualism and the hermeneutic horizon. *Journal of Advanced Nursing* **16**, 1375–1381.

Johnston M. (1982) Recognition of patients' worries by nurses and by other patients. *British Journal of Clinical Psychology* **21**, 255–261.

Katz J. (1986) *The Silent World of Doctor and Patient.* Free Press, New York.

Kitson A.L. (1987) A comparative analysis of lay-caring and professional (nursing) caring relationships. *International Journal of Nursing Studies* **24**(2), 155–165.

Krysl M. (1988) *Midwife: Poetry on Caring.* National League for Nursing, New York.

Larson P. (1981) Oncology patients' and professional nurses' perception of important caring behaviours. Unpublished PhD dissertation, University of California, San Francisco.

Larson P. (1984) Important nurse caring behaviours perceived by patients with cancer. *Oncology Nurses Forum* **11**, 46–50.

Leininger M. (1977) *Caring: The Essence and Central Focus of Nursing.* American Nurses' Foundation (Nursing Research Report) **12**(2), 2–14.

Leininger M. (1981) The phenomenon of caring: importance, research questions and theoretical considerations. In *Caring—An Essential Human Need* (Leininger M. ed.), Charles B. Slack, Thorofare, New Jersey, pp. 3–15.

Linn L. (1984) Care vs. cure: how the nurse practitioner views the patient. *Nursing Outlook* **22**, 641–644.

Llewelyn S.P. (1984) The cost of giving: emotional growth and emotional stress. In *Understanding Nurses* (Skevington S. ed.), John Wiley, Chichester.

Mayer D.K. (1987) Oncology nurses' versus cancer patients' perceptions of nurse caring behaviours: a replication study. *Oncology Nurses Forum* **14**(3), 48–52.

McCorkle R. (1984) Response (session VI). *Cancer* **53**, 2366–2373.

Melia M. (1981) *Student nurses' accounts of their work and training.* Unpublished PhD thesis. University of Edinburgh, Edinburgh.

Nightingale F. (1980) *Notes on Nursing. What it Is, and What it Is Not.* Churchill Livingstone, London.

Noddings N. (1984) *Caring—A Feminine Approach to Ethics and Moral Education.* University of California Press, Berkeley.

Nuland S.B. (1993) *How We Die.* Chatto & Windus, London.

Pearlin L.I. & Schooler C. (1978) The structure of coping. *Journal of Health and Social Behaviour* **19**, 2–21.

Phillips P. (1993) A deconstruction of caring. *Journal of Advanced Nursing* **18**, 1554–1558.

Reed J. & Bond S. (1991) Nurses' assessment of elderly patients in hospital. *International Journal of Nursing Studies* **28**(1), 55–64.

Rogers W.S. (1991) *Explaining Health and Illness. An Exploration of Diversity.* Harvester Wheatsheaf, New York.

Salvage J. (1990) The theory and practice of the 'new nursing'. *Nursing Times* **86**(4), 42–45.

Tripp. R. (1970) *The Penguin International Thesaurus of Quotations.* Penguin. Harmondsworth, Middlesex.

von Essen L. & Sjödén P. (1991) Patient and staff perceptions of caring: review and replication. *Journal of Advanced Nursing* **16**, 1363–1374.

Watson J. (1988) New dimensions of human caring theory. *Nursing Science Quarterly* **1**(4), 175–181.

Webb C. (1985) *Sexuality, Nursing and Health.* Wiley, Chichester.

CHAPTER 2

●●●

Nurses' Conceptualizations of Caring Attitudes and Behaviors

JANE DYSON

Introduction

Nursing has traditionally been concerned with caring as a principle for nursing action (Cronin & Harrison 1988) but there is still debate in the profession as to whether, or not, caring is what makes nursing unique. In professional nursing from Nightingale to the present, the concept of caring has been dominant. Cohen (1991) suggests that caring has been identified as the essence and unifying domain of nursing and supports Leininger's (1988) view that caring is the central and unifying domain for the body of knowledge and practices in nursing.

The centrality of caring in nursing is recognized by most theorists but, while recognizing this centrality (e.g. Watson 1988, Ray 1989), caring and care remain loosely defined concepts. Morrison (1989) noted that helping professions frequently employ caring as a qualitative descriptor of their function, particularly so in nursing. However, if caring is to act as an adequate descriptor, it must be clearly defined. Morse, et al, (1991) also propose that if caring really is central to nursing then it must be demonstrated and not simply proclaimed.

Defining concepts which are central to nursing knowledge and practice is not only important for the profession but also important for the clients. Kitson (1987) suggests that adequate definitions of nursing and caring are a prerequisite for defining standards of professional nursing care. Currently, no acceptable or agreed definitions have been proposed, thus the setting of standards of care is not achievable. It is vital for nurses to correct this situation if they are to be responsible and accountable for professional practice.

© 1996 Blackwell Science Ltd. Reprinted with permission from the *Journal of Advanced Nursing*, Volume 23, 1263–1269, 1996.

Defining Caring

Caring has been defined in generic terms, for example by Heidegger (1962) who considered caring to be a universal phenomenon which influences the ways in which people think, feel and behave in relation to one another. This generic sense of caring was also explored by Mayeroff (1971) who described the central ingredients of caring as knowing, patience, honesty, trust, humility, hope and courage. Some of these "ingredients" are reflected in the writings of nurse scholars. Swanson (1991) defined caring as "being with" another, as becoming emotionally open to the other's reality, giving the message that the other's experience matters to the one caring.

The knowledge of self and self-actualization is also a recurring theme in definitions of caring. Paterson & Zderad (1988) propose an existential perspective, maintaining that as a person more fully experiences being-in-the-world, their ability to express caring behaviors with self and others is enhanced. They suggest that caring in nursing is an actualizing experience, both for the nurse and the patient. Boykin & Schoenhofer (1990) assert that caring in nursing begins with knowing the self as caring, and being cared for, and then progresses to knowing others as caring and worthy of care.

The relationship between caring and loving has also been explored, for example by Campbell (1984) who perceived professional care as being a form of love. Others have suggested that love is a critical component of a caring relationship, claiming that it involves the giving of oneself to another and creating friendship through trust, love and value for each other (Clarke & Wheeler, 1992).

Morse, et al, (1991), in reviewing the literature, identified five principal categories, or ways of conceptualizing caring. These categories highlight the fundamental views adopted by the authors and include caring perceived as a human trait, caring perceived as a moral imperative, caring perceived as an affect, caring perceived as interpersonal interaction and caring perceived as therapeutic intervention.

HUMAN TRAIT

The first of these categories includes the work of Leininger (1981) who, through the methodology of ethnonursing, identified caring as primarily a cultural concept and expression. She makes clear distinctions between generic and professional caring, and caring and curing, maintaining that clients primarily value caring within the health care system. Through her work she identified 17 constructs of caring, including support, comfort, compassion, empathy, helping behaviors and activities relating to maintenance of health. Other authors have also supported this fundamental view that caring is primarily a human trait and a universal phenomenon. According to Griffin (1983) nursing is a caring profession and the process of caring involves two major aspects—activities, and attitudes and feelings underlying those activities.

Ray (1981) also identified caring primarily as a human trait and through observation of caring responses, developed four categories of caring—psychological, practical, interactional and philosophical. In a later study (Ray 1987) five caring themes were identified as being maturation, technical competence, transpersonal caring, communication and judgments/ethics. Ray (1989) supports Leininger's view relating to the importance of culture and suggests that different clinical settings will have different cultures, and therefore the expressions of care will differ. Roach (1987) asserts that nursing is the professionalization of caring, and therefore an understanding of caring is integral to nursing.

MORAL IMPERATIVE

Watson (1985) is representative of those who perceive caring to be, primarily, a moral imperative. Fundamental to her view of caring is that it is a moral ideal whereby the end is protection, enhancement and preservation of human dignity. She asserts that caring is underpinned by a moral stance that goes beyond the like or dislike of a patient and that it is not reflected in a set of techniques, but provides the stance from which one intervenes as a nurse. Within her assumptions, care and love are described as the most universal, the most tremendous and the most mysterious of cosmic forces.

From this moral imperative perspective, an objective of nursing may also be seen to be ensuring that recipients of care are not reduced to the moral status of objects, and that the purpose of care is to overcome objectivity by touching the self of the patient (Gadow 1985).

AFFECT

Bevis (1981) takes the fundamental view that caring is primarily an affect, with caring defined as a feeling of dedication to another to the extent that it motivates and energizes action which influences life constructively and positively through increasing intimacy and mutual self-actualization. According to Bevis (1981) caring has multiple purposes, with the outcome of caring being personal growth and self-actualization both for the nurse and the patient.

Fanslow (1987) also perceives caring to be grounded fundamentally in feelings, and is supported by Forrest (1989) who describes caring in terms of a mental and emotional presence that evolves from deep feelings for the patient's experience. Caring has also been described as primarily a feeling of concern, of interest, of oversight, with a view to protection (McFarlane 1976). Morse, et al, (1991) assert that, from this perspective, feelings of compassion and empathy for the patient must be present. They suggest that part of the art of nursing is the ability of the nurse to become skilled in creating the forms which express feelings of caring.

INTERPERSONAL INTERACTION

Caring as an interpersonal interaction is the perspective taken by Benner & Wrubel (1989), with the interpersonal interaction between nurse and patient being central to the caring process. Horner (1988) identifies that this is a complex process, proposing that both the nurse and patient perceive each other as unique, responsive individuals and that they respond in their being and behavior to achieve humanistic goals. Integration of communication and action in this interpersonal interaction is perceived to be of prime importance (Knowlden 1988, Weiss 1988) in the goal of achieving holistic care.

THERAPEUTIC INTERVENTION

The identification of caring behaviors reflects the final perspective proposed by Morse, et al, (1991) that caring is a therapeutic intervention. Many studies have tried to elucidate patients' and nurses' perceptions of caring in order to define what these caring behaviors are. Larson (1984) identified listening and comforting, and other psychosocial skills, as being most important from the nurses' perspective whilst Brown (1982), exploring patients' perceptions of caring, showed that the behaviors which were seen to be indicative of caring were a combination of what the nurse did and what the nurse was like as a person. Other studies have suggested that patients' perceptions focus on clinical competence and physical elements whilst nurses' perceptions focus on humanistic and psychosocial elements e.g. Mayer 1987, Keane McDermott, et al, 1987, Brown 1986). Gaut (1986), in support of the view that caring is a therapeutic intervention, concluded that caring comprises an ordered series of actions beginning with goal setting and ending with implementation, with the purpose of delivering care based on knowledge and resulting in positive change. Nurse theorists who hold the view that caring is primarily a therapeutic intervention consider caring as specific nursing actions. From this perspective nursing and caring occur regardless of how the nurse feels and feelings of caring are not a necessary prerequisite.

Other studies, which do not fall within Morse, et al's, (1991) categorization, have found that patients rate clinical competence and nurses "knowing what they are doing" as important elements in caring (Cronin & Harrison 1988) and von Essen & Sjödén (1991) identified a focus on clear information giving and communication.

In searching for a professional meaning of the concept of care, some studies have focused primarily on nurses' perceptions. Morrison (1989, 1991) identified categories of caring behaviors related to personal qualities, clinical work style, interpersonal approach, level of motivation, use of time, concern for others and attitudes. Chipman (1991) also identified behavior of a humanistic nature being central to nurses' conceptualization, and this is further supported by Clarke & Wheeler (1992) who found categories of communicating and being supportive, and the concept that caring was in some way innate.

Developing a Theory of Care

The studies and theories reviewed thus far have had little impact on the nursing profession. One could assert that this is because either the findings of studies have not been developed into coherent frameworks, or the developed theories have become so abstract and removed from the reality of nursing care delivery in today's health care environment that they provide little use to a profession which remains embedded in practice. While description of what nurses think caring means is enlightening, it is not necessarily congruent with their lived experience in the clinical setting and their professional practice, and therefore in isolation cannot provide an adequate basis for a theory of care. This author proposes that any meaningful theory of care must take into account variables which influence the nurses' thinking and practice and must be a synthesis of nurses' conceptualizations and the reality of their practice.

This paper describes a pilot study in the first stage of developing such a theory of care. It focuses on nurses' conceptualizations of caring, with a view to synthesizing these views, at a later date, with elements of professional practice.

AIM OF THE STUDY

As a pilot study for a larger research project, the aims of this study were:

1. to elicit nurses' conceptualizations of caring attitudes and caring behaviors by utilizing the repertory grid technique; and
2. to test the repertory grid technique as a useful tool in the elicitation of such constructs of caring.

Methodology

THE REPERTORY GRID TECHNIQUE

This technique was developed by Kelly (1955). It enables the focusing on individual's conceptualizations and perceptions, for example of events, people and activities, and provides a method where the emphasis is on input from the subject rather than the researcher. This also reduces researcher bias. In addition to exploring individual perceptions, the technique can provide quantitative data for analysis, complementing the qualitative nature of the method. The technique has been used successfully in a range of situations, particularly in clinical psychology, to explore individuals' understanding of events. Pollock (1986) asserts that it is a valuable tool for use by psychiatric nurses in the clinical setting and it was used by Morrison (1989) in exploring nurses' perceptions of themselves as carers.

SAMPLE

Nine qualified nurses took part in the study. They worked in a variety of clinical settings and had a range of experience (see Table 2-1). All subjects worked in hospital settings and were undertaking a post-registration degree program.

Whilst the limitations of the sample in terms of size and external validity are acknowledged, the responses are considered to give an insight and basis for further study.

PROCEDURE

Each of the subjects was given two grids to complete, one relating to caring attitudes and one relating to caring behaviors. Elements were provided as follows: (a) caring qualified nurse; (b) non-caring qualified nurse; (c) caring unqualified nurse; (d) non-caring unqualified nurse; (e) caring manager; (f) non-caring manager; (g) someone who cares about you; and (h) someone who doesn't care about you. In accordance with Kelly's procedure, identified by Fransella & Bannister (1977), subjects were asked to identify individuals who matched the role titles of the elements.

A dyadic method was used to elicit constructs. Whilst the normal method of elicitation is through triads of elements, a previous pilot study had demonstrated that the complexity of the concepts involved made elicitation through triads very difficult for subjects as they could not articulate adequate descriptors. Fransella & Bannister (1977) agree that in some circumstances, dyadic method is more successful in elicitation of constructs particularly when the given cognitive task or construct is complex.

A range of dyadic combinations was offered to subjects to elicit 10 constructs on each grid. Subjects were asked to use the same individuals, in their role titles, for each grid and the same dyadic combinations were given in order to try and achieve some consistency across the concepts of caring behaviors and caring attitudes. For each characteristic elicited, subjects were asked to identify the opposite in order to develop bipolar constructs.

A five-point rating scale was then applied, with subjects being asked to rate each of the elements (role titles) against the elicited constructs (see Table 2-2 for example). Rating the elements against the constructs in this way enabled the data within the grid to be subject to statistical analysis.

TABLE 2–1 Sample Characteristics

Years of experience		0–5		6–10		11–15	16 +	
Number in sample		2		2		2	3	
Grade		D	E	F		G	H	
Number in sample		1	3	2		2	1	
Speciality	ITU	Sugery	Elderly	Medicine		Neonatal	Admissions	Theatre
Number in sample	2	2	1	1		1	1	1

TABLE 2-2 Example of Rating Elements Against Constructs

	Caring Qualified Nurse	Non-caring Qualified Nurse	Caring Unqualified Nurse	Non-caring Unqualified Nurse	Caring Manager	Non-caring Manager	Someone Who Cares About You	Someone Who Doesn't Care About You	
Shows interest	5	1	4	2	5	2	5	1	Uninterested
Shows respect for persons	5	2	4	1	4	2	5	3	Doesn't show respect for persons
Appears unhurried	4	2	3	2	5	1	4	1	Always in a hurry

TABLE 2–3   **Themes Identified from Grid Data**

Theme	Example of Clustered Constructs
Consideration and sensitivity	Understanding, considerate
	Kind, interested
	Helpful
Giving of self	Open, loving
	Gives of self, caring, non-judgemental
	Personal
Work style	Appears unhurried
	Thinks about staff, progressive, enjoys work
	In control
	Fulfilled in their work
Motivation	Well motivated
Communication and meeting needs	Has time to listen, willing to listen, listens to problems
	Informs patients, meets patients' needs
	Listens, not abrupt
Knowledge and learning	Interested to learn
	Has knowledge
	Confident in knowledge
Individual approach	Respects persons, tolerant
	Acknowledges people, treats patients as people
	Maintains privacy, treats people as individuals
General approach/person	Easy-going, warm
	Kind, friendly, approachable
	Happy, smiling
	Open and friendly, relaxed, smiling
Honesty and sincerity	Honest, empathic
	Is honest, listens to staff
	Sincere

DATA ANALYSIS AND RESULTS

Each of the grids was subjected to cluster analysis using squared Euclidean measures. This enables the measurement of distance between constructs and allows identification of those which are closely related. The clustered constructs within each grid were then compared to identify common themes.

Nine themes were identified from the analysis of the grid data (see Table 2-3). It was clear from the data that subjects had difficulty in distinguishing between caring behaviors and caring attitudes. This is supportive of the view proposed by many authors whereby nurses commonly identify caring as a psychosocial intervention and largely ignore the physical elements of caring.

Discussion

The findings largely supported the concept that caring is a combination of what the nurse does and what the nurse is like as a person (Brown 1982). The latter, the nurse as a person, was strongly evidenced as a major component of caring, with identification of common themes of "consideration and sensitivity," "giving of self," "honesty and sincerity" and "general approach."

In support of Morrison's (1989, 1991) findings, work style was found to be a key component of caring, with subjects identifying key features such as having time for people, appearing unhurried, and being in control. Also in support of Morrison's findings were elements of motivation, personal qualities and interpersonal approach, identified as themes of "consideration and sensitivity," "giving of self," "honesty and sincerity" and "general approach," which are congruent with the findings of Brown (1982). These themes stress the importance of the nurse as a person and the psychosocial elements of care (Larson 1984). As found in other studies e.g. Larson 1984, Clarke & Wheeler 1992), caring as a therapeutic intervention was not considered to be a major component.

While self-actualization and knowledge of self as elements of caring, identified by authors such as Mayeroff (1971) and Boykin & Schoenhofer (1990), were not found in this study, the relationship between caring and loving was identified. This supports the views of Campbell (1984) and Clarke & Wheeler (1992), who claim that caring involves a form of love. While some of the constructs identified by Leininger (1981) were identified by subjects, e.g. empathy, compassion and helping behaviors, the cultural elements of care, claimed to be central by Leininger, were not evident either overtly or covertly.

In relation to the work of Griffin (1983), the "attitudes" components of care were clearly identified. However, the emotional elements and the activities elements were not articulated, other than in vague terms relating to general behavior.

Contrary to the views of Ray (1989) on the differences in clinical settings, no significant differences were found. This may be reflective of the small sample used.

The theme of "knowledge and learning" was used to categorize constructs such as "has knowledge," "confident in knowledge" and "interested to learn." Previous studies of nurses' perceptions of caring do not appear to have identified this element of caring, although it is reflective of the findings of Cronin & Harrison (1988) whereby patients, when presented with a range of subscales, rated nurses "knowing what they are doing" as very high.

The findings from the grid data did not fall directly into the categories identified by Morse, et al, (1991) but rather appeared as a synthesis of all five.

The major difficulty arising from the methodology employed was the apparent inability of subjects to distinguish between caring behaviors and caring attitudes. This makes the use of two grids, to distinguish between behaviors and attitudes, redundant. The next stage of the project therefore will employ only one grid to explore the concept of "care."

The use of the dyadic method proved successful, with subjects being able to articulate similarities and differences within the dyadic combinations offered, and therefore the elicitation of constructs was possible.

The next stage of the research project recognizes the limited sample used in this study and will use 60 subjects and a stratified sampling procedure in order to give a more comprehensive professional view and increased external validity.

Conclusions

The results from this study highlight some of the key elements in nurses' conceptualizations of care. These largely support the findings of previous studies, with the emphasis on the humanistic and psychosocial components of care. The repertory grid technique proved to be a useful method for elicitation of the constructs of caring, and the methodology employed provides direction for future studies of this nature.

It is clear that additional empirical work is needed to clarify further nurses' conceptualizations of care, and to match these against their professional practice so that a relevant and useful theory of care can be developed to provide a foundation for nursing practice, education and research.

REFERENCES

Benner P. & Wrubel J. (1989) *The Primacy of Caring: Stress and Coping in Health and Illness.* Addison-Wesley, Menlo Park, California.

Bevis E. (1981) Caring: a life force. In *Caring: An Essential Human Need* (Leininger M. ed.) Charles Slack, Thorofare, New Jersey, pp. 49–59.

Boykin A. & Schoenhofer S. (1990) Caring in nursing: analysis of extant theory. *Nursing Science Quarterly* **3**(4), 149–155.

Brown L. (1982) Behaviours of nurses perceived by hospitalized patients as indicators of care. Doctoral dissertation, University of Colorado at Boulder. *Dissertation Abstracts International* **24**(11), 4361B.

Brown L. (1986) The experience of care: patient perspectives. *Topics in Clinical Nursing* **8**(2), 56–62.

Campbell A. (1984) *Moderated Love. A Theology of Professional Care.* SPCK, London.

Chipman Y. (1991) Caring: its meaning and place in the practice of nursing. *Journal of Nursing Education* **30**(4), 171–175.

Clarke J. & Wheeler S. (1992) A view of the phenomenon of caring in nursing practice. *Journal of Advanced Nursing* **17**(11), 1283–1290.

Cohen J. (1991) Two portraits of caring: a comparison of the artists. Leininger and Watson. *Journal of Advanced Nursing* **16**, 899–909.

Cronin S. & Harrison B. (1988) Importance of nurse caring behaviours as perceived by patients after myocardial infarction. *Heart Lung* **7**, 374–380.

Fanslow J. (1987) Compassionate nursing: is it a lost art? *Journal of Practical Nursing* **37**(2), 40–43.

Forrest D. (1989) The experience of caring. *Journal of Advanced Nursing* **14**, 815–823.

Fransella F. & Bannister D. (1977) *A Manual for Repertory Grid Technique.* Academic Press, London.

Gadow S. (1985) Nurse and patient: the caring relationship. In *Caring, Curing, Coping: Nurse–Physician–Patient Relationships* (Bishop A. & Scudder J. eds), University of Alabama Press, Birmingham, Alabama, pp. 31–43.

Gaut D. (1986) Evaluating caring competencies in nursing. *Topics in Clinical Nursing* **8**, 77–83.

Griffin A. (1983) A philosophical analysis of caring in nursing. *Journal of Advanced Nursing* **8**, 289–295.

Heidegger M. (1962) *Being and Time.* Harper and Row, New York.

Henry D.M. (1975) Nurse behaviours perceived by patients as indicators of caring. Doctoral dissertation, Catholic University, Washington, DC. *Dissertation Abstracts International* **36**, 02652 B.

Horner S. (1988) Intersubjective co-presence in a caring model. In *Caring and Nursing. Explorations in the Feminist Perspective,* University of Colorado Health Sciences Centre, Denver, pp. 166–180.

Keane McDermott S., Chastain B. & Rudisill K. (1987) Caring: nurse–patient perceptions. *Rehabilitation Nursing* **12**, 182–187.

Kelly G. (1955) *The Psychology of Personal Constructs.* Norton, New York.

Kitson A. (1987) Raising standards of clinical practice—the fundamental issue of effective nursing practice. *Journal of Advanced Nursing* **12**, 321–329.

Knowlden V. (1988) Nurse caring as constructed knowledge. In *Caring and Nursing. Explorations in the Feminist Perspective,* University of Colorado Health Sciences Centre, Denver, pp. 318–339.

Larson P. (1984) Important nurse caring behaviours perceived by patients with cancer. *Oncology Nursing Forum* **11**(6), 46–50.

Leininger M. (1981) The phenomenon of caring: importance, research, questions and theoretical considerations. In *Caring: An Essential Human Need,* (Leininger M. ed.), Charles Slack, Thorofare, New Jersey, pp. 3–16.

Leininger M. (1988) Leininger's theory of nursing: cultural care diversity and universality. *Nursing Science Quarterly* **1**(4), 175–181.

Mayer D. (1987) Oncology nurses' versus cancer patients' perceptions of nurse caring behaviours: a replication study. *Oncology Nursing Forum* **14**, 48–52.

Mayeroff M. (1971) *On Caring.* Harper and Row, New York.

McFarlane J. (1976) A charter for caring. *Journal of Advanced Nursing* **1**, 187–196.

Morrison P. (1989) Nursing and caring: a personal construct theory study of some nurses' self-perceptions. *Journal of Advanced Nursing* **14**, 421–426.

Morrison P. (1991) The caring attitude in nursing practice: a repertory grid study of trained nurses' perceptions. *Nurse Education Today* **11**, 3–12.

Morse J., Bottorff J., Neander W. & Solberg S. (1991) Comparative analysis of conceptualizations and theories of caring. *Image: Journal of Nursing Scholarship* **23**(2). 119–126.

Patterson J. & Zderad L. (1988) *Humanistic Nursing*. John Wiley and Sons, New York.

Pollock L. (1986) An introduction to the use of repertory grid technique as a research method and clinical tool for psychiatric nurses. *Journal of Advanced Nursing* **11**, 439–445.

Ray M. (1981) Philosophical analysis of caring. In *Caring: An Essential Human Need* (Leininger M. ed.), Charles Slack, Thorofare, New Jersey.

Ray M.A. (1987) Technological caring: a new model in critical care. *Dimensions of Critical Care Nursing* **6**, 166–173.

Ray M. (1989) The theory of bureaucratic caring for nursing practice in the organizational culture. *Nursing Administration Quarterly* **13**, 31–42.

Roach S. (1987) *The Human Act of Caring*. Canadian Hospital Association, Ottawa.

Swanson K.M. (1991) Empirical development of a middle range theory of caring. *Nursing Research* **40**(3), 161–166.

von Essen L. & Sjödén P. (1991) Patient and staff perceptions of caring: review and replication. *Journal of Advanced Nursing* **16**(11), 1363–1374.

Watson J. (1985) *Nursing: Human Science and Human Care.* Appleton-Century-Crofts, Norwalk, Connecticut.

Watson J. (1988) New dimensions of human caring theory. *Nursing Science Quarterly* **1**(4), 175–181.

Weiss C. (1988) Model to discover, validate and use care in nursing. In *Care: Discovery and Uses in Clinical and Community Nursing* (Leininger M. ed.) Wayne State University Press, Detroit, pp. 139–149.

CHAPTER 3

●●●

Power and Caring: A Dialectic in Nursing

ADELINE R. FALK RAFAEL

A recent study of public health nurses' perceptions of the power and powerlessness they experienced in their work found serendipitously that the participants often expressed discomfort with the idea of power.[1] One nurse, for example, described her involvement in linking a family in crisis to community resources, leading to most dramatic results for the family. But she noted, "I did not feel a sense of power [in] . . . this situation. *I never feel power.*" This discomfort with acknowledging one's own power is not unique to this nurse or to this study. It has been identified in both nursing[2] and non–nursing literature and has been attributed to a societal reluctance to discuss power, particularly one's own power, openly.[3] Nurses, however, may feel this discomfort more acutely because they are predominantly women and have not been socialized to exert power and because caring is considered central to their practice, yet is perceived to be incongruent with notions of power. This article examines these concepts in an attempt to reconcile the conflict between power and caring.

Dialectic is a useful method to examine two apparently contradictory concepts. From a Hegelian perspective, *dialectic* is a logical progression of thought that exposes and examines contradictions and reconciles them through a process of thesis, antithesis, and synthesis.[4] During this process, conflicts evident in initial levels of examination are incorporated into a greater unity, allowing the development of knowledge from simple to complex.[5] An important feature of this helical knowledge development is that differences that initially appear to be related only negatively are preserved rather than destroyed.[5] Moccia[6] suggested that the dialectic is a useful form of inquiry for nursing because it both shares a similar unitary worldview with nursing and is productive in exploring the relational nature of human processes. For these reasons I have used a dialectic approach to identify three layers in the relationship between power and caring that I have labeled "ordered caring," "assimilated caring," and "empowered caring."

The first step in a dialectic examination is to identify a starting point. Although traditional conceptualizations of power and caring do not originate with the first records of human activity, I have chosen to begin with them because they predominate in the society in which nurses currently live and work and have prevailed throughout the history of

Reprinted from *Advances in Nursing Science*, 1996, 19(1): 3–17, with permission of Aspen Publishers, Inc., © 1996.

modern nursing. Traditional definitions of power and caring stem from a patriarchal perspective. To inform the dialectic examination of power and caring that follows, therefore, a brief review of patriarchy is in order.

Patriarchy

Patriarchy may be thought of as an ideology that justifies and perpetuates male dominance[7] through valuing men, their characteristics, and their activities while at the same time devaluing women and their characteristics and activities.[8] Patriarchy has not always been the prevailing ideology but rather developed over a period of several millennia to be firmly in place by about 600 BCE.[9] Volumes have been written detailing the evidence of a patriarchal ideology, and a comprehensive review of this literature is beyond the scope of this article. What is important to note, however, is the conditions that are critical for sustaining patriarchy.

Foucault's[10] analytics of power provide a useful framework for identifying those conditions. The purpose of Foucault's work was to expose the "web of unequal relationships which underlie and undercut theoretical equity posited by the law."[10(p185)] Foucault viewed power as not simply residing in individuals or groups but as an intricate web of power technologies operating throughout society.[11] His term "technologies" refers to a conceptualization of power and knowledge as inseparable. He denied that his work is a theory of power; rather, he characterized himself as having created a history of the three ways human beings are objectified, or made into subjects, in our culture: (1) dividing practices, (2) scientific classification, and (3) subjectification.[12]

Dividing practices are those that differentiate one group of people from another. The most effective dividing practices result in the confinement or exclusion of a group based on their differences. Foucault gives examples such as "the mad and the sane, the sick and the healthy, the criminals and the 'good boys.'"[12(p208)] Dividing practices have been instituted in the oppression of races, classes, and other groups that have successfully been designated as different from, and therefore less valuable than, the dominant group. It is the basis of all the "isms." To follow Foucault's thinking, the first step in perpetuating male dominance is to concentrate on the differences, rather than the similarities, between men and women by constructing the categories of masculinity and femininity. The historical exclusion of women from language, history, the priesthood, and boardrooms, as well as other social institutions, is an example of a dividing practice.

Scientific classification refers to the "modes of inquiry that give themselves the status of science."[12(p208)] As such, "scientific evidence" is generated to support and legitimize dividing practices. In relation to the perpetuation of patriarchy, *scientific classification* refers to the generation and institutionalization of gender knowledge that accentuates, exaggerates, or mythicizes the differences between men and women and provides evidence for the supremacy of men. It is illustrated in the philosophical, psychological, sociological, and medical theories of women's biological, psychological, and moral inferiority.[13]

Foucault's third mode of objectification is referred to as "subjectification" by Rabinow,[14] because it involves the active participation of an individual in the process of his or her own self-formation. Typically, however, subjectification is mediated by an external authority figure through "a variety 'of operations on [people's] own bodies, on their own souls, on their own thoughts, on their own conduct.'"[14(p11)] This phenomenon has been identified as characteristic of oppressed groups who assimilate the characteristics, practices, and values of the groups that dominate them, including the normalcy and inherent superiority of the dominant group. It is a recurrent theme in feminist literature and is described in a variety of ways—false consciousness,[15] women engaging in their own enslavement,[16] and women collaborating in their own oppression.[17] In short, women's subjectivities are molded in a way that ensures continued male dominance.

These three methods have interplayed in the construction and institutionalization of masculinity and femininity as norms in Western society. I use the term "constructed" because there is no clear evidence that real differences, other than those related to sexual and reproductive functions, exist.[7] Since knowledge is developed to maintain power,[11] it is not surprising that masculinity has been defined in a way that prepares men to dominate. Characteristics traditionally associated with masculinity include strength, aggression, mastery, independence, logic, and being unemotional, competitive, and ambitious.[18] Femininity, on the other hand, has prepared women to be dominated and has encompassed submissiveness, helplessness, dependence, tenderness, nurturance, and altruism.[18] In short, power is congruent with the characteristics of masculinity, whereas the characteristics of femininity prepare women to care.

Such gender definitions might serve a useful purpose if conforming to them did not stifle the potential of half the human race and if each were equally valued. Unfortunately, for millennia, women, and that which has been considered feminine, have been devalued. Such devaluation has been and continues to be made in the name of scientific knowledge. Although not the first, Aristotle's denigration of women has strongly influenced Western culture.[7] His pronouncements of women's biological and moral inferiority[9] validated prevailing thought and have been echoed through the ages by other respected political and religious leaders such as St. Thomas Aquinas and Rousseau.[13] Theories of Freud, Maslow, Erikson, Piaget, and Kohlberg are still being taught in higher education, including nursing schools. Often the fact that each assumed the male experience to be the norm and attributed differences among women to female inferiority is never mentioned. For approximately the last 150 years, science, primarily through medicine and psychology, has provided "scientific" evidence that women are biologically and morally inferior and suited, therefore, primarily for sexual and reproductive functions.[7]

The denigration of women and that which is feminine has been entrenched in all of civilization's major institutions.[7] It is reflected in recorded history, which, until recently, has almost completely omitted the experiences and contributions of women as well as marginalized men. Events such as the witch hunts of the 13th to 16th centuries, in which an estimated 3 million to 8 million people,[19] 85% of them women, were tortured and executed, are skimmed over in history class if mentioned at all. History of the civilizations that thrived on this continent before it was "discovered" by Columbus has not been deemed worthy of study and remains invisible in most history texts. "History," as noted in the video *The Burning Times,* "is written by the winners."[19]

Androcentric values are pervasive in Western culture and facilitate the subjectification of men and women. They are reflected in literature, classical and popular art, movies, television, advertising, and music. One of the biggest selling movies of last year, *The Lion King,* provides a current example. In this movie, the "naturalness" of male dominance is reinforced through projecting this human characteristic onto a matricentric species in which territories are passed not from father to son, but from mother to daughter.[7] Androcentric values are further reinforced through language that excludes 51% of the world's population. Although apparently great gains have been made in this area, the use of inclusive language seems often an empty gesture of "political correctness" rather than a genuine willingness to correct a wrong. There is often little awareness that the use of the generic term "man" for "human" originated at a time when women, children, slaves, and laboring men were considered less than human and propertied "man" was considered to be all that was fully human.[7]

Legal and religious systems have historically been an effective external authority in influencing the subjectification of women. Laws that enshrined women as property, restricted their participation in political or even personal decision making, and criminalized deviance from established gender roles have entrenched a pattern of male dominance as the legal norm in Western society.[7,9] Even at the end of the 20th century, media reports of judicial decisions that reflect male bias are not uncommon (eg, blaming a child for provoking her own sexual abuse). Earlier this year, a national Canadian morning show[20] reported a story of a physician that the medical association in Quebec had disciplined for "gross exploitation." The physician reportedly had sex with a female patient while she was unconscious in the operating room. What makes this story so amazing is that in the previous week a court had found the physician not guilty. The report quoted the judge as saying, "Can you blame [the doctor] for giving in to her?"

Religious systems establish a hierarchy in which men are next to God and given dominion over women and nature. Woman is conceptualized as embodying both the carnality that led to the fall of the human race and as an asexual ideal. Religious dogma strips women of control over their own sexual and reproductive functions and perpetuates male dominance as divinely ordained. An illustration of Foucault's premise that power resides in a web of social institutions and practices[11] was provided recently in the Pope's warning to politicians not to support a woman's right to choice.

Ordered Caring

It is within this context of a prevailing patriarchal ideology that the relationship between power and caring exists. In the first layer of this dialectic, power and caring are strongly aligned with masculine and feminine gender definitions. Also in the first layer of the dialectic, traditional conceptualizations of power and caring are present as polar opposites. For this reason, it is useful to examine them and their implications for nurses and nursing separately.

POWER

Power is the "natural" outcome of masculinity with its valued traits of strength, aggression, and independence and is related to having control over others and nature. A typical definition of traditional power is seen in Toffler's recent work: "the use of violence, wealth, and knowledge . . . to make people perform in a given way."[21(p14)] He proposed that power is being transformed because violence and wealth are being replaced by knowledge as the primary source of power. Whatever its source, power is associated with male supremacy and is the central value in a patriarchal culture.[7]

Nyberg[3] presented a somewhat less ruthless portrayal of power. He defined it as "the motive and capacity to accomplish plans with others."[3(p61)] Although this sounds somewhat more egalitarian, the uncertainty of whose plans are being accomplished and the consent to power that is required in his model betray a traditional view of power. In contrast to Foucault,[11] who asserted that power always exists in relation to resistance, Nyberg suggested that power is always delegated (ie, if someone has power over us, we consent to it). Consent may include obedience under the threat of reprisal, compliance, indifference, conformity, and conscious or informed commitment. He too, however, allowed for resistance, indicating that the withdrawal of consent is the final power over power.

Foucault,[11] Toffler,[21] and Nyberg[3] all acknowledged, though in varying degrees, the importance of knowledge in the generation of power. For Foucault, power and knowledge are inseparable and mutually generative. Toffler predicted that knowledge is currently becoming the primary source of power. Nyberg included knowledge in two of the four sources of power he identified: as myth in a category he calls "fiction" and as expertise in a broader concept he refers to as "fealty." He described this as a trust or loyalty that may be related to another's charisma, prestige, or expertise. Nyberg's other two sources of power include force, which may range from violence to punishment and coercion, and finance or wealth, including the ability to reward others through an organizational position.

The traditional conceptualization of power is fostered by the separation, strength, and control that are the esteemed properties of masculinity. It is this power that sustains the organizational hierarchies in which most nurses provide care and in which power is vested in certain positions and legitimized as authority over nurses. It is often not accessible to nurses for reasons of gender, position, or status vis-à-vis physicians.

Foucault[11] maintained that power is always exercised at a cost. The price of obtaining traditional power is the devaluation of that which has been labeled feminine in both men and women. For women, and nurses are mostly women, this means the denigration and denial of one's own characteristics regardless of whether one argues that femininity is biologically determined or culturally acquired. Additionally for nurses, it means rejecting the essence of nursing. Thus, nurses, to acquire power, often distance themselves from other nurses and become marginalized.[22] Such distancing may take many forms from valuing knowledge of other disciplines over nursing knowledge to aligning one's self with other disciplines rather than joining professional nursing associations. The cost of power obtained in this way is professional disunity and lowered individual self-esteem.

Nurses encounter power being exercised over them in a variety of ways. Historically nurses have experienced control of their personal and professional lives predominantly by male physician and administrator groups.[23] Examples have included or to some degree still include control over nursing practice and working environment and access to and content of education[24] as well as attire, place of residence, and freedom to marry.[25] The increasing use of unlicensed personnel, the American Medical Association proposal for "registered care technologists," and the medical lobby opposing nurses as primary health care practitioners are current examples of attempts to control nurses and nursing. Although resistance to power provides the opportunity for change, more negative consequences of administrative, medical, or gender oppression include experiences of powerlessness, low self-esteem, and horizontal violence.[1,22,26]

The relevance of traditional power to nursing is not restricted to its practitioners' personal experiences. Nurses frequently provide care in circumstances in which power has been exercised over their clients in the form of social or domestic violence. In addition, nurses frequently care for clients who are experiencing powerlessness related to their lack of control in a paternalistic health care environment, inaccessible or unaffordable health care, or disenfranchisement for other reasons. Yet within a context of being ordered to care, nurses are impotent in effecting the social and political changes necessary to transform their clients' realities.

CARING

Caring, as constructed in a patriarchal culture, is a feminine virtue designed to serve men. In contrast to the "naturalness" of power in men, caring encompasses both characteristics designated as feminine (ie, gentleness, tenderness, submissiveness, and altruism) as well as those that are in reality natural for women (ie, their involvement in reproduction and nurturance of their offspring). The latter ensures propagation of the species; the former perpetuates male domination. Both are encompassed in the traditional conceptualization of caring, and both are devalued in Western society.

Reverby[27] suggested that nursing evolved from women's historical role in caring for the community's vulnerable individuals. She asserted that caring was imposed as a duty first on women, then, as society's needs increased in times of war and epidemics, on a paid nursing work force. In her words, nurses were "ordered to care in a society that refuses to value caring."[27(p1)] Nursing practice, in other words, may be considered an exemplar of ordered caring. As such, its history should provide evidence that traditional caring is a feminine virtue and duty deemed necessary but devalued.

It is not difficult to find examples in nursing that mandate submissiveness and deference. In the mid-19th century, Florence Nightingale demonstrated that nursing care made a dramatic difference in mortality rates of soldiers in the Crimean War. Yet Palmer[28] suggested that in establishing modern nursing, Nightingale placed it under the control of a male institution, medicine. Many nurses remember being taught deference to physicians in nursing school through gestures that defied conventional social etiquette such as standing when physicians entered the room, opening doors for them, and not questioning their orders. In fact, loyalty to the physician remained an ethical requirement of the International Council of Nurses until as recently as 1973.[29] Even today nurses' language suggests deference is still required of nurses as they follow "orders" that physicians and others write.

Gentleness and quietness were required of Nightingale's nurses, and many nurses in today's work force that "trained" in the 1960s and earlier can attest to the importance attached to those virtues. It is illustrated by the motto of the first Canadian school of nursing in St. Catherines: "I see and am silent."[30] Coburn[30] believed the choice of this motto is related directly to the high value placed on the genteel character of the nurse.

Cleanliness and neatness were essentials of nursing in Nightingale's[28] time through to the 1960s. This extended well beyond the personal and environmental hygiene measures that are conducive to healing and the prevention of infection. Nurses' responsibilities in the recent past frequently included duties such as carbolizing beds and cleaning utility and linen rooms. Stories are still being told of the need to be able to bounce a dime off a draw sheet, to fold back the bedclothes in a precise regulated fashion, and to produce crisp, mitered corners. Unfortunately, I have encountered some instructional videos used in teaching nursing students basic skills today that still insist that the open end of the pillow case should face away from the door!

Nursing practice has also included attending to the comfort and promoting the health and healing of patients. In a traditional view of caring, however, this is not recognized as requiring any particular knowledge or skill; it simply comes "naturally" to women, particularly if they are adequately directed by medicine and administration. Doering[24(p30)] posited that the power relation between medicine and nursing has limited the "recognition, scope, and expansion of nursing knowledge." The lack of recognition that caring involves knowledge is, however, related not only to the power imbalance between physicians and nurses but also to gender inequity. Code[31] suggested that in a patriarchal society men have the advantageous position of declaring what counts as knowledge and who can know it. Stereotypes and "scientific research" are used to both justify limiting women's access to knowledge and discrediting what they do know. Baumgart,[25] a Canadian nursing leader, labeled this the "rightful knower status." She suggested that although nurses acquire "medical" knowledge through their practice, they must play the physician–nurse game as a pretense that they do not know what counts as physician's knowledge. Baumgart's[32] analysis of the proceedings of the Grange Inquiry into the baby deaths at the Hospital for Sick Children in Toronto illustrates, however, that the problem of rightful knower status is also a gender issue. She noted that lawyers, who were mostly male, questioned nurses about what they had experienced, in contrast to physicians, who were asked what they knew. She concluded that experience is considered inferior to knowledge in this society and that there was a message that "nurses should not know."[32(p21)]

The assumption that caring does not require knowledge is not without consequence. It quite possibly is related to the invisibility of nursing care on the hospital bill and the still-common public perception of nurse as handmaiden. The replacement of registered nurses with less skilled or, in some cases, unskilled personnel may well be less a reflection of economics than a devaluation of caring as an unskilled feminine virtue.

Just as the perpetuation of women as irrational translates into the assumption that caring does not require knowledge or expertise, "knowledge" of women as morally inferior has implications for the ethics of caring. As a patriarchal construct, caring must necessarily be devoid of an ethical component because women's moral agency is denied. This perhaps accounts for the relabeling of the International Council of Nurses' Code of Ethics in 1965 to the Code of Ethics as Applied to Nursing. Kelly asserted that the change reflected the assumption that "there were no ethical standards *unique* to nursing, but rather generally could be *applied* to nursing or any other profession."[33(p22)]

Altruism was, and some would argue still is, required of nurses. Religious imagery has portrayed women not only as submissive to men, but also as self-sacrificing servants of humanity. Such imagery may contribute both to nursing's position in relation to medicine and to nurses' historically low salaries and poor working conditions. Because of the gains that have been made with regard to nurses' salaries, particularly in Canada, it is not unusual to hear nurses express the idea that further efforts toward fair remuneration are inappropriate. Some have believed the myth that nurses' salary increases are responsible for the health care crisis and understand the "economic" necessities for replacing registered nurses with unlicensed personnel. As part of health care costs, nurses' salaries represent a very small percentage.[34] Yet other sources of health care costs remain untouched (eg, fees for medical services, price gouging of multinational pharmaceutical companies, profit margins of manufacturers who produce the increasingly sophisticated technological devices that have come to be so essential, salaries of hospital administrators, and insurance company profits). Additional evidence for the altruism expected of nurses is demonstrated by the remuneration of physicians' assistants, with varying levels of preparation not exceeding a bachelor's degree, at levels equal to or higher than nurses with advanced degrees.

There are at least two problems with ordered caring. First, as a feminine virtue it is denigrated in both men and women. Second, and perhaps just as importantly, it allows only a severely limited scope of caring, one that is devoid of knowledge, power, or ethics. It is illustrated in Liaschenko's[35] chilling example of nurses tenderly comforting psychiatric patients on their way to the gas chambers in Nazi Germany without being able to influence the social and political forces that had condemned them to death.

Assimilated Caring

From a Foucauldian poststructuralist viewpoint, power is not only restrictive, but also productive. It is always exercised in relation to resistance, and it is at that point of resistance that change is possible.[24] Assimilated caring reflects resistance to the dominant discourse concerning power and caring. In this layer of the dialectic, the notion of caring as devoid of knowledge, power, or ethics is replaced by one in which caring is a discipline grounded in science as the preferred, if not exclusive, way of knowing and governed by prevailing ethical frameworks. Although dominant conceptualizations of power have not changed, assimilated caring allows access to that power only through appropriation of traditionally male power sources.

Just as an understanding of the context in which patriarchal conceptualizations of power and caring arose facilitates an understanding of ordered caring, a review of the context in which assimilated caring developed is helpful in understanding this layer of the dialectic. Feminism represents a wide diversity of thought that is reflected in a variety of forms (eg, liberal, Marxist, cultural, radical, and others). A comprehensive review of feminism is beyond the scope of this article; rather, the discussion will be limited to those aspects of feminist thought that have informed assimilated caring.

One commonality shared by all branches of feminism is the recognition of women's oppression in a patriarchal culture. Because nurses are now and in the past have almost exclusively been women, feminist discourse is extremely relevant to nursing. Consciousness of and resistance to gender inequities that disadvantaged nursing and nurses have played an important part in nursing's development. The branch of feminism that seems to fit closely with assimilated caring is liberal feminism. It focuses on political, social, and economic equality for women (eg, the suffrage movement, equal pay for equal work, equal access to male privilege).[36] Liberal feminism has championed women's increased accessibility to universities and formerly exclusive male professions but has not challenged the male privilege of defining what counts as knowledge.

The liberal feminist focus on equality of access extends to equal access to male power. Power in assimilated caring is gained only through access to male power through assimilation of male characteristics, practices, and values. As such, the cost remains the denial of one's "femininity."

Bordo[37] noted that although young women today are pressured to retain their femininity if they wish to succeed in the traditionally male professional world, they must assimilate masculine characteristics of self-control, emotional discipline, logic, and mastery. Such assimilation is demonstrated in the slogan "The best man for the job is a woman."

Nursing again will be used as an exemplar of assimilated caring. The knowledge generated from resisting the oppression of ordered caring is a self-awareness that nursing is essentially different from medicine. Although Nightingale clearly articulated a vision for nursing that was different from medicine, it was not until approximately 100 years later that nurses began to develop what are now considered early nursing theories. Pioneers of contemporary nursing such as Henderson and Abdellah attempted to clarify the nature of nursing and rescue it from its enmeshment in medicine. To be credible in "malestream society," however, nursing could not be based on Nightingale's premise that it was a natural outgrowth of woman's work; nursing needed to be grounded in socially acceptable scientific knowledge. In short, the science of nursing became central in the development of nursing knowledge.

The acceptance of what counts as knowledge is one aspect of assimilated caring that is further demonstrated in the popularity of nursing research methodologies based on the received view. In efforts to demonstrate rationalism, assimilated caring is embedded in the nursing process, and like physicians, nurses make diagnoses. Assimilated caring is based on knowledge gained in educational institutions where nursing education is the primary focus rather than hospitals, in which nurses' educational needs are secondary to the service they provide.

Power, at this layer of the dialectic, is still only available to nurses by assimilating male and medical norms. Professionalism is a highly sought after goal in nursing despite the difficulties of meeting criteria established for advantaged men. Professional nursing standards and accreditation processes regulate assimilated caring as nursing attempts to demonstrate that it meets the criteria of self-regulation and accountability to society. Although most assimilated caring is provided in administrative hierarchies, opportunities exist for nurses to work more independently as primary care nurse practitioners. Such positions are based on advanced education that may be medically focused and may actually be sanctioned by the medical community.[23]

Assimilated caring has an ethical basis that is based on malestream ethics (eg, application of universal principles such as self-determination, beneficence, and rights-based justice).[38] Nursing codes of ethics demonstrate nursing's accountability to society. Assimilated caring is not, however, congruent with a caring ethics based on feminine virtue or a relational ethic based on women's experience because it has assimilated the dominant culture's devaluation of women, their characteristics, and their experience.

The closest characterization of assimilated caring may be the adage "If you can't beat them, join them." Nurses may "join them" for any number of personal reasons, some willingly, some begrudgingly, some consciously aware of the direction their caring has taken, some unaware that they have assimilated dominant values. Some nurses may become disillusioned and leave nursing, and some may resist and generate yet another form of caring.

Empowered Caring

As social change, influenced by liberal feminism, created an environment for assimilated caring, a broader feminist perspective underpins the tenets of empowered caring. Such a broadened feminist perspective not only recognizes women's oppression, but also values their characteristics and experiences. In so doing, it translates into these basic principles:

- both sexes are at least equal,
- this equality must be publicly recognized,
- the characteristics that have traditionally been viewed as masculine and feminine are at least equally valuable, and
- the personal is political.[7]

In other words, because the same cultural norms impinge on the bedroom and the boardroom, there is a need to take political action against injustices incurred by inequitable power relations.

Empowered caring represents the third layer of the dialectic in which power and caring are intertwined in a greater unity, rather than present as conflicting concepts. In other words, power, as well as knowledge and ethics, is an intrinsic part of empowered caring rather than being alien to caring as it is in ordered caring. Furthermore, whereas assimilated caring incorporates and perpetuates prevailing discourse on power, knowledge, and ethics, empowered caring moves beyond it.

The power of empowered caring is not limited to traditional "power over," but neither does it exclude its use as a means to an end (eg, to influence change in a health care system and society that desperately need change). Reforming, rather than simply reorganizing, health care requires the capacity to accomplish plans with others through access to traditional power sources. Although often such power sources remain inaccessible to staff nurses, several are available and may be remembered through the acronym CARE (credentials, association, research, and expertise).

Credentials are a source of power of extreme political importance in present U.S. society. As a goal in themselves, they are reflective more of assimilated power than empowered caring. However, when they are used as a means to an end, they are critical in enhancing credibility. In other words, credentials can give nurses confidence in themselves and give others confidence in nurses and nursing. If nurses are to enjoy the same credibility as members of other health care disciplines, however, their credentials must be equally valued and respected.

Association refers to relationships, not only with powerful people and organizations, but just as importantly, with each other. It includes working with other professional groups such as the World Health Organization in its pursuit of primary health care. It involves lobbying elected officials and making them aware of nursing's contributions to and potential for the improvement of health care. The power of association is realized in joining other nurses in professional associations as well as in collegiality that values and respects the expertise and experience of other nurses.

Research empowers by building nursing knowledge that in turn generates power. It is needed to make visible what nurses do to promote healing and health within and outside of the context of cure. As the population grows older, as health care continues to shift to the community, and as younger people need care for chronic illnesses such as acquired immunodeficiency syndrome (AIDS), nurses need to investigate the most effective nursing interventions to promote health. Research is needed to eliminate from nursing practice those interventions that are ineffective, even if based on tradition or the practices of other disciplines. Commitment to research involves not only doing it, but also facilitating and using it.

Expertise is closely linked to research and credentials but also develops from nursing practice.[39] Recognizing nursing expertise requires making visible nurses' contributions to healing that are often invisible to themselves and others and resisting the temptation to look outside nursing for answers to nursing questions. A recent study found that nurses perform almost 500 of the same procedures that physicians perform and for which they bill.[40] Yet because caring has not been valued in Western society and because nursing care has been upstaged by medical technology in the past 50 years, nurses often have had self-doubts about their expert contributions to health and healing. Expertise must be acknowledged by nurses themselves before they can expect others to recognize it.

Benner[39] asserted that in addition to providing a source of traditional power, nursing expertise is a source of power that often has a transformative influence on clients' lives. As such it illustrates power that moves beyond "power over" to include power that enables others. This type of power is based on respect for and connection with others and nature. Rather than exerting control over others, enabling power requires their active and equal participation.[41] In contrast to traditional power, it enhances rather than reduces personal control. Consistent with the tenets of feminism, this power has a revolutionary component that involves an awareness of and a commitment to change problematic social and cultural contexts. When power is reconceptualized in this way, nurses have access to a power within themselves that is able to facilitate the empowerment of others, whether they be colleagues or clients.

Chinn[42] offered a description of such an expanded conceptualization of power. It is characterized by valuing the personal power of each individual and is illustrated in decision making by consensus in which each person's perspective is heard and considered. Enabling power is based on respect for the diversity among people, rather than an expectation of conformity. In contrast to controlling power, which often uses force to exploit others, enabling power is characterized by nurturance of others in recognition that they are integral to one's own existence. As opposed to loyalty that may be demanded by someone who exercises power over another, enabling power shares the responsibility for decision making within the group and demonstrates a respect for the choice in self and others instead of requiring polarization in a "for or against" stance. Enabling power distributes knowledge so that all may grow, rather than hoarding it to give a few the edge. Unlike controlling power, enabling power is not invested in a position, so group leadership is free to shift as the situation demands different talents, interests, or abilities. Finally, in contrast to controlling power, which is often maintained through creation of myths, enabling power is strengthened though increased awareness of and commitment to exposing controlling forces.

The reconstruction of power is one aspect of empowered caring; the other is the reconstruction of caring. Traditional caring has been criticized as representing a division of labor that primarily serves men and their interests but has been disguised as the essence of women's nature.[35] Empowered caring values equally the characteristics that have been traditionally assigned to women and to men and is not relegated to only one sex. Thus, caring does not need to be associated with timidity and subservience but is as likely to be associated with strength and assertiveness. Nurses, caring from this perspective, are aware of the social and political forces that impinge on themselves and their clients and are willing to take political action against injustices that become evident.

Empowered caring may be viewed as ontology, epistemology, ethics, and praxis. As an ontology it may be considered a virtue, but one that is equally valued with other human virtues and not relegated only to women. Such a view marks a sharp contrast to the emphasis on separation and detachment that have characterized dominant thinking. Furthermore, an empowered caring ontology creates the opportunity for being equal in relation. It is not consistent, therefore, with deference to medical or administrative authority. Neither, however, is it consistent with paternalism. That is, empowered caring does not involve assuming the role of expert and "doing what's best" for the client. It requires active and equal participation of the nurse and client in health care decisions. Finally, an empowered caring ontology is a relational way of becoming. This reflects the notion of both the patient and the nurse being transformed during the caring relationship, a feature identified in nursing[39] and non–nursing literature.[43,44]

As an ethics, empowered caring stems from a heightened awareness of interrelatedness and emerges as a sense of responsibility toward others. As such, it is believed by some to be critical to the very survival of humanity.[43,44] The ethics of caring has been linked to feminine values[44] and criticized in that regard.[35] Noddings,[45] in response to that criticism, emphasized that these values arise from women's experiences, not their nature. In keeping with the feminist position of valuing equally the characteristics of women and men, Noddings noted, "If the ethic of care is valuable, that makes an argument for changing the experience of men, not for rejecting the experience of women."[45(p27)] Empowered caring is a relational ethics that is contextual and may at times be guided by principles but is not always driven by them.[46]

Empowered caring is *praxis*: a practice informed by various forms of knowledge. Mayeroff[43] suggested that caring without knowledge remains simply a matter of good intentions, and Watson[47] echoed this thought. In identifying the 10 carative factors that summarize the caring process, she noted that they presuppose a knowledge base and clinical competence. As Benner[39] suggested, however, knowledge is also gained through the kind of engagement empowered caring requires. In this sense, empowered caring is an epistemology and demonstrates the mutual generativity of power and knowledge. It is captured in Chinn's[42] admonition to do what we know and know what we do.

As praxis informed by various forms of knowing, empowered caring is reflected but not limited to nursing's traditional involvement in health promotion and healing. It is not restricted by setting or age and is as appropriate in intensive care units as it is in public health nursing, in assistance with birthing as it is in assisting patients to find meaning in death. Empowered caring is necessary if advanced practice nursing is to fill the existing gap in health care and provide primary health care rather than simply extend the medical model through primary care. It may well take the form of emancipatory nursing actions directed at addressing broad determinants of health and precipitating change in the social structures that maintain inequitable power relations.[48]

The relational aspect of empowered caring creates possibilities for complementary healing modalities. It is consistent with Watson's conceptualization of caring as an "energy field of its own which . . . can potentiate healing and release one's own inner power and resources by creating the expanded energy field."[49(pp176–177)] On a similar note, Quinn proposed the intentional use of the nurse's consciousness as a healing environment and suggested that therapeutic touch is an exemplar of healing modalities in which "the intentional use of expanded consciousness . . . can allow a unique, healing human–environment process."[50(p34)] As a form of caring grounded in knowledge, moreover, empowered caring subsumes the need for rigorous but appropriate research to investigate both traditional and complementary healing modalities.

The layers of the dialectic between power and caring are neither hierarchical nor chronological but rather demonstrate the helical nature of evolving as a double-stranded helix from simplicity to increasingly complex levels. In ordered caring, power and caring are seen as dualistic concepts. The conflict that is relieved at the level of assimilated caring gains power at the expense of caring values. Empowered caring represents a unity that resolves the conflict between power and caring evident in previous layers. At this level of unity, power and caring remain distinct yet intertwined concepts that, like power and knowledge, are mutually generative.

REFERENCES

1. Rafael ARF. *Content Analysis of Public Health Nurses' Perceptions of Power and Powerlessness.* Buffalo, NY: D'Youville College; 1992. Thesis.
2. Prescott PA, Dennis KE. Power and powerless in hospital nursing departments. *J Prof Nurs.* 1985; 1:348–355.
3. Nyberg D. *Power Over Power.* Ithaca, NY: Cornell University; 1981.
4. Flew A. *A Dictionary of Philosophy.* 2nd ed. New York, NY: St. Martin's Press; 1984.
5. Gadow S. Body and self: a dialectic. In: Kestenbaum V, ed. *The Humanity of the Ill: Phenomenological Perspectives.* Knoxville, Tenn: University of Phenomenological Perspectives; 1982.
6. Moccia P. The dialectic as method. In: Chinn PL, ed. *Nursing Research Methodology: Issues and Implementation.* Rockville, Md: Aspen; 1986.
7. French M. *Beyond Power: On Women, Men, and Morals.* New York, NY: Ballantine Books; 1985.
8. Gray ED. *Patriarchy as a Conceptual Trap.* Wellesley, Mass: Roundtable; 1982.
9. Lerner G. *The Creation of Patriarchy.* New York, NY: Oxford University Press; 1986.
10. Dreyfuss HL, Rabinow P. *Michel Foucault.* Chicago, Ill: University of Chicago Press; 1982.
11. Foucault M; Gordon C, trans. *Power/Knowledge: Selected Interviews and Other Writings 1972–1977.* New York, NY: Pantheon; 1980.
12. Foucault M. The subject and power. In: Dreyfuss HL, Rabinow P, eds. *Michel Foucault: Beyond Structuralism and Hermeneutics.* Chicago, Ill: University of Chicago Press; 1982.
13. Ashley JA. Power in structured misogyny: implications for the politics of care. *ANS.* 1980;5:3–22.
14. Rabinow P. *The Foucault Reader.* New York, NY: Random House; 1984.
15. Lather P. *Getting Smart: Feminist Research and Pedagogy Within the Postmodern.* New York, NY: Routledge; 1991.
16. Baker Miller J. *Toward a New Psychology of Women.* Boston, Mass: Beacon Press; 1976.
17. Sawicki J. Foucault and feminism: a critical reappraisal. In: Kelly M, ed. *Critique and Power: Recasting the Foucault/Habermas Debate.* Cambridge, Mass: MIT Press; 1994.
18. Achterberg J. *Woman as Healer.* Boston, Mass: Shambhala; 1991.
19. Pettigrew M, Armstrong M (Producers), Read D (Director). *The burning times.* Los Angeles, Calif: Direct Cinema; 1990. Videotape.
20. *Canada AM.* Toronto, Ontario: Baton Broadcasting Company; April 13, 1995. Videotape.
21. Toffler A. *Powershift.* New York, NY: Bantam Books; 1990.
22. Roberts SJ. Oppressed group behavior: implications for nursing. *ANS.* 1983;8(7):21–30.
23. Lovell MC. Feminism and nursing: daddy's little girl: the lethal effects of paternalism in nursing. *Revolution J Nurs Empowerment.* 1992;2(1):17–23.
24. Doering L. Power and knowledge in nursing: a feminist poststructuralist view. *ANS.* 1992;14(4): 24–33.
25. Baumgart AJ. The quality of work life of hospital nurses: the legacy of history. In: Attridge C, Callahan M, eds. *Women in Women's Work: An Exploratory Study of Nurses' Perspectives of Quality Work Environments.* Victoria, British Columbia, Canada: University of Victoria; 1987.
26. Attridge C, Callahan M. Women in women's work: nurses, stress, and power. *Recent Adv Nurs.* 1989;25:41–69.

27. Reverby S. *Ordered to Care: The Dilemma of American Nursing, 1850–1945.* New York, NY: Cambridge University Press; 1987.

28. Palmer IS. From whence we came. In: Chaska N, ed. *The Nursing Profession: A Time to Speak.* New York. NY: McGraw—Hill; 1983.

29. Kelly LY. *Dimensions of Professional Nursing.* 6th ed. New York, NY: Pergamon; 1991.

30. Coburn J. "I see and am silent": a short history of nursing in Ontario, 1850–1930. In: Coburn D, D'Arcy C, Torrance G, eds. *Health and Canadian Society: Sociological Perspectives.* Toronto, Ontario: Fitzhenry & Whiteside; 1981.

31. Code L. Credibility: a double standard. In: Code L, Mullett S, Overall C, eds. *Feminist Perspectives: Philosophical Essays on Method and Morals.* Toronto, Ontario: University of Toronto Press; 1992.

32. Baumgart AJ. Women, nursing, and feminism: an interview with Alice J. Baumgart. *Can Nurse.* 1985;81(1):20–22.

33. Kelly CW. *Dimensions of Professional Nursing.* 2nd ed. New York, NY: Macmillan; 1968.

34. Callan ME. Why NYSNA is leading a campaign to promote the RN. *NYSNA Rep.* 1995;26(1):14.

35. Liaschenko J. Feminist ethics and cultural ethos: revisiting a nursing debate. *ANS.* 1993;15 (4):71–81.

36. Reuther RR. *Sexism and God-talk: Toward a Feminist Theology.* Boston, Mass: Beacon Press; 1983.

37. Bordo S. *Unbearable Weight: Feminism, Western Culture, and the Body.* Los Angeles, Calif: University of California Press; 1993.

38. Bandman EL, Bandman B. *Nursing Ethics Through the Life Span.* Norwalk, Conn: Appleton & Lange; 1990.

39. Benner P. *From Novice to Expert: Excellence and Power in Clinical Nursing Practice.* Menlo Park, Calif: Addison-Wesley; 1984.

40. Griffith HM, Robinson KR. Current procedural terminology (CPT) coded services provided by nurse specialists. *Image J Nurs Schol.* 1993;25(3):178–186.

41. Gibson CH. A concept analysis of empowerment. *J Adv Nurs.* 1991;16:354–361.

42. Chinn PL. *Peace and Power: Creating Community for the Future.* 4th ed. New York, NY: National League for Nursing; 1995.

43. Mayeroff M. *On Caring.* New York, NY: Harper Perennial; 1971.

44. Noddings N. *Caring: A Feminine Approach to Ethics and Moral Education.* Los Angeles, Calif: University of California Press; 1984.

45. Noddings N. Feminist fears in ethics. *J Soc Philosophy.* 1990;21(2):25–36.

46. Carse AL. The "voice of care": implications for bioethical education. *J Med Philosophy.* 1991;16:5–28.

47. Watson J. *Nursing: Human Science and Human Care: A Theory of Nursing.* New York, NY: National League for Nursing; 1988.

48. Kendall J. Fighting back: promoting emancipatory nursing actions. *ANS.* 1992;15(2):1–15.

49. Watson J. New dimensions in human caring theory. *Nurs Sci Q.* 1988;1(4):175–181.

50. Quinn JF. Holding sacred space: the nurse as healing environment. *Holistic Nurs Pract.* 1992;6(4):26.

CHAPTER 4

●●●

Attila the Hun Versus Attila the Hen: Gender Socialization of the American Nurse

SUSAN H. CUMMINGS

From the microcosm of the health care system, gender socialization of the American nurse, 96.4 percent of whom are women,[1] closely parallels the socialization of American women in our society at large. The development of nursing as a predominantly female profession in a physician-oriented health care model mirrors the sex role socialization of women in a male-oriented society.

Gender is really about a society's perceptions of masculine and feminine attributes and behaviors. Gender is "one of the most deeply seated traits of man. We create masculinity and femininity in our ways of behaving, all the while believing we are simply acting normally."[2(p.7)] Socialization is merely the ongoing process by which all of us develop the knowledge, skills, and attitudes that help us fit in society. Sex role or gender socialization is facilitated by the transfer of expectations through family life, educational processes, and the media about how we should behave as males or females.[3] Gender socialization is fostered by (1) messages that are conveyed that gender-appropriate behaviors are different for females and males and (2) parents who interact differently with their sons and daughters, which influences development of gender-specific characteristics.

Ashley[4] describes the hospital as a patriarchal family where nurses' responsibilities encompass all "family" members including patients and physicians. Within this framework, feminine virtues—motherliness, femininity, service, and efficiency—have been valued and perpetuated by society and those providing nursing education. As each of us develops a career, gender socialization impacts our role assignment in society. Sex role socialization may lead to labor market segregation by encouraging males and females to identify sex-appropriate occupations, a phenomenon clearly evident in the history of nursing in America. Societal influences—the impact of nursing education and primary interactions with physicians who are predominantly male—have greatly impacted the gender socialization of women in nursing. The result of these influences has been that nursing is often perceived with less esteem than male-dominated professions.

Reprinted from *Nursing Administration Quarterly*, 1995; 19(2): 19–29, with permission of Aspen Publishers, Inc., 1995.

Societal Roles for Women

Role conceptions of women and women as nurses have been clearly delineated in our society. Cultural mores and mandates have caused the majority of women to react to and, in most instances, comply with societal expectations that reflect gender-specific behaviors. This socialization begins at birth, as evidenced by the fact that infant boys develop and are treated differently than infant girls.[5] The developmental outcome of female socialization in our Western culture has been to prepare women for their primary responsibilities and allegiance to their families, not for success in a career, a more masculine parameter of gender socialization. Traditionally, women have been socialized expecting to be supported financially. They have often viewed nursing as a job with a present focus rather than within a future-oriented frame of reference associated with a career. Men, on the other hand, tend to view a job as a step in a career plan.[6] Within this frame of reference, career and personal goals are seamless for men and separate for women.

Gender-socialized behaviors have also impacted achievement in nursing. Historically, achievement has been considered a male rather than a female behavior.[7] Women have been socialized to support their children and husband's successes while subordinating their own self-interests and success. The dichotomy of this situation is the masculine view of achievement, which focuses on actualization of one's own potential and the pursuit of personal rewards and recognition. This male viewpoint is analogous to the concept of achievement in professional roles,[8] which can create cognitive dissonance for women in nursing who must address both gender and professional socialization issues.

During the Industrial Revolution of the early 1800s women began the transition to roles outside the home. Nursing became a popular form of employment for women, although the word nurse often reflected episodic domestic service within a household rather than care of the sick. Paid nursing was often associated with the role of an older domestic servant.[9] This transition forced the issues of role definition as well as equality as evidenced by the women's suffrage movement that eventually resulted in equality of voting.

Between the end of the 19th century and 1920, women's position and self-image changed. Young women in the 1920s took for granted the ideals for which their grandmothers and mothers had suffered. Both world wars impacted the gender socialization of the American nurse as nurses provided care in battle zones and were expected to be independent, responsible, and accountable. These behaviors were not congruent with role expectations or acceptable behaviors experienced in the employment setting in the United States.

War's Influence

Nursing has often made its greatest strides in connection with wars, especially when progress has been viewed from a historical perspective.[10] Nurses deployed during World War I were removed from their structured practice environments and thrust into an unfamiliar situation with men at war. Many nurses in this environment developed an increased awareness of conflicts between independent nursing practice and the traditional gender socialization of the "good women." War forced nurses to examine the disparity between healing and participation in the war, and gender-based inequality with males in the face of equal danger.

War experiences provoked personal and professional growth. As a result of extensive effort and the enlistment of physician support, legislation was passed in 1920 granting nurses rank in the Army. Achievement of military rank signified that women could begin achieving equality with males in the Armed Forces.[11]

The Second World War brought the American nurse national stature. During World War II a very high percentage of nurses volunteered for military service: 75,000 of 274,405 active RNs.[10] Large sums were being spent training men for national defense but very limited funds were spent to train females who would serve as nurses. Isabel Stewart, one of nursing's most influential spokeswomen for education and Frances Payne Bolton, an Ohio Congresswoman, were instrumental in lobbying for the 1,200,000 dollars of federal funds that were allocated in 1941 to train nurses for national defense.[12]

Military nurses were stationed in approximately 50 nations scattered over the globe on multiple assignments: at the front line; in field, evacuation, and base hospitals; on hospital ships; and in the air. Flight nursing began with air transport for evacuation. Nurses were an integral part of the military structure and, for the most part, were admired and respected. Pay for male and female officers was equal, a marked change in compensation from World War I where men and women of the same rank received disparate compensation.[13]

Gender socialization impacted nurses just as it did during World War I. Nurses functioned autonomously to provide care to the wounded while simultaneously acting as handmaidens to physicians who often had less experience in military medicine than the nurses. A member of the Army Nurse Corps during World War II recalls recommendations related to patient care were not routinely heeded by physicians: as patient advocates, nurses often orchestrated patient care by communicating recommendations for care and requests for orders to physicians whom they knew as friends during night tours of duty.[13] In addition to participating in the war as nurses, women replaced many men in all types of work as they went to battle. Dependence on women's labor changed both men's and women's attitudes about women's work and women's roles.

During the Korean War and the Vietnam War, nurses again played an active part in front line care of the wounded and made tremendous contributions to the development of nursing care delivery of the wounded. Interestingly enough, appointment of men to the Armed Services Nurse Corps received legislative approval in 1966, five years after its initial introduction in 1961. Male and female nurses provided care as equals at the front line.

In summary, war favorably impacted nursing education, the value of nurses, and the development of new techniques and innovations that benefited care of both soldiers and civilians. War did not significantly impact the image of nursing as a predominantly female profession.

Feminist Movement

By the early 1970s, fueled by the feminist movement, more women attended college, and were heads of households. Societal realities legitimized two-income families and began to support women managing careers as well as families. As a result of these changes, traditional views of women were challenged: being female now included work, marriage, childbearing, career, and possibly life as head of a household. A woman's primary alignment to her family now was diluted by sharing varying allegiances.

During this period of changed role expectations for women, the right to control the practice of nursing was constrained by others as well as nurses. Gender socialization of women contributed to problematic differences in physician–nurse relationships. Nursing was still controlled by physicians who spent inordinate energy trying to convince society that nursing's subordination supported meeting the population's health care needs.[4]

The women's movement impacted gender socialization both positively and negatively. The feminist movement certainly raised women's consciousness of their situation as it related to sexual discrimination as well as job opportunities not traditionally associated with women's work. While nurses have gained from its influence, we have experienced great loss as well. The feminist movement enhanced awareness of career opportunities for women and focused on individual choices related to choosing roles; however, nursing has been negatively impacted by those in the feminist movement who omitted nursing as a viable career choice. Muff asks "we know why men view nursing in demeaning stereotypical ways, but how is it that newly conscious women are beginning to do the same?"[14(p.181)]

During the 1970s and into the early 1980s, issues affecting women often appeared on agendas at conventions and in publications. By this time many feminist nurses began to call themselves health activists.[15] Activities of these health activists centered around education, prevention, patient participation, and creating physician–nurse practices. The majority of nurses were not actively involved with feminist agendas and most feminists continued to view nurses as committed to their nurturing, caring activities, which perpetuated their status as second-class citizens. As a result both groups created lose–lose situations: nursing lost opportunities to be seen as a powerful women's group, and feminists lost potential advocates for support of their philosophies and activities.

Nursing Education

Gender socialization of women has been influenced by educational programs and strategies for nursing education. Until the middle of the 20th century, nursing education was provided within the framework of the student nurse as a member of the hospital family. Within this paternalistic framework, society viewed physicians, predominantly men, as being strong and capable of commanding respect and nurses, predominantly women, as being weak. Nurses' strong identification with feminine behaviors detracted from both physicians and society viewing them as educated members of a profession.

Apprenticeship education, a term aptly applied to education within hospital schools of nursing, was considered an appropriate method of facilitating nurses' training so student nurses would continue their traditional gender socialization.[4] The majority of nursing students attended hospital diploma programs. Students lived in the institution, were socialized to be subservient, and labored in the hospital while receiving an education. Nursing was viewed as a lower extension of medical practice in educational programs supported and managed by hospitals. Nursing students provided patient care and supported the physician's needs for assistance as he practiced medicine. Most nursing students worked long hours, learned "on the job," attended limited classes taught by physicians, and received limited clinical supervision, especially when they covered the hospital on weekends, evenings, and nights. Immediate dismissal often followed the slightest deviation from the expected behavior for students. The primary methods of learning were learning by doing and association with members of the staff who facilitated the educational process by informal socialization.[16] Men for the most part were excluded from admission to nursing schools.

Nursing knowledge that was separate from medical knowledge was literally nonexistent. Physicians diagnosed and prescribed treatment while nurses provided the care and administered the ordered medical treatments. All nursing activities were dictated by physicians. Independent nursing orders were nonexistent. Nursing was still controlled by physicians and driven by orders for medical treatment.

Nurses began to recognize that nursing had a broader role in the provision of health care. In the late 1950s instruction of nursing students was subsumed by nursing instructors. Concurrently with the assumption of responsibility for nursing education, nurses began to define a broader role for nursing with less emphasis on assisting physicians. Increased numbers of baccalaureate programs moved education for nurses into universities. Education in sciences and liberal arts provided opportunities for socialization outside of the limited confines of feminine gender socialization.

Initially, however, the apprenticeship model of education continued in clinical nursing courses. Students were filled with fear, took few risks, were dependent on physicians, and were reluctant to be self-directed or accountable.[17] Dependency was also supported by nursing instructor–student interactions and clinical experiences where hospital personnel, not instructors, controlled the learning environment. The split between those nurses who educated and those nurses who provided service was very evident. This ongoing split has begun to close with the initiation of joint endeavors that have resulted in effective partnerships between those in academic and service settings. Nurses still have much work to accomplish related to resolving the perceived dichotomy between education and service, theory and practice, thinking and doing as perceived by society as well as our profession.

Nursing Role and Practice Changes

Changes in nursing practice reflected changes in medical care and hospital management. Between 1953 and 1979 medical specialization was supported by changing technology, and the hospital industry grew into being managed as a business. Growth of the hospital industry was supported by research, dissemination of health insurance, and increased governmental support for health care. These changes resulted in supporting the emergence of more quality-oriented patient care. Specialization of medical practice developed as a result of changing technology. Transformation of nursing knowledge and nursing role functions was directly related to the transformation of medicine. Medicine's complexity made it impossible for physicians to continue to dominate the health care system. Nursing practice became more specialized and nurses began to assume responsibilities previously belonging to physicians, including analysis of cardiac rhythms and monitoring protocols. Nurses learned to be effective in caring for patients with new technology by observing and doing rather than formal continuing education.

During the late 1960s and early 1970s nurses, especially those with college preparation, assumed more responsibility for patient care and began planning nursing care as separate from medical care. The concepts of nursing as a separate discipline with a defined knowledge base and theory base were introduced into education. Nursing education, which was provided in community colleges, colleges, and universities as well as hospital diploma programs, provided opportunities for entry level as well as advanced education. The transition from diploma education to education in colleges and universities not only facilitated the development of nursing as a profession but also facilitated the development of individual nurses as educated, more empowered members of a profession. Nursing roles began to slowly change to less subservient and slightly more independent roles.

Clinical nurse specialist and nurse practitioner roles were initiated during this period, which facilitated additional independence in the practice of nursing. Nurses in these advanced practice roles are often the only caregivers who can incorporate caring, curing, and the management functions associated with the provision of quality, cost-effective health care. As these roles have evolved, nurses have become more specialized in the content focus of their practice and more generalized in their role functions. Professional nurse case managers and advanced practice nurses in clinical nurse specialist, nurse practitioner, nurse midwife, and certified RN anesthetist roles have begun to create partnerships with physicians as equals rather than subordinates. Despite the dissonance between nurses and physicians at a national level, nurses and physicians at the point of service have been working well together.[18]

Frustrations of being a woman in a male-dominated health care system are at times overwhelming. Male physicians and hospital administrators often continue to act in paternalistic ways. For many nurses the Physician–Nurse game[19] still continues. In spite of changes in education, in practice societal attitudes toward women and women as nurses have not changed substantially.

Media Images

Novels, movies, and television have continually focused on the glamour and romance of nursing as well as stereotyped images of nurses including handmaidens, battle-axes, ministering angels, women in white, nurses as ignorant or dumb, and most commonly, nurses as women.[20] Soap operas have portrayed nurses as beautiful sex objects whose sole purpose has been to provide service to physicians. These images, for the most part, have not positively impacted the population's views about how nurses behave.

Newspapers and magazines have tended to portray nurses more realistically. Nurses have not always used media to their best advantage. Media can positively support nursing. During 1990 nursing launched an image campaign that resulted in increased nursing school enrollments and enhanced opportunities for nurses.[18] Creating new realistic images of nursing, especially as nursing roles continue to evolve in an era of health care reform, will focus on (1) enhancing nurses' self-awareness, (2) actively dispelling stereotypes, and (3) positively using media to communicate about nurses and nursing.

Power and Politics

Power is a critical concept when discussing ramifications of gender socialization, as it is played out in same-gender and cross-gender relationships in health care settings. Women have learned in their roles as females, wives, and mothers to serve as a resource and support to those around them. By facilitating others' successes, women have been respected and consulted. Most men, however, have been socialized to relate to others in terms of rank and status. Families have taught females submission as opposed to dominance. Women have been socialized to believe their success is contingent on associations with power figures rather than by establishing their own power base, and by being competitive with each other for male attention rather than supporting each other.[21]

The perpetuation of the myth and reality of women's subordination to men as played out in doctor–nurse and administrator–nurse relationships—coupled with the influence of gender socialization in a society that places the value of men's work over women's—has led to less status and power for nurses, especially those who are women. As a result of gender socialization, nurses may enter power systems in health care organizations with handicaps, a potential disadvantage when one considers that by the beginning of the next century most RNs will assume leadership positions either in traditional roles or those yet to be defined at the point of service.

Power and politics are critical issues when discussing sex-role stereotypes. Feminists tell us that when the balance of power is distorted between sexes, we must ask the question "who benefits?"[22(p.40)] The majority of women in nursing have limited or no experience in roles with people working for or with them. Kanter[23] identifies two stereotypes that block women's access to power in organizations: (1) no one wants to work for them and (2) they are too bossy and controlling. Once in leadership roles women often do not support and can even be destructive to other females. Women in these roles often develop a pecking order as a power hierarchy in which they now have perceived control over others. Commonly accepted sex-role stereotypes of women include mother, iron maiden, and superwoman. Women may assume these roles unconsciously, as a result of observing women in these sex-stereotyped roles. Obviously these roles can impede attainment of personal and organizational outcomes in health care organizations, especially when they block the effective use of power and a woman's leadership potential. (See Box 4-1, "Common Sex-Role Stereotypes of Women.")

Men in nursing also cope with sex-role stereotyping in their roles as nurses. Rallis, a male student nurse, tells us how he was not prepared for how people feel about roles carried out by those of the "wrong sex."[24] He learned while conducting informal interviews about nursing with people in a shopping center that while most women approved of men being nurses, men strongly disapproved. Women perceived men as capable of being nurturing, caring nurses while the majority of men did not. Some interviewees were hostile and many assumed male nurses were homosexuals. Rallis aptly continues to remind us that it is time for all nurses to publicly recognize men as nurses and to acknowledge their contributions to nursing.[24]

Gender differences related to power are very apparent in today's health care organizations. Power is described in traditional organizations by adjectives such as control, self-reliant, secure, capable, and risk taker, while in empowered organizations power is described as delegation, sharing information, coaching, trust, and creating learning environments. McCarthy tells us that understanding the family power system that we were socialized in is relevant to our behavior within hospitals.[25] Most traditional health care organizations have been organized and managed just as families. Males within the hospital "family" traditionally have been socialized to issue orders, assign tasks, and provide a sense of direction. Females have been socialized in traditional health care settings to suggest and question rather than directly verbalizing ideas and then taking actions. Within these situations women who do not act out appropriately sanctioned roles within the organization are often attacked personally, rather than for the ideas they have presented.

The family model lends insight into the use of power by female nurses. Power, for the purpose of this discussion, is defined as the ability to accomplish tasks, mobilize resources, and utilize them to attain outcomes.[26] In our society the gender socialization of nurses, the majority of whom are women, is predicated on the premise that passivity rather than the acquisition of power is key to success, and that power is derived from personal attributes rather than accomplishments. In addition, nurses in traditional organizations who have acquired power through subversive styles may feel insecure in power positions and rarely role model positive behaviors or facilitate empowerment or development of their subordinates.

Power is used effectively in today's health care settings when those in leadership roles share power and resources, are people oriented, and build interdependent relationships that reflect the positive aspects of the gender socialization of women. Women who effec-

---

BOX 4–1 COMMON SEX-ROLE STEREOTYPES OF WOMEN

Mother
- subrogates own needs
- freely gives advice
- becomes the peacemaker
- fosters dependence
- is passive, wants recognition

Iron Maiden
- is competitive vs. collaborative
- possesses the ability to "be in charge"
- gives critical feedback
- sets rigid interpersonal boundaries
- can be unapproachable

Superwoman
- demands perfection
- won't delegate
- overcommits her time
- assumes multiple roles
- feels isolated, not supported

tively use power in health care settings recognize their innate abilities that support the effective use of power in transformed organizations. Nurse leaders who are women have learned that merely empowering others enhances one's personal power, a concept critical to individual and organizational success.

A behavioral dichotomy exists, however, as female nurses often see themselves as victims with low status and power who in turn become aggressive with each other. Ashley reminds us "women nurses are women first."[27(p.3)] Female nurses must support each other to reinforce both personal and professional competence, effectiveness, and power. Power may not be used effectively by women since its use often does not reflect learned behaviors acquired during the gender socialization process both within their patriarchal families and health care organizations.

Organizational power and politics are closely associated with each other. Kalish and Kalish[28] cite that nurses do not usually have time, energy or resources, or the will to move into active roles in either government or the workplace that involve development of positive political behaviors. All of us know from our personal experiences or observations that political behavior has both positive and deleterious effects within an organization. Politics is really about the use of power in competitive situations that involve resource availability and allocation. Group and self-interests are promoted by use of power and politics in these situations. Political behaviors often focus on building superiority and dominance, gaining support to enhance a power base, communicating or withholding information, stockpiling resources, creating obligations, and knowing the real locus of power. Men usually exhibit a greater degree of political astuteness as a result of their gender socialization related to competition and conflict resolution. Knowledge of who has real versus perceived power, formal as well as informal communication pathways, information sources, and support networks is vital to understanding and playing the political game in organizations.

Men in Nursing

Approximately 4 percent of nurses are men and that number does not appear to be increasing. During the 1970s nursing attempted to recruit male nursing students. One wonders if this recruitment was reflective of society's changing perceptions related to gender-specific occupational roles or whether nursing perceived the need for men to assume leadership positions, thereby regaining the power and status of the profession.[29]

Men in nursing often experience role strain while attempting to reconcile gender and occupational roles. Gendering of occupations is clearly evident in health care as the majority of physicians are male and the majority of nurses are female. Assumptions about gender have long been built into both of these health care professions. Williams cites that those who "cross over" upset gender assumptions associated with their work.[30] Male nurses are often suspected of not being masculine. Men in these roles often dissociate themselves from their female colleagues and accentuate their masculinity.[31] Society is only now beginning to realize that men as well as women can very successfully fulfill the nursing role.

Gender socialization has impacted men in nursing not only in practice but in their educational experiences as well. Female nurses have set men apart from women as nurses by the expectations that men will lift patients, transfer patients, and assist with male procedures. Men have been excluded from informal socialization activities on the patient care unit.[31] Men had limited opportunities to enter nursing prior to World War II. In 1941 only 68 of the 1,303 schools of nursing accepted men and four only accepted men.[32] Many schools trained men as psychiatric nurses. After the war the numbers of male nursing students increased, in part due to GI bills that financially supported education.[33]

Men are still definitely in the minority in educational programs for nursing. Most nursing instructors are enthusiastic about male students, and most male students often comment that they receive preferential treatment in educational programs.[34] Working as a male in nursing has both advantages and drawbacks. As society begins to challenge gender-specific occupations, hopefully the realization of limitless opportunities for both men and women in nursing will be realized.

Opportunities for Change

What is the next step in gender socialization? Perhaps the ideal situation in health care organizations is the creation of an archetype that supports choosing individual behaviors from those accepted as gender-specific, either male or female, that best fit a situation. Assumptions underlying this idea are (1) men and women have been socialized differently and (2) they can learn from each other. Our future success as nurses will not be determined by whether we are masculine or feminine but by our ability to blend styles and create a balance of our values. Individuals who develop a style that includes behavioral responses not usually associated with their gender socialization may act in ways that are more creative, flexible, integrative, and spontaneous. This concept is not new to nursing. Nurses who are males already role model these behaviors when they express both the nurturing and caring aspects of the nursing role as well as behaviors traditionally ascribed to men.[35]

Success in today's health care environment is not about maleness and femaleness but about who has the needed knowledge and skills and who can use them most effectively and efficiently. Individual success will be predicated on making choices about the influences and expectations created by our gender socialization as well as respecting our individual differences and using them synergistically. Developing effective behaviors irrespective of our sex role socialization could enhance our effectiveness as health care providers.

History provides a sense of continuity and connection between the past and the present. Traditional roles need not become self-fulfilling prophecies if we as nurses can learn to bridge the gap of our gender socialization. The question remains: How do we utilize our gender socialization and differences as we prepare to begin the next century in nursing?

Capitalizing on our strengths related to our own gender socialization and differences will be key to the success of nursing in the next century. Male and female talent in nursing has remained untapped due to gender socialization and resultant gender stereotyping. Our future successes may well be dictated by blending styles and creating a seamlessness within all roles in our personal and professional lives.

Today's health care organizations demand highly responsible individuals who can provide care as autonomous individuals and as team members. Eleanor Peterson, who is not a nurse, when commenting on gender socialization during a team-building leadership development experience, tells us "We are all victims of course, men and women alike because instead of learning new skills and new ways to work together, we all just repeated old roles in an old authoritarian world. . . . You can't bring about change politely. You have to be tough. . . ."[36(p.80)] Gender socialization in nursing has been an evolving process and really reflects our collective history as individuals. Creating new images will be a difficult process. It is time to break out of old molds and meld characteristics of gender socialization in our culture as we move into the 21st century.

REFERENCES

1. American Nurses' Association. *Facts About Nursing* 84–85. Kansas City, Mo.: ANA, 1985.
2. Goffman, E. *Gender Displays in Gender Advertisements.* New York, N.Y.: Harper & Row, 1977.
3. Marini, M., and Brinton, M. "Sex Typing in Occupational Socialization," In *Sex Segregation in the Workplace: Trends, Explanation, Remedies,* edited by B. Raskin. Washington, D.C.: National Academy Press, 1984.

4. Ashley, J.A. *Hospitals, Paternalism and the Role of the Nurse.* New York, N.Y.: Teachers College Press, 1977.

5. Grissom, M., and Spengler, C. *Women Power and Health Care.* Boston, Mass.: Little, Brown, 1976.

6. Kooker, M.B. "The Corporate Image of the Nurse Executive." *Nursing Management* 17, no. 2(1990):52–55.

7. Feather, N.T., and Simon, J.G. "Stereotypes About Male and Female Success and Failure in Sex Linked Occupations." *Journal of Personality* 44 (1976):16–20.

8. Epstein, C.F. *Women's Place in Professional Careers.* Berkeley, Calif.: University of California Press, 1970.

9. Reverby, S. *Ordered to Care.* Cambridge, Mass.: Cambridge University Press, 1987.

10. Donahue, M.P. *Nursing, the Finest Art.* St. Louis, Mo.: Mosby, 1985.

11. Beeber, L. "To Be One of the Boys, Aftershocks of the World War I Nursing Experience." *Advances in Nursing Science* 12, no. 4 (1990):32–43.

12. Stewart, I.M. *The Education of Nurses.* New York, N.Y.: MacMillan, 1943.

13. Thompson O., R.N. United States Army Nurse Corps (retired), personal communication.

14. Muff, J. "Why Doesn't a Smart Girl Like You Go to Medical School." In *Socialization, Sexism and Stereotyping: Women's Issues in Nursing,* edited by J. Muff. Prospect Heights, Ill.: Waveland Press, 1982.

15. Kosiba, M.A. "Identity as a Profession: An Interpretive History of Nursing's Efforts at Professionalism." Ed.D. diss., Rutgers, The State University of New Jersey, New Brunswick, 1990.

16. Bollough, V., and Bollough, B. *History, Trends, and Politics of Nursing.* Norwalk, Conn: Appleton–Century-Crofts, 1984.

17. deTourneyay, R. "Two Views on the Latest Health Manpower Issue: Expanding the Nurse's Role Does Not Make Her a Physician's Assistant." *American Journal of Nursing* 7 (1971):974.

18. Curtin, L. "25 Years: A Slightly Irreverent Retrospective." *Nursing Management* 25, no. 6 (1994):9–11, 14, 16, 18, 22, 24, 226–28, 232.

19. Stein, L. "The Doctor-Nurse Game." *Archives of General Psychiatry* 16 (1967):699–703.

20. Muff, J. "Handmaiden, Battle Axe, Whore: An Exploration into the Fantasies, Myths, and Stereotypes About Nurses." In *Socialization, Sexism and Stereotyping: Women's Issues in Nursing,* edited by J. Muff. Prospect Heights, Ill.: Waveland Press, 1982.

21. McCarthy, J.F. "Power is a Nursing Issue." In *Socialization, Sexism and Stereotyping: Women's Issues in Nursing,* edited by J. Muff. Prospect Heights, Ill.: Waveland Press, 1982.

22. La Bella, A., and Leach, D. *Personal Power.* Boulder, Colo.: Newview Press, 1977.

23. Kanter, R.M. *Men and Women of the Corporation.* New York, N.Y.: Basic Books, 1977.

24. Rallis, R. "I Want to be a Nurse, Not a Stereotype." *RN* 53, no. 4 (1990):160.

25. McCarthy, J.F. "Power is a Nursing Issue" In *Socialization, Sexism and Stereotyping: Women's Issues in Nursing,* edited by J. Muff. Prospect Heights, Ill.: Waveland Press, 1982.

26. Swingle, P.F. *The Management of Power.* New York, N.Y.: Halsted Press, 1976.

27. Ashley, J. "Power is Structured Misogyny: Implications for the Politics of Care." *Advances in Nursing Science* 2, no. 3 (1980):3.

28. Kalish, B.J., and Kalish, P.A. "A Discourse on the Politics of Nursing." *Journal of Nursing Administration* 26, no. 7 (1978):468.

29. Flanagan, M. "An Analysis of Nursing as a Career." In *Socialization, Sexism and Stereotyping: Women's Issues in Nursing,* edited by J. Muff. Prospect Heights, Ill.: Waveland Press, 1982.

30. William, C. *Doing Women's Work: Men in Non-Traditional Occupations.* Newberry Park, Calif.: Sage Publications, 1993.

31. Williams, C. *Gender Differences at Work.* Berkeley, Calif.: University of California Press, 1989.

32. American Nurses' Association. *ANA Facts About Nursing.* Kansas City, Mo.: ANA, 1950.

33. Roberts, M. *American Nursing: History and Interpretation.* New York, N.Y.: MacMillan, 1954.

34. Brookfield, G., et al. "Some Thoughts on Being a Male in Nursing." In *Socialization, Sexism and Stereotyping: Women's Issues in Nursing,* edited by J. Muff. Prospect Heights, Ill.: Waveland Press, 1982.

35. Dean, P.G. "Toward Androgyny." *Image* 10, no 1 (1977):10.

36. Strank, R. "Two Women, Three Men on a Raft." *Harvard Business Review* 72, no. 3 (1994):68–80.

CHAPTER 5

●●●

Reverse Discrimination in Nursing Leadership: Hitting the Concrete Ceiling

TIM PORTER-O'GRADY

In a time when great strides in equality and the strengthening of the value of the role of women in society have become a social priority, it is untenable to believe that there is a subtle but clearly present inequity within the ranks of the largest group of professional women in the country. Role perceptions and expectations of men in nursing by women do nothing to dispel this condition; indeed in many ways they facilitate it.

It would be inaccurate to suggest that this discrimination is intentional. Like most conditions of its kind it is quiet, unspoken, and insidious. Instead of being visually present in the consciousness of its holders, it lies just beneath the surface of the public persona of the discipline where it operates with impunity, garnering very little attention.[1]

Foundations of Reverse Discrimination

The sources of reverse discrimination arise out of the same conditions as does frank discrimination. Dependence, inequity, jealously guarded power, internal competitiveness, and the maintenance of a relatively low position on the social hierarchy all drive the syndrome.[2] When such factors exist in relationship to a specified group, they are enhanced within the group and also operate between the members of the group. When the opportunity to play out the behaviors of oppression on those that best symbolize the oppressors is presented, there is very little that can prevent internal oppressive behaviors from emerging.

The seven conditions that support this behavior are both classic and historic. They represent the foundations upon which the behaviors of discrimination build in nursing:

1. Living in the reflection of a subordinating group such as medicine where it is socially presumed that physicians provide the context and the parameters of behavior for nurses substantiates second-class citizenship.

Reprinted from *Nursing Administration Quarterly,* 1995;19(2):56–62, with permission of Aspen Publishers, Inc., © 1995.

2. The restrictive licensing of nurses and the permissive licensing of physicians reinforce the limitations on the nursing discipline and its comparative narrowness of clinical judgment and functional activity.

3. The wide range in economic value of other major disciplines and that of nurses reinforces the limited value attached to the role of the nurse.

4. The traditionally held view that nursing is "women's work," referring to the subordinating, delegated, clean up ritualism of the work of nursing, which retains a focus of mindless functionalism that belies intelligence.

5. The relative difference in the socioeconomic membership in nursing as compared to medicine indicates a "class difference" between the disciplines, resulting in a different characterization of its members and their role in decision making.

6. A variety of entry points into the profession, which do not correlate with other major disciplines, suggests that the content of education of nurses is not substantive and therefore of questionable comparative value to other more "rigorous" or eminent disciplines.

7. The lack of cohesion, collaboration, integration, and single-mindedness in the nursing profession reinforces the notions of separateness, competition, mistrust, and directionlessness that make its members easily manipulated and politically naive.

These above factors are present at varying levels of intensity between any and all members of the nursing profession. Men do not experience these conditions any more broadly than do women nurses. The weight of them, though, is more acutely identified by men in nursing than it is by their women colleagues. It happens simply because men can see the conditions' masculine origins. They cannot cope with the very male oppressiveness with which men burden women. Instead it is now directed at them out of the very masculine paradigm that they themselves emulate. It is, in fact, being discriminated against on two fronts: by one's own kind (ie, other men) and also by members of one's own profession (ie, women). Indeed the rules of relationship for men nurses are fraught with gender difficulties that often don't get enumerated. This is especially true in leadership roles.

Gender Bias and Leadership

It is expected, indeed reinforced, that men will ultimately choose to assume leadership roles in nursing.[3] The expectation is reaffirmed by the notion that there is something "wrong or suspicious" regarding the man who appreciates and resonates with rendering good patient care and ascribes to no other ambition. Even here there are degrees of acceptability with regard to the man's role. If the man works in high technology or in high intensity or acuity areas, he is looked at with more acceptability than a man who prefers the more relational or continuum roles of medical-surgical or psychiatric nursing.

However, even for the man who may aspire to administrative or leadership roles, there is a sort of schizophrenia in the support of him. While it is assumed to be appropriate for a man to move in the direction of management roles, any success in the venture is frequently attributed to the fact that he is a man and that he is somehow advantaged because he is. There is at times even a tacit indication that the fact that he does well in the role operates to the disadvantage of the women he may supervise. It is in essence a tale twice told: first, fulfilling the "natural" role for a man and in doing so automatically disabling women who may be managed by that man. Second, women are disenfranchised because the man holds the leadership position and by holding it, prevents an equally qualified woman from obtaining it, thus tacitly reinforcing a root cause of gender inequity.

This reality also plays out in the politics of the profession. It is very challenging for men to break into what could be irreverently called the "old girls club." Everyone knows how rarefied and sanctified the "old boys club" is and how exclusionary it is to women and other "undesirables." The experience also operates in reverse with just as much intensity in nursing. What makes it especially insidious is that there is no indication or intent verbalized or acknowledged by nurses to want to be exclusionary. It is simply that men do not come to mind when specific roles in leadership are available or national offices and special leadership opportunities for nurses arise. Even when the individual has made himself clearly available for such opportunities, the calls never come from those who are aware of the availability. This argument is not to suggest that there are no men in such positions. Each one, however, can tell a story of the odds, including the effort necessary to make that happen at a level of intensity not necessary for a woman under the same circumstances within nursing.

There are also occasions of tokenism that often appear in the arraying of certain work groups, task forces, or other gatherings where it would be beneficial to be able to point out the inclusiveness and the diversity of members of the profession. Men, much like the reverse where it applies to women, are included in nursing groups when it is apparent that to have a male presence is in the best visual or political interests for the group or for nursing.

The expectations of men and the problems those expectations create for men who are nurses are problematic for the discipline. In Great Britain, the expectation that men provide leadership has placed men in those positions at the great expense of women in those same roles. Only 10 percent of the nurses in England are men, yet they hold 50 percent of the leadership positions in the country. That is clear evidence that role expectations simply create an untenable set of circumstances that are difficult to break. While not quite that critical in the United States, men hold leadership positions in a greater disproportion to the number of men in the ranks of nursing.

There is a potent, hidden disadvantage to the gender favoring of men in leadership roles and that relates to the use of the masculine paradigm for decision making and for constructing responses to the need for changes in the role and use of nurses in the service setting. The tendency toward much more male-based linear techniques of decision making belies a greater need for the more feminine and appropriate meta techniques for relationship building and for making decisions. Masculinizing one more arena of health care will certainly advantage no one in the provision of health services; presuming that men are more natural at management roles does nothing but facilitate masculine notions and techniques of leadership in the workplace.

At the same time, gender bias can disadvantage decision making when the contribution of men cannot be included in significant deliberations of policy, economics, and resource use, among other topics. In the current effort at constructing meaningful health care reform, there has been a noticeable paucity of men who are nurses testifying on behalf of nursing and contributing to the conceptual shift regarding who is a nurse in the minds of legislators and policy makers.

As in all discussion regarding bias of any kind, it is hard to make a clear and cogent argument that enumerates without doubt the kind and intensity of the bias. Rather than being a clarion bell that rings for all to hear, bias is a muffled grunt that emanates from the discriminated in a wholly undifferentiated way. Since it is often so dispersed, it is hard to recognize and obtain acknowledgment so that it can be addressed directly. It is often not readily apparent even to the one discriminated against until some time later, when further thought indicates that usual circumstances don't appear to justify some exclusionary event or being barred from a role to which everyone would recognize the individual has a great deal to contribute.

Addressing Reverse Gender Bias

It must be pointed out that the profession of nursing is in a transition from one kind of reality to another. The changes in the profession, especially related to role, parallel the signposts of the women's movement. As women become more equitably related to social institutions, there is a disproportionate emphasis on enhancing opportunity for women. This is especially significant when the normative fallout for such an undertaking is somewhat disadvantaging to men. This, of course, is not just true for nursing but for all of the places where women have been actively seeking equal opportunity. It often appears that equity suffers as a result and that some of what ensues doesn't necessarily feel fair, especially to the person who was constrained by the effort.

The challenge for men in nursing is to recognize the eventuality of gender bias. While the majority of both men and women would like to believe it just isn't so, that would be naive. On the other hand, it would be of no benefit to the individual or the profession to look for gender bias in all the circumstances of one's career pathway. Therefore, certain expectations related to the possibility of gender discrimination should be attended to and should challenge the man who is a nurse to quickly follow through with an appropriate response. These four expectations include the following:

1. Gender bias is often situational. If a situation or circumstance does not feel right and something appears untenable or disadvantageous, the individual should follow up with questions related to the circumstances or situation until some clarity is established to the point of satisfaction.

2. If the bias is clear and certain, it should not be left unaddressed. If not dealt with, it is quickly repeated. Injustice and unequivocal exclusion is inappropriate if not illegal and the offended party should not fail to take action.

3. Anticipate the possibility of gender-related issues arising in the workplace. Sponsor or teach a program on gender bias with a segment that deals with male recipient discrimination so that it is made conscious and people can visualize their own actions related to the discriminatory practice with which they might most be out of touch.

4. Clearly identify personal expectations in relationships with others. Let them know your sensitivity to the issue and the arenas where you most expect to be included so that they are aware of what skill or contribution might be made by you to the group and its work.

Men often come into the profession with expectations that the relationships that they established in more male-dominated fields of pursuit can prevail in a female-dominated work arena. Nothing could be further from the truth. The behavioral patterns in a predominantly female work milieu are not the same as in male-dominated environments. Learning that lesson early in one's career can help the man who is a nurse navigate what could otherwise be a wholly negative adventure. The following five realities might be helpful to incorporate into the mixed-gender work profile:

1. Women value personal interactions and a higher intensity of communication than is often evident in male-dominated work environments. What might appear as normative interaction in a primarily female work environment may seem excessive communication in many male-controlled situations.

2. Men are historically less in touch with how they feel than with what they think. This does not suggest women think less. However, communication is more often expressive than emotionless as in many male-dominated environments. There is

often more interest in what an event or situation means than in a simply dispassionate recreation of the events as so often happens with men. Awareness of the impact of a statement or a behavior is as important in gender-mixed environments as might be the naked truth of the act or situation.

3. Traditional sociological development has led men to be quite comfortable with individual or collective competition. While competition may be just as evident among women, it is more subtle and less overt. Just as intense in female environments, competition may not be specific or clear enough for some to visualize its presence. In such an environment the outcomes of aggressive or negative competition may often result before one knows what was going on and just how it happened. The more naive persons could pay a heavy price for their lack of awareness.

4. As in any environment, there may be those with a heavy dose of gender-based anger. For a host of reasons, these individuals seek opportunities to play out their anger on hapless and unprepared members of the opposite gender in an effort to make them feel as uncomfortable as the biased person does with herself or himself. "Taking them on" in kind may be an overwhelming urge on the part of the recipient of such anger but that response rarely succeeds. Unless one feels the same intensity of genuine anger, that person is totally outmaneuvered and can simply exacerbate an already untenable situation.

5. Sexual innuendo and sex-based jokes of any kind always stimulate gender-related discomfort. The content of the joke may well be harmless. However, when the workplace depends on mutuality, colleagueship, and equity in relationships, the introduction of sexual content may change the character of the interaction, relationship, and milieu. This, then, creates a new framework for interacting into the workplace and can lead to conversations, actions, or relationships that do not reflect the appropriate character of a gender-integrated workplace.

Some Counsel for Women

A great deal of gender bias or discrimination can be eliminated by some simple evidence of role and relational sensitivity. Awareness and behavioral adjustment critically influence the kind of milieu in which men and women work together. Opportunities for the minority group can be facilitated by asking a set of simple questions in considering activities which should be undertaken by a cross section of those who make up the membership of the discipline. These seven questions are as follows:

1. In attempting to be inclusive in forming leadership or work groups have you considered men nurses as a minority that should be recommended for leadership roles?

2. When opportunities for advancement are being considered, do you equitably look at the roles of all the players, including men, as you put together the potential leadership agenda?

3. Do you assess your own feelings about men in general when assessing the character of your relationship with them so that you can manage those parts of your bias that might be impediments to an effective relationship?

4. Is there evidence that opportunity in the organization is not gender specific and is inclusive, and evidences representation from the full range of providers in the setting?

5. Has a mechanism been created that provides an opportunity to deal with gender bias and identify situations where it has been expressed so that it can be dealt with in a way that satisfies the situation and raises consciousness in the organization?

6. Are there identifiable leadership cliques in the organization that indicate a need for a "special" relationship in order to advance in the organization, which effectively eliminates all opportunity for growth or advancement unless one is subordinated to the prevailing "old boys" or "old girls" network?

7. Does the leadership of the organization encourage and facilitate cultural diversity and programs that increase, specifically, the kind and number of nurses on important decision-making bodies in health care?

Answers to the above questions can serve to effectively evaluate the kind and quality of relationships that exist in the place you work. While there are changing realities with a newer impact on the workplace, there will be growing diversity both in gender and in culture. Old practices that limit opportunity for others based on any single factor not related to competence will be increasingly unsuccessful. However, the opportunity to be subtle in one's practices never really disappears.

The challenge raised here relates to gender-specific activities, some of which exist in the most puzzling and insidious ways. The challenge to women in predominantly female environments sounds the same as must exist in any other work context. Increasing sensitivity to individual interactions and relationships with men can often help clarify and reduce any exclusions that might result from not addressing them at all.

Inclusiveness does demand some conscious work with regard to what it means to be inclusive. In nursing it is less than "natural" to think of men when enumerating opportunities for political, organizational, or social advantage or opportunity. One must cognitively acknowledge the need to be inclusive toward men in nursing just as is required with regard to any minority group. The richness and creativity of the contribution to the discipline and the delivery of health care can be enhanced through cultural and social diversity. In the case of nursing, that richness results from including men and effectively removing any impediments in the way of their using the many talents and contributions they have to continue to build an exciting and dynamic profession.

REFERENCES

1. Faludi, S. *Backlash: The Undeclared War Against American Women.* New York, N.Y.: Crown Publishers, 1991.
2. Woods, J., and Lucas, J. *The Corporate Closet.* New York, N.Y.: Free Press, 1993.
3. Ryan, S., and Porter, S. "Men In Nursing: A Cautionary Comparative Critique." *Nursing Outlook* 41, no. 6 (1993):262–267.

QUESTIONS TO PART I

. . . .

1. What do you think accounts for the differences in the way patients perceive caring and the way in which nurses perceive caring?
2. Discuss the merits of the Lazarus model of coping as it relates to your nursing practice.
3. Discuss the notion of "empowered caring" and its basic principles. How do you see it being demonstrated in your work setting?
4. Compare and contrast "ordered caring," "assimilated caring," and "empowered caring." Use situations from your own work setting to illustrate your points.
5. In describing your own professional behavior, do you align yourself with Attila the Hun or Attila the Hen? Explain.
6. To what extent has your nursing education supported "Hun" or "Hen" behavior?
7. What common sex role stereotypes do you demonstrate (if any) in your professional practice? What advantages or disadvantages have you noted?
8. How would you improve the gender socialization of both women and men in nursing?
9. In what ways have you seen men discriminated against in nursing?
10. What are your biases (if any) about men in nursing?

PART II

●●●

Leadership: Theories and Attributes

Leadership happens—not by chance, but by choice. Each time we exercise leadership, we set into motion the conscious and deliberate decision to act. Each and every day we consciously act for the benefit of our patients, and those everyday acts help make things happen for them. This is what we know how to do, and do well. But exercising leadership in a wider arena is a different story. In the organizational arena of political game playing, turf protection, and professional survival, exercising leadership is more precarious. In an organizational climate saturated with questionable alliances, dubious loyalties, and mercurial change, leadership is a philosophical orphan.

Leadership is not easy. Leadership means standing for something when standing for something is most difficult. Leadership is risk taking when playing it safe is the norm. Leadership is about conscious choices and conscious acts, because they are the right choices and the right acts. Leadership is about foresight, courage, and hope, when hindsight, timidity, and pessimism prevail. With each act of leadership we are rehearsing for our future—a future based on the conscious choice to act and go forward rather than sitting on the sidelines as bystanders, watching, wondering, and wailing about our fate. Leadership thrives when nurses choose to come together, share their beliefs, and work together for a common cause: to make their vision of the future a reality.

The readings in Part II explore the universal nature of leadership and the choices nurses have in creating their leadership roles. In the readings that follow, the holistic nature of leadership is examined as a philosophical ideology. The dimensions of transformational leadership are elaborated upon, particularly those that are relevant for nurses in today's postmodern society, as are the ethical dimensions of transformational leadership which nurses must consider in their work settings. The concluding portion of Part II focuses on the investigation of leadership styles, the behaviors of nurses in leadership roles, and their contribution to and impact on the health care environment.

CHAPTER 6

●●

The Art of Legendary Leadership

CLAIRE MANFREDI

Leadership has been a topic of interest in our society and the subject of numerous studies, particularly over the last half of the 20th century. Bass (1990) observes that there are almost as many different definitions of leadership as there are persons who have attempted to define the concept, and acknowledges over 7,500 research studies, papers, and monographs on this topic (p. xv). Over the years, leadership has been defined in terms of traits, personalities, situations, tasks, roles, power, positions, interactions, perceptions, group process, and followership (Manfredi & Valiga, 1994).

Leadership is a "universal phenomenon in humans and in many species of animals" (Bass, 1990, p. 4). How one gains an understanding of the complexities of leadership is a question often posed by those who have undertaken the task of examining the concept and communicating the process to others.

Legendary tales have been handed down from generation to generation and serve a useful role in our society. They represent accepted beliefs, values, and attitudes that give a people identity (Cavendish, 1982). They often serve as raw material for scholarly discourse in a variety of disciplines (Ashliman, 1987), and provide valuable insights into human nature and our understanding of complex phenomena. It was with this purpose in mind that the writer created the leadership legend that follows. This legend was constructed to serve as a catalyst for new and aspiring leaders as they examine and consider the complexities of leadership and prepare for leadership roles in the future.

Once upon a time, centuries ago in a tiny village far away, the Mayor who had served as the leader of the village for many years, passed away. Shortly after the burial, the town elders gathered to discuss the selection of a successor. A call went out to all of the residents in the village for volunteers to succeed the village leader. After a period of time, three candidates came forward. Since there was no job description and there were no selection criteria, the Council of Elders decided to test the leadership of the candidates by placing them in charge of the village for a period of 1 month. The candidate who was accepted by the residents and successful in leading the village for 1 month would be appointed the new leader of the village. And so the selection process began.

Candidate #1 believed that the best way to lead a village was to keep the village stable, so the word *change* was deleted from the language. The village motto became: "No need to grow; support the status quo." At the end of the month, the residents were so

Reprinted from *Nursing Leadership Forum,* 1 (2), 62–64, Summer, 1995. Used with permission of Springer Publishing Company Inc., © 1995.

bored and disenchanted they developed their own motto: "Candidate #1 must go; and so must the status quo."

Candidate #2 believed that one must create structure in order to lead. So rules were written and regulations were drafted. Unfortunately, Candidate #2 believed that rules were made for subjects only, not for leaders. So, day after day the candidate was observed violating all of the policies that had been put into place. At the end of the month the subjects created a bonfire with the 700 volumes of rules and regulations that had been generated during the brief reign of Candidate #2.

Candidate #3 believed that leaders know what is best for the general public, and that villagers cannot be trusted to make decisions or develop ideas. So for 1 month, Candidate #3 made all of the decisions and never consulted the residents of the village. At the end of the month, the villagers were finally able to make one decision: They decided they definitely did not want Candidate #3 to lead them.

Obviously, all three candidates were rejected by the villagers. When the Council of Elders gathered to consider an alternative, they began to discuss the requisite qualities and characteristics of a leader, and the role of the town leader in the future. Soon, discussion turned to argument and argument turned to heated debate. Not only were the elders unable to come to agreement about the role of the town leader, but they succeeded in generating almost as many definitions and descriptions of leadership as there were residents in this tiny village. The elders realized they needed time to examine this complex phenomenon known as leadership, so they decided to retreat to a quiet hideaway in the mountains to engage in discourse and come to resolution. They emerged 1 month later with a document entitled "The Village Leader." This document identified five roles for the leader in providing direction for the tiny village:

Leaders create visions
Leaders create climates
Leaders create conflict
Leaders create change
Leaders create leaders

One cannot help but be impressed with the wisdom of the Council of Elders in their visionary concept of the roles required for successful leaders. Most students of leadership would agree that these roles are as relevant today as they were when they were identified in that tiny village centuries ago. As one examines these roles, it becomes evident that they serve as a challenge for new leaders and those who aspire to leadership roles in the future.

Leaders Create Visions

Leaders frequently engage in the process of traveling into the future. When an individual plans a vacation, the months or weeks prior to the trip are often spent in a process the town elders might have humorously referred to as "anticipatory vacationalization." These would-be travelers envision the arrival, the setting, the climate, the activities, the people they will meet, and the places they will explore. Like vacationers, leaders dream of possibilities and envision the future. They spend a great deal of effort "gazing across the horizon of time . . ." (Kouzes & Posner, 1987, p. 9). They, too, anticipate arriving at a new and unfamiliar destination, experiencing a unique setting and climate, and exploring previously unknown territories. And, like the dreams of the vacationer, the dreams of the leader generate enthusiasm and excitement. LaPierre (1965) identifies three groups in society who bring about the diffusion of ideas: innovators (those who create the ideas), advocates (those who sell the ideas), and adopters (those who implement the ideas). In most instances, the leader is the innovator: the creator of the idea who works with followers to bring the idea to fruition. In some instances, however, the leader is the advocate or adopter: recognizing the value in the creative idea of another and working with followers to promote and implement the idea. "The leader's primary contribution is in the recognition of good ideas, the support of those ideas and the willingness to challenge the system . . ." (Kouzes & Posner, 1987, p. 8). New and aspiring leaders are challenged to be comfortable as advocates and adopters in identifying new and innovative ideas and assisting others to shape dreams into realities. Yet, they must also strive to entertain ideas about the unthinkable, the impossible, the inconceivable, the unusual, and the unimaginable. When leaders dare to dream, the visions of today can become the realities of tomorrow. "The first basic ingredient of leadership is a guiding vision" (Bennis, 1994, p. 39).

LEADERS CREATE CLIMATES

Leaders build teams and create an esprit de corps that generates excitement within followers. As Candidate #2 soon learned, leaders cannot operate in isolation, nor can they expect from followers what they themselves are unwilling to give. Dreams and visions are more exciting when they can be shared with others, and they can only be achieved through the commitment and support of knowledgeable, informed followers. Followers will go to great lengths to bring visions to fruition if they truly believe in the leader and the vision. Obviously, leaders must earn that commitment and support, and they can do so by creating a climate wherein followers can challenge ideas and are encouraged to speak the truth. The truth is not always what leaders want to hear, but it may be what they need to hear if they are to bring about the changes that will lead to a better future. Truth is related to authenticity, a concept that has been linked with leadership. Leaders are authentic when they "discern, seek, and live into truth, as persons in diverse communities and in the real world" (Terry, 1993, p. 112). Authenticity is extremely difficult for leaders who live in a society where conformity is celebrated and acquiescence is applauded. "Too many would-be leaders smooth out their rough edges and round out their sharp corners until they resemble all the other pebbles in the stream" (Safir, 1990, p. 16). New and aspiring leaders are challenged to use their rough edges and sharp corners as they strive for authenticity, and they should nurture and foster these skills in the "pebbles" they meet along the way.

LEADERS CREATE CONFLICT

Promoting and facilitating the status quo only serve to stifle creativity and impede the healthy process of change and growth. Leaders must be willing to challenge existing ideas, structures processes, and visions. They must feel comfortable raising questions, and, unlike Candidate #3, they should encourage followers to question and challenge as well. Unfortunately in a society where conflict management seminars abound and conflict resolution strategies proliferate, it is difficult to envision generation of conflict as a role requirement for leaders. Yet the well-known phenomenon of group think occurs when too little conflict exists within decision-making groups: when people are unable or unwilling to speak out (Janis, 1982). Conflict-generating strategies can be as simple as providing new information or promoting discussion of an idea or trend. Too much conflict can lead to chaos and too little conflict can lead to stagnation. New and aspiring leaders are challenged to devise innovative strategies for generating conflict, and for managing and channeling the upheavals these strategies may produce. Living with uncertainty is no easy task, yet it is essential if leaders are to eventually bring about a new order. Conflict is an antecedent of change.

LEADERS CREATE CHANGE

Candidate #1 failed to realize that one key role for a leader is that of change agent. Leaders sow the seeds of change; they initiate discussions, and engage in dialogue to stimulate thought and stretch the imagination of followers. In many respects, leaders create the window of possibility through which followers see a future crafted by the leader. The role of the leader is to work with followers to open that window to enable a changed future to emerge. Frequently, change represents a monumental threat to the status quo. "Change means movement. Movement means friction. Only in the frictionless vacuum of a nonexistent abstract world can movement or change occur without that abrasive friction of conflict" (Alinsky, 1971, p. 21). Figure 6-1 represents the relationship between conflict, status quo, and change, and can be useful tool for change agents. New and aspiring leaders need to realize that too little conflict can lead to apathy and too much conflict can lead to chaos. They must become skilled at creating a climate wherein the status quo is balanced by healthy conflict. Some degree of conflict along with a "safety net" of status quo, signals the ideal environment for change, and the ideal time for change agents.

LEADERS CREATE LEADERS

There are many people of talent and competence in our society today who would eagerly embrace leadership roles if they had reason to believe they would be supported and nurtured in the process (Clark & Clark, 1994). What, then, are we doing to prepare our leaders for tomorrow, and who is undertaking this monumental task? Leaders come from the ranks of followers (Rosenback & Taylor, 1993). The preparation of leaders for the future falls to those who are currently exercising leadership. They are charged with the responsibility of reaching into the follower ranks and grooming potential leaders who will provide a new direction and create a new order. The terms *coaching* and *mentoring* have often been associated with this process of creating new leaders. Coaches are cheerleaders; they encourage, they generate excitement, they bolster self-confidence and self-esteem, and they urge continued effort and improvement. It is often from the sidelines that coaches bring out the best in individuals. Mentors, on the other hand, play a more intimate role in the personal growth and development of a protégé. They guide, direct, open doors of opportunity, provide insight and honest feedback, and impart wisdom and knowledge. Mentors provide a prototype of one particular leadership path but never attempt to influence others in the selection of that path. Instead, after close scrutiny, the protégé may choose another path or create a path where one did not exist. New and aspiring leaders must first become comfortable with their own leadership role. It is difficult to encourage and groom others when one is in the process of learning, growing, and becoming. As the comfort level increases, the leader can seek out others and use such skills as coaching, mentoring, or both. The end result of the leader's efforts is manifested by the follower's choice of direction: selecting a new path or creating a path where none previously existed. This is the ul-

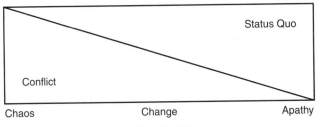

Figure 6–1 Conflict/Status Quo Model

timate indicator of success: the preparation of a new leader who will forge in a different direction, carve out a new role, and create a new order.

It seems appropriate now to bring the legend to a close. Campbell (Maher & Briggs, 1989) indicates there are two ways of living a mythologically grounded life. One is to live the "way of the village" and remain with the villagers. The other is to move out and seek adventure elsewhere (Maher & Briggs, 1989). New and aspiring leaders need not abandon the old and familiar; often they can introduce sufficient conflict to precipitate change in even the most comfortable of surroundings. However, they may wish to move on to new and uncharted territory in order to test their ability to deal with uncertainty. The challenge for the leader, then, is to decide whether to remain with the villagers and learn from the legends of the past, or move to new and unfamiliar ground and create the legends of the future.

REFERENCES

Alinsky, S. (1971). *Rules for radicals: A pragmatic primer for realistic radicals.* New York: Random House.

Ashliman, D. L. (1987). *A guide to folktales in the english language* (pp. ix–xv). New York: Greenwood Press.

Bass, B. M. (1990). *Bass & Stogdill's handbook of leadership: Theory, research, & managerial applications* (3rd ed.). New York: The Free Press.

Bennis, W. (1994). *On becoming a leader.* New York: Addison-Wesley.

Cavendish, R. (1982). *Legends of the world* (pp. 9–13). New York: Schocken Books.

Clark, K. E., & Clark, M. B. (1994). *Choosing to lead* (p. 161). Charlotte, NC: Leadership Press.

Janis, I. (1982). *Groupthink: psychological studies of policy decisions and fiascoes.* Boston: Houghton-Mifflin.

Kouzes, J. M., & Posner, B. (1987). *The leadership challenge.* San Francisco: Jossey-Bass.

LaPierre, R. (1965). *Social change.* New York: McGraw-Hill.

Maher, J. M., & Briggs, D. (1989). *An open life.* New York: Harper & Row.

Manfredi, C., & Valiga, T. (1994). Foreword. *Holistic Nursing Practice,* 9(1), vi.

Rosenback, W. E., & Taylor, R. L. (1993). *Contemporary issues in leadership* (3rd ed.). Boulder, CO: Westview Press.

Safir, W. (1990). Prolegomenon. In W. Safir & L. Safir, *Leadership* (p. 16). New York: Simon and Schuster.

Terry, R. (1993). *Authentic leadership: Courage in action.* San Francisco: Jossey-Bass.

CHAPTER 7

●●

Leadership: Can It Be Holistic?

BARBARA STEVENS BARNUM

This era is a fitting time in which to review leadership in a journal committed to a holistic philosophy. Granted, a holistic approach to leadership is a change of ideology for many of us who made a career of teaching leadership to nurse managers, but a change of perspective in itself may be renewing.

Leadership Versus Management

Until recently, the leadership literature, both in business and nursing management, focused not so much on leadership as on management. With a few signal exceptions, authors and researchers focused on the leadership behaviors of individuals holding administrative posts, that is, positional power.

Nor was that focus holistic. In contrast, the search was to identify the variables that contributed to managerial effectiveness. This perspective was to be expected because in an earlier era researchers had discovered the fallacy of trying to capture leadership by reference to the human traits and personalities of leaders. Research into whole leaders found that effective ones failed to conform to any single personality profile.

One of the final efforts in the search for a leadership personality profile was delivered by the Ohio State University study,[1] which found that leaders share only a few aspects. Namely, the leader was the one who:

- defined his or her own role and that of others in relation to goal achievement
- structured and interpreted situations to the group
- showed respect and consideration for the ideas of other group members

To reach such consensus about leaders, a subtle shift took place in the thinking of researchers. They ceased looking at the personality of the leader and switched to identifying behaviors that could be demonstrated by persons with radically different traits and styles of leadership.

The shift in perspective away from traits to behaviors led predictably to examination of job-specific behaviors, in effect completing the turnabout away from leadership to management. In this altered viewpoint, a subtle equation was struck: manager=leader.

Reprinted from *Holistic Nursing Practice*, 1994; 9(1): 9–15, with permission of Aspen Publishers, Inc., © 1994.

The manager's job behaviors were captured in many different formulas, starting with the traditional POSDCORB, an acronym for Plan, Organize, Staff, Direct, Coordinate (or Communicate), Report (or Rate), and Budget;[2] terms in parentheses represent later variations on the original 1937 theme. Newer versions of such job behavior inventories include more or fewer components, the sleekest probably being the so-called management cycle (plan, organize, and direct).

The equation manager=leader, although useful in both theory and practice, ignores those interesting leaders who function outside formal positions in organizations. Informal leaders in social groups or straw bosses on a nursing unit, for example, often get left out of the research.

For me, one advantage of the focus on tasks was that I could teach nurses how to lead with neat schematics. That is, I could teach them the tasks of management with cookbook-like prescriptions. A favorite liturgy of this era was that leaders were taught, not born. If you learned to do the requisite tasks, you could be an effective manager (ie, a leader).

Changing Times

The job-oriented approach held until recent times, when a rapidly changing environment made it impossible to educate a leader with a static checklist of job skills. Too many things started to fall through the cracks; too many managers who went by the book failed in spite of their best efforts.

In light of conditions too fluid to capture in a set of stable job variables, once again a shift in perspective away from looking at management and toward examining leadership took place. An escape? Perhaps. Leadership is a broad term, management a more limited one. In an uncertain era, one hedges at offering too many absolutes, too many pat answers. The solution: Describe the leader in broad strokes rather than in managerial job-related specifics. This represented a perfect answer for an era that defied the cookbook mentality.

The managerial prescriptions that remained were more fluid and were captured in something called strategic planning, a dance that made up the steps as it went along in response to environmental changes (often hazards). Suddenly it was not bad to be reactive instead of proactive. A manager was talented if he or she could be reactive in the right direction at the right time. It is no surprise that the ideologies changed and that transformational leadership appeared on the scene.

Transformational leadership (not management) is defined in terms of an attitude more than in relation to tasks, as an approach more than specific behaviors. The element of consistency is no longer to be found in the content of what the leader does (as in the traditional POSDCORB). Instead, with transformational leadership the constant element has shifted to context, that is, the leader's world view, his or her interpretation of what is happening in the surroundings. Surprise! We have a holistic view of leadership, one in which a leader comes from a single, coherent philosophy applied across a shifting panorama of tasks (content) and tactics (processes) whose substance may change as rapidly as today's environment.

Leadership Theory

In discussing nursing theory, I like to analyze a theory by defining elements of content, process, and context. The same system of analysis can apply to leadership theories. Transformational leadership (context), then, can be matched with a process of strategic planning (process) and applied to a shifting panorama of subjects demanding attention (content).

Burns,[3] an early formulator of the notion of transformational leadership, says that there are two kinds of leadership. Transactional leadership, the traditional kind, occurs where one person takes the initiative for the exchange (salary for services is typical here). Both parties have separate but related purposes, and their differences are the focus of the system. In contrast, in transformational leadership the leader and the followers have the same purpose, and they raise one another to higher levels of motivation and morality.

Barker[4] notes that the scientific method has fallen short in controlling and explaining world events. Therefore, a new view of humanness is emerging. People bring to the workplace a new set of beliefs and values that spring from the new paradigm.

In the old paradigm, logical decision making and rationality prevailed. Such a vision of a manager's role fit such prescriptions as management by objectives. Planning was removed and rational and counted on the future being predictable.

The new paradigm, as Barker[4] notes, relies on mutuality, affiliation, acknowledgment of complexity, ambiguity, cooperation versus competition, an emphasis on human relations, process versus task, acceptance of feelings, networking versus hierarchy, valuing of intuition, and empowerment of all employees.

The new transformational leader mobilizes others and then grows and develops together with the followers. The process is not static. As one set of needs and values is satisfied, new ones surface and contribute to the personal and professional growth of all parties.

With transformational leadership, it is easier to see results than to describe the process (remember, it is fluid). The right actions may change from day to day. The leader and the followers make sense of it all by focusing on goals and end products. In return, they develop a love of the work. In nursing, that may be seen in enthusiasm for patients and a sense of accomplishment for the care delivered.

If the leader no longer follows a pat formula, what does he or she do? The central task of the transformational leader, as Barker[4] says, is to create a vision and to build a social architecture that provides meaning for employees. In other words, in an organizational setting the leader determines how the vision will be institutionalized.

Equally important, the leader builds and sustains trust in the organization and in his or her own credibility. Furthermore, the leader recognizes the importance of building self-esteem and pride among one's followers, pride in self and in one's work.

Notice that these same qualities of transformational leadership can emerge in any group and need not be limited to organizational settings and their hierarchies. The leadership image applies in both formal and informal settings, indeed anywhere that people choose to follow a leader.

The transformational leader is less rule bound than the old-style transactional leader. But why the sudden change in leadership style? Why a switch from looking at managers to looking at leaders? The change simply fits what is happening in the world. We are in the midst of a major shift in the way the health care environment works, and we need the fluidity to interpret, create, and grow with change.

Yet even with fluidity (represented perhaps by the fast pace of strategic management), there is still a need for an anchor in the process. That is where the values of the transformational leader come in; that is where holism rears its head.

Ironically, the holism of transformational leadership takes us back to where we started: with a view of the leader as person, not as performer of a set of discrete tasks. It is not that the cyclical return is identical to the old search for personality traits. Instead, transformational leadership rests on the values and commitments that underlie both the traits and the behaviors of the leader as well as the leader's insight in interpreting what is happening today and in reading tomorrow's tea leaves as well.

A New Look at Leaders as People

Yet we cannot deny that transformational leadership returns us to the cult of the individual, a change from what the leader does to who the leader is and how he or she sees things and motivates those led. The new leader must be cut of whole cloth; who and what he or she is matter.

Not only does transformational leadership look at the leader, but it remembers that leaders are made by followers. Indeed, if we think about it, the only essential criterion for a leader is that he or she has followers. No followers, no leader; it is as simple as that. The last time workers (not followers) got much attention, however, was in the era when the unionization movement was new.

The leadership literature has often been light on the follower side of the equation. Top-down management, management by objectives, and the management cycle, to name but a few, all focused on what the leader does. So does transformational leadership, but in a different way, with effective followership being the measure of the leader's effectiveness. In that respect, transformational leadership is reminiscent of the early Ohio studies, namely that it looks at the interrelationship between the two sorts of players in the leadership game.

Transformational leadership, as I have noted, fits today. It lends a uniformity to both administrative practice and informal leadership in an era of diversity characterized by shifting meanings. It was an image whose time had come. Yet it is not fair to equate holistic leadership exclusively with transformational leadership. There are other images, other ideologies of holistic leadership.

Let's take Heider's thoughts in *The Tao of Leadership*.[5] Perhaps few philosophies can be viewed as more holistic than one based on the Tao, a system committed to the notion that all is one. In his book, Heider offers aphorisms such as the following:

> *A good group is better than a spectacular group. When leaders become superstars, the teacher outshines the teaching. Very few superstars are down-to-earth. Fame breeds fame, and before long, they get carried away with themselves. Then they fly off center and crash.*[5(p17)]
>
> *Potent leadership is a matter of being aware of what is happening in the group and acting accordingly.*
>
> *Specific actions are less important than the leader's clarity or consciousness. That is why there are no exercises or formulas to ensure successful leadership.*[5(p75)]
>
> *The wise leader is of service: receptive, yielding, following. The group member's vibration dominates and leads, while the leader follows. But soon it is the member's consciousness which is transformed, the member's vibration which is resolved.*
>
> *The relationship is reciprocal. It is the job of the leader to be aware of the group member's process; it is the need of the group member to be received and paid attention to.*[5(p121)]

Like transformational leadership, Heider's theory blurs the edges between the leader and those led. They are merged in a common cause. In a dialectic fashion, one could say that their differences are subsumed in the larger whole of the situation in which they participate.

Leadership in Diverse Roles

In this image, the best leader may not always be the most visible or the most flashy, and the best leader may not always be a manager. Indeed, in nursing some of our most impressive leaders act outside prescribed organizational roles.

I think, for example, of some of the nurses I have met who hold no managerial positions. One, for example, assesses children in cases of probable sexual abuse. Her personality and keen perceptions offer guidance and direction to both the children and the court. Another influences the lives of clients as a nurse practitioner. This nurse, who has survived innumerable bouts with cancer, has an indomitable spirit. Her enthusiasm for every moment lived is inspirational. In a sense, she has beaten the disease even though the cancer remains and she has sacrificed various body parts in her ongoing battle. If she leads the physicians with whom she works, it is with a genial tyranny. Her upbeat love of life and philosophic acceptance of its calamities offer a transformational example few patients could ignore.

Other nurses exemplify the best of leadership in traditional high organizational positions. Numerous nurse vice presidents who have learned to live in the new world of scarce resources come to mind as I write. Each has reconstituted nursing care delivery to fit the scarcity of the environment and the ever-increasing demands for quality care. Each has produced bold new designs of restructured practice. These changes, far-reaching across the nation, have shown the ability of our leaders to respond to a changing environment positively, rapidly, and successfully.

In nursing education, the leaders creating nurse-run clinics show the same ability to change from business as usual. They have reached out to those served and have returned to our roots among the people whom nursing serves. Such efforts heal the artificial schism between education and practice; this represents a return to a holistic conception of nursing and nursing leadership that spans our traditional divisions.

The growth of care delivery models outside the hospital puts nurses in positions to lead in domains far from the isolation and fragmentation of the acute care illness model. Nursing leadership may be seen in home care, long-term care, skilled nursing facilities, block nursing, and parish nursing. Many of the new domains of practice remind us of our grand origins in this country: the Henry Street settlement, frontier nursing in the Kentucky mountains, and the bold years of the early visiting nurse associations nationwide.

In the sense of holism that sees the client's life as an entirety rather than in isolated segments, nurse leaders are taking up the challenge on every front, not only expanding geographic arenas of practice but also extending notions of nursing care. Creative, vital programs prevail in all aspects of today's community health, aspects concerned with making the most of every client's life: stress management, biofeedback for pain, imaging work, industrial case management, management of lifestyle problems, and therapy for substance abuse, to name only a few. Thus the holism reflected in newer approaches to leadership is reflected in the holistic conception of the patient as well.

Spiritual Values

Another signal of renewed interest in holistic leadership may be the return to a focus on spiritual values in nursing. There was a time when nursing viewed the patient as biologic, psychologic, sociologic, and spiritual. Then the spirit part got lost when nursing, along with other health care disciplines, fell under the thrall of the scientific method. Now our theories once again look at the missing element. As Watson says, "The bold attempt to acknowledge and try to incorporate a concept of the soul in a nursing theory is a reflection of an alternative position that nursing is now free to take. The new concept breaks from the traditional medical science model."[6(p49)] Or as Clark, et al, note, "Quality care must include a spirit-to-spirit encounter between caregiver and patient."[7(p68)]

Obviously, holism means something more than the mere accumulation of parts, so that the spiritual aspect of a person—patient or nurse—cannot be seen as just something else to throw into the pot. Instead, it may be a recognition that something grander acts in the design of our leaders, followers, and patients. Spirituality is an element that resonates with the notions of Heider[5] and transformational leadership. It also represents a new conceptualization of our profession, a brave act on the part of our intellectual leaders.

Can leadership be holistic? Not only can it be, but it also must be in this tumultuous age. The leader must be a whole, unique person who is, if you will, personified by his or her work or organization. In an era when all else is in flux, there is a need for leaders who bring to a job more than the ability to perform prescribed tasks. We need leaders who bring, first and foremost, themselves, their whole being, to the leadership challenge.

The image is once again organic, with leaders, followers, and organizations growing and developing together. The holoscopic image fits, too. The group or organization becomes a reflection, an extension, of the leader. Holistic leadership? It is the only kind that will survive our times.

REFERENCES

1. Korman AK. Consideration, initiating structure, and organizational criteria—a review. In: Sorensen PF Jr, Baum BH, eds. *Perspectives on Organizational Behavior.* Champaign, Ill: Stripes; 1973.
2. Gulick LK. Notes on the theory of organization. In: Gulick LK, Urwick L, eds. *Papers on the Science of Administration.* New York, NY: Institute of Public Administration; 1937.
3. Burns JM. *Leadership.* New York, NY: Harper & Row; 1978.
4. Barker AM. An emerging leadership paradigm. *Nursing Health Care.* 1991;12:204–207.
5. Heider J. *The Tao of Leadership.* New York, NY: Bantam New Age, 1986.
6. Watson J. *Nursing: Human Science and Human Care: A Theory of Nursing.* New York, NY: National League for Nursing; 1988.
7. Clark C, Cross JR, Deane DM, Lowry LW. Spirituality: integral to quality care. *Holist Nurs Pract.* 1991;5:67–76.

CHAPTER 8

Transformational Leadership: The Feminist Connection in Postmodern Organizations

ANNE M. BARKER AND CONSTANCE E. YOUNG

Society is in the midst of a transformation from what has been labeled the modern period to the postmodern period. The modern period dates back to the time of Copernicus, which signaled the beginning of the scientific revolution. The world was perceived as being made of large, solid objects with empty space between them governed by the laws of physics and likened to the workings of a clock. In this view, it was thought that the world could be studied through controlled observations and experimentation based on the principle of cause and effect.

Beginning in this century, scientists determined that the world is, in fact, made up of minute, energetic particles and/or waves and that these are characterized by vibrations. This has led to what is known as the postmodern view of the world, characterized by wholeness and connectedness among all things. One of the best analogies for this world view is a hologram, in which each part of the picture relates to all the others and cannot be separated from the whole.

These two differing world views have had a subtle but powerful effect on our perceptions and ways of being. For instance, in the modern world view there was a reliance on objectivity and control. As the postmodern period emerged, however, there was a growing acceptance of ambiguity and uncertainty. We have come to realize that not everything can be understood and that there is more to being human than what we currently know.

In the modern period, there was a dominance of patriarchal values and assumptions. Competition, control, and manipulation characterized behaviors during this period. As the postmodern period develops, there will be an increasing emphasis on feminine values and beliefs, such as caring, nurturing, and intuition, to balance patriarchal values. Both the modern and postmodern world views are operating side-by-side and in conflict today. This is because a transition in thinking is occurring and is yet incomplete. This inevitable but slow transition, which affects how the world is viewed, is not predicted to be complete until 2010 to 2020.[1]

Reprinted from *Holistic Nursing Practice*, 1994;9(1):16–25, with permission of Aspen Publishers, Inc., © 1994.

TABLE 8–1   **New Business Paradigm**

Old Business	New Business
Single focus	Wholeness/integration
Reliance on logical analysis	Use of inner wisdom/intuition and analysis
Short-term, imposed goals	Shared, value-driven vision
Workers controlled by rigid policies/rules	Workers seeking meaning and purpose in their work
Hierarchic structure (vertical)	Network (horizontal)
Competition	Cooperation
Power-wielding	Empowerment
Subservience to technology	Technology as a tool

The Emerging Business Paradigm

Just as there is a change in world view, the assumptions of how organizations function successfully are also changing. These changes have been labeled the new paradigm of business.[2] And just as the transition of world view is not yet complete, new paradigms in organizations are emerging and are not yet ingrained in the way organizations work.

Table 8-1 contrasts the old business paradigm with the new. Again, one can see elements of both in organizations. For example, most health care organizations are still structured in a hierarchy from the top down. Currently, organizational redesigns are being considered in many health care facilities that incorporate concepts of networks and horizontal organization structures. Yet both the old and the new exist side-by-side, creating ambiguity and conflict. This conflict is likely to persist for the next several decades, making leadership and followership in organizations rife with uncertainty and mixed messages.

It is postulated by most authorities that organizations cannot survive in the next millennium without embracing the elements of the postmodern organization. Organizational structures will be characterized by networks of people versus top down delegation of authority. Cooperation, empowerment, vision, trust, and intuition will be more valued than control, competition, and power wielding. Thus it is believed that health care organizations will be changing rapidly in the years ahead not only because of health care reforms and current trends in organizational redesign but also to be successful in the postmodern period.

Leadership for the Postmodern Organization

What type of leadership is needed for the postmodern organization? The fundamental answer is that there is no one way to lead. There are no prescriptions for leadership in the contemporary and future organization. Broad, general guidelines are available to the leader, however. In a sense, today's leader needs a philosophy of leadership versus a theory of leadership with complex prescriptions.

Such a philosophy can be found in the work of Burns,[3] who first popularized the term *transformational leadership*. Burns described two forms of leadership: transactional and transformational. Transformational leadership is the less common form, with transactional characterizing most leadership situations today. Yet transformational leadership is the more desirable form.

Transactional leadership, as its name implies, is an exchange between the leader and the follower. In organizations, this exchange is generally money for service. In this form of leadership, the exchange benefits both the leader and the follower but meets only the immediate self-interests of both. The leader and follower have different goals and needs; the exchange is mutually beneficial, but their purposes are different. There is nothing inherently wrong with this form of leadership. It is simply not effective in postmodern organizations, where people are seeking purpose and meaning in their work to enhance self-esteem and self-actualization.

In contrast, transformational leadership "occurs when one or more persons engage with others in such a way that leaders and followers raise one another to higher levels of motivation and morality. Their purposes, which might have started out as separate but related, as in the case of transactional leadership, become fused." [3(p20)] Transformational leadership is moral leadership in that it has a transforming effect on both the leader and the follower, bringing out the best in each.

Transformational leaders must attend to a variety of strategies to have this transforming effect on followers, self, and the organization. Foremost, they are values brokers. They concern themselves with values in several ways. First, they provide a vision for the future that is exciting and yet feasible, one that attends to providing meaning and purpose for all involved. This vision articulates deeply held, shared values and dreams. Second, transformational leaders concern themselves with meeting the needs and motivation of followers directly. The two most important of these needs in the postmodern organization are self-esteem and self-actualization. The transformational leader helps followers understand the importance of their own values and needs by providing opportunities for dialog and by listening. The transformational leader responds sensitively to these needs and helps followers develop self-awareness. [4]

Obviously this values-oriented relationship cannot occur except in a relationship of trust and mutuality. In practice, establishing and maintaining both organizational and personal trust with others represent the fundamental strategy of the transformational leader. Only in an environment of trust can people truly be and act their best.

The Feminist Perspective

Burns argues:

> . . . over the centuries femininity has been stereotyped as dependent, submissive and conforming, and hence women have been seen as lacking in leadership qualities. . . . The male bias is reflected in the false conception of leadership as mere command or control. As leadership comes properly to be seen as a process of leaders engaging and mobilizing the human needs and aspirations of followers, women will be more readily recognized as leaders and men will change their own leadership style. [3(p50)]

A combination of factors is emerging today that calls for new leadership, leadership for which women are well suited. The changes brought about by postmodern thinking, new paradigms in organizations, and new philosophic approaches to leadership are fully in concert with feminist ways of knowing and leading. It is thus important to have an understanding of what has been learned about feminine ways of knowing and thinking.

Over the last 20 years, studies of and writings about feminist thinking have focused on the subjective experience and world view of women. In doing so, significant historical and psychosocial research has begun to paint the many-faceted picture of women. Throughout these writings is a common thread of descriptive language that reflects women's ways of thinking, feeling, and behaving. This new language is critical because "language forms the foundation of communicated meaning . . . [and is a] means of maintaining a political perspective." [5(p6)] Words and phrases of this new language include *con-*

nections, support, empathy, intuition, emotions, participation in development of others, coopera-tion, establishing and maintaining relationships, and *listening.* Without exception, this is the same language in current use for describing the organizational leadership needed now and in the future: transformational leadership.

In their classic qualitative work, Belenky, et al,[6] detail stories of how women learn, un-derstand their world, and speak. They depict a world of varying degrees of silence or voice and of self-esteem or the lack thereof and an increasing sense of ability to learn through listening and observing in the context of relationships in which there is sharing, feeling, and empathy. An outcome of this research is a detailed description of five episte-mologic categories documented from interviews and grounded in developmental changes that influence women's ways of knowing. The fifth category, constructed knowledge, is characterized by a positive sense of self and an action-oriented belief that "all knowledge is constructed, and the knower is an intimate part of the known"[6(p137)] with the incorpora-tion of context and subjective and objective frames of reference into ways of being and knowing.

The Connection of Transformational Leadership and Women

The characteristics of transformational leaders and the attributes of women, who are con-structed knowers, share common themes and meaning, albeit with different terminology. Although constructed knowledge is focused on female intellectual ability, that ability is in-extricably woven within the tapestry of the meaning of being a woman, and ways of knowing cannot be separated from ways of being. Table 8-2 compares the characteristics of transformational leaders and constructed knowers. It can be seen that transformational leaders are described as being concerned for the individual, fostering mutual trust and de-pendence, and valuing communication. Similarly, constructed knowers participate in a network or web that includes caring, moral responsibility, positive self-esteem, and use of both intuition and logic. Both transformational leaders and women seek to establish an en-vironment that generates empowerment in self and/or others. Each attribute listed in Table 8–2 is separate from and at the same time entangled with others, creating a humanis-tic and holistic orientation. The discussion below compares the characteristics of transfor-mational leaders and the attributes of constructed women knowers.

TABLE 8–2   Transformational Leadership and Feminine Attributes

Transformational Leaders	Constructed Female Attributes
Relationships: engaged	Relationships: network/web
Individual consideration	Caring
Leader as a moral agent: values and needs	Moral responsibility
Mutual dependence/trust	Reciprocity and cooperation
Communication	Integration of voices
Builder of self-esteem	Positive self-esteem
Listens to intuition, balances with analysis	Use of intuition and logic
Empowerment	Empowerment

THE WEB

The web as a metaphor for the structure of relationships and/or organizational structures is an overarching concept that helps one visualize how women view relationships and how organizations are best structured in the postmodern period. In writing about women's moral reasoning, Gilligan[7] describes that women view relationships as a web of connection. Similarly, in interviewing successful women leaders, Hegelson[8] describes the current trend toward a flatter, less hierarchic structure as a web of inclusion.

The web is a structure that "facilitates direct communication . . . by providing points of contact and direct tangents along which to connect."[8(p50)] The leader is often placed in the center of the web, providing access to multiple sources of information to and from him or her. This not only makes information available to many but also provides the opportunity for the transformational leader to make the needed connections with followers to discuss and shape values. Furthermore, the change in amount and multidirectional flow of information that occurs in a web structure has an inherent democratizing effect with the potential to generate cooperation and mutual respect, promoting both organizational and individual trust. As stated above, trust is essential for the transformational leader to be effective.

Thus the web structure unintentionally creates an organizational approach that is in accord with the attributes of women, who are constructed knowers. Feminist relationships operate within a context of equality, democracy, and connecting networks. These new, flatter organizational structures will provide women leaders with an environment in which they can easily work with and within the structure.

CARING

Caring can be defined as "the ability to imagine and be sensitive to the interior lives of others."[6(p140)] This is in stark contrast to the view of caring as an attribute equated with maternal behavior or unpaid work, a quality that has been historically devalued. In the postmodern organization, however, organizational needs for cooperation, responsibility, and involvement of all workers require that caring, as defined above, be practiced by successful transformational leaders. Recent analysis of leadership characteristics and caring in the literature implicitly references the importance of caring. For example, Billiard and Smale[9] note that the values associated with caring are needed to motivate workers and that women can be effective leaders in motivating others because they are nurturers and value-driven.

In his classic study of transformational leaders, Bass[10] found that one of their most important characteristics is individual consideration. This quality of the leader means that each person is treated as unique and special and that individuals are recognized for their talents and skills. To connect with and engage followers for a mutual purpose, the transformational leader must truly care for and be concerned with the needs and aspirations of others. Women, who are constructed knowers, demonstrate empathy toward others and are sensitive to others' needs and wants. Once again, a parallel between the characteristics of transformational leaders and the attributes of women can be drawn.

MORAL RESPONSIBILITY

Burns[3] calls transformational leadership moral leadership. By this he means that the relationship between the leader and follower is one of mutual need, aspiration, and values. Furthermore, by assuming the leadership role, the transformational leader is committed to mutual goals and change; in effect, the leader delivers what he or she has promised.

Women resolve conflicts not by invoking a logical hierarchy of abstract principles, but through trying to understand the conflict in the context of each person's perspective needs and goals—and doing the best possible for everyone involved.[6(p140)]

This process of moral reasoning and acceptance of moral responsibility is how transformational leaders must respond to be moral leaders. Transformational leaders help followers make conscious their values and needs through probing, questioning, debating, talking, and listening. Because women reason in this fashion, they can assume the mantle of transformational leadership.

RECIPROCITY AND COOPERATION

Transformational leaders foster relationships and connect with others, a skill in which women are expert practitioners. In interviewing women leaders, Rosener[11] found that women encourage participation, share power and information, and provide individual encouragement. Through participation with others in relationships of reciprocity, these women leaders were able to clarify their own values, to think out loud, and to get thorough information. Belenky, et al,[6] state that reciprocity and cooperation in relationships are based on the principle of inclusion, in which information and power are shared and in which domination is absent. Because womens' sense of self is grounded in relationships,[7,11] they seek activities in which relationships are mutual and trust is primary, where the development of others is an inherent part of those activities, and where power is shared.

Reciprocity and cooperation are fundamental to the effectiveness of the transformational leader. The reciprocity developed between the leader and the employee permits learning to be shared, recognizes the value of knowledge from both the leader and the employee, and reduces the vulnerability associated with the fear of being wrong or not knowing. Mutual respect and cooperation again build the foundation of a trusting relationship. In his work on learning organizations, Senge concurs that "a vision can die if people forget their connection to one another."[12(p230)] These connections, springing from mutual cooperation and reciprocity, are a critical force in the growth and development of women. Their value in sustaining organizational relationships is now being recognized.

INTEGRATION OF VOICES

Transformational leadership requires listening as well as talking. By valuing the information and opinions of others, the leader recognizes and affirms that leadership is more than individual expertise. It is mutual in purpose and vision.

In a study of women executives, Hegelson[8] found significant differences in the communication styles, priorities, and attributes of women and what earlier studies determined about male communication. Women executives focused on the process, as well as the outcome, of decisions and valued the ideas of others. Like the constructivist knower of Belenky et al,[6] these women engaged in real talk; that is, they listened, communicated, and thus reinforced the value of information received and used. There was an expressed belief in and a plan for taking the time to listen to the worker. The worker, the leader, and the organization benefited from this sharing of knowledge and recognition of the importance of others.

SELF-ESTEEM

Although there are many definitions of self-esteem, the common thread in each is that self-esteem is a deeply held belief in one own's worth, a valuing and respecting of one's talent and skills as unique and worthwhile. Transformational leaders are thought to have high self-esteem as well as the ability to build the self-esteem of others. Burns[3] sees the role of the transformational leader as developing and building the self-esteem of followers and eventually assisting followers to self-actualize by finding meaning and purpose in their work.

In a study of 90 chief executive officers identified as transformational leaders, Bennis and Nanus[13] found only one trait common to each: high self-confidence. They postulated that this trait is an essential ingredient for success for two reasons. First, individuals with high self-esteem can be decisive because they are confident of their abilities and strengths. Second, these individuals have a high regard for others, an essential characteristic for success.

Current understanding about women and self-esteem is conflicting. There is one school of thought that holds, because of the historical oppression and low status of women in Western society, that women generally have low self-esteem. On the other side of the debate is the work of Belenky, et al,[6] who find that women who are constructivist have learned to understand themselves, accept and value themselves, and integrate their own voice with the voices of others.

Whether women have low or high self-esteem is not the subject of this discussion. Rather, what is important is that high self-esteem appears to be an antecedent of transformational leadership. Women whose self-esteem is high (ie, those who are constructivist) can assume the role of transformational leader. In doing so, however, they have a moral obligation to followers to build the self-esteem of others through providing the environment for individual growth and achievement.

USE OF INTUITION AND LOGIC

Barnard, in a classic 1938 essay, wrote that executives are constantly confronted with information of an uncertain nature, which he referred to as "non-logical processes . . . namely those not capable of being expressed in words or as reasoning."[14(p302)] In his work, he determined that intuition is derived from many years of experience and knowledge. Written at a time when organizations were totally managed by men, his essay specifically recognized intuition as an essential ingredient in leadership. More recently, Agor[15,16] has studied the role of intuition in decision making by top executives. He found that leaders at the top of the management ladder respect and use their intuition more than those in first-level and middle management positions. Of even greater importance, he found that women score higher than men in their use of intuition.

On the other hand, female intuition has traditionally been devalued, despite the fact that intuition is acknowledged as an important ingredient in decisions made by men who are described as experts and leaders. Constructed women knowers, according to Belenky, et al,[6] use both intuition and logic within the context of a given situation. There is a balanced approach to the many related and interdependent factors involved in making decisions and in knowing. The use of intuition and logic recognizes connections between rational and nonlogical processes. This integration, balance, and connection are similar to the holistic approach advocated in nursing, in the system approach that is increasingly prevalent in organizations, and in the use of logic and intuition by the transformational leader.

EMPOWERMENT

Just as the web provides the framework for comparing the attributes of transformational leaders/constructivist knowers, empowerment may be seen as an overarching concept that connects the strands of transformational leadership and feminism discussed in this article. One measure of successful leadership in postmodern organizations is the successful empowerment of employees. Empowerment includes relationships with others nurtured by collaboration and focused on strengths, rights, and abilities in a learning process that enables others to master their environment and achieve self-determination.[17]

The ability to act purposefully and to mobilize energies, resources, and strengths connotes the linkage of empowerment with action and empathy. This is the heart of transformational leadership: empowering others to act toward a common purpose. An organization in which the structure, environment, and relationships support and sustain the individual in being empowered, in acting independently and in concert with organizational and/or client goals, also enables the transformational leader to spend the needed time reflecting on and directing the implementation of long-term goals essential for organizational survival. Thus growth and development of the individual generate growth and development of the organization and the leader. Reflecting on the definition of transformational leadership, empowerment allows for both the leader and the follower to "raise one another to higher levels of motivation and morality."[3(p30)]

Feminism and Transformational Leadership in the Health Care Environment

Western society is faced with a confluence of transformations that affect how we see the world and how organizations are led. This has tremendous impact on and implications for both health care and nursing. These transformations bring new opportunities for women leaders in organizations because emerging ways of leading are fully in concert with feminist ways of knowing and leading.

The operative word, however, is *emerging*. The reality of the health care environment, in which women are being called upon to be key players and leaders, is that it is paternalistic and hierarchic. In practice, the many reports of successful female leadership are occurring in nontraditional or entrepreneurial organizations, not in health care settings that are still characterized by hierarchic, bureaucratic structures and operations. Nursing administrators describe situations where male administrators and male physicians frequently tip the power balance in health care organizations. Issues of gender and role (ie, being female and a nurse) subtly influence communication shared and respect engendered.[18] Burns[3] states that what has kept women from leadership is not so much discrimination by men but rather the consciousness of women as the oppressed group. This reality, however, is changing.

The modern world view in which paternalistic values and beliefs predominate is ending; the postmodern world is emerging and gaining momentum day by day. Nursing leaders, a predominantly female group, need to recognize and value their unique ways of being, knowing, and leading; to place faith in their intuition; to build webs; to care; to connect; to listen; and to trust themselves and others. In doing so, nursing leaders can take their rightful place in the health care arena, side by side with their male counterparts, recognizing the valuable contributions and different perspectives of both.

REFERENCES

1. Drucker PF. The new society of organizations. *Harv Bus Rev.* 1992;70:95–104.
2. Ray M, Rinzler A, eds. *The New Paradigm in Business: Emerging Strategies for Leadership and Organizational Change.* New York, NY: Putnam; 1993.
3. Burns JM. *Leadership.* New York, NY: Harper & Row; 1978.

4. Barker AM. *Transformational Nursing Leadership: A Vision for the Future.* New York; NY: National League for Nursing; 1992.
5. Sohier R. Feminism and nursing knowledge: the power of the weak. *Nurs Outlook.* 1992;40:62–66, 93.
6. Belenky M. Clinchy B, Goldberger N, Tarule J. *Women's Ways of Knowing: The Development of Self, Voice, and Mind.* New York, NY: Basic Books; 1986.
7. Gilligan C. *In a Different Voice.* Cambridge. Mass: Harvard University Press; 1982.
8. Hegelson S. *The Female Advantage.* New York, NY: Doubleday Currency; 1990.
9. Billiard M, Smale B. Do women make better managers? *Working Woman.* March 1992:68–71, 106–107.
10. Bass B. *Leadership and Performance Beyond Expectation.* New York, NY: Free Press; 1985.
11. Rosener JB. Ways women lead. *Harv Bus Rev.* 1990;68:119–125.
12. Senge PM. *The Fifth Discipline: The Art and Practice of the Learning Organization.* New York, NY: Doubleday Currency; 1990.
13. Bennis W. Nanus B. *Leaders: The Strategies for Taking Charge.* New York, NY: Harper & Row; 1985.
14. Barnard C. *The Functions of the Executive.* Cambridge, Mass: Harvard University Press; 1964.
15. Agor WH. *The Logic of Intuitive Decision Making: A Research Based Approach for Top Management.* New York, NY: Quoram; 1986.
16. Agor WH. *Intuition in Organizations: Learning and Managing Productively.* Newbury Park, NJ: Sage; 1989.
17. Gibson CH. A concept analysis of empowerment. *Adv Nurs.* 1991;16:354–361.
18. Brown CL. *Power and Images of Nursing in the Lived World of Nurse Administrators.* Boulder, Colo: University of Colorado; 1987. Thesis.

CHAPTER 9

●●

Ethical Aspects of Transformational Leadership

VIRGINIA R. CASSIDY AND CYNTHIA J. KOROLL

The current environment of the U.S. health care culture requires a critical analysis of the ability of nursing leaders to guide the profession through an era of change. The proposed revisions of health care policy and financing have created uncertainty in all arenas. Because of this uncertainty, effective leadership is of paramount importance to ensure that the contributions of professional nursing in meeting the health care needs of the nation and in the maintenance of high-quality, patient-focused practice are recognized. The anticipated effects of health care reform on nursing education, administration, and practice call for dynamic leaders who are able to advocate, guide, and direct the followers who have entrusted them with the power to lead. These leaders must also have the ability to address the ethical aspects of proposals to increase access to health care in an environment of cost containment. Additionally, they must be cognizant of the ethical issues in refocusing health care priorities and redefining the roles of health care providers. The requirements of leadership in these times of change necessitate a clear distinction between leadership and management, an alteration in traditional leadership roles, and an evaluation of the knowledge and skills needed to address the ethical issues that arise from such changes.

Leadership Versus Management

The terms *leadership* and *management* have often been used interchangeably. Consequently, discussions of the roles, responsibilities, and relationships of leaders are often intertwined with those of managers, which may blur distinctions between leadership and management and between leaders and managers. Generally, management implies authority and regulation.[1] The power of management is determined by position and authority in the organizational structure[2] and is rigidly defined in terms of duties and responsibility. Managers serve the organization. Management focuses on organizational maintenance and routine[3] rather than on fostering an environment where growth can occur. As a result, the management process alone will be ineffective in guiding nursing into an era of health care reform.

Reprinted from *Holistic Nursing Practice,* 1994;9(1):41–47, with permission of Aspen Publishers, Inc., © 1994.

Leadership has been viewed from a variety of perspectives. For example, leaders have been identified by specific personality traits or characteristics and by descriptors of their behavior. Although no one attribute describes an effective leader, a number of specific traits appear to be common among persons with leadership ability. Three major traits described as consistent with leadership effectiveness are intelligence, personality, and ability.[4] The trait of intelligence consists of the capacity for good judgment, decisiveness, knowledge, and fluency of speech. Personality traits considered essential for effective leadership include adaptability, alertness, creativity, cooperativeness, and personal integrity. Leaders also exhibit self-confidence, emotional balance and control, and independence or nonconformity. Leaders have the ability to enlist cooperation; they are also popular, have prestige, and demonstrate interpersonal skills. Other leadership abilities include tact, diplomacy, and respect.[4]

Transformational Leadership

Leadership styles are described by the distribution of power and control between leaders and followers.[5] In contrast to the traditional view of leaders as managers of power is the concept of leaders as facilitators and mentors. Burns[6] incorporated this concept into his description of transformational leadership. He described transformational leadership as a process in which leaders seek to shape and alter the goals of followers. The process incorporates the dimensions of leader, follower, and situation. The leader seeks to motivate followers to identify and clarify motives, values, and goals that contribute to enhancing shared leadership and autonomy. Transformational leaders often exhibit charismatic traits that facilitate energy and drive toward a common vision. Followers, motivated by the charismatic style of the transformational leader, are often empowered and energized themselves. Transformational leadership is well suited to the current climate in health care because of the manner in which it actively embraces and encourages innovation and change.

Transformational leadership shifts the focus of control from leaders to followers. Transformational leaders allow followers to identify the need for control and to use control in the pursuit of goals that will benefit the group. Thus power is shared and used for the common good, not for individual motives. Power is then viewed by followers as accessible and shared. Excellence in leadership occurs when followers are inspired to take action that is not based on individual needs but rather reflects the vision and the goals of the organization.

Charisma, consideration of individuals, and intellectual stimulation are considered essential components of transformational leadership.[7] Charismatic leaders provide followers with a vision and a sense of mission that instill pride and trust and gain respect.[7] Charismatic leaders also foster inspiration, raise confidence, and communicate high expectations. Followers emulate their charismatic leaders by trusting and accepting the visions and values that are presented by these leaders.[8] Effective leadership is based on the full involvement of followers,[9] therefore, successful leaders seek opportunities to energize and empower their followers.[10] Transformational leaders are also considerate of their followers, as evidenced by interactions that include individual attention, personal advisement, and mentoring. From these interactions, followers are stimulated intellectually to explore problems and propose solutions to them.

The concept of vision is also inherent in transformational leadership. Leaders are charged with the responsibility of creating a vision and providing direction.[11] Leaders facilitate the development of a shared vision that is congruent with the goals of the organization as well as those of individuals. Development of a vision requires the clarification of shared values and beliefs. Attainment of the vision is based on the ability of leaders to assist followers in defining and accomplishing their objectives. Leaders are responsible for motivating, inspiring, and supporting followers in their pursuit of the vision.

Ethical Leadership

In comparison to other aspects of leaders and leadership, relatively little discussion is devoted to the ethical responsibilities of those who lead or to the ethical aspects of the process of leadership. Some ethical considerations are alluded to in the description of the traits that are perceived to be necessary for leaders when characteristics such as integrity[4,12,13] or overall goodness of character[14] are included among those traits. In discussions of style, appreciation for the contributions of followers and recognition of their inherent worth as individuals also imply an ethical dimension of leadership.[4]

It is important to consider the ethical dimensions of leadership for several reasons. First, professions have a duty to maintain and protect the public trust.[15] Society empowers professions such as nursing to meet its specialized needs. Such empowerment creates a moral bond between the professions and the members of the society it serves. This moral bond demands that the profession comprise individuals of integrity, be accountable for their standards of conduct, and be dedicated to upholding basic ethical principles.[15] Such requirements necessitate that leaders in the professions not only subscribe to upholding ethical principles but also create a milieu in which such principles are preeminent.

Second, institutions such as health care organizations are powerful forces that influence the quantity and quality of available health care services. Concerns about institutional efficiency and effectiveness[14] can compete with concerns about the scope and quality of the services provided. When competing concerns occur, decisions must be made to set institutional policy, goals, and priorities. Leaders who understand the ethical dimensions of making such decisions are important in shaping the structure of health care organizations and helping determine organizational ethics.[14]

Third, nurses are faced with numerous and recurring ethical issues and dilemmas in their practice. Advances in scientific knowledge and technology, the needs of the chronically ill and older adult populations, and proposals about health care rationing and resource allocation, among others,[16-19] raise ethical issues and directly affect nurses and nursing care. In such an environment, nurses need leaders who will assist them in addressing the ethical dimensions of their practice.

In one study of leadership, commitment to a high moral code of behavior modeled by the leaders' own behaviors was identified as the most important attribute for transformational leaders.[9] Transformational leaders are individuals in unique positions who have particular ethical responsibilities in upholding and protecting the public trust and in exercising their influence over followers. The influence of transformational leaders in creating a vision and shaping the goals of health care organizations has tremendous implications for the configuration of health care services in the future. Competing claims for cost containment versus quality patient care produce a myriad of ethical issues that transformational leaders in nursing will have to address with increasing frequency. In this complex decision-making environment,[14] transformational leaders will probably be called upon more frequently to support followers in addressing ethical issues and to set the standard of conduct for ethical behavior. Transformational leaders, then, must function as moral agents in fulfilling their leadership roles and responsibilities and in their relationships with followers.

Transformational Leaders as Moral Agents

The requirements for functioning as a moral agent include the capacity to act morally, the responsibility to act for moral reasons, and the obligation to maintain moral relationships.[20] The requirements provide a perspective for considering the ethical roles, responsibilities, and relationships of transformational leaders in nursing.

THE CAPACITY TO ACT MORALLY

A requirement for functioning as a moral agent is the capacity to act morally, which can be understood in the context of Rest's[21] moral competency model. Rest's model delineates the critical elements of sensitivity, judgment, intent, and behavior as the basis for moral choices and action. Sensitivity to or awareness of the ethical component of a situation is required for moral action because, if the ethical components of a situation are not recognized, the ability to act as a moral agent is lost. If the ethical components of the situation are recognized, then judgments about what ought to be done are based on perceptions of the rightness or wrongness of the situation. Once judgments are made about the ethical components of the situation, intent to act upon the situation is then determined. Intent to act involves making a decision about what morally required action should be taken. The behavioral component of the moral competency model is the execution of the morally required action on the ethical component of the situation.[21] Rest's model describes the elements needed for individuals to be able to act morally and thus assists in understanding one aspect of being a moral agent.

THE RESPONSIBILITY TO ACT FOR MORAL REASONS

The responsibility to act for moral reasons is another requirement for functioning as a moral agent. The ability to act for moral reasons presupposes that leaders have a well-defined set of moral values and that they operate from a moral value system. The development of a value system evolves over the span of a lifetime[22] and is the basis for the decisions made and behaviors exhibited by individuals. It is important that the value system of transformational leaders evolve from a moral basis rather than from other values, such as personal gain, advancement, or power for the sake of power. These other values conflict with the roles, responsibilities, and relationships of transformational leaders previously described. When other values are more of a priority, values conflicts can occur that may make acting for moral reasons difficult if not impossible.

The ongoing development of a well-defined value system is the basis for acting for moral reasons and has important implications for transformational leaders. Transformational leaders serve as role models for their followers, who will emulate their behaviors and values. They set standards for behavior within the leadership setting, help mold the values of the organization, and contribute to the development of the next generation of leaders, who must also be capable of acting for moral reasons.

THE OBLIGATION TO MAINTAIN MORAL RELATIONSHIPS

The obligation to maintain moral relationships is an element of functioning as a moral agent that can be discussed from two theoretical perspectives. One perspective for understanding moral relationships is based on ethical principles. The ethical principles of respect for autonomy, beneficence, and justice.[16] are viewed as the foundation for relationships with others. This perspective on moral relationships fits well with the concept of transformational leaders as facilitators and mentors.

The principle of autonomy is concerned with respect for others and the acknowledgment that individuals have the right to make autonomous or independent choices about their lives.[16] Ethical leaders demonstrate respect for followers by recognizing their capabilities and perspectives, treating them in an empathic manner, and viewing them as ends in and of themselves.[16,20] The dissemination of power to followers is the way in which the autonomy of followers is respected by transformational leaders. Empowering followers to create changes in areas such as role definition or standards of care is an explicit recognition of their unique and valued contributions to the organization. This empowerment is a demonstration of treating followers as ends rather than as means to ends.

The focus of the principle of beneficence is preventing harm and promoting good.[16] Specifically, beneficence addresses the idea that individuals, as members of a society, are obligated to help others and to promote the interests of others.[16] These obligations include refraining from causing intentional injury, preventing injury from occurring, and eliminating potential sources of injury. They also include promoting good by contributing to the welfare of others.[16,20] One way ethical leaders exhibit beneficence is by attending to the welfare of their followers. Beneficence is also evident in the collective use of power for the common good, that is, in proposing solutions to problems in such areas as access to health care and the quality of care.

The principle of justice addresses concerns about fair and equal treatment.[16] Fair and equal treatment refers to an unbiased and unprejudiced approach in interpersonal interactions. It also refers to the idea that individuals are given their due.[16] Transformational leaders demonstrate the principle of justice by the equitable distribution of support and resources among followers.

A second perspective for understanding the obligation of moral agents to maintain moral relationships is based on Gilligan's[23,24] work on the moral development of women. Gilligan's thesis is that morality is based on an ethic of care and responsibility in which the self is viewed from a perspective of connectedness with others. According to Gilligan, at the preconventional level of development, concern is focused on the self, feelings of powerlessness exist, and relationships are viewed as disappointing. At the conventional level of development, the focus of concern is others, feelings of self-worth emerge, and the ability to care for and protect others forms the basis of relationships. Postconventional development reflects concerns for self as well as others. At this level, the power to make choices is also recognized, and care for self and others becomes the ethical obligation in relationships.[23]

In the context of Gilligan's[23,24] work, the moral relationships between transformational leaders and followers take on special dimensions. Several aspects of transformational leadership are consistent with the development of postconventional morality as it is described by Gilligan. For example, transformational leaders challenge followers to clarify their motives, values, and goals. Such challenges can alter followers' concepts of self and relationships with others and may influence their moral development. When transformational leaders involve followers in the pursuit of goals and disseminate power to followers, feelings of powerlessness may be lessened. As feelings of powerlessness decrease, followers may be empowered to move to a higher level of moral development. When transformational leaders create a shared vision, followers are supported in the development of relationships based on mutual concern and caring. Such mutuality is the hallmark of the postconventional level of moral development. Through all these interactions, transformational leaders and followers can experience the interdependence and connectedness that characterize the different voice of women's morality.

Transformational leaders in nursing play a critical role in setting the future direction for the profession. By actively involving their followers in leadership processes, transformational leaders are ensuring the development of a new generation of leaders who can continue the pursuit of excellence in nursing. Accepting the role of moral agent is also an important requirement for nursing leaders because of increasing concerns about the ethical consequences of decisions being made about health care. Transformational leaders can be instrumental in helping define the ethical standards of the profession in a changing environment.

REFERENCES

1. Manfredi CM, Valiga TM. How are we preparing nurse leaders? A study of baccalaureate curricula. *J Nurs Educ.* 1990;29:4–9.
2. Marquis BL, Huston CJ. *Leadership Roles and Management Functions in Nursing Theory and Application.* Philadelphia, Pa: Lippincott; 1992.
3. Douglas LM. *The Effective Nurse Leader and Manager* (4th ed). St. Louis, Mo: Mosby; 1992.
4. Farley S. Leadership. In: Swansburg RC, ed. *Management and Leadership for Nurse Managers.* Boston, Mass: Jones & Bartlett; 1990.
5. Bernhard LA, Walsh M. *The Key to the Professionalization of Nursing* (2nd ed). St Louis, Mo: Mosby; 1990.
6. Burns J. *Leadership.* New York, NY: Harper & Row; 1978.
7. Bass BM. From transactional to transformational leadership: learning to share the vision. *Organ Dyn.* 1990;18:18–24.
8. Bass BM, Waldman DA, Avolio BJ, Bibb M. Transformational leadership and the falling dominoes effect. *Group Organ Dyn.* 1987;12:73–87.
9. Gevedon S. Leadership behaviors of deans of top-ranked schools of nursing. *J Nurs Educ.* 1992;31:221–224.
10. Dunham-Taylor J, Fisher E, Kinion E. Experiences, events, people. Do they influence the leadership styles of nurse executives? *Nurs Adm Q.* 1993;23:30–34.
11. Milner S. An ethical nursing practice model. *J Nurs Adm.* 1993;23:22–25.
12. Grunden E, Crissman S. Leadership skills for empowerment. *Nurs Adm Q.* 1992;16:6–10.
13. Morath JM, Manthey M. An environment for care and service leadership: the nurse administrator's impact. *Nurs Adm Q.* 1993;17:75–80.
14. Shortell SM, Kaluzny AD. *Healthcare Management: A Text in Organization Theory and Behavior.* New York. NY: Wiley, 1988.
15. Jennings, B, Callahan D, Wolf SM. The professions: public interest and common good. *Hastings Cent Rep.* 1987;17:3–10.
16. Beauchamp, TL, Childress JF. *Principles of Biomedical Ethics* (3rd ed). New York, NY: Oxford University Press; 1989.
17. Bunting SM, Webb AA. An ethical model for decision-making. *Nurse Pract.* 1988;13:30–34.
18. Quinn JC. The nurse manager and ethical choices. *J Post Anesth Nurs.* 1990;5:365–366.
19. Walleck CA. Building a framework for dealing with ethical issues. *AORN J.* 1991;53;1,248–1,251.
20. Silva MC. *Ethical Decision Making in Nursing Administration.* Norwalk, Conn: Appleton & Lange: 1990.
21. Baker PD. Moral competency: an essential element in the socialization of professional nurses. *Fam Community Health.* 1987;10:8–14.
22. Uustal DB. Values: the cornerstone of nursing's moral art. In: Fowler M, Levine-Ariff J. *Ethics at the Bedside.* Philadelphia, Pa: Lippincott; 1987.
23. Gilligan C. In a different voice: women's conceptions of self and morality. *Harvard Educ Rev.* 1977;47:481–517.
24. Gilligan C. *In a Different Voice.* Cambridge, Mass. Harvard University Press; 1982.

CHAPTER 10

● ●

Leadership in the Formation of New Health Care Environments

THOMAS KENT, JAMES A. JOHNSON, AND DAVID R. GRABER

Hospital mergers, the creation of health care networks, and other restructurings are generally undertaken to optimize an organization's financial effectiveness, that is, their formation is based on financial logic and capital considerations. The rationale for mergers and network formation usually falls into one or more of the following categories:

- Redundant activities can be eliminated, thus reducing costs such as labor and materials.
- Patient utilization and occupancy can be increased.
- Purchasing and negotiating power can be increased and leveraged.
- Costly, underfunded facilities can be shut down or more productively utilized.
- Flow of patients and patient care information can be streamlined and improved.
- Greater access to capital is secured.
- More focused investments in equipment, facilities, and training are possible.

While these are sound reasons for restructuring organizations, there is more to be gained from the opportunities created by restructurings. Not only are there direct and tangible financial results from these restructurings, but also there is great potential for additional indirect or intangible benefits. Although these less obvious benefits do positively affect the bottom line, it is usually difficult to measure their impact accurately.

Imagine the effectiveness of restructured new organizations if they could emerge with improvements in the following: trust, community perception, employees' sense of direction, intraorganizational communications, employee commitment as well as job satisfaction, and interdepartmental cooperation, to mention a few. Typically, organizations emerge from restructuring with losses in many of these characteristics. Because of the way the merger or reorganization is handled by management, we often see seriously reduced levels of trust, commitment, motivation, and sense of direction among employees. We also see communications lessened within and among departments, primarily because of fear and distrust. This often is a result of managers attempting to direct and control the change from a power vantage point and from a financial perspective.[1] Leaders go beyond a narrow focus on power and control in periods of organizational change. They create commitment and energy among stakeholders to make the change work. They create a sense of direction, then nurture and support others who can make the new organization a success.

Leaders recognize these reorganizations as "change events." Change events are situations—brief or enduring—in which a number of systems, structures, or processes are shifting or are in flux. Since these shifts are going to happen because of the reorganization, leaders use these change events as opportunities to synergize the previous organizational entities into a single high-performance organization. Positive, thoughtful, purposeful leadership can take the new organization beyond those financial results that might be predicted through management analysis.

Some managers try to minimize the effect of change on employees, communities, providers, and others who have a stake in the restructuring. They try to hide the impacts until they are inevitable: thus we see things such as surprise layoffs on a Friday afternoon. Some managers try to "manage change" by retaining information within a close circle of insiders: thus we see physicians, employees, and other groups strongly resisting restructuring moves that are made by management. These "resisters" may then create informal networks that can only undermine the realization of the valuable benefits mentioned earlier. Members of these informal networks often do this to avoid the "pain" of significant change or their loss of identity that was anchored to the previous organization. This is a problem leaders transcend by leading change, not managing it.

Experienced leaders know that in order to realize the gains possible from restructuring, significant change will be required. They also see change as an opportunity to engage the various stakeholders—employees, providers, communities—to be committed to making the reorganization a success.

Transformational Leadership and Organizational Change

The study of leadership has evolved over the years from simple lists of the factors related to effective management performance to the "Great Man" theory and the understanding of "leadership personality traits."[2] A number of theorists have focused on analyzing the behaviors of effective leaders, while others have contended that leaders' styles should be different from one situation or contingency to another.[3-6]

More recently, however, the study of leadership has sought to change the nature of the concept itself. Burns[7] differentiates between transformational and transactional leadership. Transactional leadership is an exchange of "favors" that occurs at the leader's bidding in order to accomplish the goals of the leader. The transactional leader says, "If you do this for me, I will do that for you," or, "If you do not do this for me, I will withhold certain rights and privileges from you because I have the power to do that."

Transformational leadership, Burns says, "occurs when one or more persons engage with others in such a way that leaders and followers raise one another to higher levels of motivation and morality."[7(p.20)] Transformational leaders "serve as an independent force in changing the makeup of the followers' motive base"[7(p.20)] Transforming leaders work from a set of values that is "forged and hardened" as they grow and mature from childhood to adulthood. Their behaviors create leadership through their influence on others' consciousness of purpose and value. That is, leaders engage others in order to elevate the way both leader and follower think about what they are doing. Their thinking changes regarding why (purpose) they are doing what they are doing, and regarding the importance (value) of what they are doing.

Bennis and Nanus[8] state that transformative leadership is the capacity to translate intention into reality and sustain it. Effective transformative leadership

can move organizations from current to future states, create visions of potential opportunities for organizations, instill within employees commitment to change and instill new cultures and strategies in organizations that mobilize and focus energy and resources.[8(p.17–18)]

The thrust of this work indicates that the personality of the leader is irrelevant and leaders do not change dramatically from one situation to another. In other words, whether a person is extroverted or introverted, people or task-oriented, dominant or passive, is not critical to the effectiveness of their leadership efforts. Also, their style is not situationally determined. They are not like chameleons that change color depending on things like task complexity or position power. Rather, their strengths as leaders derive from the nature of the processes they engage in with others.

Leadership Processes

There are two aspects, which are highly interrelated, to the processes that leaders employ. The first is related to the influence leaders exert over situations, and the second is related to how the leader engages others.

The first has been referred to as "culture building" by Sashkin[9] and by Wall and colleagues.[10] The transformational leader uses events to shift the thinking and valuing of people within those events, thereby shifting the nature of future events. Schein[11] suggests that leaders develop in others the beliefs and values that support high performance.

It is postulated that for this to happen (a) the leader must be clear within himself or herself what his or her own vision and values are; (b) the leader must be true to those values—so-called "walking their talk"; (c) the leader must know what must change; and (d) the leader must understand or be clear about the ethics, principles, or essential strengths the organization must possess and operate from. It is essential that all four of these factors operate in tandem.

Imagine the situation where they do not operate together. For example, a leader knows that to succeed in the newly restructured organization and to optimize its financial possibilities, people will have to relinquish their sense of departmental "turf." They will have to start cooperating more, and this means they will have to trust each other more. Open, trusting communications will be essential to the work that will follow to make the reorganization successful. A leader will take every opportunity—in meetings, in employee communication sessions, and in hallway chats—to say how important this is. Then, egregiously, the leader plans and implements an unannounced Friday afternoon layoff of 10 percent of the staff in order to meet financial objectives.

This situation is actually very common. A leader's lack of authenticity, or lack of synchrony between actions and espoused values, will often undermine organizational change. The leader's actions in the above example will normally result in dramatically reduced trust and openness and a corresponding increase in operational confusion and blaming (eg, between departments or functions).

The leader must take every opportunity to share thoughts about "the right way of doing something" (ethics and principles), what is important to the organization (values), and why things are necessary and important (purpose). Then the leader's own behavior must demonstrate those principles, values, and purpose.

The second aspect of leadership processes has to do with the interpersonal process that the leader employs when engaging others. In this article, six separate processes are delineated. Perhaps the greatest skill of the leader is to know when to employ each of the separate processes. In this sense the leader has a situational approach. However, this is a different definition of situational than the chameleon-like approach of "being" different in different situations. In fact, as is shown below, it is our contention that the leader should "be" the same from one situation to another. As such, the leader's style does not change. Rather, he or she employs different processes depending on the needs of the situation.

PROCESS #1: VISIONING

It is generally an accepted concept that effective leaders are motivated by and operate from their vision.[8-10] We define vision as a mental picture or map of where the organization is going, what it is to become, and how it will get there. The leader must have a clear sense of these facets of vision. More importantly, the leader must enable others to see this vision, reflect upon it, and modify or personalize it as appropriate. Vision in people motivates and focuses performance. Without vision a person can only follow orders or procedures. When a manager attempts to change these orders or procedures, he or she meets with resistance when there is no vision.

In the case of integrated health care systems, models and visions are still developing. Leaders must share their emerging visions with people. The more people understand the organizational journey and how they personally fit in, the greater likelihood that they will contribute to achieving the vision.

On the other hand, a lack of understanding or indifference to the vision can only lead to fear, resistance, and resentment.

PROCESS #2: COMMUNICATING FOR MEANING

Almost every interpersonal process involves communication. Specifically, here we are talking about a communication process that Bennis[8] calls "meaning through communication." Leaders are able to shift the thinking and understanding of others by developing the level of meaning that people hold. Important subjects and ideas are not treated as facts or data to be communicated objectively and without dialogue. If people are to understand something, they must engage in discourse and dialogue about it. Leaders know this takes time, and usually the more important the subject, the longer it takes.

Leaders go beyond facts and data by using values, symbols, or symbolic gestures to communicate. Communication does not occur through words alone. The leader's actions speak as loudly as his or her words. For example, to illustrate how important the community is to the organization, the network chief executive officer (CEO) might appoint citizens to planning groups during the formation of the health network. A leader will do more than to sanctimoniously announce that people are the most important resource of the organization. When consolidating redundant health care services, a leader might use normal attrition instead of layoffs to attain optimum staffing levels.

The point here is that communicating meaning is not simply a matter of sharing facts and knowledge. More importantly it involves shifting or developing the thinking of people. It challenges old ways of viewing things. It causes change by bringing about a change in the way people think about their lives and work.

PROCESS #3: CREATING POSSIBILITIES

Leaders seek to improve even acceptable situations if it will benefit the organization. They encourage creativity and continuous improvement of even effective, established processes. The key is that this effort must aid or enable achievement of the vision.

Wheatley[12] believes that disequilibrium is necessary in order for a system to grow. Growth is possible up to a point within an existing structure. Beyond that point the organization must reconfigure itself to grow further. Leaders are the pilots of this reconfiguration. They see clearly where they need to go, and they create the possibility of getting there.

When two hospitals merge, they need to look at services, costs, and quality. They must decide how to optimize services, reduce redundance, achieve optimum patient occupancy, and reduce costs. A common approach is to create a high-level management team to sort through the data and make such decisions as to which units to shut down or merge. An even worse, but still common, approach is to bring in a consultant to study the organization and make reengineering recommendations to the management team. All too often the result in both situations is little creativity in the solutions, employee hostility, reduced trust, and ongoing fear within the organizations.

Another approach is to create teams of people from both organizations who are much closer to the action—people who work in the units that are being "rationalized" or reengineered. This approach will take more training and sharing of much information; some of this information may have been previously deemed secret by management. It also involves much more effort, time, and consciousness on the part of the leader, as well as a willingness to relinquish total control over the outcomes. However, leaders understand and accept these costs in order to reap the long-term benefits of greater levels of improvement and increased employee commitment and trust.

PROCESS #4: DEVELOPING STAKEHOLDERS

We use the word *stakeholder* to define a category of people who have an investment in the organization and its success. There are many internal and external stakeholder groups involved with health care organizations, including subgroups of employees, unions, customers, suppliers, and regulatory agencies. In many organizations the stake these individuals and groups feel becomes narrowly and personally defined over the years. For example, employees may feel that they are only in it for their paycheck.

The transformational leader attempts to raise the stakes for all who are involved in the organization. When suppliers are committed to their customers, they strive to find better ways to serve the customer and to help the customer find better ways of carrying out their business. Committed employees work toward improving the methods and systems of the organization in order to help it achieve its vision.

A sense of commitment, having a stake, and "buying-in" are products of this process. The overused words of involvement, empowerment, and self-management begin to describe the process.

In a merger or network, development of stakeholders must occur at all levels of the newly structured organization. At the top, key executives must continually work to formulate, clarify, and "communicate for meaning" the direction and path for the new organization. Our experience tells us that this process should include more members of the organization than most managers typically allow.

Middle managers and professionals from the previous organizational entities can be put into teams to work together to identify opportunities for achieving the objectives of the merger and for accomplishing key projects such as integrating information systems, rationalizing services, proposing product streams, determining clinical pathways, and standardizing methods for the new organization. At lower levels, teams of people who are associated with a particular service or procedure can be created from the various organizations to standardize methods, improve procedures, and reduce or eliminate bottlenecks. All of these methods will inevitably increase employees' stake in the success of the new organization.

An interesting dynamic that leaders employ is to engage people for the specific purpose of enhancing their commitment to the vision. For example, a transformational leader might see an employee complaint as an opportunity to enhance that employee's "buy-in" and participation. Assuming the complaint has some legitimacy, in addition to taking action to resolve the situation, the leader might enlist the employee in some activity to either eliminate or improve the problem. To make this work the employee will need to grasp and understand the vision, will need to comprehend the principles and ethics that should guide problem solving and behaviors, and will need to know that the leader is supportive.

PROCESS #5: BUILDING SPIRIT AND WILL

This leadership process has two inextricably connected components—spirit and will. *Spirit* describes the leader's being or state. One might think of it as the leader's emotional condition. For instance, is the leader hyperactive, distracted, calm, patient, angry, or nurturing?

Will is related to such qualities as the leader's persistence, perseverance, and steadfastness. This process is related to the heart and soul of the leader. Will is the dynamic that creates trust among people and confidence within the organization. Trust is based on predictability, reliability, and knowledge of a person's values (which is based on behavioral experiences with that person). Leaders are unrelenting, unwavering, tirelessly steadfast, and, therefore, predictable and trustworthy.

Leaders build confidence and energy within the organization by employing what Bennis and Nanus[8] describe as the "deployment of self through positive self-regard." Leaders recognize and utilize their own and others' strengths. They nurture and develop the capabilities of others. They build rather than tear down. They reinforce rather than punish. This is not to say that they are not disciplined, or that they do not require high standards of performance. They recognize, however, that for people to excel and to go beyond previous performance, they must continually learn, stretch themselves, and, on occasion, fail. Leaders recognize that for this to happen, people must be supported, trusted, nurtured, and respected.

The process of building spirit and will may describe the quality of the leader's interactions with others as well as specific types of engagements had with others. That is, the leader interacts with others in a way that builds trust, confidence, persistence, and motivation. The leader also engages others in order to build trust, confidence, persistence, and motivation.

PROCESS #6: SUSTAINING FOCUS

Leaders cannot allow themselves or others to lose focus or become distracted from the goals and vision of the organization. In their recent book, *The Success Paradigm*, Friesen and Johnson state that "leadership is to a large degree a function of properly focusing members within an organization on a few key issues . . . in order to understand what is important for the organization to succeed."[13(p.20)] Transformational leaders relate most organizational or business conversations back to those important guidance mechanisms. In this sense, they manage or lead others' focus or attention. Of the 90 individuals in their leadership study, Bennis and Nanus report:

> All ninety people interviewed had an agenda, an unparalleled concern with outcome. Leaders are the most results-oriented individuals in the world, and results get attention. Their visions or intentions are compelling and pull people toward them. Intensity coupled with commitment

is magnetic. And these intense personalities do not have to coerce people to pay attention; they are so intent on what they are doing that, like a child completely absorbed with creating a sand castle in a sandbox, they draw others in.[8(p.28)]

The structure and financing of health care are rapidly changing, and many experienced health care executives have expressed an honest bewilderment as to what the future holds. Leaders with visionary capabilities may not necessarily divine the future of a health care organization or network. Similarly, their capacity to affect the future health care system may be minuscule or nonexistent. However, their nature and vision drive them to engage in intense activity in full faith that they can make a difference. As mentioned previously, such focus and confidence is infectious, and herein lies their unique talent to be at the forefront of the development of their organizations.

The current health care environment is almost universally described as turbulent and unpredictable. Massive layoffs are predicted in coming years in institutional settings, along with reductions in the numbers and prestige of specialist physicians. Leaders will recognize the devastating effects of such management activities and employ other means to ensure the trust, energy, and commitment of those who make the organization work. There is certainly no set formula for being a leader in the face of difficult choices and organizational upheaval. Clearly, leadership behaviors are not achieved as readily as they are prescribed.

A leader's capacity for vision, for communicating for meaning, for creating possibilities, for developing stakeholders, for building spirit and will, and for sustaining focus will be challenged by turbulent change. However, periods of dramatic change may also provide the impetus for creativity and growth. In these times, leaders will evoke and refine both their own effectiveness and that of their managers and staff.

REFERENCES

1. Kanter, R.M. "Collaborative Advantage: Successful Partnerships Manage the Relationship, Not Just the Deal." *Harvard Business Review* 72, no. 4 (1994):96–108.
2. Campbell, J.P. et al. *Managerial Behavior, Performance, and Effectiveness.* New York, N.Y.: McGraw-Hill, 1970.
3. Fleishman, E.A. "Leadership Climate, Human Relations Training, and Supervisory Behavior." *Personnel Psychology* 6 (1953):205–222.
4. Blake, J., and Mouton, R. "Theory and Research for Developing a Science of Leadership." *Journal of Applied Behavioral Science* 18 (1982):275–291.
5. Hersey, P., and Blanchard, K.H. *Management of Organizational Behavior.* Englewood Cliffs, N.J.: Prentice Hall, 1972.
6. Fiedler, F.E. "Engineer the Job To Fit the Manager." *Harvard Business Review* 43 (1965):115–122.
7. Burns, J.M. *Leadership.* New York, N.Y.: Harper & Row. 1978.
8. Bennis, W., and Nanus, B. *Leaders: The Strategies for Taking Charge.* New York. N.Y.: Harper & Row, 1985.
9. Sashkin, M. *The Visionary Leader: Trainer Guide.* Philadelphia. Pa: Organization Design and Development. Inc., 1990.
10. Wall, B., Solum, R.S., and Sobol, M.R. *The Visionary Leader.* Rocklin. Calif.: Prima Publishing, 1992.
11. Schein, E.H. *Organizational Culture and Leadership.* San Francisco. Calif.: Jossey-Bass, 1985.
12. Wheatley, M.J. *Leadership and the New Science.* San Francisco. Calif.: Berrett-Koehler, 1992.
13. Friesen, M., and Johnson, J. *The Success Paradigm.* Westport, Conn.: Quorum, 1995.

QUESTIONS TO PART II

1. Do you agree with the premise that leaders create leaders? Explain.
2. Have you been coached or mentored in your nursing career? If so, in what ways did you benefit?
3. Of the five leadership roles detailed in the Manfredi article, which one is the most challenging for you? Explain.
4. With which type of leadership, transactional or transformational, do you most identify? Explain.
5. What kind of leadership do you think is most needed in your work setting?
6. Barker and Young characterize a transformational leader as a "value broker." Discuss this characterization as it applies to your area of practice. Are any of your coworkers "value brokers?" Describe what they do.
7. Barker and Young contend that in the modern world view, paternalistic values and beliefs are ending. What are your views of this contention? Is there evidence of these changes in your health care setting?
8. Based on your own experiences, what do you consider to be ethical leadership?
9. In your health care setting, what situations have you encountered that have necessitated ethical leadership?
10. What ethical conflicts have you encountered in your work setting?
11. What are the shared values and beliefs of your coworkers? In what ways are they demonstrated in your work setting?
12. In what ways has your personal background facilitated achieving your professional goals? In what ways has it impeded your professional goals?
13. Which of the six leadership processes do you see emerging among your coworkers?

PART III

●●●

Contemporary Leadership Behaviors

To say that our present health care environment is chaotic is an understatement. Whatever light there is at the end of the health care tunnel is not yet in sight. Job insecurity, layoffs, sinking morale, compromised patient care, and organizational practices incompatible with ethical conduct all contribute to chaos in health care and to our professional vulnerability. As the chaos in health care continues, our patients' vulnerability increases and health care becomes not only more dehumanizing, but more questionable in quality.

Never before have leadership behaviors been so needed. Now, as never before, do we need to use them collectively and effectively in organizational systems that, more often than not, do not regard professional nursing seriously. Rousing ourselves from the immobilizing and demoralizing effect that these chaotic times provoke is difficult, but it must be done. Time and time again, nurses have not only shown their resiliency in adapting to change, but have proven their ability to mobilize themselves into actions that support quality care and the integrity of their practice. The road ahead is not an easy one to travel, nor is it meant to be. But using leadership behaviors collectively and effectively can make the effort all the more worthwhile.

Assertiveness, advocacy, mentoring, power, politics, change, collective bargaining, and conflict resolution are the leadership behaviors emphasized in Part III. The readings selected for Part III are, for the most part, reality-based in terms of their practical application to nurses and the health care environments in which they work. The readings provide the knowledge base that nurses need to strengthen their resolve and professionalism in their continuing efforts to improve patient care.

PART III   **Contents**

(continued)

96

SECTION EIGHT   CONFLICT RESOLUTION

CHAPTER 11

●●●

Speaking Up: A Moral Obligation

BRIGHID KELLY

Rarely do we think much of speaking up when we are among those who are likely to agree with us. However, speaking up when in the company of those with whom we know we disagree is entirely another matter. Standing up for what one believes is one of the most important aspects of personal integrity. Yet, there is reason to believe that it is very difficult, especially for nurses. We have been socialized to do what is expected. Our educational system is more concerned with conformity than with debate. Nurses, in particular, have learned to believe that one does not voice dissent. Nurses are often punished for being outspoken by their own—other nurses.

Speaking up is particularly difficult for hospital nurses because hierarchical pressures, organizational factors, and work variables influence ethical practice (Crisham, 1981; Mayberry, 1986). Holly (1993) describes how nurses' perceived inability to act on behalf of their patients results in moral distress, frustration and powerlessness. A perception of powerlessness to influence ethical decision-making is a common experience for hospital nurses (Erlin & Frost, 1991; McKinley, 1986). Dwyer (1994), in his recent article "The Ethics of Speaking Up," concludes that habitual silence in the face of perceived wrongs results in a permanent dilution of ethical values.

Being True to Self

When we say that people speak up or speak out, we imply they have assumed a position of dissent. It requires enormous courage to make a public statement that opposes a colleague's point of view. For some people defending their convictions requires a sense of right that becomes so overwhelming they are forced to take a stand. They risk ridicule, rejection, and social isolation but gain a sense of power—the power of feeling good about themselves. Such persons are often considered to be heroes, yet we all have the potential to be heroes. The courage to be a hero means taking responsibility for one's own decisions and judgments. In doing so we are conscious of our own values and standards and are willing to stand up for them.

From the moment we are born, we engage in a constant struggle between growth and stagnation. Growth means change, change means uncertainty, uncertainty means

From *Nursing Forum* 31(2):31–34. Reprinted with permission, Nursecom, Inc.

anxiety, anxiety requires new skills. Stagnation means safety, safety means dependency, dependency means self-contempt. Thus, through conflict, pain, and courage we become people we can be proud of. Why do we find it so difficult to go against the proverbial tide?

Going against the tide is not expected social behavior for women. Roles are inventions of social reality. Social interaction theorists maintain that identities are socially bestowed, socially sustained, and socially transformed (Mead, 1962; Habermas, 1990). Denzin (1978) states, "We live out every day in a complex web of recognitions and nonrecognitions" (p. 72). Moral identity cannot be separated from the social context from which it emerged. We do what is expected of us because it makes life easier. Therefore, when we occupy new roles, set forth new positions, we change the norms set by our social groups.

To be different requires courage. Courage is a virtue. It is a quality that all heroes possess. Courage is being more fearful of letting oneself down than the consequences of being different. It is saying to ourself, "Beyond this point I shall not move, because if I do I cannot live with myself." It is knowing that "going along" may appear to work in the short term but what about later? It is knowing that we live and die as individuals who in the final analysis must be alone with ourselves.

The Price of Silence

The greatest threat to being heroes is conformity. We all want to fit in, to belong: It offers us a false sense of security. Also, our society lays great emphasis upon being socially accepted. Goffman (1963) says that because "fitting in" is the rule of interaction, deviation from it is cause for special attention. We want to avoid being selected out because we have a need to act "as people of that type are supposed to act" (Goffman, p. 11). There is nothing wrong with wanting to fit in. It is a natural social phenomenon. However, when fitting in becomes more important than doing what is right, it becomes a moral problem with a huge price tag.

The prevailing value about having to "win" is another pitfall in maintaining moral integrity. When winning becomes more important than doing the right thing, we should be concerned not only about what it is doing to us, but also what message we are giving to those who look to us for example. People say "You can't win against those powers, and if you can't win why do it?" But "winning" is a separate value that has very little to do with right conduct. Doing what one believes to be right has intrinsic value apart from "winning," "looking good," or "saving face."

Research studies have found that nurses experiencing burnout are likely to perceive they have not been "living up" to their moral values (Duxbury, Armstrong, Drew, & Henly, 1984; Stone, Jebson, Walk, & Belsham, 1984). Compromising one's integrity is a major source of stress in nursing. Corroborating the prevailing attitudes does not require one to risk disapproval. "Success" depends on being well-liked. If we remain silent we appear to risk nothing. We fail to consider the price of silence. To know something is wrong and say nothing, we indirectly consent to what has occurred. In doing this we become part of the problem. If we continue to be silent about wrongs we are doomed to become victims of our own silence.

Not to speak up when we believe we ought to is to let ourselves down—when, for example, in our own experience negligence occurs, when "everyone is doing it" becomes a denial of the moral issues, or when a person is being scapegoated. To live with a lie by not speaking up results in lack of self-respect. If we do it often enough we not only damage self-esteem, but we also suffer self-alienation. Self-alienation occurs when we separate from ourselves because we have come to despise what we stand for (Gergen, 1971). It implies that we have let ourselves down. Letting oneself down can become a habit.

The concept of habit as a reinforcer of behavior is integral to health teaching. More recently, it is reemerging as an important concept in ethics. Virtue ethics is founded on the idea, of character development. The notion is that good or bad habits can change behavior and influence values in either direction. Aristotle says:

> *This, then, is the case with virtues also; by doing the acts that we do in our transactions with other men we become just or unjust, and by doing the acts that we do in the presence of danger, and being habituated to feel fear or confidence, we become brave or cowardly. . . . It makes no small difference, then, whether we form habits of one kind or of another from our youth; it makes a great deal of difference; or rather it makes all the difference. (Aristotle, 1925, p. 29).*

The Legacy of Speaking Up

Making a difference is what nurses do. But we are often kinder to our clients than we are to our young colleagues. We have the opportunity every day to make a difference not only for patients who depend upon us for guidance and information but also for our younger or less experienced colleagues. Nursing students and new graduates are particularly vulnerable to conformity (Kelly, 1992). Buckenham and McGrath (1983) assert "student nurses are groomed for subordination" (p. 104). They concluded nursing students are socialized to obedience, respect for authority, and loyalty to the team. And, both their acceptance into, and continued membership of, the health team depends upon their manifest recognition of their subordinate role. The result is often the very students who would make the best professionals are driven out of nursing because they are too assertive or just cannot put up with the "game playing." Other sources of coercion are the mistreatment nursing students receive from their "role models." A fairly recent study (Theis, 1988) revealed that lack of respect for nursing students constituted the largest number of unethical teaching acts by nursing faculty. Other sources of stress and pressure to conform were punitive instructional styles that undermine students' self-esteem and deprive them of self-confidence (Pagana, 1988; Windsor, 1987).

The point is that feeling good about oneself and having self-confidence are essential prerequisites to risk-taking. Strong leaders in nursing need a strong sense of personal integrity. They need to have confidence in themselves. We need to model risk-taking, promote self-confidence, encourage them to take risks, and give pointers on communicative strategies in confrontation. Nursing students need to learn the kind of communicative and social skills that empower them as neophyte nurses to withstand the pressure to conform to hospital systems that ultimately dilute their professional values and contribute to habits that are neither professional nor ethical.

The ability to state one's position directly and honestly without offending another is a skill. It requires an open and honest approach to others. And it requires "I" statements. The ability to say clearly "I disagree" or "I am not in accord with the policy for the following reasons" takes courage but becomes easier with practice. With regard to a clinical situation, one needs to be able to say, "I am morally uncomfortable with this decision," or in case of a particular practice, "This practice is ethically unacceptable to me." There is great power in making a moral statement. If hospital nurses today, stressed and exhausted by economic cutbacks, could word their protests about nurse–patient ratios in moral terms, it might make a difference. Hospital policies need to reflect what is right, not just what they think is safe.

Summary

The purpose of this paper was to explore the act of speaking up as a moral obligation and discuss its relationship to moral courage and habit. The difficulties of speaking up and the consequence of silence were compared to the benefits of being true to oneself and standing up for one's convictions.

Speaking up or speaking out is an act of moral courage. It often carries with it a price tag. But an even greater price tag comes with silence—the loss of self-respect. It is a matter of personal integrity. There is something sad about the inner voice that says, "I should have said something." Speaking up empowers the speaker and the receiver. And it makes us heroes. In the words attributed to Sir Thomas More in the play *A Man for All Seasons*:

> *If we lived in a state where virtue was profitable, common sense would make us good, and greed would make us saintly. And we'd live like animals or angels in a happy land that needs no heroes. But, since in fact we see that avarice, anger, envy, pride, sloth, lust and stupidity commonly profit far beyond humility, chastity, fortitude, justice and thought, and have to choose, to be human at all . . . why then perhaps we* must *stand fast a little—even at the risk of being heroes* (Bolt, 1965, p. 123).

The benefits of speaking up outweigh the risks not only from a personal point of view but for the profession as a whole.

REFERENCES

Aristotle. (1925). (translated by Ross) *Aristotle: Ethics Nicomachea.* Oxford, UK: Oxford University Press (1925, Reprinted 1990) p. 29.

Bolt, R. (1965). *A man for all seasons.* New York: Random House.

Buckenham, J., & McGrath, G. (1983). *The social reality of nursing.* Sydney, Australia: Health Science.

Crisham, P. (1981) Measuring moral judgment in nursing dilemmas. *Nursing Research, 32,* 104–110.

Denzin, N. (1978). *Sociological methods.* New York: McGraw Hill.

Dwyer, J. (1994). Primum non tacere: An ethic of speaking up. *Hastings Center Report, 24*(1), 13–18.

Duxbury, M., Armstrong, G., Drew, D., & Henly, S. (1984). Head nurse leadership style with staff nurse burnout and job satisfaction in neonatal intensive care units. *Nursing Research, 33,* 97–101.

Erlin, J., & Frost, B. (1991). Nurses' perceptions of powerlessness in influencing ethical decisions. *Western Journal of Nursing Research, 13,* 397–407

Gergen, K. (1971). *The concept of self.* New York: Holt; Rheinhart & Winston.

Goffman, E. (1963). *Behaviour in public places: Notes on the social organization of gatherings.* New York: Free Press.

Habermas, J. (1990). *Moral consciousness and communicative action.* (translated by Lenhardt, C. & Nicholsen, S.) Cambridge, MA: MIT Press (1988).

Holly, C. (1993). The ethical quandaries of acute care nursing practice. *Journal of Professional Nursing, 9*(2), 110–115.

Kelly, B. (1992). Professional ethics as perceived by American Nursing undergraduates. *Journal of Advanced Nursing, 17,* 10–15.

Mayberry, M. (1986). Ethical decision-making: A response of hospital nurses. *Nursing Administration Quarterly, 10*(3), 75–81.

McKinley, (1986). An advocacy role for the critical care nurse. *Australian Journal of Advanced Nursing, 7,* 223–229.

Mead, G. (1962). *Mind, self and society.* Chicago; University of Chicago Press.

Noddings, N. (1984). *Caring: A feminine approach to ethics and moral education.* Berkeley, CA: University of California Press.

Pagana, K. (1988). Stresses and threats reported by baccalaureate nursing students in relation to an initial clinical experience. *Journal of Nursing Education, 27,* 418–424.

Stone G., Jebsen P., Walk P., & Belsham R. (1984). Identification of stress and coping skills within a critical care setting. *Western Journal of Nursing Research, 6,* 201–211.

Theis, C. (1988). Nursing students' perspectives of unethical teaching behaviors. *Journal of Nursing Education, 27,* 102–105.

Windsor, A. (1987). Nursing students' perceptions of clinical experience. *Journal of Nursing Education, 26,* 150–154.

CHAPTER 12

●●

Anger in Nurses: Don't Lose It, Use It

PATRICIA GENTRY DROPPLEMAN AND SANDRA PAUL THOMAS

Nurses are angry, and for good reasons—heavy workloads, long hours, and lack of support from peers, managers, and administration, not to mention the sexism and sexual harassment faced by female nurses. Anger in our profession has been associated with high turnover rates, interpersonal alienation, and, ultimately, burnout.

But our anger isn't the problem. The problem is that many of us feel caught in the maelstrom of today's health care environment—tossed about by forces we have no control over.

Having conducted the largest empirical study of anger in women to date (much of which was reported in our book *Women and Anger,* Springer Publishing, 1993), we decided to take a closer look at the anger experienced by women in nursing. (We're currently conducting a separate study of male nurses and their work-related anger.) After collecting data from over 500 women, 75 of whom were nurses, and conducting a smaller, phenomenological study that's still in progress, we recognized several patterns, which we'll outline in this article (see Box 12-1, *The Women's Anger Study: Close-up on Method*). We'll discuss what nurses told us about the reasons for their anger and how they tend to express it. We'll also offer suggestions for positive anger outlets and strategies you can use in what many have described as a constant battle (see Box 12-2).

View From the Trenches

Nurses told us they saw their work environment as hostile and that working in a hospital was "like being in a war." Sue spoke of battle fatigue; Linda described herself as a "survivor." Others told us "We feel sabotaged" and "We really don't know how to fight back." They said they were tired of being treated with disrespect by physicians, managers, peers, faculty, subordinates, and patients.

Sometimes disrespect took the form of unfair or uncivil treatment. Nurses described how they were "chastised," "patronized," "talked down to," and "demeaned" in front of

BOX 12-1 **THE WOMEN'S ANGER STUDY: CLOSE-UP ON METHOD**

In 1989, a 14-woman research team led by Sandra Paul Thomas began collecting data for phase I of the Women's Anger Study. For three years they would continue collecting data with a focus on women's anger in everyday situations at home and work. From work sites, schools, and women's organizations, they recruited more than 500 female participants between the ages of 25 and 66. The subjects represented a wide range of educational backgrounds, occupations, and income brackets. Seventy-five of the women were nurses.

Phase I was primarily quantitative. The researchers used well-established questionnaires to measure variables such as anger, stress, depression, and self-esteem. The women were also asked to answer some open-ended questions about their anger.

For the past three years, phase II of the study has been in progress. This phase is phenomenological in nature. In other words, its focus is the subjects' awareness of the phenomenon (in this case, anger); no attempt is made to quantify or validate the experiences reported. The study is considered valid if it provides a thorough description of the phenomenon and the study participants agree that this description matches their experience. Validity is further substantiated if the study findings resonate with readers' own experience of anger in the workplace.

Because phase II is a phenomenological study, it differs significantly from phase I in terms of method, size, and recruitment procedures. Based on in-depth interviews, this phase involves only 60 subjects (not participants in phase I) who were selected on the basis of having experienced the phenomenon (anger) and being willing to discuss it at length.

Nine of the phase II subjects are registered nurses—including staff nurses, nurse managers, nurse practitioners, a midwife, and a nursing instructor—with 7 to 34 years in practice. Educational preparation ranges from AD to PhD. The nurses range in age from 29 to 56.

Most quotations in this article have been taken from phase II interview transcripts. Pseudonyms have been used to protect the privacy of those quoted.

others. Extreme forms of disrespect included gender and sexual harassment. As Eve saw it, "They wouldn't mouth off to me the way they do . . . if I were a male PA." Joy told us, "I saw [women] nurses being touched in ways that were just totally inappropriate . . . [and] physicians feeling they had a right to do that."

One hot button cited by several nurses is the disregard with which their clinical assessments and critical thinking are sometimes treated. They say they're tired of "not being heard."

Linda, for example, spoke of a patient who was experiencing significant pain at discharge. "I could tell she was in pain," said Linda. "This woman was not ready to go home. I related this to the charge nurse, but she would not call the doctor . . . This patient was discharged, but she ended up being readmitted to another hospital . . . [because] she had a bowel obstruction." From Linda's perspective, ". . . what's so sad is that we're educated to assess and to plan and to intervene . . . and then, for whatever reason, that assessment is rejected . . ."

Other nurses echoed Linda's sentiment. "I am most angry," explained Joy, ". . . that what I need and . . . want doesn't matter . . . It's almost like . . . [I'm] a nonentity . . . Everybody doesn't have to agree with me, but I'd like the courtesy of being heard."

One nurse went so far as to say she "had the experience as a nurse of being voiceless, of having no voice." Looking back on 30 years of practice, she realized that she had often developed a sore throat when she became very angry about work-related matters over which she felt she had no control.

Perpetual Scapegoat

Nurses are also angry that they're often made the scapegoat for others' irresponsibility. Lisa described physicians who blame "that stupid bunch of nurses" for problems arising out of their own lack of judgment. "I think someone has to relieve the pressure, has to be blamed," she explained to us, "and I think it's the nurses, most often. That's especially true in acute care and in labor situations." Lisa said she'd heard physicians telling irate families, "'I couldn't do anything about it [a fetal or maternal complication] because the nurse didn't call me,'" when, in fact, the nurse had reported "the first little flicker . . . on the fetal monitor."

Some nurses told us they were angry at coworkers who were less committed and dedicated. For example, Sally, a nurse manager, said she's angry that her nursing staff often fails to take responsibility for their professional actions, leaving her to sort out the mess that results. Another nurse expressed frustration with LPNs and aides who didn't put patients first.

"I tried to set . . . [a good] example," she told us. "I emptied the bedpans. I got patients up to the bathroom. I didn't just sit around and ask them to do things I wasn't willing to do." But when she directed aides to perform specific patient-care tasks, she said she was frequently told, "I'll do it after my break."

Unrealistic Expectations

Hospital restructuring has generated a lot of anger and frustration in nurses throughout the country. Cuts in RN staffing have left nurses feeling that their own safety, as well as that of their patients, is compromised. With fewer human resources, nurses are caring for more acutely ill patients—while hospital stays are getting shorter.

Recent graduates told us they felt unprepared for the clinical situations they encountered. Several spoke of inadequate orientations and the unrealistic expectations of hospital administrators. "Everybody expected Supernurses," explained one. "I wanted to live up to the expectation. I tried hard. But I would go home frustrated. The patient load was so heavy. I don't feel like I gave . . . [the patients] the care they deserved. I would get really angry."

Many nurses spoke of insufficient resources in terms of both personnel and time. It produced a sense that the work environment couldn't be controlled. Said one, "I knew the stuff I was taught to do, but I didn't have time to do it like I was taught to do it. It is . . . a rat race."

A new graduate told us she works from 7 AM to 7 PM on a trauma unit. She often stays an extra two hours to complete her work and help the oncoming shift because there are usually only one RN and two aides to care for 40 critically ill patients. A memo from her hospital's administration informed all nurses that they were expected to work overtime—but that they wouldn't be paid for more than 12 hours a day.

Feeling of Powerlessness

Being excluded from critical decisions, such as those concerning staffing needs, created a feeling of powerlessness among the nurses we spoke with. And much of the anger, frustration, and exhaustion they experienced resulted directly from their perceived inability to effect change. The feeling of powerlessness has been identified as a major cause of job dissatisfaction among nurses.

Why do nurses have low expectations for the level of power they're capable of acquiring? The reasons appear to be intertwined and influenced by several factors, including the socialization of women, their subsequent fear of and inexperience with risk taking, shortcomings in the traditional nursing education (specifically, lack of information about the development and use of power), and anachronistic perceptions of nursing as women's work and the nurse as physician's helper.

Nurses become angry when they know they're competent in their clinical expertise, but don't have the authority to act on it. Sue, a nurse practitioner with prescribing authority in her state, resented having to work within a system that she felt summarily dismissed her opinions. She recalled writing an order for an iron supplement based on her assessment of a patient's blood work, only to have the physician on the case cancel the order. Explained Sue, "I share my opinion, and if it's different from what the physician thinks, then it's degraded."

It's been shown that women in highly dependent, powerless positions are more likely than men in similar positions to acquiesce—that is, to give in to or agree with an authority figure even when you know he's wrong. According to Lisa Mainiero, a researcher in the area of organizational behavior, acquiescence "suggests an acceptance of the power imbalance as well as the . . . [defeat] of the individual . . . by the high power target."

Ann knew that her unit was insufficiently staffed, but despite complaints from the nursing staff, nothing was done about it until the hospital's administration heard from a physician. "It took a doctor getting upset," she explained, "to . . . make administration realize that we were functioning unsafely. It's frustrating to me that a doctor has to . . . tell [administration] 'the unit's not safe,' when the nurses are . . . [doing] that already."

Feeling powerless to change their work environments, nurses told us they waited for conditions to change—and hoped the changes were for the better. When this didn't happen, they would transfer to other units or resign their posts and move to other institutions.

Anger Turned Inward

When verbalized, anger can be used to get someone's attention. However, we found that nurses often misdirected their anger or expressed it in such extreme forms that they later felt bad about themselves and how they'd expressed the anger.

One nurse remembered screaming at her nurse manager. Another told us, "I really blow up and I start crying and I feel better it's out, but I wish I had handled it a little better." Blowups tended to make nurses feel guilty and embarrassed, and view themselves as ineffective, unprofessional, or "bitchy."

Nurses told us they often coped with anger and feelings of powerlessness in unhealthy ways. Some masked their anger with alcohol or excessive eating; others tried to vent it through smoking. Some became depressed; others somatized their feelings, experiencing physical symptoms such as fatigue.

Nurses also turned their anger against themselves through self-disparaging comments. Eve, a master's-prepared nurse practitioner, devalued her own work by referring to it as "scut work" and "taking care of the petty things." For Fran, who acknowledged that she's a perfectionist and her own worst critic, "performance equals approval." So if she doesn't receive approval, she feels she's not performing well.

Some nurses resorted to faultfinding, name-calling, backbiting, and subtle sabotage of their colleagues and superiors—a phenomenon called "horizontal violence," considered characteristic of oppressed groups. Feeling powerless to deal with those in authority (in this case, physicians, administrators, and supervisors), they fight among themselves instead of providing mutual support and empathy.

Here's one nurse's example of horizontal violence:

When I first started working here, we had a new grad on the floor . . . and I think other nurses were jealous of her. She was a baccalaureate nurse and a lot of the nurses on my floor are not . . . You could just see the potential in this girl. She was so good with the patients and she had a lot of energy . . . But other nurses would never help her. It was almost like [they were] setting her up . . . [to] fail . . . She told me, 'I really wonder if I should be a nurse. Maybe I . . . should do something else.' So I encouraged her to get off that unit. I said . . . 'You can't let other people destroy you.'

Nurses described subtle and not-so-subtle forms of sabotage, ranging from cutting remarks to withdrawal of support. Said one, "I tend to draw back . . . and give . . . the cold shoulder." Another, who described her behavior as passive-aggressive, said with a laugh, "You can cut them, but don't let them know they're bleeding until they look down."

Getting Beyond Infighting

All of the nurses told us that physicians were at the top of the hierarchy in their workplaces—and that there was a hierarchy within nursing itself, which seemed related to the amount of technology used. For example, the nurses we interviewed believe critical care nursing is perceived as a higher-status specialty than maternal–child or mental health nursing.

The different nursing factions appear to disagree on many issues. Though conflict among social groups is natural, it's not advantageous for nurses to present themselves as fragmented to those in power. Infighting within our profession results in a disunity that prevents us from pooling our resources to confront the really important issues, such as health care reform and quality patient care.

Some nurses regard assertive coworkers as uncaring. As one of them put it, "Nurses who speak up do not have the qualities that nurses should have." Others, however, told us anger empowered them—that it motivated them to take action to protect their rights and support their patients.

Ann spoke of being outraged when a physician refused to give a maternity patient an epidural because she only had Medicaid coverage. She confronted the physician's discrimination and successfully advocated for her patient, who was ultimately given the epidural.

Linda's anger helped her speak up for herself when she alone was charged with a medication error for which at least one other person should have been held responsible. Fueled by her anger, she explained to the director of nursing that although she was in error when she administered potassium to a patient who'd been taken off the supplement, the outgoing nurse hadn't flagged the change in orders in the Kardex or the chart—and she'd forgotten to tell Linda about it at shift report. The hospital's error reporting form was subsequently revised to accommodate shared responsibility. And hospital policy was modified to put more red flags into effect when changes were made to a patient's medication regimen.

One nurse told us that when her unit's nursing staff banded together to make changes, they were empowered. "We feel like we have our unit back in our control again, which is the way it should be," she explained. "You [the nurses] should have some control over what happens and why and how."

Turning Anger Into Empowerment

Of the nearly 600 women we studied in the two phases of our investigation, we felt that those who seemed least angry—and most empowered—had a few things in common:

First, they worked to channel their anger to develop their power (see Box 12-2, *Using Anger Effectively*). Though women are socialized to view power as a negative, coercive force, fear and coercion aren't instruments of power; they're instruments of oppression. As the biographies of great nurses such as Margretta Styles, Luther Christman, and Hattie Bessent demonstrate, leaders with a healthy concept of power empower those around them. In fact, Dr. Styles wrote of aspiring to provide leadership that "engages the full person of the follower, resulting in a relationship of mutual stimulation and elevation."

Second, they viewed anger as a protective and helpful ally. Anger is often a signal that our rights and values are being jeopardized. It may motivate us to take action and restore our own power.

As one nurse said of her anger, "I see it as a red flag that says, 'something just happened here—you were violated.' If I acknowledge my anger instead of trying to stuff it, I can identify solutions . . . " So when you feel yourself getting angry, take a deep breath, survey the situation, identify the problems, and think proactively.

Third, they were politically active at the local or national level. Anger can serve as a powerful catalyst in tackling problems. Coalitions of nurses can be effective in making policy changes. In the spring of 1995 thousands of nurses, mobilized by anger, took to the streets of our nation's capital. They marched down Pennsylvania Avenue to the White House to protest hospital staffing cuts and advocate better patient care. They expressed their anger toward eroding nurse-patient ratios, replacement of RNs with unlicensed personnel, and the shortening of hospital stays for critically ill patients. (Many organizations, including professional unions and national associations, banded together to support the march.)

The New York State Nurses Association (NYSNA), outraged over these same issues, launched an aggressive media campaign on television, subways, and commuter trains to inform the public about this health care threat. Thousands of consumers responded to their slogan, "Every patient deserves an RN, not an imitation," and called NYSNA for information on how to demand appropriate care by RNs. And Indiana nurses have been instrumental in supporting Pam Carter, state attorney general, in her investigation of unlicensed, unqualified personnel performing nursing procedures.

BOX 12–2 **USING ANGER EFFECTIVELY**

Helplessness and powerlessness, feelings which accompany poor self-esteem, foster inappropriate expressions of anger. But self-esteem can be bolstered and anger expressed constructively. Here are a few tips:

- Learn to give yourself credit for your knowledge and competence.
- Take responsibility for your mistakes and successes.
- Define your goals, develop strategies to meet them, and be persistent in pursuing them.
- Address issues, not emotions.
- Commit to affirming and supporting your peers.
- Watch out for scapegoating, blaming, or disrespectful treatment of fellow nurses, and be prepared to intervene on their behalf in appropriate ways.
- Take time to take care of yourself—even when you're on the unit.

Fourth, they took action. They were willing to use their professional association's lobbying force, to pursue legal avenues when necessary, and to send documentation to the medical malpractice board, the state board of nursing, or the Joint Commission on Accreditation of Healthcare Organizations.

Suppressing our anger, somatizing it, masking it with food or drugs, or expressing it in a hostile way won't help us achieve the changes we want. But our anger can act as a liberating force if it's channeled into productive political action or problem solving on the unit. When we speak out about injustices and join together to solve our problems in an environment of mutual respect, we'll find that anger can empower us to take actions that enrich our lives and the future of our profession.

SELECTED REFERENCES

Carlson-Catalano, J. Invest in yourself: Cultivating personal power. *Nurs. Forum.* 29(2):22–28, Apr.–June 1994.

Duldt, B. W. Anger: An occupational hazard for nurses. *Nurs. Outlook* 29:510–518, Sept. 1981.

Lernet, H. G. *The Dance of Anger: A Woman's Guide to Changing the Patterns of Intimate Relationships.* New York, Harper & Row, 1985.

Mainiero, L Coping with powerlessness: The relationship of gender and job dependency to empowerment strategy usage. *Adm. Sci. Q.* 31:633–653, 1986.

Muff, J. *Socialization, Sexism and Stereotyping: Women's Issues in Nursing.* Prospect Heights, IL, Waveland Press. 1982.

Munhall, P. Women's anger and its meaning: A phenomenological perspective. *Health Care Women Int.* 14:481–491. Nov.–Dec. 1993.

Schort T. M., and Zimmerman. A. *Making Choices, Taking Chances: Nurse Leaders Tell Their Stories.* St. Louis. MO, Mosby, 1988.

Smith, M., et al. Under assault: The experience of work-related anger in female registered nurses (in press). *Nurs.Forum.* 1996.

Thomas, S. P., and Jefferson. C. *Use Your Anger: A Woman's Guide to Empowerment.* New York, NY, Pocket Books, 1996.

Thomas, S. P., ed. *Women and Anger.* New York, NY, Springer Publishing. 1993.

Valentine, P. Feminism: A four-letter word? *Can.Nurse* 88(11):20–23, Dec. 1992.

CHAPTER 13

Nursing Advocacy: An Ethic of Practice

NAN GAYLORD AND PAMELA GRACE

Introduction

In a recent article, "The nurse as patient advocate," Ellen Bernal, a hospital ethicist, provides a thought-provoking account of the problems that the nursing profession faces in the area of patient advocacy.[1] We believe, however, that Bernal makes erroneous assumptions about nursing's intent: the first is that, for nurses, patient advocacy is defined only as patient rights advocacy; the second is that patient advocacy for nurses is inseparably linked with freedom to practice. We deny that nursing is trying to establish patient rights advocacy as a vehicle to reach autonomy of nursing practice, and we assert that patient advocacy has a much broader meaning for nurses than only patient rights.

It is true that autonomy of practice is one of the goals of the nursing profession, and achievement of this goal is necessary for enhancing patient care because it secures direct access to nursing services for clients and makes nurses accountable for these services. However, the debate over nursing autonomy includes many more issues than can be found in the nursing advocacy literature referenced by Bernal and used to support her propositions. Among the issues confronting nursing as a developing discipline are: educational preparation for entry into professional practice, direct reimbursement for services, and prescriptive privileges for advanced practice nurses. However, professional autonomy is not the subject of discussion in our paper. Instead, we would like to analyze the concept of advocacy as it applies to nursing and, therefore, have accepted Bernal's challenge to define "patient advocacy more precisely."[1] In the following we will examine how patient rights advocacy differs from patient advocacy as understood by the nursing profession. Both historical and contemporary perspectives of nursing advocacy will be presented to provide support for a broader definition of advocacy. Case studies will be utilized as examples of nursing advocacy.

Patient Rights Advocacy

Bernal maintains that, to the nursing profession, patient advocacy means the responsibility of protecting patient rights and interests in the health care setting. Patient advocacy, as discussed in the nursing literature, is advocacy with a broader meaning than that presented in her article. She derives her definition from a selection of nursing literature but has not fully interpreted some of the cited authors' viewpoints. Her truncated interpretations have limited the scope of the advocacy role for nurses only to the protection of patient *rights*. She assumes correctly that there are inherent difficulties for nurses acting in adversarial roles when attempting acts of patient rights advocacy, either within the institution in which they are employed, or with other pertinent hierarchical systems. She views this as problematic for nurses because it pits them against their employers, and perhaps against physicians with whom they must work. For this reason she asserts that nurses may not be the best persons to act as patient rights advocates, but such constraints pose problems for any provider of care employed by the hospital, including physicians, pharmacists, patient advocates, and hospital ethicists. Nevertheless, our main task at this juncture is not to discover who may be most suited to patient rights advocacy roles, but rather to delineate what we believe patient advocacy to mean in the context of the nursing care of individual patients.

In many respects, Gadow's[2] views on nursing advocacy are closest to what we, as nursing professionals, believe patient advocacy by nurses actually to be. It involves the nurse and patient in a much more intimate, interpersonal relationship. Gadow defines this relationship as "existential advocacy." It is the interaction of nurse and patient in such a way that it allows the person to understand "the unique meaning which the experience of health, illness, suffering, or dying is to have for that individual." This is a holistic approach to patient care. It does not preclude patient rights advocacy but recognizes it as only part of the existential advocacy role for nurses.

The ideal of such an "existential advocacy" as espoused by Gadow[2] stems from the assumption that "freedom of self-determination is the most fundamental and valuable human right." For the purposes of existential advocacy, then, the patient is the one who decides what is in her or his "best interests" in any situation; also stressed is the idea that this type of nursing advocacy helps to enable persons to

> . . . authentically exercise their freedom of self-determination. By authentic is meant a way of reaching decisions that are truly one's own—decisions that express all that one believes important about oneself and the world, the entire complexity of one's values.[2]

The authenticity is gained because it is the total person who is regarded and with whom the interaction occurs. Such a viewpoint necessarily takes into consideration that an individual's whole range of values, including any contradictions and any changes in values brought about by the new situation, must be included in the evaluation of any possible courses of action (including inaction) for or by the person. Gadow summarizes "existential advocacy" as "the effort to help persons become clear about what they want to do." Nursing, then, should be "distinguished by its *philosophy* of care and not by its care *functions*," functions being specific tasks performed by the nurse. She suggests that the

> . . . philosophical foundation and ideal of nursing is that of advocacy—not the concept of advocacy implied in the patients' rights movement in which any health professional is potentially a consumer advocate, but a fundamental, existential advocacy for which the nurse alone, among all the health professionals, is uniquely suited, and which is as distinct from consumer advocacy as it is from paternalism.[2]

Why, then, is the nurse the best person to act as advocate in this model? The answer appears to be that the nurse sees the patient as a whole, rather than as discrete physically or mentally diseased parts. Gadow explains:

> Nursing care because of its immediate, sustained, and often intimate nature, as well as its scientific and ethical complexity, offers ready awareness for every dimension of the professional to be engaged, including the emotional, rational, esthetic, intuitive, physical, and philosophical.[2]

Because such interrelationships exist between patients and nurses, failing to advocate is synonymous with failing to practice well.

Kohnke's[3] definition of advocacy for nurses also bears resemblance to Gadow's model, although at first glance, it appears to corroborate Bernal's[1] assertion that, "The primary role of advocacy (for nurses) is defined as the protection of patients' rights and interests." Kohnke's full definition, however, reads: "Advocacy is the act of informing and supporting a person so that he can make the best decisions for himself." Therefore, in Gadow's, Kohnke's, and our views, a nurse's interest in patients' *rights* is an incidental part of the broader advocacy undertaking necessitated by nursing's philosophy of practice.

Part of Bernal's[1] argument is that the patient advocacy role for nurses is a new one within the profession. She discusses Florence Nightingale and the origin of nursing's identity since her time. She states that Florence Nightingale "brought order and greatly improved conditions to military hospitals." However, Bernal wrongly assumes that Florence Nightingale supported the military ideal of "unquestioning loyalty and obedience to the nurse's training school, hospital, and physician's orders; protection of the patient's faith in the physician, even in cases of physician error or incompetence." In actuality, Florence Nightingale challenged the military system and the conditions it produced. She stated in a letter home from the Crimean War (now exhibited in the Florence Nightingale Museum, St. Thomas' Hospital, London) that, "It is a current joke here to offer a prize for the discovery of anyone willing to take responsibility." She believed nursing practice should be based on research and she kept judicious statistics on her care of patients in military hospitals (1858), surgical patients (1863), and workhouse infirmaries (1867, 1869). After an analysis of data in 1871, Nightingale accused the medical staff of complacency regarding the high mortality rates in the lying-in hospitals:

> It is a lamentable fact that the mortality in lying-in wards from childbirth, which is not a disease, approaches closely to the mortality from all diseases and accidents together in general hospitals, and in many instances even greatly exceeds this mortality.

Her espousal of "military ideals" could have been derived from her zealous concern for the sanitary conditions that were required in the mid-nineteenth century for a patient to heal. To say that nursing graduated from "military language to advocacy language"[1] distorts Florence Nightingale's patient advocacy role in the Crimean War and in her care of other patients. She clarifies her role in *Notes on Nursing*:

> It is often thought that medicine is the curative process. It is no such thing; medicine is the surgery of functions, as surgery proper is that of limbs and organs. Neither can do anything but remove obstructions; neither can cure; nature alone cures. Surgery removes the bullet out of the limb, which is an obstruction to cure, but nature heals the wound. So it is with medicine; the function of an organ becomes obstructed; medicine, so far as we know, assists nature to remove the obstruction, but does nothing more. And what nursing has to do in either case, is to put the patient in the best condition for nature to act upon him.[4]

Patient advocacy, then, for Florence Nightingale was "putting the patient in the best condition" so that nature could do its work. "Putting the patient in the best condition" means understanding what the best condition is for that individual. The best condition for each patient is defined by that patient and dictates the ensuing nursing actions.

To further her argument, Bernal[1] states that, over the past two decades, nurses' perceptions of their primary allegiance has shifted from physicians and hospitals to patients. This assumes that patients' welfare was not formerly the nurse's primary concern, but that total obedience to hospitals and physicians was the only course open to the nurse. One of the first legal cases involving a nurse occurred in 1929 and reinforces the notion that the nurse's responsibility is to the patient and not to the physician.[5] Nurse Somera gave medication that was verbally ordered, and verified by the physician, but the medication turned out not to be what was intended by the physician. The medication was one inappropriate as a surgical anaesthetic and the patient subsequently died. The nurse was found guilty of homicide through reckless imprudence and the two attending physicians were absolved. Whether the medication or the patient's disease was the cause of death did not affect the court's decision, and the nurse would have served time in jail had a pardon not been granted. This case exemplifies the fact that nurses were responsible, even in the early part of the century, for their professional actions. Even if this nurse suffered retribution for both her and the physician's professional inadequacy, society demanded that the nurse should take responsibility for her own actions in relationship to her patients' welfare. To say allegiance to the physician or hospital has changed in only the past two decades would have to ignore this precedent set 65 years ago.

Gerald Winslow,[6] although initially seeming to concur that "patients' rights advocacy" is the type of advocacy modern nurses are bent on adopting, in the end supports our inclination to believe that the attitudes of past nurses have been inaccurately described by Bernal. He suggests that it is misleading to assume that nursing's loyalty to physicians and to the institutions employing them (which might be said to resemble a military model of attitudes), means that patients were of secondary concern to these nurses. The reason that nurses were encouraged to be loyal to physicians and to hospitals by nurse educators and nursing leaders was that it was presumed to be detrimental to the patient's health and healing process not to be able to be assured that they were getting the best treatment. He notes:

> It is one of the myths of a later generation that nurses of the past never questioned loyalty to the physician. In speeches, journals and books, leading nurses complained that loyalty to the physician often was not deserved . . . And the difficult moral dilemmas faced by nurses were usually discussed in terms of conflict of loyalties.[6]

Curtin and Flaherty[7] reinforce the broader definition that has been proposed of advocacy by the nurse. They state:

> The nurse–patient relationship is determined by the patient's needs and the nurses response to them. The foundation of the relationship is advocacy in the sense that the nurse ". . . defends, vindicates, . . . is friendly to, . . . upholds . . ." [Curtin and Flaherty derive this from Webster's Dictionary definition of advocate.] The purpose of the relationship is among other things, to maintain or to return control of his life to the patient. However, the form of the relationship varies. So relationship, by nature, is dynamic—a living interaction that changes, grows, contracts and, in this instance, ends. The needs of the patient, the knowledge and ability of the nurse, and environmental circumstances all influence the form of the relationship. So, a nurse is a patient advocate when her practice helps alleviate suffering or when her practice promotes respect for patients as persons.[7]

Patient Advocacy: A Nursing Approach

Patient advocacy by nurses does not necessarily mean that nurses have a special moral sensitivity or moral point of view in regard to patient care. The case study described by Curtin and Flaherty, and quoted by Bernal,[1] reveals a nurse in a patient care dilemma within the hospital setting. A surgeon refused to inform the patient, a 68-year-old widower, of his diagnosis, yet the nurse was asked continual questions by the patient about his own health. Curtin and Flaherty report that the

> . . . *nurse has a moral duty to be honest in answering the patient's questions although it is unlikely that nurses will do so as long as physicians have the professional and institutional power to coerce and punish them.*

This may be a moral duty of the nurse but it does not require a special moral sense to see that a patient's rights are violated. Any other health professional would make the same assessment, but whether the violation is justified or not requires a critical analysis of the situation. Some nurses may have the knowledge and ability to act as direct patient rights advocates and may have this as their primary role in certain settings. Most nurses do not possess the skills to intervene with patient rights infringements, but part of the nursing advocacy role would be to initiate the institutional procedure for intervention.

Nurses in the United States are legally obliged to act as patient advocates and report suspected cases of child abuse (all states) and elder abuse (some states). Situations beyond their own expertise frequently arise, are recognized by nurses, and relevant referrals are made. Hospital ethics committees and patient representatives are appropriate sources of referral for such difficult and potentially adversarial conflicts. They too, though, may suffer from the same constraints as hospital employees that nurses do. Therefore, ideally, such representatives and committee members should be persons not employed by the institution. Hospital employees and health professionals should be included when involved in the particular case being reviewed.

Case Study

If nurses are not considered to be patient advocates, then who will assist the patient in the realization that the care being delivered is not optimal and present means to rectify such problems? This is not to say that nurses are the only professionals that may be patient advocates within the health care arena, but they are frequently the members of the team with a holistic approach to the patient's care. Part of this holistic role is the coordination of care for a patient. This entails transmitting vital information to other health care providers, thus ensuring each member has the data necessary to make an accurate assessment of the patient's needs or requirements. Such an undertaking, which includes the patient's input, is an aspect of nursing advocacy as described in this paper. The following examples are offered to illustrate nursing advocacy in action. The first describes a discrete act of advocacy of which the patient may not ever be aware. The second is more demonstrative of the broader definition of advocacy as stated by the previously mentioned nurse authors.

EXAMPLE I

If the pulmonary specialist prescribes a maximal dose of theophylline, and, subsequently, the infectious disease specialist orders erythromycin as the antibiotic of choice without knowledge of the former prescription, complications can ensue. The nurse informs the latter physician of the previous prescription because it has not been completely processed and is not reflected in the records or perhaps because the physician did not read the chart. Such information forwarded by the nurse allows the physician to prescribe a safer alternative treatment. This enables fulfilment of the nurse's ultimate goal, which is promotion of the patient's well-being as the patient's advocate.

EXAMPLE 2

Mr L. is a 59-year-old patient with quadriplegia from a car accident four years ago. He maintains some gross motor ability in his arms but does not have effective use of his hands. His wife has cared for him at home in between sporadic hospitalizations for a variety of problems associated with his quadriplegia. His present four months' hospital stay is for treatment of a large sacral pressure sore, which necessitated plastic surgery repair with a skin graft. On the plastic surgeon's order, Mr L. is to remain flat on his back on a special bed that evenly and continuously distributes and reduces pressure, thereby promoting healing and preventing further skin breakdown. Additionally, this patient is ventilator dependent since his accident.

Mrs L. is now refusing to take care of her husband at home. Attempts have been made to wean Mr L. off the ventilator in order that a nursing home placement may be secured. Mr L. can manage through the day while off the ventilator, but has insufficient neuromuscular function to breathe effectively through the night without ventilatory assistance. He can, however, talk with the aid of a special device and can make his wishes known. His main and most pressing desire is to sit up. He does not care whether this means to sit up in the bed or to sit up in a chair; he just wishes to change his position once in a while.

The nurses relayed this information to the various physicians involved in Mr L.'s care, but all defer to the plastic surgeon, Dr A., who is adamant that Mr L. may not sit up, as this risks the breakdown of his perfectly healed, skin-grafted buttocks. Mr L. knows that he is at risk of further skin breakdown. He has discussed this with the nurses at length and is able to give an account of what another skin breakdown might mean. However, he also understands that conditions in the hospital differ from those at home where frequent changes of position were not possible because moving Mr L. requires the effort of two people. Mr L. is willing to take the risk of sitting up in order to improve the quality of his life, and has been encouraged to speak to Dr A. about his wishes, but he has been unable to do so since Dr A.'s visits are cursory and it is noted that he leaves before Mr L. can present his case. Dr A. has been approached on several occasions by nurses who attempted to ensure that Mr L.'s wishes were known. On one of these occasions it was revealed that the reason Mr L. could not be allowed to sit up was that the bed the hospital provides is an inferior copy of the one that meets with Dr A.'s approval and, therefore, he cannot trust it to keep the weight off Mr L.'s sacral area when he is in the upright position. One of the nurses then asked, "Can Mr L. never be permitted to sit up?" The nurse was told, "Not while the patient is on this bed." This same nurse then made a series of inquiries to discover if it would be possible to obtain the approved bed for Mr L., and this bed was subsequently ordered. After placement on his new bed Mr L. was allowed to sit up for periods of time. Thus, Mr L. was enabled in his quest for self-determination and improved quality of life, via the advocacy action of a nurse.

This, admittedly, is an extreme case but the authors would like to pose the question: If the nurse had not been able to advocate for Mr L., who else would have been in the position to do it? Much of what is wrong here lends itself to a discussion that is not necessarily focused on rights so much as on the holistic practice of nursing care or as on patient advocacy as we have defined it.

Summary

In conclusion, patient advocacy is not merely the defense of infringements of patients' rights. Advocacy for nursing stems from a philosophy in which nursing practice is the support of an individual to promote his or her own well-being as understood by that individual. This is congruent with historical and contemporary theories of nursing practice and with the nursing literature.

REFERENCES

1. Bernal EW. The nurse as patient advocate. *Hastings Cent Rep* 1992;**22**(4):18–23.
2. Gadow S. Existential advocacy: philosophical foundations of nursing. In: Pence T, Cantrell J eds. *Ethics in nursing: an anthology.* New York: National League for Nursing, 1990:41–52.
3. Kohnke MF. The nurse as advocate. *Am J Nurs* 1980;**80**:2038–2040.
4. Nightingale F. *Notes on nursing: what it is and what it is not.* London: Harrison, 1859.
5. Grennan E. The Somera case. In: Pence T, Cantrell J eds. *Ethics in nursing: an antholoqy.* New York: National League for Nursing, 1990:188–191.
6. Winslow GR. From loyalty to advocacy: a new metaphor for nursing. *Hastings Cent Rep* 1984;**14**(2):32–40.
7. Curtin L, Flaherty J. *Nursing ethics: theories and pragmatics.* Bowie, MD: RJ Brady, 1982.

CHAPTER 14

●●

Managed Care and the Nurse's Ethical Obligations to Patients

JUDITH A. ERLEN AND MARY PAT MELLORS

Managed care is a system of care delivery that strives to provide a cost-effective and efficient comprehensive package of health services to specific groups of people, namely those individuals who are enrolled in the health plan (Himali, 1995; Iglehart, 1994; Moccia, 1989). The package of services includes both wellness and illness care. The assumption underlying this type of comprehensive package is that the cost of health care can be reduced if the emphasis is placed on keeping people healthy, decreasing the length of hospital stays, and providing coordinated at-home care.

Frequently, discussions about managed care focus on cost control. From a nursing perspective that has meant that there have been work redesign programs and layoffs. The work of nurses has been redistributed so that fewer nurses cover a larger number of patients while nonprofessional patient care assistants provide much of the direct patient care.

The professional nursing staff has been reduced because there are fewer inpatients. Nurses are expected to delegate patient care responsibilities to the appropriate staff. The nonprofessional patient care staff, as well as nurses, are being cross-trained so that they can do several different jobs. These changes are proposed to increase flexibility and to provide the necessary patient care services within a managed care framework.

The impact of these changes is being felt by nurses, patients, and families. There are concerns that the quality of patient care is declining, that nurses do not have as much time to spend with individual patients, and that patients' families are shouldering much of the responsibility for care once patients are discharged.

Nurses take pride in the fact that caring is central to its mission. Yet, in a world where the emphasis is on cost control and on doing more with less, caring seems to be receiving limited attention. Nurses are doing or are delegating the physical and technical aspects of their patients' care. But what about the other concerns that patients have? Are the emotional, social, educational, and spiritual needs of patients being identified and addressed?

The challenge for nursing, as a result of the changes brought about by managed care, is how to fulfill its ethical obligations of fidelity and due care. This article discusses these ethical responsibilities and the impact that managed care is having on the fiduciary rela-

---

Orthopaedic Nursing, 14(6), pp. 42–45. Reprinted with permission of the publisher, the National Association of Orthopaedic Nurses.

tionship between nurse and patient. Four strategies that nurses can use to fulfill their ethical obligations are presented:

1. Engaging in personal reflection
2. Communicating and collaborating
3. Protecting patients' rights
4. Evaluating patient outcomes

Ethical Issues

FIDELITY

Fidelity, or promise keeping, forms the basis for the special relationship that nurses have with their patients. Nurses have an implicit promise to provide care to patients. There is a pledge of loyalty, reliability, faithfulness, and trust. The expectation of patients and their families is that nurses will be there when patients require help with their health care needs.

The nurse–patient relationship is built on a promise of trust rather than on a contractual arrangement. There is no need to specify what is expected of the various parties as one does in a contract. The use of a contractual model to describe this nurse–patient relationship has the tendency to make the relationship too simplistic when, in fact, this relationship is very complex (Beauchamp & Childress, 1989).

This fiduciary relationship is grounded in the ethical principles of respect for persons and beneficence (Beauchamp & Childress, 1989; Veatch & Fry, 1987). Respect for persons means that people matter. Patients are not reduced to objects but are instead viewed in their wholeness and as having inherent worth and dignity. They are unique and are in charge of their own lives. People know what they desire and what is in their own best interests.

Nurses have particular responsibilities to promote the well-being of their patients, ie, beneficence. They are to treat patients as they ought to be treated and to help those who are ill (Drane, 1988). The proper end of nursing is good patient outcomes.

Thus, the nurse–patient relationship sets up obligations that one has to the other; there are expectations. Nurses see themselves as being responsible and accountable to the patients for whom they are providing care. Patients expect that nurses will act in accord with their interests, and that nurses will not abandon them whenever they need help. Both parties expect that each will be honest and will disclose information that is essential for appropriate care of the patient. Each expects to be treated with respect.

This reaching out to and connecting with the other, nurse to patient and patient to nurse, helps to form a bond or a closeness between nurse and patient (Benner & Wrubel, 1989). This caring relationship fosters communication between nurses and patients. Compassion, genuine concern for the other, and humaneness are of central importance.

DUE CARE

The goal of nursing, to promote the well-being of patients and their families, is a moral purpose (Curtin, 1979). Toward that end nurses are to use their knowledge and skill to provide the care that is appropriate for and required by patients.

Due care enjoins nurses to provide care according to the standards that have been set by the profession. This requires an ongoing critical appraisal of one's professional nursing practice by self and others (Jonsen, 1977). This process enables nurses to improve their knowledge and skill so that patients and their families benefit. Nursing care that meets or exceeds the expected standards should result in a "beneficial outcome" (Jonsen, 1977, p. 32) and help to promote patients' "legitimate interests" (Beauchamp & Childress, 1989, p. 194).

To further these patient goals means that nurses have to optimize their care. It is not enough to provide only the minimal level of care. Doing only the minimum suggests that patients are not harmed and that they are not put at risk rather than suggesting that nurses are engaged in a positive action of promoting patients' well-being.

Due care requires nurses to use critical thinking skills to make judgments, ie, to make prudent decisions. These judgments and decisions assist nurses to act responsibly. Such actions result in doing good. Patients are neither neglected nor abandoned. Thus, when nurses provide due care they are fulfilling their professional responsibility.

Impact of Managed Care

Managed care is a paradigm shift in the delivery of health care (Himali, 1995). The focus is on keeping patients healthy and preventing illness, thereby reducing the need for high-tech care. Patients are not hospitalized as readily and more care is delivered on an outpatient basis.

From a nursing perspective fidelity and due care can be threatened by managed care. Nursing's primary responsibility is to provide quality patient care; yet, managed care and its emphasis on cost containment seem to be interfering with the implementation of this duty of the nurse.

Reducing and controlling costs is a two-edged sword. On the one hand, constraining costs benefits those who are paying for the services. On the other hand, cost controls can harm those who are receiving the services. Less service may be available, the service may be less accessible, or there may be less time for each patient.

Work redesign, a reallocation of nursing staff, and an increasing use of unlicensed assistive personnel are occurring (Crawley, Marshall, & Till, 1993). As a result of these changes, nurses find themselves in a conflict: how to provide quality care within the boundaries of managed care.

Managed care policies and practices are based on the usual or typical patient and not on the individual. In most instances the identified length of stay for a particular patient condition or disease and the prescribed services are appropriate. However, each patient's situation is unique and particular; each patient "is a statistic of one" (Jonsen, 1977, p. 33). Therefore, guidelines proposed by managed care do not always apply in each person's situation.

In addition, nurses have been taught to focus on the individuality of the patient, to consider the wholeness of the patient, and to develop a plan of care with the patient to address specific needs and concerns. This means that patients make decisions as to the risks and benefits in accord with their situation and values. However, keeping this focus within a managed care environment presents a challenge for nurses because of the use of critical pathways for monitoring the progress of care.

Case Example

Nurses frequently encounter situations in their practice similar to the one that follows. These situations are disquieting to nurses and are challenging them to think differently about nursing and the proper goals of patient care.

Peter has been a staff nurse on this particular orthopaedic unit for 5 years. Until recently there was always an adequate number of nurses to care for the patients regardless of the census. Then the hospital administrators began to make changes which, at first, seemed rather minimal. No new nurses were hired; some nurses were transferred to other departments: and some nursing positions were eliminated.

Over time, the number of professional staff on Peter's unit was reduced, although the average daily census has remained the same. There are nonprofessional patient care providers where there once were nurses. These nonprofessional patient care providers are retrained nurses' aides and other ancillary support staff who are now being used in expanded roles.

Peter is concerned because he is being pulled in many directions at one time. He never seems to have enough time to adequately prepare patients for procedures or for discharge. He believes that patients would do much better if only there were the resources to address their needs.

In this case Peter is questioning the quality of care that his patients are receiving. Peter is aware that the staffing changes could potentially put his patients at risk. The nurses are involved in nursing functions, as well as nonnursing tasks related to patient care. Selecting which of these activities to delegate to others is of immediate concern to Peter. He recognizes the importance of carefully assessing the abilities of those who work with him so that he can delegate patient care responsibilities appropriately. Likewise, Peter recognizes his responsibility to patients to treat them with dignity and respect and to work with them in meeting their needs. He knows that patients look to nurses for support and help with their problems and that they expect that nurses will answer their questions honestly.

As the professional nurses on Peter's unit are being asked to do more with less, they wonder how they can individualize their care. How can they completely assess their patients, make the necessary decisions about their care, and delegate the patient care responsibilities appropriately?

Strategies

What should nurses, such as Peter, do to fulfill their promise to patients and families to provide due care within a managed care environment? Four strategies are discussed below.

I. ENGAGE IN PERSONAL REFLECTION

Nurses need to reflect on their personal experiences and examine their personal values and beliefs regarding patient care (Drane, 1988). This introspection enables one to come into closer contact with who one is and the reasons for choosing nursing as a career.

The importance of examining one's character lies in the fact that personal qualities and characteristics determine whether the nurse–patient relationship is an ethical one grounded in fidelity. Quality care follows from a relationship based on fidelity as the promise that nurses have made requires competent, compassionate care.

Additionally, nurses have a responsibility to maintain their competence (American Nurses Association, 1985). They need to continually assess their ability to function within this new care delivery system and the change in staff and skill mix. Nurses are accountable to communicate performance deficiencies to their supervisor so that educational programs may be implemented to address these needs. This ongoing assessment means that nurses can better assure that they are keeping their promise to provide due care.

2. COMMUNICATE AND COLLABORATE WITH HEALTH CARE TEAM

Providing quality patient care cannot be done in isolation; communication and collaboration are essential (Baggs, 1993; Johnson, 1992). The basis for this collaborative process lies in the joint commitment to providing due care and in the respect health care professionals have for each other's perspective.

Within a managed care environment, communication and collaboration are particularly important because patients have shorter hospital stays. To promote the patient's well-being, all care providers need to be involved in the planning. This planning ensures coordinated care that is provided in a timely manner.

Since nurses are working with more nonprofessional assistive staff, there is a need to be very clear about what patient care tasks need to be done and how they are to be done. Nurses have the responsibility to delegate care to others; however, this has to be done prudently and thoughtfully. Staff need to be assigned responsibilities that are within their abilities.

Communication has to extend beyond the health care team and include the patient and family. Nurses need to ensure that patients and families are involved in this process. Including patients demonstrates respect for them and recognizes their inherent worth.

3. PROTECT PATIENTS' RIGHTS

Patients expect and are entitled to good care. However, the changes created by managed care are causing nurses to be concerned that the quality of patient care may be decreasing when there are fewer professional nurses to provide care.

The *Code for Nurses* (American Nurses Association, 1985) admonishes nurses to protect patients when their care and safety are jeopardized. Thus, there is a need to monitor the level of care that is being given. If the care is not appropriate or particular care providers are inadequately prepared, nurses have a responsibility to bring such matters to the attention of the appropriate person.

For nurses, speaking out to protect the patient's right to good care translates into advocacy for patients. However, advocacy brings with it certain risks. Raising questions and concerns about the quality of care being given and the changes in care delivery may not be very popular with administrators. As such, nurses may feel threatened that they will be replaced. Therefore, documentation is necessary when addressing quality of care issues. Additionally, policies and procedures need to be developed so that nurses know what process to follow when they are addressing quality-of-care issues.

4. EVALUATE PATIENT OUTCOMES

There is a need for ongoing review mechanisms to determine if the nursing care being delivered is meeting and/or exceeding standards. "The health care system can no longer just state that quality care is being given" (Frost, 1992, p. 64). Achievement of nursing process and nursing outcome criteria have to be assessed, using all relevant quality assurance criteria and indicators.

Clinical indicators such as rates of infection, medication errors, patient falls, and IV administration errors attributable to nursing care have to be documented. Documentation via critical pathways can ensure that patients do not receive inadequate care in the name of cost containment. The information gained from evaluating patient outcomes enables nurses to know if their care is appropriate.

Summary

Managed care is having a direct effect on the implementation of the nurses' ethical responsibilities to their patients. This new health care system has altered the nurse's primary direct care role in many institutions. Changes in the reimbursement system have led to nonprofessional patient care providers carrying out nursing activities and nurses assuming nonnursing tasks.

These changes are confusing and they signal a serious departure from the traditional history and authority of nurses at the bedside. They have the potential to jeopardize the well-being of patients. Every time a nursing activity is delegated, one or more caregivers is added to the equation. This diminishes the nurse's opportunity to develop a trusting professional relationship with the patient.

To fulfill their ethical responsibilities to patients within a managed care environment, nurses need to be aware of the changes that are occurring, as well as recognize the implications of these changes on quality of care and patient outcomes. Nurses have to act responsibly so that patient care is not compromised.

REFERENCES

American Nurses Association (1985). *Code for nurses with interpretive statements.* Kansas City, MO: Author.

Baggs, J. G. (1993). Collaborative interdisciplinary decision making in intensive care units. *Nursing Outlook, 41,* 108–112.

Beauchamp, T. L., & Childress, J. F. (1989). *Principles of biomedical ethics* (3rd. ed.). New York: Oxford University Press.

Benner, P., & Wrubel, J. (1989). *The primacy of caring: Stress and coping in health and illness.* Menlo Park, CA: Addison-Wesley.

Crawley, W. D., Marshall, R. S., & Till, A. H. (1993). Use of unlicensed assistive staff. *Orthopaedic Nursing, 12*(6), 47–53.

Curtin, L. L. (1979). The nurse as advocate: A philosophical foundation for nursing. *Advances in Nursing Science, 1*(3), 1–10.

Drane, J. F. (1988). *Becoming a good doctor: The place of virtue and character in medical ethics.* Kansas City. MO: Sheed & Ward.

Frost, M. H. (1992). Quality: A concept of importance to nursing. *Journal of Nursing Care Quality. 7*(1), 64–69.

Himali, U. (1995). Managed care: Does the promise meet the potential? *American Nurse, 27*(4), 1,14,16.

Iglehart, J. K. (1994). Physicians and the growth of managed care. *New England Journal of Medicine. 331*(17), 1167–1171.

Johnson, N. D. (1992). Collaboration—An environment for optimal outcome. *Critical Care Nurse Quarterly, 15*(3), 37–43.

Jonsen, A. R. (1977). Do no harm: Axiom of medical ethics. In S.F. Spicker & H.T. Engelhardt, Jr. (Eds.). *Philosophical medical ethics: Its nature and significance* (pp. 27–41). Dordrecht-Holland: D. Reidel Publishing Company.

Moccia, P. (1989). 1989: Shaping a human agenda for the nineties: Trends that demand our attention as managed care prevails. *Nursing and Health Care, 10*(1), 15–17.

Veatch, R. M., & Fry, S. T. (1987). *Case studies in nursing ethics.* Philadelphia: Lippincott.

●●

Dirty Hands: The Underside of Marketplace Health Care

WANDA K. MOHR AND MARGARET M. MAHON

Advocacy has long been recognized as central to the nurse–patient relationship. Indeed, advocacy is a primary motivating factor for the pursuance of a health care profession. The centrality of advocacy as a moral principle suggests that nurses and other professionals recognize that conflict between professionals involved in patient care and the subordination of the good of the patient to an ethic of utility are real possibilities. In the American Nurses Association code of ethics,[1] the concept of advocacy is clearly stated in principle 3, in which the professional nurse must "safeguard the client and the public when health care and safety are affected by incompetent, unethical, or illegal practice of any person."[1(p3)] The American Nurses Association has developed standards of nursing that specify the nurse's responsibility to foster environments that are congruent with therapeutic goals.[2] In addition, various Nurse Practice Acts provide for and set a standard in which registered nurses will report any unethical or unprofessional conduct or exposure of patients to risk of harm.

Legal requirements, standards of practice, and ethical directives exemplify cherished professional ideals and represent "ought" statements that constitute guidelines for registered nurses. These documents were formulated by professional leaders and experts with the assumption that these moral "oughts" could indeed be adhered to autonomously by individual practitioners. Thus, evaluations of ethical practice are based on the premise that individual practitioners can follow these guidelines.

This assumption that nurses can indeed fulfill their professional mandate of advocacy and ethical directives underlies nursing education and practice acts. Little formal consideration is given to the consideration of impossible "oughts" or guidelines that place the professional actor in compromising moral situations. Yet given some of the changes that have taken place in the increasingly complex health care "industry," the question of choices, morals, ethical practice, and the specifics of what individual practitioners and professionals can effect must be reevaluated. This article explores the idea of seemingly unattainable moral behavior, specifically challenged with the moral dilemma that is known as "dirty hands."

Reprinted from *Advances in Nursing Science* 19(1), pp. 28–37, 1996, with permission of Aspen Publishers, Inc., © 1996.

Dirty Hands

One of the most intractable problems in moral philosophy is how to act morally in apparently immoral situations. Problems of this kind have been labeled by some as "dirty hands" situations, because the circumstances are such that the agent is left with a "moral stain" after taking an action.[3] These situations differ from most moral dilemmas in that those commonly encountered are cases in which there is no right act open to an agent; every option is simply wrong. Dirty hands cases are those instances in which one agent is morally forced by someone else's immorality to do what is, or otherwise would be, wrong. A key element of dirty hands situations is not only the choice between two options, but also the role of immorality in creating situations that necessitate and justify acting with dirty hands. The classic case that is frequently invoked is that described in William Styron's[4] novel *Sophie's Choice,* in which the protagonist is forced by a Nazi officer to choose which of her two children is to be condemned to the gas chamber. She must make the choice or both children will be gassed.

Stocker argued that the justifying or necessitating circumstances of this kind of decision making are themselves immoral and that they are immoral in a particular way: "They are violations of moral autonomy and selfhood—and this in a particularly vicious way. The agent is immorally coerced to take part in, perhaps even to help implement an immoral project."[3(p20)] Thus, two essential features of dirty hands exist: There is a moral conflict, and one is morally compromised in doing what is morally justified or perhaps even required. The concept of dirty hands has particular relevance for the profession of nursing today. In health care environments that are increasingly driven by market forces, unwary practitioners can unwittingly find themselves in circumstances where they must commit acts that can be justified, even obligatory, but are nonetheless wrong.

Situations—Unfettered Marketplaces

In the 1960s health care was not called an industry.[5] By the mid- to late 1980s, it had become the nation's largest industry.[6] During that time manufacturing was in decline, and major corporations were moving their operations to developing countries. By 1986 other investor-owned corporations had acquired 20% of acute care hospitals, and in 1990 proprietary chains owned 80% of chronic care facilities.[5] Community pharmacy is likewise corporatized, with more than 70% of the U.S. prescription market being controlled by corporate empires such as Wal-Mart or pharmacy benefits management firms.[7]

This transformation of health care into an enormous industry, which Relman[8] called the "medical industrial complex," has diminished the function of health care encounters as therapeutic and has increased their role as a profitable provision of service. This shift has commodified health care provision, made it into a lucrative business, and subjected it to the same performance standards as any other business enterprise. Health care has entered the brand name era. Various organizations compete to attract patients to a logo or image in much the same way that computer and soap companies attract their clients. Health services are now "product lines," administrators seek to "corner markets," and faceless investors look for return on equity based on the profitable manipulation of the interaction between the health care provider and the health care consumer.

In this world of corporate enterprise, where Darwinian rules apply, it is inevitable that the business of health care is subjected to the same pressures that face any other business—survival being the priority issue. In such a competitive environment managers or administrators have no choice but to view health care encounters as business transactions. Forced into mean and competitive markets to make sufficient money to meet payrolls, retire bond debt, or provide acceptable profit margins, they must do so mainly by cutting costs and expanding reimbursable services. To do so in a labor-intensive industry without affecting the quality of care is extremely difficult. Patients are sometimes offered disincentives for seeking care, so that fewer costs are incurred or so that greater monies will accrue from those procedures that still generate substantial profit. Fewer people must be employed to reduce payroll expenses; market shares must be increased to generate more income.

Nothing is inherently evil about the idea of application of marketplace principles to health care delivery, nor is there anything to fault about the idea of cost containment initiatives. Correcting inefficiencies and eliminating unnecessary expenditures are worthy and appropriate enterprises. These goals, however, should not be achieved at the expense of the moral foundation of the health care system itself. When such a situation does exist—when the competitive dynamics of the invisible hand transcend a commitment to operate within socially responsible parameters—the stage is set for the compromise of values and the possibility of being left with dirty hands.

Such a situation did exist during the 1980s when nurses and other professionals were placed in morally compromising positions. One of the authors has researched and written extensively on what has become known as the "for-profit psychiatric hospital scandal."[9-11] Certain large investor-owned chains were investigated by state and federal authorities for illegal and unethical conduct in 1991. Complaints about these institutions included

- Excessive medication and therapy
- Questionable and potentially abusive therapies
- Exorbitant charges and charges for services never rendered
- Overly aggressive and deceptive marketing
- Bounties paid to professionals and marketing personnel to deliver paying patients to treatment facilities
- Holding patients against their will without medical justification
- Isolating patients from families, friends, and legal counsel by withholding telephone, mail, and visitation privileges
- Falsifying diagnoses to match insurance benefits
- "Dumping" patients regardless of their condition once insurance benefits were exhausted, and
- Unnecessary hospitalization of patients whose conditions could have been treated in a less restrictive environment.[12]

Investigations based on these complaints continue, and hundreds of lawsuits have been filed on behalf of patients who believe they were mistreated, cheated, or damaged by inappropriate incarceration in these facilities.

Some of the material that follows has been reported elsewhere,[10] and it is based on interviews conducted with nurse informants who discussed their struggles to advocate for their patients within deviant work environments. Nurses too often found themselves unable to take appropriate action on behalf of patients because they were frightened that they would lose their jobs. They were also subjected to intimidation tactics that included being threatened with legal action if they spoke out. Several nurses in this study who spoke out against abusive conditions did in fact have suits filed against them for slander by hospitals and professionals associated with hospitals.[10]

Deviant Decisions, Deviant Environments, or Both?

Alleged psychiatric hospital fraud, abuse, and unethical behavior first came to national attention in 1991. These abuses were at the center of much of the subsequent suits of for-profit psychiatric hospitals by the Texas State Attorney General's office and resulted in both federal and state investigations of major psychiatric hospital chains. The Texas State Senate Interim Committee on Health and Human Services reported, "Many of these problems festered without attracting attention from state agencies responsible for addressing them, and violations of state law and agency rules went unpunished."[12(p6)] If the problems they referred to took place over time and in a systematic manner, it is reasonable to assume that nurses and other professionals within the organization would have some knowledge of them. However, it took a state investigation and complaints of patients and families to bring these abuses to light and for any action to take place.

At issue for the profession is whether nurses who were confronted with these problems were in fact aware of them and whether or not they fulfilled their advocacy responsibilities to the patients in their care. It was not known whether they stayed and struggled with their situations or whether they simply left these environments by quitting. To date there has been scant attention paid in the nursing literature to these events and the resulting problems with respect to the profession or with respect to the effects of any exploitation or abuse on patients.

During the course of the research on which this article is based, nurses were questioned as to what actions they took, if any, when they realized that they were in situations that posed multiple ethical contradictions for them, in particular those that required them to engage in patient advocacy. Nurses reported experiences of pain and suffering that occurred during their employment when they came to realize that they were working in deviant circumstances. This suffering most closely approached the concept of angst, an idea that has been best developed by existentialist philosophers. The existentialists describe angst as an encompassing attitude that entails a range of emotions or moods—sometimes anguish, sometimes anxiety, and sometimes dread.[13] Sometimes angst is used to refer to excruciating distress or suffering, sometimes to an all-embracing extreme fear of everything or a fear of oneself, including one's own emotions or identity. One poignant example of this came from a nurse who reported the following:

> #019: So, what did it all mean, it was just an intimidation, it was unbelievable. And in fact when I verbalized it to you, I know it happened, you know? But it sounds so unreal. So, no, we could not [advocate]—there'd be times, getting back to your original question, we could not be advocates of patients [because] we were told immediately that was the way it was. . . . That's what we were given—statistics. Not that this was how we helped individuals, but this was our average daily census, our FTE [full-time equivalent] to patient ratio, our profit margin, always the statistics. There was no room for treatment issues. And we were comparing [how] much money . . . that we have here. . . . That's what we were given, national statistics. . . . There was no room for people. Or human concerns. And that's what it all meant.[10]

Themes of fear and powerlessness in the face of the "corporate embrace"[14] were reported by another:

> #017: We went through God knows how many administrators. In fact there were some jokes about the "administrator du jour." We were taken [over] during the last year and a half I was there. We were bought by a major corporation, which came in with an administrator who was eventually fired. But who was—let me put it kindly— who was a tyrant . . . who didn't know very well how to deal with hospitals or anything about health care but how to be a dictator. It was organized totalitarianism, no, it was totalitarian chaos. . . . We were like doormats getting chewed out on a weekly basis like children. And it was always, you know, that we were not making enough money, that we had to keep down staffing, that we have to look at ways to reduce expenditures, and that there was no way that we could ask at this point in time for anything for our patients. That we needed to put our heads together and if we were not

better managers, essentially we would not be there. So the message was conveyed to us so very strongly that we didn't even dare. One time we sat at the conference table, we needed some copies made, the copy machine was broken, so we wouldn't even ask to go make them on the outside. [Laughter] It sounds silly, it sounds, you know, stupid. I look back and I tried to talk to my colleagues and remember if it was really that way. We were, it was, and what we had also amazingly enough, was scare tactics. We were individually asked to report our colleagues if we saw something that they were doing or saying against the hospital. And not promoting the hospital or saying negative things about the hospital. . . . It was a reward system, and sometimes it was a punishment system. If you don't go by, you know, what we are saying, you know, you won't be here—essentially that was the message. And people were fired right and left without going through the guidelines of the policies and procedures. They were there one day, and one day they were told to leave. It happened to several program directors. Of course, we were told that we were working for a good corporation and jobs were hard to come by, which is true.[10]

The Dangers of Dirty Hands

Dirty hands, then, is the moral quandary of working within externally imposed parameters that directly counter the provision of high-quality patient care and the principle and value of beneficence. Goffman[15,16] suggested that in situations that present these kinds of threats to integrity or values, people often engage in a form of avoidance as a self-protective strategy. One form of avoidance is to simply stay away from the circumstance. But if people are unable to do so, and must remain in the noxious situation, they must find a way to ensure that their interactions within those circumstances are as structured or predictable as possible to avoid negative encounters. This means restricting the range of activities associated with their positions, and the safest way of doing this is to focus only on one's fragmented job and to ignore its many ramifications. Lifton[17] called this phenomenon "psychological doubling," which he described as a conscious or unconscious division of the self into two functioning wholes in such a way that each part functions as an entire self.[17(p418)] One nurse who engaged in this form of resistance called it "going into my place."[10] Another described the process as "focusing on what you have to get through to do your job and put the rest away. Off somewhere where it won't get in the way."[10]

Two nurses who found that they had to protect themselves from the grief, anxiety, and rage that they said were beginning to overwhelm them related the following:

> *#001:* But I was stuck, so I just went to work and did what they wanted, almost everything they wanted. . . . It was like I was there but I wasn't. I was doing these functions, like passing [medications] and writing on charts and sitting in the treatment team meetings, but I'm sorry to say I wasn't nursing. I stayed away from the patients as much as I could because I thought that I really didn't want to get involved. I guess it was a feeling that if I got to feeling like they had a human relationship with me, then I would start to feel myself, and I didn't want to do that. If I felt something, then I would get angry at the situation, and somehow things would go badly for me. So I just kind of pretended . . . and it kept me from feeling. I just did things, you know— things? It wasn't that hard to do either, because everyone was kept pretty busy doing things. You just did yours for the minute and then on to the next, and before you knew it the day was over and you could go home.[10]

Another nurse reported that she engaged in similar disengagement in her work setting during which she simply attended to what had to be done to get through her shift:

#020: After $4\frac{1}{2}$ years I believe I have just learned to put my frustrations in a box and put them aside and say, okay, now I've got to set up the 9:00 [medications] . . . I've got to take off the orders. You learn to stifle it, the rage. You learn to put aside your feelings and your expectations and your hopes and dreams and get on with the business at hand.[10]

In these two responses, nurses related that when there was no escape, they could avoid or at least attenuate the meaning and emotional impact of remaining at their job. Even as they found themselves in these circumstances, they tried to bring some semblance of structure to their jobs in an attempt to maintain a vestige of order where disorder seemed to be the rule. And (because statistics do not feel and charts do not bleed) these nurses removed themselves to an FTE corporate world. This retreat represented an impersonal defection in which they could relate more to tasks than to people.

Other nurses relating the same phenomenon described "splitting off one part of another," "becoming a different person at work," and "becoming anesthetized."[10] These are interesting phrases because they communicate the kind of "splitting off" that Lifton[17] described in his studies on psychological doubling. He found that most people feel poorly equipped to make a conceptual restructuring of their accustomed picture of the world to make it fit dimensions that are alien to their lifelong learning. In other words, to feel forced to function in a world that is antithetical to one's beliefs is very difficult and can be psychologically damaging. As a means of dealing with their situations, they focus on "little lumps" of reality, engaging in a form of dissociative emotional distancing or "dehumanized behavior."[17(p7)] This emotional distancing involves a bypassing, a suppression, or a stifling of components of full psychic functioning. Certain aspects of psychic functioning, such as empathy, are shunted aside. The person's relationships to others become stereotyped, rigid, and above all inexpressive of interpersonal mutuality. Lifton maintained that certain occupations require a certain amount of selectively "dehumanized" behavior, among which he listed nursing and medicine. Without this mechanism, he maintained that emotional reactions would interfere with "the efficient and responsible performance of what has to be done."[17(p214)]

Nevertheless, the psychologically damaging aspect of this experience emerged when nurses talked about their feelings of guilt. They discussed being caught in the middle, blaming themselves on the one hand and knowing on another level that another choice could have been made, as illustrated in the following:

#030: It makes me sick to think of it now. It's like I was put in the position of the "I was just following orders" defense. Just by virtue of staying, I mean I wouldn't even have had to do anything overt. All I can say is that when my eyes were opened and I saw what was going on it scared me to death, and I was scared the whole 9 months, a constant grating of every nerve in my head being on edge. I was scared of a lot, but most of all I was scared I was going to become sucked in.[10]

The above examples were chosen from nurses' narratives to illustrate the deviant environments that can lead to dirty hands situations. These nurses' experiences foreshadow what may have profound implications for the profession of nursing and its future. As administrators with advanced financial training decide which workers are to carry out what tasks according to predetermined methods, nurses will lose more and more autonomy. Marx[18] observed that workers' loss of autonomous decision making, discretion, and creativity within the work process has the potential to result in a pervasive source of alienation. Deskilling and alienation are the underside of what appears on the surface to be rationalized managerial control over the work process.

Toward a 21st Century Research Agenda

There is little question that health care has undergone substantial structural and qualitative changes and that it has become megabusiness in the mold of Fortune 500 companies.[5,19] An unfortunate aspect of those changes may include deviant or criminal activity that creates an ethos that can compromise professionals and those under their care.[9–11,20] Mills[21] proposed that such deviance is a ubiquitous feature of business culture, being more the rule than the exception: The widespread existence of such deviance was underscored by research reporting that over 65% of Fortune 500 companies were charged with corporate crimes in 1975 and 1976.[22]

Organizational theorists have long believed that huge bureaucracies can lead to "legitimate" abandonment of personal responsibility in the support of organizational goals.[23] Because corporations shape the symbolic field in which employees find themselves situated, they also can shape employees' definitions of situations. Organizational goals (sometimes deviant) become virtually identical to employee goals, leading to dirty hands situations.

The authors propose that dirty hands is a phenomenon that has been insufficiently examined in the nursing ethics literature and that should be placed on the ethics research and theory development agenda. In rarefied discussions of moral conflicts, too often the focus is more on the dilemma in the abstract, the principles, or the conflict rather than on the complex contextual factors that give rise to and influence those decisions. In addition, the personal and moral toll as well as the effect on the profession and subsequently on health care itself is rarely played out. Ethics has also become the stepchild to "real research," which is outcome and intervention oriented and geared to what can or cannot be funded in a competitive atmosphere. But elegant outcomes studies benefit no one if they cannot be implemented in hostile and unsupportive environments or in environments that are threatening.

We argue that in situations in which one's own position becomes threatened, such as in difficult job markets or during situations of deprivation, the pull of self-preservation becomes strong. In addition, the tug of loyalty to one's group can sometimes result in a temptation to "go along and get along" in order to avoid negative sanctions. Thus, when "doubling" or "ethical numbing"[24] becomes a structurally normative practice as a result of an environment in which individuals are pressured to follow institutional agendas that conflict with personal agendas, the dangers are not to be underestimated. The disturbing aspect of this doubling or numbing for the profession as a whole is that such mental manipulation has the potential of becoming a maintenance behavior. That is, this form of avoidance, if it becomes a systematic practice, has the potential for making anyone who works with people regularly perceive and treat them as nonhuman, as statistics, commodities, or interchangeable pieces in a large and profitable numbers game. It might easily lead to a diminished sense of responsibility for those same people, who are no longer cognitively represented as human.

It might also lead to an attenuation of a sense of responsibility for one's own actions with respect to those who are now nonhumans, which Lifton called a "we're just running the trains" mentality.[17(p400)] What starts out as a protection against feelings of anxiety, frustration, and rage toward the feeling that one has become an insubstantial human widget in a vast bureaucracy actually becomes what it started out to prevent. In a tragic dialectic, the reaction against dehumanization itself becomes dehumanization. Those who would be susceptible to this staining are within our own ranks. They are our own colleagues. Even more vulnerable are the people for whom nurses are pledged to care and advocate. As a profession we owe it to the vulnerable among us to address and study the issue of dirty hands and the contexts that lead to this moral staining and to develop strategies that mitigate morally crippling environments.

REFERENCES

1. American Nurses Association. *American Nurses Association Code of Ethics with Interpretive Statements.* Kansas City, Mo: ANA; 1985.
2. American Nurses Association. *Standards of Psychiatric and Mental Health Practice.* Kansas City, Mo: ANA; 1982.
3. Stocker M. *Plural and Conflicting Values.* Oxford, England: Oxford University Press; 1990.
4. Styron W. *Sophie's Choice.* New York, NY: Random House; 1979.
5. Salmon JW. A perspective on the corporate transformation of health care. *Int J Health Serv.* 1995;25(1):11–42.
6. Wohl S. The medical industrial complex: another view of the influence of business on medical care. In: McCue JD, ed. *The Medical Cost-containment Crisis: Fears, Opinions and Facts.* Ann Arbor, Mich: Health Administration Press Perspectives; 1989.
7. Rodwin MA. *Medicine, Money and Morals.* New York, NY: Oxford University Press; 1993.
8. Relman A. The new medical industrial complex. *N Engl J Med.* 1980;303:963–970.
9. Mohr W. The private psychiatric hospital scandal: a critical social approach. *Arch Psychiatr Nurs.* 1994;8(1):4–8.
10. Mohr W. Multiple ideologies and their proposed roles in the outcomes of nurse practice setting: the for-profit psychiatric hospital scandal as a paradigm case. *Nurs Outlook.* 1995;43(1):35–43.
11. Mohr WK. *The Nature of Nurses' Experiences in For-profit Psychiatric Hospital Settings.* Austin, Tex: University of Texas at Austin; 1995. PhD dissertation.
12. *Texas State Senate Interim Committee Report on Private Psychiatric Substance Abuse and Medical Rehabilitation Services.* Austin, Tex: State of Texas Department of Health and Human Services; 1992.
13. Barnes HE. *An Existentialist Ethics.* New York, NY: Knopf; 1967.
14. Woolhandler S, Himmelstein DU. Extreme risk—the new corporate proposition for physicians. *N Engl J Med.* 1995;333:1706–1707.
15. Goffman E. *The Presentation of Self in Everyday Life.* Garden City, NY: Doubleday-Anchor, 1959.
16. Goffman E. *Asylums.* New York, NY: Doubleday-Anchor, 1961.
17. Lifton R. *The Nazi Doctors: Medical Killing and the Politics of Genocide.* New York, NY: Basic Books; 1986.
18. Elster J. *Making Sense of Marx.* New York, NY: Oxford University Press; 1987.
19. Brown P, Cooksey E. Mental health monopoly: corporate trends in mental health services. *Soc Sci Med.* 1989;28:1129–1138.
20. Luske B, Vandenburgh HW. Heads on beds: toward a critical ethnography of the selling of psychiatric hospitalization. *Per Soc Prob.* 1995;7:203–222.
21. Mills CW. *The Power Elite.* New York, NY: Oxford University Press; 1956.
22. Clinard M. Corporate ethics and crime: a view of middle management. In: Ermann MD, Lundman DJ, eds. *Corporate and Governmental Deviance.* New York, NY: Oxford University Press; 1986.
23. Weber M. *The Protestant Ethic and the Spirit of Capitalism.* New York, NY: Scribner's; 1904(1958).
24. Drucker PF. Corporate takeovers—what is to be done? *Pub Interest.* 1986;8:23–24.

CHAPTER 16

●●●

Uncommon Decency: A Case Study in Collegiality

LEAH L. CURTIN

A few days ago, my friend Ida* told me the following story over lunch. Her 50-year-old sister, who was otherwise in good health, went into a hospital for "routine" gallbladder surgery. An error was made, and the hepatic duct was cut above the juncture with the common bile duct. The surgeon tried to correct the error by creating a new duct. The surgeon also chose not to "worry" the patient and her family by telling them of this mishap. Unfortunately, the newly created "duct" did not hold and bile was soon collecting in the patient's abdomen. As her condition deteriorated, her family became alarmed—especially Ida, who is a recently retired, master's-prepared clinical nurse specialist.

When her sister's surgeon wanted permission to "go back in to see what was wrong," he still did not mention the error that had occurred in the first surgery. Because she was so concerned, Ida insisted upon a consult, who explained what had happened, advised her that her sister's abdomen was filling rapidly with bile, and urged her to act quickly because few patients survive such an error. Ida made arrangements to fly her sister (the consult did not believe that she would survive an extended ambulance transfer) to another city where experts would attempt to repair the damage.

Ida flew to that city very early the next morning to consult with the physicians who would be caring for her sister only to learn that their lead surgeon was on vacation and could not be reached. They referred her to another team of experts who, they promised, would agree to take her sister's case—but these surgeons practiced in yet another hospital. They made the referral, but arrangements had to be made to transfer her sister and her sister's records to this new hospital, the helicopter pilot had to be notified that the patient was to be taken to a different hospital—and all of this had to be done right away, and she couldn't even find a pay phone.

Taking her heart in her hands, Ida asked someone to direct her to the nursing office. She went in and started to tell her story. "I'm a retired nurse, and I need some help," she said, and then she began to cry.

Personnel in the nursing office rallied to her support. One found some tissues for her. Another gave her a spare office to use, helped her contact all the people she had to reach,

*Not her real name

and let her use the nursing office phone number for essential call-backs. Still another nurse brought her coffee and sandwiches, and then one of the nurses even drove Ida to the receiving hospital. Thus, Ida was there when her sister's helicopter arrived at 4 o'clock that afternoon.

"I was a mess," she said. "I'd only had a few hours sleep in the last week. I was dressed in blue jeans and sneakers. I'm sure I looked like a little old lady in tennies. I didn't know any of these nurses, but they came through for me. They were wonderful. When I tried to express my thanks for what everyone in the nursing office had done for me to the nurse who drove me to the hospital, she touched my hand and smiled a smile I'll remember for years. 'We'll be praying for your sister,' she said."

Reflections on Our Relationships . . .

On the face of it, showing consideration for one's colleagues does not seem to be a terribly difficult proposition. It truly does not require much more energy to be kind than to be indifferent. And it is so much more life-giving!

Nonetheless, it seems that fewer and fewer of us are able to manage it. Indeed, we behave worse toward one another than we ever have before—or so it seems to me. Particularly in a case like this where malpractice undoubtedly could rear its ugly head, we tend to keep as far away as possible from those in trouble lest we somehow be implicated or perhaps it is simply a sign of the times: hard times foster self-absorption that translates into indifference.

What is particularly curious about all this is that so much has been written about collegiality in recent years. It is almost as if reducing the collegial relationship to published print has left us less capable of actually responding to one another. Bombarded by polysyllabic platitudes, we simply do not "hear" the message behind the words, see the human needs before our eyes or, finally, feel so deeply.

Thus, those who choose to be what has become (regrettably) uncommonly decent can do an inestimable amount of good. Indeed, they can set even cynical strangers to speculating on the possibilities of the human heart.

Nurse/Nurse Relationships . . .

Professions, and thus collegial relationships, trace their origins back over 2,300 years to ancient Greece: to the Pythagorean school of philosophy, to be exact. Among their works can be found the Hippocratic Corpus, a collection of 72 books (not by a single author) that contain prescriptions and proscriptions about the behavior of physicians from which the ancients extrapolated "The Hippocratic Oath."

In his study of the Hippocratic Oath, historian Ludwig Edelstein characterized those duties that physicians undertake toward patients as an ethical code, and those assumed toward colleagues as a covenant.[1] William F. May notes that, "Physicians undertake duties to their patients, but they *owe something* to their teachers. . . . Toward their patients they relate as benefactors, but toward their teachers they relate as beneficiaries."[2] And one may well ask, "Who is my teacher?"

The rapid growth of knowledge—and its rapidly shrinking half-life—forces professionals to recognize their own limits and capabilities. Nurses know that they must rely upon and incorporate the research, experience, and knowledge of other nurses in their own practice. Clearly—and ever more clearly as we move to seamless networks—the very structure of work forces us to practice interdependently, ie, to depend on the professional expertise of colleagues, to rely on their judgments and to place trust in their competence.

The Ethics of a Profession . . .

The ethics of a profession not only delimit the role and scope of its activities and pre-scribe the nature of the relationship that should pertain between its members and the lay public, but also establish obligations professionals owe to one another and to their pro-fession.[3]

The ethical principles that guide collegial relationships derive from several sources.[4] Before it is anything else, the collegial relationship is a human relationship; therefore nurses' mutual humanity forms the fundamental framework for relationships among peo-ple who happen to be members of the same profession. First and foremost, collegial rela-tionships should be characterized by exquisite respect for the person of the other: what Heidigger called "The I—Thou" relationship.[5]

The second source of the ethical principles that underlie professional relationships stems from the essential nature of the services they provide, and thus the special obliga-tions society imposes on those who would earn their living by providing for some of the most fundamental and personal needs of human beings. In fact, the very word "profes-sional" (Latin: *profitere*) means "to promise publicly"—and among those promises is a commitment to share information to the good of client and public. That is, unlike busi-nesses that are rewarded for hoarding information (patents, trademarks, copyrights), pro-fessionals are rewarded for sharing information (publication, teaching, consulting). It is expected—and it is essential to the public good.

The third source of the principles that are to guide collegial relationships derives from the professional bond itself: that special kinship born of membership in the same profes-sion. That kinship flows from the shared experience of what it means to be a nurse, of what it feels like to practice nursing—with all its tragedies and triumphs, frustrations and achievements.[6]

We happen to be members of a profession that, by its very nature, brings us into con-tact with a great deal of human suffering. Not only do we have *contact* with suffering, but we also are *expected to respond* to it with both competence and compassion. And that is a very special drain, one that only those who have experienced it can understand. With the understanding comes an obligation to respond to the human needs generated by the stresses of practice.

Not only can collegial relationships help one survive the rigors of practice, but they also can and do *enable* one to be a professional (specifically, a nursing professional) through identification with others and through finding again the dilemmas of others within oneself. Collegial relationships—though they often are formalized into rules about the handling of incompetent colleagues, peer evaluation and review, and professional courtesies—do not tell one how to act so much as they teach one *how to be*.

The discovery and understanding of oneself as a professional inevitably results from one's experience of other professionals. As nurses discover, emulate, and create their pro-fessional personas, they discover, add to, and create their profession. Far too often, we think of "the profession" as an organization or a set of texts or even as a faculty of nursing. *Yet, this is not so: a profession exists* only *in its practitioners and in its practices.* Organizations, books, journals, faculty members and the like may represent the profession, but its practi-tioners *are* the profession.

To the extent that we nurture—teach, guide, correct, and support—one another, we give life to the profession. As Ida recounted her story, I was reminded that there are still thousands (maybe millions) of life-giving nurses in practice today . . . and hope springs anew!

REFERENCES

1. Edelstein, Ludwig. *Ancient Medicine,* edited by Owsei Temkin, and C. Lillian Temkin, (Johns Hopkins University Press. 1967) p. 46.
2. May, William F., *The Physician's Covenant,* (The Westminister Press, 1983) p. 110.
3. Veatch, Robert. *The Ethics of Professional Relationships* in Warren T. Reich (ed.), *The Encyclopedia of Bioethics,* (The Free Press 1978) pp. 178–179.
4. Curtin, Leah, and M. Josephine Flaherty, *Nursing Ethics: Theories and Pragmatics,* (R.J. Brady Company, 1982) p. 126.
5. Heidegger, Martin, *Existence and Being,* (The Henry Regnery Company, 1949) p. 287.
6. Curtin and Flaherty, *op cit.,* p. 127.

CHAPTER 17

●●

Are You At Risk for Disciplinary Action?

ALEXIA GREEN, CADY CRIMSON, LOUISE WADDILL,
AND ONEY FITZPATRICK

What's your image of a nurse who is brought up for disciplinary action for violating state law or regulations? Do you envision a new graduate overwhelmed by the responsibilities and pressures of the profession?

That's a widely held view—but it's a misconception. In a study of nurses in our state, Texas, who violated the nurse practice act (NPA), we found that three-quarters had been in the profession for more than six years. In fact, most had been in nursing 11 years or more. Clearly, experience alone doesn't prevent nurses from breaking the law.

Sometimes nurses incur disciplinary action because of willful misconduct, such as stealing medications. But often, action is prompted by a mistake that stemmed from a lack of knowledge or a lapse in vigilance. If you, like many nurses in these changing times, have moved to a new institution or practice environment, you may be at greater risk than you think for making such a mistake.

Here we'll review some of the most common missteps leading to NPA violations and offer a few common-sense tips on how to avoid them. We'll also present a profile, based on our research findings, of the "typical" disciplined RN—a profile you may find surprising. And you'll hear comments from disciplined nurses themselves on how their careers and lives have changed.

Ignorance of the Law

Sometimes, a nurse may violate a provision of the NPA or other law or regulation simply out of lack of knowledge. But ignorance of the law is no defense against disciplinary action.

Know your state's NPA. Their exact content varies, but all NPAs provide a general definition of nursing practice, outline the scope of practice, and differentiate nursing from other professions. They also set forth requirements for licensure and grounds for disciplinary action.

To ensure compliance, the NPA establishes a regulatory body, usually called the board of nursing, and outlines its roles and functions, which include licensing, promulgating rules governing nursing practice, and carrying out disciplinary action. State boards work together, and all belong to the National Council of State Boards of Nursing, which develops licensure examinations and maintains a data bank on disciplined practitioners.

As important as the NPA itself are the rules adopted by the board of nursing. These rules generally carry the weight of law and are enforceable under the regulatory authority of the board. Such rules may include the standards of professional nursing practice, unprofessional conduct rules, rules regarding use of nursing personnel and delegation of nursing tasks to unlicensed personnel, and continuing education requirements, among many others.

If you don't already have copies of your state's current NPA and the board's rules, write the board to request them. Since the NPA is statutory law, enacted by the state legislature, it's usually written in legalese, so it's not the easiest or most exciting document to read. Fortunately, some state nurses associations, such as Texas's, have prepared annotated versions of NPAs, with explanations of the acts' provisions. Ask your state's nurses association whether it has published an annotated NPA.

If you're a traveling nurse, or you live near state lines and are licensed and practicing in more than one state, remember that laws vary. You must know the NPA and regulations in each state where you practice.

It's also worth noting that you must inform your board of your change of address if you move. Amazingly, many nurses fail to do this. Consequently, they don't receive their license renewal forms and therefore forget to renew their licenses. Most boards will take disciplinary action or at least levy a fine against the nurse who practices with an expired license. And a hospital won't hire or continue to employ a nurse with a lapsed license.

Depending on your practice setting, there are other laws and rules that govern your practice. Such rules may be promulgated by agencies such as the state health department, department of mental health and mental retardation, and other state licensing bureaus, and may include home health licensing regulations, long-term care standards, and hospice criteria, among myriad others. Often, these rules address the requirements for and the responsibilities of the RN in a particular setting. You're responsible for knowing and complying with the rules that apply to your practice setting. Frequently, violation of such rules constitutes a breach of professional standards as defined in the NPA or nursing board rules. Your employer should have current copies of the rules that apply to your setting. If not, you can obtain copies from the regulatory agencies.

Going in Unprepared

Nurses appear most at risk of violating the NPA when they're new to their position or practice setting. Most of the disciplined nurses in our study (see Box 17-1, *Profile of the Disciplined Nurse*) had worked for their employer for less than a year.

Many nurses' errors involved IV therapy or medication administration. The nurses failed to follow established procedures for administering drugs or treatments. Although the "Five Rights" of medication administration always apply, there are details that vary between institutions or settings, such as who is authorized to give particular classes of medication, how PRN medications are charted, what to do with unused medications, and who can provide medications when a patient is going home. A nursing board may view failure to follow the hospital's policies and procedures as unprofessional conduct, even if one nurse's actions would have complied with policy at other hospitals.

BOX 17-1   PROFILE OF THE DISCIPLINED NURSE

From our study of 476 disciplined RNs in Texas, in which we reviewed board records, a profile of the "typical" disciplined nurse emerged: a white female, age 44, with more than a decade of experience in the profession. At the time of her violation, she worked full-time as a staff nurse in a medical-surgical or critical care unit or emergency department. In other words, she resembled in many respects a typical member of the general RN population. Her violation involved failing to administer medications or treatments responsibly.

However, when we compared the disciplined nurses to a like number of randomly selected RNs who hadn't been disciplined, we saw some differences. Though the women predominated in both groups, there were three times as many men among the disciplined nurses. (The reason for this is unclear, but at least one study has found that men more often cite nursing's advantages as a career than a need to nurture or care as their reason for entering the profession and that men tend to choose high-risk practice areas such as critical care.) Disciplined nurses alto tended to have less education. More disciplined than undisciplined nurses had associate degrees and fewer had baccalaureate degrees. And most disciplined RNs were in their current positions three years or less.

In many respects, this profile closely resembles that revealed in a 1992 study by M. D'Ann Murphy of the Colorado Department of Regulatory Agencies in Denver of nurses disciplined by that state's board of nursing for medication errors. In both studies most disciplined RNs had an associate degree, were employed in a hospital at the time of the incident, and were 40 to 44 years of age. And in both, a great majority of nurses had been with their institutions three years or less, with most in their first year of employment.

A third study of disciplined nurses, by Joanne Supples of the University of Colorado Health Science Center School of Nursing, also in Denver, provides further insight into how nurses come to face disciplinary action. The study focused on self-regulation among nurses in the Southwest. As in our group, the most common practice mistake was a medication error. But Supples also found that nurses most likely to be reported to a nursing board chronically engaged in substandard practice, didn't cooperate with managers and colleagues, and had "no problem recognition, remorse, or desire to change." Another interesting finding was that an employee's tenure at an institution influenced how far the institution was willing to extend itself to help her. Supples concluded that nurses with less time on the job lack social solidarity—that is, they haven't yet developed relationships with co-workers or managers that would allow them to ask questions and confide concerns. Also, a hospital (or its employees) may expect a new nurse to perform like an experienced one, with minimal guidance. When the new RN falls short, co-workers may even "push her to fail" by expanding their expectations.

Little research is currently available that has examined advanced practice nurses (APNs), but a 1993 study by the National Council of State Boards of Nursing revealed that nurse anesthetists (CRNAs) were more likely than other APNs to be disciplined for abuse of drugs or alcohol. Other APNs were more likely to have committed practice-related violations, such as medication errors or inaccurate or incomplete assessments. These findings closely correlate with those on APNs in our study.

Many disciplined RNs in our study said that their downfall was assuming that a policy or procedure was the same as it had been in their previous work setting. Only after an incident did they learn there were different expectations (such as about when to notify a supervisor or physician) or different equipment or documentation required in the new setting.

Don't make the same mistake. Before accepting a new position, be sure you're comfortable with your new employer's orientation program. The orientation should include a review of the job description and policies and procedures as well as time to ask questions. Attend the entire orientation, and when something is unclear, don't hesitate to ask for clarification.

Also review on your own your new institution's (or new unit's) policies and procedures, especially any that aren't covered in depth during orientation. These should be available on your unit in a designated area.

Once on the job, remember that no nurse can know everything or be competent in every skill. If you feel you're not prepared to perform a particular procedure or care for a certain patient or group of patients, ask for appropriate continuing education or training or refuse the assignment. Simply say, "I haven't had the opportunity to perform that procedure before. Could you please give me assistance?" or "I don't have the experience or training to provide quality care to that patient."

Even if you haven't changed employers or practice settings, you can put yourself at risk by not keeping your knowledge and skills up to date. One nurse disciplined by our board had failed to stay abreast of proper technique for drawing blood samples from a subclavian line. The nurse reinjected part of the withdrawn sample back into the patient, which is known to risk infection and injection of air or thrombus.

To keep out of trouble, keep current. Attend continuing education programs, read the nursing literature, review new institutional policies, and participate in your state or specialty nursing organization. Many states and certifying bodies require nurses to earn a given number of continuing education credits for license or certification renewal.

Failure to Assess or Document

Another frequent cause for disciplinary action among the nurses we studied was failure to assess a patient, or consequent failure to take care measures that might have stabilized the patient or prevented complications. We all know that patient assessment is one of our primary responsibilities. Today, ongoing assessment is more important than ever, with patients more acutely ill and hospital stays shorter. Yet in the course of our busy shifts, it's easy to neglect to do thorough followup assessments.

Poor charting, like inadequate documentation of assessment, may lead to improper care decisions, jeopardizing patients. Many nurses in our study were disciplined for consistently failing to chart or for falsifying or destroying patient records. Such offenses typically come to light when another clinician finds that the patient's condition doesn't match the nurse's recorded assessment findings.

Nursing boards may see inappropriate or inaccurate documentation as a sign of disregard for the patient's safety and welfare. Falsifying assessment findings may be particularly hazardous to the patient, and so may draw especially strong sanction. But even a simple error of omission may make it difficult to defend your care to a nursing board—or, for that matter, to a jury in a malpractice case. Certainly, complete documentation of assessment, care measures, and patient responses takes time, but it's your best defense against lawsuits and complaints to the nursing board. (See Box 17-2.)

Looking the Other Way

You probably know that impaired practice due to chemical dependency or mental illness and such "unprofessional" activities as stealing medication, supplies, or equipment from the hospital or personal items from the patient are grounds for disciplinary action. But you may not be aware that you may have a duty under state law to report such conduct by others to your supervisor, the peer review committee, the peer assistance program, or the board of nursing (depending on the law's stipulations). In states that have such mandatory reporting requirements, failure to do so may violate the law and draw disciplinary action (see Box 17-3, *Picking Up the Pieces*).

BOX 17–2 **DISCIPLINED FOR BAD PRACTICE: A CASE IN POINT**

The vast majority of nurses conscientiously maintain good nursing practice and obey the law. But one case of nurse misconduct that recently occurred in Texas shows why states have boards of nursing and disciplinary powers. It also vividly illustrates how an RN can make numerous violations in a single incident when she disregards policy, procedures, and practice standards.

The nurse was caring for a patient, whom we'll call Mr. Mendez, who'd been transferred to her medical-surgical unit from the ICU two days before. An LVN reported to the RN that Mr. Mendez, who had a traumatic head injury and was in a stabilization halo, was becoming agitated and attempting to get out of bed. After instructing the LVN to tell Mr. Mendez to "be still and not get out of bed," the RN went on with other activities. A short time later the LVN again reported that Mr. Mendez was trying to get up.

Without assessing him, the RN flipped through the chart and found an order for Mr. Mendez's ICU stay for "Pavulon (pancuronium bromide) for agitation." Although the order had been discontinued when Mr. Mendez was extubated and transferred to the med-surg unit, the RN, without calling the physician, rewrote the order on the current order sheet. She then instructed the LVN to administer the pacuronium. The LVN did administer the drug, but, fortunately, gave it IM, sparing Mr. Mendez from respiratory arrest.

The RN exhibited a blatant disregard for care standards and hospital policy as well as the patient's safety. She didn't assess Mr. Mendez, she falsified his medical record by writing a physician's order, and she failed to assure the safe administration of a medication. The RN was immediately fired and subsequently reported to the nursing board for investigation. At her hearing, held within six months of the incident, she could describe neither the mechanism of action of pancuronium nor the risks and necessary precautions of administering neuromuscular blockers. She'd taken no medication review course and, although terminated from her employment, appeared not to understand the seriousness of her actions.

In order to protect the public, the board suspended her license, thus preventing her from working as a RN, until she completed courses in nursing jurisprudence, medication administration, and pharmacology. After she completed these courses, she was allowed to practice nursing, but had to work under strict supervision of another RN for three years.

One nurse in our study who was disciplined for such inaction recalled,

This was a devastating incident for me. I was charge nurse and an RN working with me took a drug meant for a patient—the patient was allergic to the med and we were to destroy the drug [per hospital policy]. The nurse took the drug, with my knowledge, for her own use. Since I did not stop this or report it, I was disciplined the same way she was, with a reprimand to my license.

In our study, we found that abuse of drugs and alcohol and mental illness continue to figure in NPA violations. Certain behavior seen in our study—particularly involving charting—can tip you off to a colleague's chemical dependence problem. For example, the coworker may sign out a drug on the narcotic records, but fail to document giving it to the patient in the medication administration record or nursing notes. She may sign out drugs to a nonexistent patient or one who no longer needs pain medication. Or she may often report spilling or otherwise wasting a drug. In our study and others, meperidine was the medication most often diverted by nurses.

Sometimes nurses, out of ignorance, fail to notice these warning signs—or, out of denial, they don't acknowledge them. But one chemically dependent nurse who had been disciplined told us, "Nurses should be informed of the high potential for alcohol or drug abuse within the profession due to the high levels of stress involved. They should be aware that emotional makeup and inability to cope with stress can result in abuse."

BOX 17–3 PICKING UP THE PIECES

In our study, the most common sanction used by the nursing board (given to 43% of disciplined RNs) was a warning. Typically, this penalty was issued for a minor, first-time violation. About one-quarter (26%) of disciplined RNs were given reprimands with stipulations, such as having to practice under the supervision of another nurse, lasting one to five years. And about one-fifth (19%) had their licenses revoked. The remainder received suspensions and other penalties.

Although nurses in our study found the investigation and disciplinary process was stressful, most said they were treated fairly. Most believed their investigation had been conducted in a professional manner and that they had been afforded due process by the nursing board. But about one-third felt otherwise. Based on their comments, it's clear that these nurses felt devastated by the experience.

The nurses we examined underwent the process of professional and personal transformation that Sally Hutchinson of the University of Florida, Miami, identified in her 1992 study of disciplined nurses in that state. Like those Hutchinson studied, our nurses began with "assuming a stance" after being confronted with the incident. Their stances covered a spectrum ranging from taking complete responsibility to placing blame squarely on others. One nurse, for example, described a lack of managerial skills leading to an incident. Another spoke of her ex-husband's alcohol problem as "causing my lack of professionalism." Still another said, "I would have felt much more satisfaction if all parties involved could have discussed the issues to try and determine what led to many poor errors in judgment, not just on my part." Finally, there was the nurse who alleged "posturing by administration who needed a scapegoat ... I was handy."

We also found that nurses went through what Hutchinson calls "re-visioning," a process of reflecting on and integrating the various aspects of their experience. For some nurses, this resulted in more profound self-awareness. Said one, "I finally know I cannot work around drugs and will have to find employment in another area where drugs are not involved."

Most of the nurses continued to practice following disciplinary action, with most of these continuing to work as staff nurses. But almost one-third were unemployed or inactive. Of those remaining active, most had left the employer for whom they worked at the time of the incident. Nearly one-third still work in hospitals, but a significant number had migrated to geriatric nursing or long-term care facilities. More than 6% worked in geriatrics following disciplinary action, compared to less than 4% of the larger RN population.

Some nurses, it seems, will never recover from the often far-reaching professional, financial, and personal consequences of disciplinary action. One nurse told us, "This pain will never go away ... My status has gone from viable employment to food stamps and homelessness ... Overall, the whole incident has left me emotionally devastated. This lasted seven years, resulting in my bankruptcy, losing everything I owned, especially my dignity."

Others, however, saw brighter prospects. These included nurses who left the profession. Said one, "I am not able to handle the stress of nursing and my therapist suggested I not work [in the profession]. I am now, joyfully, a full-time homemaker and love it." Another told us, "Current employment is much more rewarding. Pleasant surroundings, make lots of money, am enjoying life again."

Those who stayed in nursing, too, were often optimistic about their future. Almost one-third planned to pursue additional nursing education. One nurse, who had been disciplined for not reporting a co-worker's drug diversion, told us how, with the help of colleagues, she'd successfully faced the crisis. "The head nurse and clinical director of my station were very supportive of me. The other nurse was fired from the hospital, but I did not lose my charge nurse position. Even though I had been an RN for over eight years at the time of the incident, it has completely changed the way I practice nursing. So in that respect I would have to say that the whole incident was a positive learning experience for me." Responses like this suggest that disciplined nurses who continue to embrace the nursing profession rather than distancing themselves grow both professionally and personally.

Mental illness in a colleague is often difficult to miss, our study suggests. In many cases, a nurse exhibited bizarre behavior, such as dramatic changes in mood that endangered patients.

Lessons To Be Learned

Many nurses in our study said they hoped its findings would help prevent others from violating the law and having to go through the painful process of disciplinary action. We share that hope.

Our study and other research have shed light on who violates the NPA and what the most common causes are for violations. Individual nurses, hospitals and other employers, and nursing schools can all learn from these insights. For example, if you accept a position in another hospital or a different practice setting, you may want to make an extra effort to learn and follow policies and procedures.

Hospitals may want to reevaluate their orientation programs and consider more detailed orientations focusing on medication administration and documentation. Nursing schools similarly may want to place more emphasis on proper drug administration and precautions for avoiding errors.

Most nurses consistently provide good patient care and will never have to face disciplinary action. But in this time of rapid change and greater stress, all of us will have to strive to maintain nursing's record of excellence. It's more than a matter of law—it's a duty to your patients.

SELECTED REFERENCES

Green, A., et al. *Disciplined Professional Nurses in the State of Texas: A Profile and Comparison to Nondisciplined RNs.* Austin, TX, The Board of Nurse Examiners for the State of Texas, 1994.

Hutchinson, S. Nurses who violate the nurse practice act. Transformation of professional identity. *Image J. Nurs Sch.* 24:133–139, Summer 1992.

Murphy, M. D. Individual characteristics of nurses who committed medication administration errors. *Issues* 13(1):11–13, 1992.

National Council of State Boards of Nursing. Advanced nursing practice discipline survey results. *Issues* 14(2):1–10, 1993.

Perkins, J., et al. Why men choose nursing. *Nurs. Health Care* 14:34–38, Jan. 1993.

Supples, J. Self-regulation in the nursing profession: Response to substandard practice. *Nurs. Outlook* 41(1):20–24, Jan.–Feb. 1993.

Willmann, J. *Annotated Guide to the Texas Nursing Practice Act.* Austin, Texas Nurses Association, 1994.

CHAPTER 18

Mentoring in the Career Development of Hospital Staff Nurses: Models and Strategies

DIANE J. ANGELINI

Enhancing the career development of hospital staff nurses may be the greatest human re-source challenge facing hospital organizations as they move into the 21st century. Pro-grams such as precepting and internships have assisted in developing nurses during their beginning orientation into professional practice. Yet, the career development efforts for staff nurses beyond completion of such programs are much less definitive.

At the present time, two-thirds of employed nurses practice in hospital settings (Aiken, 1990). In general, the welfare of American nursing seems tied to professional staff nursing practice in hospital settings. What mentors and mentoring circumstances exist for staff nurses in hospital settings have rarely been documented. The collection of more extensive data on mentoring and staff nursing has been advocated (Jowers & Herr, 1990; Just, 1989; Hinson, 1986; Hagerty, 1986). Researchers have concentrated interest primarily on other nursing groups (White, 1988; Holloran, 1989; Kremgeld-Barrett, 1986). The focus of such re-search has provided limited understanding of the staff nurse's experience with mentoring.

Mentoring surveys and inventories have been used, yet no real qualitative data on mentoring and staff nursing have been generated before such survey development. Little is known about the extent to which staff nurses or others serve as mentors to other staff nurses (Hinson, 1986). The purpose of this exploratory, descriptive study was to identify perceived mentoring experiences of staff nurses working in various hospital settings, de-scribe mentoring strategies and career development as viewed by staff nurses, and de-velop models that depict mentoring and emergent variables.

Review of Literature

The theoretical framework for this study encompasses female development, career devel-opment theory, and mentoring as related to nursing.

FEMALE DEVELOPMENT

Mentoring is an interpersonal phenomenon (Gilbert & Rossman, 1990) and exists within a social context (Kram, 1988). Thus, female development as it relates to life's social experiences and interpersonal relationships is key to the background of female mentoring experiences. The importance of connectedness and relationship-building efforts are documented by both Belenky, Clinchy, Goldberger, and Tarule (1986) and Gilligan (1979,1982). Miller (1986), in describing a new psychology of women in line with the works of Belenky, et al, and Gilligan, described critical aspects of female development such as maintaining connections with others, and being able to maintain affiliations and relationships. Hennig and Jardim (1977) reflected that most adult women have not been socialized to actively engage their environment, including the work environment. Women tend not to seek goals that threaten important affiliative relationships, so crucial to the dominant female thread of connectedness.

CAREER DEVELOPMENT

The concept of career development is viewed as a developmental life process the context of which is determined by two measures, ie, the individual and the environment in which the individual exists (Vondracek, Lerner, & Schulenberger, 1986). The work environment plays a key role in an individual's life as do organizational and societal forces. The interest in women's development has sparked new importance in career development for both individuals as employees in organizations and for organizational life (Gallos, 1989). Another part of the organizational environment critical to an individual's career development is the employee peer group that can influence one's career (Hall, 1980).

Betz and Fitzgerald (1987) note that women face unique barriers in their development of a career, and they achieve far lower levels of rewards. Lack of role models for women in strong career pursuits is evident and in the past, women have had to rely on both male and female influentials (Betz & Fitzgerald, 1987). Vondracek, et al, (1986) acknowledged that little is really known about how women feel relative to their career situations.

MENTORING AND STAFF NURSING

Within the literature on career psychology of women, mentoring has gained notoriety (Campbell-Heider, 1986; Shapiro & Farrow, 1988; Roberts, 1987; Bolton, 1980). Women have underused mentoring relationships as an important career advancement strategy and have lacked models and skills for successful mentoring relationships (Campbell-Heider, 1986). Yet, women represent more than 49% of the American workforce (Chao & Malik, 1988) and 96.7% of all employed nurses are women (Facts About Nursing, 1986–1987). Darling (1985) defined mentoring as a process in which a person is guided, taught, and influenced in one's life work in critical ways. She defined mentoring as a broader, more inclusive term focusing on the process, not solely on the interaction with people. Darling considered people mentors as a limiting definition for mentorship.

Kram (1988) suggests the following two types of mentoring functions: career functions, which enrich career advancements; and psychosocial functions, which enhance competence, identity, and effectiveness in a professional role. She suggested that young people seek peer relationships because the mentor–protege relationship is often unavailable to most people. Arthur and Kram (1989) have also suggested a notion of individual organizational reciprocity, ie, a method of matching the environmental needs of both parties. Gilbert and Rossman (1990) identified particular aspects of mentor functions that are different when women mentor women. These related to creating new images of women and using the relationship to empower women and sponsorship.

Three research studies focusing on mentoring and staff nursing include works by Stachura (1989), Just (1989), and Hinson (1986). Stachura used a descriptive design for a study of staff nurses and professional socialization. The study indicated that the most common professional socialization relationship involved a staff nurse from the same work unit and that the relationship was promoted by caring for patients.

Just (1989) looked at mentors and self-reports of professionalism in hospital staff nurses. From this study, a modest positive relationship between presence of a mentor was found relative to self-reports of professionalism.

Hinson's study (1986) looked at identification of the mentor relationship in the career of a staff nurse. The major findings showed that staff nurses have mentors and mentors contribute to the career development of nurses. However, the exact nature of the mentoring relationship was unclear. She recommended further studies to determine the essential characteristics of a mentor for the staff nursing group and how a mentor relates to career development for staff nurses.

Methodology

This study represented an exploratory, descriptive study qualitative in nature using grounded-theory method. Grounded theory provides a method for investigating previously unresearched areas and for discovering a new point of view in certain situations (Stern, 1980). Constant comparative method is concerned with generating and suggesting categories, properties, and hypotheses about general problems (Strauss & Corbin, 1990). Selected probe questions were used to facilitate the interview process.

Triangulation of the following four data sources was used to gain perspective on mentoring and staff nursing: audiotaped face-to-face interviews with staff nurses; audiotaped face-to-face interviews with their respective nurse managers regarding organizational and environmental issues of career development in the hospital work setting; biographical data and career history questions; and document analysis of job descriptions, philosophies, and mission statements of each institutional setting.

Verbatim audiotaped interviews were transcribed and content analyzed. Constant comparative analysis was applied to transcribed data. Coding of data was ongoing as data were collected. Memo writing was also used.

Data analysis used coding of data and the generation of categories leading to conceptual models explaining the topic of mentoring as perceived by hospital staff nurses. Inter-rater reliability on 22 data items by two independent reviewers was noted to be 91% and 71% agreement.

The population consisted of 37 female staff nurses and 8 female nurse managers representing four acute care hospitals, both teaching and nonteaching, in two northeastern states. The mean age of the staff nurses was 38.2 years with an age range from 25 to 55 years. The median age was 37 years. All nurses worked 32 hours or more per week and worked in medical surgical clinical settings only, and had a minimum of 5 years nursing experience.

The educational background of the hospital staff nurses consisted of 10 prepared at bachelor's level, 14 with diplomas, 11 with associate degrees, and 2 with master's degrees in nursing. The year of graduation from the basic educational program in nursing ranged from 1954 to 1987.

The average number of years that the hospital staff nurses were employed in their current employment was 12.2 years. In two institutions, a clinical advancement program or clinical ladder was operational.

LIMITATIONS OF THE STUDY

Only female staff nurses representing various medical surgical units and their female nurse managers were sampled. No federal or military hospitals were included in this sample, and because most of the data were collected in the northeast portion of the United States, it does not account for any regional differences. One gender is explored and the study looked at only white women. Other study limitations included data collection technique that employed a single investigator, and use of one interview contact per subject only.

Findings: Structural Model of Mentoring

A structural model of mentoring as perceived by hospital staff nurses developed from the data (Fig. 18-1). Three main categories of mentoring influentials emerged, ie, environment, people, and events. The data from staff nurses and nurse managers support a broader base of mentoring influences than that of a single-mentor model.

ENVIRONMENT AS MENTORING INFLUENCE

The category of the environment was defined as an acute care institution or work setting in which hospital staff nurses are employed. The environment comprised the following four subcategories: barriers, nonbarriers, expectations, and rewards. Barriers were defined as hindrances encountered in the interaction within the hospital organizational climate. Barriers included value conflicts, limited advancement and recognition opportunities, lack of support at the unit level, and unsafe work conditions.

Nonbarriers were viewed as those items which enhanced or made possible a more positive interaction within the hospital organizational climate. Forty-nine percent of the nurses mentioned these items, and they included employee recognition programs, nursing judgments being valued, nurses viewed as key players in the health care system, and job opportunities beyond the unit level.

Expectations of the hospital environment were what staff nurses anticipated as being provided for them by the hospital organization and were mentioned by 54% of the staff. These included educational opportunities, as well as tuition reimbursement to advance such opportunities. Other items encompassed support for career changes and transitions, and flexible scheduling to accommodate the continuing education needs of staff.

Rewards were both materialistic and psychic, ie, both internal and external rewards. They were noted by 84% of the nurses. Items included financial rewards, ie, compensation, as well as psychic rewards including feeling satisfied with their care to patients and families, as well as working with competent people at the unit level and having a chance to serve as a consultant to other nurses.

PEOPLE AS MENTORING INFLUENTIALS

The category of people was defined as including both primary and secondary influentials who were used by staff nurses employed in acute care hospitals. Primary influentials were those people with whom nurses had relatively frequent contact and included peers who were hospital staff nurses and nurse managers on the unit in which they worked. Both groups were mentioned by 95% of the staff nurses sampled.

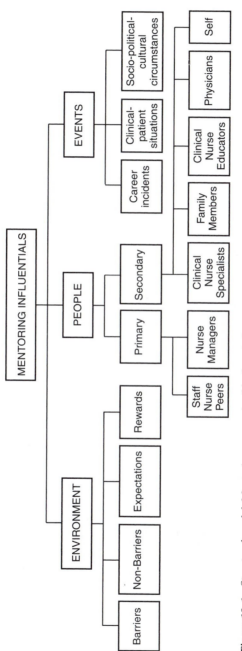

Figure 18–1 Structural model: Mentoring as perceived by hospital nurses.

Secondary influentials were those people with whom staff nurses had minimal or less frequent contact either in or outside the work setting. They included family members, clinical nurse specialists, physicians, clinical nurse educators, and aspects of self-mentoring.

INFLUENTIAL EVENTS

The category of events was defined as occurrences experienced by hospital staff nurses which were perceived to be critical to career development. These events occurred both in and outside the work setting and were both related and unrelated to nursing. Within the category of events the following three subcategories were noted: career incidents, clinical patient situations, and socio-political-cultural circumstances.

The subcategory of career incidents, included those events considered critical during one's tenure in nursing. Career incidents were mentioned by 73% of the nurses. A sample of items in this subcategory included: initial employment as a new graduate, moving from one unit or facility to another, first off-shift experience, first time taking charge of the unit, and failing state board exams.

Clinical patient situations, the second subcategory, were related occurrences experienced by staff nurses during their hospital career and were noted by 54% of the nurses. Because only nurses employed in medical-surgical settings were interviewed, the following examples of patient situations related exclusively to medical or surgical clinical scenarios with patients. These included code blue situations, both successful and unsuccessful resuscitation attempts, dying patients (especially young dying patients), patients who were suffering, and critical trauma patients in which ethical issues needed to be considered. A code blue event included:

> I think that every time I've been to a code blue situation, especially working on the cardiac floor (unit), has been a mentoring experience. Something different every time, different people running them . . . you try to improve with each one that you do, know more about what you are doing, know the drugs better that you're giving. Just try to make it run smoother each time. . . . At each one that comes, you remember the last one you went to before.

The third subcategory, socio-political-cultural circumstances, included occurrences experienced by staff nurses external to the hospital work setting and were mentioned by 10.8% of the nurses. Data elements included larger social factors such as the influence of the women's movement and family illnesses.

In general, the subcategories of barriers, nonbarriers, and expectations under environment and the subcategory of clinical patient situations under events were further subdivided as to teaching versus nonteaching institutions because the percentages in these subcategories were neither decidedly high nor low. However, no real differences were noted between teaching versus nonteaching hospitals for these selected subcategories.

Findings: Process Model of Mentoring

The structural model of mentoring, as perceived by hospital staff nurses, reflects a kind of topology of influentials thought to be salient to mentoring at the staff nurse level. However, mentoring seemed to be more than just structural and was described as a dynamic, interactive process in which mentoring influentials interacted in the career of hospital staff nurses. Mentoring demonstrated not only a structural model but also a process model with specific phases leading to selected career development outcomes (Fig 18-2). Mentoring emerged as a dynamic process in which people as mentors as well as events and the environment interplay to become the key mentoring influentials for the staff nurse employed in an acute care hospital setting.

FOUR PHASES OF PROCESS MODEL

In response to this dynamic interaction, a four-phase process model of mentoring as perceived by hospital staff nurses emerged (see Fig. 18-2). Phase 1 consists of mentoring influential characteristics including environment, people, and events plus the subcategories under each. Phase 1 is connected to phase 2, mentoring dimensions, signaling a strong linkage and movement across the model. Positive or negative influences of each mentoring characteristic, ie, people, the environment, or events seemed to be factors in the facilitation across the process model. For example, if a staff nurse encountered barriers versus nonbarriers in the environment or if she worked with a nurse manager who had a positive versus negative influence, or if a staff nurse's exposure to key events was positive or negative, this could contribute toward advancement or limited progression within the model. Combinations of influences, eg, events and people mentoring occurring simultaneously, needs further exploration.

Phase 2 is mentoring dimensions and includes the following three constructs: structure-specific dimensions, setting-specific dimensions, and profession-specific dimensions. Any one of these dimensions could apply to each of the mentoring characteristics. As an example, events could be related to both structure and setting-specific dimensions and not just the dimension of profession. However, one dimension may be dominant for a selected category, ie, environment being structure-specific, people being setting-specific, and environment being profession-specific.

These dimensions lead to phase 3 of the model which consists of mentoring strategies provided by others for the staff nurse. These mentoring strategies subdivide by category but are represented as a composite, because they may occur simultaneously. These strategies are interconnected and assist the flow of mentoring toward the three crucial career development outcomes in phase 4. These outcomes include positive interaction within the organizational climate, development of career-building relationships, and facilitation of career transition points. The flow of this mentoring process model is predominantly horizontal across all phases. Yet the flow may become interrupted along the process to become more interactive, as necessary. However, each phase seems to move predominantly toward achievement of the career development outcomes. No readiness factor emerged regarding progression in the process model. However, the amount of exposure to mentoring influentials or combinations thereof, as well as their positive or negative influence, may tend to advance or limit individual progression toward completion of career development outcomes in the model.

Responses of Nurse Managers and Document Analysis

Data from interviews with nurse managers supported data findings noted by staff nurses. The following salient themes emerged:

The influence of the hospital environment on staff nurses
Staff nurses' need for assistance with clinical problem-solving
The work nurse managers perform to promote career advancement for staff nurses
The need for support and socialization for hospital staff nurses
The influence of staff nurse peers

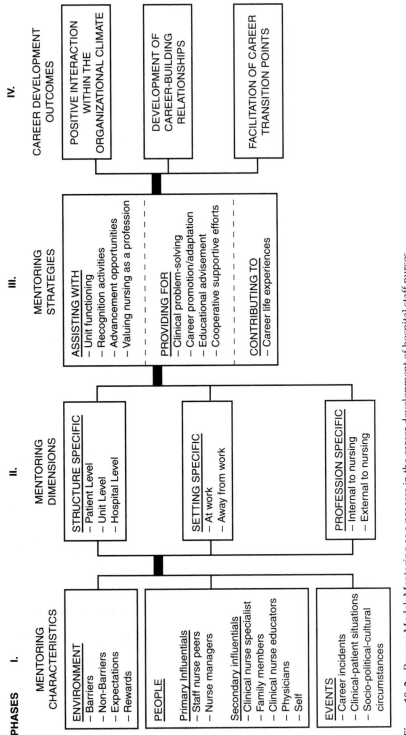

Figure 18–2 Process Model: Mentoring as a process in the career development of hospital staff nurses.

Document analysis of descriptive items in hospital mission statements, nursing organization philosophy statements, and staff nurse job descriptions was performed. The descriptive items from hospitals and nursing documents attest to some of the data elements noted in the audiotaped interviews with staff nurses and nurse managers.

The documents of teaching hospitals stressed the importance of the environment, education, and use of peers. The documents of nonteaching hospitals described similar elements. However, the number and breadth of such elements in the documents from nonteaching hospitals were limited. Educational descriptors seemed equivalent between both types of institutions.

Findings: Mentoring Strategies Provided by Staff Nurse Peers

Although the environment and events were identified as mentoring influentials, people, specifically peers and nurse managers, provided the most salient mentoring strategies for hospital staff nurses. The mentoring strategies provided to staff nurses by their nursing peers were identified as assistance with clinical problem solving, providing cooperative/supportive efforts, and promoting career adaptation. Clinical problem-solving involved the sharing of clinical information, assisting in clinical decision-making, reviewing clinical events, and assisting during difficult or critical patient situations. Relative to cooperative efforts, mentoring strategies were used to provide confidence-building behaviors including nurturing, providing positive verbal feedback, and availability and approachability as a team player.

Within the strategy of promoting career adaptation, the following mentoring behaviors were identified: socializing to the unit, acting as preceptors, assisting with unit or job transitions, and assisting with career goals.

Findings: Mentoring Strategies Provided by Nurse Managers

The mentoring strategies provided by nurse managers were identified as educational advisement, career promotion, and cooperative efforts. References to both current and past nurse managers were noted. Educational advisement included behaviors such as providing for challenging projects and opportunities, sharing educational knowledge and/or information, and encouraging educational classes and programs.

Relative to career promotion, nurse-managers assisted staff nurses with opportunities to transfer to other units, promoted clinical advancement and recognition, discussed career decision making with staff and promoted involvement in professional organization. The third mentoring strategy was cooperative efforts which included easing work transitions, allowing for risk taking, providing for unit organizational support, and for unit organizational consistency over time.

Conclusions

Mentoring takes on primary importance at the clinical bedside.

Mentoring, for hospital staff nurses, is a multidimensional process involving the environment, people, and events as mentoring influentials, not a single mentor model.

Peers and nurse managers served as the primary influentials for the mentoring of staff nurses.

Mentoring influences were noted through both positive and negative data as perceived by staff nurses.

Staff nurses perceived mentoring to be a large part of their career development.

No difference was found for teaching hospitals versus nonteaching hospitals regarding how mentoring was perceived.

The issue of gender with female staff nurses and female nurse managers revolved around relationship-building.

Implications for Clinical Nursing Practice

Because the largest number of nurses employed in the United States work in hospital settings, these exploratory findings relative to mentoring and hospital staff nurses have major implications. Assisting nurses in their career development and positively modifying their perceptions of mentoring seem vital to improving the nursing workforce at the bedside whether in a teaching or nonteaching institution.

Data suggest that people as mentors are critical at the clinical level (at the bedside) to assist staff nurses in the mentoring process.

Educational training, inservices, and continuing education for peers and nurse managers, as well as other hospital influentials, could upgrade the general awareness level of mentoring influentials. Providing them with the information on how mentoring occurs (process) and who and what influentials exist (structure) can provide a beginning step in addressing mentorship needs.

Specific educational strategies could focus on exploring the role or relationship-building; reviewing positive and negative experiences of staff nurses relative to environment, people, and events; and upgrading the awareness level of career transitioning and the facilitation of the career process for staff nurses.

Because the influence of peers on peers is significant, developing a peer mentorship program to facilitate mentoring seems appropriate. Rewarding peers either monetarily, through promotion in a clinical ladder advancement program, or with job enrichment would assist in promoting peer mentoring. Expecting staff to mentor each other and use key mentoring strategies may do more for the career development of staff nurses than almost anything else.

Development of the nurse manager in his or her role as mentoring influential is key. Nurse managers need development in their own career guidance skills to effectively develop staff nurses as employees.

Working with influential hospital personnel at all levels would assist in modifying the hospital organizational climate and environmental influences affecting staff nurses. Adjusting these influential environmental constructs by enhancing them or reducing negative perceptions could foster a more positive interaction within the organizational climate for staff nurses in hospitals.

Recommendations for Further Research

Among the recommendations possibly generated from this study, the following are suggested for further exploration and research:

1. Use study results to prepare a tool to survey a larger number of hospital staff nurses across the country relative to mentoring.

2. Examine whether male nurses show the same degree of relationship-building and connectedness with peers and nurse managers as evidenced by female nurses.

3. Using a larger sample size, determine how positive and negative mentoring influences impact progression along the process model.

4. Explore whether this mentoring model is consistent for nurses with less than 5 years experience in hospitals or for nurses who are employed less than 32 hours per week. Would their perceptions differ as to content or intensity?

5. Replicate and validate structural and process models of mentoring for other professionals in the United States as a mini-theory on mentoring.

Summary

Because two-thirds of employed nurses practice in hospital settings in the United States, the perceptions of these nurses on the influences of mentoring in their career are noteworthy. Mentoring for hospital staff nurses is multidimensional, situational, and relational occurring in an environment perceived to be influential. Mentoring models and strategies advance hospital staff nurses toward crucial career development outcomes.

ACKNOWLEDGMENTS

Special thanks to Dr. Joseph Cronin and Dr. Veronica Rempusheski, formerly Nurse Researcher, Beth Israel Hospital, Boston, MA.

REFERENCES

Aiken, L. (1990). Charting the future of hospital nursing. *Image: The Journal of Nursing Scholarship, 22*, 72–78.

Arthur, M., & Kram, K. (1989). Reciprocity at work: The separate, yet inseparable possibilities for individual and organizational development. In M. Arthur, D. Hall, & B. Lawrence, (Eds.). *Handbook of Career Theory*. (pp. 292–312). Cambridge, England: Cambridge University Press.

Belenky, M., Clinchy, B., Goldberger, N., & Tarule J. (1986). *Women's ways of knowing*. New York: Basic Books.

Betz, N., & Fitzgerald, L. (1987). *The career psychology of women*. Orlando, FL: Academic Press.

Bolton, E. (1980). A conceptual analysis of the mentor relationship to the career development of women. *Adult Education, 30*, 195–207.

Campbell-Heider, N. (1986). Do nurses need mentors? *Image: The Journal of Nursing Scholarship, 18*, 110–113.

Chao, G., & Malik, S. (1988). A career planning model for women. In S. Rose & L. Larwood, (Eds.). *Women's Careers*. (pp. 105–129). New York: Praeger.

Darling, L. (1985). Mentors and mentoring. *Journal of Nursing Administration, 15*, 42–43.

Gallos, J. (1989). Exploring women's development: Implications for career theory, practice and research. In M. Arthur, D. Hall, & B. Lawrence, (Eds.). *Handbook of Career Theory*. (pp. 110–130). Cambridge, England: Cambridge University Press.

Facts About Nursing. (1986–1987). Kansas City: American Nurses Association.

Gilbert, L., & Rossman, K. (1990). *Gender and the mentoring process*. Paper presented for the Symposium, Women Mentoring Women: New Theoretical Perspectives and their Application. Annual Meeting of the American Psychological Association, Boston, MA.

Gilligan, C. (1979). Woman's place in a man's life cycle. *Harvard Educational Review, 49*, 431–446.

Gilligan, C. (1982). *In a different voice. Psychological theory and women's development*. Cambridge, MA: Harvard University Press.

Hagerty, B. (1986). A second look at mentors. *Nursing Outlook, 34*, 16–24.

Hall, D. (1980). Potential for career growth. In M. Morgan (Ed.). *Managing Career Development*. (pp. 87–89). New York: D. Van Nostrand.

Hennig, M., & Jardim, A. (1977). *The managerial woman*. New York: Doubleday.

Hinson, D. (1986). *Identification of the mentor relationship in the career of a staff nurse.* Unpublished master's thesis, University of Utah.

Holloran, S. (1989). *Mentoring: The experience of nursing service executives.* Unpublished doctoral dissertation. Boston University.

Jowers, L., & Herr, K. (1990). A review of literature on mentor protege relationships. In G. Clayton & P. Baj, (Eds.). *Review of Research in Nursing Education.* (Vol III, pp. 49–77). New York: National League for Nursing.

Just, G. (1989). *Mentors and self-reports of professionalism in hospital staff nurses.* Unpublished doctoral dissertation, New York University.

Kram, K. (1988). *Mentoring at work.* Lanham, MD: University Press of America.

Kremgeld-Barrett, A. (1986). *Women mentoring women in academic nursing faculty.* Unpublished doctoral dissertation, Boston University.

Miller, J. (1986). *Towards a new psychology of women* (2nd ed.). Boston: Beacon.

Roberts, P. (1987). *Female Mentor Relationships.* Unpublished doctoral dissertation, The Wright Institutes, Berkeley.

Shapiro, G., & Farrow, D. (1988). Mentors and others in career development. In S. Rose & L. Larwood (Eds.). *Women's Careers.* (pp. 23–39). New York: Praeger.

Stachura, L. (1989). *Mentoring and other professional socialization relationships of registered nurses after entry into practice.* Unpublished master's thesis, Madonna College, Lavonia, MI.

Stern, P. (1980). Grounded theory methodology: Its uses and processes. *Image: The Journal of Nursing Scholarship, 12,* 20–23.

Strauss, A., & Corbin, J. (1990). *Basics of qualitative research.* Newbury Park, CA: Sage.

Vondracek, F., Lerner, R., & Schulenberger, J. (1986). *Career development: A life-span development approach.* Hillsdale, NJ: Lawrence Erlbaum.

White, J. (1988). The perceived role of mentoring in career development and success of academic nurse-administrators. *Journal of Professional Nursing, 4,* 178–185.

CHAPTER 19

●●●

An Analysis of the Concept of Empowerment

CHRISTINE M. RODWELL

Introduction

Concepts have been described by many authors in a variety of ways. At its simplest level a concept may be defined as an idea, a mental image of reality, or an abstraction (King 1988, Meleis 1991). Meleis (1991) states that a concept is a term or label used to describe a phenomenon or a group of phenomena. In a theory the concepts are therefore seen as the building blocks and elements essential to the foundation for scientific theories—and are therefore also fundamental to research and theory development.

It is thus a useful exercise to analyze a concept in current use in nursing in order to define and clarify its meaning for the intellectual advancement of the profession (Rodgers 1989). Indeed the profession has been criticized for failing to analyze and operationalize its concepts (variables) in nursing research and to clarify and exemplify concepts fundamental to the nursing metaparadigm (Batey 1979, Jacobs & Huether 1978, Schultz & Meleis 1988). The recent works of Benner (1984) and Schön (1990) delineate the need for clarification of the metaparadigm through qualitative approaches.

A number of analysis tools exist and most appear to have their foundations in Wilson's (1969) framework. While Walker & Avant (1988) and Meleis (1991) favor this approach, critics argue that this analysis method is empirical in its orientation, favoring reductionism in an attempt to isolate the apparent essence of the concept. It is also argued that this form of analysis is static in its approach and is not congruent with the broader social context of nursing (Rodgers 1989).

This paper will, however, use the published tool ascribed to Walker & Avant (1988) with the exemption of the contrary, invented, and illegitimate cases in line with the philosophy of Rodgers (1989), whose view is that these cases present too static a view of the concept under discussion. Instead these functions will be addressed in the form of related concepts. The social context of the concept for nursing will be addressed in the final section on implications for practice.

Aim of the Analysis

A concept that is considered significant within a culture will be used often (Rodgers 1989) and many authors agree that empowerment is a popular word in nursing (Maglacas 1988, Chavasse 1992). An extensive literature review identifies that the concept is widely used in society and in health care contexts, including mental health (Rogers 1990, Malin & Teasdale 1991), health promotion (Gott & O'Brien 1991, Yeo 1993, Rissell 1994), women's health and the feminist movement (Mason, et al, 1991; Parker & McFarlance 1991), empowerment of students (Chavasse 1992, Clay 1992, Manthey 1992), empowerment of children (Kalnins, et al, 1992), empowerment of single parents (Labonte 1989, Newton 1989), community empowerment (McMurray 1991, O'Neill 1992), and the empowerment of people with AIDS (De la Cancela 1989). The contemporary nature of the literature is evident.

The literature is multifaceted and diverse including writings from educational, organization, environmental, sociological, psychological, and feminist ideologies. Uses of the term seem to be extensive, therefore an objective analysis using a synthesis of Walker & Avant's (1988) and Rodgers' (1989) analysis tools will be undertaken to examine the attributes, characteristics, and uses of the concept. Kemp (1985) argues that clarifying definitions and meanings will enhance communication within the profession, and Rodgers (1989) suggests that clarifying the common usage and definitions will enable the concept to be used more effectively.

If a concept is clearly and analytically defined it will contribute to the development of nursing's knowledge base, which Mason, et al, (1991) see as the key to nursing's power and credibility as a profession and within society. At a personal level, Kemp (1985) suggests that concept analysis will promote critical and conceptual thinking and enhance the attainment of intellectual goals.

Uses of the Concept, Existing Definitions, and Parameters

The *Shorter Oxford English Dictionary* (1989) defines the verb "to empower" as to invest legally or formally with power, to authorize, to license; to impart power; to enable, to permit.

The *Random House Webster's College Dictionary* (1991) defines "empower" as to give official or legal power or authority; to endow with an ability or to enable. The suffix "ment" is defined as a result, act, or process and thus by adding the suffix "ment" to the verb "empower," empowerment becomes a noun defined as the process or result of empowering.

Analysis of the verb "to enable" further enhances the meaning of empowerment. The *Oxford English Dictionary* (1989) defines "enable" as to authorize, to empower, to make possible or effective.

Etymological investigation of the derivation of empowerment leads us to the word "power." The Latin word *potere* means to be able and the ability to choose, and is also linked to the word "potent" meaning powerful, cogent, persuasive, and having or exercising a great influence. The Middle English 1250–1300 verb *pouer(e)* or *poer(e)* also means to be able, as does the Anglo-French verb *poueir* or *poer* (*Random House Webster's College Dictionary* 1989).

Synonyms for "empowerment" are located in *Roget's Thesaurus* (1982) and include: to make possible, commission, permission, authority, ability, enable, authorize, endow with power, allow, capability, potentiality, and to arm. Many of these terms appear throughout the literature review and will be discussed in the text.

In simple terms, the concept of empowerment would appear to be the process of enabling or imparting power transfer from one individual or group to another. It includes the elements of power, authority, choice, and permission. Empowerment may also be viewed as the result or product of the process of empowering.

Concepts are continually subject to change and therefore data sampling for the concept analysis addresses a broad time span in order to evaluate both the historical development and the contextual usage of the concept. Similarly, reviewing literature from many disciplines allows similarities in the use of the concept across a broad field of concern (Rodger 1989). Literature is included from British, American. Canadian, Australian and New Zealand authors, offering a range of cultural variations. The various meanings are addressed in the following discussion, using themes as derived from the initial dictionary definitions. Each section will be summarized.

POWER

An apparent dichotomy appears to exist between the concepts of empowerment and power. Grace (1991), Malin & Teasdale (1991) and Zerwekh (1992) all offer contemporary studies suggesting that contradictions exist for nurses who use empowerment strategies in practice.

Grace (1991), in a qualitative study including 21 health promotion nurses in New Zealand, analyzed the contradictions and inconsistencies surrounding the use of the notion of empowerment within the discourse of health promotion. She argues that there is an empowering/controlling dichotomy in health promotion practice, as the system effectively constructs the individual as a health consumer in accordance with the model of consumer capitalism.

Malin & Teasdale (1991), also using a qualitative approach, discuss the tensions which exist between the concepts of caring and empowerment. In this British study it is argued that caring includes altruism, control, and paternalism as related concepts and that this aspect of the nurses' function is at odds with the idea of empowerment which places the patient in a partnership relationship with the nurse. Since caring is considered fundamental to nursing, does this mean that empowerment has no role to play in contemporary nursing?

Zerwekh's (1992) research of 95 American public health nurses concludes that the apparently contradictory activities of empowerment and coercion often coexist in helping relationships. These studies suggest a relationship between power/control and empowerment as evidenced by the dictionary definitions. Hence some analysis of power/control as it is embedded in empowerment may clarify the issue.

Chandler (1991) states that power and empowerment connote very different meanings and yet there has been little distinction made between these concepts in the literature. From a feminist perspective Bookman & Morgan (1988) see empowerment as a process aimed at changing the nature and distribution of power in a particular cultural context. Empowerment is widely understood in feminist circles as a more appropriate approach to power than traditional male models. French (1980) states that the patriachal form of "power over" is inappropriate and that the feminist form of "power to" is fundamental to empowerment.

Mason, et al, (1991) suggest that empowerment includes enabling people to recognize their strengths, abilities, and personal power and includes power-sharing, respect for self and others as part of the process. Wheeler & Chinn (1989) believe that empowerment entails commitment to both self and others and Zerwekh (1983), cited in Zerwekh (1992), states that power originates in self-esteem developed through love, responsibility, opportunities for choice, and perceived meaning and hope.

Transferring Power

Empowerment is therefore seen as a process of transferring power and includes the development of a positive self-esteem and recognition of the worth of self and others. Empowerment thus has a personal and individual element and has a cyclical nature; as Chavasse

(1992) states empowerment is a state arising from valuing others and no one can value others unless they value themselves. Nurses cannot therefore empower unless they themselves are empowered. Weis & Schank (1991) suggest that the profession does not value its professional roots, which may explain why nursing does not enjoy empowerment.

In the management literature, empowerment is seen as delegating authority and sharing power. Large organizations provide a forum for authority and sharing power. They also provide a forum for the use of power and empowerment. There is much evidence of managers attempting to share power by participative management techniques, networking, and quality circles (McClelland 1975, Manthey 1992). However, in a qualitative analysis of 56 staff nurses' perceptions of empowerment, Chandler (1991) found that power, delegation, and authority were not identified as elements of the concept. The participants viewed empowerment as enabling others by increasing resources, capabilities, and effectiveness and stated that empowerment was derived from interactions such as counseling, supporting, and comforting.

It would appear that there is dissonance between administrative and practitioner perception of empowerment. Practitioners appear to value the interpersonal process element of empowerment, whereas managers see empowerment as returning power and control to the practitioners.

Malin & Teasdale (1991) suggest that it is in the mental handicap arena that the belief in the empowering role for nurses is most clearly expressed. Empowerment implies that the nurse maximizes patients' independence and minimizes their dependence using "normalization" principles (Wolfensberger 1972). Malin & Teasdale (1991) see enormous moral and political dilemmas for nurses within their caring and empowering roles. Perhaps these dilemmas exist even more strongly in mental health care. The Mental Health Act (1983) empowers the police to remove a person they consider to be mentally disordered and in need of immediate care and control to a place of safety (Rogers 1990). Thus the Act empowers a non–mental health professional with a legal mandate to make a judgment about a person's mental state. This takes us back to the patriachal form of power (French 1980) and in this example empowerment is used synonymously with "power over."

Josefowitz (1980), cited in Hokanson Hawks (1992), helps us to understand this dichotomy when she distinguishes between power in terms of forcefulness (ability to control) and effectiveness (the capacity, ability, and the means) to achieve objectives. The idea of effectiveness is more congruent with the element of power embedded in empowerment in this paper.

Health Promotion

In the health promotion literature there is frequent reference to power and control within the process of empowerment. The Alma Ata Declaration that health promotion is the process of enabling people to increase control over and to improve their health (World Health Organization 1978) underlines current health promotion practice. Green & Raeburn (1988) see empowerment and enablement as similar concepts and they see enablement as returning power, knowledge, skills, and other resources to the individual, community, or population.

Similarly, French (1990) sees community empowerment as a process by which health educators try to enable people to increase control or at least a sense of control over their lives and their health. At the heart of this process is the empowering of communities—their ownership and control of their destinies and endeavors. Empowerment appears to be about changing the power base.

The literature also suggests a partnership relationship in this shifting power base. Salvage (1990) argues that the ideology of partnership is at the root of the fundamental reform movement in the "new nursing." Citizen participation is recurrent in the literature and authors suggest this is intrinsic to health promotion philosophy (Tones 1986, French 1990, Gott & O'Brien 1991). However Godbout (1981) states that, consciously or not, citizen participation usually ends up as consolidating the power of professionals or bureaucrats and not as a way to empower the community. O'Neill (1992) states that the only way for a community to acquire influence is to have a strong sense of autonomous power and a position of power.

Grace (1991) states that the language of enabling is misleading, and although the empowerment process attempts to position the community as being in control the professional often has an *a priori* agenda which is directive, controlling, and strongly implicated in the ensuing action. Grace (1991) does not mean to imply a misguided professional approach; she merely seeks to raise questions about the frequently made assumption that those in an empowering role do not have an *a priori* agenda. As she states, it is the health professionals who control the determinants of health.

Power as it is embedded in empowerment is important as it may explain the contradictory processes described at the beginning of this section by Grace (1991), Malin & Teasdale (1991), and Zerwekh (1992).

Contemporary nurse theorists also see power as embedded within the nurses' role. For nurses, expert power implies having the necessary knowledge, competence, and skill to perform effectively one's role within the context of caring (Benner 1984). King (1981) identifies power as a concept within the social system of her conceptual framework; Parse (1981) also discusses "powering" as fundamental to the metaparadigm of nursing.

ENABLEMENT: PROCESS OR PRODUCT?

The etymological derivation of "empowerment" suggests "to be able" or "to enable" as meanings of the word. Chandler (1991) defines "to empower" as "to enable to act."

The psychology, education, health promotion, and management literature all incorporate enablement in their definitions and usages of empowerment. Current health promotion ideology accepts empowerment as enabling and supporting people to set their own health agendas and to take control of their health status through skills development and critical consciousness raising. Indeed Yeo (1993) and Rissell (1994) see the ethic of empowerment as fundamental to health promotion. Zerwekh (1992), on parental empowerment, says it is enabling a parent to develop personal capacity and authority to take charge of everyday family life.

Bredeson (1989) sees empowerment as a process of providing people with opportunities and resources needed to understand and change the world (cited in Hokanson Hawks 1992). Mason, et al, (1991) see empowerment as a mutual process of sharing and development. The educational literature perceives empowerment within the facilitative role of the educator (Schön 1990). The issue is therefore: Is empowerment a process or a product? The dictionary definitions imply that it may be either but most sources appear to suggest a process orientation.

Mason, et al's, (1991) research demonstrated that education is an effective vehicle to empower nurses, and D'Onofrio (1992) says that the application of professional theory is the key to empowerment for practitioners.

In a *Nursing Management* editorial (1989) a cyclical process–product approach is offered in a discussion of change as a means to empower people. It is argued that people are empowered during the process of successful change and that once change is complete people remain empowered. Mason, et al, (1991), in a continuation of the discussion relating empowerment and change, identify a product definition. Empowerment is seen as an energizing experience, that mobilizes resources and enables change in creative ways. When one is empowered one experiences a sense of hope, excitement, and direction.

Empowerment is therefore an enabling process or a product arising from a mutual sharing of resources and opportunities which enhances decision making to achieve change.

CHOICE

Professionals in all spheres talk of empowering individuals and groups. Labonte (1989) reminds us that if the Latin root of power, *potere,* also means the ability to choose, then this is ironic as one cannot empower anyone because to presume to do so strips people of the ability to choose. Groups and individuals can only empower and motivate themselves.

Empowerment is a popular phrase in the 1990s and its essence is embodied in such political endeavors as The Patient's Charter (Department of Health 1992) and even the Tax Payer's Charter (Inland Revenue 1992). In the last two decades the issue of choice has been raised in the health care arena. particularly emphasizing freedom of choice, rights to information, acceptance of responsibility, and accountability for health by individuals.

In 1976 a British government document exhorted patients to modify their lifestyles in health-enhancing ways and to accept responsibility for their health and ill health (Department of Health and Social Security 1976). Many authors have criticized this approach to health promotion as a form of "victim blaming" and have emphatically denied its philosophy (French 1990; Downie, et al, 1990). The community health movement and women's health groups of the 1970s were seen as raising social and political issues related to health care (Grace 1991). The consumer movement in health care is also a reflection of a grassroots desire for empowerment, and the current health service reorganization is presented as a plan to respond to demands for patients to have greater choice of service (Department of Health 1989a).

Chavasse (1992) suggests that in the present economic climate, self-reliance and self-care are seen as being cheaper than a reliance on health services. Viewed from an egalitarian point of view it is also more desirable. Grace (1991), however, argues that empowerment can be viewed as a health establishment response to demands for increased control over health by members of the community.

Advocates of radical health promotion approaches see choice as a key issue (Tones 1986; Green & Raeburn 1988; Mason, et al, 1991). Zerwekh (1992) sees empowerment as a helping process which enables people to take charge of their lives, deliberately making choices and believing the future can be influenced. Tones' (1986) self-empowerment model emphasizes rationality and free choice as well as decision-making, self-concept, and life skills development. Empowerment as choice is also implicit in the *New Public Health* (Ashton & Seymour 1988) and the Health for All Strategy (World Health Organization 1981).

Choice is embedded in the empowerment process. Recent health education campaigns have emphasized the need for people to make "healthy choices." However, choice is not equally available to all people; choice is constructed and constrained by many factors; however, while health promotors emphasize the principles of voluntarism—the freedom to make any choice (Tones 1986)—it is clear that some choices are assumed to be better than others. There is also an implicit assumption that healthy choices are synonymous with rational choices and this is not always the case.

Concepts Linked to Choice

Some authors argue that linked to choice are the concepts of responsibility, authority, and accountability (Manthey 1992). Responsibility means being able to respond and responsibility needs to be allocated and accepted. Authority means the right to act in areas where the individual has and holds responsibility. Accountability is the retroactive review of decisions made to determine whether actions taken were appropriate. Manthey (1992) argues that acceptance of responsibility is what opens the door to authority and power. Related to these issues is decision making, as making choices implies that there are decisions to be made. Clearly if groups or individuals are to be empowered they must perceive responsibility and accountability for their actions. O'Neill (1992) states that the only way for a community to acquire influence is to have a position of power.

The logical consequence is to agree that if educated people choose to act in an unhealthy way then, providing it does not impinge on the freedom of others, this must be seen as an acceptable goal of health promotion (Tones 1986). It is often hard for health educationalists to accept such an outcome. Tones (1986) addresses this point in his self-empowerment model, emphasizing the decision-making process via modifying self-concept/esteem. Empowerment centers on enabling individuals to develop an awareness of the cause of their problems and a desire to take actions. French (1990) states empowerment is enabling and supporting people to set their own health agendas, implemented in ways decided by themselves.

The choice is therefore with the individual, who, given the power, authority, skills, and willingness to act, may choose to accept empowerment.

SUMMARY

Findings from the literature review correspond with the original dictionary definitions identified at the beginning of this paper. Empowerment is a helping process whereby groups or individuals are enabled to change a situation, given skills, resources, opportunities, and authority to do so. It is a partnership which respects and values self and others—aiming to develop a positive belief in self and the future. Enablement is about changing the nature and distribution of power which recognizes that power originates from self-esteem. The individual has the power and freedom to make choices and to accept responsibility for actions should he wish to do so. Empowerment involves a partnership and mutual decision making.

Defining Attributes

The defining attributes as derived from the literature are:

1. A helping process
2. A partnership which values self and others
3. Mutual decision making using resources, opportunities and authority; and
4. Freedom to make choices and accept responsibility

Based upon the defining attributes listed above, it is possible to give a theoretical definition of empowerment.

In a helping partnership it is a process of enabling people to choose to take control over and make decisions about their lives. It is also a process which values all those involved.

Development of a Model Case

Walker & Avant (1988) state that the model case should be a pure example of the concept. A model case for empowerment is described below.

A health visitor is involved in an educational program aimed at "healthy eating" with a group of unemployed single mothers. Using the medium of discussion groups to generate a mutual exchange of ideas, the aims of the group are defined. The mothers believe they possess knowledge about appropriate nutritional intakes for themselves and their children, but they express a desire to develop skills to enable them to save time and money on food.

With the aid of the health visitor the group identifies appropriate agencies who may provide help to the group, such as the community dietitian and local food stores. Using literature provided by the health visitor the group contacts other local groups involved in similar projects to discuss practical issues. The group reforms itself into a self-help (client-directed) group, identifying its own agenda and determining its goals and resources. The health visitor remains as a member of the group, who respects the contribution she is able to make as a nurse and educationalist. Conversely, the health visitor benefits from observing and experiencing the dynamics of a client-directed group.

This demonstration case contains all the defining attributes of empowerment. The health visitor is involved in a helping process with the mothers. By enabling the group to identify their own needs and set their own agenda, she encourages mutual decision making and a sense of freedom to make choices. The mothers use her experience as a health visitor and use her as a resource to gain the authority and opportunities needed to develop the group. The health visitor values the group's self-motivation and learns from its dynamics. The partnership nature is evident. The group is empowered by accepting responsibility for the running of the group.

Related Concepts

Related concepts are those concepts which convey similar or associated meaning with the concept under analysis (Rodgers 1989). The related concepts as derived from the literature review are listed below.

Autonomy
Responsibility
Accountability
Power
Choice
Advocacy
Motivation
Authority

Antecedents and Consequences

Respect is an important antecedent to the empowerment process (Tones 1986, Manthey 1992). Nurses must have an awareness of and respect for an individual's beliefs about his/her destiny, which are often rooted in issues such as locus of control (Rotter 1954, cited in Niven 1989), learned helplessness (Seligman 1975) and health beliefs (Janz & Becker 1984). Similarly, trust is an important prerequisite to empowerment (Hokanson Hawks 1992) and trust should be mutual. The empowerer must trust individuals' ability to make decisions, accept responsibility, and act for themselves (Manthey 1992).

While Mason, et al, (1991) and D'Onofrio (1992) propose education as an important vehicle for empowering individuals, Chandler (1991), in a study of 267 staff nurses, demonstrates that emotional support is the most relevant antecedent.

Finally, health care professionals cannot empower people; people can only empower themselves. However, the empowerment process can provide the resources, skills, and opportunities to develop a sense of control. Antecedents thus include motivation, participation, and mutual commitment to the process (Labonte 1989, O'Neill 1992).

The antecedents are as follows.

Mutual trust and respect
Education and support
Participation and commitment

Labonte (1989) reminds us that it is self-awareness and resources that self-empower, not the services provided; similarly the product is embedded in the process. The results of empowerment include enhanced self-esteem (Tones 1986; Mason, et al, 1991), the ability to set and reach goals (French 1990), and a sense of control over life and the change process (French 1990; Mason, et al, 1991; Zerwekh 1992). Mason, et al, (1991) state that empowerment is a confirmation of one's values, dreams, and abilities. They state that it is an energizing experience, creating a sense of hope, excitement, and direction. The consequences may thus be described as follows.

Positive self-esteem
Ability to set and reach goals
A sense of control over life and change processes
A sense of hope for the future

Empirical Referents/Operationalization of the Concept

Empirical referents provide a means of measuring the defining attributes and are the events that demonstrate the existence of the concept (Walker & Avant 1988). Given both the multidimensionality of empowerment and its process nature, it is difficult to operationalize, and thus in line with other published work an attempt will not be made to operationalize it (Gibson 1991). An appropriate means of generating further knowledge about empowerment for nursing would be to use a qualitative approach such as ethnographic or phenomenological research.

Implications for Practice

Green & Raeburn (1988) state there is little evidence that true empowerment is practiced by health care professionals. However, using the previously identified critical attributes the author will address the fundamental issues at the "macro" and "micro" levels of health care contexts. The area of health promotion in nursing will be used to discuss the issues.

Nursing appears to have enthusiastically accepted empowerment as part of its role (Hall 1987, Gott & O'Brien 1991) and it is clearly identified as intrinsic to nursing's health education function, both by the Strategy for Nursing (Department of Health 1989b) and the training recommendations (United Kingdom Central Council 1986). Similarly at practice level, changes to nursing care delivery such as the nursing process and primary nursing ensure that nurses work more closely with people to set shared, relevant, and realistic goals, which are fundamental tenets of the Health for All 2000 Strategy (World Health Organization 1981). Indeed a recent study into health education practice in acute wards indicated that the way in which nursing care is organized has a key influence on nurses' health education practice (Maben, et al, 1993).

Recent political reforms of the health service have attempted to address some of the critical attributes of empowerment, namely: patients' rights to choose, mutual decision making, and acceptance of responsibility. These aspects are discussed by the World Health Organization (1984), who describe health promotion as a unifying concept which recognizes the need for change by synthesizing personal choice and social responsibility. *Working for Patients* (Department of Health 1989a) is presented as a response to the demands of patients to have a greater choice of service.

In an ideal world it is suggested that patients should retain autonomy for decision making during treatment and accept responsibility for decisions thus made. It is recognized that patients (or clients as they are now known) will need help and information to do so. While this ideology sounds most laudable it is at the practice level that one must examine its practicality.

Perhaps the questions one needs to address are: To what extent do patients have autonomy? To what extent do they want autonomy? Are health care professionals ready to use empowerment strategies?

Salvage (1990) questions the extent to which patients actually wish to become partners in a therapeutic relationship. Ideally one may argue that the nurse puts her knowledge and skills at the disposal of the patient, whom she trusts to make responsible decisions. However, one could argue that this is not empowerment in its true sense as it does not include all the essential attributes.

If health care professionals adopt a positive approach to health they need to accept that health may not be a central concern for all people; some may choose not to heed the advice given for attaining better health (Gott & O'Brien 1991). Similarly it would appear that many health care professionals have difficulty in accepting patients' rights not to conform. If empowerment includes "freedom to choose," Delaney (1991) asks are we promoting or impairing health by seeking compliance?

PROFESSIONAL POWER

A key element in empowerment is the relinquishment of professional power. Both Barrow (1988) and Chavasse (1992) question whether nurses are ready to relinquish their control in patient encounters and to enter into shared partnerships with clients. Gott & O'Brien (1991) argue that nurses have too little autonomy and too little authority within the health care system and hence have no power to relinquish. Gibson (1991), however, says that nurses need to realize that they are powerful by virtue of both their expertise and sheer numbers, and that this power should be used for the benefit of the client.

Gott & O'Brien (1991) also suggest that nurses appear to perceive their health promotion role as communicating to patients what their risks of specific diseases are, then further communicating what patients should do to reduce these risks. Hence nurses are unwittingly colluding in a victim-blaming approach. Maglacas (1988) identifies that nurses need to develop new skills in enabling and empowering people to achieve self-care and self-help, and promoting positive health behaviors. Nurses need to cast aside the influence of a nurse training system which rewards conformity and discourages creativity, which is disempowering for nurses. While there is evidence that these skills are being addressed in the Project 2000 (UKCC 1986) curriculum and in postregistration studies, it must be accepted that these initiatives will take time.

Finally there has been tremendous emphasis on a lifestyle intervention approach, both at British government level and in nurses' health promotion roles, and there is a growing awareness that interventions cannot be solely aimed at the individual without addressing the broader social, political, and environmental context in which the individual lives (Ashton & Seymour 1988, Delaney 1991). There have been frequent calls for nurses to become more political (Delaney 1991) and it is the author's premise that this is fundamental to developing the nurse's empowering role.

CONCLUSION

The analysis of empowerment indicates that it is a significant concept as it is used broadly within nursing and in related professional practices (Rodgers 1989). The discussion has indicated a major role for empowerment in nursing. In order for empowerment to exist, nurses need a management structure and an educational process which supports and encourages the development of attributes essential for empowerment.

Professional nurses are firmly placed in a position of close contact with consumers of health care and are therefore able to make a significant impact on the lives and health of many individuals. It is essential therefore that the nursing profession develops an intrinsic philosophy of valuing and empowering its members in order that nursing can take charge of its practice and empower its clients.

REFERENCES

Ashton J. & Seymour H. (1988) *The New Public Health.* Open University Press, Milton Keynes.

Barrow R.N. (1988) Response to the keynote speech: health for all—nursings' role. *Nursing Outlook* **36**(2), 71.

Batey M. (1979). Conceptualisation: knowledge and logic guiding empirical research. *Nursing Research* **28**, 324–329.

Benner P. (1984) *From Novice to Expert: Excellence and Power in Clinical Nursing Practice.* Addison-Wesley, California.

Bookman A. & Morgen S. (1988) *Women and the Politics of Empowerment.* Temple University Press, Philadelphia.

Bredeson P. (1989) Redefining leadership and the roles of school principals: responses to changes in the professional worklife of teachers. Paper presented at the annual meeting of American Educational Research Associates, San Francisco.

Chandler G. (1991) Creating an environment to empower nurses. *Nursing Management* **22**(8), 20–23.

Chavasse J.M. (1992) New dimensions of empowerment in nursing and challenges. *Journal of Advanced Nursing* **17**(1), 1–2.

Clay T. (1992) Education and empowerment: securing nursing's future. *International Nursing Review* **39**(1), 15–18.

De La Cancela V. (1989) Minority AIDS prevention: moving beyond cultural perspectives towards sociopolitical empowerment. *AIDS Education and Prevention* **1**(2), 141–153.

Delaney F. (1991) Getting the message across. *Nursing* **4**(43), 10–25.

Department of Health (1989a) *Working for Patients.* HMSO, London.

Department of Health (1989b) *A Strategy for Nursing: A Report of the Steering Committee.* Department of Health Nursing Division, London.

Department of Health (1992) *The Patient's Charter.* HMSO, London.

Department of Health and Social Security (1976) *Prevention and Health: Everybody's Business.* HMSO, London.

D'Onofrio C.N. (1992) Theory and the empowerment of health education practitioners. *Health Education Quarterly* **19**(3), 385–403.

Downie R.S., Fyfe C. & Tannahill A. (1990) *Health Promotion: Models and Values.* Oxford University Press, Oxford.

French M. (1980) *Beyond Power: On Women, Men and Morals.* Abacus, London.

French J. (1990) Boundaries and horizons, the role of health education within health promotion. *Health Education Journal* **49**(1), 7–9.

Gibson C. (1991) A concept analysis of empowerment. *Journal of Advanced Nursing* **16**, 354–361.

Godbout J. (1981) Is consumer control possible in health care services? The Quebec Case. *International Journal of Health Services* **11**, 151–167.

Gott M. & O'Brien M. (1991) The role of the nurse in health promotion. *Health Promotion International* **5**(2), 137–143.

Grace V.M. (1991) The marketing of empowerment and the construction of the health consumer: a critique of health promotion. *International Journal of Health Services* **21**(2), 329–343.

Green L.W. & Raeburn J.M. (1988) Health promotion. What is it? What will it become? *Health Promotion* **3**(2), 151–159.

Hall D. (1987) *The Concept of Primary Health Care.* Keynote address, Primary Health Care Workshop, Winnipeg.

Hokanson Hawks J. (1992) Empowerment in nursing education: concept analysis and application to philosophy, learning and instruction. *Journal of Advanced Nursing* **17**(5), 609–618.

Inland Revenue (1992) *The Tax Payer's Charter.* HMSO, London.

Jacobs M.K. & Huether S.E. (1978) Nursing science: the Theory-Practice linkage. *Advances in Nursing Science* **1**(1), 63–73.

Janz N.K. & Becker M.H. (1984) The health belief model: a decade later. *Health Education Quarterly* **11**, 1–47.

Josefowitz N. (1980) *Paths to Power.* Addison-Wesley, Reading, Massachusetts.

Kalnins I., McQueen D.V., Backett K.C., Curtice L. & Currie C.E. (1992) Children, empowerment and health promotion: some new directions in research and practice. *Health Promotion International* **7**(1), 53–59.

Kemp V. (1985) Concept analysis as a strategy for promoting critical thinking. *Journal of Nursing Education* **24**(9), 282–284.

King I.M. (1981) *A Theory for Nursing* 2nd ed. John Wiley & Sons, New York.

King I.M. (1988) Concepts: essential elements of theories. *Nursing Science Quarterly: Theory, Research and Practice* **1**(1), 22–25.

Labonte R. (1989) Community and professional empowerment. *Infirmiere Canadienne* **85**(3), 23–28.

Maben J., Latter S., Macleod Clark J. & Wilson-Barnett J. (1993) The organisation of care: its influence on health education practice on acute wards. *Journal of Clinical Nursing* **2**(6), 355–362.

McClelland D. (1975) *Power: The Inner Experience.* Irvington, New York.

McMurray A. (1991) Advocacy for community self-empowerment. *International Nursing Review* **38**(1), 19–21.

Maglacas A.M. (1988) Health for all. Nursing's role. *Nursing Outlook* **36**(2), 66–71.

Malin N. & Teasdale K. (1991) Caring versus empowerment: considerations for nursing practice. *Journal of Advanced Nursing* **16**(3), 657–662.

Manthey M. (1992) Issues in practice: empowerment for teachers and students. *Nurse Educator* **17**(4), 6–7.

Mason D.J., Backer B.A. & Georges C.A. (1991) Towards a feminist model for the political empowerment of nurses. *Image: Journal of Nursing Scholarship* **23**(2), 72–77.

Meleis A.I. (1991) *Theoretical Nursing: Development and Progress* 2nd ed. Lippincott. Philadelphia.

Newton J. (1989) Empowerment for isolated parents. *Open Mind* **38**, 12–13.

Niven N. (1989) *Health Psychology: An Introduction for Nurses and Other Health Professionals.* Churchill Livingstone, Oxford.

Nursing Management Editorial (1989) Empowerment: change = change: empowerment. *Nursing Management* **20**(6), 17.

O'Neill M. (1992) Community participation in Quebec's health system: a strategy to curtail community empowerment? *International Journal of Health Services* **22**(2), 287–301.

Oxford English Dictionary (1989) 2nd ed vol. V, Clarendon Press. Oxford.

Parker B. & MacFarlane J. (1991) Feminist theory and nursing: an empowerment model for research. *Advances in Nursing Science* **13**(3). 59–67.

Parse R. (1981) *Man-Living-Health: A Theory of Nursing.* John Wiley & Sons, New York.

Random House Webster's College Dictionary (1991) Random House. New York.

Rissell C. (1994) Empowerment: the holy grail of health promotion? *Health Promotion International* **9**(1), 39–47.

Rodgers B.K. (1989) Concepts, analysis and the development of nursing knowledge: the evolutionary cycle. *Journal of Advanced Nursing* **14**(4), 330–335.

Rogers A. (1990) Policing mental disorder: controversies, myths and realities. *Social Policy and Administration* **24**(3), 226–236.

Roget's Thesaurus of English Words and Phrases (1982) Longman, Harlow.

Rotter J.B. (1954) *Social Learning and Clinical Psychology.* Prentice-Hall, Englewood Cliffs. New Jersey.

Salvage J. (1990) The theory and practice of the new nursing. *Nursing Times* **86**(4), 42–45.

Schön D.A. (1990) *Educating the Reflective Practitioner.* Jossey-Bass, San Francisco.

Schultz R. & Meleis A. (1988) Nursing epistemology: traditions, insights and questions. *Image: Journal of Nursing Scholarship* **20**(4), 217–221.

Seligman M.E.P. (1975) *Helplessness.* Freeman, San Fransisco.

Shorter Oxford English Dictionary (1989) Volume 1, A-M. Clarendon Press, Oxford.

Tones B.K. (1986) Health education and the ideology of health promotion: a review of alternative approaches. *Health Education Research* **1**(1), 3–12.

United Kingdom Central Council (1986) *Project 2000: A New Preparation of Practice.* UKCC, London.

Walker L.O. & Avant K.C. (1988) *Strategies for Theory Construction in Nursing.* Appleton & Lange. Norwalk.

Weis D. & Schank M.J. (1991) Professional values and empowerment a role for continuing education. *Journal of Continuing Education in Nursing* **22**(2), 50–53.

Wheeler C.E. & Chinn P.L. (1989) *Peace and Power.* 2nd edn. National League for Nursing. New York.

Wilson J. (1969) *Thinking with Concepts.* Cambridge University Press, London.

Wolfensberger W. (1972) *The Principle of Normalisation in Human Services.* National Institute of Mental Retardation. Toronto.

World Health Organization (1978) *Alma Ata Declaration.* WHO. Copenhagen.

World Health Organization (1981) *Globai Strategies for Health for All by the Year 2000 (Health for All Series No. 3).* WHO. Geneva.

World Health Organisation (1984) *Health Promotion: A Discussion Document on the Concepts and Principles.* WHO. Ottawa.

Yeo M. (1993) Toward an ethic of empowerment for health promotion. *Health Promotion International* **8**(3), 225–235.

Zerwekh J. (1983) Empowering the no longer patient. *Washington State Journal of Nursing* **54,** 12–16.

Zerwekh J.V. (1992) The practice of empowerment and coercion by expert public health nurses. *Image: Journal of Nursing Scholarship* **24**(2), 101–105.

CHAPTER 20

••

Delegation Versus Empowerment: What, How, and Is There a Difference?

CHARLES R. MCCONNELL

Janet, the unit manager of the radiology department of Community Hospital, felt she was experiencing work overload in a number of respects. The unit had recently been expanded physically and in the number of technologists and support staff, and the hospital had recently launched an all-employee educational effort as part of the implementation of total quality management (TQM).

As part of her TQM education, Janet had recently heard a great deal about employee empowerment. She rather casually wondered how empowerment differed, if at all, from delegation. Delegation she accepted as a fairly basic management process she believed herself to have been practicing for as long as she had been in management.

To help deal with her perceived overload and also to help expand staff members' capabilities, Janet decided to delegate the data-gathering for the department's monthly activity report. She selected Allen, a technologist of several years who seemed capable and who had sufficient time available. Janet instructed Allen in how to approach the task. Allen had no questions about what he was supposed to do, and he expressed no feelings one way or the other about picking up this particular task. Janet told Allen that she needed his first rough figures in two days.

Three days later Janet had not received any numbers. When asked, Allen told her he had not had the chance to do it but he would get it started right away. He seemed in no particular hurry to tackle the report. That same day Janet accidentally overheard a portion of a conversation between Allen and another technologist in which Allen said, "... her lousy statistics, and I think she ought to do it herself. After all, it's *her* job, not mine."

Janet found herself thrown into doubt about what she was supposed to be doing as a manager and especially about how she might be expected to change her approach to certain management processes under TQM. She felt she had delegated as she had always done. Sometimes it worked, but sometimes it failed and she had to try again with a different employee. She began to wonder whether she was missing something about this thing

Reprinted from *Health Care Supervisor*, 14(1), pp. 69–79, 1995 with permission of Aspen Publishers, Inc. © 1995.

called "empowerment," and all at once her lack of instant success with Allen caused her to feel inadequate as a manager.

Janet had fallen into one of the more common traps of the TQM era. She had been distracted by labels that left her confused about the nature of some basic management processes.

Getting Things Done Through People

The basic task of supervision, often cited as a simple definition of management, is *getting things done through people.* If the supervisor could accomplish all of the work of the department alone, there would be no need for other employees. However, because the supervisor is responsible for ensuring the completion of more work than can be done alone, it is necessary to place some of that work in the hands of others.

It follows also that the supervisor is ordinarily not the only person in a group who is capable of planning, thinking creatively, making decisions, and generally behaving responsibly. There is, within any given work group, a wealth of capability that will be largely wasted if it is allowed to lie undeveloped.

Because there is often more work to be done than a single person can do, work is given out—delegated—to various members of a work group. For a number of reasons having to do with efficiency and consistency, a single individual, a member of the broad class of employees known as "management," is made responsible for seeing that the work gets accomplished.

Work is delegated in different ways, the most fundamental of which we rarely think of as "delegation." In its most basic form, delegation occurs when an individual is assigned a job to do on some regular basis. If, for example, supervisor Jane says to billing clerk Susan, "Your job is to operate this terminal and follow this procedure and produce bills that will then be mailed out," Jane is giving Susan the authority to do a given amount of work for which Jane is responsible. Jane is delegating to Susan, although this may be described as *structural delegation,* because it involves communicating the basic elements of a job to an employee.

We generally think of delegation in terms of assigning an employee tasks that lie outside of that person's job description, that is, beyond the understood structure of the job. Thus we ordinarily regard delegation as involving the assignment of something "extra" to an employee. By delegating we are asking employees to do things that by and large may not be perceived as part of their regular assignments.

Most people working in management believe they understand delegation and practice it regularly. Delegation has been talked about and written about for as long as management has been considered a legitimate pursuit in its own right. Why, then, does it appear that we have traded in the concept of delegation for something called "empowerment?"

Delegation "Out," Empowerment "In"?

Technically, delegation and empowerment are the same. As may be verified in any comprehensive dictionary or thesaurus, the two words are actually synonyms for each other. Therefore, any differences between them are largely perceived differences, brought about mostly by years of misuse of "delegation" and the present overuse, misuse, and abuse of "empowerment" as one of the "in" terms of present day management and more specifically as part of the language of TQM.

Delegation is both a *process* and a *condition*. It has long been seen as the process only, the act of handing off an assignment to a subordinate. In fact, some of the more complete thesauruses even list the phrase "passing the buck" as one of the more loosely applied synonyms for delegation. What has happened all too often is that an assignment is simply passed to a subordinate who is not adequately prepared to take it on. Proper delegation requires preparation that includes not only complete instruction but also conscientious attention to issues of employee motivation. Proper delegation takes time, but more often than not managers hand off assignments to subordinates under the pressure of limited time. It is under time pressure when the manager is most likely to feel the need to delegate, but it is the wrong time to attempt to do so.

The condition of delegation, under which an employee incorporates new tasks and expands in knowledge and responsibility, is neither more nor less than what people are presently referring to as empowerment. However, because of years of misunderstanding and improper use, the word delegation has become tarnished, and for a great many people it is apparently tarnished beyond all redemption. Another, shinier term was required.

There is a phenomenon at work that one might describe as The Great Management Word Game. This is surely related to some extent to the political correctness movement in which terms that are more generally acceptable replace others that have accumulated some baggage. Thus we speak of "reengineering" or even "reinventing" the corporation, even though the descriptions of downsizing, right-sizing, or reorganizing previously reflected the essence of the same process. Similarly many now contrast the synonymous words *management* and *leadership* as though the differences they would attribute to these terms were actually real. (A seminar brochure recently proclaimed, "Be a *leader*, not just another manager.")

Similarly, it is possible to clearly identify the essence of today's total quality movement under four or five labels applied to past quality improvement efforts. A label, however, does not define the process or guarantee that it will be properly applied. If a process is not being effectively applied, calling that same process something else will do nothing to ensure its proper application. In concept, reengineering is simply reorganizing done correctly; leadership is no more than management done correctly; empowerment is no more than delegation done correctly. Delegation became tarnished because of chronic misuse and abuse. If not conscientiously applied, the term empowerment will become similarly tarnished.

The essence of a process lies not in what it is called but rather in how it is applied.

Delegation Failure: A Common Occurrence

That one person can do only so much and still do things well is true for anyone after a point. Even the tasks and problems that flow naturally to the supervisor can add up to a workload that is often too great for one person. People differ greatly from each other in their capacity to take on additional responsibilities. Some can absorb an astonishing number of tasks, but even these people have their limits. And when individuals' limits are exceeded, the stage is set for delegation failure if the process is not approached reasonably and rationally.

CONSEQUENCES OF DELEGATION FAILURE

Delegation failure is a management shortcoming that leads to undesirable consequences in a number of dimensions.

The nondelegating or improperly delegating supervisor is hurt by delegation failure. This person will often suffer the results of work overload while demonstrating to higher management that he or she cannot effectively delegate and thus cannot control the job. Of course some supervisors are very good at absorbing more and more and seeming to keep up, but eventually the work days get longer and some tasks get attended to only superficially or perhaps not at all.

The supervisor who covers many bases at high speed and puts in extra hours as a matter of routine may briefly appear to be an energetic, highly productive individual. Although occasional bursts of such activity are in order and sometimes downright necessary, in the long run the supervisor who adopts the workaholic pattern will impress nobody. Also, the workaholic supervisor is compounding the risk of stress-related health problems.

If limited to effects on the supervisor, delegation failure might be easier to accept in that its perpetrator would also be its sole victim. However, most of the consequences of delegation failure accrue to the employees of the nondelegating supervisor. The supervisor who fails to delegate properly has denied the employees the opportunity to learn and grow. Minus this opportunity the employees experience little or no challenge, and they are denied more interesting work experiences and greater task variety.

Employees who do not have the chance to be challenged and to learn and grow often become bored and generally demotivated. In this kind of environment certain employees, primarily those who seek challenge and aspire to higher positions, will decide to seek their futures elsewhere. Eventually the department is left with mostly those who are not driven to seek advancement or interesting experiences but are rather held by the nominal bonds of job security. It is demonstrated time and again that the employees who are the first to leave the stifling environment created by the nondelegating supervisor are those employees who the organization should be most interested in retaining.

Delegation failure can also negatively affect a department's image. Once acquired, a reputation for lack of timeliness, for lack of creativity, or for unreliability can be extremely difficult to shed and can outlast the reign of the nondelegating supervisor and make life difficult for the next supervisor.

WHY DELEGATION FAILURE?

There are a number of reasons for delegation failure. The most common among these is a lack of time to delegate properly. Too often the supervisor takes a short, narrow view of delegation and sees it primarily as a means of getting some relief from part of the workload. The perceived need to delegate is then experienced most acutely when the supervisor's time is in shortest supply. Some give in and attempt to delegate to obtain some immediate relief.

Proper delegation, however, is a time-consuming process. Done correctly, it requires *more* time and attention on the supervisor's part in the short run. Delegation's potential time-saving payoff lies weeks or months in the future. The time one puts into proper delegation today is at best an investment in potential future gains. In brief, supervisors often feel the most pressure to delegate at precisely the time when they are least prepared to delegate properly.

Delegation will also fail if it is driven primarily by the supervisor's selfishness. There has to be a sense of ownership developed in an employee who is expected to take on a new task. If the employee cannot come up with a reasonable answer to the reasonable question, "What's in it for me?," the truth of the matter will quickly make itself felt: I'm doing this job only because the boss didn't want to do it. Employee resistance or resentment kills the process when it is perceived that the supervisor is simply "passing the buck" or handing off the undesirable work.

A number of other causes of delegation failure may be found in the personality and character of some supervisors. A supervisor who is insecure may fear competition from subordinates or may be unwilling to share the credit that goes along with a job well done. In most organizational settings such supervisors' fears and uncertainties are unfounded.

Indeed, in many instances exactly the opposite of what the supervisor fears can be true. That is, the subordinate who does an outstanding job with a delegated task can make the entire department—including the supervisor—look good.

Old habits are frequently encountered reasons for failing to delegate properly and fully. Most supervisors' earliest working years were devoted completely to the *doing* of work. Some never get completely beyond that old mindset even though as supervisors they have spent years supposedly *directing* the doing of work by others.

Another common reason for the failure to delegate is the feeling that available employees simply cannot handle increased responsibility. A classic situation presents itself: You hesitate to trust someone with more responsibility because you do not know whether he or she can handle it, yet the only way you will ever find out is to try. This uncertainty, and the attendant risk of failure, causes many supervisors to hold back when they should be reaching out.

What Is Actually Delegated

We have heard and read time and again about the delegation of responsibility. However, in the strictest sense, every reference to delegated responsibility is incorrect. Delegating actually means giving away something—specifically, task performance authority—to someone else. If, for example, you delegate your department's monthly activity report to a trusted employee, you have given away that task in that you no longer perform it. But the responsibility for that task remains yours. Should your trusted employee let you down and either bungle the report or not do it at all, you remain responsible for those results.

You can and should, of course, make an employee to whom you have delegated responsible in turn to you. Then if the task is bungled or ignored, the employee must answer to you, although you still must answer for the situation to *your* manager. Therefore, when a task is delegated, it is authority that is delegated. Task performance authority rests with only a single level, but task responsibility is replicated at each level involved in the delegation.

The key to delegation, and thus to empowerment, is equivalent authority and responsibility. That is, the person who is made responsible for performing the task must be given sufficient authority to complete the task. When one is fully responsible for a task without having full authority, we find that the job gets done only when one begs or borrows resources or assistance outside of normal channels. Indeed it is fairly common practice for an individual who is made responsible for completing a given task to discover that it cannot be done without the assistance of someone who reports to a different manager but that no arrangement has been made for assistance.

Although responsibility without full authority can present difficulties, it is usually possible to get the job done with imagination and creativity if the disparity between responsibility and authority is not too great. In fact, a small to modest amount of this imbalance can challenge and stimulate some employees. However, if the disparity is large, the job becomes more and more difficult and eventually impossible.

Task Authority: What Can Actually Be Delegated

The supervisor's job is made up of managerial or supervisory tasks and technical tasks. The latter can be delegated; the former cannot.

The supervisor cannot delegate, for example, decisions to hire, fire, promote, demote, or to grant pay increases, and cannot delegate disciplinary actions or performance evaluations. In brief, the supervisor cannot legitimately delegate functions that can be described as personnel actions. It is possible to obtain staff involvement in at least two of the afore-mentioned personnel activities, however. Consider the supervisor who assigns a trusted, long-term subordinate to do screening interviews of job candidates. The interviewer may talk with six or seven applicants, for example, and pass along to the supervisor the apparently strongest two or three possibilities. Concerning performance evaluations, the supervisor may wish to obtain the input of other staff as part of a peer-review process. But whether interviewing or evaluating, it should remain clear that the actual decision on a potential hire or possible evaluation score is the supervisor's alone.

It is also possible at times to delegate limited portions of departmental planning, budgeting, and development of departmental policies and procedures. Doing so reflects commonsense management; the people who will live with these plans, budgets, policies, and procedures should be able to participate as much as practical in their development.

One can generally delegate everything that falls outside of personnel actions and the other few exceptions cited above. That is, all of the supervisor's nonsupervisory work can potentially be delegated.

Bringing Person and Task Together

Giving a job that needs doing to the next employee who passes by is an invitation to failure. Some effort must be expended in examining the nature of the task relative to the qualifications and experience of the available people. Delegation is a highly imperfect process. Whenever one brings together a task with a person who has not previously performed it, there is a risk of failure. If we absolutely knew every delegation would work perfectly, there would be little chance of growth and challenge would be absent. Each task must be realistically assessed for what it involves, and person and task must be carefully matched.

Some common sense rules should apply in selecting someone to take on any particular task. Specifically:

- Delegate a task only to someone who you feel can be trusted to give it a fair shake in terms of attitude and effort. There is little point, for example, in giving additional work to a person who has so far only impressed you as a dodger of "extra" effort.
- Delegate only to someone you believe is ready to assume some authority and perhaps grow a little. Avoid delegating, for example, to an employee so new to your department that he or she has not yet demonstrated a complete grasp of the position's basic duties.
- Delegate only to people who report directly to you. If, for example, you have two assistant supervisors and a secretary reporting to you but your entire department includes 25 people, there are three people to whom you can delegate work, not 25. Any delegating to the rank-and-file staff should come from the assistant supervisors. Never bypass your subordinate supervisors by delegating directly to their employees. Doing so only undermines your own chain of command and reinforces with the rank-and-file that they can bypass their supervisors and deal directly with you.

Preparing the Person

For each delegated task, the chosen employee needs certain information. Using the radiology department's monthly activity report of the opening example, Janet's possible directions to Allen are provided along with the general descriptions of eight bits of information the employee should be given.

1. *The complete definition of the task.*

   "If you agree and we can get together on a reasonable process, you're going to be providing most of the statistical information for our monthly activity report."

2. *The results expected.*

   "I'd like you to assemble all of the statistical information that goes into the report, once per month."

3. *When the task starts.*

   "We'll begin with the September report, which gives you nearly four full weeks to prepare."

4. *The duration of the task.*

   "Consider the duration indefinite, since this is a monthly report and as far as I know it will be required of us monthly for the foreseeable future."

5. *How much time the task should take.*

   "Once you're completely familiar with how this is done, it should require about two hours each month."

6. *The procedure for performing the task.*

   "We've never had a written procedure for this, so the first couple of times we can go through it together and we'll document the primary steps as we go."

7. *The motivational aspects of the task; "what's in it" for the employee.*

   "This should give you a little variety, a bit of a break from some of the other things you do all the time. Also, this could help you prepare for the possibility of one of the senior tech positions someday. After all, the senior techs get more into administrative matters."

8. *The authority assigned.*

   "You'll eventually be doing the whole report yourself, so you're free to adjust your schedule on your customary data collection day, and you can sign as preparer of the report and I'll sign off as department manager."

Examining Your Delegation Performance

Maintaining too much control over an employee can destroy the effects of delegation. Why delegate if you will then monitor the employee's every move? Conversely, too little control can be damaging in that a task can go far off track. Employees differ greatly from each other. All tasks are not the same in magnitude or difficulty. The combinations of employees and tasks seem practically limitless, so the supervisor cannot regard every pairing of person and delegated task in the same way. It is necessary to know the employees well enough to have a sense of how closely any individual's activities will have to be supervised.

There is also the danger of destroying the benefits of delegation by pulling a task away from an employee at the first signs of shaky performance. We should consider an apparently shaky performance as an early indication of the possible need for additional instruction and supervisory support. Actually pulling back an assignment should be the last resort, following all reasonable efforts to get performance back on track.

We must also be aware of the need to delegate whole, definable tasks, not just pieces. Employees to whom we delegate need to have a sense of accomplishing something, hopefully completing something, and individual motivation will usually be much stronger if they can see how tasks fit together and they can point to the specific results of their efforts.

Be aware of the need to delegate "good stuff," not simply the boring or dirty jobs that you clearly do not want to do. Proper motivation depends a great deal on whether an employee is interested and challenged or is convinced that this latest delegated task is simply the "scut work" the boss did not want to do. The supervisor must be aware that some employees perceive an extremely fine line dividing delegation from dumping.

The successfully delegating supervisor will go to some lengths to openly acknowledge the employees' contributions. As some supervisors will shy away from delegating because they fear losing credit to subordinates, so will certain others who may delegate take credit for what is actually done by the employees. Truly effective supervisors realize, however, that subordinates' successful performance also represents supervisory success.

Probably the most important dimensions of a supervisor's delegation performance reside in the extent to which the supervisor has provided the employee with the freedom to fail. One of the surest ways to destroy delegation is to punish a subordinate for making a mistake. However, people do not learn and grow without making mistakes. Every mistake has to be treated as part of the growth experience; no mistake should be allowed to inhibit further attempts to learn and grow. Each employee should be prepared with all reasonable guidance and assistance before tackling a delegated task, but if something goes wrong, what follows should be constructive correction and support, not negative repercussions.

Empowerment

There is probably no concept associated with the TQM that is as widely misunderstood as empowerment. Empowerment is one of the truly "in" words of the decade of the '90s, whether we are speaking of employees relative to their work, parents relative to their children's education, residents relative to their community, or others who could benefit from active input in determining their own destiny.

Much of the misunderstanding of empowerment probably arises from two conditions. First, empowerment is presented as though it is something new and different. The ongoing "word game" that continually gives us new names for older, tarnished concepts does not tell us that it is simply delegation done correctly, so we are expecting something not previously encountered. Second, the root word of empowerment—power—immediately raises the expectations of those who believe empowerment to be something brand new. Some interpret this as power coming into their hands, the automatic authority to address issues they could not previously address and to make decisions in their own way.

Although empowerment and proper delegation are the same process, we cannot deny their semantic differences. Even when one ignores the decades of tarnish on delegation, the word "delegation" cannot stand up to "empowerment" in connotation. On all counts empowerment is the "better" word, carrying the far more favorable connotation. It is in all instances the preferred word, but because of the difficulties noted above, it is frequently misunderstood.

At a fairly basic level, empowerment has initially been taken by some as the authority to "do their own thing." In TQM education the essential customer focus of all business— service to internal as well as external customers—frequently takes some time to establish. The empowerment concept, however, is readily taken up in its misunderstood form, and some employees slide right past the issue of customer focus and fix on what they can personally obtain from TQM. Thus we have the example of the hastily assembled employee team that went to work on determining how to implement 12-hour shifts in their unit, not because it was thought that a new scheduling pattern might enhance patient care but rather because most of the unit's staff wanted for themselves a schedule of three 12-hour shifts per week. Similarly, there was the individual who expressed the belief that he was now free to alter his starting and quitting times to better accommodate attendance at his second job.

The empowered employee must in fact have in common with the empowered manager a strong customer focus, and it should be a given that customers, in their own particular priority order, are the primary concern. If the empowered employee is given a certain amount of decision-making authority, this must consist of the authority to deliver certain expected results. The empowered employee is self-directed, but only within the limits of the general direction and expected results provided by the manager.

Thus we are able to return to the contention that empowerment and proper delegation are one and the same. The manager provides instruction, assistance, support, resources, expected results, and overall direction that may well have been developed with the employee's participation, and the employee operates freely within those boundaries to deliver what the customers need.

Not everyone wants to be empowered. Some people simply do not want their jobs to get any larger, and we get nowhere with talk of increased job interest and increased opportunity to learn and grow. As supervisors have discovered frequently over the years, not every employee is a reasonable candidate for delegation. Some employees want no more responsibility than they presently have. Some wish only to put in their workdays and collect their pay, and some will be sufficiently resistant to change that they see attempts to expand or enrich their jobs as threatening.

The resistant employee is a supervisor's special challenge. It can be extremely satisfying to turn around the attitude of someone who has been chronically resistant to change and perhaps distrusting of management. This is not readily accomplished. All employees are equally deserving of the supervisor's attention and respect, but not all will respond to the supervisor in the desired manner.

It is expected in every TQM implementation that a proportion of employees will never completely "buy in." There will be some who will not respond but will rather continue to do their jobs as always. What is the supervisor to do with such employees?

The answer, not always welcome, is to accept those particular employees for what and where they are. When an employee resists delegation, the supervisor's initial reaction should be to reassess the supervisor's own approach to ensure that the delegation is honest and thorough, that it represents empowerment in the finest sense of the word. If the delegation approach withstands rigorous scrutiny and the employee continues to resist, the supervisor should move on to another employee.

Eventually the employee who resists will be left to simply perform in the same manner. As long as the resistant employee is performing at or above the minimum standard of the job and will not respond to the encouragement to do more and better, there is little the supervisor can do except focus on other employees. The resistant employee will be passed over for delegated assignments. By thus forfeiting the opportunity to learn and grow, this employee will essentially be self-limited as far as promotional opportunity is concerned.

A Sense of Ownership

A large proportion of delegation's failures are due to motivational problems. The process is too often treated as simply handing off work to a subordinate for the sole purpose of getting it done. Little is done to instill a sense of task ownership in the person to whom the work is delegated.

Task ownership arises when a willing employee who is asked to take on something new is properly instructed, encouraged, and included in determining exactly what needs to be done and planning how it should be done. Call it delegation or call it empowerment, without a sense of ownership the employee's reaction is still likely to be, "After all, it's *her* job, not mine."

CHAPTER 21

●●●

Staff Nurse Work Empowerment and Perceived Control Over Nursing Practice

Conditions for Work Effectiveness

HEATHER K. SPENCE LASCHINGER AND DONNA SULLIVAN HAVENS

The frustrations experienced by professionals working in bureaucratic settings have been well documented in both the sociological and professional nursing literature.[1–5] The rigidity of hierarchical rule-bound structures, particularly in hospital settings, has been blamed for nurses' inability to sufficiently control the content of their practice. This lack of control over practice or the authority to act on one's knowledge and expert judgment frequently is offered as an explanation for reported work dissatisfaction among nurses. Indeed, lack of autonomy often is identified as a prominent reason for nurses leaving the profession.[6]

In the past decade, numerous strategies have been proposed to improve nurses' control over both the content and context of their practice, such as work redesign initiatives, professional practice models, and shared governance structures. The goals of these approaches are consistent with the ideas of Rosabeth Moss Kanter,[7,8] who maintains that people are empowered to reach organizational goals if their work environments are structured in ways that provide access to information, support and resources necessary for getting the job done, as well as access to opportunities to learn and grow. It is logical to expect that nursing work environments structured in this way would be highly supportive of control over nursing practice. Although Kanter's original research was in the business setting, relationships described in her theory have been supported in nursing studies.[9–22] The purpose of this study was to use Kanter's theory to examine the relationship between staff nurses' perceptions of work empowerment and the degree of control over their nursing practice. In addition, relationships among perceived work empowerment, control over practice, work satisfaction, and effectiveness were examined.

Kanter's Theory of Structural Power

In her theory, Kanter[7,8] argues that work behaviors and attitudes are shaped in response to an individual's position and the situations that arise in an organization, as opposed to individual/personality predispositions and socialization experiences. For Kanter, power is a structural determinant that affects organizational behaviors and attitudes (Fig. 21-1).

Power is obtained from the ability to access and mobilize support, information, resources, and opportunities from one's position in the organization. Access to these empowerment structures is influenced by the degree of formal and informal power an individual has in the organization. Formal power evolves from having a job that affords flexibility and visibility and is relevant to key organizational processes. Informal power is determined by the extent of an individual's networks and alliances with sponsors, peers, and subordinates, both within and outside of the organization. Those with sufficient power are able to accomplish the tasks required to achieve organizational goals and have the ability to empower those around them, creating effective work units within the organization. Conversely, individuals in positions that limit access to power and opportunity structures perceive themselves to be powerless. These individuals believe that they lack control over their fate and are dependent on those around them. According to Kanter,[7]

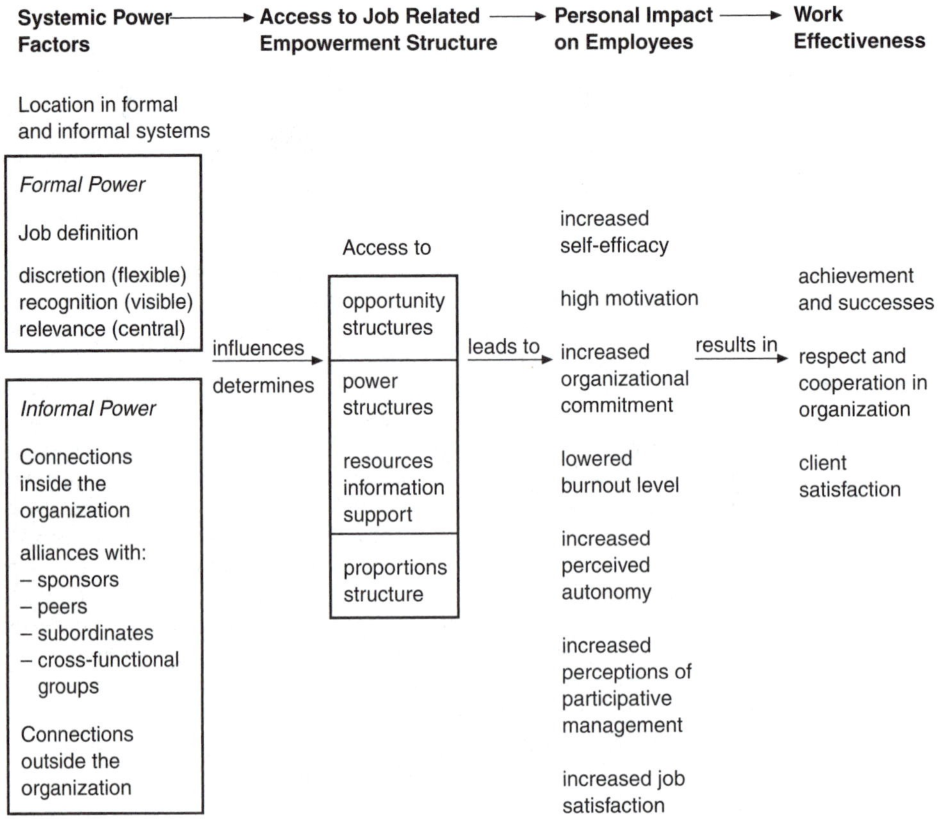

Figure 21–1 Relationships of concepts in Rosabeth Kanter's structural theory of Power in Organization.

they are more rigid and rules-minded and are less committed to the achievement of organizational goals.

Related Research on Kanter's Theory

In 1986, Chandler was the first nurse researcher to test Kanter's theory and found that 268 staff nurses perceived power in their jobs to be low, which she interpreted to be a reflection of the nonempowering nature of their work environments. Chandler also did extensive psychometric analyses of the instrument used to measure work empowerment, the Conditions for Work Effectiveness Questionnaire.[12,13] As part of an ongoing program of research in the Faculty of Nursing at the University of Western Ontario, 16 independent studies have generated considerable empirical support for the theory. In all of these studies, staff nurse empowerment scores have been moderate, suggesting the need for more access to opportunity, information, resources, and support in nursing work environments. Staff nurses' perceptions of work empowerment have been found to be significantly related to commitment to the organization,[9,14,15] burnout,[16] job autonomy,[11] participation in organizational decision making,[17] job satisfaction.[18,19] leadership style,[20] and level in the hierarchy.[21,22] Recently, the impact of formal and informal power on perceptions of work empowerment has been studied. Formal and informal power have been found to be significant predictors of access to work empowerment structures in seven recent studies.[11,14,17–20]

In all studies within this program, staff nurses who perceived their immediate managers to be influential and powerful in the organization also perceived themselves to be empowered in their work setting. These findings support Kanter's notion that "power begets power" because powerful managers are more likely to share their power with coworkers and thereby increase the productivity of their organizational units. In studies of nurse managers, perceptions of job empowerment have been found to increase significantly with level in the organizational hierarchy[21] and to be strongly related to self-efficacy for performing managerial roles.[19]

Control Over Nursing Practice and Nurse Work Satisfaction

Recent efforts to restructure nursing work environments to increase nurses' control over the content and context of their work evolved from an acute nursing shortage in the United States that threatened patient care quality. Research and anecdotal reports on why nurses were leaving nursing were consistently identifying nurses' dissatisfaction with working conditions that limited their autonomy or authority to act on their knowledge and clinical judgment within their domain of practice. Several researchers established significant relationships between work autonomy and nurse job satisfaction. Colgrove[23] found that perceived work autonomy had a direct effect on work satisfaction, which in turn had a direct effect on how patients experienced their care from the nursing staff.

A variety of professional practice models have been designed and implemented to address these concerns. The common goal of these models is to create structures that involve nurses more extensively in participation in decision making with regard to matters that affect both direct patient care and indirect contextual matters that have an impact on their practice. Shared governance systems as proposed by Porter-O'Grady[24] and collaborative professional practice models advocated by Aydelotte[4] and Milton, et al,[25] are examples of models that have been implemented to achieve greater control over nursing practice in the past decade. Recent reports of the outcomes of these efforts are positive. Kreitzer found that congruence between preferred and actual decisional involvement was significantly related to both work satisfaction and organizational commitment.[26] Mancini found higher job satisfaction in nurses working in a hospital with a shared governance system in place than in another without a shared governance system, particularly in regard to autonomy, task requirements, and organizational policies.[27]

Thus, evidence exists in the literature to support the link between work conditions and the ability of nurses to exercise control over their practice. However, the links between structural power factors, perceived control over practice, work satisfaction, and effectiveness have not been explored from Kanter's theoretical perspective.

The vice presidents of nursing in each participating hospital provided a list of 200 randomly selected names of staff nurses and their work addresses. The questionnaires and a letter of explanation were distributed through the hospital mail system in each hospital and returned by regular mail in a researcher-addressed stamped envelope. A follow-up letter and a flyer to be posted on all work units were sent 3 weeks later. As is often the case with mail surveys, the return rate was low (33%), with 127 nurses returning usable questionnaires.

The Conditions of Work Effectiveness Questionnaire was used to measure perceptions of access to sources of work empowerment described by Kanter: 1) information, 2) support, 3) resources, and 4) opportunity. The four subscales are summed to yield an overall measure of perceived work empowerment (range, 4–20). Formal and informal power were measured by the Job Activities Scale and the Organizational Relationships Scale, respectively. Gerber's Control over Nursing Practice Questionnaire[28] was used to measure nursing work autonomy or control over issues within the nurse's scope of practice. Gerber maintains that the tool is particularly relevant for measuring current conceptions of professional nursing practice and has used the Control over Nursing Practice Questionnaire in a variety of studies to measure outcomes of an implemented professional practice model.[29] Global measures of job satisfaction and work effectiveness contained in Bass's Multifactor Leadership Questionnaire were used to measure these variables.[30] Alpha reliability coefficients for scales used in this study were acceptable, ranging from 0.76 to 0.95 (Box 21-1).

Findings

Eighty-nine percent of nurse respondents were female; age ranged from 23 to 63 years (mean [M] = 42.1 years; standard deviation [SD] = 8.9 years). Forty-two percent were baccalaureate prepared, 24.8% were diploma prepared, 20.8% were associate degree prepared, and 12.6% were master's prepared. The mean years of nursing experience were

---

BOX 21-1 METHODS

Design: Descriptive correlational mail survey with 3-week follow-up
Sample: 127 randomly selected nurses from 2 urban Southeastern U.S. teaching hospitals
Measures: Conditions of Work Effectiveness[7]
          Job Activities Scale
          Organizational Relationships Scale
          Control over Nursing Practice[28]
          Job Satisfaction Scale[30]
          Work Effectiveness Scale[30]

16.31 (SD = 9.9 years), with an average of 5.76 (SD = 5.64 years) in their current position. Fifty-nine percent of the respondents worked in general medical/surgical units, 34.5% worked in critical care, and 6.7% worked in staff education roles. Demographic characteristics did not differ significantly between the two groups.

The nurses' mean scores on the total the Conditions of Work Effectiveness Questionnaire and subscales (opportunity, support, information, and resources), the Control over Nursing Practice Questionnaire, and global measures of work satisfaction and work effectiveness are presented in Table 21-1. The work empowerment scores are within the range of found in previous studies in Canadian settings, suggesting that American nurses perceive their work environments in a similar way. Nurses in both settings perceived themselves to be moderately empowered with only the opportunity subscale averaging over the midpoint of the 5-point scale (M = 3.03). Consistent with the Canadian studies, access to resources was the lowest Conditions of Work Effectiveness Questionnaire subscale (M = 2.38). Perceived formal and informal power were also moderate (M = 2.92 and 2.97, respectively). Similarly, nurses thought they had a moderate degree of control over their practice (M = 4.46). Nurses in this sample were only somewhat satisfied with their jobs (M = 3.70), although they rated their own and their organization's effectiveness higher (M = 4.6 on a 7-point scale). The two groups did not differ significantly on the key study variables, and the data were thus aggregated to test the hypotheses proposed for study.

Correlations among study variables are presented in Table 21-2. Perceived work empowerment was strongly related positively to perceptions of control over nursing practice ($r = 0.625$, $P = 0.000$), supporting Kanter's contention that access to empowering work structures such as opportunity, information, resources, and support enable workers to exercise control over their work and better accomplish organizational goals. Correlations between the Conditions of Work Effectiveness Questionnaire subscales and the Control over Nursing Practice Questionnaire all were significant and of similar magnitude (range, $r = 0.51$–0.58). Interestingly, the highest correlation with control over practice was with infor-

TABLE 21–1 **Mean Scores for the Conditions of Work Effectiveness Questionnaire (CWEQ) Subscales, Empowerment, Control over Practice, Work Satisfaction, and Work Effectiveness**

Subscales	Hospital 1 (n = 60)		Hospital 2 (n = 67)		Total Sample (n = 127)	
	M	SD	M	SD	M	SD
CWEQ						
Empowerment[†]	11.00	2.58	10.81	2.68	10.90	2.62
Opportunity*	3.10	0.79	2.97	0.67	3.03	0.73
Support*	2.74	0.77	2.71	0.77	2.72	0.77
Information*	2.78	0.78	2.76	0.77	2.77	0.77
Resources*	2.39	0.66	2.37	0.75	2.38	0.70
Formal power	2.90	0.54	2.94	0.54	2.92	0.54
Informal power	2.93	0.69	3.00	0.61	2.97	0.65
CONP	4.46	1.13	4.45	1.31	4.46	1.12
Satisfaction[‡]	3.69	1.61	3.71	1.52	3.70	1.56
Effectiveness[‡]	4.75	2.58	4.48	1.31	4.60	1.26

M = mean; SD = standard deviation; CONP = Control over Nursing Practice Questionnaire.
*Score range 1–5
[†]Score range 4–20
[‡]Score range 1–7.

TABLE 21–2 **Correlations Between Empowerment, Control over Practice, Satisfaction, and Work Effectiveness***

Subscales	Control over Nursing Practice	Work Satisfaction	Work Effectiveness
Empowerment	0.63	0.66	0.57
Opportunity	0.57	0.62	0.58
Information	0.55	0.50	0.44
Support	0.58	0.63	0.51
Resources	0.51	0.57	0.47
Formal power	0.46	0.52	0.40
Informal power	0.66	0.58	0.45

*All correlations significant at $P = 0.001$ one-tailed probability.

mal power ($r = 0.65$, $P = 0.000$), which may suggest that nurses who have developed strong alliances in the organization increase their credibility and are thus afforded more autonomy. In a regression analysis, the three power variables (formal and informal power and overall empowerment) were found to explain 48.5% of the variance in control over practice ($R^2 = 0.485$, $F(3,122) = 38.3$, $P = 0.000$). However, formal power did not add significantly to the prediction after taking into account overall access to empowerment structures and informal power. These findings are similar to previous results in which formal position power was not found to add to the prediction of other dependent variables such as job autonomy[11] or perceptions of shared decision making.[16]

There were strong positive correlations between access to empowerment structures and overall work satisfaction ($r = 0.656$, $P = 0.000$) and perceived work effectiveness ($r = 0.566$, $P = 0.000$). These findings corroborate those of Whyte,[20] who found a strong positive relationship between perceived work empowerment and another measure of job satisfaction.[31] Separate regression analyses revealed that perceived empowerment and control over practice in combination were significant predictors of both work satisfaction and perceived work effectiveness ($R^2 = 0.515$ and $R^2 = 0.58$, respectively; $P = 0.000$). The standardized regression coefficients suggested that although access to work empowerment structures and control over practice were equally important for work satisfaction, control over practice was considerably more important to the prediction of perceived work effectiveness ($\beta = 0.156$ and 0.645, respectively). The latter finding highlights the importance of decisional control in the practice domain for effective nursing outcomes.

The pattern of relationships between study variables and demographics also are worthy of attention. Male respondents scored higher on all study variables—although significantly higher only on informal power and perceived access to information. Critical care nurses scored significantly higher than nurses on general medical/surgical areas on both the total empowerment scale and all subscales, as well as on work satisfaction. Although critical care nurses scored higher on perceived control over their nursing practice and effectiveness than those on medical/surgical areas, the differences were not significant.

Limitations

The hospitals involved in this study were selected based on their willingness to participate and therefore may not necessarily be representative of other acute care settings. The experience of participants in these hospitals may differ from those in nonacute care, nonteaching, or rural settings. Both institutions were experiencing restructuring changes, and consideration must be given to the effects such changes may have had on perceived access to support, information, resources, and opportunity under these circumstances. A follow-up study at another time would provide an opportunity to examine the effects of changing environments. However, the support for predicted relationships strengthens the results and somewhat offsets these limitations.[32]

Discussion and Implications for Nurse Administrators

The findings of this study further support the validity of Kanter's theory in nursing settings. In this study, perceptions of access to opportunity, support, information, and resources showed a similar pattern to previous studies, with nurses reporting the least access to resources, followed by support and information. These nurses believed that they had greatest access to opportunity structures. As in previous studies, nurses perceived themselves to be only moderately empowered in Kanter's sense of the word. Considering the strong correlations observed between perceived access to these work empowerment structures and perceptions of job satisfaction and work effectiveness, redesign of nursing work environments to increase access to opportunity, information, support, and resources seems warranted. The findings also provide empirical support for claims in the theoretical literature about the benefits of professional nursing practice models. The strong correlations between work empowerment and perceived control over nursing practice suggest that contrary to the beliefs of some authors,[33] work autonomy is an important factor in nursing work.

Nursing administrators can use the results of this research by examining workplaces for structural factors that act as barriers to staff nurses access to power sources described by Kanter. Although the work of staff nurses is fundamental to the provision of patient care, neither the position of staff nurse nor staff nurses themselves have received the visibility or recognition commensurate with the centrality of their role in achieving organizational goals. McDermott[17] suggests that recognition programs to reward and celebrate achievements of nurses at all levels should be instituted through such mechanisms as organizational newsletters, local newspapers, and award ceremonies for both individual and group achievements. Involving staff nurses in the development of these systems is necessary to ensure that the methods of recognition are meaningful and rewarding for the recipients. Regular, specific, and timely positive feedback also is a simple and effective way of recognizing contributions. McDermott also suggests that one way of highlighting the significance of nursing contributions in the organization would be to have staff present "stories" or exemplars of care at hospital board meetings to illustrate the clinical expertise, the nursing judgment, and the skills of involvement demonstrated by nurses in providing care for patients. Nurse administrators also might facilitate the dissemination of these stories to the public through arrangements with public relations departments.

Job redesign to increase access to work empowerment structures would create environments that support true professional practice because nurses who feel empowered are more likely to provide more effective and efficient care. Fralic[34] asserts that the essence of professional nursing practice must be preserved when introducing new care delivery models, and Clifford[35] warns us that professional practice is impossible without support systems that remove barriers between nurses and patients. Commenting on new models of care delivery, Clifford maintains that although professional nurses must oversee tasks of nonprofessional workers, they always must be in a position to use their knowledge and expertise on behalf of the patients, arguing that clinical decision making and expert judgment "cannot be delegated nor substituted by lesser prepared personnel."[35] Care systems and structures that maximize the use of the clinical expertise of nurses are critical to achieving this aim.

Practicing nurses must have input into the design of their work environments if such structures are expected to empower nurses in their practice. To influence control over the context of nursing work environments, Kanter recommends spreading formal authority through such mechanisms as participative management, shared governance, decentralization and the development of autonomous work units. Evan, et al,[36] describe a whole-system shared governance model that emphasizes point-of-care decision making and the importance of alliances in new models of care, evoking Kanter's notions of giving staff the "support, information and opportunity to make the majority of decisions in the service arena." Staff nurses' access to information about organizational activities can be increased through such mechanisms as "information hot-lines" established on voice mail or electronic mail systems. Having information about plans and events that affects one's job is crucial, particularly in times of uncertainty, and guards against the spread of unfounded rumors and concerns. Sharing information openly and honestly builds trust in the organization.

Kanter warns that the mindless downsizing undertaken by many organizations in an attempt to cuts costs and improve effectiveness may result in remaining feelings of frustration and a sense of blocked development among staff members. She recommends nontraditional options for career growth and development, such as the creation of cross-functional programs, problem-solving teams, and participation on special task forces and committees that allows people to form new relationships, learn new skills, and gain recognition by having the opportunity to demonstrate their abilities. Job exchange programs with other areas in the organization would help form cross-functional alliances in the informal system that Kanter maintains are important sources of empowerment. An environment in which opportunity for staff learning, growth, and development is expected, rewarded, and valued will greatly augment staff nurses' sense of access to opportunities to learn and grow. Trofino[37] recommends making educational programs available to all nurses, regardless of content, and the creation of organizational policies that support educational leaves or other educational incentives, as examples of initiatives that empower nurses by challenging their thinking. Creation of career ladders within positions affords nurses another means of gaining recognition for increasing levels of expertise.

Visibility of nurse managers at all levels in the clinical setting is an important indicator of support and gives clinical nurses' the opportunity to demonstrate their clinical expertise and be recognized for their skills. Clifford[38] maintains that by talking to nurses, asking questions, and listening to staff nurses' perspectives of the work setting, nurse executives can gain valuable insight into the current reality of nursing practice environments. Finally, it is crucial that all levels of nursing management must be committed genuinely to a shared vision fostering empowered behavior in staff because, as Senge warns, ". . . empowering people in an unaligned organization can be counterproductive."[39] The impact of these and other strategies that increase perceptions of job-related empowerment is likely to be a more efficacious work group and improved client care. Further discussion of empowerment strategies can be found elsewhere.[10,40]

Kanter's model of organizational empowerment is potentially useful for nurse administrators concerned with the recruitment and retention of autonomous professional nurses. When relationships proposed by the theory are supported by the data, program planning to create organizational structures outlined by Kanter will be strengthened by a solid research base. The current program of research provides more insight into the nature of power in nursing organizations and assists in the understanding of the acquisition and use of power by nurses to better influence the healthcare system and control of nursing work.

Recommendations for Further Research

Based on the limitations of this study, further research is needed to explore factors that influence work empowerment and its relationship to work effectiveness. Further exploration seems warranted to examine such notions as the role of sponsors and alliances in influencing professional and personal growth, organizational commitment, or other valued outcomes. Investigation of factors that may mediate the relationship between perceptions of work empowerment and work effectiveness, such as self-efficacy, achievement orientation, and other personality factors, would provide a more stringent test of Kanter's contention that organizational factors are more important than personality predispositions in determining work behaviors and attitudes. Such studies would be of value to both nursing and healthcare organizations and contribute to a systematic body of knowledge for nursing administration which, according to Jennings,[41] has suffered neglect for the past two decades.

Summary and Conclusions

The results of this study support Kanter's suggestion that work environment structures have an impact on factors that influence employees' work effectiveness, such as control over professional nursing practice and work satisfaction. Attention to work structures that influence these factors rather than focusing on the attributes of the people in the positions, may be a more fruitful approach to creating more effective and efficient health care organizations. Reengineering initiatives to provide quality care at reduced costs must include structures that allow empowered staff members to best manage their work within highly effective teams. The findings of this study are both relevant and timely for nursing administrators faced with work environment constraints that demand doing more with less, yet preserve the essential elements of professional nursing practice.

REFERENCES

1. Corwin R. *Militant Professionalism: A Study of Organizational Conflict in High Schools.* New York: Appleton Century and Crofts; 1970.
2. Scott R. Professionals in bureaucracies: areas of conflict. In: Vollmer H. Mills D. eds. *Professionalization.* Englewood Cliffs. NJ: Prentice Hall; 1966:265–274.
3. Kanter RM. The impact of hierarchical structures on the work behavior of women and men. *Soc Problems.* 1976;23:415–430.
4. Aydelotte M. The path toward professional autonomy. *Milit Med.* 1982;147:1048–1057.
5. Styles M. Conflict and Coalition Strengthen Nursing as a Profession. *Orthop Nurs.* 1988;7(6):9–11.
6. Meltz N. *The Shortage of RN: An Analysis in a Labor Market Context.* Toronto. Canada: Registered Nurses Association of Ontario; 1988.
7. Kanter RM. *Men and Women of the Corporation.* New York: Basic Books; 1977.
8. Kanter RM. *Men and Women of the Corporation.* New York: Basic Books; 1993.
9. Wilson B. Laschinger HKS. The relationship between power and opportunity of staff nurses and organizational commitment. *J Nurs Adm.* 1994;24(4S):39–45.
10. Laschinger HKS. Shamian J. Staff nurses' and nurse managers' perceptions of job-related empowerment and managerial self-efficacy. *J Nurs Adm.* 1994;24(10):38–47.
11. Sabiston JA. Laschinger HKS, staff nurse work empowerment and perceived autonomy; testing Kanter's theory of structural power in organizations. *J Nurs Adm.* 1995;25(9):42–50.
12. Chandler G. *The Relationship of Nursing Work Environment to Empowerment and Powerlessness.* Salt Lake City. UT: University of Utah; 1986. Doctoral dissertation.
13. Chandler G. Creating an environment to empower nurses. *Nurs Manage.* 1991;22(8):20–23.
14. Dubuc L. *Job Empowerment and Commitment in Military Nursing: An Extension Study.* London. Ontario. Canada: University of Western Ontario; 1995. Master's thesis.

15. McDermott K. *The Relationship Between Registered Nurses' Perception of Job-Related Empowerment and Organizational Commitment: A Replication Study.* London Ontario, Canada: University of Western Ontario; 1994. Master's thesis.
16. Hatcher S, Laschinger HKS. Staff nurses perceptions of job empowerment and level of burnout. *Can J Nurs Adm.* 1996;9(2):74–94.
17. Kutzscher L. *Staff Nurses' Perceptions of Power and Degree of Participative Management: A Test of Kanter's Structural Theory of Power.* London. Ontario. Canada: University of Western Ontario; 1994. Master's thesis.
18. Huffman J. *Staff Nurses' Perception of Work Empowerment and Control over Nursing Practice in Community Hospital Settings.* London. Ontario. Canada: University of Western Ontario; 1995. Master's thesis.
19. Whyte H. *Staff Nurse Empowerment and Job Satisfaction.* London. Ontario. Canada: University of Western Ontario; 1995. Master's thesis.
20. McKay C. *Staff Nurses' Job-Related Power and Perceptions of Managerial Transformational Leadership.* London. Ontario. Canada: University of Western Ontario; 1995. Master's thesis.
21. Goddard P. *Power Perceptions of Middle and First Line Nurse Managers: A Test of Kanter's Theory of Structural. Power.* London, Ontario, Canada: University of Western Ontario; 1993. Master's thesis.
22. Haugh E. Laschinger HKS. Power and opportunity in public health nursing. *J Public Health Nurs.* 1996;13(1):42–49.
23. Colgrove SR. *The Relationships Among Nursing Unit Structure, Autonomy, Professional Job Satisfaction, and Nurse-Patient Interaction in Ambulatory Care Clinics.* Augusta, GA: Medical College of Georgia: 1992. Doctoral dissertation.
24. Porter-O'Grady T. Shared governance and new organizational models. *Nurs Economics.* 1987;5(6):281–287.
25. Milton D, Verran J, Murdaugh C. Gerber J. Differentiated group professional practice. *Nurs Clin North Am.* 1992;27(1): 23–30.
26. Kreitzer MJ. *Impact of Staff Nurse Participation in Decision-Making on Job Satisfaction and Organizational Commitment.* Minneapolis. MN: University of Minnesota; 1990. Doctoral dissertation.
27. Mancini VT. *The Relationship Between Shared Governance Management Structure and Registered Nurse Satisfaction: A Comparison of Two Hospitals.* Amherst. MA: University of Massachusetts; 1990. Doctoral dissertation.
28. Gerber R. Murdaugh C. Verran J. Milton D. *Control over Nursing Practice Scale: Psychometric Analysis.* Poster presentation at the National Conference on Instrumentation in Nursing: September 1990; Chapel Hill. NC.
29. Verran J. Murdaugh C. Gerber R. Milton D. *Measurement of Control over Nursing Practice Among Individuals and Groups.* Poster presentation at the CGEAN Annual Meeting: June 1992: Las Vegas, NY.
30. Bass BM, Avolio B. *Transformational Leadership Development: Manual for the Multifactor Leadership Questionnaire.* Palo Alto, CA: Consulting Psychologists Press; 1990.
31. Whitley M, Putzier DJ. Measuring nurses' satisfaction with the quality of their work and work environment. *J Nurs Care Qual.* 1994;8(3):43–51.
32. Serlin R. Hypothesis testing, theory building and the philosophy of science. *J Counc Psych.* 1987;34(4):365–371.
33. Schwartz R. Coping with unbalanced information about decision-making influence for nurses. *Hosp Health Serv Adm.* 1990;35(4):547–559.
34. Fralic M. Creating new practice models and designing new roles. *J Nurs Adm.* 1992;22(6):7–8.
35. Clifford J. Fostering professional practice in hospitals: the Boston Beth Israel experience. In: Aiken L. Fagin C. *Charting Nursing's Future: Agenda for the 1990s.* Philadelphia. PA: JB Lippincott; 1992.
36. Evan K, Aubry K, Hawkins M, et al. Whole systems shared governance: a model for the integrated health system. *J Nurs Adm.* 1995;25(5):18–27.
37. Trofino J. Nurse empowerment for the 21st century. *Nurs Adm.* Q. 1992;22:20–24.
38. Clifford J. The myth of empowerment. *Nurs Adm Q.* 1992;16(3):1–5.
39. Senge P. *The Fifth Discipline.* New York: Doubleday Currency; 1990.
40. Gorman S. Clark N. Power and effective nursing practice. *Nurs Outlook.* 1986;34(3):129–134.
41. Jennings BM. Nursing research: a time for redirection. *J Nurs Adm.* 1995;25(4):9–11.

CHAPTER 22

●●

The Power of One Vote

Motivating Women to Political Action

GLORIA STEINEM*

The best role of an outside agitator is to serve as an excuse for all of you to come together and discover that you didn't need anybody from the outside in the first place. You have all the energy and ideas and creativity that you need right here.

We meet together to look at the world *as if everyone mattered.* Today, women are striving for legal equality. Yes, we have legal identity as citizens now, but we still do not have legal equality. We are really simply trying to give each other the power to make our own choices, to be fully human, to be fully dignified, and to live in mutual respect.

For people who don't know what feminism means, it is what the dictionary says: the belief—I would say the fact—in the full social, economic, political equality of women and men. Given this definition, the majority of both women and men will agree they are feminists. But people who really believe that a normal male/female relationship is 60–40 or 70–30 are going to be very threatened by 50–50, even though that's all we're talking about.

Becoming active in a social justice movement may feel very new and scary, like you're out at the edge of the earth with the wind whistling past your ears. However, I would remind you that women's cultural pattern of activism is the reverse of men's. That is, men are rebellious when they are young and get more conservative as they get older, while women are more conservative when we're young and get more radical as we get older.

Caring About and Working Toward Humanity

Each of us is a miracle of nature, a unique combination of heredity and environment that could never have happened before in history and could never happen again. Perhaps in the years to come, whole human futures will not be determined by the single, infinitesimal elements of race or class or sex, and we can be, finally, the unique individuals, the unique miracles, we really are. There is also the magic of discovering that we are not

*Adapted from a speech by Gloria Steinem. The views expressed are those of the author and not necessarily those of the editorial staff at *Nursing Policy Forum.*

alone, that there are examples and role models and heroes in the past who can inspire us into the future.

By not looking at the world as if everyone mattered, and as if all of history mattered, we—women and men, whatever our race, whatever our age—denigrate or ignore the concerns of females of all races and the concerns of many racial groups of men. For example, we don't consider child rearing as all that important because it is a female, soft, nonhard science ... nonconquering. It is marginalized by how much we pay to do it—which is nothing. We don't even count child rearing and work done in the home in our GNP, even though it is 40% of the work that goes on in this country.

The importance of child rearing is seen in the studies of Good Samaritans, the people who risked their lives to save Jews during World War II even though they, themselves, were not Jewish. There has been a lot of research that has tried to figure out what it was about these people that was different. Was it class? Was it religion? Was it family structure? We're beginning to discover that their single most often shared characteristic was that they were not abused as children. There is a natural human empathy to another member of the same species if not cut off by abuse. There is a leap of empathy, saying that could be me ... I will help that person.

Until we take this "female" area of child rearing seriously, we will continue to miss the key to so many of our problems. I think, in my old age, I'm going to end up as an old lady in tennis shoes marching around with a big sign that says, "The only form of arms control is how we raise our children." Because as long as we are raised with violence, we will believe there are only two choices—to be the victim or the victimizer—and we will use whatever weapons are available.

The Power of Our Vote

Obviously, the issues we're talking about go much deeper than party labels, but most are effected by decisions made in the political system. This year is the most crucial election of my lifetime, because an extremist, antiequality group has taken over one of our two major parties—a first in history. There is a huge gender gap, the biggest in history, on issues and on candidates.

Only 39% of eligible voters in this whole country voted in the last election—less than any other democracy in the world. We can register and vote, but we have been conned into believing our votes don't matter. We have been conned into believing that politics is dirty so that you and I won't get into it. It's up to us—we really can change this. We should have voter registration and signups as part of everything we do, every class, every dance ... it is absolutely crucial. We are not respecting ourselves if we don't use our power of the vote. In this election year, voting is not the most we can do, voting is the least we can do.

Trials and Tribulations

Another area we must consider and understand that is crucial to building the kinds of coalitions and groupings we need to make—and the kind of vision we all have to have as individuals to solve our problems—is the gendered nature of history. We have not understood the racist nature of what we study and what we don't. We have not understood that racism and sexism are actually interdependent. So even at our best, we laundry list issues. We say, let's talk about women's equality, as if all women were white, or let's talk about racial equality, as if all blacks were men, and then we start saying which is more important. The point is that both issues are inextricably intertwined.

It's impossible to be a feminist without being an antiracist because we're not just talking about *some* women, we're talking about *all* women. But it is also true that there is common cause with men of color because these two caste systems are so intertwined that they can't be fought separately. In order to maintain any degree of racial "purity," and thus racism, women's freedom must be restricted; thus racism is dependent on sexism in a long-term, anthropological way.

When we begin to see the degree to which we have been taught a very, very limited kind of history—usually by those in positions of power—it's literally maddening to understand how much we have missed and how poorly we base our decisions because we are not looking at reality. The past 5,000 years or more have been devoted to getting females and other less powerful groups to feel that our powerlessness is natural, inevitable, making us feel that our security and our interests lie in attaching ourselves to a member of the superior group, and fighting with each other.

Fortunately, women can't be our own worst enemies, if only because we don't have the power to be. We're not the ones who are typically hiring and firing, deciding what goes on in Congress, and making the policies. But we are socialized, and we need to recognize that a group of women together will often punish the strong member of the group—just as a group of men together will punish the weak member. It's the way the gender roles are policed. Once we recognize it, we can begin to do something about it. But the most amazing thing to me is that there are women now, against all odds, who take joy in each others' accomplishments, who do support each other, and who are more likely to vote for other women.

There also is an effort to make men, in general, in every race, feel threatened by women in power as if it were a zero sum game. This hierarchical view, this nationalist view, is the old paradigm that's with us still. It makes men feel as if they are supposed to be superior, and it curtails women's humanity even more. It's as if you took a full circle of human qualities, the 100% of human qualities, and arbitrarily said two-thirds are masculine and one-third are feminine. Men are missing less, but they're missing some of their whole human self.

Changing History

MOVING ALONG THE CONTINUUM

Progress lies in the direction we haven't been. So for women, it may lie in becoming more assertive, more daring outside the home. It might be deciding to run for office yourself, organizing your neighborhood to get out to vote, or going to county commission meetings. For men, it may lie in becoming more expressive, more creative, more able to talk about emotion, more nurturing toward children and active inside the home. But both of us are trying to create the full circle of ourselves.

We're halfway there. We've learned—and we've convinced the majority of the country—that women can do what men can do, but we have yet to learn that men can do what women can do. And so many women, the majority of women, have two jobs, one outside the home and one inside the home. Women can't be equal outside the home until men are equal inside the home, until men are caring for babies and little children as much as women are.

Yet there are a lot of people who are experimenting with communal values and with different values in all kinds of ways. For example, one-third of Americans are now using nontraditional healing methods. It's as if people who have a change in consciousness are beginning to reach critical mass. I find wherever I go, this is happening. It's not because it's me, it's not because it's the women's movement. It's a changed paradigm. It's about hope. We're hungry for change. There's not enough leadership, but it's so important we realize that we're not alone.

The problem for women of all races is that we don't have a community in which we're equal and fully human. Women are the one oppressed group who will never have a country, we'll never have a neighborhood of our own. So we especially need to make small psychic families, groups in which we meet once a week. You can call it a consciousness raising group, a rap group, a book club, a meeting club, a quilting bee . . . . It doesn't matter as long as it's a place where you can tell the truth and say this "unsayable" thing and hear six other women say, "You feel like that? I thought only I felt like that." Then you realize that if six unique people can have a similar experience, something political is going on here. If we get together, we can fix it.

In general, we need to think of the circle of completing ourselves—not outstripping other people, but completion of our unique selves. For instance, the golden rule works very well for men or people with power: You should treat other people as you want to be treated. But for women of any race, for men of color, for poor people, for people who have internalized their oppression and believe that they're not somehow full human beings, we have to reverse the golden rule. We have to learn how to treat ourselves as well as we treat other people.

Celebrating Ourselves and Others

Whatever side of the circle we are on, we are just together trying to complete that circle of full humanity, and to give each other the power to make choices. It matters less what choice we make than that we have the power to make a choice.

We can't turn back—we've seen ourselves and others being reborn. We've glimpsed that uniqueness and that humanity. You may feel like you've stood in the same place, but if you look back over the great social justice movements in this country, you'll see that it was really a spiral and we have come a very long distance. If we look at each other and trust each other, take each other seriously, really listen with respect to each other, we will discover how much power each of us has.

Even the most cynical, hard-nosed physicist now admits that the flap of a butterfly's wing here can change the weather hundreds of miles away. Each of us has incredible power. The art of behaving morally is behaving as if everything we do matters—because everything we do *does* matter. Together, we make one hell of a butterfly.

REFERENCE

Pearlstein, S. (1996. January 30). Angry female voters a growing force. *The Washington Post.* pp. A1, A5.

ACKNOWLEDGMENTS

Special thanks to Gloria Steinem and Diana James for their time and cooperation in the development of this article. We also would like to acknowledge the valuable assistance of Dr. Lynne Carroll, Cynthia Cornish, and Richard Culver of Salisbury State University.

●●

CHAPTER 23

The Legislative Process

KATHLEEN SMITH

It has been said for a democracy to function successfully its citizens must be willing to participate in their government. The First Amendment of our Constitution, adopted in 1791, guarantees us the freedom of speech, the right to assemble, and the right to petition the government. Therefore, lobbying policy makers to make our interests and concerns heard is a key component of our democratic government.

Participation in government takes many forms. The single most important activity of citizens in a successful democracy is exercising the right to vote. Voting implies an understanding of the issues concerned and the potential impact of election of the candidates. Other activities in which citizens may involve themselves include working on campaigns; participating in organizations to promote or oppose certain legislative issues; contacting legislators about issues; and providing testimony at hearings. Citizens can even be involved in helping to originate and encourage the passage of specific legislation.

Much of the professional life of nurses is and will continue to be influenced by legislation at both the state and national levels. For this reason, it is imperative that nurses take on the responsibility of citizenship. For example, the nurse practice act in each state controls nursing education and practice. These laws can be amended, totally rewritten, or eliminated in the state legislature.

In addition, any law involving not only health care, but also general education and social issues, may well have an impact on nursing, sometimes only because they affect the patient populations with which nurses work. On the national level, previous or existing legislation such as Medicare, Social Security, welfare reform, insurance reform, health professionals' education programs, public health service programs, promotion of managed care, health research funding, and labor relations all have effects on nursing practice.

While nurses are becoming more sophisticated in the legislative process, they have not yet reached their full potential of influence as individuals, as members of a profession that numbers over 2 million, and as members of other "power" groups. This is in part due to a lack of knowledge of the process itself and results in the lack of understanding of the ways they can make their power felt and the appropriate time to take action.

This article proposes a remedy for that situation by (1) presenting an overview of the structure of the federal government and the legislative process and (2) providing the basic information needed to get involved in politics and policy making.

Orthopaedic Nursing, 14(5), pp. 58–63. Reprinted with permission of the publisher, the National Association of Orthopaedic Nurses.

Structure of the Federal Government

The three branches of the United States government include the executive, the judicial, and the legislative.

EXECUTIVE BRANCH

Included in the executive branch are the offices of the president and the vice president as well as the federal departments and agencies. The duties of the executive branch include recommending legislation, such as President Clinton's sweeping health care reform proposal, the Health Security Act of 1993, administering laws, and signing or vetoing legislation.

Current executive branch policy is usually presented to a joint session of Congress and to the nation by the president in the State of the Union address each January. Within the executive branch of government, responsibility for health policy lies with the Department of Health and Human Services (DHHS).

JUDICIAL BRANCH

The chief function of the judicial branch of the government (the court system) is to interpret laws and sometimes change laws within its jurisdiction.

One of the checks and balances in our system of government gives Congress the authority to supersede an unpopular Supreme Court decision by enacting new legislation. This has often been talked about in relation to the Roe v Wade abortion decision, but to date the Court's ruling stands.

LEGISLATIVE BRANCH

The legislative branch of government consists of the Congress whose primary responsibility is to make laws. It is called the "heart of the government" because of its responsibility to listen and respond to the needs of the people.

Our federal legislature is bicameral, meaning it has two chambers, the House of Representatives and the Senate. While the House has the constitutional responsibility to originate legislation that deals with raising revenue and spending it, sole authority rests in the Senate to approve the ratification of treaties and nominations by the president, including federal circuit court and Supreme Court nominations.

How a Bill Becomes Law

Nurses have long been involved in the drafting of health policy and the procedures to carry them out within their employer organizations. In much the same way, national health policy is crafted. At the federal level, however, such "policies" are written in the form of laws passed by the Congress. The "procedures" for carrying out these laws are expressed in federal regulations and published in the *Federal Register.*

A bill faces difficult odds in wending its way through the House and Senate. For example, in the 103rd Congress, which was in session during calendar years 1993 and 1994, 9,822 measures were introduced, but only 2,037 were made law. The only measures assured of passage are those that provide annual funds to keep the government operating.

Otherwise, it takes strong White House support or the support of a substantial number of lawmakers for a bill to survive.

A bill can be introduced in either house of Congress, or it can be introduced in both houses simultaneously. Anyone can initiate a bill. It is a citizen's demand for action, originated by an individual who takes his complaints or ideas to a legislator; or it can be put forth by a special interest group.

Obviously, the larger and more politically active the group is, the better chance it has of being heard. If there are a number of such groups, representing even more citizens (ie, voters) with an interest in the issue, they may come together as a coalition in support of or in opposition to a legislative proposal and have even more clout.

In addition to individuals and special interest groups, some common originators of bills are a governmental administrator, agency or department, a delegation of citizens in a legislator's district, a legislative committee, or the legislator himself.

Many more citizens involve themselves in responding to legislation that has already been introduced than are involved in getting it introduced in the first place.

Committee Structure

Much of the work of Congress occurs in the 20 committees of the House and 20 committees of the Senate. Each committee has jurisdiction over certain areas of public policy. Committees are further divided into subcommittees: 86 in the House and 68 in the Senate. Virtually all bills are sent to these panels after introduction, and many die there as a result of inaction.

SENATE

The two major committees in the Senate having jurisdiction over health care and overseeing the activities of the Department of Health and Human Services are the Finance Committee's Subcommittee on Health with jurisdiction over Medicare and Medicaid, and the Labor and Human Resources Committee which authorizes programs under the Public Health Service Act. These programs include federal funding of nursing education and research, National Institutes of Health programs, the Centers for Disease Control and Prevention, and the Food and Drug Administration.

HOUSE OF REPRESENTATIVES

In the House of Representatives, two major committees are primarily responsible for health issues. The Commerce Committee's Subcommittee on Health and the Environment authorizes the programs under the Public Health Service Act. The Ways and Means Committee's Subcommittee on Health has jurisdiction over the physician and nurse practitioner reimbursement part of Medicare and shares jurisdiction for Medicare hospital insurance with the Commerce Committee.

In both houses, the Appropriations Committees' Subcommittees on Labor, Education, and Health and Human Services are responsible for yearly appropriations for health items in the federal budget, except Medicare. Other committees in both houses, such as the Budget Committees, affect health care issues in their work.

Subcommittee Work

Once a committee takes up a bill, it usually holds public hearings. At this time the members of the committee hear testimony from the bill's sponsors, expert witnesses, administration officials, and special interest groups. Written testimony can be submitted for the record if the group or individual is not asked to participate at the hearing.

The next step in the process is for the bill to go to "markup," which is a committee session during which the legislators go over the proposal line by line and vote on changes. The committee then considers the bill. The outcome is either to approve the bill (report it out to the full committee) with or without amendments, some of which can change the nature of the bill completely, to "kill" the bill, or to draft a new bill to accomplish the same goal, but in a different manner.

The subcommittee to which a bill is referred is the first place where its fate can be influenced. If the bill is never put on the committee agenda or is not approved, it will generally not proceed further. The chairman has the power to keep the bill off the agenda or to introduce it early or at a favorable time.

To get the desired action, interested persons/groups begin their legislative action at this point. All members of the subcommittee, and especially the chairman, are important targets for the individuals or organizations that want to see the bill move forward.

Individual members of these organizations whose legislators sit on the subcommittee may be asked to contact their legislator because of the influential position he or she has over the fate of the legislation at this point. Letters, phone calls, telegrams, fax messages, and personal contact are used to reach the chairman and other committee members.

Committee Work

The same process outlined for subcommittees takes place at the full committee level, the next step in the legislative process for a bill that is reported out of the subcommittee. Opportunity for citizen/organization action occurs in the same way, focusing this time on the chairman and members of the full committee.

A bill surviving committee action is then scheduled for action "on the floor," meaning the total membership of the body. Under certain circumstances, amendments may be proposed at this stage and are approved or rejected by the majority of those assembled.

After a bill passes one chamber, it is sent to the other for a complete repetition of the process it went through in the first chamber.

Conference Committee

If the bill passed by the House and the one passed by the Senate are not the same, or if the bill has been amended by the second house after passing the first, and the first house does not agree with the amendments, the bill is sent to a conference committee.

This committee consists of an equal number of members of each house and usually includes members from the committees that originally handled the bills. Once the members of the conference committee are named by the leadership, opportunity for citizen action begins again.

The conference committee attempts to work out a compromise that will be accepted by both houses. Sometimes, however, the two houses are not able to arrive at a compromise and the bill dies, but usually an agreement is reached. The conference report issued by the committee when they achieve a compromise, is sent to both chambers for vote. The compromise bill must be approved by each chamber before it is sent to the White House for signing by the President.

Presidential Action

After passing both houses, the bill goes to the president. If he approves it or fails to take action within 10 days, the bill becomes law. If Congress adjourns before the 10 days in which the president should sign the bill, it does not become law. This is known as a "pocket veto." The president may veto the bill and return it to the house of origin. A two-thirds affirmative vote in both houses is necessary to override the veto. Voting on a veto is often along party lines.

It is difficult and time consuming to translate an idea for legislation into statutory law with such a complicated system of checks and balances, which the due process of law provides in a democratic government such as the United States. Law makers are also subject to extreme political pressure from within the government as well as from the influence of lobbyists.

Federal Regulatory Process

Action on a bill does not end with its passage. Laws are usually written very generally, because too much specificity makes them obsolete too rapidly. After a law is passed, it is sent to the particular federal agency that is responsible for writing the regulations to implement the law. These regulations are as important as the law itself: they have the force of law and they spell out the specifics of how it will be carried out.

It is possible to influence legislation at this point also and to strengthen or weaken the intent of the law. The opportunity to contribute to the development of regulations is available to interested organizations, which may make recommendations for individual appointments on advisory committees or offer informal participation and cooperation.

Becoming Knowledgeable

A number of ways exist for nurses to become more knowledgeable in matters of legislation. The American Nurses Association and its constituent state groups take a very active role in the legislative process.

Many specialty nursing organizations, such as NAON, devote significant resources for the legislative issues that affect their membership and its specific patient population. The major legislative activities of nursing associations are discussed at the local chapter level.

In addition, members are kept informed about legislation through the written materials of the organizations. Major nursing journals and newsletters routinely report key national legislative efforts and even those on the state level that have particular significance.

Another way for nurses to become more informed is by reading the newspaper. Feature articles, news stories, and editorials may not include more narrow pieces of legislation that are of special interest to nurses, such as reauthorization of the Nurse Education Act or funding for the National Institute for Nursing Research, but broader bills will be reported on, such as changes in the Medicare and Medicaid programs and welfare reform.

Some newspapers list the major bills in the state legislature and in Congress, the action taken on those bills, and their current status. The votes of legislators on particular bills may also be occasionally reported. This information enables the readers to follow the path of a bill and to see how their legislators vote in general. The League of Women Voters and other political action groups can also be a source of such information.

One of the first pieces of information that one needs to become familiar with is the names of their own legislators. One way to begin is to call the local municipal building or the County Clerk's office. A local or state League of Women Voters branch is also a good source, as is the district and state nurses' association. The state nurses' associations are usually headquartered in the state capital.

Registration and voting are, of course, important, since voters are more influential than their nonvoter counterparts.

The Process of Lobbying

The increasing complexity of public issues has forced law makers to rely heavily on the expertise and opinions of professional and trade associations, and business, labor, and industry groups. Such expertise is provided by lobbyists, who are paid representatives of interest groups, many of which, depending on the size and contribution power of their constituencies, wield considerable power in legislative bodies.

It is important to remember that individual citizens can also "lobby" for or against legislation. Although there is a certain mysticism about the process of lobbying, it is quite simply an attempt to legitimately influence legislators to promote or suppress proposed legislation.

Influencing the law making process involves educating the legislators and staff members who decide what issues to consider in a given congressional year and who vote on those issues as they move through the legislative process. This process of influencing, or lobbying, is nothing more than educating, marketing, and selling. These are not foreign concepts to nurses who spend their days educating patients and colleagues, marketing ideas to physicians to get appropriate orders written, and selling good health habits or practices to patients. There is no special skill set required of nurses who decide they want (or need) to involve themselves in the legislative process.

There are numerous ways lobbyists try to influence legislators. Much is accomplished on the basis of direct contact in personal meetings and semisocial gatherings. Lobbyists provide information and introduce resource people to the legislators and their staff. They are also valuable in keeping their interest group informed about any pertinent legislation and aid the group in effective action.

One way that individuals "lobby" is through membership in a professional association that establishes a legislative agenda and works as a group, either independently or in coalitions with other like groups, to advance it. For nurses, supporting these organizations with dues and making their opinions heard through the various mechanisms available are ways of indirectly influencing the legislative process.

However, to effectively influence a specific piece of legislation, multiple lobbying strategies need to be employed. NAON's Government Relations Committee, with approval of the Executive Board, typically prepares a letter outlining the association's official position with regard to a specific piece of legislation that it is interested in. The letter is distributed to all members of the subcommittee or full committee of the congressional body to which the measure has been referred.

However, the individual members of those committees are more strongly influenced by what their own constituents tell them about a bill than they are by anything else. This is where individual citizens become critical to the process and to their specialty association's ability to truly influence legislation.

At this point, more direct lobbying techniques are necessary, such as communicating with legislators. Communication can take several forms, such as letters, phone calls, and personal visits.

Preparing for Contact

Learning to effectively communicate with legislators is essential to achieving positive results. While legislators want, and often need, to hear from their constituents, their time is limited. Carefully planned and organized contacts are usually the most effective.

Before contacting legislators, it is important to do some preparation on the issue at hand AND on the legislator. With regard to the latter, their party affiliations and whether they have an interest in or any prior knowledge about the issue are important to know.

Their local offices can be contacted: they are usually listed in the blue pages of the telephone book. Simply tell the staff what the issue is and ask if the legislator has taken a position on it or not. To call their office in Washington, dial 202-224-3121 for the Senate information operator and 202-225-3121 for the House operator. They connect callers to their legislator's office and will provide the direct phone number for future reference.

In terms of being prepared on the issue, that can be as simple as reading the newspaper or other news media and keeping abreast of the issue in other publications.

Communicating by Letter

While this section focuses on writing a letter to a Congressional representative, you may want to write to your representative in the state assembly, the city council, the governor, mayor, town council representative, or even the president of the United States. The essentials of developing a letter to influence a policy maker are the same regardless of the intended recipient.

For members of Congress, letters can be mailed or sent via facsimile to the legislator's office. This is especially helpful if time is critical. Their fax numbers are available from their offices.

The inside address and salutation should look like this . . .

For a Senator:

> The Honorable _____
> United States Senate
> Washington, DC 20510

> Dear Senator _____:

For a Representative:

> The Honorable _____
> U.S. House of Representatives
> Washington, DC 20515

> Dear Representative _____:

> *or*

> Dear Congressman _____:

> *or*

> Dear Congresswoman _____:

Identify yourself immediately in the opening paragraph:

- As a constituent, by showing in your letter exactly where you reside
- As a health care professional, including any relevant information that may be helpful, such as where you work and the type of work that you do, the patient population you deal with
- As a member of a large group or coalition, such as NAON or your state nurses' association, which suggests strength in numbers. It may be important at times to differentiate between issues which are your own from those of any associations you belong to, however. If the association has not taken an official position on an issue, do not imply you are representing the opinion of the association

Give enough of your background to identify yourself as an expert on the specific issue you are requesting. At the end of the paragraph, state your issue and the reason you are writing.

General Guidelines

In terms of discussing the issue, there are several rules.

Rule 1. Be Specific. Use the actual bill number if you know it. Share your position on the issue and why you have come to that position. Ask for his or her position on this issue. If you can, include information on the local impact of a specific proposal. Tell the Member what you want done, eg, do you want him to cosponsor the bill to add support to it? Do you want to urge hearings on the matter? Do you want a particular vote? Look for the Member to make a commitment and ask for a response.

Rule 2. Be Brief and to the Point. Legislators and their staff have very little time and long letters and documents will not be read. Keep letters to one page and limit yourself to one issue per letter. Pare down support material to a concise fact sheet, double spaced, using bullets and accurate statistics and information easily seen "at a glance." Such material will be kept and referred to as necessary.

Rule 3. Be Constructive. Don't whine. If you think a particular bill is the wrong approach, explain what you think is the best approach.

Rule 4. Be Persistent. One contact probably will not be enough. Call the office a week or so after you have sent a letter to ask if it was received and to discuss it further with the appropriate staff member. (Staff members are assigned different types of issues. Typically, you will want to speak to the Legislative Assistant [L.A.] for Health.) Ask for an appointment to discuss it with the legislator when he or she is in town. Keep the heat on!

Rule 5. Be Courteous. It is not wise to threaten any kind of action if you don't get what you want from the legislator. If a vote is contrary to your position, politely tell the Member how you feel.

Rule 6. Keep in Regular Contact. This need not be time consuming and is important in relationship building. Send a note of thanks for a specific vote or for some activity that was held locally. Such behavior makes asking for something later a lot easier.

Rule 7. Report Back. Let your organizations know what you have done. If you receive a reply letter from your Member of Congress indicating support, the association leadership can use that letter in Washington to ensure that support. Sometimes Members say they cannot support a measure because they haven't heard from their constituents. Knowing that letters were sent and having copies can be very helpful.

Rule 8. Say Thank You. Say thank you for time spent in a meeting or on the phone, or for a vote on your issue.

CLOSING THE LETTER

In closing the letter, establish yourself as a source of information and offer your assistance as a resource for more information . . . and prepare to be called if your issue becomes a hot topic. Invite the Member or the staff to your workplace if that would help illustrate your point.

FORM

In terms of the form your letter takes, typed personal letters are more suspect than handwritten ones. Members say handwritten letters are the only way to ensure that a personal letter is, in fact, personal. The next best thing would be to print the letter on personal stationery.

YOUR LETTER COUNTS

It cannot be stressed enough how much YOUR LETTER COUNTS! Sometimes specific letters are read by the Members on the floor of the House or Senate; some letters are shared with colleagues if they illustrate a point particularly well. Members are told every day how much correspondence came in to both the district and Washington offices on a particular topic. Your voice will be heard. Don't forget to spread the word to others with whom you work or network. Urge them to write as well.

The Personal Visit

Personal visits with legislators and staff members are a very effective means of grassroots lobbying. It is generally wise to be on time, to stick to the agreed-upon time frame, dress appropriately, be friendly and polite, greet the legislator with a firm handshake, and keep the visit short.

As with letter writing, it is important to identify yourself as a nurse and to offer to be a resource in the area of health care with which you are most familiar. Also identify early in the meeting the purpose of your visit. Present the facts in an orderly manner, be succinct, and avoid jargon or too many statistics.

It is thoughtful to comment on any of the legislator's bills or votes of which you approve, and it is appropriate to ask if he or she has taken a position on the issue you are there to discuss.

Most of the guidelines for letter writing are also applicable to personal visits, including telling the legislator or staff member what you want the legislator to do and asking when you might have an answer on the legislator's position on your issue.

If you are asked a question you cannot answer, do not lie; simply promise to get the information and provide it to them at a later date. This is one way to establish yourself as a reliable source of information that could improve your access to your legislator in the future.

At the end of the meeting, establish agreement on when you should follow up and with whom, and then do so. Leave a one- or two-page fact sheet that summarizes the issue and your position and that includes the name and phone number of a contact person if there should be a need for further information. Leave behind your business card as well. Remember the value of "thank you." Follow up after the meeting with a letter thanking the legislator or staff member. Take this opportunity to reiterate your position, and include any information requested during the meeting.

Telephone Calls

Phone calls are best for obtaining information. Lobbying calls should be kept very short. Ask to speak to the legislative assistant handling health issues as that is the person who can give you the best indication of the member's position on the issue.

Summary

From the foregoing, it can be seen that nurses are major stakeholders in legislation. Whether acting as individuals or as part of a group, such as NAON, they can make and have made an impact on the political scene.

These are years of rapid change in health care. Nurses face many challenges and have many opportunities to participate in and influence the formation of health care policy. Nurse citizens can become very effective in their lobbying efforts, whether on the federal, state, or local level, when they are armed with information about the key players and the processes and their belief in what nursing can contribute to the health care system.

As nursing activist Peggy Chinn has said, "For the remainder of this century, the most worthy goal that nurses can select is that of arousing their passion for a kind of political activism that will make a difference in their own lives and in the life of society" (Solomon, 1986).

BIBLIOGRAPHY

Redman, E. (1973). *The dance of legislation.* New York: Simon & Schuster, Inc.

How our government works. (1985. January 28) *U.S. News and World Report.*

deVries, C.M. & Vanderbilt, M.W. (1992). *The grassroots lobbying handbook: Empowering nurses through legislative and political action.* Washington, DC: American Nurses Association.

Solomon, S.B. (1986). *Key concepts in public policy.* New York: National League for Nursing.

CHAPTER 24

••

Labor Laws Working to Protect You

BARBARA E. CALFEE

Has your knowledge of labor law been put to the test yet? If you're like most nurses, you understand your legal responsibilities to patients, but don't know whether the law protects you in the workplace until:

- You're fired.
- You must fire someone else.
- You feel discriminated against.
- You confront sexual harassment.
- You try to understand how your overtime wages are calculated.

The time to brush up on labor law is now, *before* you're involved in a problem related to termination, discrimination, sexual harassment, or wages. In this article, I'll review the labor laws that protect you and provide examples of related cases.

Termination

One of the most painful work-related experiences you'll ever deal with is losing your job. As inpatient days are decreasing, the ranks of hospital nurses are thinning. If you're not already a casualty, you may be threatened by layoffs daily.

A nurse who loses her job—and with it income and self-esteem—isn't the only one affected: The nurse-manager who breaks the news faces stress, and the health care institution must worry about wrongful-termination lawsuits. So whether you're an employer or employee, you need a good grasp of laws concerning termination.

Most states have a policy known as *employment at will*, meaning that an employee may be fired for a good reason, a bad reason, or no reason at all—so long as the termination doesn't break a law. Although this sounds favorable to employers, recent federal and state legislation and court decisions have restricted the employer's ability to terminate at will.

FEDERAL STATUTES LAY THE FOUNDATION

More than three decades ago, Congress laid the cornerstone for eliminating discrimination in the workplace and since then has strengthened its base with additional federal statutes. Let's look at the building blocks.

- *Civil rights.* In 1964, Congress passed Title VII of the Federal Statutory Restrictions of the Civil Rights Act. This law prohibits an employer with 15 or more employees from discriminating against employees because of their race, color, religion, sex, or national origin. Penalties range from reinstating the employee's job and lost wages to civil fines, punitive damages, and payment of attorney fees.
- *Age.* The Age Discrimination in Employment Act of 1967 prohibits employers from terminating employees 40 years of age or older strictly because of age. But an employer may terminate someone over 40 for reasons unrelated to age or if he can show that age legitimately affects job performance. So requiring airline pilots to retire at age 60 is permitted because health risks associated with aging could impair their performance. Clearing the cockpit of workers who may have major medical problems, slowed reflexes, or diminished eyesight helps ensure public safety.
- *Pregnancy.* The Pregnancy Discrimination Act of 1978 protects women affected by pregnancy, childbirth, or a related medical condition. A woman must be evaluated the same as other applicants and employees—strictly on her ability to work. If she's medically able to work, she can't be fired, refused a job or promotion, or forced to take a leave because she's pregnant. And if she can't work because of pregnancy, she's entitled to take disability leave, then return to her job when she's able to resume working.
- *Disabilities.* In 1990, Congress passed the Americans with Disabilities Act (ADA). This act bars discrimination against disabled people in areas of employment, travel, and access to private services, such as restaurants and shopping malls. Rather than simply asking employers to overlook a disability, the ADA compels employers to give the disabled special consideration.

  Giving a disabled person special consideration doesn't mean an employer must hire a candidate *because* she has a disability. However, if she's the most qualified candidate, he must hire her and accommodate the workplace for her disability. For example, if she uses a wheelchair, he must remove obstacles from the area to allow her to move about freely. If the employer hires someone other than the disabled candidate and she challenges his decision, he may need to justify his action to the Civil Rights Commission.

  In the following case, a nurse challenged her dismissal because of a disability (Box 24-1).

BOX 24–1

The claim.   A nurse with a back injury could perform only light-duty nursing tasks. After 8 weeks of successfully carrying out her assignments, she was fired without explanation. She sued her employer, stating that the facility had discriminated against her because of her disability.

The ruling.   The court ruled that the employer's actions were discriminatory—the deciding factor was that no one had complained about the nurse's job performance during her light-duty assignments.

Tuck v. HCA Health Services of Tennessee, Inc. 7 F.3ed 465 (Tennessee 1993)

STATE STATUTES ADD STRENGTH

Backing up federal legislation, your state also may have laws that protect workers against discrimination. Some have passed laws that protect employees based on marital status, sexual orientation, personal appearance, political affiliation, source of income, or place of residence. Many states also restrict the employer's options in the following situations.

- *Whistle-blowing.* Most states prohibit employers from retaliating against employees who report or try to report the employer for illegal acts. The intent of whistle-blower laws is to encourage employees to report law violations, unsafe conditions, and dangers to the public. In some states, though, reporting the problem to corporate headquarters or nongovernment organizations doesn't provide immunity—to be protected, you must report the problem to a government agency.
- *Workers' compensation.* Most states prohibit employers from discharging employees because they've filed or intend to file workers' compensation claims. An employer found to have threatened, harassed, or terminated an employee for filing a claim can face severe penalties.
- *Drug testing.* In the case of drug screening, potential employees have fewer rights than current employees. Employers generally have the authority to administer pre-employment drug tests. However, most states prohibit employers from testing current employees without good cause or unless the employee performs safety-sensitive duties, such as operating a train or bus. When employee testing is permitted, state laws may dictate how to protect the employee's privacy, obtain and handle test specimens, present test results in court, and perform follow-up testing.

  Because nurses have access to drugs, testing may be allowed when the employer suspects drug abuse. The state Civil Rights Commission, the American Civil Liberties Union, or a local law school clinic can help you find out whether your state supports drug testing for nurses. If you're concerned about a coworker who's drug-impaired, contact your state nurses association for information about obtaining legal help or addiction counseling; many state boards of nursing have a program to help nurses overcome addiction. Participating in such a program may enable a nurse to retain her license.

WHEN OTHER LIMITATIONS APPLY

Employer/employee agreements, union contracts, and court rulings also may affect your employer's ability to terminate you. For example, some private-duty contractors and home health care agencies require employees to sign contracts when they're hired. If you've signed such a contract, it may spell out the conditions under which your employer may terminate you.

If you belong to a union, you may be protected by a collective bargaining agreement that requires your employer to prove good cause for terminating you. An employer whose workers are protected by a union contract must understand and adhere to its restrictions for termination because breaching the contract could nullify the entire agreement.

Case law based on court decisions also limits an employer's ability to fire an at-will employee if:

- *The termination would violate public policy,* meaning that it would go against the public good. For example, if an employer fired a nurse because she refused to do something illegal, the courts wouldn't uphold her termination. The following case shows what happened to a nurse who was fired for serving public policy (Box 24-2).

BOX 24–2

The claim. A nurse who believed that her patient was dying because of improper treatment reported her concerns to her nurse-manager, who told her to "stay out of it." The nurse was then fired for becoming too involved in the case. Claiming that her license would have been jeopardized if she'd done nothing on her patient's behalf, she sued for wrongful termination.

   The ruling.   Stating that the nurse's role as patient advocate served public policy, the court ruled in her favor.

Kirk v. Mercy Hospital Tri-County, 851 S.W.2d 617 (Missouri 1993)

- *The termination would violate an implied-in-fact contract.* Even without a written contract, employer/employee communications may imply that the employee can be terminated only for a good reason. For example, a conversation in which a nurse-manager assures a staff nurse of job security may later be interpreted as an implied-in-fact contract.

   The validity of implied-in-fact contracts has driven employers to protect themselves against lawsuits for wrongful termination. Some have reworded their policy manuals, and many ask employees to sign a statement saying they realize their employment is on an at-will basis.

- *The termination would violate an implied covenant of good faith and fair dealing.* A few states recognize a third exception to the at-will doctrine: They assume that good faith and fair dealing permeate every employment contract. A court in such a state may determine that certain unwritten terms of employment are implied and valid. For example, in California employers who terminate employees just before they become vested in the company pension plan have been found guilty of violating a good-faith covenant. To determine if your state recognizes such a covenant, contact your state Civil Rights Commission, a law school clinic, or an attorney.

Discrimination

To a degree, discrimination in the workplace is legal if it's based on legitimate business needs. When employers hire, promote, and make other management decisions, they legally discriminate against unqualified applicants. Discriminating against employees or applicants because they belong to a protected class, however, is prohibited.

   Two theories of discrimination are recognized under federal law:

- *Antidiscrimination* prohibits discrimination against someone in a category protected by federal and state laws. If you're a nurse-manager, look at the questions applicants are asked to ensure that your institution's hiring process isn't discriminatory. Asking about age, race, and other factors isn't illegal, but you'd have a hard time proving that the information obtained wasn't used in the selection process if a rejected candidate files a complaint. For this reason, avoid asking about factors that don't relate to the position you're trying to fill.

   Consider these examples: Asking "How old are you?" could cause a problem if the candidate is over 40 and feels you've discriminated against her because of age.

BOX 24–3

The claim. A skilled-nursing facility refused to hire a nursing assistant applicant because he was male. Five years later, the applicant sued for sex discrimination, so the facility finally offered him a job.

    The ruling. The court ordered the facility to pay the plaintiff what he would have received in salary if he'd worked in the position for 5 years; a job offer 5 years later wasn't considered adequate compensation for the earlier discrimination.

Little Forest Medical Center of Akron v. Ohio Civil Rights Commission, 631 N.E.2d 1068 (Ohio 1993)

However, asking "Are you over 18 years of age?" establishes that she's of legal working age without risking age discrimination. Employers also must use caution when developing preemployment screening tests. The courts view tests as discriminatory when they're weighted against applicants in a protected class. The following case shows an example of gender discrimination (Box 24-3).

- *Affirmative action* requires that institutions take steps to reverse the effects of past discrimination. Although not every federal law protecting workers requires affirmative action, your institution may voluntarily engage in such a program. For example, the ADA doesn't require a quota of disabled employees in the workplace, yet some employers seek disabled applicants anyway.

Sexual Harassment

Taking larger strides against gender-based discrimination, the Equal Employment Opportunity Commission (EEOC) ruled in 1980 that sexual harassment is a form of discrimination. Since then, sexual harassment cases have been defined as either quid pro quo harassment or a hostile work environment.

Quid pro quo harassment means an employee must choose between yielding to sexual demands or losing job benefits, promotions, or employment. (*Quid pro quo* is the exchange of one thing for another.) According to the EEOC, "unwelcome sexual advances, requests for sexual favors, and other verbal or physical conduct of a sexual nature" constitute harassment when:

- Submission to such conduct is an explicit or implicit condition of employment.
- The employee's submission to or rejection of such conduct is used as the basis for employment decisions affecting that person.

Sexual harassment is discriminatory when it becomes a problem for workers of one sex but not the other. For example, a male manager harassing a female employee discriminates against her because he excludes male employees from the same harassment. In order to successfully litigate a harassment claim, an employee must prove that:

- The employee belongs to a protected class (in essence, everyone is protected because of gender).
- The employee was subjected to unsolicited, unwelcome, and offensive sexual conduct.

- The harassment wouldn't have occurred if the employee were of the opposite sex.
- The employee's refusal of sexual advances has negatively affected her compensation, working conditions, or privileges of employment.

A *hostile work environment* means the workplace is so intimidating or offensive that an employee regularly suffers from sexual incidents, comments, or conduct. For example, continually enduring a manager's demeaning and offensive language before colleagues alters the employee's conditions of employment so that she feels unwanted or unwelcome and may even become emotionally ill.

To sustain an action against the employer, the employee must prove that:

- The employee belongs to a protected class.
- The behavior in question wasn't solicited, desired, or encouraged.
- The defendant's activities are offensive to employees of one sex only (sexual harassment laws are based on discrimination, so no remedy exists for an environment that's offensive to both).
- The behavior persists to affect the employee's psychological well-being and is a term of employment.

A recently recognized form of sexual harassment is *reverse harassment*. This occurs when an employee is passed over for advancement or a pay raise because another employee is having an affair with a manager and receiving preferential treatment. Although the complaining employee probably hasn't been subjected to sexual advances, she's been professionally harmed by her manager's involvement with another employee. Because the concept of reverse harassment is still in its infancy, the courts are grappling with how to treat it—some have categorized it as unfair, and others have ruled it illegal.

Wage and Hour Law

Two federal laws—the Fair Labor Standards Act (FLSA) and the Equal Pay Act of 1963—govern wages and are enforced by the U.S. Department of Labor. The FLSA spells out the requirements for minimum wage, overtime, and child labor. The Equal Pay Act requires equal pay for equal work, yet it also allows an employee with superior education or extensive experience to earn more than someone else who's doing equal work. Because states also have wage and hour laws, you should become familiar with your state's requirements regarding pay and overtime—they may provide for benefits above and beyond what the federal laws guarantee. In the following case, the court examines the fine line between equal pay and equal work (Box 24-4).

BOX 24–4

The claim.   Nurse practitioners sued because they received lower pay than physician assistants who performed similar tasks. They claimed they should receive equal pay for equal work.

   The ruling.   The court held that physician assistants had more training and expertise in medical diagnosis and treatment. They also took night call in rotation with physicians, which the nurse practitioners weren't required to do. Consequently, the court justified the pay differential—to receive equal pay, workers must perform the exact same job.

Beal v. Curtis, 603 F.Supp. 1563 (Georgia 1985)

CALCULATING OVERTIME

By far, the biggest concern nurses have regarding wage and hour issues is how their over-time pay is calculated. Because health care institutions may be calculating overtime wages improperly, the U.S. Department of Labor is currently looking into the institutions' calcu-lation methods. To understand how you're paid for overtime, you first need to answer these questions.

- *Who can collect overtime pay?* To determine who's eligible to collect overtime wages, the FLSA makes distinctions between *exempt* and *nonexempt* employees. Adminis-trators and managers are usually exempt, meaning they can't collect overtime pay no matter how many hours they work. Staff nurses, however, are generally consid-ered nonexempt hourly employees entitled to collect overtime pay.

  But two issues cloud the nonexempt status for nurses: In 1994 the U.S. Supreme Court ruled that nurses who direct other workers may be supervisors and thus con-sidered exempt. In addition, some nurses receive a flat salary regardless of the hours they work. The distinction between exempt and nonexempt employees is be-coming increasingly complicated, so check with your employer, your collective bar-gaining agent, or the U.S. Department of Labor, Wage and Hour Division, to re-solve any doubts you have.

- *What's the basis for calculating overtime?* To calculate overtime pay, you must first un-derstand how your institution structures time. Health care facilities may compute overtime on a 7-day or 14-day period. However, don't assume that receiving pay-checks every 2 weeks means that your overtime is calculated on a 14-day basis. Check with your human resources department to find out which method your em-ployer uses.

  Generally, workers on 12-hour shifts have their overtime calculated on a 7-day cycle. An employer using this cycle must pay one and a half times your regular rate for any time over 40 hours worked in the 7-day period, regardless of your shift or pay schedule. Averaging hours over 2 or more weeks isn't permitted. So if you work 30 hours one week and 50 hours the next, you must receive overtime pay for the 10 additional hours worked in the second week, even though the average hours worked are 40 for each week.

  For employees working 8-hour shifts, overtime may be based on a 14-day cycle. If your employer uses this cycle, you probably signed a form agreeing to calculation on this basis when you were hired. Overtime calculated on a 14-day cycle is any time worked beyond 8 hours in one workday or 80 hours in the 14-day period. So if you work one 9-hour day in a 14-day pay period, you're due 1 hour of overtime pay; if you work an 8-hour shift on each of the 14 days, you're entitled to 32 hours of overtime pay.

  The U.S. Department of Labor requires a long-lasting or permanent commitment to calculating overtime over 14 days. Although an employer may avoid paying overtime wages if he switches from a 7-day to a 14-day calculation, the government prohibits it.

  An especially hot topic for nurses is working through breaks and lunch without receiving overtime pay. If you work through any authorized break period or stay late to complete documentation, your employer must pay you for the time worked.

THE LAW AND YOU

The law is constantly changing. To understand how changes affect your rights in the workplace, stay abreast of recent court rulings, laws, and changes in state statutes. If you believe your rights in the workplace have been violated, consult an attorney who's familiar with labor law.

SELECTED REFERENCES

Calfee, B.: *What Do I Do? Who Do I Call?* Cleveland. ARC Publishing, Inc., 1996.

Collins, D.: "Can't You Take a Joke? Sexual Harassment in Healthcare," *Revolution: The Journal of Nurse Empowerment.* 5(3):68–74, Fall 1995.

Zuffoletto. J.: "OR Nursing Law: At-Will Employment." *AORN Journal.* 57(3):708–713, March 1993.

CHAPTER 25

●●

The End of Collective Bargaining for Nurses?

PATRICIA C. MCMULLEN AND N.D. CAMPBELL-PHILIPSEN

Earlier this year, the U.S. Supreme Court decision, *National Labor Relations Board (NLRB) v. Health Care and Retirement Corporation of America,* No. 92-1964, raised serious doubts as to whether nurses retain any collective bargaining power when they engage in patient care activities. (See Box 25-1.) On May 23, 1994, Justice Anthony M. Kennedy wrote the majority opinion that licensed practical nurses (LPNs) employed by Heartland Nursing Home in Urbana, Ohio were considered "supervisors" who acted in the "interest of their employer" when performing patient care duties. As a result, they were *not* eligible for protection under the amended National Labor Relations Act (NLRA), the law that guards against unfair labor practices and defends union activities and actions by employees. This finding reversed the position supported by the National Labor Relations Board—the agency which enforces the NLRA and provides a forum for employee grievances—and gave nurses across the country pause.

While this case dealt with LPNs who were the senior managerial people on the premises—an unlikely situation with employers other than nursing homes—many registered nurses (RNs), whether unionized or not, are concerned that they, too, will be affected. For, although LPNs are considered technical employees, the Board applied the identical supervisory test that it uses for professional RNs because the duties of both types of nurses at Heartland were virtually the same. (See 306 NLRB 68, 69, n. 5.) In fact, RNs in almost any setting are likely to find that they meet at least one of the 26 criteria for "supervisors" as determined by the NLRA. And, in the wake of the landmark 5–4 Supreme Court decision, a number of registered nurses are wondering if they are losing control of their professional practice—and their autonomy.

With approximately 20% of nurses in hospital settings currently being represented by unions, several questions come to mind: Can nursing's voice still be valued in designing and sustaining work environments that promote the delivery of high quality patient care? What other avenues of redress can nurses utilize if they experience employee–management problems, such as hospital downsizing or cross-training of nonprofessionals to carry out nursing functions under the supervision of remaining professional staff? Will members of the profession ever be able to gain back their leverage and collectively bargain in the future?

BOX 25–1 COLLECTIVE BARGAINING

COLLECTIVE BARGAINING is a procedure with the objective of reaching enforceable agreements between an employer and the representative of an organized group of employees (as opposed to an individual) concerning conditions of employment (e.g., hours, wages, grievances) that requires parties to deal fairly and openly with a shared goal of stabilizing labor and encouraging the free flow of commerce.

(Source: NLRA Sec. 8(5), 29 USCA Sec. 158(5))

The answers to these questions lie in fully exploring the history and facts behind the Supreme Court decision—as well as the opposing positions on the continuing collective bargaining controversy.

The NLRA: Protecting Employees' Rights?

Enacted on July 5, 1935, the NLRA (ch. 372, 49 Stat. 449) initially afforded *all* employees the right to organize and engage in collective bargaining activities with their employers, without fear of reprisal or interference. When employers realized that supervisory personnel also were allowed to collectively bargain, they argued in support of an amendment that would exclude these individuals because of the potential conflict within management.

Twelve years later, employers got their wish: Congress passed the Labor Management Relations Act of 1947, which amended the NLRA to exclude from coverage "any individual employed as a supervisor" (61 Stat. 137-138, codified at 29 U.S.C. 152(3)). However, at the same time, the amended Act expressly included "professional employees" within its protections.

What is the difference between these two types of workers? "Professional employees" are defined in the NLRA as individuals whose work is "predominantly intellectual and varied in character," and involves "consistent exercise of discretion and judgment." The term also applies to those whose work produces a result that "cannot be standardized in relation to a given period of time," and requires knowledge "in a field of science or learning . . . acquired by a prolonged course of specialized intellectual instruction and study in an institution of higher learning or a hospital" (29 U.S.C. 152(12)(a)).

Some examples of professional employees who are within the realm of the Act's protection include pharmacists, physicians, lawyers, faculty members, social workers, architects, and engineers. (See cases cited in 114 S.Ct. 1778, 1789, FN6-FN12.) In addition, this group includes individuals, such as nursing students, who are "performing related work under the supervision of a professional person to qualify himself to become a professional employee" (29 U.S.C. 152(12)(b)).

On the other hand, employees are considered "supervisors" under the amended NLRA if they meet three conditions. First, they must have the authority to perform one of 12 criteria, including hiring, transferring, suspending, laying off, recalling, promoting, or discharging other employees. In addition, employees must be able to assign, reward, discipline, or direct other workers, adjust their grievances, or effectively recommend such action. Second, this type of employee authority must require the use of independent judgment and not simply be routine or clerical in nature. And, third, the employee's activities must be "in the interest of the employer." (See 29 U.S.C. 152(11).) (Box 25-2)

BOX 25–2 **WHO IS A SUPERVISOR?**

The 26 factors listed below have been considered by the Courts in making the fact-specific determination as to whether a nurse is a supervisor or a covered employee under the National Labor Relations Act:

1. Does the employee recruit or refer, interview, screen, or hire workers?
2. Does the employee orient and/or train new workers?
3. Does the employee inform employees of new policies and procedures?
4. Does the employee prepare or revise work schedules?
5. Does the employee assign staff to patients?
6. Does the employee call off-duty workers or transfer employees to cover understaffing?
7. Does the employee recommend transfers?
8. Does the employee grant time-off?
9. Does the employee direct or re-direct workers?
10. Does the employee approve time cards and overtime?
11. Does the employee evaluate other workers' performance in writing?
12. Does the employee recommend pay adjustments?
13. Does the employee recommend or grant promotion?
14. Does the employee adjust grievances or make effective recommendations for adjustments or grievances?
15. Does the employee discipline or recommend discipline of another worker?
16. Does the employee issue, sign, and communicate disciplinary action to workers?
17. Does the employee suspend, discharge, layoff, or recall workers, or effectively recommend any of these motions?
18. How many people work for the employee in question?
19. Is the employee's superior always on call?
20. Does the employee attend supervisory meetings regularly?
21. If called to testify, would workers or other supervisors regard the employee as a supervisor?
22. Does the employee order supplies or have purchasing authority?
23. How many levels of supervisions exist within this particular department?
24. What percent of time does the employee spend performing non-supervisory functions?
25. Is the employee paid differently than other workers?
26. Does the employee receive any benefits or privileges not granted to non-supervisory workers?

Under the Board's test for supervisory status, however,

a nurse who in the course of employment uses independent judgment to engage in responsible direction of other employees [during patient care activities] is not a supervisor. Only a nurse who in the course of employment uses independent judgment to engage in one of the activities related to <u>another employee's job status or pay</u> *can qualify as a supervisor*

(114 S.Ct. 1778, 1782).

Moreover, according to the Board, nurses who act "for management not only in formulating but also in executing its labor policies" are the only ones who meet the NLRA's third condition, "in the interest of the employer" (114 S.Ct. 1778, 1782 (citing 67 S.Ct. at 795)). As demonstrated in a number of cases over the past 20 years, the NLRB has maintained that nurses who provide patient care are acting within the professional nature of the discipline and not in the interest of their employers. The Supreme Court decision surrounding this case illustrates that this phrase is not clearly defined in the amended National Labor Relations Act and continues to be open to interpretation.

The Facts of the Case

The NLRB's stance that nurses who assign patient care and exercise independent judgment can still be considered nonsupervisory personnel has gained a large following over the years—so much so, in fact, that *NLRB v. Health Care and Retirement Corporation of America* was initially decided in favor of the Board, the petitioner. To better understand the appeals process and the eventual Supreme Court decision, let us look at the nature of the original grievance.

In January 1989, four LPNs who were employed at Heartland Nursing Home—a nonunionized facility—complained to its corporate headquarters about a number of concerns shared by nurses at the institution. These issues included

> *disparate enforcement of its absentee policy, short staffing, low wages for nurses' aides, the [nursing home] unreasonably switching its prescription business from one pharmacy to another, which increased the nurses' paperwork, and management's failure to communicate with employees.*
>
> *(139 LRRM 1175)*

These nurses—who were among the senior ranking employees on duty after 5 p.m. during the week and at all times on weekends—had not been previously disciplined, and each had been employed at the nursing home for many years. Management from the corporate office visited the Urbana facility and met with them on more than one occasion. In fact, administrators even implemented some changes, such as hiring more aides and increasing the salaries of the aides, based upon their investigation of the complaints.

On March 2, 1989, a corporate management representative met with employees at Heartland to inform them of the results of their investigation. During this meeting, he noted that four nurses—two of whom were original complainants to corporate management—were "crossing their arms and rolling eyes in response to comments" (139 LRRM 1176). From this body language, the representative concluded that those clinicians "conveyed an attitude of 'resistance to change . . . to . . . make Heartland of Urbana a good facility'" (139 LRRM 1176). Based on his observations and perceptions, he decided to fire the nurses, stating they were terminated because of their "attitude" toward management (139 LRRM 1177).

One of the nurses who was fired then filed a complaint with the NLRB. She alleged unfair labor practices and that all four nurses had been illegally terminated for engaging in activity protected under the NLRA. Keep in mind that employees do not need to be in a union to file an unfair labor practice grievance, as these nurses did. One such grievance even might be that an employer is not permitting employees to organize a union.

Battling It Out in Court

What happened next? Over the next five years, the nurses, the NLRB, and Healthcare and Retirement Corporation of America—the parent corporation of Heartland Nursing Home—were embroiled in determining the definitions of "supervisor," "professional employee," and "in the interest of the employer." The case was appealed again and again by both parties until its petition for review was selected by the U.S. Supreme Court justices. This, in itself, was no small feat: Less than 3% of all such petitions are accepted by the Court (Chen, 1992.)

STEP ONE: HEARING BEFORE AN ADMINISTRATIVE LAW JUDGE

While the NLRB contended that the nurses had been unfairly disciplined, Health Care and Retirement Corporation of America argued that the LPNs were supervisory personnel and were, therefore, not covered under the amended NLRA. They based their argument on the fact that the LPNs were responsible for adequate staffing, made work assignments, supervised nursing assistants, resolved aides' problems and grievances, and assisted in the aides' performance evaluations.

What were the findings of the Administrative Law Judge (ALJ)? After considering both sides, he found that while the nurses gave certain kinds of orders to aides, and the aides executed the orders, the LPNs exercised that authority in a limited fashion. In fact, the nurses' primary responsibility was to ensure that the needs of the residents were met. Moreover, if nonroutine matters arose, the nurses called the administrator and the director of nursing at their homes. (See 306 NLRB 69, 72.)

Because the nurses' supervisory work did not "equate to responsibly directing the aides *in the interest of the employer*" and their focus was "on the well-being of the residents rather than of the employer," the ALJ ruled that they were not supervisors and, therefore, covered under the Act (306 NLRB 68, 70). Likewise, the NLRB found that the LPNs were employees and, therefore, were able to file a grievance. (See 306 NLRB 63, 63, n. 1.)

STEP TWO: APPEAL OF THE FINDINGS OF THE ALJ

Although the Administrative Law Judge ruled in favor of the four nurses on the definition of "supervisory employee," he found they had not been the victims of unfair labor practices. The general counsel prosecuting the case against Heartland Nursing Home filed exceptions with the NLRB, asking that the Board find unfair labor practices. The NLRB determined that the ALJ was incorrect, stating that the employer had discriminated against the nurses for engaging in concerted protected activity in violation of the NLRA. As a result, Heartland was ordered to reinstate the nurses with back pay and to stop engaging in unfair labor practices.

STEP THREE: APPEAL TO THE SIXTH CIRCUIT

Health Care and Retirement Corporation of America then appealed to the Sixth Circuit Court, claiming that the clinicians were disciplined because of an uncooperative attitude, not because of protected activity. Rather than addressing the issue of unfair labor practices, the circuit court judge reversed the NLRB decision and ruled that the four nurses did not come under the protection of the NLRA at all.

Why? Citing earlier cases as precedent, the judge found that the NLRB's test for determining supervisory status was inconsistent with the statute. In addition, the Court of Appeals held that the NLRB wrongly excluded patient care activities from being classified as supervisory in nature and that this exclusion had not been provided for under the Act.

To remedy this problem, the court determined that the test for whether a nurse is a supervisor will be the same as for any other employee in any other field. In essence, nurses who have discretion and meet any *one* of 26 functional tests used by the Courts—from recruiting employees to recommending promotion of others—will be considered "supervisors" and, therefore, be unable to file a grievance with the NLRB. (See 987 F.2d 1256 at 1259, 6th Cir. 1993.)

At the time of the ruling, the Court of Appeals also noted that "there is a history of conflict between the Board and the courts concerning the supervisory status of nurses employed at nursing homes" and concluded that "it is the courts, and not the Board, who bear the final responsibility for interpreting the law" (Ibid. at 1260).

STEP FOUR: APPEAL TO THE U.S. SUPREME COURT

To resolve the conflict between the National Labor Relations Board and the Court of Appeals, the U.S. Supreme Court was charged with deciding whether the Board's test was rational and consistent with the amended NLRA. On February 22, 1994, the Supreme Court heard arguments by the NLRB and Health Care and Retirement Corporation of America. And, on May 23, 1994, they reached a decision.

Five Justices—Anthony M. Kennedy, Sandra Day O'Connor, Antonin Scalia, Clarence Thomas, and Chief Justice William H. Rehnquist—held the majority opinion that the LPNs were indeed supervisory personnel who should be excluded from NLRA coverage. The other Justices—Ruth Bader Ginsberg, Harry A. Blackmun, John Paul Stevens, and David H. Souter—filed a dissenting opinion.

The Majority Opinion

In the 5 to 4 decision that affirmed the Court of Appeals, the Supreme Court concentrated on certain aspects of the case at hand. It did not address whether the activities of the nurses were collective bargaining or whether management's activities would have constituted a violation of the Act. (See 62 Law Week 4371.) The Court also declined to address the tension in the law resulting from the fact that "professional employees" are within the Act's protections simply because the NLRB did not argue it. Rather, the Supreme Court confined its opinion to interpreting the phrase "in the interest of the employer" and limited itself to the narrow determination that the NLRB's prior exclusion of patient care activities as supervisory in nature was inconsistent with the meaning of the NLRA.

After deliberation, the Court found that patient care is a nursing home's business because the patients are its customers. Additionally, it concluded that the NLRB must apply the same supervisory test to nurses as to other employees, noting that the Board had not used that test in this case, but had relied instead on the phrase "in the interest of the employer." Justice Kennedy also pointed out that because "the Board's interpretation of [that key phrase] is for the most part confined to nurse cases, our decision will have almost no effect outside that context" (114 S.Ct. 1778, 1785).

The Dissenting Opinion

Justice Ruth Bader Ginsberg disagreed with the majority decision, stating,

> The Court's opinion has implications far beyond the nurses involved in this case. If any person who may use independent judgment to assign tasks to others or direct their work is a supervisor, then few professionals employed by organizations subject to the Act will receive its protections.
>
> (114 S.Ct. 1778, 1792, 1793)

In her dissent, she touched on the purpose of the Act's definition of "supervisor," stating that it was "to limit the term's scope to 'the front line of management,' the 'foremen' who owed management 'undivided loyalty' as distinguished from workers with 'minor supervisory duties'" (114 S.Ct. 1778, 1786 (citing from Senate Report at 5, Legislative History 411)). Justice Ginsberg also addressed the overlap between the two types of authority—managerial and professional—and referred to remarks from *NLRB v. Res-Care, Inc.*:

Most professionals have some supervisory responsibilities in the sense of directing another's work—the lawyer his secretary, the teacher his teacher's aide, the doctor his nurses, the registered nurse her nurse's aide, and so on (114 S.Ct. 1778, 1788 (citing from 705 F.2d 1461, 1465. (CA7 1983)))

Arguing that the authority of nurses often arises from their superior skill, training, and experience, rather than flowing from management, Justice Ginsberg added:

Through case-by-case adjudication, the Board has sought to distinguish individuals exercising the level of control that truly places them in the ranks of management, from highly skilled employees, whether professional or technical, who perform, incidentally to their skilled work, a limited supervisory role. I am persuaded that the Board's approach is rational and consistent with the Act. I would therefore uphold the administrative determination, affirmed by the Board, that Heartland's practical nurses are protected employees."

(62 LW at 4375)

Where Do We Stand Now?

Although the Supreme Court decision was close, it obviously weakens the Board's authority to protect the activities of professional nurses. This decision will make it harder for nurses, and possibly other professionals, to unionize. It represents a significant withdrawal of NLRA protection for nurses.

"We are very concerned about the Court's decision because of its potential impact on registered nurses (RNs)," said Virginia Trotter Betts, JD, MSN, RN, president of the American Nurses Association (ANA), in a statement the day following the ruling.

[This decision] comes at a time of great cost-cutting in the healthcare industry. Nurses are being asked to do more with far less. Now is not the time to tell the frontline caregivers in hospitals that they can be fired for complaining about management decisions that are detrimental to patient care

(Werning, 1994).

How, then, do nurses deal with the legal realities? After all, the recent decision handed down by the Supreme Court will ensure that similar cases will be scrutinized more closely than ever before.

For now, future grievances should continue to be brought to the NLRB. Keep in mind, however, that an initial investigation of these grievances will include assessment of the nurse's "employee" versus "supervisory" status. For a case to be valid, the National Labor Relations Board will have to show substantial evidence that nurses do not perform any of the 26 supervisory functions—or, if they do, that their authority is merely routine or clerical in nature and not considered independent judgment.

In addition, because of the Supreme Court decision, activities based on patient care interests are not excluded from management interests. Therefore, nurses are likely to be deemed supervisors if they perform these functions in situations which are not simply "incidental to the performance of patient care services" (their normal professional duties). This determination of a nurse employee's status will be made on a case-by-case basis.

Remember, too, that the Supreme Court did not base its decision on the kind of work being done by the nurses, but on *whether the work was in the interest of the employer.* Other aspects of being a supervisor were not considered because the NLRB did not argue them. The exception that professional employees can organize and form bargaining units still exists, and it still applies to nurses unless they fall into one of the 12 statutory criteria.

A nurse who could argue that supervisory work was incidental to his or her professional duties could be "exempt" as a professional, and still be able to bargain collectively. On the other hand, a nurse manager or a nurse working at a small institution—as most nursing homes are—is very likely to be designated a "supervisor" in the future. The ability of these nurses to organize or bargain collectively appears to have been eliminated by this case. They are considered part of management, rather than employees, for bargaining purposes under the NLRA.

Where Do We Go From Here?

Of course, nurses who wish to maintain NLRA protection by avoiding any of these responsibilities will find it next to impossible in many settings. These activities often arise from professional expertise and cannot be performed adequately by those without it. Indeed, nurses who are concerned with patient care are not likely to abandon professional responsibilities such as patient assignment, monitoring of aides, or evaluating peers, in an effort to protect their collective bargaining rights.

So, what can be done? Unfortunately, modification through the Courts, if any, is usually a slow process. Future cases with distinguishing facts may encourage the Courts to create exceptions to this holding as it stands—or even to overrule it.

However, there is other action that can be taken. The Supreme Court majority opinion noted "if Congress wishes to enact the policies of the Board, it can do so without indistinction" (62 LW 4374). Here, the Court is telling nurses, as well as others concerned about the protection of employees in the United States, to seek changes by convincing their elected representatives to modify existing statutes or to enact new ones.

In addition to contacting senators and representatives in Congress, nurses also can write to their state nursing associations and request information on any proposals or plans under development. For example, the ANA—along with other labor representatives—is creating legislative language that would amend the NLRA and remedy the Supreme Court's decision. The amendment, which only relates to employees of health care institutions, would allow the NLRB to continue to determine on a case-by-case basis whether health care workers are supervisors or professional or technical employees (Ketter, 1994).

While the full impact of the Supreme Court ruling remains to be seen, one thing is certain: The controversy between issues of patient care, the definition of "professional employee" and the meaning of "in the interest of the employer" has only just begun. It is a positive sign for the collective bargaining rights of professional nurses that the dissent in this closely split Supreme Court decision presented a potent argument for future cases.

REFERENCES

Chen, A.C. (1992, October). Equal justice under law: Beneath the robes of the Supreme Court. *Healthcare Trends & Transition*, 4(1), 24–26, 78.

Ketter, J. (1994, October). Employers use Supreme Court decision against RNs: ANA devises legal, legislative strategies. *The American Nurse*, pp. 1, 7.

NLRB v. Health Care & Retirement Corp, of America, 114 S.Ct. 1778, 128 L.Ed.2d 586, 62 USLW 4371, 146 LRRM (BNA) 2321, 128 Lab. Cas. P 11.090 (U.S., May 23, 1994) (NO. 92–1964)

Werning, S. (1994, November/December). Supreme court decision prompts nursing action [Trends in Transition]. *Healthcare Trends & Transition*, 6(2), 4–5.

CHAPTER 26

●●●

Technology, Deskilling, and Nurses: The Impact of the Technologically Changing Environment

RUTH G. RINARD

A recent article in the *New York Times*[1] described the changing environment of health care practice. Increased competition between managed care organizations, shorter hospital stays, radical reorganization of delivery systems, and the downsizing of hospitals all figured into the picture. Nurses have wondered how these pressures of rationalizing and commodification of health care would affect them. Indeed, the California State Nurses Association has mounted an advertising campaign to highlight their concerns: "Hospitals and HMOs are cutting care to make record profits. Patients are paying the price. Just ask any nurse who provides direct care."[2(p199)] Despite appeals to the public in the name of safety, informal talk among nurses uncovers basic, deep fears that the changes will lead to the substitution of less skilled, less trained, and less well-paid workers to accomplish tasks now done by nurses.

But these concerns are not new. Since World War II the nursing environment has experienced several distinct waves of technological change. Each change produced debates, fears, and even anguish about the nature of nursing skill and its valuation. Although these concerns about skills and internal histories of the profession have often been read as a part of a story about new roles, increasing education, and research in nursing, a less positivistic, less internalist stance reveals another story. It is the story of the fragmentation and deskilling of nursing under the impact of massive technological changes introduced since the Second World War. It is the story of the production and reproduction of social relations within an increasingly corporate capitalistic health care environment. It is the story of the creation and re-creation of gendered jobs.

This article examines the question of deskilling in nursing since 1950. It will address four concerns. First, did the impact of technological change in this period lead to

Reprinted from *Advances in Nursing Science,* 18(4): pp. 60–69, 1996 with permission of Aspen Publishers, Inc., © 1996.

deskilling? And if so, how did it occur, and how was consent to deskilling obtained? Third, what attempts, if any, were made to forestall the process, and how successful were they? And finally, can anything be learned by nursing from this story of the impact of and responses to technological change?

Theoretical Concerns

The story of the technological changes that swept across nursing in the past 50 years and the response to them lies at the intersection of three distinct bodies of literature: the history of technology, labor process theory, and gender studies. Concepts from each of these fields will be explored and then applied to an examination of the transformation of nursing under the impact of technological change.

TECHNOLOGY

Technology has held an important place in U.S. culture. Indeed, our identity and national character have been intimately associated with the application of scientific knowledge to practical problems. In the narrow sense, American fascination with technology encompasses machines and innovations. But in a wider sense it also includes the systematic organization of tasks. Americans have generally regarded technical innovations as arising spontaneously and rather inexplicably from the genius of the inventor. Even mass efforts are seen as largely exogenous, dependent on American character. Because of this, historical explanation is often inadequately considered in the literature on technology, and the explanation of changes often relies on a more or less crude technological determinism.[3,4] Thus, technology seems to take on a life of its own, as if it had an internal dynamic that, when unleashed, explains social changes tautologically.

In addition to this unexplained causal determinism in the older literature of technology and medicine, the choice of technologies is often obscured as well. One is led to assume that a particular technology was introduced because it was more efficient, more rational, or more cost-effective than the technologies it replaced as is *ipso facto* demonstrated by its adoption in the first place.[5] Little, if any, attention is given to the fact that alternate technological pathways might have been present or that social factors or government largesse might influence the adoption of a particular technology regardless of cost, efficiency, or rationality. Yet a few studies have highlighted just such factors.[6,7] They suggest that the introduction of technology and accompanying social changes are not rooted in some positivistic essence of technology, but rather that technology itself, and the responses to it, are determined by social forces in the culture at the time, including the important social relations of production. In periods of change, choices exist both about the shape of technology and its relationship to worker skill.[8]

The literature on the history of technology thus offers several insights pertinent to a study of nursing's response to the introduction of technology. First, technology is not confined to the introduction of machines. It includes changes at the site of production, in the transfer of production between work stations, and in the coordination of the two. The dramatic increase in the numbers and types of drugs used by nurses is similar to the introduction of machines in manufacturing. The development of specialized care units and their equipment is similar to batch processing. In industry, critical care information systems are similar to automated manufacturing. All these activities represent the introduction of technology into nursing.

The history of technology also suggests that the introduction of technologies and the response to them are influenced by the structure of social relations surrounding their use.

While technologies have a material base, their meaning, use, and skill valuations have more to do with historically determined cultural and social forces.

LABOR PROCESS

Recently, American labor economists have been primarily concerned with the creation of high-wage jobs. They have not often, however, used Marxian concepts in their analysis. English economists have made more use of the perspective to look at the labor process—the relationships people enter into as they transform raw nature into useful goods. The labor process involves both relations with others at the point of production in the hospital or community and the practical activities including technologies that create useful goods like wellness. Within a Marxian analysis of capitalism, it is through the labor process that the distinctive relations of capitalistic societies between those who produce the necessities of life and those who live off the product of others, between those who produce a surplus and those who expropriate it, are maintained. As technological changes occur in the drive to accumulate capital, there is a corresponding drive to recreate the social relations of production. So one of the questions to be asked is how, as the technological changes are introduced into nursing, are the social relations of a capitalistic society maintained?

In *Labor and Monopoly Capital*, Harry Bravermann[9] looked at these issues. He argued that the introduction of mechanization and automation in combination with modern management techniques has led to a deskilling of work. Using the efficiency studies of Taylorism, job components were increasingly separated and each subjected to the rigors of closer management scrutiny. As jobs were subdivided, ever-tighter policies specifying each step were introduced. The eventual result was a separation of the conception of a job from its execution. The traditional skill content of jobs was destroyed and a homogenous, degraded working population created. Intensity of work increased, and social relations of production were maintained during technological change. Wagner[10] applied these ideas to the rise of hospital nursing to show how deskilling occurred with the embrace of Taylorism.

Bravermann's work has been critiqued by a number of authors[11,12] and most extensively by Burawoy[13] in *Manufacturing Consent*. He showed how workers are inclined to accept deskilling to gain relative satisfaction in the game of making it on the shop floor, thereby obscuring and mystifying the expropriation of unpaid labor. He showed how the creation of an internal labor market served to diffuse resentment toward management and redirect it toward coworkers. He showed how skill devaluation involved in the consent to technological change maintains the social relations of production.

GENDER

Studies from a gender perspective have added much to the understanding of nursing.[14,15] But integration of the insights drawn from feminism with those from studies of capitalism, while beginning, has not yet been fully achieved.[12,16] Two aspects of gender studies of work as they relate to labor process theory are important in this study.

The first concerns the description of skill. Are there ways in which the description and valuation of skills are gendered? To what extent are tacit skills, skills acquired by women *qua* women in their domestic and social lives, outside of the workplace? What skills have been construed as naturally feminine, and do they include or exclude emerging technologies? And if skills are gendered, how does that affect a deskilling process? Tantalizing suggestions about these issues can be found in Benson[17] and Wood.[18]

A second aspect of gender studies concerns the creation of consent to technological deskilling. In introducing new technology, does management use gender construction developed in the wider culture to secure acquiescence to deskilling? Sturdy, et al,[11] and Knights and Willmott[12] explored this perspective.

Method

A content analysis of the *American Journal of Nursing*, the first and foremost nursing journal in the postwar period, was undertaken in 5-year intervals. The content examined included advertisements and recruitment notices as well as published articles and regular departments. Changes were noted in types of articles, in the introduction of new departments, and in the changing character and appeal of advertisements and recruitment notices. Its purpose was to provide a historical and empirical look at the technologies introduced and nurses' responses. Such a content analysis is necessary to hear the voices of ordinary nurses and nursing leaders as they responded to technological changes, defined objective skills, and defended tacit ones. It provides a way to understand how nurses, as women, accepted, rejected, and finally consented to technological change. On the basis of this content analysis, a rough periodization was constructed. The first period, from 1950 to 1960, was characterized by the introduction of medical techniques and a myriad of new drugs. A second period, from 1965 to 1980, saw the introduction of electronic machinery and specialized care units. The third period, from 1980 to the present, introduced technologies to control, streamline, and predict care.

Results

1950 TO 1960

The flavor of the immediate postwar period found its way into the pages of the *American Journal of Nursing*. The fascination with the technology that won the war was apparent. Ads for Plexitron drip chambers drew on atomic imagery. The chambers produced a "flashball" when squeezed.[19] Television broadcasts of surgical procedures caused a gee whiz excitement.[20] But the threat of the Cold War also had the American Medical Association advertising in the *Journal* against national health insurance as socialized medicine.[21] It was a period when social roles narrowed. The marriage age dropped, and many nurses left the profession for childbearing. Good personal adjustment and absence of conflict with coworkers were proclaimed the criterion of good nursing. Nurses, like other women, were targeted by advertisements in the *Journal* as consumers of a vast array of new products—Jell-O, frozen orange juice, Dacron uniforms, cellophane tape, and Gerber's baby food.

What technological changes were introduced during this period? The first and most important was the introduction of new medicines. In 1950 advertisements for medicines were confined to Dermassage, Desitin, Riasol for psoriasis, and baby formula. By 1955 the number of medicines available had grown enormously. Penicillin and Ilotyan antibiotic drops were advertised.[22] Archromycin—the easy-to-take medicine with its "special dropper etched to measure each dose quickly"[23(p137)]—competed for the nurse's attention with tetracycline and Terramycin. The new psychoactive drugs, reserpine and chlorpromazine, it was hoped, would transform mental hospitals.

Use of intravenous (IV) fluids increased in this period.[24] In some states venipuncture was not considered appropriate for the nursing role. In other states it was done by a special team of nurses during the day and by doctors and residents at night. Large quantities of IV fluids were used—1,000 mL over 4 hours, 3,000 mL during one shift. Intravenous carts that could care for 8 to 10 patients at a time were developed. A nurse could spend most of her time starting, stopping, and adjusting these rapid infusions.

With new methods for separation and preservation, blood products became available. Use went up dramatically. In one hospital the assistant director of nursing was responsible for drawing blood promptly when community volunteer donors appeared so as "not to keep them waiting."[25(p320)] Albumin, fibrinogen, and gamma globulin were available in 1955. A patient might be given 20 to 30 transfusions as a source of protein for body repair over several days.[25] The technology of blood products and their transfusions drastically changed the labor process experienced by ordinary nurses.

Still other devices were introduced in this period. Electric call bells, pneumatic tubes, and intercoms changed nurses' relationships with patients and other hospital departments. Since many new drugs including penicillin were given intramuscularly every 2 hours, increased use of these drugs meant increased demand for sterilizing and resharpening needles for reuse. The number of autoclaves expanded, with one for each service area.[26] Oxygen therapy with tents became widely used. Oxygen was pumped from wall units directly into incubators, also a new piece of equipment, for "convenient infant care" before concerns developed about retrolental fibroplasia.[27]

What was nurses' response to these technological changes? The separation of tasks entailed by the changes made many fear that the hospital was turning into a factory and the nurse into a technician. One letter writer exclaimed: "The assignment methods . . . make the average nurse more of a robot than a woman. This system puts nursing on the factory level. Her assignments are her assembly line. . . . [It] makes the nurse all hands, little head and hardly any heart."[28(p4)] Another letter writer wondered "if the patient has any feeling . . . that he is on an assembly line?"[29(p258)]

The changes also brought a sense of loss for many nurses. One nurse wrote, "There is something tragic in a nurse who has failed to find anything to replace that lost vision. She rather resembles a player piano—mechanically perfect, but without the something that makes the music come alive "[30(p342)] Advertisements for lotion echoed the same theme: Pictures portraying "oxygen in every room," "plenty of antibiotics," and "new and greater x-rays" were dismissed with the caption, "But what is the state of the patient's back so long as he lies in bed?"[31(p34)] Another nurse wrote, "What has become of the old-fashioned nurse? Nurses are not ready today to give comfort—they'll give a pill, or a needle, or keep charts, yes, but that seems to be the extent of their duties. Actually, anyone can master skills, but nursing is a true vocation."[32(p260)] The sense of loss was connected with the decline of "personal bodily care" for "the patient's sake."[33(p804)]

There was a widespread sense that nursing skill, a tacit agreement of personalized caring associated with feminine identity, was threatened by new technical demands and the subsequent separation of tasks and fragmentation of work. Cultural expectations for women at this time simply did not include being called on to understand the working of new devices or to take responsibility for troubleshooting their problems. One recruitment ad for Yale New Haven Hospital made this cultural norm explicit: "Do it yourself isn't just for men. If you think this is a silly ad, you're right."[34(p616)] The dilemma as one writer put it was, "How can we mechanize the procedures as far as the patient's door, and personalize them within the room?"[35(p1099)]

How did nursing leaders respond to the dilemmas posed by technical change? If old craft traditions and tacit skills learned by women *qua* women in their roles in families and communities were being undermined, perhaps it was possible to reclaim them by seeking to objectify them in the language of the social sciences. Articles in the *Journal* speak to this process. The skills of talking with patients were emphasized.[36] An editorial asserted, "We believe the application of social skills is the essential part of professional nursing."[37(p45)] As nursing moved into higher education, differentiation between a "technical" nurse and a "professional" one depended on the ability to discuss tacit skills in a social scientific jargon. Nursing leaders, through strong logical positivistic leanings, seem to have believed that naming tacit skills in suitably academic language gave those skills an objective reality. They seem to have believed that simply naming was enough to reclaim lost skills and forestall changes in the labor process brought by technological change. Given their positivistic framework, they could not see that tacit skills and technological changes depended on underlying social relations. Perhaps the social scientific redefinition of tacit skills only served to fragment nursing and reproduce gendered skills.

Management and manufacturers of the new technology also promoted a gendered accommodation to the new changes. The appeal was the same as that to housewives for consumer goods in the postwar period. Alevaire, a bronchial nebulizer, was advertised as like a detergent. New drugs were presented as conveniences like the baby formula and toothpaste that nurses bought as wives for their families. New devices like the Circolectric bed and the Aeroflush sanitary disposal were convenient time savers like vacuums and washing machines. And just as possession of appliances and gadgets gave housewives reflected status by what it revealed about their husband's income, so management's recruitment ads tried to lure nurses with the promise of reflected status to the hospital with the newest radiology equipment or surgical suites.

1965 TO 1980

In the 1960s and 1970s, new nursing environments were created by a different sort of technological change—the organization of specialized care units. Machines of all kinds—dialysis units, cardiac monitors, fetal monitoring and automatic recording devices—were associated with the development of these units. The rapidity of these changes, with the exception of a couple of articles, was almost unnoticed in the pages of the *American Journal of Nursing*. However, comments in letters and advertisements amply document the change. The editorial for the one issue with articles on technology declared,

> *If the nurse has an uneasy feeling about today's wondrous machines, some of which seem to be encroaching on her practice, she's not much different from other people. Much as it is* <u>natural</u> *to resist them, we'll have to get used to them because they're here.*[38(p67)]

What to make of them because they were here is another matter. Some thought the significance of the recording machines lay in reduced disputes with physicians: "The nurse and the physician can ascertain simultaneously . . . the vital signs."[39(p69)] Others marveled at the degree of individual variation the machine revealed. Still others saw more clearly that the new machines required new learning and new responsibility.[40(p76)] Dialysis nurses pointed in this direction by talking of "technical nursing observation" skills.[41(p83)] But this view was editorially dismissed:

> *Today's machines, especially electronic ones, are forcing us to see machines in a new perspective. Since we* can't *be expected to be expert in electrical engineering, we have no choice but to leave that to others and keep our focus on the patient to which the machine is attached* [italics added].[38(p67)]

Although the official view in the *Journal* left no room for new valuations of skills, ads and letters spoke to the pervasive reality of technological change. One Pacquins ad from 1960 was particularly striking.[42] All previous Pacquins ads showed gracefully draped, polished, ring-adorned hands.[43] But this one showed unpolished hands holding a syringe ready for injection. Earlier recruitment ads had stressed new equipment or new surgical suites as belonging to the hospital. Now recruitment ads emphasized special technical skills belonging to the individual nurse. Letters give evidence of increased conflict between nurses around workplace-generated valuation of skill. One letter writer snidely remarked, "Knowledge of family and community will be lost in the pursuit of higher knowledge that says—this is an inverted T wave."[44(p246)] A few writers even spoke of the creative uncertainty within limits that the new machines afforded as an antidote to the deskilled drudgery of most nursing work.

The period from 1965 to 1980 saw the creation of highly technical new work environments but also a studied refusal to look seriously at them. This refusal, it seems, was grounded in the belief that objective skills had already been defined and that feminine nature left no room for other new skill evaluations.

1980 TO 1990

The technological changes from 1980 to 1990 involved attempts to control, streamline, and predict care. They ranged from institutionwide computerized information systems to novel organizational structures to linkages between segments within health care. These technological changes, spurred by government-imposed cost control measures, are still in progress. Once again, very few of these changes appeared in the pages of the *Journal*. There were a few scattered references to early health maintenance organizations as news items but no discussion of their implications for the labor process of nursing. Similarly, ambulatory care centers raised concerns about the survival of the nursing role in this setting. How, one writer worried, could you have an identity if you were not delivering nursing services or writing care plans?[45]

What was more apparent in the pages of the *Journal* was the cost of the disjunction between the social scientific attempt to describe tacit skills and the real environment of the labor process. An editorial proclaimed that "nursing is coming into its own" but acknowledged at the very end that "nurses themselves say they are under stress."[46(p1587)] A letter writer complained that she was a "coma specialist" performing automatic, unconscious tasks.[47(p1588)] Still another called herself an "artificial nurse": "You want to assess and plan and meet psycho-social needs," she wrote, "and this is what you get in a shift—checking IVs, refusing meds, O masks, pain shots, housekeeping stuff, and dealing with docs."[48(p248)] Yet an article on stress in nursing did not explore causes in the technological changes affecting the work environment itself, but rather offered tips on "how to make it work for you" through jogging, relaxation exercises, and expression of feelings.[49(p912)]

Discussion

The story of the impact of technological change on nursing from 1950 to 1990 is thus a story of deskilling. The introduction of new machines and equipment and of specialized care units and electronic monitoring and the transformation of nursing by information system technology continues to radically alter daily routines of nurses. This change was experienced by nurses as a deskilling in the Bravermannian sense. The tacit empathic and relational skills that had been acquired in the process of forming a culturally acceptable feminine identity were difficult to articulate. But their objectification in the language of social science did not render them less gendered. Furthermore, the fact of naming these socially constructed tacit skills made it more difficult for nurses either to see or to value other skills introduced or demanded by technological change.

Only as the hold of feminine cultural identity loosened in the 1970s and wider models became possible were nurses able to acknowledge, and in some cases even value for themselves, new technical skills. But because skills are not primarily objective categories, but are rather a system of socially valued activities and attributes, glimmering recognition of new skills by nurses themselves was not enough.

Many of the new technological skills had formerly been the exclusive province of the largely male medical staff. As the skills crossed gender lines, they became devalued, merely technical things that anyone with a little training could do. The feminine cultural traits of patience, observation, and orderliness were now attached to the very same tasks. And the task itself became transformed into one suitable for women.

But the cultural valuation of technological innovation also played a significant role. Once a technological procedure was removed from the realm of novelty and performed more routinely, it became less interesting, even dull. It was no longer a cutting-edge skill. Even when it was apparent in the 1980s and 1990s that the naive, optimistic faith in technology of the 1950s was no longer viable and that technology had created unanticipated problems, solutions proposed by nurses were regarded not as valued innovations, part of the march of progress. They were viewed as minor tinkering. And when practical solutions to human predicaments relied on relational skills to discern distress, to comfort, and to motivate patients caught up in complicated medical procedures, they were evaluated on both technological and gender grounds. Against the technology *cum* gender landscape, nursing activities continued to be less valued on both counts.

Implications for the Future

The story of the changes in the work environment for nurses caused by the successive waves of technological change from 1950 to 1990 has implications for nursing as it continues to confront technological change. The major implication is that a logicopositivistic view of knowledge and skills has limited flexible responses to changed work environments. Historically, it has provided an inadequate basis for a response on several counts. First, it assumed that the content of tacit knowledge can be fully objectified. As letters of the time indicate, however, few who experienced deeply a loss of skill felt that their work had been fully or adequately represented in the new academic jargon. Because skills are dynamic social constructions, it may not be possible to exhaust tacit meanings and translate them into objective language. Second, the professional legitimation of nursing through social science research was simply too narrow a part of cultural discourse to provide the hoped-for result. Third, the belief that nursing skill had been objectified, which was fostered by the positivistic assumptions about knowledge, prevented a serious examination of technological change. It encouraged ignoring huge parts of nurses' experience in the labor environment.

Finally, the positivistic stance towards knowledge, accelerated by nursing's move to the academy in the 1960s, resulted in a static view of feminine nature. It could not be conceptualized as a more fluid social entity that might have provided nursing with more flexible responses to technological change. Adopting the view of knowledge as a social construction will allow us to see skills and their valuation as part of a broader historicosocial process, within which nursing exists, that includes changing concepts of technology, labor process, and gender. This view will, it is hoped, give us the understanding and flexibility to deal with continuing technologically produced changes in our environment.

REFERENCES

1. House budget committee, 24 to 17, approves 7-year plan to wipe out federal budget deficit. *New York Times.* May 11, 1995:A1, A6.
2. Gordon S. Cutbacks or caregivers: is there a nurse in the house? *Nation.* 1994;258:199–204.

3. Kranzberg M. *Technology and Culture.* New York, NY: Shocken; 1972.
4. Hughes T. *Development of Western Technology since 1500.* New York. NY: Macmillan; 1964.
5. Sigerist H. *A History of Medicine.* New York, NY: Oxford University Press, 1961.
6. Smith M. *Harpers Ferry and the New Technology.* Ithaca, NY: Cornell University Press; 1961.
7. Noble D. *Forces of Production: A Social History of Automation.* New York, NY: Knopf; 1984.
8. Cockburn C. *Brothers: Male Dominance and Technological Change.* London, England: Pluto Press; 1983.
9. Bravermann H. *Labor and Monopoly Capital: The Degradation of Work in the Twentieth Century.* New York, NY: Monthly Review Press; 1974.
10. Wagner D. The proletarianization of nursing in the United States, 1932–1946. *Int J Health Sci.* 1980;10:271–290.
11. Sturdy A, Knights D, Willmott H. *Skill and Consent.* London, England: Routledge; 1992.
12. Knights D, Willmott H. *Gender and the Labour Process.* Brookfield, Vt: Gower, 1986.
13. Burawoy M. *Manufacturing Consent.* Chicago, Il: Chicago University Press; 1979.
14. Melosh B. *The Physician's Hand.* Philadelphia, Pa: Temple University Press; 1982.
15. Reverby S. *Ordered to Care.* Cambridge, England: Cambridge University Press; 1987.
16. West J. *Work Women, and the Labour Market.* London, England: Routledge; 1982.
17. Benson S. *Counter Cultures: Saleswomen, Managers, and Customers in American Department Stores, 1890–1960.* Urbana. Ill: University of Illinois Press: 1986.
18. Wood S. *The Degradation of Work? Skill, Deskilling and the Labour Process.* London, England: Hutchinson: 1982.
19. [Advertisement]. *Am J Nurs.* 1955;55:514.
20. McConnel M. Surgery on television. *Am J Nurs.* 1950;50:227–278.
21. Shafer G. Compulsory health insurance for Americans? No! *Am J Nurs.* 1950;50:542–543.
22. [Advertisement]. *Am J Nurs.* 1955;55:32.
23. [Advertisement]. *Am J Nurs.* 1955;55:137.
24. Anderson B. Nursing service and the law. *Am J Nurs.* 1955;55:438–439.
25. Crews H. Small hospital blood bank. *Am J Nurs.* 1955;55:320–321.
26. Edelson R. Organizing the nursing service for a new hospital. *Am J Nurs.* 1955;55:198–201.
27. [Advertisement]. *Am J Nurs.* 1955;55:219.
28. [Letter]. *Am J Nurs.* 1950;50:4.
29. [Letter]. *Am J Nurs.* 1950;50:258.
30. [Letter]. *Am J Nurs.* 1950;50:342.
31. [Advertisement]. *Am J Nurs.* 1950;50(9):34.
32. [Letter]. *Am J Nurs.* 1955;55:260.
33. Lesser M, Kearns V. Nursing and bodily care. *Am J Nurs.* 1955;55:804–806.
34. [Advertisement]. *Am J Nurs.* 1955;55:616.
35. Brandt P. Work can be vacation too. *Am J Nurs.* 1955;55:1099.
36. Peplau H. Talking with patients. *Am J Nurs.* 1960;60:964–966.
37. [Editorial]. *Am J Nurs.* 1960;60:45.
38. [Editorial]. *Am J Nurs.* 1965;65:67.
39. George J. Electronic monitoring of vital signs. *Am J Nurs.* 1965;65:68–71.
40. Imboden C, Wynn J. Coronary care area. *Am J Nurs.* 1965;65:72–76.
41. Tsurk C. Hemodialysis for acute renal failure. *Am J Nurs.* 1965;65:80–85.
42. [Advertisement]. *Am J Nurs.* 1960;60:1727.
43. [Advertisement]. *Am J Nurs.* 1955;55:25.
44. [Editorial]. *Am J Nurs.* 1970;70:246.
45. Engelke M. Nursing in ambulatory settings: a head nurse's perspective. *Am J Nurs.* 1980;80:1813–1815.
46. [Editorial]. *Am J Nurs.* 1980;80:1587.
47. Pillette P. Caution: objectivity and specialization may be hazardous to your health. *Am J Nurs.* 1980;80:1588–1590.
48. Pope M. Thoughts from an artificial nurse. *Am J Nurs.* 1975;75:248–249.
49. Scully R. Stress in the nurse. *Am J Nurs.* 1980;80:912–917.

CHAPTER 27

●●

The Seven Basic Rules
for Successful Redesign

TIM PORTER-O'GRADY

It certainly should come as no surprise to anyone that at this time in our history, everything is changing.[1] The global shift from the industrial age to the social technical future is well under way.[2] The impact of the transformation is being felt in both the workplace and social settings. There simply is no place to hide from the scope and intensity of the changes confronting every society and political structure on the globe.

The problem with the current change being experienced is that no one can really cope with its rate, scope, or intensity. Changes we never expected or desired become conditions of our lives and force us to confront what they bring to us and challenge us to accommodate them within our values and our lives.[3]

New realities are affecting work, its structure, and the design of new models. Some of the realities emerging that indicate the need for new approaches to work and work relationships are:

- The emergence of the computer as the primary vehicle for managing information and disseminating it as necessary to inform and connect people in all kinds of environments;
- The rise of information as the new architecture for organizations linking people and information in a way that allows people to function well, no matter where they are located;
- The requirement to build different work relationships in light of the impact of information technology on the way we manage systems, people, processes, and outcomes;
- The necessity to build on the "point of service" and construct the organizational supports around the worker and customer to facilitate rather than impede that relationship;
- The need for new, yet fewer leadership roles that require a higher level of competence and confidence than what often was acceptable in the old paradigm;

- Now there are higher levels of expectation from those who do work: both competence and interdependence rank high as appropriate behaviors for the worker in the emerging paradigm.

The leader in today's world must be comfortable with the ambiguities and conflicts that being in a state of change engenders. She or he must be able to harness the energy of change and use it to keep the organization focused on the work and purposes of the system.[4] Furthermore, the leader must be able to produce sustainable change that reflects a commitment to consistent application of the principles and rules of good change. In the earnestness to produce results quickly, the leader often can sacrifice those processes and principles which undergird real and meaningful change. Understanding the basic rules of effective change and applying them consistently can mean the difference between solid change and a passing fad.

Rule 1: No Exceptions

The change the world is experiencing leaves no one untouched. It will affect the way people do things and the way they view themselves as citizens of the world.[5] From newborns to the very old, the global changes will affect the way people live their lives, interact, and manage their affairs on a daily basis. Children now learn the intricacies of technology with Sega™ or Nintendo™ even before they can speak in full sentences.[6] The elderly receive their government checks through electronic transfer and do their banking over the phone, and most people now prefer to use the computerized teller machine because it is faster and does everything the human teller normally does. From communication to work products, technology is changing everything and everyone.

What is critical in the emerging role of the leader, in these circumstances, is to communicate successfully to all people that they are affected by transformation and are therefore required to respond to it at some level in their lives. No more can people say or act as though they are exempt from the vagaries of change. Change demands that we all recognize the transition and respond to it, engage it, and give it the form necessary to derive both meaning and direction from it.[7]

The notion that somehow these changes do not apply to certain individuals has been historically rampant in many work organizations. Health care facilities have been notorious for accommodating those who do not seek to embrace the necessary changes and thus, make it difficult for those who do. These people hold hostage those who seek to make change work well. They imprison their work group to their reaction to the change and increase the difficulty in building the necessary changes in the organization.

This is not a very successful strategy for constructing the future of health care. It no longer is optional to withdraw from the work of change or to actively work against it. There is no room or time to tolerate those who do not wish to engage the demands of a changing health care system. With the changes that are occurring in health care, there is no time to oppose the dynamics that are forcing health services to reconfigure themselves in newer ways to respond to a changing payment and service marketplace.[8]

There must be a level of honesty in the organization if it will successfully undertake the kind of changes necessary to position itself in a radically changing health care system. The organization can no longer afford to "carry" those who do not or cannot support the necessary redesign which improves a health facility's service and cost framework for a changing marketplace. Those who have had trouble embracing changes in the past will be challenged greatly by these circumstances. Leaders will have to use creative strategies to engage staff members in the change process or, if not, help them make other choices about their roles and their lives.[9] There are some fundamental expectations that must be clear in the new work milieu:

- The real significance of any change must be communicated broadly and clearly to as many people in the organization as possible.
- No more secrets. Everyone is a stakeholder and has a right to know what is really going on.
- No more myths about information confidentiality. Information rarely is as confidential as we think it is. If two or more people know something, it is no longer confidential. Just how many people does it take to make information no longer confidential? It is the patient's rights we must protect, not confidentiality.
- All people are required to respond to the changes that confront them. No escape points are allowed in the organization.
- Everyone must give notice of their response to specific changes in the organization. Every participant must respond to the change and indicate to their colleagues what that response is.
- The leader must be clear that the message regarding response must be followed up by action that is congruent with embracing the change. If certain staff members find this difficult, it must be addressed and strategies must be defined to assist them to engage the changes or to make the decision to leave.
- Everyone needs options. All persons should be aware of what their options are in relation to necessary changes. Participating in building toward the future will be the ticket into it. The roles that people may play always are subject to change. Staff members must be flexible about how they contribute to making the changes successful.

These are very exciting times in health care. It is rare that one has such a clear opportunity to participate in writing the future script for health. One of the rules of engagement regarding change is that you must be present to respond well. If we are not present during the dialogue and the design, the design unfolds anyway; it is simply missing the contribution of those who are not at the table.[10] That is a tragedy for all involved. When key stakeholders are not involved in planning change, there is a lasting negative impact on the whole organization. Those essential to the dialogue must be fully immersed in it.

Rule 2: Read the Signposts

As American health care moves toward a new paradigm, it simply is not possible to see the end of the redesign road, and it will not be possible for some time.[11] The complexities involved in making the change preclude a solid image of what the system will look like "down the road." It is not important that we know anyway.

The complexity of great change can be overwhelming. There simply is too much to be able to visualize in one sweeping view. Forces at work are changing the core processes and structures to which we have become fully accustomed.[12] It is not possible to enumerate what will happen to either process or structure with any great clarity at any given moment in the change process.

The one skill that is imperative during times of great social change, however, is the ability to read the signposts. Through discernment, the leader gets a sense of how the changes converge to indicate the direction in which they are leading. The leader can use the insight to give more form and substance to the change and ensure that change activities are congruent with the character or direction of change.

To understand these signposts:

- Look beyond health care: read about and visualize the trends in a global context affecting what and how we do things.
- Enumerate the driving forces for the change, be they economic and financial, social and cultural, process and structure, or any other combination.
- Personalize the changes to the organization's culture or service and ask questions as to how well organizational practices reflect the changes.
- Read the futurist authors in health care and other journals so that the landscape of the future begins to take shape. With new insights, the leadership can begin to design for the future rather than react to it.
- Convene a leadership futures group to put form to the dialogue and focuses the perceptions of the future on the organization, system, or affected discipline.
- Translate the views of the future into action plans and work processes. Indicate how far the organization is from the desired changes and what has to be done to incorporate them into the organization's own work.

If we are to be ready for the future, we must see what the indicators tell us and build on what can be discerned reasonably.[13] Leaders will not always be right in what they see, but if they are critical in their analysis of the signposts, they will be substantially correct. True leadership is seeing the challenges ahead, identifying the risks, and moving carefully but confidently through them. Openly engaging the processes of change makes all the difference and ensures a place at the table as the changes move from concept to reality.

Rule 3: Construct a Vision

People need more than good process to give meaning to their energies, their work. They need to find meaning in what they do. If meaning cannot be found in their work, giving it direction and value, people will construct it outside the work they do. The problem with defining one's value solely through their work processes is that when functions and activities change, transforming the people is nearly impossible because their meaning is found only in those processes. Devoid of other sources of meaning, they tenaciously cling to things they know how to do now.[14]

An essential role of the leader is to help people find meaning in the purposes for work, not just in the work itself. The meaning for work should go beyond mere task and function. It is here that the organization's vision becomes critical. A vision is full of meaning and purpose; rather than tell what an organization does, it says what it is. An organizational vision gives people both meaning and direction sufficiently full of value that they are willing to commit their energies and their work to it.[15]

A vision takes people beyond their work and places them squarely in the middle of completing an important work that affects the quality and value of life and the direction of humankind. It has spiritual as well as work implications and allows every person to see his/her role in the context of the purposes to which it is directed. It is pivotal to finding meaning in all the efforts of work.

There are some unique considerations for constructing a viable vision:

- A vision cannot be constructed unilaterally. Every stakeholder at every level of the organization must participate if ownership of the vision is to be obtained throughout the organization.
- The vision has to be of sufficient breadth to obtain wide-ranging commitment to it. It should be of such strength that people have little difficulty endorsing it with their behavior.

- Vision statements must be brief, clear, and understandable. They have to be acted on, so vision statements must be practical and readable by anyone. Vision statements that are too long, ethereal, and abstract lose the people to whom they are directed and cannot be translated into action.
- Vision must be applied in the places where the organization does its work. If it does not take form at the point of service, it does not matter where else it does.
- A particular vision is never permanent. The stakeholders should periodically revisit the vision they have constructed and validate its relevance and update it in ways that are more congruent with the reality of the time.

People want to identify with something that provides meaning and direction for their lives. This is no different at work than in any other part of life. There must be a reason for doing what we do that lies beyond the work itself. If organizations are to get the partnership, equity, accountability, and ownership that is required for sustaining the organization, the vision must lead the way. Everything that relates to the work and the support of work activities then becomes valuable. Having a clear vision creates a sustainable context within which people can commit to achieving the outcomes that validate the meaning to which everyone attaches the results of their own work.

Rule 4: Empower the Center

The word empowerment is bandied about a lot in the current redesigned organization. Simply defined, empowerment is the recognition of the power already present in a role and allowing it to be appropriately expressed.

Increasingly, organizations are becoming aware that they cannot obtain the changes that are necessary without involvement of people at the center of the organization: those closest to the point of service or care. In this "high tech" world, it is becoming increasingly clear that the work of those closest to the customer (patient) have the greatest impact and play the most important role in representing the organization.[16] Indeed, much of the work of redesign is placing service providers at the center of the system and rebuilding the structures and supports around that role.[17] It is clearer every day that the old design of the organization around provider systems actually impedes the effectiveness of the organization. It is only when artificial structures and processes not directed to supporting the patient–provider relationship are removed that the purposes of the system can be achieved fully.

There is much more dependence on structures that support empowerment today than at any time in history. The growing dependence on the knowledge worker makes this person central to the organization's health. What is critical is the development of empowerment that results in staff investment in true point-of-care decision making. People must own their own decisions and be accountable for the results of their actions. The organizations of yesterday spent more time talking about empowerment than actually creating it. Hierarchical structures work against the effective empowering of persons other than those already in the power pyramid. To create real loci of empowerment, much of the decision-making power present in the management track must be reallocated.[18] This is a very challenging process for the leadership. Organizations have worked for years to build the kind of power structure that now must be dismantled to build new, more effective power relationships in the organization.

Some foundations on which empowerment builds in the emerging health care system are:

- Ownership of work is foundational to accountability and the achievement of outcomes. Staff members must know that they are accountable for their own work.
- Empowerment is not something one gets from someone else. It is a recognition and application of the power already present in a role.
- Empowerment demands performance. Outcomes indicate the effects of empowerment and are the foundations of measuring its success.
- Roles and expectations must be clear at the outset for all players in the organization. Ambiguity of roles and expectations is the enemy of successful empowerment.
- Genuine empowerment means the freedom and authority to make decisions that affect what is done. Management-driven approval structures actually impede the appropriate expression of empowerment and should be avoided.

There is a temptation to halt the development of true empowerment at the talking stage. There currently is precious little real empowerment happening in U.S. organizations. The challenge for leadership is to build truly empowering processes and structures and then genuinely support them when in place. To sustain empowerment, tolerance, patience, and perseverance will be necessary to endure the pain of learning, growing, and personal behavior change on the part of both leadership and staff.[19]

Rule 5: Construct New Architecture

New roles and work behavior cannot be reinforced unless the organizational structure in place supports and sustains them. Many leaders talk about building empowerment processes and creating opportunities for workers to participate in critical decision making. The problem is, however, that simply permitting the behavior and expecting it from staff members does not ensure that it is obtained or sustained. The structure of the organization must be designed in a way that makes the desired empowered behavior the modus operandi of the system.[20] That means addressing organizational relationships, structure, interactions, power loci, and supports for the empowered expectations that leadership hopes become a part of the functioning system.

Structure tells everyone how the system is supposed to function. It shows the world how the design of the organization supports its processes.[21] Although structure itself does not reinforce behavior, it is one of the pillars that supports desired action and creates a milieu that encourages the advancement and permanence of desired behaviors.

It must be remembered, too, that structure itself must be fluid in providing context to performance. As the design of service and work change to reflect a changing work market and environment, structure also must be adaptive and flexible. It must be able to provide a safe context for the behavioral changes and role shifts of the staff. Nothing is or should ever be cast in stone. A structure that is permanent and inflexible ultimately becomes an impediment to essential change.[22] However, structure evolves successfully over time, and the maturation of structure requires attention to change and the ability to build newer components as the organization matures in its behavior and in achieving outcomes. From centralized organizations to self-organizing systems: from hierarchy to self-directed work teams is quite a journey. No system can get to either the requisite behaviors or the supporting structures for this shift in work expectations overnight. Building and linking the pieces of organizational change along a continuum of growth and transformation is essential for sustainability.

It is good to remember some basics when creating supporting structure for effective redesigned workplaces.

- All supporting structure should be built around the point of service in organizations. Any structure that does not will eventually impede the work done there.
- The role of the manager is to support not parent the staff. Developing the staff's ability to appropriately express the power they have and to become self-directed in the interests of the patient and the organization is the primary role of the leader.
- The structure should be lean and simple. There should be no more than two layers of decision making; that which operates at the point of service and that which integrates the system. It is becoming increasingly clear that more than those two categories of structure diminish the effectiveness of the organization.
- Structure should discipline process. If there is a way for individuals to ignore or "game" the system to their own advantage or to fulfill some need for control, structural efficacy begins to break down relationships and belief in the system. It does not take much manipulation of structure to create cynicism and alienation throughout the organization.
- Consistent application of the supporting structure for empowerment and the attendant behaviors is critical for building trust and commitment. If the words of empowerment, shared governance, investment, and ownership are not supported consistently by appropriate responses, creditability and belief in them diminishes.

There is a lot of discussion about the appropriate structures needed to support decentralized and reengineered workplaces. From whole systems models to the continuum of service structures, new designs are being explored.[23] The basic principles of design call for simplicity and a configuration of structure that supports the places where the organization does its work and lives out its mission. In supportive structures, staff, through their own initiative and judgment, are engaged fully in those activities that result in efficient work and healthy outcomes.

Rule 6: Always Have a Plan of Action

One of the great difficulties of health systems is the ability to act in concert and move in the same direction collaboratively and consistently. Individual and unilateral agendas affect organizational viability and effectiveness. Although it is great to have a clear agenda, if it does not integrate the organization's purpose and activities, it simply does not work. Compartmentalization of strategy, standards, practices, and initiatives is one of the single greatest contributions to organizational dissemination and to poor goal congruence in health care.[24]

There must be evidence that everyone's activities are fulfilling the purposes and goals of the system. Every person should be able to evidence how what they do is contributing to the success of the system and to the future of their roles and work.[25] There is a symbiotic relationship between the success of the system and the opportunities for career advancement. There is no "us" and certainly no "them" in systems any more (and I suspect that there never really was). Everyone is a stakeholder in the success of a system; if it fails, its people fail to thrive. Congruence takes on special significance in these circumstances.

Clear goal development and convergence of all activities around those goals is essential to the integrity of systems. It is surprising to see health systems busy implementing many programs and plans in their departments, services, and disciplines without any clear notion of how they support the future core mission and goals of the system. In a transforming health system, all work must be constructed from the perspective of the new paradigm for health care, otherwise they are simply shortsighted.

Many systems simply "fashion surf" through the current "buzz programs" and innovations without ever asking whether they fit and take the organization where it needs to go to thrive.[26]

Some principles to keep in mind regarding goal construction are as follows:

- Goals must always be consonant with the direction of change. Developing goals that do not fit the emerging future is an exercise in futility.
- Getting commitment to goals at every level of the system means assuring that stakeholders are involved in both their construction and their implementation.
- There should be few goals in an organization. However, the goals should be significant and important to the future of the enterprise so that people want to converge around them and commit their energies to their achievement.
- Goals should be understandable and clear. The language of goals must be such that everyone in the organization can understand them within the context of their own role.
- Goal statements should be brief and clear, not ambiguous and uncertain. Goals give clear and concise direction to the organization regarding the activities that lead to creating the preferred future. They never need to be complicated.
- All evaluation mechanisms will use goals as their centerpiece. Performance in any role is judged in context of the goals to which work energy is directed. It is goals that give work its direction and therefore, goals serve as the foundation for measuring effectiveness.
- Goals serve as the foundation for all plans and actions. Work and strategy plans reflect the goals to which they are directed, and thus validate the goals themselves. All plans can be adjusted to the extent that they do not facilitate achievement of the goal to which the plan is related.

In the course of building effective organizations, leaders often can get lost in the complexity. Most of the rules or principles that guide work and relationships are not complex. That is not to suggest that there are not elaborate issues with which people in organizations have to deal. It does suggest, however, that the application of clear principles to the issue can help the individual manage the complexity and stay focused.

Plans simply provide a template, a map, that the individual can use to move along the pathway to a desired outcome. The role of leadership is to help staff stay focused on the outcome and to adjust the pathway when it does not support the goal and to validate those processes and activities when they do facilitate goal achievement.

Rule 7: Evaluate, Adjust, Evaluate Again

One of the greatest challenges in any change is knowing precisely where the group is in the midst of the change event. People get so caught up in the change events and activities that the change becomes an end in itself. Staying focused on both the reason for the change and its outcome can be difficult when people are "up to their eyeballs" in work. Just to cope with the onslaught of the elements of change, individuals often focus just on what lies in front of them at the time they are working. Although that may be comforting, it is not a very successful strategy.

All focus must be on the desired outcome. All activity must be a subset of the outcome to which it is directed.[27] When working in complexity, it is better to continue to see the whole than get caught simply enumerating its parts. Of course, that is easier said than done.

It is for this reason that defined moments for reflection and evaluation must be built into the process. Leadership must make opportunities available to assess where the individual and the group is in light of the goals to which their work is directed. Effectiveness does not require being needlessly intense or complicated about evaluation.

Evaluation should be built into the activities of the staff.[28] Staff members should be aware of the established time frames for assessing where they are in their work and change efforts. Both goal and activities need to be examined to make some critical assessment of the intensity of the relationship between their activities and the results of their efforts.

The challenge is found in making evaluation moments a part of the work activities of the team members. The frequent cry of the staff is "I have no time. I'm too busy doing the work." The problem with that argument is that the more time they spend doing work (that they either had no part in defining or that does not clearly relate to some previously understood goal, or results in no measurable outcomes), the more time they spend in activity for which there is no defined value.[29] As organizations tighten up resource use and look more critically at the cost–quality relationship, the more important evaluation of work will become. Building that into staff work will be a critical work imperative over the next decade in the increasingly outcome-oriented organization.

Evaluation always has some consistent characteristics that make it invaluable for both leadership and staff:

- Define time parameters for evaluation in advance. Make it an important part of staff meetings and interaction.
- When constructing goals and clinical processes, make sure that the evaluation indices are identified at the same time the outcome expectations are defined.
- Evaluation should be a staff-driven function. Staff members should define the evaluation elements related to their work efforts. Ownership is essential to accountability.
- Performance always should be tied to outcome achievement. Incremental evaluation of progress develops insight and commitment to goal achievement and strengthens the level of performance.
- Problems identified in the evaluation processes do not escalate if they are responded to at the time they are identified. Goal achievement is facilitated and duplication is reduced.
- The need for external "checking" and approval mechanisms are eliminated when regular incremental evaluation is imbedded in the activities of the stakeholders and incorporated as a part of the expectations of work.

Evaluation is simply a tool, nothing else. Its purpose primarily is to measure the congruence between activities and their outcomes. The more simply and more frequently evaluation measures are used, the more effective and efficient work and relationships are. Much redundancy, duplication, expense, and unnecessary work can be eliminated if good regular and basic evaluation is undertaken at the point of service by the stakeholders.

Conclusion

These seven rules for effective change are neither complex nor demanding. They reflect a way of approaching work rather than creating additional obligations for the work. They provide a context to the undertaking and demand a discipline to the activities and outcomes of the workplace. Their consistent application ensures most benefit and helps all workers see the meaning and value in their efforts in a way that can be defined and made visible and real to them. One of the great problems in the workplace has been the lack of ownership and investment in the processes and products of work from those on the front lines. Engaging them with some good structure and healthy process provides a frame for that ownership.

Increasingly, work will demand the full and conscious engagement of all the people in organizations. The tools they use to clarify their contributions will be critical to the health of the organization and to the purposes to which it is directed. Consistent applications of these rules of change will significantly contribute to achieving and advancing that work.

REFERENCES

1. Bergquist W. *The Postmodern Organization: Mastering the Art of Irreversible Change.* San Francisco, CA: Jossey-Bass; 1993.
2. Beneveniste G. *The Twenty-First Century Organization.* San Francisco, CA: Jossey-Bass; 1994.
3. Kidder R. *Shared Values for a Troubled World.* San Francisco, CA: Jossey-Bass; 1994.
4. Bartlett C. Ghoshal S. Changing the role of top management: beyond strategy to purpose. *Harvard Bus Rev.* 1995;72(6):79–84.
5. Devereaux M. Johansen R. *Globalwork.* San Francisco, CA: Jossey-Bass: 1994.
6. Rheingold H. *The Virtual Community: Homesteading on the Electronic Frontier.* New York: Addison-Wesley; 1993.
7. Negroponte N. *Being Digital.* New York: Knopf; 1995.
8. Coile R. Transformation of American Healthcare in the Post Reform Era. *Healthcare Executive.* 1994;9(4):8–12.
9. Bennis W. *Why Leaders Can't Lead.* San Francisco, CA: Jossey-Bass; 1990.
10. Kritek P. *Negotiating at an Uneven Table.* San Francisco, CA: Berrett-Koehler; 1994.
11. Bohm D. Edwards M. *Changing Consciousness.* New York: Harper-Collins; 1991.
12. Beckhard R. Pritchard W. *Changing the Essence: The Art of Creating and Leading Fundamental Change in Organizations.* San Francisco, CA: Jossey-Bass; 1992.
13. Drucker P. *Managing for the Future: The 1990s and Beyond.* New York: Truman Tally Books/Dutton; 1992.
14. Block P. *The Empowered Manager.* San Francisco, CA: Jossey-Bass; 1991.
15. Beckham D. The vision thing. *Healthcare Forum J.* 1994;37(2):60–70.
16. Bennett A. Making the grade with the customer. *Wall Street J.* 1990 Nov 12:1.
17. Peters T. *Liberation Management.* New York: Harper and Row; 1992.
18. Adams F. Hansen G. *Putting Democracy to Work.* San Francisco, CA: Berrett-Koehler; 1993.
19. Byham W. *Zapp! The Lightening of Empowerment.* New York: Harmony Books; 1991.
20. Elliott C. Leadership without bosses: shared leadership in the creation of a health network. *Healthcare Manage Forum.* 1994;7(1):38–43.
21. Galbraith J. *Designing Organizations.* San Francisco, CA: Jossey-Bass; 1995.
22. Mink B. Downes E. Owen K. *Open Organizations.* San Francisco: Jossey-Bass; 1994.
23. Porter-O'Grady T. Managing along the continuum: a new paradigm for the clinical manager. *Nurs Adm Q.* 1995;19(3):1–12.
24. Argyris C. *Knowledge for Action.* San Francisco, CA: Jossey-Bass; 1993.
25. Kochan T. Osterman P. *The Mutual Gains Enterprise.* Boston. MA: Harvard Business School Press; 1994.
26. Beckham D. The longest wave—fad surfing. *Healthcare Forum J.* 1993;36(6):78–82.
27. Leavenworth G. Quality costs less. *Business Health.* 1994;12(3):7–11.
28. del Bueno D. Evaluation: myths, mystiques, and obsessions. *J Nurs Adm.* 1990;20(11):4–7.
29. Hall B. Time to nurse: musings of an aging nurse radical. *Nurs Outlook.* 1993;41(6):250–252.

CHAPTER 28

●●●

Understanding the Seven Stages of Change

JO MANION

As a nurse, you handle change successfully every day: new patients and families, new ways of providing care, new or improved equipment, a new group of physicians. So what's the big deal? You know how to cope with change. Or do you?

Change today is different. Experts tell us that there's more change going on now than ever before. It's happening faster; it's more complex; the implications are more serious; and the shelf life of our solutions is shorter. Change occurs on several levels: personal, professional, organizational, and societal. Many times we experience changes on all these levels simultaneously.

When change becomes overwhelming, a typical response is the holding action. We find ourselves saying, "If I can just make it through next month, my life will get back to normal" or "As soon as things slow down I'll get caught up." It's time to recognize that this thinking represents the "good old days"—and the good old days are gone.

To deal effectively with change, you need to realize that every change involves psychological adaptation, a period of transition. And transitions can be tough, even when the change is something you really want—a promotion, a reassignment, a new job. Before you can experience the new beginning you must go through an ending and an in-between time of adjustment.

This takes considerable energy, and when multiple changes are happening at the same time, you can easily run out of reserves. Such an emotional drain sometimes leads to unwise and even unsafe actions.

Organizational change usually creates additional problems. It's been estimated that as much as 50% of an employee's energy goes into coping with organizational change. Most organizations aren't good at tolerating such a reduction in productivity. Experts also point out that healing the grief that accompanies change can take a long time—up to a year, in some cases. Most organizations don't have that kind of patience. Because they're expected to remain productive and positive throughout the change, employees feel anger and resistance toward the authority figures with whom they work—and another source of fatigue develops.

Your strongest antidote to the trauma of change is an understanding of the sequential nature of the process. A model that I and other nurses have found helpful is the mood curve developed by S. A. Spencer and J. D. Adams (Figure 28-1). In their extensive work with people navigating transitions, Spencer and Adams identified seven stages their clients went through when confronted by a major change. Here's what each stage involves, and its specific application to nursing situations.

Stage 1: Losing Focus

Expect some confusion and disorientation during this stage. You may be uncertain about boundaries and expectations. Decisions are especially difficult. On the positive side, this stage usually passes quickly and, as the following example demonstrates, may not require specific interventions.

A man who'd been a military nurse for 22 years was forced to retire during a recent downsizing. He and his family experienced disbelief and anger at this unexpected change. He became forgetful and had trouble making decisions. At first his wife worried that something was physically wrong with him. But when she talked with other military spouses who were experiencing the same change, she realized that her husband's condition was quite common. As the newness of the change receded, his forgetfulness and indecision gradually disappeared.

Stage 2: Minimizing the Impact

At this stage you're likely to deny the impact or pretend the change isn't significant. You may feel the need to "put a good face on it," telling others that you're doing just fine, that the change is "no big deal." You may even believe this yourself. That's understandable. You probably still haven't figured out how this change will fully affect you; instead, you're just getting through it day by day. Slowly, however, you'll begin to recognize the impact of the change and your need to deal with it.

The staff nurses in one patient care unit had experienced major changes over the previous three years. They lost two nurse managers in a short time; had a turnover of key, experienced nurses; relocated the unit twice; and added a major new physician practice to the service. These nurses took great pride in their reputation as the hospital's "star performers." They were constantly being recognized for their reputed ability to deal with change. They responded by directing their energy toward shrugging off the difficulties. As a result, they stayed in this stage too long. Their productivity and commitment gradually disintegrated and when they "hit bottom," they hit hard.

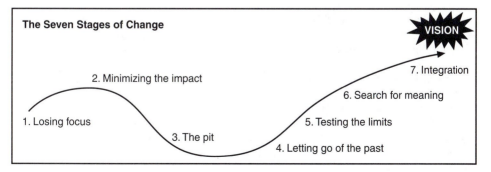

Figure 28–1 The Seven Stages of Change.

Stage 3: The Pit

This is the lowest point on the mood curve (see illustration); anger, discouragement, resentment, and resistance are common. Expect difficulty dealing with these emotions, especially if the people you're angry with are your supervisors. Because you might not feel safe expressing your feelings, you could end up directing them toward people around you who have nothing to do with the change. Or you might direct them inward, especially if you brought the change upon yourself. For instance, you may have sought that promotion or asked for this new responsibility. Even if the change is positive, you may find yourself unprepared for the intensity of these negative feelings.

The nurses from the patient care unit described in the previous stage fell into a deep pit, made worse by the length of time they'd stayed in the first and second stages. They exhibited anger, hostility, and despair. In fact, they were so worn out that they had no energy to counteract the effects of the changes they were experiencing. So their morale and the quality of care suffered.

Stage 4: Letting Go of the Past

This is a more positive stage. Your energy starts to return and you begin to see the end of the change process. The disruptive emotions are behind you—or so it seems. Because these emotions don't always unfold in a clean, progressive fashion, something can happen that drags you back into the pit. Don't be discouraged. You probably won't stay there as long as before.

You have two main tasks during this stage. First, let go of the past. Until now you've probably focused on how things used to be. Accept the fact that the change won't go away. Second, start looking ahead and preparing for the future. Use the optimism and renewed energy that you're feeling.

A small group of nurse educators had worked as a team for over four years. Now they were being redeployed to clinical services and were interviewing for positions in specific clinical areas. Most of the team was still in stage 3, but two of them had secured new positions and were at stage 4. When members of the same group are at different stages, problems can develop. Those at stage 3 resent the optimism of those at stage 4; those at stage 4 grow impatient with their colleagues' resistance and anger.

Stage 5: Testing the Limits

At this point, the sadness you felt during the previous stages has faded and your optimism is more energizing. You have many more good days now than bad. You find you're ready to test and push yourself. Your focus is on trying your new coping skills and dealing with the situation in a more creative way. You feel alive again.

If you're an introvert, you may be surprised to find yourself more open and talkative about your experiences. If you're extroverted, be careful not to irritate others around you by repeatedly recounting your experiences.

During an educational program, hospital employees were discussing the changes their institution was undergoing. Among those present were staff members whose patient care units were scheduled for restructuring, plus others whose units had been restructured for several years. The first group reported feeling discouraged, resentful, and resistant (stage 3); the second group, excited about what they'd accomplished, wanted to share their

BOX 28–1 TIPS FOR GETTING THROUGH THE STAGES OF CHANGE

1. Losing focus
   - Expect some forgetfulness.
   - Use to-do lists.
   - Ask for clarification of expectations and temporary lines of authority.
2. Minimizing the impact
   - Tell yourself the truth about what's happening. List the gains and losses associated with the change. Be honest about what you're losing or giving up.
   - If others offer help but you're not ready to accept it, respond in a way that leaves the door open for their support at a later date.
   - Take one step at a time.
   - Don't stay in this stage too long—but don't try to end it precipitously either. Start gathering your courage for the next stage, which is the most difficult.
3. The pit
   - Expect to feel angry, discouraged, and resentful. If you know what's happening inside you, you're more likely to keep your equilibrium.
   - Let yourself experience the feelings. Suppressing or denying them will make it more difficult for you to deal with change in the future.
   - Find a safe place to express your feelings, preferably with someone who can listen comfortably without taking them on or trying to talk you out of them.
   - Develop a positive vision of what things will be like when you've finished this transition, then think of it often. People with a clear vision have an easier time getting through the pit.
4. Letting go of the past
   - Say good-bye to the past, either formally or informally. You might do this with a "letting-go" ritual. An example of such a ritual would be to review what was positive about the past, recount good memories, and then bury it. Or it may be more appropriate to have a graduation party.
   - Allow some sadness and longing for the way things used to be.
   - As you look ahead, think of what you'll need to adjust to the change—new skills and new approaches, for example. Consider specific ways to obtain them.
   - Take care of yourself. Celebrate the small successes.
5. Testing the limits
   - Seek new experiences and ways to use the skills you've gained.
   - Spend time with people who have experienced the same change or loss.
   - Talk about the past only with those who will listen and not become impatient.
   - Associate with people who are encouraging and supportive.
6. Search for meaning
   - Spend time reflecting on your experiences since the change occurred. Sort through your feelings. Ask yourself: "What have I learned that I didn't know before?"
   - Look back to how you handled the different emotional stages. Notice which were particularly difficult and give yourself a pat on the back for getting through them.
   - Find others going through the same experience. Listen carefully to see if you can offer any support.
7. Integration
   - Appreciate reaching this final stage. (It doesn't always happen.)
   - Recognize how far you've come and the skills you've learned along the way.

experiences and answer questions. But instead of being supportive, they were inadvertently acting superior to those who were still facing change.

Stage 6: Search for Meaning

As you continue this journey of transition, you gradually reach the point where you can look back over all the difficulty and discomfort and recognize what you learned along the way. Even if the change was painful, you now see meaning in it. With newfound confidence and freedom, you may find yourself wanting to reach out to others who are still in the early stages of the change experience.

Caren found herself unexpectedly out of work as a result of her hospital's declining patient census, so she and another nurse started a consulting business. Despite some success over the next year and a half, Caren decided the business wouldn't make enough money to support them both. She returned to work at the same hospital but in a different department. During subsequent cuts, Caren's supervisor sought to allay any anxieties about losing her job again.

Caren responded, "I'm really not afraid. I've learned that I can survive losing my job. It isn't easy, but I know I can manage."

Stage 7: Integration

By this stage the transition is complete. The change—once a strange and frightening prospect—has now been integrated into your life. You may not realize how far you've journeyed unless you look back from time to time. Your vision is in front of you, orienting you toward the future. Unfortunately, you may not reach full integration of one major change before being called on to deal with another. This is especially true in today's rapidly changing health care environment.

In one hospital, multidisciplinary patient care teams were formed as part of a restructuring effort. After several years on the same team, members had integrated this change into their lives to the point where they sometimes forgot what things were like before the change. Periodic opportunities for growth and development helped the team maintain its progressive vision. The members even accepted more and more responsibility for their work.

Coping with change may be your biggest challenge in the years to come (Box 28-1). It calls for resilience, adaptability, and flexibility. Make no mistake: Change is hard work. But by understanding the key principles for managing the process of change and the emotions it evokes, you're likely to handle it in a healthy and productive manner. After all, it's not as if you've never faced change before.

SELECTED REFERENCES

Bridges, W. *Managing Transitions: Making the Most of Change*. Reading, MA, Addison-Wesley, 1991.
————. *Transitions: Making Sense of Life's Changes*. Reading, MA, Addison-Wesley, 1980.
Connor, D. *Managing at the Speed of Change: How Resilient Managers Succeed and Prosper Where Others Fail*. New York, NY, Villard Books, 1993.
Manion, J. Managing Change: The Leadership Challenge of the 90's. *Seminars for Nurse Managers*. Philadelphia, PA, W. B. Saunders Co., Dec. 1994.
Naisbett, J., and Aburdene, P. *Megatrends 2000: Ten New Directions for the 1990's*. New York, NY, William Morrow & Co., 1990.
Spencer, S. A., and Adams, J. D. *Life Changes: Growing Through Personal Transitions*. San Luis Obispo, CA, Impact Publishers, 1990.

CHAPTER 29

●●●

Surviving Organizational Change

RUTH DAVIDHIZAR

Modern health care organizations are constantly undergoing change to keep up with technology, new federal regulations, new information, changes in personnel, budgetary problems, and a myriad of other factors. People are spending fewer days in the hospital than ever before. Businesses are taking a more active role in the health care their employees receive. Sage, chief executive officer (CEO) of Memorial Health Care System in South Bend, Indiana states, "Health care reform is here. And it's going to continue regardless of what happens in Washington."[1]

Health care managers, whether they are department heads, administrators, supervisors, or directors get the brunt of any change since they must plan the change, often convince the employees of the need for the change, serve as a change catalyst, assist employees to implement the change, and see the change through to completion. It is the managers that must deal with the difficulties that accompany the change process and with the concomitant stress.[2,3]

Stress is often like an invisible epidemic that accompanies change. In most organizational changes, everyone involved in the change process experiences some stress. Some managers and employees wish that change would slow down so the stress would be less. Some wish the change would go away altogether and thus stress might be eliminated. However, since neither of those are possible, employees often look for a person to blame for the stress. Frequently, the blame is directed at the administration. Since higher management usually has its hands full, it is the managers who relate with the employees and who often are the best available targets of blame for employee stress. Consequently, many managers find themselves in what feels like the middle of an epidemic of stress.

Instead of reacting to the stress in ways that make it even more intense, the manager must be able to confidently handle both personal stress and that of employees. Managers need knowledge about change, about the stress change may cause, and about how stress induced by change can be dealt with by the manager and employees. It is also important to understand the feelings of loss that accompany change.[4] Instead of behaving in ways that create additional stress, managers can improve their methods of reacting and become aware of and thus avoid basic mistakes managers and employees make in responding to change induced stress.

Reprinted from *Health Care Supervisor,* 14(4), pp. 19–24, 1996, with permission of Aspen Publishers, Inc., © 1996.

Drivers of Change

While many factors affect the reshaping that is occurring in health care organizations today, technology, information, and people are of major importance. These three factors can be called drivers of change.

TECHNOLOGY

By many measures, the U.S. health care system has been phenomenally successful in recent years. Clinical, diagnostic, and therapeutic advances; leadership in biomedical research; unrivaled clinical facilities; and the development of the latest medical technology are all hallmarks of the system.[5] It has been said that approximately 80% of the world's technological advances have occurred since 1900.[6] As technology advances, the rate of change will continue to increase and, in fact, an accelerating rate of technological change for the future is basically guaranteed.

Managers do not need to learn all of the intricacies of technological advances. However, managers must be experts in assisting employees to adapt to the new technology and to cope with the stress that accompanies change.

INFORMATION

A second driver for change is information. Information availability is accelerating at a phenomenal rate. There has been more information produced in the 30 years between 1965 and 1995 than was produced in the entire 5,000-year period from 3000 B.C. to 1965.[6] Some suggest that in modern times the amount of information available in the world is doubling every five years. In addition, with the advent of such items as interactive computers, cellular phones, and television hooked to satellites broadcasting around the world, knowledge is reaching more people than it ever reached before. A better informed population means better chances for change. Since change and stress are connected, organizational life will only get more stressful.

PEOPLE

In addition to technology and information, people are also multiplying rapidly. Within the short span from 1860 to 1935, the population of the world doubled from one billion to two billion. Then by 1975 it doubled again, to four billion. It is estimated that by the year 2040 there will be 10 billion people on the earth.

As the number of people increase so does change. People make more things, have more creative ideas, and compete for depleting resources. Additional people accelerate change. The relationship between change, stress, self-esteem, and coping has been the subject of research studies. Stein asserts that self-image influences an individual's reaction to stressors.[7] It is also accepted that individuals who experience a loss or decrease in self-esteem when faced with a change in life are more likely than others to utilize negative coping outcomes.[8] Thus, the self-image of employees is another important factor if the manager is to help in the adjustment to change. It cannot be overstated that even though many actions performed by employees are requirements of their job position, recognition is a powerful motivator and boost to morale and self-esteem.[9]

Common Mistakes in Coping With Organizational Change

ASSUMING MANAGEMENT SHOULD KEEP YOU COMFORTABLE

Some employees feel that "caring management" should keep stress in the workplace to a minimum. They interpret "caring" to mean operating within the boundaries of employees' comfort zones. Thus management would be making it easier on employees, not harder.

This is certainly not true. High stress and heavy pressure may provide the best proof that management's heart is in the right place. Minimizing job stress is a cruel and heartless option these days. Management can best show caring by doing what works in the end and gets the best results. "Caring management" is best defined as doing what needs to be done to keep the health care organization alive. Survival is not necessarily a comfortable process, but it sure beats the alternative.[6]

EXPECTING SOMEBODY ELSE TO REDUCE YOUR STRESS

Since higher management appears to employees to be the source of change, it may also seem fair to hold them responsible for the stress. Here again appearances are deceiving. Top management moves are often reactions. More than likely the organization is simply trying to respond to outside forces, like stiffer competition.

If employees think that the actions have been bad and management should "fix" things, that will also mean more change. It is likely top management did not make a mistake and things make sense from their point of view. Employees should not count on anyone else to relieve their stress. Rather, each person should be put in charge of managing his or her own pressure. The chances are the individual is the only one that can lighten the psychological load.

SHOOTING FOR A LOW-STRESS WORK SETTING

Employees and managers should not fall into the trap of believing there's such a thing as a low-stress organization that is on track to survive. Just the opposite is true. There is a lot of evidence today to suggest that slow-changing organizations are going to end up in more trouble. By buying a little time now, the organization can end up living close to the edge.

Employees and managers know that the stress of a rapidly changing organization can be difficult and upsetting. What cannot be known is how much more stress would be experienced if the organization failed to change. The hard truth is that the stress of high-velocity change is here to stay. It is now that the decision to change should be made.[8]

TRYING TO CONTROL THE UNCONTROLLABLE

Some employees and managers get worked up about trying to influence matters that are totally beyond their control. Energy is fruitlessly expended trying to control the uncontrollable. There comes a point where one must say, "If you cannot beat them, join them." It is better to admit to lack of control and to "go with the flow." When the inevitable is resisted, frustration and stress increase.

Human nature is to "go down fighting," so it is a common reaction to stress to try to gain control of the change situation. Individuals try to steady the unsteady work world back to where it used to be. Unfortunately, the more resistance there is to change, the less energy there is for efforts that will really produce a payoff. The changes occurring in health care cannot be controlled. In fact, individuals often have little ability to control the pace of change. It is better for managers and employees to keep in step with the organization's intended rate of change and to march with the cadence that is being called for by the people in charge.

FAILING TO ABANDON THE EXPENDABLE

It is important to know when to abandon the expendable. In order to take on new duties, old duties must be given up. Things that were significant before will become less significant now and in the future. This may mean that one's job needs to be reengineered to eliminate unnecessary steps, to get rid of busy work, and to unload activities that fail to contribute enough to the organization's current goals.

It is easy to find employees who, although focused on doing things right, are failing to do the right things. These employees are holding on to assignments that no longer exist and holding onto priorities that have changed over time. It may take some time for the employee to realize that there are no accolades for doing old jobs well. It is a new game with new rules, and they must adapt in order to stay on the job. Efforts must be focused on doing the right things and not doing the things that no longer matter.

FEARING THE FUTURE

Many employees and managers are troubled about the future. Employees often worry about what is coming next, and how that will effect them. Will they measure up to the demands of change and the job as it will be tomorrow? Will they still be around when the next group of employees is laid off? If they are laid off, how will they get their careers back on track?

Now is the time for serious mind control. Instead of worrying about bad things that might happen, it is better to get busy trying to create a desirable future. The best insurance policy for tomorrow is to make the most productive use of today. Even in the midst of change it is possible to trust and maintain a philosophy of "Everything turns out for the best." There is no decent argument for giving in to fear of the future.

PICKING THE WRONG BATTLES

In a situation with many issues of conflict and many causes to support, it is very important to respond only to issues that are important. Some issues are not worth the energy and time it would take to get one's way in the end. Only crusades of potential future importance must be selected. Things can be evaluated by asking "Will this be important five years from now?" Under this magnifying glass many causes become frivolous.

Some persons set themselves up for stress and failure by pursuing lost causes. These are the employees who are determined to "defend the undefensible." They throw themselves across the tracks in a hopeless attempt to stop the freight train of reality. Picking the wrong battles is a sure road to burnout and to possibly being fired. The key is to pick battles big enough to matter, yet small enough to win.

PSYCHOLOGICALLY UNPLUGGING FROM YOUR JOB

Some employees and managers have worked hard at their jobs, have mastered them well, and feel in good control of matters that affect them on the job. It is important to fall in love with a job and to keep the romance alive. However, change can totally undo both the tasks that were done before and the feeling of control. The job can lose its sparkle and change can become a wedge between the employee and the job of the work.

It is important to avoid psychologically unplugging from the job. One cannot really afford to quit caring. It may be that different things are cared about, but commitment makes individuals emotionally stronger. Commitment to a job makes for happiness.

AVOIDING NEW ASSIGNMENTS

Some individuals try to minimize stress by shying away from new, unfamiliar duties. Performing the old duties is safer and easier. However, living in a world of change means that sticking with the old is only a delay tactic and sets one up to be a prime target for bigger problems in the future. Avoiding the new is a short-sighted strategy for managing personal stress.

It is only by jumping in and accepting tough new assignments, that the important edge can be maintained on the job. Without this edge it is easy to become "inexperienced" in the new techniques and therefore easily dispensable on the job. One should not assume that it is less stressful to "ease into" the new situation. One of the best ways to reduce stress is to get better quicker, to have updated skills, and thus be highly employable.

Change is a must in health care organizations today.[11] Consequently, the stress felt by many employees in health care organizations is spreading like an epidemic. The manager is in a key role to try to decrease anxiety and turmoil that accompanies the stress of change.[12]

Developing a greater tolerance for constant changes in the work setting is key to being both a satisfied employee and a satisfied manager in a health care organization today. The uncertainty and instability of the health care scene are here and will not go away. In order to cope with this stress, it is important to be able to flex to fit the immediate demands of the situation and to strategically use coping mechanisms that will help one cope with stress.[13] Support systems to reduce stress and the importance of connectedness to others cannot be overemphasized. Thus, both managers and employees should look at renewing ties with old friends and strengthening bonds with family. Besides listening and offering support, these people often can share advice on how to weather an organizational storm.

The most important part of stress reduction, however, is prevention. Obviously, prevention is better than having to come up with a cure. In addition to a positive attitude, techniques such as eating right, getting enough sleep and exercise, saying nice things when talking to yourself, using relaxation techniques, and cutting down on caffeine will help manage stress and contribute to an easier adjustment to change in the workplace. It is also important to practice optimism and positive expectancy. Hope is a muscle and should be developed. Above all, play and have fun: humor can lighten one's personal load.

REFERENCES

1. Sage, D. "A Prescription for Change." *Pulse* (Winter 1995):1.
2. Davidhizar, R., and Kuipers, J. "How To Plan and Implement Change." *Advancing Clinical Care* (May/June 1989):38–39.
3. Kaplan, S. "The Nurse as Change Agent." *Pediatric Nursing* 16, no. 6 (1990):603–605.
4. Davidhizar, R., and Bowen, M. "Change: How to Prepare for Loss." *Today's OR Nurse* (1990):30–32.
5. Cooper, P. "A Challenge to Change." *Healthcare Trends and Transitions* 4. no. 3 (1993):27–29.
6. Pritchett, R., and Pound, R. *A Survival Guide to Stress of Organizational Change.* Dallas, Tex.: Pritchett & Associates, 1995.
7. Stein, K. "Structure of the Self and Stability of Self-esteem." Ph.D. diss., University of Michigan, 1988.

8. Roberts, J., Browne, G., Brown, B., et al. "Coping Revisited: The Relation between Appraised Seriousness of an Event, Coping Responses, and Adjustment to Illness." *Perspectives in Nursing* 19, no. 3 (1987):45–54.

9. Davidhizar, R. "Breaking the Barriers to Change." *Advances for Administrators in Radiology* (1994):49–52.

10. Boyd, M. "Is It Time to Decide?" *Modern Maturity* (1993):80.

11. Boyd, M. "When Change Is a Must." *Modern Maturity* (1995):78.

12. Steele, P. "Surviving Organizational Change." *Nursing Management* (1994):50.

13. Davidhizar, R. "Coping with Difficult Changes." *Today's OR Nurse* (1994):53–54.

CHAPTER 30

●●

Thriving in Chaos: Personal and Career Development

JANE NEUBAUER

The massive amount of complex, continuous change throughout the world, including the health care industry, is affecting careers, jobs, community, family, and self. The effects and demands of these changes have been eloquently presented by Peters,[1] Handy,[2] and others. Theories for coping with change abound. One theory of change has been profoundly stated by Eric Miller from the Tavistock Institute: "The essence of the long term solution to the management of change depends on helping the individual to develop greater maturity in understanding and managing the boundary between his own inner world and the realities of his external environment."[3(p.6)] In other words, the only thing one can manage is oneself. Self-management is a skill that can be developed to assist in *thriving in chaos* if one engages in a program of personal development. (For definitions of italicized words used throughout this article, see Box 30-1 entitled "Terminology.")

The developmental focus in organizations has been on designing a vision, setting goals, managing stakeholders, and building teams. Consistent energy has not been committed to personal development. Personal development includes self-assessment, learning about one's reactions, getting feedback, setting goals, and caring for self. It is really about learning to learn. In Rodgers's words,

> If an individual engages in a life long experience of personal growth, he/she is a fully functioning person. One is then able to experience all feelings, is open to all sources of feedback, is engaged in the process of being and becoming oneself, and lives completely in the moment.[4(p.288)]

As the challenges of our work and personal lives demand "fully functioning people," there is no choice but to commit to personal development, thus complementing organizational development.

One model for actualizing personal development is derived from the Chinese characters for change, which are interpreted in two thoughts: danger and opportunity (Fig. 30-1). This article will develop these two aspects of change, arguing that individuals must first deal fully with the dangers of any change and its effect on them before they can move on to take full advantage of the opportunities available to them. This means taking full per-

---

Reprinted from *Nursing Administration Quarterly*, 19(4), pp 71–82, 1995, reprinted with permission of Aspen Publishers, Inc., © 1995.

BOX 30–1   TERMINOLOGY

A plan for Monday:	an emergency plan to put in place if one loses a job
Go to hell $:	money to maintain life if one loses one's job
Hot buttons:	ideas, words, thoughts that trigger excessive feelings and reactions possibly based on personal historical meaning
Jobs for life:	the concept that if one worked hard in a job, it would last a lifetime
Leak:	feelings that are communicated to others when one does not want them to be
Steering rather than rowing:	keeping focused on strategy rather than the operational work involved
Stop the chatter:	alter the list of thoughts and ideas that goes on constantly in the mind
Story:	the description of a real event including feelings and learning gained
Team or job "dies":	loss of team members or job identity experienced as a death
Thriving in chaos:	the ability to thrive in the midst of multiple, unpredictable changes
Warmth and light:	the balance of support and challenge that assists others to grow

---

sonal responsibility for personal and career development. The goal is not only to survive the chaos but also to thrive in it. The model with various aspects of danger and opportunity can be seen in Figure 30-2, and will be referred to throughout the article.

Dangers

It is important to deal first with the dangers inherent in any change, thus enhancing readiness to take advantage of the opportunities. This section will explore the various aspects of the dangers inherent in change. Threat and the necessary grieving processes, as well as survival techniques and self-care, are reviewed.

THREAT AND GRIEVING

People have initial reactions to change, depending on how directly the change affects them as well as their perception of the meaning of the change to their lives. Many reactions are related to loss and fear and the resultant threat to the person. Even positive changes signify the loss of something. Initial reactions to loss pose a sense of threat, which sets off the grieving process as described by Kubler-Ross.[5] The knowledge of these processes has been used when working with patients and families consistently but rarely applied to either

——— Dangers

——— Hidden opportunities

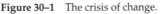

Figure 30–1   The crisis of change.

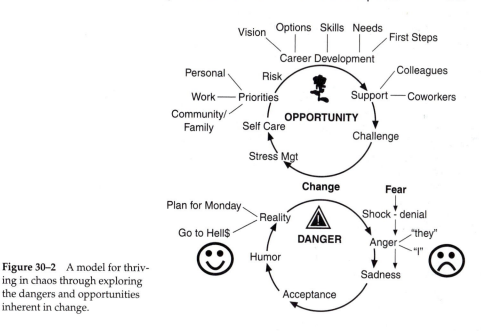

Figure 30–2 A model for thriving in chaos through exploring the dangers and opportunities inherent in change.

coworkers or self. The theories of grieving or dealing with death are as applicable when one experiences the loss of such things as a job, a position, personal status, a work partner or team, or simply undergoes a change in work routine.

The steps in the grieving process include shock, denial, anger, sadness, and acceptance. Individuals must progress through the stages of grieving, once they have experienced a loss, in order to move on to take advantage of the opportunities the situation offers. Some people internalize the anger and blame themselves while others externalize the anger and blame "them." Either way, it is crucial to identify a method for expressing the anger so that one can move on to sadness. Some people never allow themselves to reach the sadness stage and remain stuck at the anger stage, quite often based on an incident that may have happened years ago. Unfortunately, there are those who spend their entire lives as angry victims blaming others for their lack of opportunity.

Moving through the levels of the grieving process takes time and energy. Finding a safe place to acknowledge threat and loss and recognize and express the feelings can be helpful. Expressing anger and sadness is not necessarily encouraged in work environments. But acceptance often comes when one is assisted to look at the positive as well as the negative aspects of a specific change, including the exploration of feelings.

There are various methods for acknowledging and moving through the grieving process. A few ideas include the following:

- Write the story in a journal, including feelings.
- Tell someone the story and your reactions.
- Write a letter to someone with whom you are angry even if you decide not to send it.
- Use your creativity—paint a picture, compose a song, write a poem.
- Take a long walk and cry.

Sometimes counseling can be necessary. If one does not actively engage in the grieving process, anger can remain, affecting one's future work and general perception of life.

Knowledge of the grieving process is common among health care professionals but the recognition that it is necessary for self and coworkers is not common. Commitment to working through the anger and sadness oneself and assisting colleagues when the timing is right is crucial to managing the changes individuals and groups are involved in every day. One person was heard to say, "I've learned to move through the circles faster."

REALITY

Acceptance evolves as one moves on to accepting reality as it is, not as one wishes it would be. The essence of reality in the health care industry today seems to be the acceptance of the loss of *jobs for life* and giving up the paternalistic role of the employer to provide for employees for life. "The average American can expect to hold eight jobs over the course of their working lives and four of those will terminate involuntarily."[6] Taking advantage of the opportunities in the job market today is dependent on people accepting the loss of *jobs for life* and giving up the belief that someone else will take care of them. In addition, leaders are beginning to realize that success in a top job concerns both chemistry and competence. Chemistry is very tenuous and can go wrong at any time.

Development of *a plan for Monday* is the first step to surviving reality. People who have accepted the loss of *jobs for life* and recognize that success in a leadership position concerns both chemistry and competence will have formulated several ideas regarding their plan of action if asked to leave their job next week. Once they have dealt with the fear of "What would I do?" and have made a plan with several options, the fear will never be as intense again. Some options often included in a plan are:

- Return to school.
- Stay home with the kids for a while.
- Enjoy the summer.
- Take a sabbatical and learn something new.
- Try another clinical area.
- Retreat for a while and reflect.
- Travel.
- Spend some time with family.
- Find another job immediately.

Some people believe that trying to fight for one's job, once key stakeholders have decided the chemistry is wrong, is a waste of energy. Filing lawsuits is an option but may hamper any future job search by affecting references. The grapevine is often the most powerful reference, not the formal ones listed; managing one's public image is critical to being able to take advantage of future opportunities. Dealing with the grieving and then moving on to focus available energy on the future are found to be more healing and more productive.

Requests for support during the transition are appropriate. It is important to seek advice regarding requests one might make of the organization if asked to leave. Some thoughts are:

- Financial compensation
- Health insurance
- Outplacement service, which might help with resumé, networking, self-assessment
- Secretarial and telephone support
- Tuition payment
- Moving expenses

Proactive career managers try to stay one step ahead and attempt to be aware before others feel the chemistry has gone wrong. Support might be sought before one is asked to leave a job but when there is a sense that the chemistry has begun to go wrong. If the organization wants a person to leave, it is often willing to agree to multiple requests. Support for oneself so as to get on with one's life is an appropriate method of taking care of one's self.

When first confronted with this model, many people say, "But how will I live?" That's why *go to hell $* is needed. Money to live on for a period of 6 to 12 months is essential to thriving in this chaotic work environment where *jobs for life* are no more and one is valuable for the fit with the team, not just skills. Many people say, "But I can't save any money, I spend every cent I earn." Saving can be done, and a successful career manager starts small and does it over a period of several years. The plan might include decreasing one's cost or standard of living to allow more flexibility. It is not mandatory to spend every salary increase and get oneself trapped in a life style; but a person can move out of a trapped life style. The security of knowing how one would live allows freedom to take risks and do the job more creatively rather than hanging on to the job to pay the mortgage. This personal security may, in fact, allow one to contribute more to the organization because of a willingness to take more risks. By adding increased value, job security could be increased.

"Take this job and shove it" is an option an individual might exercise if a decision is made to leave the organization *and* some *go to hell $* is available for support. A person might feel he or she has had enough of the job, is out of ideas on how to solve the organization's problems, or has been asked to implement decisions beyond what personal values allow. (Awareness of values and clarity about areas open for compromise are critical to this option.) Having *go to hell $* allows choices and puts a person in control of his or her own life. Making a choice to stay in a job feels very different from feeling stuck in a job.

SELF-CARE

Self-care is the transition stage, moving from danger to opportunity. It is critical to survival before one can really move to thrive, not just survive in the chaos. Stress management is a major part of self-care. In the 1970s, Hans Selye[7] described the body's production of adrenaline when stressed. This response can be positive or negative depending on both the intensity of the perceived threat and the individual's reaction to it. Selye reminds us that our bodies have evolved from individuals who had to fight or run from physical danger and that the body continues to create adrenaline when frightened to allow the person to fight or flee. However, the modern stimulation is usually no longer physical danger and the modern life style does not include the physical activity to allow the body to rid itself of the adrenaline produced. Therefore, more psychosomatic illnesses exist now than at any time in the past and are directly or indirectly related to the adrenaline buildup in the body. In fact, Americans are described as addicted to stress because they move at such a pace as to keep their adrenaline constantly at a high level.[8] As the speed and intensity of the changes are not predicted to decrease, the body's response will be to continue to produce excessive amounts of adrenaline. The health of the body suffers unless methods are found to rid the body of excessive adrenaline.

Many courses and books on stress management have been written. The principles of stress management recommended fall into two categories: work off the adrenaline with exercise three times a week and slow down the body and mind with some type of relaxation, such as breathing or yoga. Relaxation is an attempt to *stop the chatter* in the mind; to stop the endless list of things to do, say, and things that scroll through the mind constantly.[9] Self-care includes development of supportive relationships, both personally and at work. An assessment of personal relationship networks and a plan for how to fill gaps can be helpful, using a mind map to illustrate relationships.

A crisis or a change in life or job is often an opportune time to alter life styles and improve coping mechanisms. This will happen only if goals are set and a plan developed. Changes in life style and habits are not easy to make; it is important to celebrate little wins and successes. The body cannot sustain this level of stress without permanent effect; the time is now to make a few adjustments as one moves on to opportunities in this chaotic world.

Opportunities

At the top circle in the model (Fig. 30-2), the individual moves from just surviving to thriving in the midst of the surrounding chaos. The first step is to identify priorities, including values and lifetime dreams. Next, a major aspect of opportunity is career development, which includes vision, options, identification of skills one has and those one needs to acquire, and first steps to begin the process of career management. A lifetime commitment to self development is suggested with specific ideas for follow-up. Finally, the importance of support and challenge to coworkers is suggested.

PRIORITIES

Identifying one's priorities about self, family, work, and community helps one to move into career development. Values clarification exercises can be helpful. One method is to write a personal obituary as one would like it to be and then to develop goals for life to assist with life goal achievement. Using creativity activities such as visualization,[10] mind maps,[11] or magazine collages to bring the beginnings of a life vision to the forefront can be helpful and fun. These activities can stimulate the subconscious desires that are often lost when using only words.

Specifically, identifying lifetime goals regarding relationships, children, power, status, money, location, community, and work is important. It is difficult to divide personal and family life from career. Once the life values and goals are identified, attempting to prioritize them can be enlightening. These priorities can even dictate one's time management. Developing a balanced life is important to maintaining a perspective on various aspects of work and home life.

It is easy at this point to say, "My life is set, my dreams don't matter, I have no choices." But if a person is aware of his or her dreams, it is just possible that some of them can be achieved. One person who works in a hospital records department saw the ocean for the first time at 44 years of age. She said, "I love it and I am going there every year!" She rarely eats out or buys many clothes, but she does travel to the ocean every year. Awareness of one's dream is the first step to achievement.

Objectively observing one's life style and daily life activities and reflecting on how the day is spent can be enlightening. Life is made up of a series of days. Successful life managers know what they like to do, what gives them pleasure, and what causes them anxiety. Awareness of these issues can assist a person in beginning to design life to spend time doing what one enjoys and avoid that which causes anxiety.

CAREER DEVELOPMENT

The components of career development include vision, options, skills, needs, and first steps (see Fig. 30-2). Various aspects of these will be explored.

Vision

Much of the work on vision may have been completed when working on priorities for life. The vision for work should further explore the world of work. Reviewing results of creativity exercises, describe the ideal job in detail:

- What activities are taking place?
- What kinds of people are there?

- How much power and control does the person have?
- Are the power and influence in the organization, at the state or national level?
- Is status important?
- How much money does the person have?

Other questions important to each individual can be explored. Honesty with oneself is critical so that a picture emerges on which to base a plan.

Options

The options for how to fill work time are many. Handy describes four kinds of work and says people must contribute to each to have a balanced life. Work necessary to sustain life includes paid work for time (wages) or results (contract), homework to maintain life, gift work to contribute to the community, and learning work to develop the self. Another perspective for how to view life's work includes recognition of the Third Age when people who reach their 40s and 50s may choose to contribute through various approaches. One person may choose a new career but keeps at the old one part time to earn money. Another person may have saved some money and works part time as well as volunteering and doing some writing or teaching. Handy calls this a portfolio career. If variations on the current work life are wanted, a dream must be developed and acknowledged and a plan devised.[12]

To maximize choices, a person must learn and practice the survival skill of having *go to hell $*. From the perspective of options, the plan for money management can move from reactive to proactive. Many books have been written on the topic of money management.[13] Managing money is complex and anxiety producing but it is necessary to allow realization of dreams as well as provide security. It takes plans and commitment to make it happen. It is puzzling why people will not attempt to fix their $25,000 car but will try to self-manage several hundred thousand dollars worth of assets. Financial management consultants are available to assist with short-, intermediate-, and long-term financial goals. They will suggest developing a plan with short-, intermediate-, and long-term goals and reviewing it yearly. Other steps to follow yearly include:

- Evaluate money status (count assets and debts).
- Note progress from last year.
- Analyze budget compliance.
- Revise goals.

Being aware of the jobs that are available by reading advertisements and using networks are important for a career manager. Recruiters can be a good source of information about jobs as well as changes in the market and current salaries. Networks should not be superficial and require keeping in touch with 10 to 20 people around the country. Through the network one can keep informed, keep a broad perspective, and might be offered an opportunity never dreamed of. These relationships must be "real," though, and not just superficial chat. Connecting people with other people who have a common interest is not forgotten and often rewarded. Meeting new people at events can add to the network as one works to expand contacts, especially beyond nursing.

Job Success

One major option is to decide whether or not to remain and be successful in the current job. Making a choice is a totally different perception as compared to feeling "stuck" in a job. If the choice is to remain in the current job, then success in this job becomes the primary career development strategy. A person should keep focused on job success until the day he or she walks out the door. There are four key aspects to job success. They are as follows:

- Being clear about *what* one is attempting to do.
- Having a specific action plan about *how* to complete the work.
- Identifying and working with key *stakeholders*.
- Measuring and marketing the *outcomes.*

It is quite easy to confuse the *what* and the *how* aspects, especially if one has been heavily involved in operations. Being clear about *what* one is trying to do includes keeping focused on vision and goals. To keep focused on vision and strategy rather than get bogged down in operations is a major premise of Bennis[14] and this is sometimes referred to as *steering rather than rowing.* Communicating the vision and the plan everywhere is the other aspect of the vision thing. Peter Vaill says the leader must "purpose" for the organization constantly.[15] Identifying five or six key measurable goals and articulating them so as to add value to the organization help people be clear about priorities and keep focused. Use can be made of the five to six key goals principle so as not to try to do too much and confuse people about what the priorities are. It is possible to become bogged down in both operations and process, thus accomplishing very little. Time management can then be applied by checking to see if time is being spent on tasks that will meet the goals.

Once clarity has been established regarding the goals, a plan and appropriate follow-up must be developed. Senior executives delegate much of the operation to subordinates and then allow freedom for people to get on with implementation as long as the identified goals are being met. There are many good plans that are never completed. Suggested steps to goal achievement include the following:

- Be specific about who, what, when, and where.
- Hold people accountable to the plan.
- Communicate what is happening to everyone.
- Celebrate small wins to help people see progress.
- Stop often to reflect, identify success and next steps.

Managing the stakeholders who are key to the executive's success is important. The executive might begin by identifying the boss's five goals and then become a part of the accomplishment of these goals. It is important to recognize that if the boss's goals are different there are now 10 goals to meet. Clarifying the boss's goals and expectations regularly and asking for what is needed to accomplish the goals set the agenda for the working relationship. Getting feedback from the boss regularly can help clarify progress and concerns. However, senior executives do not always allot much time for feedback processes, so the nurse executive may need to manage the feedback process himself or herself. One person wrote a one-page report of goal achievement, problems, and future goals to her boss quarterly and asked for comments. She received feedback and suggestions.

Other key stakeholders for the senior nursing leader are physicians, staff nurses, and colleagues. Developing and actively managing a relationship with key physicians and colleagues is essential. Job failures can result because the nursing leader becomes caught up in focusing on nursing issues and does not proactively manage other relationships or spend enough time being a team player. Others make the mistake of focusing too much on corporate work and not enough on leading nursing. Getting the balance right and managing it are critical.

Finally, connecting achievements to measurable outcomes for patients and the organization is important. The nurse leader should always be describing how nursing adds value to the organization. At the organizational level, nursing is a *how*, not a *what*. The goals of the organization are patient outcomes, customer satisfaction, and financial success. Nursing is one of the most important operational mechanisms for achieving organizational goals, but it is often necessary to make these connections for people. One can market success in annual reports and presentations by using four or five consistent "sound bites" with accurate data attached (ie, "x unit saved 5% last year, which was $250,000"). Use of nursing jargon can make it difficult for nonnurses to understand achievements and relate them to outcomes. Communication throughout the organization in simple language regarding achievement is essential. Job success is essential to career management.

Skills and Needs

Assessment of current skills and identification of learning needs for the future are major tasks. Box 30-2, "Career Development: The Questions," lists five key questions to assist with development of a plan for career management. A few words about each step follow:

1. Where have I been? An assessment of skills acquired through experience.
2. Where am I now? Skills and qualities I have.
3. Where do I want to get to? What knowledge and skills will I need for my ideal job?
4. How do I get there? This is a plan for meeting needs I have identified.
5. How will I know if I have arrived? An assessment of my own plan and a revision of the plan.

Significant progress on a plan can be made by working through these five questions in some depth. Ongoing self-assessment is the key to career management.

First Steps

It is critical to begin an action plan assessing the current state of one's career plan. There are many choices. A few ideas are listed:

BOX 30–2 CAREER DEVELOPMENT: THE QUESTIONS

1. Where have I been?
   - How has my life gone?
   - What are the highs and lows?
   - What are the chapter titles?
   - What is my background, my previous experience, and what have I learned?
2. Where am I now?
   - What successes have I had in my current job.
   - What skills and qualities do I possess?
3. Where do I want to get to?
   - What kind of person do I want to be?
   - What is my vision of the future?
     —personal
     —family
     —community
     —work
   - What do I like to do?
   - What kind of role do I wish to fill?
   - What skills and qualities do I need to gain?
4. How do I get there?
   - What experiences do I require in order to learn what I need to learn? What learning programs do I need?
   - What experiments do I need to try?
   - What kind of help do I need, and from whom?
5. How will I know if I have arrived?
   - How will I evaluate my learning?
   - What measures do I need to assess myself?
   - What feedback do I need and from whom?

Source: Hennessey, D., and Gilligan, J. H. "Identifying and Developing Tomorrow's Nursing Trust Directors." *Journal of Nursing Management* 2, no 1(1994): 37–45.

1. Assess where one is in the grieving process and plan one intervention to assist movement.
2. Initiate a plan for survival:
   - Develop a *plan for Monday.*
   - Assess current financial situation and make a plan.
   - Assess current self-care regime and plan to improve.
3. Identify life priorities and dream about the ideal.
4. Assess current status of career management:
   - Be sure of job success.
   - Get the work vision clearer.
   - Assess skills and needs.
5. Make a commitment to personal development and learning.

Support and Challenge—Self

The necessity for personal development was discussed as the premise for this article. Finding opportunities to get support and challenge is the essence of personal development. Critical aspects of this process include reflection, creativity, and self-awareness.

Leaders must learn how to empower others and create opportunity for those around them. This begins by a simple but very difficult change in style. If the goal is to empower others, one can ask questions to assist them to find their own answers rather than giving advice and telling them what to do. Giving advice illustrates how clever the individual is, but does not empower the other person. Development of leaders to interact with others in a nondirective, facilitative way is the essence of such empowerment. A change in style can only take place by practicing in an environment of learning and support such as a peer learning group, where the focus is on helping others learn.[17] Good leaders function essentially as consultants once the vision and key goals are established.

REFLECTION

Successful people make a lifelong commitment to continuous learning about themselves and the world around them. Change is occurring so fast that the ability to learn is maybe becoming more critical to success than past experience. It is said that the rate of learning must be greater than the rate of change. The first principle of continuous learning is reflection. In this process, several questions are asked of oneself:

- What am I really trying to do?
- What is happening now (the *story*)?
- How do I feel about it?
- What are my analyses and conclusions?
- What have I learned from this experience? (both the actual incident and telling the *story*)
- What am I going to do now?

Schön describes reflection in professional practice as a method for professionals to assess, learn, and alter their practice.[18] Neubauer[17] and Margerison[19] describe learning networks or sets, which are groups where reflection and learning by individuals and assessment of group process are the focus. The important task is that one find a method to review, think, reflect, and plan. This could be personal through a journal or a tape, with another person one can trust (ie, colleague, mentor, professional, friend) or a group of colleagues, a continuous quality improvement team, or a learning network.

The principle of reflection is that others listen to the *story* without interrupting so as not to change the agenda of the storyteller. There must be enough trust among the participants that each person can be honest with the *story* and with feedback. The emphasis is on asking questions to assist the person to learn, not solving the problem or giving advice. Learning this process is critical to behavior change if one wishes to empower others. The feedback to participants should be a balance between support and challenge—*warmth and light*. If too much support is given, a person is overprotected and there seems no need to grow and change; but if a person gets too much challenge, he or she defends rather than being open to learning.

A place and time to reflect seem to be the things that busy executives need the most. Many are bright and good problem solvers and are not afraid to disclose about themselves, but only a few take the time for the processes. Learning will not take place unless one makes the time for the processes.

CREATIVITY

New solutions must be found to old and new problems, and the traditional left-brain, rational approach to problem solving is not working very well. It is critical to find ways to enhance and develop creativity. Tapping into the "right brain" offers images, color, rhythm, and intuition, which may produce a new idea for solving an old problem. Our education and our work in the western, rational culture have not developed these abilities.[11] Painting, dancing, or making music will help rediscover childhood creativity. These are good activities to gain some balance in one's life and develop creativity at the same time. Use of stories, pictures, mind maps, and models helps others see the big picture and often shifts their thinking.

SELF-AWARENESS—THE ROAD TO AUTHENTICITY

Awareness of values, feelings, history, fears, anxieties, joys, wants, and needs is essential to being authentic. Leaders must be sure that they are aware of their own personal needs so that their motives are clear to them. Knowing one's *hot buttons* is essential. Colleagues know what makes one anxious or angry, and they often use this knowledge during interactions. Leaders must know and accept their dark side. Otherwise these things *leak* all over their work. Self-awareness is a lifelong process.

Self-assessment tests are helpful. Completing one every year and repeating some assessments once in a while can be revealing, as the results may change or a new insight gained. Getting feedback from various people, including some with whom one does not work, is essential to developing a personal picture. Work colleagues are usually working from their own agenda. Just telling one's *story* often gives insight.

The major result of self-awareness is that one is assisted in continuously evolving a vision and plan that help in finding environments that make the most of strengths. This seems to be the best alternative, as few people change significantly after childhood. A person who failed in one job situation often flourishes in another.

Support and Challenge—Colleagues and Coworkers

Once the nurse executive has mastered the process of allowing danger and opportunity to be a part of his or her conscious life, it is then possible to facilitate the processes for others. The challenge is accepting the need to assist staff to work through the grieving, especially if it is related to a project the leader is committed to. Not arguing, trying to fix it, or talking others out of their feelings may be the most difficult challenge a leader can have. Often, an outside consultant can be helpful at this point to facilitate discussion. Every staff member from environmental services worker to executive should be offered opportunities for career and personal development as well as financial planning. General equivalency diploma (GED) programs for service workers and basic financial planning for staff nurses can be some of the most rewarding development programs to initiate for staff. Organizations can no longer offer *jobs for life,* but they can offer skills to *thrive in chaos.*

In the world of the 21st century, environments must be created where people can learn by taking risks, reflecting on experiences, getting the proper balance between support and challenge (*warmth and light*), and being successful. Leaders cannot create these environments for others unless they are a part of one themselves.

REFERENCES

1. Peters, T. *Thriving on Chaos: A Handbook for Management Revolution.* London, England: Macmillan, 1988.
2. Handy, C. *The Age of Unreason.* London, England: Arrow Books, 1989.
3. Miller, E. *From Dependency to Autonomy: Studies in Organisation Change.* London, England: Free Association Books, 1993.
4. Rodgers, C. *Freedom To Learn.* Columbus, Ohio: Charles E Merrill, 1969.
5. Kubler-Ross, E. *On Death and Dying.* London, England: Routledge & Kegan Paul, 1990.
6. Richman, L. "Getting Past Economic Insecurity." *Fortune* 131, no. 7 (1995): 103–7.
7. Selye, H. *The Stress of Life.* New York, N.Y.: McGraw-Hill, 1976.
8. Longfellow, L. *STRESS: The American Addiction: How to Break the Habit.* Prescott, Ariz.: Lecture Theatre, Inc., 1984.
9. Nuernberger, P. *Freedom from Stress.* Honesdale, Pa: Himalayan International Institute of Yoga and Science and Philosophy of the USA, 1981.
10. Gawain, S. *Creative Visualization.* New York, N.Y.: Bantam Books, 1982.
11. Buzan, T. *The Mind Map Book.* London, England: Pan Books, 1994.
12. Handy, C. *The Age of Paradox.* Boston, Mass.: Harvard Business School Press, 1994.
13. Ross, R. *Prospering Women.* New York, N.Y.: Bantam Books, 1984.
14. Bennis, W. *On Becoming a Leader.* London, England: Hutchinson Business Books, 1989.
15. Vaill, P. *Managing as a Performing Art New Ideas for a World of Chaotic Change.* San Francisco, Calif: Jossey-Bass, 1990.
16. Hennesaey, D., and Gilligan, J.H. "Identifying and Developing Tomorrow's Nursing Trust Directors." *Journal of Nursing Management* 2, no. 1 (1994): 37–45.
17. Neubauer, J. "The Learning Network: Leadership Development for the Next Millenium." *Journal of Nursing Administration* 25, no. 2 (1995): 23–32.
18. Schön, D. *Educating the Reflective Practitioner.* San Francisco, Calif: Jossey-Bass, 1988.
19. Margerison, C. "Action Learning and Excellence in Management Development." *Journal of Management Development* 7, no. 5 (1988): 43–53.

CHAPTER 31

●●●

Collaborative Conflict Resolution

WILLIAM UMIKER

A study by DiStephano and Maznevski[2] led to the conclusion that training in collaborative conflict resolution was essential to effective team performance. They found that without debating, negotiating, disagreeing, questioning, probing, and differences of opinion, there was little group decision making. Change efforts in general (and increased productivity or cost-cutting in particular) require confrontations, and confrontations are healthy as long as they culminate in win–win solutions. Collaborative conflict is when the participants attack problems rather than each other, and the problems are resolved through honest and open discussion. Collaborative conflict builds healthy relationships and helps to disclose information, to challenge assumptions or perceptions, to understand problems, and to make good decisions. Negotiation, mediation, and arbitration are special forms of conflict handling and should also feature collaborative techniques.

Dysfunctional teams either suppress conflicts that then fester and eventually disrupt working relationships, or employ adversarial conflict in which the proceedings are competitive rather than cooperative. Adversarial conflict may feature anger, hostility, humiliation, or rancor.

The Six Major Causes of Conflict

The etiology of a conflict is not always apparent. Often there is a covert issue that is hidden by a less important, overt factor. Other situations are murky because the cause is multifactorial. Here are the six most common causes.

1. Unclear expectations. People may not know what they are expected to do, how it is to be done, and what the results can be. Policies and rules can be ambiguous. For example, a policy concerning sexual harassment may not spell out what exactly constitutes sexual harassment.

2. Poor communication. Conflicts attributed to ill will are frequently the result of communication short circuits, especially poor listening, hastily scribbled memos, or garbled e-mail messages. Faulty perceptions or assumptions give rise to misun-

---

Reprinted from *Health Care Supervisor,* 1997; 15(3), 70–75. © 1997 Aspen Publishers, Inc.

derstandings. We all can cite personal examples of hurt feelings and broken friendships that resulted from distortions or half-truths.

3. Lack of clear jurisdiction. When limits of power are not spelled out, turf and authority disputes may erupt. Conflicts may arise over funds, space, time, personnel, or equipment. Squabbles over work and vacation schedules are common.

4. Incompatibilities or disagreements based on differences of temperaments or attitudes. These are often complex conflicts with overlays of race, religion, nationality, age, politics, ethics, or values. As an example of the latter, animal caretakers may disagree about how some animals are being treated. We are all familiar with examples of conflicts based on some of the first items listed.

5. Individual or group conflicts of interest. There may be chronic friction between departments or shifts. For example, disagreements arise between the purchasing department and a unit manager.

6. Operational or staffing changes. Whenever there are organizational or functional changes, conflicts are bound to arise.

Dangers of Escalating and Suppressed Conflict

When conflict is permitted to escalate, the parties become impatient, angry, or frustrated. They turn their attention from problem solving to attacking the other person. Blame and threats spew forth, and issues proliferate from one to many. Old grievances emerge to compound the situation. The relationship is damaged, and the bitterness leads to thoughts of how to get even rather than how to solve the initial problem. Eventually the parties may enlist supporters from among the bystanders, resulting in the formation of opposing cliques.

When an organization attempts to suppress conflict, the consequences include chronic complaining; decline in productivity, attendance, morale, and loyalty; increased stress; and possibly sabotage or violence.

Basic Strategies for Coping With Conflict

Each of the following strategies is appropriate for certain situations. Face your next conflict by picking the right one.

AVOID

Action here may be to deny that there is a problem, to physically escape, to pass the buck, or to procrastinate. The problem remains unresolved. This "gunnysacking" results in the buildup of anger that eventually explodes.

Avoidance can be appropriate when it is not your problem, when there is nothing you can do about it, when it is not worth the effort to face, when additional information is needed, when you or the other individual is emotionally upset, when potential disruption outweighs the benefits of resolution, or when the situation will probably ameliorate if you can wait it out.

FIGHT

There are several booby traps in this aggressive approach. You can lose! Even if you win a skirmish, your opponents may regroup and return to the fray, wait for another opportunity to retaliate, or become saboteurs. This strategy is used when quick action is needed, such as enforcement of safety regulations. It also may be appropriate when ethical or legal violations are involved.

SURRENDER

Nonassertive people often succumb to this, thus building up internal frustration as self-esteem erodes. This strategy is appropriate when the other party is right, when it does not matter to you, when you have little or no chance to win, when harmony and stability are especially important, or when giving in on a minor item means winning a more important one later.

COMPROMISE

This partial-win strategy is often what you must settle for. Compromise permits each party to get part of what they want, so there is some satisfaction for both parties. Most union–management disputes are settled in this manner.

On the negative side, neither party gets everything it wants. In addition, compromise may involve game playing, with each side pumping up its demands or disguising them. A common error is to adopt this alternative prematurely, without making a greater effort at collaboration. This strategy is appropriate when opposing goals are incompatible, when a temporary settlement to complex issues is needed, when time constraints call for an expedient solution, or when discussions have stalled.

COLLABORATE

Collaboration is defined as problem solving, working together to find solutions that satisfy both parties. This win–win approach is usually the best alternative but often requires creative solutions because the best answer is one that neither side originally considered. The basic principle is to turn conflict from an attack on individuals to a mutual attack on the problem, such as "How can we solve this in a way that satisfies both of us?" An added benefit of this approach is that it builds positive relationships.

Negative aspects include the length of time often required, frequently a delay of decisions, and frustration when no consensus is reached. This strategy is usually the best one, especially when the issue is too important to be settled any other way, when commitment is sought via a consensus, or when different perspectives are to be explored.

Preparations for Collaborative Confrontation

Analyze the situation by answering these questions:

- What do I want to accomplish, and what is the most I will give up?
- What do I think the other person wants? What covert goals might the other person have?
- What false assumptions or incorrect perceptions might the other person have
- Which strategy should I use?
- What are my "hot buttons," and what should I do if they are pushed?
- If I plan to use a collaborative approach, what special precautions should be taken?

Get psyched up for the event by using these three techniques:

1. *Success imagery.* Visualize a successful confrontation. Picture your body language, hear your words and voice tone, and envisage a successful outcome. Athletes and professional speakers have used this technique with great success.

2. *Self-talk.* this is the process of converting negative thoughts to positive ones when talking to yourself. All of us cary on a constant inner dialogue. When we are in a passive mode, these internal conversations are negative and pessimistic; our subconscious mind conjures up statements such as, "I could never say that" or "She'll just blow me away." Let your positive affirmations take control. Say to yourself, "I will be in control." Avoid weak statements such as "I'm going to try to stand up to her next time."

3. *Rehearsing.* After you have selected your dialogue and its appropriate body language, rehearse the anticipated encounter over and over. Do it in front of a mirror. Verbalize out loud. Still better, get a friend or relative to role play with you. Don't be satisfied until your performance is down pat.

The Confrontation

Confrontations are seldom as bad as anticipated, especially when you prepare beforehand. Here are some practical tips for holding a collaborative type of confrontation:

- Avoid sitting across from the person. This invites opposition. Sit next to each other or at right angles. Still better, take a stroll side-by-side.
- After outlining the problem, move on to areas of agreement. To do this, start with questions you are certain will be answered affirmatively. It is then easier to get a yes to more controversial questions. For example, "Steve, don't you agree that we must put team goals before our individual agendas?"
- Be an attentive listener, asking lots of questions and keying in on what the other person is saying. Be empathetic. Respect the other person's feelings, but still feel free to respond in a manner of your choosing.
- Often it pays to ask exactly what it is that the person wants. You may be pleasantly surprised to find that what she wants is less than you were prepared to offer. On the other hand, don't neglect to say what it is that you want.
- Let the person know that you hear and understand—both content and feelings. Validate feelings with something like, "As I understand it, Joan, you're angry because I asked one of your assistants to give me a hand with my project. Is that it?" Validating has two benefits. It clarifies the problem and lets the person know that what he or she is saying is important.
- Seek a bigger pie instead of dividing the pie up. This means finding a win–win solution.
- Emphasize that you can't change the past and should concentrate on the present and the future.
- Stay cool and avoid rhetorical or emotional escalation. When upset, people tend to exaggerate. This increases anxiety and makes problem solving more difficult. When forced into a corner, say "You're making me uncomfortable" or "I find myself getting upset, Steve. Let's take a 10-minute break, OK?"
- Let the other person save face. He or she must come away with something.

Confronting an Angry Person

We may provoke anger in others when we criticize, pressure, threaten, deny, irritate, or deride—anything that attacks self-esteem. Almost anyone can be provoked into anger if the stimulus is intense enough, but each of us has a different threshold. Some associates are supersensitive. They may have explosive tempers on very short fuses. Some use anger to get out of unpleasant assignments. These individuals take everything personally. They quickly and angrily charge favoritism or discrimination. Here are some tips for coping with an angry person.

- Do not lose your cool. Never shout or even raise your voice. Avoid any threatening gestures or aggressive body language. Never touch. When you are angry, do not say a word until your emotions are under control.
- Do not make comments about the other person's anger or tell them not to be angry, such as "Why don't you calm down?" This just does not work. Do not patronize or lecture.
- If a person walks into your office and you sense that she is angry, greet her in a friendly fashion. *The person who speaks first sets the mood.*
- Listen to the other person's outburst without interrupting. This has a powerful calming effect. Make certain that you understand the problem. *The person who listens best usually comes out a winner.*
- Do not become defensive or argumentative.
- Empathize by paraphrasing what the other person is angry about and why he or she feels that way.
- Ask questions. *The person who asks the most questions controls the agenda and the direction of the dialogue.* The key question is "What do you want me to do?" Determine exactly what the other person wants and satisfy that want if possible. If not, offer your solution.
- Assure the other person that something will be done.

Conflict can be made less painful and more productive if the collaborative approach is used. Planning for confrontations and the application of a few commonsense communication principles can help supervisors to become more expert in this essential skill.

REFERENCES

1. DiStephano, J., and Masnevski, M.L. "Process and Performance in Multicultural Teams." *Harvard Business Review* 3 (1996): 10.

CHAPTER 32

● ●

Negotiating Skill for Health Care Professionals

WILLIAM UMIKER

At its worst, negotiation is battling with opponents; at its best it is an interaction that enables both parties to gain what they want—a win/win outcome.

Managers and self-directed teams negotiate with vendors and may participate in negotiations with external customers over services and charges. They negotiate with internal customers (other departments and individuals) and with members of their own work groups over schedules, salaries, assignments, work hours, and overtime. Because of more cross-functional activities, health care professionals now deal less with their superiors and subordinates and more with colleagues. In other words *horizontal* negotiations are now of paramount importance.[1]

The Three Basic Forms of Negotiation

THE POWER PLAY—"GOTCHA"

This is a form of combat in which one side makes an unfair offer and expects the other side to counter with an equally unfair demand based on the presumption that the stronger party will eventually triumph. This authoritarian approach is based on marshalling enough power to overwhelm the opponents. "I'm king of the castle and you're the dirty rascal."

People who play this game bring their big guns with them to the negotiating table. They may have prestigious titles, approval authority, powerful friends, or professional expertise. These Sherman tanks are aggressive and condescending. They try to humble those who fail to fall in line. They make their opponent fully aware of their influence by posturing—dropping names, exaggerating past successes, and threatening (eg, "Here's what will happen if you don't . . ."). A very few have charisma, which is a powerful nonverbal form of persuasion.[2]

They think it naive to believe that being cooperative will work. A few really want to hurt the other party. What they seek, of course, is a complete victory with no concessions. At-

Reprinted from *Health Care Supervisor,* 14(3), pp.27–32, 1996, with permission of Aspen Publishers, Inc., © 1996.

tempts at this kind of dominance often meet counter-dominance, and attempts to bully one's way through by sheer nerve and aggressiveness are usually ineffective in the long run.[3]

There are several ways to respond to power plays.

- Develop a thick skin. Don't take the nasty things you hear personally.
- Don't be intimidated. Be assertive. Going hat in hand to throw yourself at the other person's mercy is not a very effective option.[3]
- If a person tries to intimidate you with technical jargon, speak right up; "I need you to put that in one-syllable words."[4]
- Consider requesting that a third-party mediator be appointed.[5]
- Respond to threats with "Why would you want to do that?"[2]

HAGGLING—TAKING POSITIONS

This is still the most common kind of negotiating. Both sides play their cards close to their chest and seek to get win/lose outcomes through gamesmanship. Each side adopts a fixed position.[6] Taking a position means that one is inflexible and reluctant to compromise. This often leads to nonresolution: "This is what we are offering. Take it or leave it."

When negotiators bargain over positions, they become locked into defending those positions to save face. This makes it difficult to modify their stance, thus reducing the possibility of agreement. The negotiations become contests of will rather than problemsolving exercises.

On the other hand, taking an interest permits flexibility, give and take, and new positions. It can result in compromise or a win/win outcome.

Traditional haggling, in which each side argues a position and either makes concessions to reach a compromise or refuses to budge, is not the most efficient and amicable way to reach a wise agreement.

R. Fisher and W. Ury[7(p.1)]

Here are some of the tactics used by hagglers.

- Never make your best offer at the start.[6]
- Ask for more than you expect to get.[2]
- Create an obligation by giving them a little something.[2(p.49)]
- Make them feel guilty: "Your proposal doesn't sound very fair to me," or "I take that remark personally."[2]
- Offer options that are all favorable to you.
- Manipulate. Manipulators exaggerate their requests so they can settle for less, or they promise more than they know they will deliver. Artfulness in concealing intentions may yield short-term gains, but manipulation and deceit sooner or later catch up with almost everyone.

COLLABORATION—PROBLEM SOLVING

Most people want to end up with a good deal while preserving goodwill with the other party. With collaboration you achieve your goals while helping others achieve theirs. These are win/win outcomes. They dispense with power tricks and traps in favor of a more transparent approach.[6]

Collaboration is based on the premise that you make the pie bigger rather than fighting over the size of each party's slice. In other words, the negotiators add value to the package rather than seeking concessions from each other. The insightful negotiator points out the benefits of various options that the other person had failed to realize.

Collaboration is really creative problem solving in which both parties work as partners rather than as opponents. The more creative they are, the better the end results. For example, two work units may be having arguments over the use of a sole copier. Supervisor A agrees to grant priority to supervisor B in return for permission to use the graphic computer software that is under the control of supervisor B.

A special form of collaboration is that advocated by the Albrechts.[6] When using added value negotiating (AVN) instead of one option, multiple ones emerge. With multiple options to choose from. the parties are very likely to find at least one that meets all of their needs.[6] Deliberations feature empathy, fairness, and assertiveness. One-upmanship is eliminated; dignity and self-respect are preserved.

Preparations for a Negotiation

Like any worthwhile activity, planning is essential to successful negotiations. Too often we walk into a negotiation unprepared. Since each person has different interests, being prepared helps one to understand these different interests.

THE WISH LIST

You must know what you want and what you are willing to concede. Try to find out what the other side wants, how badly they want it, what they are likely to propose, and what cards they hold.

DATA

Effective negotiators have the necessary data. These may be copies of laws, policies, protocols, or written and unwritten guidelines. Negotiators must have up-to-date information gleaned from formal and informal communication channels. Nothing will shoot down a proposal quicker than a valid document that proves that what has been proposed violates a law or the organization's mission statement.

Information must be organized and presented in a concise understandable fashion. This often requires handouts, graphs, charts, and other visual displays.

COMPLETE A PLAN OF ACTION

Several steps should be taken before negotiating. You should sketch out the possible options you can offer, prepare your opening remarks, and prepare the arguments you can make to maximize the positive aspects and to counter the other person's arguments. Before meeting, review your approach with an associate or mentor. Then try to pick the best time and place for you for the meeting.

Major Steps in a Negotiation

STEP 1: CLARIFY INTERESTS

Interests may be objective (special service, sharing of equipment, turnaround time) or subjective (goodwill, long-term relationships).[6] Ask the person with whom you are negotiating how the situation is viewed and what is important. Paraphrase the message you get and ask if you have interpreted the view correctly. Then, state your view. Don't proceed until these viewpoints and desired outcomes are crystal clear.

STEP 2: FOCUS ON PERCEIVED POINTS OF AGREEMENT

Center on points of agreement and work from there. Only after covering each of these should you get into the problem areas.

STEP 3: FORMULATE POSSIBLE OPTIONS—THE MORE THE BETTER

Verify that each deal offers a different way to balance interests through a different arrangement of the value elements.[6] Articulate the benefits of each option to the other person.

Don't get stuck believing that your solution is the only good one. Be gracious; if the person has a valid argument, say so.

STEP 4: AGREE ON THE BEST OPTION

If you can't reach complete agreement, be willing to compromise, *but not until you have explored all win/win solutions.* If things stall, call for a break or a postponement. Psychologists report that 20 to 30 minutes of steady negotiating is the limit without an interruption.[1]

In some situations it is best not to make a definite commitment. Each of you may need more information or to consult with other individuals. View the initial meeting as an exploratory session.

- -

BOX 32–1 GENERAL TIPS FOR MORE EFFECTIVE NEGOTIATION

Do

- State objectives or interests, not positions. Make certain that you understand the other party's interest.
- Regard the other person not as an enemy but as a partner in problem solving. Attack the problem, not the other person.
- Remember that the other person is usually willing to accept a solution if you can make it sufficiently attractive. Phrase requests in terms of the other person's best interest.
- Listen carefully for what is said, what is not said, and watch the body language.
- Keep things simple. Distill your ideas into a few sentences.
- Anticipate objections.
- Know what you can give.
- Present several options.
- Model openness and compliance and act as if you expect the other party to do the same.
- Remain assertive but not aggressive.
- Remember your veto power. You can always say no or walk away.

- Use your body language. A simple shudder when the other person makes an offer may change the offer in your favor.
- Persist when you know you are right.

Avoid

- Putdowns, sarcasm, gloating, cynicism.
- Manipulation and dirty tricks.
- Distortions, exaggerations, or falsehoods.
- Revealing that you have been taken by surprise.
- Rushing the negotiating process.
- Jumping at the first offer; you can almost always do better.
- Making just one offer.
- Giving away the store. Don't be a pushover.
- Trying to score all the points. Your position is strengthened and cooperation is much more likely if you accede to some of their ideas.
- Allowing the other party to pick the best parts from all the deals in order to make a new one—"cherry picking."[6]

- -

STEP 5: PERFECT THE DEAL

It's important to refine the selected deal, to make sure it's balanced in terms of total value, and to ensure that each of you is comfortable with it.[6]

STEP 6: WRAP IT UP

Just as a sales associate focuses attention on closing a sale. you too should review what has been agreed upon, and document it. Rindler[5(p.81)] provides this useful list of closing tips:

- Agree on exactly who is going to do what—and when.
- Get commitments for deadlines for completing specific responsibilities.
- Get it in writing. A carefully typed statement demonstrates commitment and provides a reference for the future when memories get hazy.
- Decide how long results will be monitored, what will be measured, how, by whom, and for how long. What will constitute a successful outcome?
- Discuss a series of "what happens if."
- Help the other person sell the agreement to associates and superiors.

The boxed item lists several things one should and should not do when involved in negotiation. (Box 32-1)

Barriers to Successful Negotiation

FEARS

There may be fear of loss of friendship or future cooperation. Some people cave in quickly because they just don't have the stomach for any kind of disagreement. Others may be inflexible or demanding because they fear that someone will take advantage of them.

SECRECY

Some negotiators mistakenly think that they will win more often if they withhold information.

ULTIMATUMS AND DEADLINES

Avoid making these types of threats yourself unless they are absolutely necessary. However, sometimes the threat to walk out of a bargaining session will get results.

ANGER, GUILT INDUCTION, RIDICULE, OR TEARS

These are seldom indicated. Experienced negotiators are not moved by these gimmicks, but these responses may be effective when dealing with novices.

BRINGING ALONG A TEAM

While team efforts have some advantages, such as augmented expertise and mutual support, there are problems. Showing up with a cadre of supporters may suggest that you lack the ability to handle the process by yourself. Sometimes one member of your group makes a remark that hurts your case or may even disclose disunity among the group's members. Also, the team approach takes longer and is more likely to end without a consensus being reached.

TOO MUCH RELIANCE ON DATA

Statistics are good if valid and not redundant, but reliance on them backfires when the other party points out flaws or comes up with more recent or more impressive data.

DELAYING TACTICS

Repeated and unnecessary delays not only postpone needed action, but also erode the spirit of cooperation and can be very frustrating.

REFERENCES

1. Goddard, R.W. "Negotiation: How to Win by Forgetting about Winning." *Training* 21 (1984).
2. Dawson, R. *Secrets of Power Persuasion.* Englewood Cliffs, N.J.: Prentice Hall, 1992.
3. Cohen, A.R., and Bradford, D.L. *Influence without Authority.* New York. N.Y.: Wiley, 1990.
4. O'Brian, J.D. "Negotiating with the 'Big Kids.'" *Supervisory Management* 39 (1994):10.
5. Rindler, H.S. *Managing Disagreement Constructively.* Los Altos, Calif.: Crisp. 1988.
6. Albrecht, K., and Albrecht, S. *Added Value Negotiating: The Breakthrough Method for Building Balanced Deals.* Homewood, Ill.: Business One Irwin, 1993.
7. Fisher, R., and Ury, W. *Getting to Yes: Negotiating without Giving In.* New York. N.Y.: Houghton-Mifflin, 1988.

QUESTIONS TO PART III

. . . .

ASSERTIVENESS

1. In thinking about speaking out on an important matter in your health care setting, what factors do you consider when you are deciding about whether or not to speak up?
2. In assessing the ways you get angry, what aspects are effective and what aspects are ineffective?
3. What is the most difficult thing for you to handle when anger is directed to you?
4. Think about one situation in which you handled anger effectively. What specific behaviors made it so?

ADVOCACY

1. Of the definitions of advocacy cited by Gaylord and Grace, which definition comes closest to your philosophy of nursing care? Explain.
2. In their article on advocacy, Gaylord and Grace attempt to define patient advocacy more precisely. In your opinion, did they succeed? Give your reasons.
3. In what ways do you fulfill your ethical obligations to patients in your work setting?
4. In your opinion, is the philosophy of managed care compatible or incompatible with your ethical obligations to patients? Explain.
5. Presuming that you or your coworkers have experienced or witnessed the "dirty hands" dilemma detailed by Mohr and Mahon, what actions were taken to resolve this dilemma? Did these actions help or hinder the resolution of the dilemma?
6. How collegial are you with your coworkers? In what ways do you demonstrate collegiality?
7. In today's managed care environment, is it possible to be collegial? Explain.
8. How knowledgeable are you about the laws governing your nursing practice? If not, discuss your reasons.
9. Have you worked with anyone who has been disciplined? What were the circumstances?

MENTORING

1. Have you worked with a mentor in the development of your professional career? If so, were mentoring functions primarily focused on career development or on psychosocial functions? Describe.
2. What aspects of mentoring *not* identified in the Angelini article did you experience?
3. In what ways does the mentoring process model apply to you and your professional development?

POWER

1. What is your concept of empowerment? In what ways is it similar to or different from Rodwell's analysis of empowerment?

2. In what ways do you empower your patients? Are you comfortable in allowing them to make decisions about their care?

3. What problems have you encountered in delegating tasks to others? Are they similar to or different from the delegation problems in McConnell's article?

4. Describe the way you prepare to delegate a task to another person. Is your preparation compatible to those outlined by McConnell? If not, in what ways do they differ?

5. What conditions would increase your work satisfaction and effectiveness?

6. What would you like to tell your nurse manager with regard to empowering you and your coworkers?

POLITICS

1. Do you believe that your vote matters? What would you say to someone who is skeptical about one vote making any difference?

2. What does the future hold for this country if only a minority of voters vote during an election year?

3. What do you think needs to be done to increase the number of people voting?

4. In what ways have you been involved in the legislative process? If you haven't been involved, what prevents you from doing so?

5. What gaps are there in your knowledge of the political process?

6. What do you consider the most important piece of legislation regarding nursing practice and/or health care before either your state legislature or Congress?

COLLECTIVE BARGAINING

1. In what ways have labor laws protected you? Elaborate.

2. What do you think about nursing's present collective bargaining efforts?

3. What problems, in your opinion, do nurses continue to have about collective bargaining?

4. Describe the advantages and disadvantages of belonging to a collective bargaining unit.

5. What would you like changed in the way nurses use collective bargaining?

6. How have the recent rulings concerning nurses and collective bargaining affected your practice?

CHANGE

1. What, in your opinion, makes the changes taking place in nursing today different from those in the past?

2. Which of the seven basic rules listed in the Porter-O'Grady article is the most significant for you?

3. What is your plan of action as your health care facility changes?

4. What aspect of dealing with change gives you the most problems? How are you dealing with it?

5. Of the seven stages of change detailed by Manion, at which stage do you most frequently find yourself? What do you think accounts for this?

6. Of the tips for getting through the stages of change, which do you find most helpful? Which do you find least helpful? Explain.

7. Of the common mistakes made in coping with organizational change, which one are you most susceptible to? How did you remedy the situation?

8. What opportunities have you taken for your own self-care during periods of change and/or stress?

CONFLICT RESOLUTION

1. What is your usual method of dealing with conflict? Is it effective in resolving conflict? Elaborate.

2. How do you prepare yourself for dealing with a conflict situation? In what ways has it been effective or ineffective?

3. Describe your style of negotiating. In what ways is it similar to or different from those described in Umiker's article?

4. Which one of the three forms of negotiation cited by Umiker, appeals to you the most? State your reasons.

5. What appeals to you about negotiating with someone? What does not? Elaborate.

PART IV

●●

The Organizational Setting

Health care organizations can be dangerous to one's health. What nurses are experiencing in these turbulent times borders on the toxic. Without the certainty of checks and balances that lend perspective to rapid change, it is understandable that nurses perceive themselves as members of an endangered profession. Both newcomers and veteran nurses alike are finding themselves in the midst of an organizational siege mentality that, in effect, holds nurses captive to their particular organization's "whim of the week." Is working in this kind of environment for the faint of heart? Hardly.

To keep victimization at bay in this "organizational zoo," nurses need some sort of a professional survival kit—one that would contain a collection of observational and listening skills ("What do I *see* and *hear* around me?"); a ready knowledge base ("What do I *know* about what I see and hear?"); and a set of adaptive intervention skills ("How do I *respond* to what I see, hear, and know?"). No 90-day warranty comes with this survival kit, nor is there any guarantee of success. But using the skills it contains can give nurses a "jump start" on their journey through the embattled organizational maze of which they are a part.

Part IV is divided into three sections: organizational assessment, the organizational setting, and organizational behaviors that directly affect nurses in their work settings. The readings on organizational assessment begin with a satirical look at organizations and their similarity to zoos. The problems faced by the animals in the zoo offer revealing parallels to the zoo-like atmosphere often seen in health care organizations. In the readings that follow, the assessment of factors that contribute to the development of healthy and unhealthy organizations are discussed, as are selected factors that should be considered in assessing an organization's structure.

In the organizational setting section, the focus is on issues and concerns directly related to the three major actors within the setting: nurses, patients, and management. Among the topics featured in this section are the customer in the health care environment; patient-focused care; shared governance; managed care; reduction in force; and the measurement of patient outcomes.

The last section of Part IV, organizational behaviors, concludes with readings devoted to those behaviors that adversely affect the morale of nurses in their health care settings. Unless these potentially dysfunctional behaviors are recognized and effectively dealt with, the use of defensive, distrustful, and self-protective behaviors will continue unabated, making the work climate in the already embattled health care setting all the more intolerable.

PART IV **Contents**

●●●

SECTION THREE ORGANIZATIONAL BEHAVIORS

CHAPTER 33

●●

The Organization Zoo: A Fable

JOHN G. BRUHN AND ALAN P. CHESNEY

The observation of animal behavior has always been an accepted method for gaining a better understanding of human behavior. As a biologist, Morowitz utilized insights gained from studying ecology to help him understand the behavior of individuals in organizations.[1] He observed that individuals in organizations play dual roles: functional roles determined by their job descriptions and ego roles determined by their psychological needs. Ego roles lead individuals to make ego niches in the organizational structure for themselves. Individuals' egos often are more apparent in organizations than their jobs.

During their many years of working in bureaucratic organizations such as universities and hospitals, the authors observed numerous similarities between human behavior in organizations and animal behavior in zoos. Indeed, in some instances, human behavior has been observed to be so animalistic and egoistic that the interventions required to stop or change behavior are similar to those humans might use with their pets. Sharing experiences with colleagues led us to believe that our experiences were not unique and that they existed in many different kinds and sizes of organizations. We hope that by sharing the following fable with readers, we will help them gain greater insights into collective behavior at work, both productive and nonproductive, and some of the ways in which people create their own problems.

Our fable takes place in a moderate-sized zoo; not all of the possible animals are present in this zoo, but those common to most zoos are represented. In zoos, placards on the cages identify the animals and give a few facts about them; in organizations, name plates on doors and desks and organizational charts provide some information about the employees. Who they are becomes most apparent, however, when one observes their behavior, especially when the zookeeper or boss is away.

The Fable

One day, the zookeeper was gone. The myna birds, known for picking up words from patrons of the zoo, said, "Let's organize; let's organize." The gorillas beat their chests, the chimps jumped up and down, the lions roared, the hyenas laughed, and the peacocks spread their tail feathers—all signifying approval. The majority of animals were unenthu-

Reprinted from *Health Care Supervisor*, 14(3), pp. 13–20, 1996, with permission of Aspen Publishers Inc., © 1996.

siastic; the ostrich buried its head; the seals, otters, and sea lions busily raced one another from one end of their pool to the other; the bears slept; the hippos took a mud bath; and the mountain goats ranged, outside of hearing, on the top of the ridge. Since it never requires a majority to get anything started, the minority decided to form an organization. The animals knew they had as much right to be in charge as the zookeeper. If necessary, they could always call upon the Humane Society to protect their rights.

LEADER

Who would be the leader? The giraffe, who had the best perspective of the zoo, suggested that an election be held. The zoo's prima donna, the peacock, felt best qualified, the bison felt most experienced, the lion believed he had the "presence" of a chief executive officer (CEO), and the gorilla knew he could intimidate most any one; but the chimps, who heard all of the campaigning, laughed and jumped up and down, because they knew that in this age of political correctness, the leader would have to be either a black or brown bear. All the animals believed their leader should be a known entity from within their own ranks, not a rare or endangered type, and certainly not a farm animal. The black bear was elected CEO.

STRUCTURE

The next issue was the type of organizational structure they would have. They considered the pyramid, but discarded it because the bear's managerial style was to roam around the organization rather than sit at the top. The rectangle was discarded because it required the animals to take sides. The circle was discarded because all of the animals could not get around a table. The animals wanted a futuristic organizational structure. They heard about quality circles from the zoo patrons and, since patrons were their clients, they listened. The zoo patrons expected quality service; with the diverse ways in which service in the zoo was provided, the animals thought quality circles most closely resembled the type of organization they should have. Quality circles were formed, each with a leader. The gorillas, chimps, orangutans, and all of the water animals formed a quality circle that provided entertainment for the patrons; it was important that these animals liked to perform. The peacocks, lions, elephants, bears, tigers, and hippos formed a quality circle whose service was to appear for photographs. Since most of the animals in this circle liked to sleep, their pose for photographers was always natural. Some animals didn't fit in quality circles with others because they were too ugly (hyena, bison, rhino), too large (giraffe), too remote (mountain goat), too unfriendly (turtle, ostrich), or wouldn't talk to patrons (parrot). These animals were named supervisors and directors.

ORGANIZATION COMPONENTS

Some members of organizations are independent, competitive, and seek individual rewards; new organizational structures that stress teams, quality circles, and task groups make it difficult to satisfy their ego needs. Indeed, the animals in the zoo have a variety of egos. Animals are kept in cages not only to protect the patrons but also to protect the animals from each other's egos. But cages didn't keep the animals from forming an organization, albeit different from the formal organization of which the zookeeper knew he was in charge.

Every organization needs an advisory committee. The animals selected the bison, the oldest and most experienced, to chair the committee. The myna birds and parrots were named to head up public relations and the giraffe, who knew everyone's business, was charged with fund raising. The black bear, as CEO, commanded the full attention of the advisory committee as he laid out goals and objectives for the organization. The advisory committee was to help promote the zoo to patrons, obtain financial support for improvements and the acquisition of new types of animals, and lobby for animal rights. The bear explained that the animals had adopted a mission statement that they would provide the best entertainment, photographic opportunities, and human-sensitive animals of any zoo in the country. Other zoos might be larger, have more exotic animals, or even have a special zoo for children, but this zoo was unique because it tried harder.

The zoo organization seemed to work well. The animals let the zookeeper believe he was in charge, and he was, when it was time to feed the animals and clear out the patrons so everyone could sleep.[2]

PROGRAMS

By listening to and watching the patrons, the animals quickly learned important words that would help make the new organization a success: "benchmarking," "diversity," "change management," "pay for performance," and "outplacement" were used frequently to help the animals choose a course of action. Since only the words were learned, they took on new meanings at the zoo.

The black bear created teams that were charged with implementing the new words. The birds were charged with benchmarking. They flew out of the zoo, observed other organizations, and brought back ideas about how to be more productive and how to measure zoo performance. Soon, the bear was measuring popularity to determine which animals were most popular with the patrons and therefore most productive.

The hoofed animals were put in charge of diversity. They studied the variety of animals in the zoo and concluded that certain farm animals should be included. They brought in horses, sheep, cows, and pigs because these animals were underrepresented in the zoo population. Although they did not contribute to the photographic or entertainment value of the zoo, it was hoped that, in time, these animals would learn how they could contribute.

Because the bear, as CEO, wanted to introduce change gradually, he chose the reptiles to form a team on change management. The reptiles moved slowly, under cover, and since they were almost noiseless, could surprise the animals with new ideas. Originally, the reptiles resisted change, but they learned from the chameleon, who changed colors to fit its environment, that it was important to please the boss. Soon the reptiles were presenting workshops to the other animals on how to become peak performers. The snakes carefully monitored change so that whatever changes occurred, their own niche in the organization was not threatened.

One day, the water animals, sea lions, seals, otters, and dolphins approached the bear with a new concept called "pay for performance." The idea was to distribute the organization's scarce resources to the animals on the basis of the value of each animal's contribution to the organization's goals. The logic of this system, with its emphasis on rewarding those animals who were most important to the organization's success, led to a new and improved reward system, which was designed to motivate the animals to be more productive. The water animals, who were both entertaining and photogenic, benefited greatly from the new plan. Unfortunately, the elephants, hippos, and rhinos, who had a greater need for rewards (food), found that they were getting less and less.

All of these changes meant that some of the animals were not needed for the efficient operation of a first-class zoo. The bear, therefore, needed to develop an outplacement program. The big cats were placed in charge of this function. The tigers, lions, jaguars, and cougars, being hunters, were able to get rid of dead wood in two ways. The small animals disappeared at night without a trace. The larger animals—the old bison, the elephants, hippos, and rhinos—were outplaced by being sold to circuses.

PROBLEMS

The zoo was running very efficiently. The programs had been fully implemented, and the zoo was gaining a national reputation. People came from all over the country to see the model zoo run by the animals. But the new zoo was not without problems.

Basically, there were two problems, which the bear and those who reported to him considered minor. First, the humans who worked at the zoo were getting tired of doing all of the scut work, such as feeding the animals and cleaning the cages. Second, the level of distrust and lack of respect among the animals was increasing. Everyone was fearful of the big cats: if they were seen in your area you might be the next candidate for outplacement. Many animals were jealous of the sea lions, otters, and dolphins, who had the most glamorous jobs and the best pay. Most of the zoo animals distrusted the reptiles who changed opinions as the need arose. No one liked the new farm animals, who were common, or the cleft-hoofed animals, such as the bison, giraffe, gazelle, and antelope, who were perceived to be strong supporters of their farm cousins. Because the birds, led by the owls, hawks, and eagles, were always away from the zoo, looking for prey and conducting studies, the other animals could reach them only by carrier pigeon.

Change and Challenge

The black bear gained national attention as a CEO. He had many speaking engagements and traveled frequently but failed to delegate authority to his line officers when he was gone. The black bear received many awards for being successful in getting the organization established. The President of the United States named him Animal of the Year, and the Humane Society put his picture on their poster. As the zoo flourished, the bear felt that he had met his goals as a CEO. Therefore, he began to look around for his next career opportunity. He wanted to be Commissioner of Wildlife, but no black bear had ever held such a high-level government job. Instead, he was recruited by the San Diego Zoo to be chair of the Zoo Board. This job would give him exposure working with zoos throughout the world, recruiting outstanding and unique animals to San Diego. The San Diego Zoo also had a bachelorette black bear who was looking for a mate. The snake, who overheard the bear's telephone conversation about the job offer with the San Diego Zoo, spread a rumor that the bear was leaving.

Almost immediately, speculation arose about who should take the bear's place. Some animals wanted another bear; others wanted an animal like the lion or tiger, who would be more aggressive; some wanted the myna bird who could be told what to say; and still others wanted an animal who had more of the "presence" of a CEO, like the parrot or peacock. Therefore, the animals decided to retain a search firm to assist in the search for a new CEO. The search firm advertised the position widely. Female, ethnic, minority, and disabled animals were encouraged to apply. The birds spread the word about the CEO vacancy in their travels as representatives to the annual meeting of the Zoo Animals of America (ZAA). However, no other zoos in America had established such a viable organization and it appeared that, in order to recruit a CEO to fill the shoes vacated by the bear, the search would have to be broadened to the international level.

The search firm received applications from the panda bear in China, the koala bear in Australia, the dancing bear in Russia, the kodiak and polar bears in Alaska, and the sloth bear in South America, but all were rejected by the zoo animals for various reasons. Japanese zoos had a reputation for having successfully implemented total quality management and for providing first-class service to patrons. Therefore, the search firm identified a Japanese ape as the next CEO. The ape was smaller than its American counterpart, was polite, energetic, experienced in animal and human relations, knowledgeable about technology, and totally dedicated to quality service. The ape's philosophy was that productivity and trust go hand in hand. He quickly established a set of values for the zoo that were based on a concern for the zoo as a whole. He called it the "Z" organization.[3] The zoo was no longer a hierarchy or a bureaucracy: it was like a clan or community where all the animals worked together with pride to provide the best possible service to zoo patrons. The big cats stopped their outplacement activities because turnover and incompetency had become almost zero. Small animals were as important as large animals. Jealousy, fear, and turfism were greatly minimized. The subversive reptiles always seemed to find roles as informants and facilitators of gossip.

The ape's motto for Z organization was "Our future is your business." Under the ape's leadership and philosophy, Z organization tripled the number of its patrons in one year. As the number of zoo patrons and the zoo's income rose, it was logical that the Board of Directors consider expansion. More cage space was needed for the animals, and special accommodations were needed for aging, ill, and disabled animals. A new exotic and rare animal section, a petting zoo for children, and new food booths for patrons who liked to feed themselves and the animals were needed. A capital campaign was launched with the gorilla as campaign chair. Using gorilla tactics, the campaign goal was exceeded. As the zoo expanded in size and complexity, the Z organization experienced growing pains. Someone was needed to oversee change in the organization. The ape named the skunk to the new position of director of the Office of Organizational Change and Evaluation. The skunk immediately inquired about how the zoo could become accredited and outlined policies for workloads, promotion, and annual evaluations. New forms and policies proliferated, and the need for new animals to monitor them grew accordingly. Soon, the entire skunk family was employed. The Evaluation Office evaluated everyone in the organization, everyone in the organization evaluated the Evaluation Office, and everyone evaluated everyone else.

Everyone in the zoo thought change was good also. Every six months, all the animals changed cages. Some animals carried change a bit further. The reptiles, led by the snakes, attempted to form a union. The big cats proposed the creation of a satellite zoo. The farm animals were now sufficiently integrated into the zoo to want to start an independent group that would inform patrons about their unique history and culture, and requested funds to assist them in this effort. Some animals petitioned to bring back the outplaced rhinos, hippos, elephants, and bison now that the zoo was more affluent and diversified. And the ostrich, llamas, and deer took a leave of absence to take a continuing education course to learn about what their role should be in a changing zoo. All the proposed changes overwhelmed the zookeeper, who resigned to return to teaching zoology at a small college.[4]

Now What?

The real test for the survival of Z organization and the ape's tenure as CEO was at hand. In order to sustain the success of the zoo, the ape decided to make a major investment in new technology, which would replace the humans who had been relegated to menial jobs. The push for technology involved a large outlay from the capital campaign fund with the promise that cost savings in the future would provide an excellent return on the dollar. E-mail, voice mail, local area networks, imaging, teleconferencing, and automated information systems were installed. The CEO could now communicate easily with all the animals without going through the chain of command. However, many animals resented the investment in computers. There was substantial resistance from the older animals who hoped their retirement would precede pressure to learn the new technology. The reptiles thought the money should have been spent on more or better food and on air conditioning for the cages, and that the zoo was sending the message that computers were more important than animals.

Downsizing

In the midst of this expansion into an information super highway, the zoo experienced a dramatic decrease in revenue due to two external factors: decreased state and local funding and increased state and federal zoo regulations. The national and state political climate of downsizing led legislators to cut zoo budgets. The ape tried to appeal to local and state politicians for additional support, threatening to close the animal nursery and reduce the daily ration of food to the animals, but to no avail. Meanwhile, the federal government began regulating zoos. They required zoos to implement birth control to reduce their size, they discouraged the replacement of animals who retired or died, and they restricted zoos to no more than two animals of each kind. Every zoo was to demonstrate its cost-effectiveness and submit plans for "right sizing." Children throughout America became upset at the effects of these interventions. They began to write letters to their legislators and planned marches accompanied by their pets. Smaller zoos closed or were bought out by larger zoos. Older animals retired from zoos to enter second careers. The federal government promised that zoos would continue to be important and formed a new office called the Animal Protection Agency. A moose, who had recently lost his job due to "right sizing," was named director.

The process of "right sizing" was traumatic for the zoo. Travel and operating funds were curtailed sharply. Programs were discontinued; the owls, hawks, and eagles could no longer go outside the zoo for prey; and travel to meetings of the ZAA was eliminated. Paranoia and fear became common at the zoo. Those animals who could accepted job offers from circuses, wild animal farms, and foreign zoos. Seals and sea lions departed for Walt Disney World, and many birds accepted contracts at Busch Gardens.

The ape began to lose popularity. As animals became critical of his investments, he began to centralize control of the zoo. The ape said his greater control of the zoo was for everyone's benefit. He still professed to operate a "Z" organization, but began to surround himself with fewer and fewer advisors. The external advisory committee to the ape was told that everything was under control and that turnover of animals was normal. The ape met with department heads and other leaders in an effort to convince them that the zoo was on the right track. However, these meetings were not informative. Increasingly, the ape withheld information from the animals for fear that he would be blamed for the problems. In the long run, this strategy proved disastrous. The animals called a meeting of the senate, took a vote of no confidence, and pressured the ape to resign. The ape filed a grievance with the zoo's Equal Employment Opportunity (EEO) officer, a turtle, in a futile attempt to regain his job.

The turtle moved so slowly that a new CEO was named before the ape had obtained another position. The Zoo Board decided the new CEO must be a female, because no female had ever been CEO in the zoo. A dolphin was elected because of her superb ability to communicate with two- and four-legged animals as well as her balanced philosophy of work and play. The dolphin named more sea animals to positions because she believed they had been underrepresented in zoo bureaucracies. Almost immediately, the reptiles began to spread rumors of sexism and favoritism. The myna birds said, "Here we go again; here we go again." The gorillas beat their chests, the chimps jumped up and down, the lions roared, the hyenas laughed, and the peacocks spread their tail feathers. They all knew the moral of this fable: "The more things change, the more they stay the same."

From Zoo to Workplace: A Short Leap

In the parable we have exaggerated animal behavior to show the importance of ego niches that people make for themselves in the organizational structure. Individuals' egos are often more apparent than their actual jobs. Therefore, change is difficult in organizations because change threatens the ego niches that people have made for themselves. We are willing to change almost any aspect of an organization or a job as long as it doesn't threaten our ego niches. Change will be resisted with great force in organizations where the ego needs of employees are not well meshed with the organizational goals.

The parable illustrates the difficulty supervisors have in juggling individual egos, organizational needs, and change. Supervisors need to be alert when an organization engages in change as a strategy for avoiding the more difficult task of changing the culture of an organization or the skills and attitudes of employees. The appearance of change can be a means of avoiding conflict. In these situations supervisors will observe that the more things change, the more they stay the same.

The zoo at first appears to be unlike a human organization and yet the behavior described occurs in various degrees in all organizations. The advantage of the parable is that it changes a supervisor's perspective of an organization. The parable causes one to look at the workplace with a sense of humor and also points out the absurdities of fad and fashion. It is easy to lose our most valuable asset as managers, which is our sense of humor.

REFERENCES

1. Morowitz, HJ. *Ego Niches: An Ecological View of Organizational Behavior.* Woodbridge, Conn.: Ox Bow Press, 1977.
2. Bruhn, J.G. "Managerial Indecisiveness: When the Monkeys Run the Zoo." *Health Care Supervisor* 8 (1990):55–64.
3. Ouchi, W.G. *Theory Z.* New York, N.Y.: Avon, 1981.
4. Blanchard, K., Onchen, W., Jr., and Burrows, H. *The One Minute Manager Meets the Monkey.* New York, N.Y.: Quill, 1989.

CHAPTER 34

●●●

Diagnosing the Health of Organizations

JOHN G. BRUHN AND ALAN P. CHESNEY

Organizations are living systems with their own needs and life cycles. Like other living things, they experience change and conflict as they grow and develop. Sometime during their life cycles, most organizations become ill and need treatment and rehabilitation.[1] Some organizations, like people, become chronically ill but continue to function until their eventual demise, other organizations successfully conquer acute episodes of illness, and still others appear to be "genetically" favored and rarely experience illness.

Most of us work in organizations that are relatively healthy. However, the concept of a healthy organization is idealistic. Organizations are never fully stable, they never maximize their potential, and they never achieve complete harmony. Yet, most managers and leaders want to make their organizations more healthy and, therefore, successful in their mission.

It is a common myth that the leader determines an organization's health and success.[2] Kelley[3] points out that a leader's effect on organizational success is only 10 to 20%; followership is the factor that makes for success. Yet Bolman and Deal[4] stress that neither the leader nor the followers, but the interaction between the two, makes a workplace healthy. It is how the psychodynamics of an organization are managed, and the capacity of its leaders and followers to repair broken relationships, that influence an organization's health.[5]

Numerous authors use the metaphor of health or sickness to describe organizations. This metaphor for understanding organizations offers at least three advantages; first, we know from the World Health Organization's (WHO) definition of health that health is not simply the absence of disease. WHO defines health as a state of complete physical, mental, and social well-being and not merely the absence of disease or infirmity.[6] The second advantage is that it focuses on processes not products. The literature on health and particularly health promotion identifies biological, psychological, and social processes by which a person may become sick or healthy. Third, the health paradigm has a strong behavioral component. Behaviors such as smoking cessation, exercise, diet modification, and stress management improve our chances of remaining healthy. It is the authors' premise that examining the health of an organization will provide valuable insights into how an organization may become dysfunctional.

Reprinted from *Health Care Supervisor*, 13(2), pp. 21–33, 1994, with permission of Aspen Publishers, Inc., © 1994.

It must be noted from the outset that an organization may be sick or dysfunctional and yet productive. In many organizations there is a time lag that allows organizations to continue to be productive while they are in declining health. However, eventually sick organizations become unproductive. The advantage of examining the health of an organization is that eventually health will predict productivity. If the illness is acute, productivity may not suffer at all. However, when the illness is chronic and untreated, productivity is threatened.

While it might be argued that it is essential only for insiders or members of an organization to decipher their organization's health, it usually takes an outsider's inquiries to stimulate insiders' awareness of their organization's behavior.[7] Usually the assistance of an outsider's analysis is solicited when leaders experience their organization's declining health. Unfortunately, when leaders are a part of the reason for their organization's declining health, and do not recognize it, organizational members may seek the advice of outsiders without the leaders' knowledge. Informal feedback about an organization's culture can be used for constructive change instigated by insiders. This could involve pressure from organizational members for a change in leadership.

It is the authors' experience that members of organizations that are experiencing a period of dysfunction, especially when the leader is part of the problem, often reach a state of helplessness and seek informal advice and guidance from sources outside their organization. Informal advice from outsiders is used by members of sick organizations to make decisions, whether the advice assists individuals to leave for other jobs or work for change within the organization. It is also the authors' experience that sick organizations more often meet an early demise rather than experience rehabilitation and revitalization because symptoms of unhealthiness are not recognized or are denied by leaders.

The purpose of the present paper is to describe an approach whereby an objective assessment can be made of an organization's health without a formal request for consultation from an organization's leader. The approach proposed involves observing the behavior of organizational members in a variety of work situations, obtaining information on the organization's leadership history and performance, eliciting the organization's mission and goals as perceived by members at different levels of the organization, and inquiring about the satisfaction, accomplishments, and morale of members at different levels of the organization. Such a cursory assessment of organizational health can be of benefit to persons who are considering accepting a job or making other contractual relationships with an organization. An assessment is also necessary if one is to diagnose and prescribe a remedy for a "sick" organization.

Similarities and Differences Between Individuals and Organizations

The major difference between individuals and organizations is that an organization has the potential for being immortal. People grow old and die of natural causes. Organizations die, but for different reasons. More important, individuals are more or less coherent beings. They function because of the smooth integration of numerous organs, but these organs are coordinated by unconscious means. Organizations consist of many independent organisms that are coordinated by sets of similar needs, but they consist of autonomous individual consciousnesses.

The similarity between organizations and individuals is that they are both influenced greatly by internal and external events. We use words like morale and pride to describe both individuals and organizations because they define these entities' approaches to existence. These words describe a real but intangible aspect of both individuals and organizations that is connected with their ability to survive and flourish.

Human spirit may be broken by adversity, by a lack of nourishment, and even by punishment for the possession of admirable qualities such as creativity, enthusiasm, honesty, directness, self-confidence, and initiative. Organizations and individuals can be broken by adversity. The business climate changes, the government cuts funding, a highway blocks a restaurant entrance, a war starts, a hurricane sweeps in, a loved one is taken by accident or disease. Often, however, in the case of both individuals and organizations, something damages the spirit. An organization, because of faulty leadership, can destroy the internal climate, that is, office politics determines who gets promoted, honesty is punished and sycophancy encouraged, new ideas are devalued, and the tried and true are elevated to immutable law. However, organizations do not always respond to adversity by becoming sick. Some organizations are able to increase their resistance to disease, to adapt to changes in the environment, and to become more healthy as a result of coping with adversity. Recent changes toward total quality management made by Ford, General Motors, and Chrysler serve as examples of organizations that have survived adversity. Each may survive as a healthier organization by virtue of its response to adversity.

Characteristics of Healthy Organizations

A healthy organization has been defined as one in which the individuals and groups that comprise it reach homeostasis or equilibrium in their capacity for growth.[8] Albrecht and Albrecht[9] have said that a healthy organization is one in which the authority structure, value systems, norms, reward systems, and sanctions operate to support the success of the organization, its environment, and the well-being of its personnel. Health may be defined differently by members of an organization and those outside it because health is a value-laden term; values are reflected in how we perceive and interpret behavior. The state of an organization's health, therefore, is, to some extent, perceptual. However, people act on their perceptions, and the resultant behavior can be constructive or destructive. We can learn a lot about beliefs and values in an organization by examining its employees' behavior.

Certain key characteristics, collectively, make an organization healthy (Figure 34-1). The culture or environment of an organization provides the context for organizational behavior. The tone set by the culture influences employee behavior. Organizational culture is established largely by the leaders of an organization. When leaders change, the culture also changes; even when new leaders attempt to maintain the same culture, it never is exactly the same. Changes in employees also modify an organization's culture.

Lyth[10] outlines some measures of organizational health such as productivity, morale, and loyalty. She notes that task-effective organizations tend to be healthy for their members. Efficient task performance is rewarding and increases confidence and self-esteem. Healthy organizations provide the opportunity to confront and work through problems, deploy people's capacities to the fullest, provide independence without undue supervision, demonstrate visible relationships between effort and rewards, avoid using repressed defenses to deal with anxiety, and permit members to exert realistic control over their life in the organization.[10]

A healthy organization has a clear mission and a set of consistent principles that frame it and distinguish it from other organizations, but it is its values that provide the how and why for people in the organization to behave as they do. An organization that values democracy, autonomy, and entrepreneurship empowers individual employees to share their talents, skills, and ideas in helping the organization achieve its goals and stay focused on its mission. An environment of open communication and sharing of information conveys to all employees that the leaders are not the only persons in the organization who have good ideas. This provides for a work environment of trust and encourages creativity and innovation.

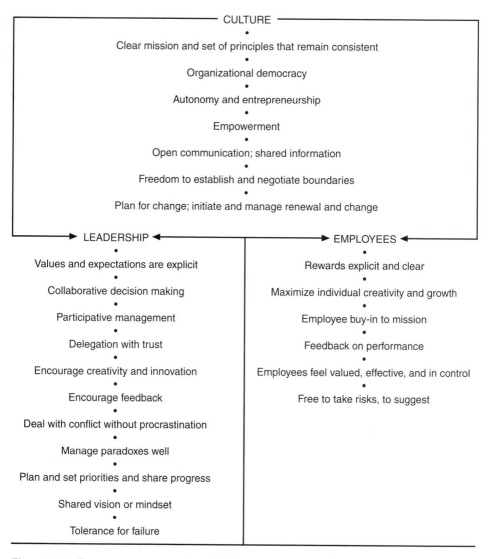

Figure 34–1 Characteristics of healthy organizations.

A healthy culture is more team-oriented than territorial. This does not mean that healthy organizations are not competitive, they are, but they provide freedom to negotiate boundaries in order to accomplish organizational as opposed to individual goals. Every employee in a healthy organization is an investment and, as such, when permitted to grow and develop, helps strengthen the entire organization. Finally, healthy organizations plan for, rather than wait for, change. Indeed, healthy organizations initiate change, encourage change and renewal, and, as a result, change usually can be directed and the effects of change can be controlled.

Hewlett-Packard builds its philosophy around trust. Hewlett-Packard uses three methods for remaining innovative and healthy. First, managers are reviewed on their ability to manage people. Second, employee input is obtained through communication sessions. Third, employees are encouraged to speak up when they feel that things aren't right.

Hewlett-Packard puts these words into action by operating on "guidelines" rather than on rules and regulations.

Another example of a healthy organization is Aetna, which strives to create an environment that is conducive to people wanting to work there. Aetna is proactive on workplace issues. They have developed elder care programs, a management advisory council, alternative staffing programs, and hiring and training programs for the historically unemployed. Aetna pays its employees well, which is a necessary but not sufficient condition to being a healthy organization. It is the additional programs that help Aetna remain healthy.

DePree[11] said that chief executive officers (CEOs) should create an organizational environment that is kind to the user. Organizational leaders should make their values and expectations explicit. Employees in a healthy organization know what is expected of them and know how they can contribute to the organization's goals. It is important that leaders share their vision with employees. Visions can only become realities if they are adopted by all the employees in an organization. Consistency and congruency in a leader's values convey feelings of both stability and direction in an organization. Much is written about management style as an essential factor in shaping the environment of the workplace. Collaborative decision making, participative management, delegation of authority and responsibility, and the encouragement of feedback by the leadership sends employees the message that they are valued, trusted, and empowered. Good leaders also permit failure and the chance to try again.

The leaders of a healthy organization plan, set priorities, and monitor their progress toward achieving goals. They are proactive problem solvers who consistently manage boundaries and paradoxes, thereby preventing the need to resolve conflicts that divert managers and others from their primary tasks. A healthy organization has few "fires" to put out because the leadership ethos has an effective fire prevention program.

The measure of leadership is in action, not in words. There are many leaders who can speak eloquently about participative management, visions, delegation of authority and responsibility, and proactive problem solving. However, there may be large gaps between words and deeds. Leaders who surround themselves with only a few "trusted" associates (many of whom have more than one title), who are constantly focusing on the failures or failings of individual employees, who begin discussions by accusing rather than questioning, and who make decisions on the basis of incomplete or incorrect information, are leaders of sick organizations regardless of what they profess.

Employees directly contribute to maintaining a healthy organization when they are valued and feel in control and effective at their jobs. Employees feel invested in an organization when they feel free to take risks and can contribute ideas for the organization's improvement. Employees in a healthy organization are encouraged to be creative, to learn new skills, and to assume greater responsibilities. This is reinforced when employees are given feedback on their performance and employee rewards are made explicit. Employees want to continue to work in a healthy organization where they are happy, productive, and receive rewards.

The reward system in healthy organizations starts with compensation and benefits, but it does not stop there. Organizations reward employees by valuing their input and by developing programs that are designed to meet both personal and organizational needs. Programs such as employee assistance, child care, elder care, flex time, and personal leave are examples of how healthy organizations reward employees.

How Organizations Become Unhealthy

Kets de Vries and Miller[12] point out that troubled organizations have symptoms and dysfunctions that combine to form an integrated syndrome of pathology. Pathology may be a mixture of neurotic styles. These authors note that parallels can be drawn between individual pathology, that is, the excessive use of one neurotic style, and organizational pathology, resulting in poorly functioning organizations. The personality of the leader can influence the structure, strategy, and culture of an organization. Not all unhealthy organizations are run by neurotic leaders. However, the personality of the leader, especially if the leader is concerned with the centralization of power, can create a gestalt that reflects throughout the organization. Organizations can easily recruit leaders and managers with similar styles; therefore, there will always be a danger that the lack of diversity may give rise to organizational pathology.

Organizations become sick through neglect and lack of preventive maintenance, through inflexibility and intolerance of change, and through the arrogance of power and insensitivity of the leaders to the needs of employees. Organizations rarely become sick suddenly; symptoms, if neglected, accumulate over time until the organization becomes incapacitated. Symptoms of dysfunction are often more observable to people outside an organization than to those within. Figure 34-2 lists some symptoms of unhealthiness in organizations.

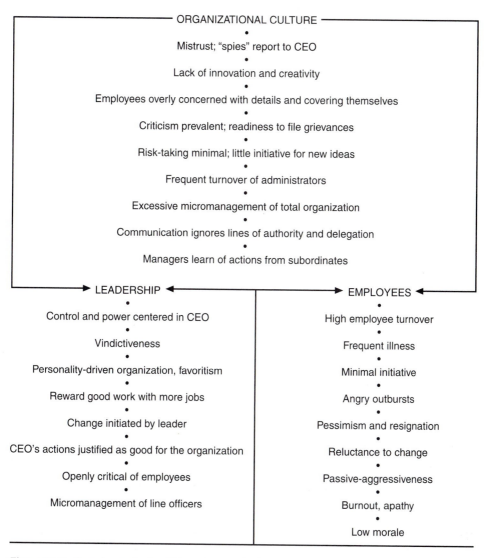

Figure 34–2 Symptoms of unhealthiness in organizations.

A culture of mistrust in an organization and evidence that the CEO and top management check up on people produce an atmosphere in which employees cover themselves, take minimal risks, and do only what is necessary to do their jobs. This kind of atmosphere puts people on guard to protect their turf and creates a defensive climate. Criticisms and grievances are common, because people lack loyalty to others or to the organization. Employee comments about the organization, their jobs, and the leadership may be the best clue that the organization is sick. When many employees take the role of a victim, then the organization is unhealthy. Such comments as: "I'm stuck here," "It's just a job," "That new guy with good ideas won't last long," "We will never get a raise," "It's not my job to think," "The CEO won't give up control," and "It's no use trying to change things here" are examples of comments that have an underlying theme of victimization. Whether these comments are a product of experience or simply self-fulfilling prophecies is not a critical issue because in either case, the organization is sick.

Other clues to an unhealthy organization include frequent turnover of managers and administrators, the reputation of the CEO as a micromanager, communication patterns that ignore the organization chart, a lack of innovation and creativity, and strong resistance to change and upholding of traditional patterns of authority that are based on centralized control at the top of the organization.

Organizations become sick when they serve the psychological needs of the leader. Some leaders become blinded by power and the need to satisfy their own egos and ignore the realities of an organization.[13] These leaders fashion a personality-driven organization where they reward and favor employees who cater to their needs and are vindictive toward employees who do not. Other leaders cultivate a small group of close associates who do only what they know the leader wants and expects. As a result, these leaders are reinforced by their own thinking.

Leaders who do not permit line officers in an organization to do their job without close supervision stifle the organization and the line officers. Leaders who treat their line officers like staff convey the message to all in the organization that control and power are centered in the CEO. In sick organizations, leaders may continue to exert tight control while advocating empowerment or total quality management. Since these innovations are not modeled by the leader, employees distrust the CEO's sincerity. Thus, a vicious circle is established where management and employees distrust each other and neither party will take the risk of trusting the other.

Perhaps the most significant symptoms of organizational sickness are manifested by leaders and managers who cannot effectively cope with difficult boundaries or issues and therefore identify certain people in the organization as the problem. The "identified" persons are treated as "devils" or "scapegoats" and marked for dismissal with the rationale that a new person will be able to solve the existing problem. A second symptom is the rewarding, by leaders and managers, of good work with more work. An organization that only lets employees know they are valued by giving them additional jobs is indicating that its reward system is unhealthy. The message sent to employees is, don't do an outstanding job; you will only be rewarded with more work. Overworked people do not and cannot perform at their peak. Indeed, over a sustained period, overworked people put themselves at risk for personal health problems. This further illustrates the insensitivity of unhealthy organizations to the social and psychological needs of its employees.

Employee behavior is often the most obvious way to diagnose an unhealthy organization; it is not difficult to ascertain attitudes of anger, apathy, low morale, pessimism, and passive–aggressiveness from employees. Organizations that have high absenteeism and turnover rates are unhealthy. Employees in unhealthy organizations show little loyalty toward the organization, little enthusiasm for their work, or little optimism about their jobs. If the atmosphere at work is grossly vindictive, there may be a reluctance to communicate in order to protect their jobs.

Cycles of Sickness and Health

Sick organizations do not necessarily decay, decline, and die. Some organizations live protracted yet sick lives. Sick organizations have an impact on the people who work in them. Some sick organizations may, indeed, attract and retain sick employees; the organizational culture and the employee's needs may become enmeshed and reinforced. In fact, in some family businesses, family dynamics in the form of rivalries and jealousies are played out to the point at which family members leave the business or open directly competing ventures.

We spend the bulk of our daily lives at work. Work becomes a place where we play out many of our goals and aspirations as well as problems. Organizations, like people, can become addictive and foster addictive (dysfunctional) behavior.[14] For example, in dysfunctional organizations communication is often indirect, vague, confused, and ineffective. Gossip, triangulation, secrets, and extensive written memos help avoid face-to-face interaction, confrontation, and intimacy. Such a culture fosters dishonesty, creating "in" groups, tension, defensiveness, and controlled feelings.

Healthy organizations, on the other hand, tend to remain more or less healthy with occasional crises. Healthy organizations tend to select their employees with careful attention to philosophy, past work records, and personal goals. Since healthy organizations are team-oriented, their employees usually have good interpersonal skills. Healthy organizations tend to stress group goals and successes; it is unlikely that an employee who is highly competitive and needs constant individual recognition and rewards would be selected to be part of a healthy organization. Open, direct, and honest communication fosters a group spirit, and destructive behavior usually is prevented by positive group pressure or early intervention.

Healthy and unhealthy organizations are influenced by their leaders. Both types of organizations look for leaders who will promote the organization as it is. Healthy organizations usually attract healthy leaders, and unhealthy organizations usually attract unhealthy leaders. However, mismatches occur when a healthy leader becomes the head of an organization that he/she discovers is unhealthy. The leader who attempts to change an unhealthy organization is likely to be met by strong resistance. It is unlikely that a healthy leader would stay long in an unhealthy organization. Unhealthy leaders may not be known until they have been in a leadership position for awhile. Unhealthy leaders who have been unsuccessful in a prior job may have been given good references by supervisors who wished to be rid of them. However, when unhealthy leaders are detected, it usually does not take long for a healthy organization to close ranks against them. Votes of "no confidence," petitions, and pressure from board members, politicians, or the public can lead to their termination.

The leader is not always the problem in an unhealthy organization or, if the leader is a problem, it is not always feasible to change leaders or to change their behaviors. Howell and colleagues[15] suggest ways to "neutralize" the negative impact of a leader, such as peer support groups. It is difficult for members of an organization to provide substitutes for negative leadership, because leaders who are concerned with control will doubtlessly prevent innovations that would circumvent or inhibit their ability to control. Unfortunately, members often find it easier to leave an organization than to try to modify it.

Degrees of Organizational Health

The health of organizations is relative and is subject to change by the internal and external forces that act upon it. Figure 34-3 shows the key elements in the process of maintaining organizational health. The interaction between leadership styles and organizational culture is more obvious in organizations where decision-making power is centralized. Kets de

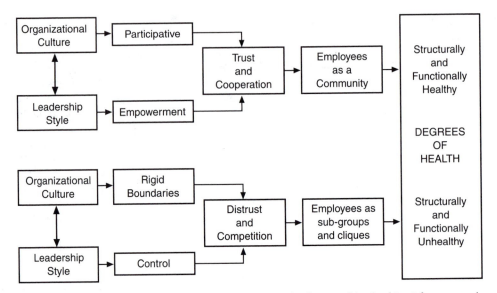

Figure 34–3 Effects of interaction between organizational culture and leadership style on organizational health.

Vries[16] has described five constellations of how the personality or management style of the leader can impact an organization's culture. A suspicious style can lead to a paranoid culture and organization. A depressive, dependent style can result in an avoidant culture and depressive organization. A dramatic, narcissistic leader can create a charismatic culture and an impulsive, venturesome organization. A compulsive leader can create a bureaucratic culture and a controlling organization. Finally, a detached leader can create a politicized culture and schizoid organization. While these are pure prototypes, they exemplify how the structure of an organization can be influenced by the personality of its top manager.

The more centralized an organization, and the more power given its leaders, the greater the impact of their personality on the culture and structure of the organization.[13] Healthy organizations have a mixture of personality types; unhealthy organizations are more likely to be described by one of the five prototypes. In healthy organizations employees know how to get along with their coworkers and leaders in ways that benefit the organization.[3] The best followers treat the organization as a "commons." This attitude helps in organizational relationships. A community culture is established in which employees not only try to maximize their own self-interest but also help to facilitate the interests of coworkers. Healthy organizations demonstrate "a web of relationships" among all levels of workers that is based on trust, credibility, and honesty. In Hirschhorn's[5] terms this would be an "open system." To maintain a healthy organization, leaders must develop strategies of management that are neither too open nor too closed. In healthy organizations, boundaries are interdependent; they must be managed carefully to allow negotiations yet not create distrust. Thus, the degree of healthiness of an organization is fluid. The challenge to the leadership is to keep the organization on the side of healthiness more often than on the side of unhealthiness.

While organizational environment or culture is a powerful variable that affects the performance of an organization, excellent organizations become "peak performers" largely because they employ excellent individuals.[7] People who are peak performers will be attracted to work with other peak performers in organizations where peak performance is the norm.

How an Organization Solves Problems

One approach in diagnosing an organization's health is to ascertain the process by which the organization solves problems and resolves conflicts. The process or method of resolution will convey much about the leadership style and organizational climate of the organization. Table 34-1 shows six aspects of problem solving or conflict resolution that assist in diagnosing an organization's health. In healthy organizations, problems or conflicts are openly discussed and identified so that they can be brought to the appropriate manager for resolution. There is no motivation to keep problems or conflicts hidden in a healthy organization, as this would undermine morale and the cohesive atmosphere of the working environment. In healthy organizations, the parties involved in a problem or conflict actively work to resolve it rather than refer it to management for solution. It is rare that the CEO becomes involved in solving problems in a healthy organization unless the issue is one of concern to the total organization. Even then, it is likely the CEO will ask for the input of all employees in the resolution. Perhaps one of the most important points in the process of resolving problems in a healthy organization is the attitude and behavior of employees following the resolution of a problem. A healthy organization is resilient and adaptive; it is not concerned with personalities or holding grudges. The work of the entire organization transcends the problems of individuals and groups. Organizations that repair themselves acknowledge good and bad experiences openly and directly, and employees have the attitude that they can learn from both failures and successes.[5]

An observer of an organization can readily elicit the process by which problems and conflicts are resolved and will be able to diagnose the relative health of an organization from this inquiry. Since "health" is an ideal, it is rare that one would find a completely healthy organization; it is likely, however, that a "sick" organization would be detected. The purpose in diagnosing an organization is to determine its usual patterns of behavior. Healthy organizations have the ability to adapt to fluctuation and change and return to their usual, stable pattern of functioning. Sick organizations, on the other hand, become sick because they are not flexible and adaptive. The health of an organization cannot be controlled by its leader or its culture. A flexible organization should not assume that success (or health) is a state of stable consensus.[18] Leaders and managers in a flexible, adaptive, or healthy organization need to let the type of problem or conflict determine the resources they will use to correct it rather than use a common approach or common set of problem-solving tools to solve all problems or conflicts.

TABLE 34–1 **Approaches to Conflict Resolution in Healthy and Unhealthy Organizations**

Approach	Healthy Organizations	Unhealthy Organizations
Identification of problem	Open discussion	Attempt to hide or minimize problems
Behavior of parties involved	Bring to attention of management	Defensive, scapegoating
Parties' motivation for solving problems	Improve morale and working relationships	Fear, retribution
Degree that parties are involved in resolution	Participative	Reluctant, cautious
Involvement of CEO in resolution	Rare	Usual
Working climate after resolution	Adaptive	Resentment, grudges held

Changing Diagnoses

Just as the health of organizations is relative, what constitutes a healthy organization is also relative. Drucker[19] points out that a new type of organization is emerging; we are entering a period of change from command-and-control organizations (the organization of departments and divisions) to information-based organizations (the organization of knowledge specialists). The organizational chart of the information-based organization will be flatter, with decentralization into autonomous units; task forces will be assembled to solve specific problems. The entire organization, to accomplish such a restructuring, will have a cohesive and common vision, bonding the decentralized units together. The health of an organization will be determined by the health of its various units and their ability to contribute to the mission and goal of the entire organization. The information-based organization will need to adopt a new set of values, structure, and behavior. Schein said,

> My sense is that the various predictions about globalism, knowledge-based organizations, the information age, the biotech age, the loosening of organizational boundaries, and so on have one theme in common—we basically do not know what the world of tomorrow will really be like except that it will be different. That means that organizations and their leaders will have to become perpetual learners.[7(p.361)]

REFERENCES

1. Kimberly, J.R., et al. *The Organizational Life Cycle.* San Francisco, Calif.: Jossey-Bass, 1980.
2. Bennis, W. *Why Leaders Can't Lead.* San Francisco, Calif.: Jossey-Bass, 1990.
3. Kelley, R. *The Power of Followership.* New York, N.Y.: Doubleday, 1992.
4. Bolman, L.G., and Deal, T.E. *Reframing Organizations.* San Francisco, Calif.: Jossey-Bass, 1991.
5. Hirschhorn, L. *The Workplace Within: Psychodynamics of Organizational Life.* Cambridge, Mass.: MIT Press, 1988.
6. World Health Organization. *The First Ten Years of the World Health Organization.* Geneva, Switzerland: World Health Organization, 1958.
7. Schein, E.H. *Organizational Culture and Leadership.* 2d ed. San Francisco, Calif.: Jossey-Bass, 1992.
8. Clark, J.V. "A Healthy Organization." In *The Planning of Change,* edited by W.G. Bennis, et al. 2d ed., New York, N.Y.: Holt, Rinehart and Winston, 1969.
9. Albrecht, K., and Albrecht, S. *The Creative Corporation.* Homewood, Ill.: Dow Jones-Irwin, 1987.
10. Lyth, I.M. "Changing Organizations and Individuals: Psychoanalytic Insights for Improving Organizational Health." In *Organizations on the Couch,* edited by M.F.R. Kets de Vries, et al. San Francisco, Calif.: Jossey-Bass, 1991.
11. DePree, M. *Leadership Is an Art,* New York, N.Y.: Dell, 1989.
12. Kets de Vries, M.F.R. and Miiler, D. *The Neurotic Organization.* San Francisco, Calif.: Jossey-Bass, 1984.
13. Kets de Vries, M.F.R. *Prisoners of Leadership.* New York, N.Y.: Wiley, 1989.
14. Schaef, A.W., and Fassel, D. *The Addictive Organization.* San Francisco, Calif.: Harper & Row, 1988.
15. Howell, J.P., et al. "Substitutes for Leadership: Effective Alternatives to Ineffective Leadership." *Organization Dynamics* 19, no. 1 (Summer 1990): 21–38.
16. Kets de Vries, M.F.R., et al., eds. *Organizations on the Couch.* San Francisco, Calif.: Jossey-Bass, 1991.
17. Garfield, C. *Peak Performers.* New York, N.Y.: Avon, 1986.
18. Stacey, R.D. *Managing the Unknowable.* San Francisco, Calif.: Jossey-Bass, 1992.
19. Drucker, P.F. *The Ecological Vision.* New Brunswick, N.J.: Transaction, 1993.

CHAPTER 35

●●

"Sizing Up" the System

ELEANOR C. HEIN

All living organisms have structure. Structure gives an organism form, allowing various parts of the organism to interact with each other and function as a whole.

Organizations resemble and often act as living organisms. Like living organisms, organizations can expand and contract, merge with other like systems, reshape themselves and move on, often assimilating and/or discarding whatever or whomever lies in their path. In whatever "new" form they may acquire, all organizations continue to have one thing in common: they require a way of functioning with and relating to their various interconnected parts. Structure provides that function.

In the past, organizations were perceived as relatively stable and constant systems. In today's health care system, however, organizations are increasingly fluid and variable. Previous ways of functioning have given way to "the bottom line." Budget sheets, fiscal reports, cost-containment projections, and profit margins seem to have a life of their own, often overshadowing the vibrant center of any organization—its people. New terms are being coined and included in the "new" organizational vocabulary. "Sound bite" euphemisms such as "downsizing," "reshaping," "strengthening effectiveness," "release of resources," "repositioning," and "career change opportunity" are being used to obscure the unpleasant realities that are taking place in many health care settings. While these "sound bites" seem innocuous, they are a cosmetic overlay masking a more ominous meaning: being laid off or terminated.

The changes within the health care system that have and will continue to emerge make it even more essential that nurses learn to "size up" their own health care setting. While "sizing up" a particular health care setting is not a panacea for solving its problems, doing so can alert nurses to changes that may be coming. Anticipating and preparing for the inevitability of change can help nurses use the system more adroitly for the benefit of their patients and their own professional survival.

Formal Organizational Structures

Organizational structures have two coexisting forms: formal and informal. Both types of structure contribute to the goals of the organization. Whether both facilitate or impede an organization's goals is an essential task to any undertaking that involves "sizing up" the system.

The key components of a formal organization are clarity, control, and centrality. *Clarity* involves the degree to which formal organizations clearly arrange and describe their practices, procedures, and task responsibilities. Each element of an organization's structure and its relationship to other elements of the organization must be clearly depicted and understood. Organizational charts serve that purpose. Similarly, all task responsibilities, procedures, and standards of practices must be clearly outlined and described. Job descriptions and procedure manuals are two examples that serve this purpose. Everyone within the organization must understand what they do, what their task and procedural parameters are, what the process of answerability is, what measures of quality care are in place, and how what they do helps to achieve the goals of the organization. Clarity is often obscured as organizational changes begin to outpace an organization's ability to communicate those changes to its members.

The second component of formal organizations is *Control*. In formal organizations, control is direct and extends into every aspect of organizational life. Control is funneled through chains of command and lines of authority. Chains of command are made up of people who have been given positional authority, that is, the right to act by virtue of the position given them by the organization. The right to act involves the use of authority and the assumption of responsibility that accompanies the use of authority. When both qualities are used, they exert influence in monitoring the implementation of organizational decisions. When people who serve as the links in the chain of command exercise organizationally sanctioned authority and responsibility, they are using *legitimate power*. Whether legitimate power is used for purposes of reward or punishment, people in positional authority are accountable to the organization for the way that power is used.

Centrality, the third component of organizational structure, involves the location and concentration of authority. The decisions that are made for a majority of people within the organization are made by a relatively small number of individuals. It is this small number of people that sets into motion the chain of command and its lines of authority. Conversely, an organization whose concentration of authority extends decision-making from "the few" to "the many" is viewed as a decentralized organization. Overall governance, chains of command, and lines of authority continue to exist, but it is the individual accountability of each staff member that is the hallmark and the concern of decentralized organizations. In such organizations, qualities such as flexibility, respect for an individual's ideas, and suggestions for changes in policy and procedures are valued and encouraged. As a result, these valued qualities help to increase overall motivation and job satisfaction among the staff in decentralized organizations.

How an organization governs itself, the manner in which it achieves its goals, and the changes that result, generates a good deal of anxiety when organizational structures are altered and/or are perceived as unclear. Trying to anticipate these changes can be daunting. Here are some questions to raise and consider in terms of your health care facility:

- Does it have a centralized or decentralized concentration of authority?
- Have you reviewed the organizational chart? Has it been modified or altered to reflect changes in structure? Are various professional groups or departments identified in the chart?
- Is the concentration of authority used efficient? Is it effective? Which is more valued by the facility?
- How long does it take to change a policy or procedure? Is the facility responsive to change?
- Does everyone you work with know who comprises the chain of command? Do they use them or circumvent them?
- Is the chain of command used by your coworkers to implement change?
- What kinds of decisions are made by nurses in positional authority? How are these decisions made? By whom?

- How are new policies and procedures monitored?
- Does everyone you work with know to whom they are accountable?
- In what ways do your coworkers contribute to decision-making processes?
- Who holds legitimate power? How many are nurses?
- Is your organization open to new ideas?
- Does your health care facility have recurring problems? What are they? Is there an attempt to correct the problems?
- What threats to centrality, control, and clarity do you perceive?
- In what ways has restructuring, downsizing, or mergers changed the organizational structure?
- How has your health care facility supported nursing staff during these changes?
- What is the greatest barrier to change?
- Is there a job description for your position available? Is it clear? Concise?
  - Does your job description contain performance standards?
  - Are the criteria for performance standards included in your job description?
  - Does your job description reflect the philosophy of nursing of your health care facility?
  - Does your job description specify the frequency and number of performance evaluations, and by whom they are given?
- What kind of help can you expect in order to do your job well?
- Are the values of your health care facility similar to yours?

TYPES OF COMMUNICATION

The knowledge explosion together with the technological innovations that comprise the "information highway" make communication, especially within organizations, an even more complex process than it already is. While messages and/or memos sent from one part of an organization to another may seem reality based, it is the receiver's *perception* of that reality that can become problematic for an organization. Breakdowns, distortions, and misunderstandings are typical of faulty communication exchanges that are unclear, selectively heard, misread, or skewed when emotional reactions overshadow thoughtful responses. In formal organizations three common types of communication are generally used: downward, upward, and lateral.

Downward communication is a traditional form of communication used in most organizational settings. The flow of this type of communication is from top to bottom, as from a director of nursing service to the nursing staff. Downward communication serves to inform, to establish limits on the staff's use of power, to instruct staff about their job performance, to exert influence, and to help coordinate activities with the organization.[1] Because the physical distance between the sender and the receiver in organizations is often great, distortions in downward communication frequently occur. Common forms of downward communication include written memos, computer-generated memos, procedure manuals, and performance appraisal interviews. Although these are typical forms of communication, each may lend themselves to psychological distancing and differences of opinion and responses between those in positions of authority and those who are not.

Communication that is directed from the bottom to the top—from nursing staff to the director of nursing service—is called *upward* communication. This type of communication is relied upon the most by those in positions of authority because it serves as the data base from which decisions are made about the working environment and health care facility's future goals and objectives. In health care facilities, upward communication acts as a reporting system used by the nursing staff to inform those in positions of authority about what is happening. It is from this data base that decisions can be made about staffing patterns, orientation programs, the implementation of new procedures, and ways to contain costs. Other examples of upward communication can include nursing staff meetings, grievance procedures, written progress reports, and one-to-one discussions.

While, in theory, upward communication can facilitate improvements within the system, in reality it is a particularly vulnerable type of communication when the nursing staff do not consider their information worth sharing ("What difference will my suggestion make!"), feel that they have no access to or are misunderstood by the director of nursing service ("Have you ever tried to get an appointment?"), and, as a result, choose to withhold communication altogether ("If they want it, they can come and get it!").

Lateral communication takes place among and between staff members at the same organizational level. This type of communication is best demonstrated by the staff's sense of team spirit. Lateral communication is used to facilitate achievement of organizational goals. As such, it serves as the basis for teamwork in coordinating various groups and individuals within the health care facility. Generally speaking, the use of lateral communication also saves time and energy; coworkers can discuss matters that concern them, plan projects, formulate ideas, and make suggestions for the improvement of a particular unit. The end-of-shift report, nursing staff meetings, and interdepartmental meetings are some additional examples of lateral communication. Trust, respect, and nondefensiveness are behavioral qualities that must be operative if lateral communication is to be effective.

Because the communication process in organizations is complex and often problematic, taking a good look at how an organization keeps its members informed is all the more essential. Some questions to raise and consider in terms of your health care facility are:

- What formal channels of communication are used?
- What forms of communication are used to convey its rules, policies and procedures?
- Does it have a way of checking on whether staff members have read its directives?
- What forms of upward communication are used by the nursing staff? Are these channels used regularly by the nursing staff?
- Do your coworkers withhold information from the people in the chain of command? What do you think the reasons are?
- What common forms of lateral communication are used?
- What do you consider to be the major problem in how formal communication is used?
- Where is important organizational information posted on your nursing unit?
- Are the various forms of written communication clear and orderly?

LEADERSHIP

Two characteristics of behaviorial leadership theories are choice and control. When a person chooses to use a certain type of leadership, that person is selecting an overall method of implementing specific behaviors that will, when used, accomplish a task or realize a goal. The overall pattern of behavior used in these situations is called a *leadership style*. While leadership styles may vary, the selection of a leadership style signals the amount of control a person exercises when that style is being used.

For example, if, in large, complex health care facilities, task achievement and procedural efficiencies are valued over human needs, then the most likely style of leadership used would be an *authoritarian* style. A person using this style of leadership exerts control by making all the decisions and assuming the responsibility for the group in achieving a task. The freedom a group has to participate in decision-making processes is very limited or nonexistent. Task achievement is the overriding concern of the person using an authoritarian style of leadership.

A *laissez-faire* style of leadership is the opposite of authoritarian leadership style. Little, if any, control is exerted. Decision making and other group processes are left to the group with minimal, and in some cases, no direction. Responsibility for task achievement is abdicated by the person using this style of leadership. As a result, the group's process becomes inefficient and its outcomes are of poor quality.

Midway between these two opposing styles is the *democratic* leadership style. Control, decision making, and responsibility are shared between the style user and the group members. While some efficiency may be sacrificed in this group endeavor, the group members commitment to the task and their satisfaction with both the process and the outcome are high.

In recent years, *transformational leadership theory* has emerged as a response to the rapid changes taking place in the health care system. The major premise of this theory involves the ability of a person (ie, the transformational leader) to share a vision of the future with coworkers. In doing so, the transformational leader helps coworkers prepare for the changes that await them.[2] Transformational leadership has also been described as moral leadership because its effect transforms the people who are engaged with each other. Through their interactions, each person brings out the best in the other.[3] Part charismatic, part inspirational, the person who uses transformational leadership offers individualized attention, collegiality, and intellectual stimulation to group members as they work together to achieve a common goal.

Determining who, within a health care facility, uses effective leadership is pivotal to job satisfaction and patient welfare. Here are some questions to raise and consider:

- What is the predominant leadership style used by your nurse–manager? By your supervisor? Are the styles appropriate for the task, situation, or staff?
- Are any of the nurses in positions of authority using transformational leadership? If so, in what ways do they demonstrate it?
- To what extent does control play a part in the leadership style used by your nurse–manager? By your supervisor?
- Is your nurse–manager flexible in the use of her style of leadership? In other words, does your nurse–manager adjust her leadership style to meet the needs or tasks of the nursing staff? If not, how do your coworkers respond?
- What do your coworkers do in support of the leadership style used by your nurse–manager?

POWER

Power is the ability to influence and change the behavior of others in order to achieve a specified end. Each nurse has potential power: an intrapersonal energy source that is released and exchanged through personal relationships. But potential power must be put to use in some fashion. How it is used stems from a clear understanding of both the types and sources of power. Three types of power commonly seen and used in formal organizations are legitimate power, reward power, and coercive power.

The source of *legitimate* power within an organization is positional; that is, it is a position of power granted and delegated by the organization. It is the position itself that has power, not the person in that position.[4] When a nurse–manager makes a request of the nursing staff, that nurse–manager is activating legitimate power. When the nursing staff comply with their nurse–manager's request they are acknowledging the legitimate power used by their nurse–manager.

Reward power is based upon the way an organization rewards its members for their efforts. It is often used to spur increased job performance. People holding legitimate power are in a position to grant any number of rewards. Promotions, attractive work assignments or hours, and public commendations are among the many available rewards that can be given. It is equally persuasive when rewards are deliberately withheld, giving nurses the message that they are not valued, that they may have done something wrong, or that they are perceived as no longer useful in their work setting.

Coercive power is another persuasive type of power. Its source is fear. When the lack of compliance is an issue in the eyes of the legitimate power holder, that person can exercise coercive power to force compliance. The threat of transfer, unexplained shift changes, demotion, formal reprimand, and denying vacation requests are some of the more overt ways coercive power can be used. Covert methods are also used. They can include ignoring a person, belittling or intimidating someone, and publicly embarassing or correcting a person's comments in front of others. Veiled, hinted at, or implied comments suggesting some form of threat are often sufficient in achieving the desired effect. In whatever manner overt or covert methods of coercive power are used, one thing is clear: their intent is compliance through fear.

How health care facilities exercise legitimate, reward, and coercive power should be of special concern to nurses whose jobs may be at risk during changes taking place within their health care facilities. The use of fear to intimidate or to force compliance is a sad commentary on the state of an organization's integrity and effectiveness. While many health care facilities use reward power evenhandedly, it is the use of fear that makes nurses especially vulnerable during organizational change. Here are some questions to raise and consider in thinking about your health care facility:

- Who, within the formal organizational structure, has the most power?
- Is nursing as a whole, viewed as powerful within your facility?
- Does your nurse–manager use legitimate power evenhandedly?
- What abuses of legitimate power have you seen on your nursing unit?
- What kinds of reward power are given? Who gives them?
- Is reimbursement provided for nurses' continuing education? For workshops?
- What are the effects on the nursing staff when they are not rewarded or when rewards are less than expected? Does it effect quality of work?
- In what ways has coercive power been used?
- Have there been any negative effects in attempts to challenge the use of coercive power?
- Is your nurse–manager openly critical of a nurse or the nursing staff?

CULTURE

In every culture there is a learned pattern of norms, values, beliefs, customs, language, and symbols that are shared by people within that particular culture. How each culture expresses its learned pattern of behavior distinguishes one culture from another. In expressing and sharing these patterns of behavior, each culture preserves its history, determines its present, and sets the stage for influencing and shaping its future. As del Bueno asserts: "Culture is a pattern of basic assumptions or behaviors that have worked in the past and are taught to new members as the correct way to perceive, to think, to feel and to act."[5]

Each health care facility has its culture. Over time, a pattern of norms, values, customs, and beliefs is developed, shared, and preserved. When entering a particular culture of a health care facility, new members must learn what these patterns and expectations are and adopt them as the appropriate way to perceive, think, feel, and act within that facility.

In formal organizational structures, culture is conveyed through an organization's physical and social environment and its customary practices. Each of these elements has a norm and a value attached to it: a norm, in that each element within the health care facility's culture has a rule of conduct attached to it, and a value, in that there is a belief about that element's essential worth.

When a nurse enters a health care facility for the first time, the cultural imperatives are immediately communicated. The message comes across clearly: "You must...," "You should...," "You can't...," "You can...," "You will...," "You need to...," "Please remember to...," "This is how...," "This is what...." With these consistent dictates, the intended behavior is learned and internalized. Whether or not the culture of a health care facility is perceived as stifling or inviting by its newest members depends on the extent to which those new members can determine which cultural elements are facilitating or impeding their professional growth and development. Here are some questions to raise and consider in thinking about your health care facility:

- Is adequate security provided? Are the parking lots and entryways well lit?
- What is the overall noise level?
- Is there a quiet place for the nursing staff to use for relaxation, other than the cafeteria? Is it adequate? Are there adequate rooms for conferences?
- What provisions are made for a patient's privacy?
- Is the area for the preparation of medications and intravenous fluids quiet and convenient? Room to chart? Is the nurses station noisy or quiet?
- What provisions are made to relieve high levels of stress among the nursing staff?
- How would you describe the social environment?
- Does your health care facility's values include the active participation of nurses in planning changes?
- What cultural messages did you receive when you were being oriented?

Informal Organizational Structures

When a formal organization fails to satisfy the needs of its members, an informal organizational structure will emerge. Informal organizational structures meet peoples' needs in a way formal organizations do not. Their existence greatly influences, positively or negatively, how a formal organization meets its goals.

As people interact and increase their social contacts within the formal organization, they learn about the impact organizational decisions have on their lives. When members express dissatisfaction with the conditions of their work environment, experience the withholding or lack of information they need to do their work, and have minimal collaborative opportunities, a common bond is formed between them. This common bond unifies them and is the basis from which they choose to act on situations directly affecting them.

The aim of informal groups is to seek ways of satisfying the needs and interests of its members. But they do so in a loosely organized way. Informal groups offer a supportive climate and provide its members with recognition, status, and close personal contact.[6] Though their structures and responsibilities are less clearcut and organized, informal organizational groups develop their own communications network, form their own leadership, encourage their members to recognize and use their potential power and, over time, develop their own culture.

Because informal organizations are a collective response to deficits within a formal organization, they represent a truer picture of the actual working structure of a formal organization. Recognizing the importance of a health care facility's informal structure is an essential component in adjusting to life within an organization. Here are some questions to raise and consider:

- Is there an informal structure or group in your health care facility?
- What appear to be the common bonds and interests that unify this informal group?
- What differences are there between the formal and informal structures within your health care facility?
- How does the informal structure function? Does it have any goals? Any responsibilities? Any power?
- Which gives the most accurate picture of your health care facility, its formal structure or its informal structure?
- Are there informal groups that socialize outside of your health care facility?
- Do your coworkers like and get along with each other?
- What supportive measures are offered through your health care facility's informal structure?

TYPES OF COMMUNICATION

Social interaction generates communication. In health care facilities, the informal free-flowing exchange of communication is known as "the grapevine." The grapevine's network spreads rapidly from the more powerful to the less powerful. It reaches every corner and level of the health care facility and provides a rich source of information to its members. In doing so "the grapevine" serves as the link between members' desire to achieve need satisfaction and the health care facility's need to achieve its goals.

Ribeiro cites two forms of communication used in informal groups: gossip and rumor. Within informal groups, grapevining takes the form of gossip. Gossip is generally limited to the individuals who are known to the group. Usually such gossip is judgmental and unsubstantiated.[7] In contrast to the often slow, sometimes hesitant and impersonal methods of communicating used by formal organizations, "the grapevine" is quick, lively, influential, personal, and flexible. However troublesome the grapevine may appear to some, it cannot be ignored. If members do not receive credible information from their health care facility, then "the grapevine" will take over and provide its own interpretation. While grapevines can often be distorted or inaccurate, there is enough truth in their message that they cannot be easily dismissed. Generally speaking, messages spread by the grapevine network are correct 75% of the time.[8] Although spreading rumors about a health care facility through "the grapevine" can have deleterious outcomes, they are not a negative factor in getting the "real" message across. New ideas and policies can be "floated" to gauge group members responses.

While nurses must learn to use formal channels of communication, they must also observe and listen to their coworkers' informal ways of communicating. In doing so, they learn how the members of a formal organization use and respond to its informal communication network and what its impact is on others. Here are some questions to raise and consider:

- Who sits with whom at meals and at coffee breaks day after day?
- Which people carpool together or socialize together?
- Which subgroups interact with ease? Avoid each other?
- Who among your coworkers always supports new ideas? Criticizes new ideas?
- Who among your coworkers neither supports new ideas nor offers constructive criticism?
- Who speaks out in the various subgroups?
- Is there a grapevine in your health care facility? How accurate is it?

- Who are the persons who seem to have all the "latest news?" Do they share their sources of information? Where do they share it?
- How does your informal group deal with rumors concerning restructuring, downsizing, layoffs, and mergers?
- In what ways does the informal group support each other in the face of rumors that may threaten job security?

LEADERSHIP

Leadership does not occur in isolation. It is an interactional process that involves and needs people communicating with each other. In that process, communication is the medium of exchange that allows a person who uses leadership to influence and guide others toward the achievement of a goal. Leadership is what nurses do best when they influence and guide patients toward achieving their health care goals. During this interactional process, patients come to rely on, respect, and value their nurse's expertise. As a result, nurses become increasingly influential in patients' eyes.

The same is true for the members of informal organizational structures. The appointment of leaders in formal and informal organizational structures differ. In informal organizational structures, interactional processes are relied upon to determine who is perceived by the group as the most able in facilitating the satisfaction of their needs. Effective communication skills, accurate information, the ability to establish and sustain interpersonal relationships, and expertise that the group members respect and value, all contribute and enhance that person's ability to influence others. The group's interactional processes provide the conditions that foster a nurse's use of transformational leadership. A nurse's ability to share ideas and a vision of the future with coworkers helps them become a more cohesive group, one that becomes increasingly more committed to the goals they have formed for themselves.

As the informal group's needs change, so does its leadership. So long as the informal group's members perceive that progress is being made in satisfying its needs, its leadership will remain the same. When those perceptions change, the influence of that person in a leadership role will diminish or end.

How leadership is used within the informal structure of a health care facility is an important factor to establish. Here are some questions to raise and consider:

- Do you see leadership emerging in your coworkers?
- Do you compliment your coworkers when you see them demonstrate leadership effectively?
- When was the last time you were told that something you did was done well?
- In what ways does your informal group use and/or rely upon the leader in your informal group?
- Are any of your coworkers using transformational leadership?
- Is leadership among your coworkers shared or is one person consistently in the leadership role?
- Do the nurses using leadership in your informal group collaborate easily with the group? Are they creative and promote new ideas? What is management's response to their efforts?

POWER

For leadership to be effective, it must be accompanied by the use of power. Whether power is perceived as a means to an end, or persuading others to do something, or the ability to change behavior, its use is a reality in today's health care environment. While the uses of power in formal organizational structures are relatively clearcut, the uses of power in informal organizational structures are less so because its source depends primarily on intrapersonal and interpersonal factors. Power is intrapersonal, since the desire to acquire power must first come from within. It is interpersonal because its use must also be perceived by others in one's group. Two types of power that are operative in informal organizational structures are expert power and referent power.

Building professional credibility involves demonstrating a solid knowledge base and an equally solid base of clinical skills. This is the source of *expert* power. When members of the nursing staff in a health care facility perceive that their coworker is competent—that is, that the coworker has valid knowledge, skills, and the ability to use them well—that nurse has achieved expert power in the eyes of coworkers.

Referent power is more subtle. It stems from a person's ability to attract others on the basis of perceived personal qualities. These qualities may include a good sense of humor, thoughtfulness, integrity, and honesty. Whatever this person's qualities may be, they are qualities that others admire and value. It is understandable then, that a person with referent power is in a key position to influence and persuade others.

Associating with nurses who have expert and referent power is a good way to begin the process of developing one's own power base. Consistent efforts to update one's knowledge and skills base will increase a nurse's continued marketability and expert power. Networking with other nurses helps a new coworker gain access to more information, ideas, and knowledge about the unwritten rules in a health care facility and the people in that facility who have a power base. Learning about what it takes to acquire expert and referent power are essential activities in one's professional development. Here are some questions to raise and consider:

- Who among your coworkers do you consider has expert power? What specifically leads you to that conclusion?
- How do your coworkers respond to a coworker who is acknowledged to have expert power? How do people in positional authority respond?
- What are you doing to achieve expert power?
- Do your coworkers seek you out for help with a particular skill or piece of knowledge?
- Who, among your coworkers, do you feel has referent power? What specifically leads you to that conclusion?
- In what ways do your coworkers relate to the person with referent power?
- What kind of influence do you perceive this nurse has upon your coworkers?
- Are those nurses you have identified as having both expert and referent power in fact one and the same person? Different persons? Are they a part of the informal group or are they in positional authority?
- Are you consciously associating with those coworkers who have expert and referent power? If so, what impact has this association had on your professional practice?

CULTURE

In many health care settings, the informal culture is unobservable, unofficial, unwritten, and often unexpressed. Invisible boundaries exist that may not be apparent until one tries to cross them. Over time, the norms of the informal culture are learned and adopted by its new members. Organizational taboos ("We never discuss union matters with any administrator"), rituals ("We always have coffee during morning report!"), and "sacred cows" ("The hospital administrator is always right") are a part of a health care facility's culture and do not take long to discover. While formal organizational structures, for example, may require formality in addressing physicians, informal structures may be very casual in this regard.

It is through the informal culture that one learns the difference between what an organization *says* it values, and what, in reality, it *does* value. Informal cultures attempt to promote interpersonal harmony and cooperation among its members, since these are a rich source of recognition and support. Interpersonal social encounters also provide a valuable source of learning about the "nooks and crannies" of the health care facility. Learning how to adapt and function within an "informal" culture without a misstep will take time, not to mention good observational and listening skills. Here are some questions to raise and consider in regard to your health care facility:

- What "sacred cows" have you discovered?
- What topics are "off limits"? How did you discover them?
- What kind of policies or rules seem to be set in concrete?
- What rituals are helpful? Not helpful? Why?
- Were you readily welcomed into your informal group or are you still considered an outsider?
- Being considered a member of the group means. . . . . ?
- What does being an outsider in your health care facility mean to you?
- How does your group interact with or treat a perceived outsider?
- What is the morale among your coworkers? Is there a high staff turnover? Apathy? Frequent illnesses? High stress levels? Minimal initiative? Reluctance to make any changes? How are your coworkers dealing with these factors?

REFERENCES

1. Marquis, B.L. and Huston, C.J. (1992). *Leadership roles and management functions in nursing: Theory and application.* Philadelphia: J.B. Lippincott, 277.
2. Tappen, R.M. (1995). *Nursing leadership and management: Concepts and practice.* (3rd ed.) Philadelphia: F.A. Davis, 100.
3. Barker, A.M. and Young, C.E. (1994). Tranformational leadership: The feminist connection in post modern organizations. *Holistic Nursing Practice,* 9(1), 21.
4. Tappen, 346.
5. del Bueno, D. (1986). Organizational culture: How important is it? *Journal of Nursing Administration,* 16(10), 16.
6. Strader, M.K. and Decker, P.J. (1995). *Role transition to patient care management.* Norwalk, Conn.: Appleton and Lange, 265–266.
7. Ribeiro, V.E. and Blakeley, J.A. (1995). The proactive management of rumor and gossip. *Journal of Nursing Administration,* 25(6), 43.
8. Strader and Decker, p. 438.

BIBLIOGRAPHY

Bruhn, J.C. and Chesney, A. P. (1994). Diagnosing the health of organizations. *Health Care Supervisor,* 13(2), 21–33.
Bruhn, J.C. and Chesney, A.P. (1995). Organizational moles: Information control and the acquisition of power and status. *Health Care Supervisor,* 1995, 14(1), 24–31.
del Bueno, D. (1986). Organizational culture: How important is it? *Journal of Nursing Administration,* 16(10), 15–20.
Marquis, B.L. and Huston, C. J. (1992). *Leadership roles and management functions in nursing: Theory and application.* Philadelphia: Lippincott-Raven.
Ribeiro, V.E. and Blakeley, J.A. (1995). The proactive management of rumor and gossip. *Journal of Nursing Administration,* 25 (6), 43–50.

Strader, M.K. and Decker, P.J. (1995). *Role transition to patient care management.* Norwalk, Conn.: Appleton and Lange.

Tappen, R. M. (1995). *Nursing leadership and management: Concepts and practice.* (3rd ed.) Philadephia: F.A. Davis.

Willey, E. L. (1987). Acquiring and using power effectively. *Journal of Continuing Education,* 18 (1), 25–28.

CHAPTER 36

●●●

The Current Healthcare Environment: Who Is the Customer?

BARBARA S. HEATER

Arguments will be presented that indicate that current healthcare financial incentives pose threats to the obligation of healthcare institutions to function as service organizations and maintain the patient as prime beneficiary or primary customer. Historically, the customer of the hospital has shifted from the patient to the corporation with changes in financial reimbursement to hospitals.

The purpose of this article is to caution professional nurses about the various customers competing for the role of prime beneficiary of health care and the pressures on the nurse to value meeting institutional goals over clinical treatment outcomes of patients. Throughout nursing's history and the different environments for providing care, nursing has placed the welfare of the patient above all other good. Will nursing continue to view the patient's needs as primary?

This article presents definitions of customer, consumer, and provider and identifies the customer of health care in five different reimbursement environments: pre-Medicare, Medicare retrospective payment, prospective payment (DRGs), healthcare reform, and managed care. Additionally, the author will address classifications of organizations and concomitant organizational obligations and consumers' concerns.

Customers, Consumers, and Providers

Germane to a discussion of the customer of a healthcare organization is a definition of customer. *Webster's College Dictionary* (1991) defines customer as "a person who purchases goods or services" (p. 336). A consumer is defined (by the same dictionary) as one who acquires commodities or services. A broker is "an agent who buys or sells for a principal on a commission basis" (*Webster*, p. 174). According to Chaney (1991), provider includes the individual members of professional disciplines as well as the corporate institutions where health care is provided. Chaney adds "the basic ethical obligations of all providers are

From *Nursing Forum* 31(3): 31–34. Reprinted with permission, Nursecom, Inc.

similar because all are engaged in the special activity of caring for patients" (p. 260). Thus patients have a right to expect institutions, such as hospitals or HMOs, to put patient interests above all other interests.

The Customer of the Hospital Pre-Medicare

Prior to the Medicare legislation of 1966, the financial responsibility for health care was borne by either the individual who received the care or an employer-sponsored insurance plan. With this method of payment to the hospital, the customer was the patient who was free to choose a different provider for hospital services. Hospital finances were managed carefully to keep costs to the patient low and thus make the hospital more attractive to patients.

The Customer of the Hospital in the Medicare Years

In 1966, Title XVIII (Medicare) and Title XIX (Medicaid) of the Social Security Act established reimbursement for hospitals based on reasonable cost plus a 2% fixed fee. For a period, rich and poor and young and old received similar if not the same treatment (Stevens, 1986) and the hospital was reimbursed for the costs of caring for the elderly and the poor. Under this retrospective cost reimbursement method, there were few incentives to manage finances efficiently. A high volume of patients with long lengths of stay benefited the hospital. Based on the assumption that physicians and patients would want the latest technology and the highest level of comfort and services that money could buy, hospitals invested large amounts of money to make themselves attractive to physicians and potential patients.

Since physicians control admissions to hospitals, physicians were viewed as the buyer of services or customer of the hospital (Harris, Hicks, & Kelly, 1992). Based on the assumption that physicians controlled patients' decisions about hospital choice, recruitment of physicians superseded recruitment of patients. Research indicates that patients have always been less passive about choosing their hospitals than is commonly believed (Folse, 1984; Kurz & Wolinsky, 1985). Despite the evidence from the research literature, physicians became the primary customer of the hospital with patients the secondary customers.

The Customer of the Hospital Under DRGs

The Social Security Amendments of 1983 eliminated the retrospective cost-plus-fixed-fee reimbursement for Medicare and Medicaid patients. Instead, a prospective payment system based on a fixed price per diagnosis-related group (DRG) was established for inpatient services. Essentially, a hospital was paid a preestablished price for a patient's hospitalization based on that patient's diagnosis. If the hospital's costs for treating the patient were less than the reimbursement for the pertinent DRG, the hospital retained the surplus. The risk to patients as consumers was that of decreased services during shortened hospital stays. Several authors have validated that decreases in services since DRGs have resulted in poorer patient outcomes (Fitzgerald, Fagan, Tierney, & Dittus, 1987; Fitzgerald, Moore, & Dittus, 1988; Jette, Harris, Cleary, & Campion, 1987; Keene & Anderson, 1982). When services to patients decrease and clinical outcomes worsen, the patient is no longer a customer, not even a secondary customer. Forced to operate in a market economy, health care organizations and providers have had difficulties meeting obligations to patients (Garrett, Klonski, & Baillie, 1993).

On the other hand, if the patient's treatment cost more than the hospital's reimbursement, the hospital suffered a loss. The risk to hospitals was that of assuming the financial risk for decisions made by physicians. In an attempt to limit their financial risk, hospitals began to monitor and influence decision making and resource use by physicians.

This monitoring and influencing of decision making has led to discussions about the deprofessionalization of medicine. O'Connor and Lanning (1992) argue that the key characteristic of a professional is autonomy in decision making. Chaney (1991) argues that throughout history, the healing relationship between physician and patient was based on the trust the patient placed in the physician. Pellegrino and Thomasma (1988) maintain that

> providers are ethically obligated to put the good of the patient first. The good of the patient is the most fundamental norm of the physician–patient relationship. Physicians cannot interpose other priorities, such as research goals, their personal self-interests, or institutional goals, if these conflict with the good of the patient.

Under the prospective payment system, the identification of the customer is difficult. Both the patient and the physician posed financial threats to viability of the institution. Survival of the institution became the customer or prime beneficiary; hospital self-interest was primary.

The Customer of the Hospital During Healthcare Reform

The customer of health care during healthcare reform became the general public, who demanded higher quality and lower costs since they believe they pay either directly or indirectly. Since the early 1990s, legislative activity across the country has been aimed at responding to the demands for the reform of health care. The pressure for reform stems from the needs of the underinsured and the uninsured as well as the skyrocketing costs (Thomasma, 1995). Decreasing the costs of Medicare and Medicaid by decreasing reimbursement to providers while increasing the volume of patients receiving services is viewed as essential. Private insurance companies, like the federal and state governments, have suffered from the skyrocketing costs of health care and have responded like governmental payers. The rising cost of private health insurance premiums has hurt employer-purchasers of healthcare benefits in their competition in foreign markets. Employers have reacted by asking employees to pay a larger share of the premium and larger deductibles when using services.

Provider groups are preparing for reform in health care with the concomitant decrease in reimbursement by examining strategies such as less expensive care providers and other cost-cutting strategies. One healthcare reform proposal for cutting the cost of health care is combining providers and insurers in one organizational structure; managed competition or managed care are the terms used to describe this structure (Reinhardt, 1994).

The Customer of the Hospital Under Managed Care

According to Thomasma (1995), managed care is "the definition of an interventionist healthcare system that emphasizes social control through organized competition. The idea is to push providers and hospitals into networks, such that the old fee-for-service will be far down the food chain" (p. 151). In a managed care system like a health maintenance organization (HMO), a flat annual capitation payment is assessed, with those who enroll eligible to receive all healthcare services with only a modest copayment at the time services are received. Managed care has grown, especially in young healthy populations and in employee groups whose employers present few choices for healthcare insurance. An estimated 45 million people had enrolled in managed care by 1993, up from 12.5 million in 1983 (Schroeder, 1994). By the year 2000, it is anticipated that 60% of all employees along with their dependents will be covered by managed care (Chilingerian, 1992).

The goal of managed care is forcing regional rivals to compete for patients on both the amount of the capitation and copayment as well as the quality of care (Reinhardt, 1994). The outcomes of treatment will need to be monitored carefully since powerful incentives to limit care are intrinsic to care providers with predetermined revenues. Managed competition is regulated by statute through sponsors. However, sponsors might be corporate personnel departments more interested in cost containment than quality. The identity of the customer will blur more under this financial mechanism than any previously discussed. Healthcare professionals fear that the customer of health care will be viewed as the corporate office where decisions regarding employee healthcare benefits are made.

Organizational Classifications and Concomitant Responsibilities

The general public has a right to expect that an organization's operationalized mission will be congruent with the way society classifies that organization. Blau and Scott (1962) classified all organizations into four mutually exclusive groups according to prime beneficiary: mutual benefit, business, commonwealth, and service.

The membership of mutual-benefit organizations is the prime beneficiary with the goal of improving benefits to members. An example of a mutual-benefit organization is a labor union. Dues-paying members expect the officers of the labor union to focus on members.

In a business organization the goal of making a profit serves the prime beneficiaries, the owners, or stockholders. The officers of the business organization, hired by the owners or stockholders, report regularly to the owners or stockholders. Mechanisms such as external auditors' reports to the owners or stockholders serve to protect the interests of the prime beneficiaries. Failure to make sound business decisions or make a profit usually results in termination of the errant officer(s).

The general public is the prime beneficiary of commonwealth organizations. All local, state, and federal offices fall in this category. The goals of democratic control by the public and efficient administration are essential in commonwealth organizations to ensure that the general public remain the focus of this type of organization.

The prime beneficiaries of a service organization are the clients who seek services. The major problem is keeping the client, not employees or others associated with the organization, as the prime beneficiary. This is particularly true of healthcare organizations. Made vulnerable by lack of medical knowledge and perhaps the stress of serious illness, patients depend on the integrity of professionals for information and guidance in decision making. The question arises as to whether healthcare professionals will be free to make decisions or guide patients' decision making in the best interests of patients or one of the many other customers, such as employer groups, third-party payers, or health maintenance organizations. An additional concern is where on the continuum of well-being officers of the healthcare organization would place the best interests of the patient.

Consumers' Concerns

The American public has expressed grave concerns about the cost and quality of health care. The costs and outcomes of health care affect everyone in the nation as taxpayers and as purchasers of goods and services. The costs of employee healthcare benefits are passed on to consumers and affect the ability of American business to compete in foreign markets. O'Connor and Lanning (1992) have argued that healthcare organizations must operate as businesses in order to achieve greater efficiency and lower costs for buyers. Greater efficiency has necessitated the end of autonomous decision making by physicians and greater accountability to the public.

Greater public accountability would be advanced by Hegyvary's proposal (1991) that the outcomes of patient care reflect the interests of patients/consumers, providers, purchasers, payers, and the public. The four categories of outcome evaluation suggested include clinical, functional, financial, and perceptual. Employers and insurers want the most value for the dollar, while hospitals want clinical outcomes to reflect the highest professional standards. Nurses and physicians use evaluation of clinical and functional outcomes to judge effectiveness of treatment for a given patient and for knowledge building in the disciplines (Jones, 1993). Patients want option-outcome information prior to making decisions about their own course of treatment and selection of providers. Inlander (1990) has questioned why patients haven't demanded truth in healthcare laws requiring providers to support recommendations for treatment with evidence and cost information sooner.

Maraldo's (1990) prediction that consumers would take over the power base in decision making currently occupied by physicians and hospital administrators seems less likely in a managed competition environment. Instead of taking over the power base in decision making, most people will be thrust into cut-rate health maintenance organizations by their employers. Clancy, Himmelstein, and Woolhandler (1993) argued that competition would disempower patients and clinical professionals while at the same time empowering corporate providers. Shore (1994) defined managed care as making the best use of resources in the delivery of health care to individuals. Yet Clancy and colleagues have asserted there was little evidence that managed competition would result in savings of healthcare dollars.

Business Customers and Healthcare Customers

Providing health care to patients results in the payment of money to an institution, a hospital, or a physician at some point in time. The fact that the care may have been paid for by the government, the patient's employer, an insurance company, or managed care tends to blur the identity of the customer relative to who must be satisfied with the services and the outcome. Both the tradition and ethics of health care require that the purchase and payment for services be regarded as different from a commercial transaction (Chaney, 1991).

Differences between business customers and healthcare customers exist mainly due to differing levels of customer independence. People seeking health care are especially vulnerable and dependent on others who possess the knowledge and skills the individual seeking care doesn't have. In commercial transactions, buyers of services and goods approach sellers from a position of equality and independence with the ability to seek other sellers. In a business transaction the seller is simply held to the duty to tell the truth; however, in interactions with patients, providers are held to a higher standard because of the trust patients place in providers of health care. Patients are not usually in a position to compare healthcare providers for quality and price. In a managed care system, patients who are in a position to compare healthcare providers for quality may be denied the opportunity to compare and then choose a provider. Additionally, patients risk more than a commercial buyer; the patient's life may be at stake in the experience with the healthcare provider.

Conclusion

The notion that any group, other than patients, is a primary customer of the hospital presents a dilemma for professional nurses. This article raises issues about the competing demands of hospitals within the context of the hospital as a service organization forced to operate as a business.

Liedtka (1992) has pointed out that the major obstacle to hospitals serving customers other than patients is the strong professional values of nurses. While the nursing literature suggests that professional values develop from the nature of the nurse–patient relationship (Fry, 1989; Yarling & McElmurry, 1986), Liedtka argues that these values developed as a result of practice in an environment free from financial constraints and administrative interference. Implied in Liedtka's argument is the belief that the cost-containment and administrative directives inherent in managed care will reshape professional practice. Professional nurses must examine their values and their beliefs about practice and make choices. Will nurses choose to allow institutions to reshape professional nursing practice and the nurse's view of the patient as primary customer of healthcare institutions? Raines (1994) asserts that professionals must possess "courage or a willingness to act—even if against public opinion, authority, tradition, or current standards, with acknowledgment of the possible outcome of the choice" (p.7).

REFERENCES

Blau, P., & Scott, W. (1962). *Formal organizations: A comparative approach.* San Francisco: Chandler.

Chaney, H. (1991). Practical approaches to marketing. In M. Ward & S. Price (Eds.), *Issues in nursing administration* (pp. 252–267). St. Louis, MO: Mosby Year Book.

Chilingerian, J. (1992). New directions for hospital strategic management: The market for efficient care. *Health Care Management Review, 17*(4), 73–80.

Clancy, C., Himmelstein, D., & Woolhandler, S. (1993). Questions and answers about managed competition. *International Journal of Health Services, 23*(2), 213–218.

Fitzgerald, J., Fagan, L., Tierney, W., & Dittus, R. (1987). Changing patterns of hip fracture before and after implementation of the prospective payment system. *JAMA, 258,* 218–221.

Fitzgerald, J., Moore, P., & Dittus, R. (1988). The care of elderly patients with hip fracture. *The New England Journal of Medicine, 319,* 1392–1397.

Folse, M. (1984, November). Marketing staffs give hospitals a shot in arm. *Advertising Age,* p. 14.

Fry, S. (1989). Toward a theory of nursing ethics. *Advances in Nursing Science, 11*(4), 9–22.

Garrett, T., Klonski, R., & Baillie, H. (1993). American business ethics and health care costs. *Health Care Management Review, 18*(1), 44–50.

Harris, C., Hicks, L., & Kelly, B. (1992). Physician-hospital networking: Avoiding a shotgun wedding. *Health Care Management Review, 17,* 17–28.

Hegyvary, S. (1991). Issues in outcomes research. *Journal of Nursing Quality Assurance, 5*(2), 1–6.

Inlander, C. (1990). Truth in medicine. *Nursing Economics, 8,* 196, 198.

Jette, A., Harris, B., Cleary, P., & Campion, E. (1987). Functional recovery after hip fracture. *Archives of Physical Medicine and Rehabilitation, 68,* 735–739.

Jones, K. (1993). Outcome analysis: Methods and issues. *Nursing Economics, 11,* 145–152.

Keene, J., & Anderson, C. (1982). Hip fractures in the elderly: Discharge predictions with a functional rating scale. *JAMA, 248,* 564–567.

Kurz, R., & Wolinsky, F. (1985). Who picks the hospital: Practitioner or patient? *Hospital and Health Services Administration, 30,* 95–106.

Liedtka, J. (1992). Formulating hospital strategy: Moving beyond a market mentality. *Health Care Management Review, 17*(1), 21–26.

Maraldo, P. (1990). The nineties: A decade of search of meaning. *Nursing and Health Care, 11,* 11–14.

O'Connor, S., & Lanning, J. (1992). The end of autonomy? Reflections on the postprofessional physician. *Health Care Management Review, 17,* 63–72.

Pellegrino, E., & Thomasma, D. (1988). *For the patient's good: The restoration of beneficence in health care.* New York: Oxford University Press.

Raines, D. (1994). Moral agency in nursing. *Nursing Forum, 29*(1), 5–11.

Reinhardt, U. (1994). Managed competition in health care reform: Just another American dream, or the perfect solution? *The Journal of Law, Medicine & Ethics, 22,* 106–120.

Schroeder, S. (1994). The latest forecast: Managed care collides with physician supply. *JAMA. 272,* 239–240.

Shore, M. (1994). Managed care—turbulent wave of the future. *Harvard Mental Health Letter, 10*(10), 4–6.

Stevens, R. (1986). The changing hospital. In L. Aiken & D. Mechanic (Eds.), *Applications of social science to clinical medicine and health policy* (pp. 80–99). New Brunswick, NJ: Rutgers University Press.

Thomasma, D. (1995). The ethical challenge of providing healthcare for the elderly. *Cambridge Quarterly of Healthcare Ethics, 4,* 148–162.

Webster's College Dictionary. (1991). New York: Random House.

Yarling, R., & McElmurry, B. (1986). The moral foundation of nursing. *Advances in Nursing Science, 8*(2), 63–73.

CHAPTER 37

●●

Patient Focused Care: Improving Customer Satisfaction While Reducing Cost

JEAN PHILLIPS TRUSCOTT AND GAIL MARCHIGIANO CHURCHILL

Although it is doubtful that comprehensive, nationwide health care reform will be seen during the 104th Congress, it is still one of the most important domestic concerns confronting Americans. Indeed, public demands for affordable, quality care; government sanctions on delivery systems to contain costs; and the lack of access to services for millions of uninsured citizens have all had an impact on the ways hospitals operate and care is delivered.

To compete more effectively in the ever-changing health care environment, institutions across the country are considering a number of new strategies—including the concept of *patient focused care.* Described as "a kaleidoscope turning, rearranging the mosaic-like interconnections of people and processes that make up the modern hospital to form an entirely different pattern" (Manthey, 1994, p. 9), this delivery system aims to improve customer satisfaction and quality of care while reducing cost.

Since its first implementation in 1989 at Florida's Lakeland Regional Medical Center, patient focused care has been gaining popularity nationwide. Over the past five years, proponents have converted one or more units within health care facilities so "resources and personnel are organized around patients rather than around various specialized departments" (Sherer, 1993, p. 14). Concord Hospital, a 295-bed acute care facility in Concord, New Hampshire, is one such example.

Through *patient focused work transformation (PFWT)*—a restructuring strategy that combines both work redesign and reengineering techniques—this hospital is continuously improving quality of care and enhancing efficiency by eliminating resource waste within the delivery system. For example, key elements—including preadmission testing, discharge planning, and surgical and pharmacy services—are being reengineered to support the new patient focused environment. With such services moving closer to the bedside, all aspects of inpatient care delivery are being assessed as part of work redesign.

Certainly, this intense and complex process is a formidable task, requiring years of commitment—from the design stage, to implementation, to evaluation. Moreover, the

---

dedication of all departments is necessary for success. Mediocrity cannot be tolerated at any level.

While Concord Hospital continues to meet client needs and to contain costs in a patient focused environment, other institutions may wonder whether this delivery system is the answer in these difficult times. As nursing leaders, you also must carefully consider your own willingness to direct or to participate in such a process. Can you help design a vision for professional nursing that embraces change? Do you have the commitment necessary for this long-term project? Indeed, for optimal results, you and your colleagues must share a strong belief that even though every crisis period has a certain amount of risk involved, tremendous opportunity also abounds.

Embracing Change

LOOKING BACK TO UNDERSTAND THE FUTURE

To maintain leadership roles in these dynamic times, it is crucial that nurses understand how and why change has occurred—and continues to occur—in our nation's health care facilities. Relman (cited in Wenzel, 1992) identified three periods that have emerged as revolutionary in U.S. health care, particularly in relation to policy.

The first, a time of *expansion* beginning in the 1940s, was characterized by a rise in the numbers of hospitals, physicians, and technical advances. In addition, more and more citizens were covered by health insurance plans—especially for hospitalization. The National Institutes of Health also increased funding for basic research. And during this period, policy decisions were directed to growth.

These changes' inflationary nature inevitably led to a stage of *cost containment* in the early 1980s. This era was highlighted by the development of Medicare's prospective payment system, based on a number of diagnostic related groups (DRGs). Additional federal regulation appeared in the form of peer review organizations (PROs). At this time, managed care also began its rapid growth, and changes in health insurance—such as copayments, deductibles, second opinion requirements, and better coverage in ambulatory and extended care—surfaced.

The third phase, *assessment and accountability,* began in late 1989. This period had a number of landmarks, including the passage of the federal Omnibus Budget Reconciliation Act which mandated the use of a Resource Based Relative Value Scale (RBRVS). Most recently, a move toward managed care organizations and capitated payment systems has occurred, shifting the financial risks of providing health care from insurers to providers.

As more hospitals face the challenge of remaining profitable in light of increased competition, declining resources, and revenue reductions, it is clear that they can no longer use traditional cost control methods to survive in the health care marketplace. By changing the fundamental ways they operate and deliver care to reflect a patient focused approach, however, institutions not only can provide efficient, quality care, but also maintain their competitive edge.

Restructuring

THE KEY TO SUCCESS

Patient focused care, an outcome of inpatient hospital restructuring, requires significant organizational changes. For example, traditional hospital departments, structured as virtually independent "silos," must be realigned so that patient needs, rather than the department's preference, are the focus of services. In turn, these services should be brought to patients whenever possible, instead of vice versa. Therefore, leadership at the executive level must also consider itself open to review and readjustment as the process completes its full cycle.

Before beginning a restructuring process, however, the organization must have a sound, clear vision. Without this critical element, it cannot remain effectively centered during the difficult transition period that will follow. Moreover, without a vision, inappropriate compromises can result in less than optimal outcomes for the institution.

A critical step in the early part of the restructuring process is the selection of internal staff who will guide the teams and provide support. It is imperative that these key individuals are credible leaders across disciplines, have strong group process skills, and share the organization's vision. Depending on the time frame allotted for results, some institutions also may use consultants to drive the process more rapidly or to provide an additional resource for change management. Together, these individuals will help to revamp the highly compartmentalized organizational structure of the facility, moving services closer to the bedside and reducing the number of care providers interacting with each patient.

Traditionally, hospitals have had discrete functional services such as housekeeping, pharmacy, and the laboratory. Unfortunately, this specialization has led to more fragmented, costly care and less than ideal customer service. For example, Lathrop (1993) describes that during a typical three-to-four day inpatient stay in a large hospital, a patient may interact with 50 to 60 employees—and the average 500-bed hospital has as many as 350 job classifications. In addition, the hospital care delivery system according to Porter-O'Grady (1993) is "not based on the needs of the patient; it reflects the needs and conveniences of the provider" (p. 7). Two situations readily illustrate the problem: It is not uncommon for the x-ray department to summon a patient just as the meal tray arrives or for the ECG technician to be delayed while a patient is experiencing chest pain.

Such compartmentalization also breeds process complexity and raises costs. Hospitals using a patient focused care approach, on the other hand, have redeployed clinical, administrative, and support services—including basic laboratory, pharmacy, admitting/discharge, medical records, and housekeeping—to patient units from central departments. In fact, a primary goal of the patient focused design is to provide 70 to 90% of all services on the unit (Wakefield et al, 1994). Only those services which have expensive equipment or highly skilled personnel remain centrally located. To achieve this objective efficiently, patient focused units typically are larger and contain similar patient populations.

PROCESS REENGINEERING

A major element of restructuring, process reengineering makes breakthrough changes in the systems associated with the delivery of care so services are aligned with patient needs. Besides this gain in customer service, however, reengineering aims to improve measures of performance, including profitability, market share, and reductions in cost.

Teams—comprised of information management staff, who possess knowledge of the institution's systems and technology, and specially trained hospital employees, sometimes called process experts—consider their options and weigh alternatives carefully. Because process reengineering is not "jury rigging an existing system so that it works better" (Hammer & Champy, 1993, p. 31), but a radical redesign resulting in a new system, team members starting the project do not know what the final result will be. A common approach, however, is to answer the question, "If we could start from scratch how would we do this? . . . Then do it that way, and throw away everything else" (Stewart, 1993, p. 42). Considering this, it is no wonder that Whetsell (cited in Bergman, 1994) contends "the best time to begin reengineering is when an organization is still doing well and has time and resources to commit to it" (p. 32).

An example of the effectiveness of reengineering can be seen within Sentara Bayside Hospital, a 157-bed acute care hospital in Virginia Beach, Virginia. Staff turned to this reorganization tool to reduce the time and number of steps patients must take to complete preadmission testing. As a result, the process now takes an average of 40 minutes—versus the previous 120 minutes (Box 37-1) (Berdick & Humphries, 1994).

WORK REDESIGN

Another component of restructuring—work redesign—often is a difficult organizational change because it directly involves people and their jobs. Focusing on the question, *Who does what?*, this procedure requires a careful examination of patient care needs and the types of jobs that will most effectively and efficiently meet those requirements. Although work redesign models vary from institution to institution—and across services—patient focused care units most often contain cross-trained personnel, self-managed work teams, and empowered, accountable staff (Figure 37-1).

Cross-training usually includes four broad categories of generalists: professional, clinical/technical, support, and administrative. The professional category includes registered nurses, physical and occupational therapists, clinical dieticians, and social workers. A clinical/technical generalist may be a respiratory therapist, electrocardiogram technician, or a nonprofessional trained to perform a variety of clinical skills, such as phlebotomy and basic nursing, respiratory, and physical therapy procedures. On the other hand, a support generalist assumes the more nonclinical tasks, like housekeeping, dietary, supply management and transport, and an administrative generalist is involved with admissions, insurance verification, coding, completion of medical records, and unit secretarial duties.

BOX 37–1   REENGINEERING AND TQM/CQI

Like Total Quality Management (TQM) and Continuous Quality Improvement (CQI), reengineering analyzes the way an organization does business while identifying opportunities for improvement. Often, when reengineering ends, TQM can be used to continue the process.

Relationship	TMQ/CQI	Reengineering
Process	Continuous process improvement, making small incremental gains over time.	Major breakthroughs and radical, dramatic changes that provide significant gains quickly (6–12 months).
	Focuses on existing processes.	Examines existing processes and cuts across boundaries. Discards the old process.
Timing	Takes a long, long time.	Eight weeks to design a new process; several years to reengineer a hospital.
	Is continuous.	Periodic rather than continuous.
Outcome	Focuses on customer satisfaction.	Greater emphasis on improving performance: profitability, market share, reduce costs.

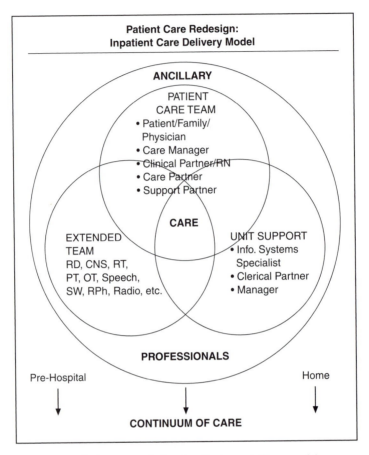

Figure 37–1   Patient care redesign: Inpatient care delivery model.

The goal of cross-training is to decrease the number of caregivers who interact with patients. On patient focused units, clinical generalists are cross-trained to meet most of a patient's needs. Additionally, any skill that is cross-trained requires that competency be established and then maintained through ongoing assessment and education. While this technique can produce role ambiguity and a loss of professional identity, Watson (cited in Manthey, 1994) points out, "it is not a single skill or set of skills alone that makes a professional. It is the unique combination of skills, knowledge, and ability . . ." (p. 11).

Besides cross-trained providers, patient focused units rely on multidisciplinary teams to consistently work with the same physician and care for similar types of patients. Both the specific number and mix of individuals on a team vary from hospital to hospital and must be carefully analyzed based on the needs of patients and the ability/expertise of professional and technical staff.

Similarly, the role of the nurse may vary substantially between patient focused units and institutions. Without exception, work redesign alters the role of the professional nurse and increases the need for RNs to be skilled in managing various levels of assistive personnel while understanding the responsibilities of delegating nursing care (Barter & Furmidge, 1994). For example, on some units, RNs are cross-trained to do ancillary tasks and function under the principles of "do it yourself" whenever possible (Brider, 1992). Other patient focused areas ascribe more to the principle of selecting the right person for the job (Zimmerman, Crosier, & Taylor, 1993). On these units, part of the care team is comprised of RNs working with individuals—either unlicensed assistive personnel (UAP) or certified nursing assistants (CNAs)—who are cross-trained.

Another characteristic of this phase of restructuring is the major paradigm shift toward empowering staff. Indeed, patient focused hospitals provide all levels of employees with the opportunity for increased responsibility and the authority to meet patient needs with established accountability for patient outcomes. Some of the responsibilities that empower staff on patient focused units include multidisciplinary collaboration and the development and use of practice guidelines, critical paths, and care maps to standardize patient care processes. The provision of care, which extends across a continuum from an episode of care to an episode of illness, is another characteristic responsibility.

Borfitz (1993) reports how three patient focused care hospitals have broadened their scope of care. At the University of Utah Hospital in Salt Lake City, for example, teams are responsible for managing care from preadmission through postdischarge, and they oversee that care across multiple care sites. Leveraging, a system also employed by some patient focused care hospitals, allows staff to spend an optimal portion of their work time at the high end of their skill level. In other words, staff are empowered to function at a level most consistent with their education and training.

Indeed, the essence of work redesign is "pushing responsibility and authority to act further down in the organization" (Borfitz, 1993, p. 14). With patient focused hospitals, the rigid, static structure of the hierarchical pyramid is being replaced by a flatter structure with a very small, well-defined top leadership group. Smith (cited in Borfitz, 1993) relates that "employees, referred to as associates, are encouraged to take risks and cross departmental lines to identify problems and experiment with solutions to them" (p. 14). On many patient focused care units, teams perform evaluation, supervision, and problem resolution. Decision making is decentralized and requires that staff have responsibility for decisions affecting cost and the quality of care (Moore & Komras, 1993).

Implementing the Plan

A DEMONSTRATION IN NEW HAMPSHIRE

While the concepts of process reengineering and work redesign may be implemented separately, many experts believe the best system for organizing work activities features a combination of the two—in sequential order. In the case of Concord Hospital, this complete restructuring effort, termed *patient focused work transformation*, continues to concentrate on the human side of health care—and not merely follow a set process.

What factors influenced this facility's decision to restructure? How was the model implemented? What were some of the problems encountered? And what type of evaluation was designed?

MAKING THE DECISION

Like many other institutions across the nation, Concord Hospital faced declining patient stays and changing admission patterns. Although the facility maintained a position of financial strength, it soon became clear that the belt-tightening of past years simply would not bring about the results needed for continued successful operation in the future. In addition, it was obvious that this facility was organized hierarchically and functionally by departments . . . and, thus, was fragmented from the patient's perspective. A significant portion of staff time was nonvalue added—that is, spent waiting for telephones to ring and elevators to arrive.

When considering potential options, Concord Hospital made a conscious decision not to terminate employees as a result of any restructuring efforts. Indeed, the commitment of the organization remains that no one would be without a job. All changes would be voluntary or realized through attrition.

In addition, the facility continues to be committed to its philosophical values. First and foremost, the hospital believes in playing a strong role within the community, centering on collective responsibility and working in partnership with others to assure a continuum of care. Leadership and management support, as well as the empowerment of staff, are crucial. Developing customer and physician partnerships, while emphasizing cost management and information sharing, also are paramount. Other values include a commitment to individual and team involvement, to work process improvement and information management, and to education, training, and development of staff.

In searching for a long-term solution, Concord Hospital identified major systems problems, and this necessitated that a systems approach be applied. Consistently in the literature, the idea of restructuring the total hospital system emerged as appropriate. For this facility, patient focused care was the option of choice. This delivery system would help the facility not only meet its philosophical goals, but also better compete in the capitated, managed care marketplace of the future.

To assist teams and expedite the process, Concord Hospital interviewed several consultant groups. Key issues for selection were:

a. Fit in with the values of the organization

b. Demonstrated success with all dimensions of the project process

c. Have positive post-project references

d. Maintain a reasonable cost

Also, organizations involved in hospital restructuring across the country were contacted. Fairly extensive dialogues occurred, and information was willingly shared in all instances. In fact, the candor of others facilitated Concord's decision-making process.

No restructuring effort is a "low risk" project—especially when an active organization is involved. At Concord Hospital, redesign affected the daily work of 1,200 employees and 200 physicians, a community of 35,000, and a service area of 100,000—necessitating careful review and consideration of all options. Clearly, the cost, whether measured in direct dollars (consultation, education and training, committee support, facility modifications) or indirect costs (organizational chaos as well as staff, physician, and community confusion, resistance, and anger toward change) is high.

Upon reflection, the hospital realized that while PFWT requires the involvement of all employees throughout the process, the commitment of senior management was, and is, essential. Indeed, without their dedication and support—often over an extended period of time—change will not occur. It is hoped, therefore, that by becoming immersed in the restructuring effort, these individuals not only will better understand the process, but also feel a sense of ownership and advocacy that will lead to a successful implementation.

PUTTING THE PLAN INTO ACTION

The move to patient care redesign proceeded in four phases: Vision, Design, Develop, and Demonstration. A critical first step in beginning the restructuring process was to create the *vision*. Without an understanding of the plan's goal, the daunting task of restructuring simply would not have been possible. The work is too hard, the issues too diverse, the opportunities for sabotage too available.

At Concord Hospital, creation of a vision that reflected the values of the organization was the responsibility of senior management. Others involved in the process were leaders of the medical staff and members of the project group that would assume responsibility for guiding the vision.

This mission—to "provide high quality, cost-effective health care, delivered in a caring and professional manner, to meet the needs of the community"—was shared in detail at multiple meetings of hospital and medical staff so all who would become stakeholders in the process could understand the direction of the organization. In fact, the CEO led many of these sessions, reinforcing his commitment to the vision and restructuring process.

The vision statement became the foundation for the *Design* Phase. Overarching priorities for the outcome of this stage were:

a. To minimize travel time for patients and staff

b. To decrease the numbers of staff with whom the patient interacts

c. To increase the time available for all staff to meet patient needs

d. To leverage work to the greatest extent possible

A group of 30 patient care and support department directors were charged with designing a template for inpatient care that emphasized teams (see Figure 37-1). For optimum health outcomes, the model was applied across the entire continuum of care, from prehospital to home.

Staff involvement, which was supported by the organization in time and dollars, began during the *Develop* Phase, where the model was customized. One unit was selected for demonstration: Orthopedic/neurosurgery. To improve the transition to a patient focused care environment, hospital and unit staff were involved on all committees, which addressed, collectively, all aspects of daily activity at the unit level. The input of staff doing the work is crucial in decision making. Among the recommendations made by staff during the Develop Phase were some facility modifications which, while minimal in terms of expense, created a more positive work flow for nurses and created improved access points for both staff and patients to unit support facilities.

During this phase in the process, four new patient care positions were identified—Care Manager, Clinical Partner, Care Partner, and Support Partner. The roles of care manager and clinical partner were held by registered nurses while those of care partner and support partner were nonprofessional assistive positions.

Responsibilities of the care manager included case management functions, collaboration with clinical partners, family, and physician, as well as coordination of daily discharge planning. The clinical partner assessed patients, developed plans of care and discharge plans, and coordinated the team. Tasks performed by the care partner included performing phlebotomy and simple dressing changes, as well as assisting with procedures, while the support partner was responsible for supply management, dietary functions, housekeeping, and transportation.

Concord Hospital made the decision that since these positions were new, staff had the option to apply for them or to become assigned to another position in the organization for which they were qualified. All who applied were interviewed, and this was followed by a careful selection process.

Staff who opted not to apply or who were not selected for the new roles were reassigned to traditional remaining units (those areas not yet involved in PFWT). Some individuals did not apply because they were close to retirement. In these cases, "bridges" were created to assist them. Of the staff who went to other units, some reapplied and were selected when those areas went through the PFWT process.

In addition, a number of licensed practical nurses (LPNs) on the transformed unit elected to return to school to become registered nurses. Those opting to continue their education were paid a full salary—and tuition—by Concord Hospital. Still other LPNs accepted positions as pharmacy technicians. While the surgical technologist program at Concord was offered as another career avenue for licensed practical nurses, none chose that option.

A key challenge to the Develop Phase was to carefully plan which services would be deployed to a unit based on patient population. Some questions included: *Would respiratory care be a factor on this particular unit? Is the volume of work such that moving the function would make sense? Does the volume of radiography justify the expense of replicating services on a patient focused unit?*

Each organization has unique needs in relation to relocating services. The space for services deployed at Concord Hospital came from those patient care areas after a careful analysis of the number of beds actually required. Facility modifications, therefore, were modest and made fairly easily. It also was an organizational decision that the centralized departments would apply their existing quality assurance standards to the skills performed in the decentralized location—ensuring the same standard of care was being applied.

Keeping in mind that the transition from traditional delivery system to patient focused care environment often can be obstructed by a culture that does not want to change, as well as by perceived threats to professional autonomy, Concord Hospital relied on communication, leadership, and education to accomplish its goal. During the Develop Phase, it was essential that resource issues involving education, transition of work to the new model, coverage of existing daily work during training, and the readiness of staff to learn—and of others to teach—were thoroughly assessed. It is not possible to overemphasize the need for attention to detail on these crucial factors.

Communication. To enhance information sharing and understanding, a special newsletter was created and an open meeting was held weekly for managers. In addition, town meetings were conducted by the CEO four times a month—around the clock—and a job fair was held, allowing staff in all departments access to information about the newly available roles and what support would be available to them for transitioning. When staffing patterns were posted and the selections of employees were made, morale was a challenge. Providing ongoing opportunities for open, honest dialogue, while allowing for discussion to clarify misconceptions and rumors, became critical. These communication enhancements continue to support the implementation process as PFWT diffuses to other units.

Although the anxiety and fear created by restructuring an entire organization cannot be eliminated by ongoing communication, it can be successfully managed through quality leadership and the commitment of the facility to transitional education needs. However, developing and maintaining an atmosphere of trust through consistent modelling of desired behaviors across *all* levels of the organization is essential.

Leadership. Indeed, excellent leadership skills are a crucial factor for success of any project. The leader certainly must have vision for what the model will become and passion for the concepts of patient focused care. He or she should be a strong, empowered communicator and empathetic listener—in addition to being mature, clinically sound, respected, and committed to the model and staff.

To overcome potential cultural barriers to change—such as fear of the unknown and high costs/low returns, lack of clarity and trust, too little involvement, and loss of job security—skilled management is required. Certainly, for optimal results, there must be strong and visible leadership, a frequent and interactive presence on the part of senior management, and face-to-face support from consultants or internal management development staff, educators, and others who can "walk the talk" of change.

Education. At Concord Hospital, a Develop Phase committee coordinated the education and training component of work redesign. Although the training cycle varied somewhat, the overall process occurred over a 12-week period. "Team training," a component of the education plan, addressed the complex issue of how individuals on the teams would work together on a daily basis.

Clearly, significant resources need to be committed to the didactic education pieces; however, it is equally important that there be resources to support implementation. PFWT is a *process,* not a "light switch" operation. Ongoing support of all staff is, again, a critical success factor. Whether RN staff are addressing delegation and conflict resolution or non-professional staff are accepting the challenges of cross-training, the work group as an entity is new. Often, the numbers of staff involved are large, and the dynamics of work groups, tasks, and skills will remain a challenge for an extended period of time.

Reviewing the intricacies of complex change theory with those involved in providing the support, as well as for the staff experiencing the transformation, is extremely important. All involved, including senior management, unit leadership, and clinical staff, need to relearn sophisticated, current change and chaos theory to know what "normal" is and where they fit. Trust and teambuilding take time—and they are built on successes. Remember, support around even the smallest accomplishment needs to be provided.

Keep in mind, too, that learning curves will vary depending on the baseline knowledge and skills of those assigned to the unit as well as with the quality of the leadership available. Importantly, support must be committed to assist leaders and staff on a daily basis since the requisite skills on the transformed unit require successful application and ongoing practice. Failure to attend to this key element will diminish an otherwise successful transformation.

The final phase, *Demonstration,* also includes ongoing improvement. Although it is the "last" phase, nothing is ever complete. Refinements continue to be made as Concord Hospital diffuses PFWT to other units: Oncology has recently been transformed, Pediatrics is scheduled to deliver services within a patient focused care system in July, and Telemetry should be "live" in August.

Staff continue to benefit from the initial efforts of the Orthopedic/neurosurgery unit—and modify their plans according to assessments of what worked and what did not. Decisions must be data driven, not intuitive.

Additionally, it is vital that staff feel supported as they make this transition and that problem solving is ongoing and facilitated. To reinforce the complexity of the project and to ensure that seemingly simple pieces of the patient focused puzzle do not threaten to affect successful implementation, leaders must commit to the model and show visible support to staff. Management also must keep in mind that more staff are needed on a temporary basis during demonstration and for support of the education process. And leaders should realize that new roles require clarification over and over again.

To this end, daily team planning meetings on units are essential. When they do not occur, work does not happen well. Likewise, clinical competency reviews for all staff need to be ongoing, and close communication between central departments and the transitioned units must occur. Moreover, physicians should be involved at every possible juncture to increase opportunities for collaboration.

EVALUATING QUALITY OF CARE AND PATIENT OUTCOMES

As with any project, measurement indicators must be identified and must be shared. Without known indicators, neither staff nor management will realize whether success has been achieved. At Concord Hospital, the indicators that were identified and continue to be measured are patient, staff, and physician satisfaction; clinical outcomes; and financial performance.

The data in these areas has been collected since the GO LIVE date of the demonstration unit—May, 9, 1994. Some elements are measured daily while others are collected weekly, monthly, or quarterly. Data is reviewed formally on a monthly basis. To date, there has been no diminution of clinical outcomes and a gradual decrease in length of stay (LOS) has occurred in some diagnoses. Because Concord Hospital's critical pathway implementation has just begun, the impact of these changes are expected to be long-term. However, it has been noted that physician satisfaction with the model rises and falls depending on staff satisfaction. While staff satisfaction reflects the delivery system's newness and their own evolving skills, both continue to improve over time.

The organization's senior management recognizes the long-term benefit of patient focused work transformation and that the organization is still involved with the expenses of supporting multiple or dual systems (traditional and PFWT) during the transition. Therefore, full cost savings have not yet been realized. Predictions are for cost savings of 10% in operations by year three, the first year all inpatient areas will be functioning as PFWT units.

Despite the continuing challenges, Concord Hospital remains committed to creating a patient focused care delivery system within its walls. Indeed, staff feel the vision is solid and the plan will work.

Preparing for the Future . . . Today

As Concord Hospital has found, the issue of restructuring health care organizations requires making hard decisions about how to best meet the needs of patients while containing cost. To achieve success, hospitals—foremost—need a vision. Like other corporations, their strategies must be directed to provide a marketable, quality service at a reasonable cost. Patient focused care provides that opportunity.

The nursing community must be prepared to create a vision that is inclusive rather than exclusive—and to participate fully in the intense process of change. Those for whom control continues to be both an issue of style and of substance had best update their resumes. The restructuring organization will demand only your best, your most creative, efforts. Staff will need, and should be able to expect, that your commitment will be complete.

Yet, it is a formidable task. No one has all the answers, but the reality is that change is linear and never ceases. As an optimist reminds us, take time to look outside, anticipate change. Change before you have to. And create the future, do not simply react to it!

REFERENCES

Barter, M., & Furmidge, M. (1994). Unlicensed assistive personnel. Issues related to delegation and supervision. *Journal of Nursing Administration, 24*(4), 36–39.

Berdick, E., & Humphries, V. (1994). Hospital re-engineers to improve patient care. *Health Care Strategies Management, 12*(11), 13–14.

Bergman, R. (1994). Reengineering healthcare: A new management tool aims to transform the organizational processes—and stir discussion. *Hospitals & Health Networks, 68*(3), 28–30, 32–34, 36.

Borfitz, D. (1993). Patient-centered care: A new structure on old foundations. *Decisions in Imaging Economics, 6*(3), 12–17.

Brider, P. (1992). The move to patient-focused care. *American Journal of Nursing, 92*(9), 26–33.

Hammer, M., & Champy, J. (1993). *Reengineering the corporation: A manifesto for business revolution.* New York: Harper.

Lathrop, J.P. (1993). *Restructuring healthcare: The patient-focused paradigm.* San Francisco: Jossey-Bass.

Manthey, M. (1994). The patient focused approach: Professional identity and the multiskilled approach. *Journal of Nursing Administration, 24*(10), 9–11.

Moore, N., & Komras, H. (1993). *Patient-focused healing.* San Francisco: Jossey-Bass.

Porter-O'Grady, T. (1993). Patient-focused care service models and nursing: Perils and possibilities. *Journal of Nursing Administration,* 23(3), 7–15.

Sherer, J.L. (1993). Putting patients first: Hospitals work to define patient-centered care. *Hospitals,* 67(3), 14–18.

Stewart, T. (1993). Reengineering the hot new managing tool. *Fortune,* 128(4), 41–48.

Wakefield, D., Cyphert, S., Murray, J., Uden-Holman, T., Hendryx, M., Wakefield, B., & Helms, C. (1994). Understanding patient-centered care in the context of total quality management and continuous quality improvement. *Journal of Quality Improvement,* 20(3), 152–161.

Wenzel, R. (Ed.). (1992). *Assessing quality health care: Perspectives for clinicians.* Baltimore: Williams & Wilkins.

Zimmerman, J., Crosier, J., & Taylor, S. (1993). Support service assistants: Redesigning roles for patient-centered care. *Stanford Nurse,* 15(1), 3–6.

CHAPTER 38

●●

Helping Your Patients Manage Managed Health Care

SUZANNE GORDON AND TIMOTHY MCCALL

Although most of your patients, family members, and friends know that the healthcare system is changing dramatically, few understand the profound implications of its wholesale shift to managed care. Nurses will be key in helping patients and other members of the public comprehend the new healthcare landscape and respond to it effectively.

It's important for all healthcare providers to have a clear grasp of what managed care is, how Health Maintenance Organizations and other forms of managed care save money, and what the implications are for quality patient care. The more each of us understands this system, the better able we'll be to fight its excesses and work for a model of healthcare delivery that serves both caregivers and those they care for.

The transition to managed care has been touted as the "solution" to all our healthcare woes. Advocates contend it will lower costs, while improving quality. But the laudable goal of managing care—coordinating a fragmented and wasteful system, and emphasizing primary care and preventive services—is a far cry from the corporate model that manages cost, while quality, at best, is a secondary consideration.

Today's HMOs are very different from the pioneering not-for-profit plans started by progressive groups in the early 1970s. The initial cost savings in HMOs were an unanticipated side effect of the tighter organization of medical care, often under one roof, and a greater emphasis on prevention. As healthcare expenditures skyrocketed in the late '80s, however, lowering costs became the central focus.

Employers started looking to reduce the premiums they were paying and managed care was seen as part of the solution. Insurers and for-profit corporations rushed to meet this need by forming their own HMOs, but with a crucial difference: gone was the philosophical commitment to better care and in came the obsession with the bottom line and, with it, the need to police the behavior of patients and caregivers. Today 9 out of the top 10 largest HMOs—and all of the newer ones—are for-profit.

Since the demise of the Clinton health care plan in 1994, the corporate version of managed care has become the *de facto* solution to our healthcare crisis. By the end of 1995, U.S. HMOs were predicted to have 56 million subscribers. Another 70 million Americans will have more traditional insurance retrofitted with managed care features, such as preferred providers and utilization review.

Thus, millions of Americans will depend for one of their most critical needs—health-care—on for-profit corporations. These companies, by law, owe their primary allegiance to shareholders, not to patients; their legal mandate is to maximize profit.

Indeed, these corporations have become some of the most profitable companies in America, with revenues in the largest HMOs reaching astronomical heights. A recent story in the *Wall Street Journal* discussed the multibillion dollar surplus that for-profit managed care plans have amassed and that they simply don't know how to invest. CEO salaries and stock options for the top seven for-profit HMOs averaged seven million dollars in 1994. Leonard Abramson, the CEO of U.S. Healthcare, has amassed over half a billion dollars in company stock.

Even the terminology for the percentage of premiums spent on medical care—the medical loss ratio—reflects the orientation toward maximizing profit. According to the *New York Times*, the large *not-for-profit* HMO, Kaiser Permanente of California, spent all but 4% of its 1994 revenue on patient care. U.S. Healthcare, a large *for-profit* plan, spent less than 73 cents per dollar on care. The rest went for administration, advertising, executive salaries, and shareholder dividends. The lower the "medical loss ratio"—that is the less spent on patients—the more attractive a plan is to potential investors.

In Florida, in an effort to save money, the state government invited essentially all comers to start HMOs to care for indigent patients covered by Medicaid. Only after a series of blistering investigative reports in Fort Lauderdale's *Sun Sentinel* exposed substandard care and deceitful and coercive marketing tactics did the state investigate and then decertify 21 of the 29 plans. Several of the plans had spent more than 50% of premium dollars on profit and administration. One Miami HMO had spent 77%, leaving only 23% for patient care.

To generate this level of profit, HMOs have had to dramatically reduce costs. Their methods include:

- *Changing the way caregivers are paid.* Under the traditional fee-for-service system, the more the doctor did, the more the money flowed. One need look no further than to the literally millions of unnecessary tonsillectomies and hysterectomies performed in the '50s and '60s to see how this reimbursement system led to excessive, and costly, intervention.

  The not-for-profit HMOs that dominated until the late 1980s paid doctors a straight salary. Today, however, HMOs have pioneered what is called "risk sharing." Under risk-sharing arrangements, physicians' reimbursement (and increasingly that of nurse practitioners) is dependent on how much it costs to care for their patients. According to a recent series of articles in the *New England Journal of Medicine*, most HMOs employ a strategic mix of bonuses and penalties to encourage parsimony. Bonuses are sometimes tied to limiting particularly expensive services such as specialist referrals or MRI scans.

  An increasingly common method of risk-sharing known as capitation (literally "by the head") involves paying doctors a monthly fee per patient and making them responsible for some or all of the medical expenses patients incur. In the most extreme version, common in California and increasingly in other areas of the country, every lab test, specialist referral, and hospitalization comes directly out the physician's pay.

  The bottom line is that most HMO physicians are paid *more* if they do *less*. This pits the economic interest of doctors against the well-being of their patients. In essence, greedy physicians stand to benefit enormously by denying helpful, but expensive, services. Well-intentioned doctors who had the bad luck, or some would say the poor planning, to have many gravely ill patients, could find themselves with little or no compensation at the end of the year. According to one of the *New England Journal* studies mentioned above, by Harvard Medical School professors David Himmelstein and Stephanie Woolhandler, "An internist with 1,500 U.S. Healthcare patients might take home more than $150,000 from bonuses and incentives, or nearly nothing."

- *Changing the type and balance of doctors who work in the plan.* HMOs hire a greater percentage of primary care doctors and fewer specialists. To weed out those doctors who spend too much on patient care, HMOs use a technique called "economic credentialing." Under many HMO contracts, doctors can be dismissed with no explanation, little warning, and no recourse. Since HMOs, rather than physicians, now control patients, the loss of a major HMO contract may mean the loss of one's livelihood.

  Holly Roberts, an obstetrician in New Jersey, explains the phenomenon. Several months ago, a representative from a major HMO appeared in her office carrying two charts. One tracked how many Caesarean sections contracting physicians performed, the other how many days their patients stayed in the hospital. "They told me that the only thing keeping me in the system was my low C-section rate," she said. "But if I didn't get my patients out of the hospital sooner, they would have to eliminate me from participating in the system. After that meeting, I realized it was either my profession or my patients' getting out."

  As a result of this kind of pressure, a peculiar thing happens in our medical system. Physicians who were trained to care for the sick begin to view their patients as liabilities. "A patient with bilateral breast cancer walks into your office," one internist told us recently, "and you can't help thinking what this is going to do to your cost profile. This is a terrible thought to have when someone is sick." Sighing, she added, "They're turning us into people we don't even like."

- *Erecting barriers to limit the use of services.* In order to cut down on usage, HMOs set up a series of hoops patients must jump through. The primary care provider serves as the gatekeeper, deciding who may or may not see a specialist. Getting an appointment with one's doctor, or with a specialist if it's been approved, can take weeks, even months. Visits to emergency rooms and many other services must be preapproved. Enrollees who are dissatisfied with a decision limiting care may not be told of their right to appeal. Those who appeal may find themselves in a morass of red tape, waiting hours on hold or trying to wend their way through the bureaucracy to reach the right person.

- *Cherry-picking—selectively enrolling lower risk patients.* HMO television ads depict radiant young people at weddings and christenings and mountain-biking—seemingly everywhere but in the hospital. Marketing materials tend to focus on services, such as discounts on health club memberships, that are likely to be attractive to younger, healthier patients. Commercials never seem to feature seriously ill people or the frail elderly lauding the care they receive.

  In July, 1995, for example, the *Orange County Register* reported that University of California–Irvine Medical Center chief Philip DiSaia, M.D., sent a memo to physicians, stating that their HMO could "no longer tolerate patients with complex and expensive-to-treat conditions being encouraged to transfer to our group."

  According to a 1994 survey conducted in Boston, Los Angeles, and Miami, 53% of enrollees in managed care were less than 40, compared with 43% in fee-for-service. One recent survey found that those most likely to be dissatisfied with managed care, due to long waits for services and other barriers to care, were the sick and the disabled. These more expensive patients might be expected to opt out of their HMOs more often, further facilitating cherry-picking.

- *Limiting "nonessential" services.* HMOs routinely refuse to pay for nonessential services, but the definition of what is nonessential can be debated. Few would argue about cosmetic surgery, but what about promising experimental treatments such as bone marrow transplants in cases of advanced breast cancer? Long-term psychotherapy is another example of a service that is extremely difficult to obtain in a managed-care setting.

- *Denying payment retrospectively.* Even patients who have obtained preapproval for services may find their HMO refuses to pay the bill. A child in California received approval for surgery, but her father learned after the surgery that the services of the anesthesiologist had not been approved and would not be paid for. The same applies to emergency room visits if the condition turns out not to be an emergency. In other words if crushing chest pain turns out to be a symptom of a heart attack, fine. However, if it's indigestion, the patient is stuck with the bill, even if it took the staff two hours and 14 tests to figure that out. According to Dr. Toni Mitchell, Director of Emergency Care at Tampa General Hospital, "This is a new type of cost-shifting, a way for HMOs to shift costs to patients, physicians, and hospitals."

- *Limiting the number and length of hospitalizations.* Many operations that traditionally took place in hospitals are now performed in the lower-cost outpatient setting. Pressure is applied to caregivers and patients to limit the length of hospitalizations. Witness the current controversy over so-called "drive-through deliveries," in which women are discharged from the hospital less than 24 hours after giving birth.

- *Reducing time with the caregivers.* Doctors' appointments now often last less than ten minutes and time with nurse practitioners, while somewhat longer, is also being reduced. The math is simple: The less time a provider spends with each patient, the more patients each provider can follow and the fewer providers the HMO needs to hire. In Northern California, Kaiser Permanente has increased the patient panels of primary care physicians from 2,000 to up to 2,700 patients.

The Consequences of the Move to Corporate Managed Care

Its proponents say that managing care can improve quality in many important ways. For instance, removing the financial incentives to overtest and overtreat has cut down on the rates of unnecessary, and potentially dangerous, surgeries and other medical interventions of doubtful value. Some of the problems of the fragmented and, at times, redundant care that is so typical of our medical system in the last decades will at least theoretically be improved by coordinating all care through a single primary care provider. HMOs have also, on average, done a better job of obtaining routine preventive services such as Pap smears and mammograms.

But quality, under corporate-controlled managed care, has suffered in many other ways. As scores of anecdotes demonstrate, HMOs are denying potentially valuable treatments and diagnostic procedures. A New Jersey teenager is refused the expensive growth hormone treatments that would allow him to grow to a normal adult height. A 29-year-old Florida mother of four dies of cervical cancer after months of misdiagnoses. A 4-year-old girl in New York City bleeds to death after receiving inadequate care following a routine tonsillectomy.

In 1987, a 60-year-old man called his private doctor with symptoms suggestive of a stroke. His doctor instructed the man to meet him in the emergency room right away. He was immediately admitted to the hospital where a CAT scan revealed he had indeed suffered a stroke. Several days of intravenous blood thinners averted further damage, and the man eventually had a full recovery of function.

Eight years later, the same man went to his HMO doctor complaining of a partial loss of vision, a symptom highly suggestive of a recurrent stroke. No tests were obtained and the man wasn't hospitalized, although the doctor mentioned that a stroke was a possible cause of his symptoms. That night, his wife called the HMO stating that he seemed worse and had become nauseated. She was told the nausea was due to nervousness and that a visit to the emergency room was unnecessary. Two days later, after the police picked him up for driving his car on the sidewalk, he was hospitalized, where tests revealed he had suffered a series of strokes. At the time of this writing, more than a month later, he is still hospitalized with disabilities that might have been prevented.

Before managed care, the American healthcare system was already burdened by administrative waste. Now this phenomenon has become more exaggerated. A suburban Boston internist complained that his four-doctor practice had been forced to hire three full-time employees just to keep up with the paperwork from the various managed-care companies.

John O'Brien, CEO of Cambridge Hospital Community Health Network, laments that at a time when he needs more clinical staff to care for increasingly sicker hospitalized patients and the greater burden of the uninsured, he is forced to hire more administrators.

> For hospitals to comply with utilization review and the other complexities of the payment system, we need more and more administrators and utilization-review staff to insure that we get paid. This inevitably drains resources away from direct patient care.

To compensate for lower per-patient revenues in the age of managed care, hospitals throughout the country have cut pharmacists, registered nurses, and laboratory personnel from their staffs. These cuts directly compromise care. A nurse may now follow eight patients on a medical ward instead of four. Since less acutely ill patients are denied admission to the hospital, those eight patients will, on average, be much sicker than in the past. And since the most experienced nurses are also the most expensive, chances are that "nurse" may, in fact, be a nurse's aide.

A recent study in the *Journal of the American Medical Association* discovered that many potential drug errors are spotted by skilled nurses at the bedside and thus prevented. Similarly, when state and federal health officials investigated University Community Hospital in Tampa, Florida—where a surgeon amputated the wrong foot, another operated on the wrong knee, and a poorly trained aide inadvertently killed a patient by disconnecting him from a ventilator—they discovered that skilled nurses had been removed from the critical patient-safety loop.

The rush to get hospitalized patients, including some who are acutely ill and unstable, out the door as fast as possible has also led to problems. New mothers may not have had the time to learn proper breastfeeding technique. Neonatal complications like jaundice have been shown to be dramatically higher. "They don't care whether patients are exhausted or fainting in the bathroom," according to obstetrician Holly Roberts. "Unless they're hemorrhaging or have a high fever they want them out."

The disincentive for primary care providers to refer to specialists can lower quality. A Boston woman who was denied a recommended surgical referral for a breast biopsy by her primary care gatekeeper was, three years later, diagnosed with breast cancer so advanced that two operations could not remove it all. After X-ray therapy, her chance of long-term survival is estimated to be 40 to 50%.

Perhaps no area of medicine has taken a bigger hit in managed care than mental health. According to interviews with numerous therapists, case managers routinely pressure mental health practitioners to prescribe drugs instead of more expensive psychotherapy, even in cases where neither the caregiver nor the patient favors medication. From the HMO's standpoint, therapy can almost always be viewed as optional. Difficulty coping, low-level chronic depression, or patterns of destructive relationships tend not to turn up in mortality statistics or in malpractice awards likely to affect the corporation's bottom line.

Cutting the length of the average visit threatens two of the hallmarks of the original HMOs: primary care and preventive services. Harried clinicians may not be able to elicit the information necessary for accurate diagnosis or to teach patients about their diseases and medications. Time is also required to instruct patients about things like diet, exercise, and stress reduction—vital elements of preventive medicine. Less time together may also damage the relationship between caregivers and patients.

"I don't trust them at all," says the wife of the stroke victim mentioned above, referring to the doctors at her HMO. Her comments reflect one of the most fundamental problems of the new system. How can rapport—itself therapeutic—be established when the patient worries that the caregiver's primary allegiance is to the corporation and to his or her own economic survival?

This fundamental shift in the caregiver's allegiance is exemplified by the gag rules now common in managed-care contracts. Here's an example:

> Physician shall agree not to take any action or make any communication which undermines or could undermine the confidence of enrollees, potential enrollees, their employers, their unions, or the public in U.S. Healthcare or the quality of U.S. Healthcare coverage.

One of the most disturbing consequences of such a gag rule is that providers may not inform patients of a medically viable treatment alternative that the plan will not pay for.

On December 1, 1995, Dr. David Himmelstein, the Harvard Medical School professor who coauthored one of the *New England Journal of Medicine* studies mentioned earlier, and a primary care doctor at Cambridge Hospital, received a letter from U.S. Healthcare, stating that his contract was being terminated. No cause was given. Three days earlier, he had appeared on "The Phil Donahue Show" where he criticized HMOs. Since managed-care companies routinely ask doctors whether they've ever been terminated by another plan when making hiring decisions, Dr. Himmelstein's prospects for working with other HMOs could be jeopardized.

The biggest consequence of the move to managed care, however, may be what it hasn't done. For years, the United States healthcare system has been characterized by haves and have-nots and managed care has done nothing to address the problem of the 40 million uninsured Americans. If anything, the increased financial strain on hospitals has meant the closing of public and smaller institutions which had previously offered some free care. Indeed, even among the haves, managed care is leading to increased stratification.

The rule of thumb in HMOs is that the squeaky wheel gets the grease. Well-informed, assertive patients are often able to get care that would otherwise be denied. Some HMO enrollees, whether because of shyness, a lack of sophistication, or a physical incapacity from illness, are unable to advocate for themselves. They may be stuck with whatever their HMO doles out—or fails to dole out.

Arthur L. Caplan, Director of the Center for Bioethics at the University of Pennsylvania, reports attending a board meeting of a large Minneapolis HMO where the subject was enrollee appeals of service denials.

> *The questions [the board members] asked were not "How much does it cost?" or "Will it work?," but rather "Does the person have a lawyer?," "Are they likely to be in touch with the media?," "Is this someone who's going to be persistent or just go away?," and "Can they make trouble for us in the community?*

He added, "This is a poor way to make benefit determinations."

What RNs and Other Healthcare Providers Can Do

HMOs and other forms of managed care are steadily becoming the dominant force in American healthcare, and the for-profit sector of managed care now dominates the industry. Since the primary mission of for-profit HMOs is to make money, patients and their families and caregivers will need to become more assertive and government regulation of the industry will be required to ensure that a minimum standard of care is maintained. (See Box 38-1.)

The following areas in particular demand legislative action:

- Full disclosure of reimbursement methods. All methods of reimbursement to caregivers, including bonuses and penalties, must be revealed to potential enrollees. Similarly, patients must be made aware of all required preauthorization and utilization-review measures designed to limit the use of services. HMOs must disclose the percentage of premium dollars devoted to marketing, administration, executive salaries, and profits.
- Gag rules should be outlawed. Providers must be able to disclose to patients *all* information relevant to their medical care.
- Marketing excesses, such as occurred in Florida, must be penalized harshly.
- Patients with grievances must receive timely decisions on appeals. There should be a mechanism both within plans, and another independent of plans, to settle differences.
- For some reasonable copayment, patients should be given the option of consulting clinicians outside the plan.
- An emergency should be defined as the presence of symptoms that a reasonable layperson would interpret as needing immediate attention. No preapproval should be required in potentially life-threatening situations.
- Comparative data which reflect quality and satisfaction on medical outcomes, patient satisfaction, and yearly turnover rates for both patients and clinicians should be made available. Responsible independent researchers should be provided the opportunity to measure quality of care, as their data would tend to be less biased.

Many of the healthcare delivery problems the United States is currently experiencing would be remedied by adopting a single-payer system like Canada's—a solution favored by many nurses, activist nursing organizations, and unions. A single-payer system would provide universal access, preserve choice of providers, eliminate the incentives to undertreat, and cut administrative costs to a fraction of what they currently are. In 1994, the effort to forge a new healthcare system was derailed largely as a result of the efforts of many of those who are now profiting enormously from the shift to corporate managed care. However, as the number of uninsured Americans grows and the public becomes more aware of the problems of for-profit HMOs, our next opportunity to achieve real healthcare reform may come sooner rather than later.

BOX 38–1 THE TEN STEPS THAT FOLLOW ARE A GOOD BEGINNING:

1. Inform patients, friends, and the general public about how managed care works, what you are seeing it do to your job, and how it is affecting your ability to provide quality care.

2. Be willing to share this information with the media, perhaps anonymously if your job would be imperiled, and with your political representatives.

3. Nurse practitioners should refuse to sign managed-care contracts that reward them financially for denying care.

4. Encourage consumers to carefully read all materials from HMOs before signing up. Tell them that advertisements only highlight a plan's advantages. Suggest to your generally healthy patients and friends that they evaluate the coverage as if they were ill and needed to use the HMO's services. A discount on membership to a health club is great, but how is the coverage for visiting nurses, physical therapy, and hospice care?

5. Stress the value of assertiveness when dealing with managed-care plans. Suggest that patients ask doctors and nurse practitioners if their contracts contain gag rules or financial incentives to deny care. Inform patients that all HMOs have formal grievance procedures. Managed-care plans count on the fact that many patients, frustrated by repeated denials, will simply give up. Tell consumers that persistence often pays off. If necessary, they should consider escalating to legal action or to contacting the media. Remember Arthur Caplan's observations of the board meeting at a big HMO.

6. Underscore the importance of not delaying needed care while waiting for approval (or after it's been denied). Patients should be instructed that in the case of a true emergency, they should call or go to the nearest hospital even if it's not on the approved list. Consumers can too easily become prisoners of their HMOs—even when they could get the care they need first and worry about how it will be paid for later.

7. Provide realistic advice to elderly patients who are currently being aggressively wooed into Medicare HMOs. They should consider whether short-term cost savings are balanced by increased long-term risks. The stroke victim discussed earlier, for example, had given up his regular Medicare coverage to avoid paying the supplemental premium. Many of us have experienced that elderly patients are among the least assertive healthcare consumers. They should honestly assess whether they will be able to get the care they need in a system where patients often have to fight for it.

8. When you hear stories about patients being denied needed care, encourage the people involved to go public. Patients should contact their political representatives, the chair of their legislature's health committee, their state insurance commissioner, or their state's department of health, as well as the media. The public spotlight on individual cases where mothers and their newborns were discharged prematurely has been the major impetus for legislation to stop drive-through deliveries.

9. Be a whistle-blower. Be willing to leak inside information that substantiates managed-care abuses. For example, someone working for Kaiser Permanente provided the group Consumers for Quality Care with a copy of the HMO's 213-page "Southern California Region Business Plan for 1995–1997" which included provisions to tie physician bonuses to denials of care. The subsequent furor in the press led Kaiser to reverse the policy.

10. Encourage your patients, family members, and friends to be politically involved. According to a study released in November, 1995 by the Center for Health Care Rights in Los Angeles, most states do not provide adequate protection for HMO enrollees. "In every area of consumer HMO law, but especially in the areas of access; quality of care; grievance procedures; the collection, analysis and release of quality of care data; and the provision of HMO information to enrollees and the public, the study found that critical legal and regulatory issues were not addressed."

CHAPTER 39

●●●

Managed Care: Employers' Influence on the Health Care System

KAREN T. CORDER, JANET PHOON, AND MARJORIE BARTER

Health care consumers and purchasers are demanding accountability for quality, cost, and accessibility of services from the health care industry and its providers. Kerfoot and Helsinger (1994) state:

> *The pressure to treat patients in the least invasive, most appropriate environments has resulted in excess capacity in hospitals and has led to the consolidation of patient care units and even the merging of hospitals into integrated health care networks (p. 280).*

The reform momentum has increased over the past few years as the focus of health care shifts from acute care, inpatient hospital services to community-based services that span the continuum of health. According to Riley (1994), the payers of health care have organized the demand side of the economic equation of supply and demand, and are now forcing change on the provider/supplier side. The providers/suppliers of health care are responding by organizing what has been a disjointed and fragmented supply side of health care into integrated systems. Integrated systems coordinate care throughout a continuum of health services. Managed care is an integration of providers and payers into one organized system designed to control costs by monitoring access to care and use of services to a designated population.

To appreciate the impact managed care is having on the current health care system and how it will affect the future, the American public, especially frontline health care providers, must consider the evolution of our health care system. It is necessary to know who the key players are and the roles each plays in the health care system's evolution. However, no one player can affect the changes needed to make our current system more efficient. Each is important as a part of the whole system, but the system must be greater than the sum of its parts. Change in any one or two areas will not be effective without collaboration from all parts of the system. The ultimate goal must be a healthier citizenry and a healthier system. To achieve this, each player must participate in health care reform. The

Reprinted from *Nursing Economic$*, 1996, Volume 14, Number 4, pp. 213–217. Reprinted with permission of the publisher, Jannetti Publications, Inc., East Holly Avenue, Box 56, Pitman, New Jersey, 08071-0056.

key players of the U.S. health care system include consumers, providers of care, employers, insurers, and local, state, and federal governments.

The reorganization and restructuring currently underway throughout the country can lead to a more efficient health care system. The key to its long-term success will be the collaborative efforts of all key players to make quality, cost-effective, and accessible health care a reality. Managed care must be implemented in a broad systems context, rather than a narrow cost-cutting context to successfully reform the out-of-control health care system. To understand the forces driving managed care, it is necessary to look at the role employers play in the health care system.

Employers Influence Providers

Much of the literature has covered the need for reform from the perspective of providers (usually physicians), insurers, hospitals, managed care organizations, and the government—especially concerning Medicaid reimbursements. One player who is rarely presented, especially in the nursing literature, is the employer.

To educate and advocate for patients and all consumers of health care services, health care providers, especially nurses, must understand the history of our health care system. If nurses do not understand the impact employers have on health care organizations, they cannot be proactive change agents for health care reform.

Nurses' lack of knowledge about the health care system is demonstrated by scare tactics aimed at the public. Unionized nurses and other health care workers are fighting a losing battle when they attempt to stop health care facilities from restructuring. A proactive, professional stand based on an understanding of the forces driving health care reform would better serve professional nurses. Using knowledge and professional power to work with all health care providers will help create the new health care system that is so desperately needed.

Health care providers must consider patients' insurance before they prescribe a plan of treatment. They must ask:

- Who are my patients?
- Are they employed?
- Who are their employers?
- What kinds of benefits do they have?
- Do those benefits include services delivered by advanced practice nurses or other nonphysician providers? If not, why not?
- Are patients covered by Medicare or Medicaid? Are they medically indigent?

If providers understand why these questions are important, they will begin to see another dimension of the complex health care system. Health care providers, especially nurses, should understand why these issues are important. Care delivery and, often, quality of care, are linked to the patient's ability to pay.

Managed Competition

All employers deal with customers who are aware of competitors' goods, services, and prices. To obtain and retain customers, employers rely on the quality of their goods or services, not just on price or availability. If an employer can provide an affordable, quality product that can be distinguished from a competitor's product, that employer will retain customers and a competitive edge. Control of rapidly rising health care costs has been targeted by business and by government as critical to remaining competitive in a global market.

Managed competition, as a purchasing strategy, is designed to obtain maximum value for consumers and employers as they acquire health care. The goal of managed competition is to divide providers in each community into economic units to motivate them to develop efficient delivery systems (Enthoven & Kronick, 1989). Efficient delivery systems are not found in the traditional fee-for-service or third-party reimbursement systems. However, efficient means of delivering health care are seen in managed care models (Fox, 1993).

Managed care can play a role in making managed competition a reality. As health care facilities try to decrease costs and maintain or increase revenues, efficient use of services must be maintained so as not to compromise quality care. Managed care delivery systems attempt to provide the customer with quality services that are efficient and cost effective. The managed care industry has been at the forefront of educating employers and patients on how to obtain better health care, maintain good health, and better use the health care system in the United States because it focuses on wellness and not just illness (Benes, 1992).

As consumers and employers are required to pay more for health care, they begin to ask valid questions:

- What services are offered?
- How accessible are those services?
- How accessible are the health care providers?
- How is quality of service determined?
- Are resources used appropriately?
- Are prices fair and competitive?

In response to these questions, health care providers (through the managed care system) must show, in the form of outcomes research data, how their services, rather than those of a competitor's, are better suited to meet patients' and employers' needs. Measurable outcomes must be developed and implemented to evaluate all services offered. These measurable outcomes, when compared to community or national standards, help determine the level of quality to be expected, and encourage competition between providers and networks.

Background

Proponents insist managed care systems can reduce health care costs. Employers are a primary driving force behind reducing costs. To understand the need for cost reduction, it is necessary to consider the history of the American health care system, especially since World War II. An understanding of how the health care system evolved from 4.5% to over 14% of the gross domestic product within 50 years reinforces the importance and complexity involved in changing and reforming the out-of-control health care system (Ginzberg, 1994).

Attempts to reform the health care system have been ongoing long before President Clinton's call for national reform, and efforts to improve health care continue even after the national reform agenda was tabled. Government influence on the health care system goes back to Teddy Roosevelt's national health insurance proposal in 1912. FDR's national insurance proposal was not included in the Social Security legislation of 1935 because of lack of public backing and opposition by the powerful American Medical Association (Ginzberg, 1994).

As early as 1929, Blue Cross, a private nonprofit health insurance system, offered a community-based prepayment plan to guard against the high cost of hospitalization. As Blue Cross grew rapidly during the war, commercial for-profit health insurance companies entered the scene and began offering experience-based premiums to employers. These premiums were less expensive to employers in industries with low frequencies of illness or accidents and who had a young, healthy workforce. To counter the competition, Blue Cross changed from community to experience-based premiums, making insurance less affordable to the elderly, high risk, and chronically ill (Ginzberg, 1994). Health insurance became a fringe benefit for the employed.

The state of our current health care system evolved over a relatively short span since World War II, during which time labor unions were able to bargain for health care benefits after the federal government agreed that receiving benefits would not violate the existing wage freeze. The federal government allowed employers to treat health benefits premium payments as nontaxable business expenses, and exempted employees from income tax liabilities (Ginzberg, 1994). This encouraged employers to provide health care to all workers and subsequently created a large pool of individual health care consumers who were unconcerned about the price of services.

During the 1950s, it became apparent that the private health insurance industry, founded on employment, would not cover retired or disabled employees (Ginzberg, 1994). Some of those most in need of health care coverage were no longer covered. The federally backed Medicare and Medicaid programs did not begin until 1966. A tax-based insurance system, Medicare was designed to provide health care coverage for Americans over age 65. The Medicaid program was set up to provide access to health care for certain categories of the poor, especially women and children.

Until the passage of Medicare and Medicaid, hospitals and physicians treated the poor for nominal rates or for free. Although advances in medical technology were causing health care prices to rise, many hospitals were restricted in their choice of capital improvements or purchases because of limited funds. Loans were hard to come by and charity care depleted revenues. With the implementation of Medicare and Medicaid, money was no longer restricted. Because of government backing to pay the costs of treating the elderly and the poor, incentives to contain costs were almost eliminated. Health care costs began climbing at increasing rates which surpassed most other industries.

Employers Want Proof: Outcomes Data Needed

Employers were rightfully concerned about rising health care costs. Health care benefits costs soared, taking money away from the business itself, and decreasing companies' local and global competitive edge. To counter the increasing costs in the 1980s, employers began restricting benefits and shifting costs of health insurance to their employees through required deductibles, nominal copayments, and/or partial premium payments. This cost shifting decreased employers' expenses minimally.

Limiting benefit options and shifting costs to employees did not slow health care spending. Employers then began to look closely at the type and quality of the health care benefits they were purchasing, and began pressuring insurers and managed care organizations to provide basic benefits at affordable prices, with guarantees of quality service and care.

To meet the demands of employers, managed care organizations (MCOs) began standardizing quality measurements through the National Committee for Quality Assurance (NCQA). The NCQA, founded in 1979 as a joint effort of the Group Health Association and the American Association of Foundation for Medical Care, reorganized in 1990 and expanded its program of voluntary accreditation for MCOs with emphasis on quality measurement systems (Lipson, 1993). It was believed that nationally recognized and validated accreditation standards for MCOs would simplify the selection process for employers (Lipson, 1993). The NCQA relationship with MCOs is similar to the relationship between the Joint Commission for Accreditation of Healthcare Organizations (JCAHO) and acute care hospitals. In fact, JCAHO started a managed care accreditation program in 1988 but abandoned it in 1990.

Several major MCOs and employer groups, along with the NCQA, worked together to develop a set of standardized measurements for identified quality indicators. The Health Plan Employer Data and Information Set (HEDIS) assesses the overall quality and resource use in a health plan and focuses on outpatient care and preventive measures that keep employees out of the hospital (Morrisey, 1993). Employers are provided standardized data that can be compared and evaluated across health plans. Most employers are demanding that their health plans provide HEDIS information (Kertasz, 1994).

Outcomes projects are changing health care delivery by affecting medical practice and health care costs. Alter and Holzman (1992a) state, "The point of outcomes research is to determine the most appropriate care for all patients" (p. 10). Outcomes research attempts to improve health care by identifying best treatments and helping eliminate those treatments that are ineffective or unnecessary. A strong motivator behind outcomes studies is the search for greater value and cost effectiveness in health care.

Medical care is already improving due to implementation of outcomes data. One HMO, for example, found that educating parents about their child's condition kept emergency room use down compared with emergency room use by parents unfamiliar with their child's condition (Alter & Holzman, 1992b). Decreasing emergency room use for nonemergent events can substantially reduce health care costs.

While researchers are looking for optimal ways to treat disease, outcomes data are also being used to monitor health care quality. United HealthCare Corporation is working to ensure that physicians are providing care consistent with practice guidelines (Alter and Holzman, 1992c). Current research is also looking at the outcomes of patients covered by managed and nonmanaged health plans, and which types of providers produce the most favorable results for both medical and mental health illnesses.

The Health Policy Corporation of Iowa is developing a demonstration project that will partner employers and providers in continuous quality improvement in areas such as cardiac care, maternal and infant care, mental health, and substance abuse treatment (Alter & Holzman, 1992c). Members spend half their health care dollars on these interventions. Health Policy Corporation administrators believe they will improve outcomes by identifying what works and what does not, especially in these areas that show wide statistical variations in quality. Another example is the case of New England physicians who were alerted to geographic variations in tonsillectomies and subsequently decreased the rate of surgeries (Alter & Holzman, 1992c).

Large employer groups are joining forces to investigate practice patterns before entering into contracted agreements with insurers, networks, and providers. Comparing results provides concrete information and evidence that providers and insurers can present to consumers and employers to show their level of quality for a particular price.

Employers are using outcomes research and cost information to help choose the best providers for their employees. Quality indicators that will help reduce employer liability as they direct their employees into managed care networks are being identified. Employers do not have the expertise to evaluate clinical quality. They hire managed care companies to evaluate provider networks. The managed care company must perform internal audits to comply with NCQA standards. If the managed care company conforms to industry standards, it will have more leverage in competing for managed care contracts with employer groups. This also gives the MCO more credibility as they audit the provider networks. Presenting audit results allows employers to compare their providers and managed care company against the competition.

Employers have used similar processes to assess the competition and identify marketing strategies to determine where to focus business interests. Employers have used health care quality data processes to collect information on costs, morbidity, and mortality rates of providers. Data are analyzed and presented to various provider groups. The increased awareness of, and activity related to, appropriate data collection have provided information which can be used for managerial decision making. This information lets providers know where they stand among their peers in the community and helps create a competitive market.

While individual providers have not had the tools or systems to demonstrate quality characteristics, employers are hoping that managed care companies will develop a database using large populations to draw conclusions about the effectiveness and efficacy of medical treatments and communicate this quality information to providers (Lipson, 1993).

Conclusion

The American health care system is very complex. Constructive change can occur only when each part of the system is realigned appropriately. Health care providers must begin thinking about being "health care advocates"—a more encompassing stance than "patient advocate." As Porter-O'Grady (1995) states, "Looking at health care as health practice rather than medical practice will call for a significant change in the orientation of physicians to their own role" (p. 38). Nurses, especially in advanced practice or in community-based settings, must incorporate health care advocacy and a systems perspective into their practice.

As the public becomes more aware of the cost shifting and begins to pay ever-increasing costs out-of-pocket for their health care benefits, and as employers' health care costs continue to rise (even with some of the burden placed on employees), pressure will mount for providers and insurers to reduce costs and become more accountable. To make reductions, true reform must come into play, and more effective systems must be expanded. Nursing administrators will be required to make radical changes in care delivery to significantly decrease costs while demonstrating quality outcomes to managed care organizations. Nursing administrators and advanced practice nurses must develop a community-based orientation and seek avenues for partnership with employers to develop and provide preventative and wellness services. Health education and case management are examples of services that might assist employer groups to control health care costs.

REFERENCES

Alter, J., & Holzman, D. (1992a, September). Interest in outcomes research is growing rapidly. *Business and health: Special report,* 8–13.

Alter, J., & Holzman, D. (1992b. September). How outcomes projects are changing medicine. *Business and health: Special report,* 16–21.

Alter, J., & Holzman, D. (1992c. September). Studies look at many facets of health care. *Business and health: Special report,* 14–16.

Benes, R.J. (1992). Strategies for health care reform highlight managed care meeting. *Quality Review Bulletin,* 18(10), 348–350.

Enthoven, A., & Kronick, R. (1989). Consumer choice plan for the 1990's: Universal health insurance in a system designed to promote quality and economy. *New England Journal of Medicine,* 320(1), 29–37.

Fox, J.C. (1993). The role of nursing in public policy reform. *Journal of Psychosocial Nursing,* 31(8), 9–12.

Ginzberg, E. (1994). *The road to reform: The future of health care in America.* New York: The Free Press.

Kerfoot, K., & Helsinger, I. (1994). Managing mergers: The nurse manager's challenge. *Nursing Economic$,* 12(5), 280–282.

Kertasz, L. (1994). Kaiser releases HEDIS information. *Modern Healthcare,* 24(28), 6.

Lipson, E.H. (1993). What are purchasers looking for in managed care quality? *Topics in Health Care Finance,* 20(2), 1–9.

Morrisey, J. (1993). HEDIS standards get upgrade. *Modern Healthcare,* 23(51), 62–64.

Porter-O'Grady, T. (1995). Reengineering in a reformed health care system. In S. Smith Blancett & D.L. Flarey. *Reengineering nursing and health care.* Gaithersburg, MD: Aspen Publishers, Inc.

Riley, D.W. (1994). Integrated health care systems: Emerging models. *Nursing Economic$,* 12(4), 201–206.

CHAPTER 40

●●

After Reduction in Force: Reinvigorating the Survivors

CHARLES R. MCCONNELL

Your health care organization has recently experienced its first layoffs in many years and the most significant reduction in force (RIF) in its history. Unfortunately, given the present state of health care in America and the real and impending impact of financial cutbacks on health care organizations in general and hospitals in particular, the foregoing statement is probably more real than hypothetical for a great many readers. We are all well aware that layoffs are the order of the day as one organization after another reengineers, restructures, right-sizes, down-sizes, reorganizes, or, to use another term that is creeping in to nudge reengineering aside in places, repositions.

It goes without saying that a considerable amount of thought and effort are required in structuring and implementing a reduction in a manner that will be as fair as possible to all concerned while supporting the primary responsibility for delivering top quality health care. However, the effort associated with this significant undertaking cannot stop simply when the staff who have been appropriately identified for separation have been released. For those at all levels who remain with the organization—and in the vast majority of work force cutbacks the people who remain are far more numerous than those who leave—the implementation of the RIF is the beginning of a completely new work situation in what will, and what in fact must, become a dramatically different organizational culture. Although many will tend to seek a "business as usual" state of affairs following a staff reduction, they will find that this is not possible.

What Follows Reduction in Force?

A major RIF will forever alter many employees' beliefs and attitudes concerning their employment. Consider the following:

- For many years health care workers saw reductions occur in manufacturing and commercial industry in their areas while feeling relatively safe against the likelihood of ever having to share the experience. For a long time we felt fairly certain

Reprinted from *Health Care Supervisor,* 14(4), pp. 1–10, 1996, with permission of Aspen Publishers, Inc., © 1996.

that, as an absolutely essential service, we would remain untouched by the severe economic concerns that plagued other industries.
- Many health care organizations long enjoyed a sense of employment security that has now been severely—and for all practical purposes permanently—damaged.
- Health care workers have been forever awakened to the hard fact that health care is subject to many of the external forces from which we believed it was relatively protected. That is, we now see that forces beyond our control can cause permanent changes to health care whether we do or do not seek these changes ourselves.

The immediate reactions to a health care organization's RIF can include the following:

- Many employees may at first—and permanently, if positive steps are not taken— feel more like a cost of doing business than valued members of a work organization: They view themselves as simply another purchased commodity of which the organization will henceforth purchase less.
- Employee commitment to the organization will tend to erode as perceived employment security is diminished.
- Employee morale will be automatically reduced.
- Some key staff that the organization desires to retain may resign to seek employment in environments they may perceive as more stable, further impacting the morale and outlook of those who remain.
- Managers and supervisors, with their thinking still bound by former ways of doing things, may attempt to compensate for lost staff by increasing the use of overtime and temporary help. They will experience additional frustration as controls are placed on hiring and on the use of overtime and temporaries.

In the time immediately following a RIF, there is a severe risk of cost reduction becoming universally perceived as a higher priority than people. It is true that successful cost control is an essential element of survival; the health care organization that cannot adapt to financial reality will not survive to employ anyone. People, however, still remain the driving force. It is people working together who must bring the organization into line with financial reality, yet the same organization's continued existence then and forever will depend on people serving people.

What necessarily follows any RIF is a revitalization of the remaining work force. An organization cannot and should never attempt to simply "lay off" a number of employees and call upon those who remain to close ranks and continue as before. All who remain have a more difficult and more responsible task looming before them, and the organization's top management should endeavor to provide all of the support and assistance that can reasonably be provided in making the transition to a leaner, more purposefully directed organization.

The Necessity of Reducing the Work Force

Although the scenarios have differed to some extent from state to state, health care provider organizations across the nation have been experiencing reductions in revenue from most payment sources. Further significant revenue shortfalls will likely be occurring because of additional limitations placed on reimbursement levels by most payers, although primarily by Medicare and Medicaid. This should come as no surprise to those who have been aware of the budget and health care debates continually raging at all levels of government. The simple fact of the matter is that the health care system is being forced by external circumstances to drastically reduce the amount of money spent to deliver service. But since the demand for service remains as high as ever and in many respects continues to grow, the system is called upon to accomplish more results with less resources.

Consider the circumstances of one particular institution, a large teaching hospital. This hospital's modest financial circumstances and generally good fiscal health sustained operations for several years during which costs rose at more than twice the rate than its income increased. This hospital employed a delaying tactic used by many not-for-profit organizations by annually reallocating modest reserves of various sorts to bring the current year into line, while avoiding any attempt at serious cost cutting—until the reserves ran dry during the same year that serious cuts in Medicare and Medicaid occurred.

Thus, following literally decades of fiscal performance that was at a break-even or better level, the hospital faced a projected loss of such significance that two or three such years together could render the organization insolvent. Not the least of top management's concerns was the task of communicating the facts of their situation truthfully and believably to a work force that had never experienced layoffs, had never felt more than token pressure to contain costs, and had been conditioned by years of experience to believe that costs and revenue would somehow always be made to balance.

One should hope that realistic cost containment activities, pursued as a normal course of business, might help an organization avoid or at least lessen a massive financial crunch of the kind just described. However, the problem remains the same regardless of its immediate magnitude and must be dealt with. The communication issues are difficult enough when faced squarely with realistic data on a year-to-year basis; they become all the more difficult when the work force has been conditioned to believe that nothing serious is amiss.

In brief, when a RIF is planned and before the cuts occur, the work force must be given every opportunity to understand why this is going to happen. The more openly the employees have been treated all along and the more frankly they have been advised of the organization's real circumstances on a continuing basis, the easier it will be to communicate that *why*.

Any RIF, while preferably designed and recommended by senior management and the medical staff leadership and approved by the board of directors, should proceed only after all other reasonable efforts to reduce costs have been explored. Specifically:

- All realistic short-term savings opportunities should be identified and implemented.
- Maximum effort should be expended to reduce staff through attrition before the actual reduction by freezing hiring in most positions and as far as possible transferring existing employees into areas of greatest need.
- Overtime should be severely curtailed, essentially reserved for true emergencies only and approvable by only a select few. Also to be curtailed is the use of temporary help (along with overtime, agency temporary help can tend to increase under staff reduction pressure if not closely monitored).
- Supply inventories should be reduced to levels conforming with the true needs indicated by reduced levels of activity.

It must be stressed that no matter how much cost control effort precedes a RIF, the reduction itself is never the end of the process. For the organization's continued financial viability and effectiveness, it becomes the job of all employees to pursue continuous cost control in concert with continuous quality improvement if the organization is to prevail as a quality provider of health care.

The Employees Who Remain

A RIF instantly establishes two entirely different groups of employees: those who leave and those who remain. Except in rare instances, those who remain far outnumber those who leave. Judging from many of the health care staff reductions that have occurred in recent years, it is not unusual for the "survivors" to outnumber those leaving by eight, nine, or ten to one.

Management must recognize that the manner in which it deals with the reduction's survivors has a considerably greater bearing on the organization's future than how the terminations attendant to the RIF have been addressed. Those who have departed are gone, probably forever, but the survivors are there and are critical to the organization's future.

Stress and stress-related fear among those who remain following a RIF is natural, predictable, and essentially universal throughout the organization. A fully understandable feeling among survivors is the fear that they may be the next to go.

It becomes necessary to unite the survivors into a forward-moving team and to motivate them to work harder in a leaner, more efficient, and yet initially a completely alien, situation. Through a concentrated and continuing communication program the survivors of the reduction need to learn several things:

- why they remain and what will be expected of them; why the old organization is gone forever, and how they can help shape the new organizational culture that will be emerging;
- that as the survivors of the reduction they are among the best in their occupations, and that that is essentially why they are still in place; and
- that a future in which continually doing more with less will remain critical to organizational survival and continued employment.

Immediate and Natural Reactions to RIF

The issues emerging in the wake of a RIF are all essentially people issues. The major issues that surface usually include:

- the short-term loss of good talent in the form of productive employees that the organization would wish to retain. At special risk are valuable "free-agent" employees, those professional and technical employees whose primary loyalty is to an occupation and whose movement between organizations may be governed more by labor market circumstances than by ties to a specific organization or group;
- an immediate drop in productivity, precisely at a time when productivity increases are needed for the sake of long-term survival. This occurs because morale has dropped and employees are preoccupied with issues of security and concern for their future.
- increases in the use of sick time, health care benefits, on-the-job accidents, medication errors, and other lapses in quality. These are often experienced during and after a RIF, again owing to employees' concern for their employment.

During and after a reduction, there may be a fully understandable tendency to cut all financial corners and curtail all possible expenditures in an effort to save jobs and achieve an acceptable financial position. However, this may be precisely the time for the organization to be devoting money and effort to developing new sources of income and to ensuring the increased flexibility, adaptability, and effectiveness of the remaining work force.

Employee Motivation Following RIF

Under normal circumstances—without the direct prospect of a reduction in the work force and with each employee's reasonable expectation of continued employment—job security and wages are not particularly active motivating forces. Rather, they are potential dissatisfiers; as long as wages and job security are perceived as "reasonable," the concern for them is secondary. However, when they are disturbed—when raises are eliminated, for instance, or when security is perceived as threatened—these become factors in heightening employee dissatisfaction, which in turn negatively impacts motivation.

It becomes necessary to help the surviving employees reestablish a measure of equilibrium with their altered surroundings and achieve a relative sense of security. An employee who may come to work each day wondering "Will I be next?" will be neither effective nor productive. As long as an employee is preoccupied with personal survival, individual productivity will decline at the time its improvement is needed more than ever.

It is necessary to communicate with employees fully, completely, and repeatedly until they understand the following:

- Nobody—neither the organization nor a labor union—can absolutely guarantee continued employment, which frequently plays upon fears and uncertainties attendant to downsizing.
- A certain amount of stress is inevitable regardless of what management does following a RIF, but stress can be energizing as well as debilitating and can serve as a spur to improvement.
- A future emphasis on improved productivity is essential to survival as an organization.
- Employees' aggregate job performance is the organization's best survival guarantee, and as far as individual employees are concerned, their performance is their own best job security.

The most potent motivating forces—some say the only true long-run motivating forces—are inherent in peoples' work. These forces are largely opportunities: the opportunity to learn and grow, to do interesting work, to contribute, to feel a sense of accomplishment and worth. However, these motivators can work only when employees are able to feel relatively secure and reasonably compensated. Management needs to provide conditions under which all employees can become self-motivated and then act on that belief.

Attendant to employees' motivational needs, the organization might also consider the creation of incentive programs and other flexible awards to encourage and acknowledge innovation, commitment, and enhanced productivity. Overall, top management should at all times let employees know what is expected of them and tell them exactly how this desired behavior will be rewarded.

Changes in Supervisors' and Managers' Roles

Any significant RIF includes the elimination of some positions and the combination of positions responsible for managing the work of others. In the presence of a generally "flatter" management structure—that is, overall fewer levels from top to bottom—supervisors and managers are likely to find their roles enhanced. They will essentially assume new roles, roles that are more challenging and that require more direct decision making.

The individual who directly supervises others will be the organization's primary conduit for communications with staff. At each management level, the supervisor is always a critical link in the movement of information up and down the chain of command. The supervisor is the primary communicating link between each direct reporting employee and the rest of the organization. It is through the supervisor that the individual employee receives assignments, evaluations and performance feedback, praise and criticism, information about the organization's fate and future, and information about nearly all other aspects of employment.

The supervisor's role is critical. As the one member of management who the employee knows best and the one whose role it is to be the employee's communicating link, the supervisor influences the attitudes and outlooks of a significant portion of the organization. Thus *as the individual employee views the supervisor, so too is he or she likely to view the organization.* In other words, if a supervisor of 15 people is seen as distant, uncommunicative, and uncaring, so too are 15 people likely to see the total organization as distant, uncommunicative, and uncaring. Since the size of direct reporting work groups generally increases following a RIF and flattening of the organization, the influence of the individual supervisor becomes even more significant.

Some of the supervisor's key concerns following a RIF are:

- the need to be conscious of employees' motivational needs and to work to control turnover both immediately and over the long term;
- the need to function as a strong advocate for the staff, to achieve the best for those who must leave as well as for those who remain;
- the need to begin preparing to work with the survivors, helping them to internalize the dramatic change well before the reduction is fully implemented;
- the need to actively encourage employee participation more than ever before, stressing involvement and drawing all possible employees into the decision-making processes. More than ever the supervisor's focus needs to be "we," never "I" or "you";
- the need to fully implement the principles of total quality management (TQM), developing and utilizing employee teams to the fullest possible extent;
- the need at all times to communicate, communicate, communicate, remaining in touch with employees' fears and concerns even when some of the answers have to be "We simply don't know yet, but we'll keep you informed."

Assistance in responding to these and other concerns can be provided to supervisors and middle managers in part through enhanced educational opportunities, a number of which are described in the following section.

Education and Training Following Staff Reduction

It has been almost a foregone conclusion that an organization's education function is among the first to be cut during lean times. The traditional treatment of the education function implies that education is seen as a "frill," that it is dispensable often to a greater degree than most other functions. Since education departments are usually small and a cutback usually removes one or more full-time positions, education in terms of percentage of staff reduction is frequently harder hit than many other activities.

No staff reduction rationale is more counterproductive than the across-the-board cut in which every department is expected to surrender an equal percentage of staff. Yet this rationale is frequently applied out of a misguided sense of "fairness" that suggests the pain must be equally borne by all.

Some functions are simply more valuable at certain times than are others. In a manufacturing company that is reorganizing in response to a declining market share, for example, it could be folly to reduce staff in marketing and new product development since this may be precisely the time to be enhancing and reemphasizing these functions. Likewise in many health care organizations, it can be shortsighted to reduce the resources allocated to education as part of a RIF that leaves in its wake a dramatically increased need for education.

Following a RIF, it is necessary to assist all remaining employees to become more flexible and adaptable. To that end, an enhanced program of continuing education is strongly recommended for all employee levels, that is, for supervisors and managers as well as nonmanagerial employees.

MANAGEMENT EDUCATION

The organization needs to provide assistance to those who supervise the work of others and who, following a RIF and perhaps even complete reengineering, may find their scope of responsibility increased. The organization should consider providing management education to include the following two types of programs:

1. An orientation program for new supervisors, both for those new to management within the organization as well as those entering management for the first time. This program may also serve as a refresher in basics for those for whom a need is expressed or indicated.

2. Management development programs, with either individual classes or multisession offerings as appropriate, addressing several "how-to's." These are enumerated in the box titled "How-to's for Management Development Programs" (Box 40-1).

An area of constant emphasis in supervisory and management training, running through most of the programs presented for these people, should be the importance of the

---

BOX 40–1 HOW-TO'S FOR MANAGEMENT DEVELOPMENT PROGRAMS

- How to improve one's personal effectiveness as a supervisor
- How to delegate work and appropriately empower staff in the new environment
- How to utilize corrective processes in dealing with problems of employee performance and conduct
- How to enhance employees' ability to adapt to the demands and requirements of their new environment (largely motivational concerns)
- How to deal with certain employee issues that arise from time to time (problem employees as well as employee problems)
- How to maintain effective communications upward, downward, and laterally
- How to conduct interviews and make the best possible, fully legal employee selection decisions when necessary
- How to effectively manage day-to-day in spite of an ever expanding body of law affecting the employment relationship
- How to develop and work with a departmental budget and effectively control costs at the department level
- How to protect your employees' and your organization's best interests during union organizing
- How to make effective decisions in a realistic manner
- How to organize, develop, and run effective empoyee teams—while keeping them legal
- How to enhance productivity at the department level
- How to guide employees through change
- How to effectively manage time
- How to make the transition from traditional management to effective leadership
- How to write effective letters and memos
- How to organize and conduct productive meetings
- How to develop and deliver effective presentations

individual supervisor being visible and available to staff, constantly reinforcing the supervisor's key role in each employee's relationship with the organization.

EMPLOYEE EDUCATION AND TRAINING

Individual department orientation and on-the-job training that have long been a fact of organizational life should continue in full force following a staff reduction. In addition, a number of practices involving education and training should be considered for their potential to assist the reinvigoration of the remaining work force.

With appropriate orientation and on-the-job training, some employees who have been offered transfer as an alternative to layoff may be allowed a normal probationary period during which to attain standard performance (assuming the presence of the basic qualifications for the job). An employee offered a transfer should be strongly urged to accept the new assignment as it will likely be the sole alternative to layoff.

A program of *cross-training* should be undertaken between, among, and within certain departments as appropriate. Each employee cross-trained will enhance the work force's flexibility as well as increase the individual's potential value through improved flexibility and versatility.

Programs should be planned and developed for the education of *multiskill specialists*, those generally technical employees who are qualified to work in more than one area (for example, a phlebotomist who is also a specimen processor, a licensed practical nurse who is also an electrocardiogram technician, or a secretary/receptionist who is also a medical office assistant). Multiskill specialists enhance their own potential job security while providing greater flexibility to the organization.

Enhanced *tuition assistance benefits* should be considered for employees who wish to advance themselves by pursuing education in occupations for which the organization has identified current and projected needs.

The organization might also make available *remedial education* in certain basic skills (for example, reading and basic mathematics) to assist employees who have otherwise demonstrated the capacity to seek advancement through self-improvement.

Wherever possible, the organization should pursue a policy of promotion from within, providing all reasonable assistance and preparation for employees who wish to advance themselves.

Resistance to Change: Coping With Dramatic Paradigm Shifts

A RIF in a health care organization involves a forced paradigm shift that affects workers in a dramatic and considerably disturbing fashion. For many years health care providers have been locked into a particular paradigm, clinging especially to a number of assumptions about the manner in which care must be delivered in a hospital setting. As a reduction approaches and the visible signs such as deliberate slowdowns in filling open positions or hiring freezes begin to emerge, much of the resistance of supervisors and managers to delays in filling positions will center around the contention that quality of care will suffer without the one-for-one replacement of departing personnel. The extremely strong paradigm at work here is that which assumes that our present way of delivering care is the best and most efficient way, that cost and quality exist in a direct relationship so if we take cost out (in this instance, remove staff), quality will automatically decline, and, therefore, since we would never willingly or knowingly deliver poor quality care, we believe we have to have the staff whether the money to pay them exists or not (Implicit in this argument is the belief that the answer lies in more money for the system or, at the very least, money diverted from other parts of the system: "Cut *their* program, not mine").

For a number of complex reasons the cost of health care has grown far more rapidly than any other significant societal cost for a considerable number of years. Steps are now being taken to stem that alarming growth by simply reducing the amount of money allowed to flow into health care. In doing so, the government and other third-party payers are forcing health care out of its age-old paradigms, quite literally making health care providers look for ways of accomplishing the same ends at much less cost. Yet the strength of the old way of doing things hampers an ability to quickly find a new way.

When we are forced into unwanted change, we typically respond through a grieving process. (Actually, it is not change itself that we resist so much as being changed.) Loss and uncertainty prevail. Those who survive a staff reduction may even experience guilt over having done so. There is considerable trauma experienced by those who leave the organization involuntarily, but the trauma is just as great for those who remain. Those who remain have to make the painful adjustments that organizational survival requires.

The survivors of a RIF typically perceive dwindling control over their work circumstances. Therefore, every effort should be made to keep all employees advised of the organization's circumstances. Employee communication and involvement are critical in establishing the future direction of the work force that remains following a reduction. To ensure maximum possible communication and involvement, management should:

- Hold regular employee meetings to answer questions and to explain where the organization is going.
- Make necessary changes rationally, whenever possible calling upon the participation of affected employees.
- Seek regular employee feedback by way of surveys and other means so as to be continually aware of employee concerns.
- Continually explore new business strategies and other potential means of enhancing the organization's value to the community and its financial viability as an organization.

For some who leave, a staff reduction seems like the end of the world, at least for a while. Many who remain also tend to see the dramatic changes forced upon them as marking the end of the world as they knew it. Since none who survive, neither line managers nor rank-and-file, can control what happens to the organization, it is indeed the end of the world as many knew it. But for the survivors, it can also be the beginning of a challenging new world.

CHAPTER 41

Shared Governance: Nursing's 20th-Century Tower of Babel

ROBERT G. HESS, JR.

Solve your personnel shortages, boost staff morale, slash costs, enhance multidisciplinary collaboration, improve clinical outcomes. Cited in the nursing literature, these are but a few of the soaring testimonials and promised resolutions that come with implementing a new model of professional nursing governance. But despite the fact that nursing publications have been besieged with articles about models that empower nurses, nursing administrators still are hard-pressed to differentiate one nursing governance innovation from another—beyond rearranged organizational charts and structures, that is.

The waters become that much murkier given the fact that nurse researchers have failed to empirically link any change noted after implementing a governance model to patient or staff outcomes, or to provide hard evidence that successful programs can produce similar results from one setting to another.

It gets worse; there is little agreement on some very key issues: What is shared governance? What exactly is altered by it? And how do we measure the change? This ambiguity contributes little persuasion—beyond a leap of faith—to enlist support from hospital administrators and to fuel staff enthusiasm for new programs.

Recognizing that any innovation that endeavors to enhance professional practice and bolster staff retention also must effect a bottom-line savings, nurse researchers have attempted to demonstrate the cost-effectiveness of shared governance models.[1-5] But these reports, as in past studies,[6-9] merely defined governance via anecdotes, making it nearly impossible to link specific programs to outcomes. In the absence of common measures, the results have provided little justification for the use of scant resources to implement new programs or even to continue the old.

In Search of Common Ground

Governance permeates so many facets of an organization that it cannot be viewed unidimensionally. Rather, an accurate definition must be derived from many angles. But defining governance is like nailing Jello™ to a wall—no easy task. But more than labels and slogans, it really asks the question, "Who rules?"[10] In more theoretical terms, according to Peabody,[11] governance is a fused phenomena—a multidisciplinary concept that portrays the distribution of control, influence, power, and authority in an organization. In entrepreneurial endeavors, it is easy to nail down—the owner rules. However, in current health-care institutions sovereignty is far more complicated.

Shared governance can be defined broadly as a nursing management innovation that legitimizes nurses' decision-making control over their professional practice while extending their influence to administrative areas previously controlled by management. Shared governance programs have not only shifted the balance of control by professionals and administrators over their respective clinical and administrative areas, but also have redistributed their influence over more global organizational spheres regarding information, authority, goals, and conflict.

What's All This Babble About?

Nurse administrators have used labels, such as shared, collaborative, professional, and participatory governance to describe, what are in fact, dissimilar programs that share just one common thread—an intention to augment nurses' sphere of influence within the organization. However, these models typically emphasize clinical practice. They address the enhancement of staff participation in decisions about patient care and limited management functions, such as scheduling, patient care assignments, and quality assurance monitoring—problematic areas that managers would just as soon delegate. But are staff nurses and administrators speaking the same language?

A survey of 1100 registered nurses from 10 hospitals was conducted from June 1993 to April 1994 to find out just how hospital-based nurses defined governance and to develop an instrument that could be used to measure distribution of governance and the progress of innovation in this area in any hospital. Administrative nurses—experts in innovative hospital-based governance models—along with staff nurses validated the items that formed such an instrument: The Index of Professional Nursing Governance (IPNG) (Box 41-1). The instrument demonstrated excellent feasibility, reliability, and validity throughout testing. (Cronbach's reliability for the overall instrument was 0.97; construct validity was assessed by factor analysis, factor subscale intercorrelations, known groups technique, and convergence between the IPNG and a measured, related phenomena.) The distribu-

---

BOX 41-1 THE INDEX OF PROFESSIONAL NURSING GOVERNANCE

Ninety items in six categories (dimensions) were derived from the literature of management, organizations, professionals, and nursing. The six dimensions included:

- Control over professional practice;
- Influence over organizational resources that support practice;
- Formal authority granted by the organization;
- Committee structures that allow participation in decision making;
- Access information about the organization;
- The ability to set goals and negotiate conflict.

The items simultaneously encompassed unit, departmental, and institutional levels.

tion of governance was found to be correlated with decentralization, the degree to which organizational members participate in organizational decision making, which was measured by the Index of Centralization.[12] The moderate correlation showed that the IPNG measured something different than decentralized decision making, a concept that has been erroneously mistaken for governance.

Analysis of the entire sample's responses revealed that the nurses held a different view of governance than had been advanced in consultant and editorial rhetoric, extrapolated from 160 articles and abstracts from the last 20 years. Out of the six significant aspects of governance, control over professional practice, was found to be the least important—it barely made the list at all. Instead, professional nurses revealed that control over nursing personnel and influence over resources that affect clinical practice were more relevant indicators in defining governance (Box 41-2).

The importance of control over nursing personnel probably reflected that sample's realization that in labor-intensive facilities such as hospitals, the organization's product—patient care—is derived mainly from the work of its nursing staff. For hospitals in which they work, nurses are an important organizational resource. Additionally, the importance of control over resources is consistent with other traditions of organizational study such as resource dependency theory, one of the only theories that has generated research into organizational governance.[13-20] However, by far the most important implication is that when dialogue about governance takes place between nurse administrators and the rest of the hospital nursing community, the two groups are speaking different languages.

Total scores from each hospital formed a continuum of governance, suggested by earlier nurse researchers,[21-23] that ranged from governance dominated by administrators to governance shared between management and staff members. Hospitals with a reputation for strict bureaucratic control had low scores. Hospitals with a track record for empowering nurses—including a magnet hospital with a long-standing tradition of participative

---

BOX 41-2　HOW NURSES DEFINE AND PRIORITIZE ORGANIZATIONAL GOVERNANCE AS PROFESSIONALS

A. Control over nursing personnel, including hiring, promoting, evaluating, and terminating nursing personnel; recommending and adjusting salaries and benefits; creating new positions; formulating unit budgets; and conducting disciplinary action.

B. Access to information about management, nurse, physician, and patient opinions of nursing practice; unit budget and expenses; nursing department goals and objectives; hospital financial status, compliance with regulatory agencies, and strategic plans.

C. Influence over organizational resources, including monitoring and securing patient care supplies; recommending, consulting, and enlisting support of hospital services outside of nursing; and determining daily assignments and regulating flow of patient admissions, transfers, referrals, placements, and discharges.

D. Participation and creation of decision-making committees that address policies and procedures, clinical practice, staffing/scheduling and budgeting, goals and objectives at the nursing unit and departmental levels; policies and procedures at the hospital-wide level; and collaboration among multidisciplinary groups.

E. Control over nursing practice, including writing patient care standards; monitoring quality of care and products used in care; setting and adjusting staff levels and determining qualifications and ongoing education requirements for nursing personnel; writing policies and procedures for direct patient care; and incorporating research into practice.

F. Formulation of philosophy, goals, and objectives of the nursing department and hospital; negotiation of conflict among nurses, physicians, other hospital service personnel, nurse managers, and hospital administrators; and creation of a formal grievance procedure.

management and a community hospital that had implemented a state-funded shared governance model—scored high. These high scores indicated a hospital environment in which the distribution of governance was shared between administrative and staff nurses.

As expected, the study successfully measured shared governance status regardless of reputation, and transcended simple labels placed on programs. This was clearly illustrated in a self-proclaimed "shared governance hospital," whose scores grouped it with the traditionally governed institutions. The hospital's scores were incongruent with its reputation, suggesting that some shared governance innovations might not involve sharing at all, but merely a change in the name of the game,[24] or perhaps, in this case, where one nurse administrator insisted that control over clinical practice had been turned over to the staff, a program that promotes sharing only what the staff perceives as less important in terms of governing the organization in which they work.

Back to Earth

This study has contributed an instrument for measuring the professional nursing governance of hospital-based nurses. The instrument can provide baseline data before the implementation of governance innovations and evaluative data of its progress and effects afterward. The IPNG provides a means of comparison and verification of governance situations among hospitals and among nursing groups or units within a hospital. Because these comparisons include six areas of governance, the IPNG may be useful in establishing benchmarks during organizational change. The bottom line? The IPNG provides the first opportunity to comprehensively measure governance as an independent variable that may affect outcomes.

What's Ahead?

Nurses have been willing to implement shared governance, despite the fact that the benefits of these models still are speculative. As the consequences of early implementation are being evaluated, there still is little research outside of single institution-specific studies to support the continued popularity claimed in anecdotal literature. Although several outcome studies[7,8,25-29] have reported favorable changes for nurses in autonomy, job satisfaction, collegiality, retention and turnover rates, and cost effectiveness, the governance variables are imprecisely and variously defined, thereby limiting the conclusions that can be drawn from the results.

The real dilemma is that cost/benefits of shared governance have yet to be quantified in spite of clear research opportunities. There is an urgent need to collect data because researchers speculate that any changes for shared governance are not realized for several years.[7,33]

Innovative governance models such as shared governance are appealing to nurses. Nevertheless, nurse executives have little empirical justification to persuade hospital administrators to modify existing governance arrangements in a healthcare climate that is already short of resources. Without a common measure of governance, it has not been possible to compare models and outcomes. The instrument generated in this study may offer a means to identify the best programs and the evidence to justify continued innovations in governance.

REFERENCES

1. Daly BJ, Phelps C, Rudy EB. A nurse-managed special care unit. *J Nurs Adm.* 1991; 21(778):31–38.
2. DeBaca V, Jones K, Tornabeni J. A cost-benefit analysis of shared governance. *J Nurs Adm.* 1993; 23(7/8):50–57.

3. Iacobellis J. *Nurse Manager Cost/Quality Strategies.* San Jose, CA: San Jose State University; 1993. Masters thesis (microfilms AAC1353025).

4. Minors SP. *A Twelve Group Time Series Analysis of Job Satisfaction and Financial Effects of Nursing Shared Governance.* Atlanta, GA: Georgia State University; 1993. Doctoral dissertation (university microfilms AAC9319132).

5. Wong R, Gordon DL, Cassard SD, et al. A cost analysis of a professional practice model for nursing. *Nurs Econ.* 1993; 11(5):292–297.

6. Johnson LM. Self-governance: treatment for an unhealthy nursing culture. *Health Prog.* 1987; 5:41–43.

7. Ethridge P. Nurse accountability program improves satisfaction, turnover. *Health Prog.* 1987; 5:44–49.

8. Pinkerton S. Evaluation of shared governance in a nursing department. In: Stull MK, Pinkerton S, eds. *Current Strategies for Nurse Administrator.* Rockville, MD: Aspen; 1988:141–150.

9. Jenkins J. A nursing governance and practice model: what are the costs? *Nurs Econ.* 1988; 6(6):302–311.

10. Dahl RA. *Who Governs? Democracy and Power in an American City.* New Haven, CT: Yale University Press; 1961.

11. Peabody RL. *Organizational Authority.* New York: Aetherton Press; 1964.

12. Hague J, Aiken M. Relationship of centralization to other structural properties. *Adm Sci Q.* 1967; 12(6):72–91.

13. Zald MN. The power and functions of boards of directors: a theoretical synthesis. *Am J Sociol.* 1969; 75:97–111.

14. Pfeffer J. Size and composition of corporate boards of directors. *Adm Sci Q.* 1972; 17:218–228.

15. Allen P. The structure of interorganizational elite cooptation. *Am Soc Rev.* 1974: 39:393–406.

16. Pfeffer J, Nowak P. Joint ventures and interorganizational interdependence. *Adm Sci Q.* 1976; 21:398–418.

17. Pfeffer J, Salancik, GR. *The External Control of Organizations: Resource Dependency Perspective.* New York: Harper & Row; 1978.

18. Burt R, Christman KP, Kilburn HC Jr. Testing a structural theory of corporate cooptation: interorganizational directorate ties as a strategy for avoiding market constraints on profits. *Am Soc Rev.* 1980; 45:821–841.

19. Burt R. *Corporate Profits and Cooptation: Networks of Market Constraints and Directorate Ties in the American Economy.* New York: Academic Press; 1983.

20. Burt R. *Structural Holes: The Social Structure of Competition.* Cambridge, MA: Harvard University Press; 1992.

21. Blouin AS, Pelletier M. Integrating a nursing shared governance model into the hospital corporate culture. In: McDonaugh K, ed. *Nursing Shared Governance: Restructuring for the Future.* Atlanta: KJ McDonaugh & Associates; 1990:227–238.

22. Wake M. Nursing care delivery systems—status and vision. *J Nurs Adm.* 1990: 20(5),47–51.

23. Havens DS. *Analysis of the Nature and Extent of Implementation and Projected Implementation of a Model Proposed to Support Professional Nursing Practice in Acute Care General Hospitals.* Baltimore, MD: University of Maryland; 1990. Doctoral dissertation (university microfilms 91-100096).

24. Hess RG. Shared governance: innovation or imitation. *Nurs Econ.* 1994; 12(1):28–34.

25. Howard DC. Outcomes of shared governance on staff nurses. *J Nurs Adm.* 1987; 17(12):9.

26. Pinkerton S. An overview of shared governance. In: Pinkerton S, Schroeder P. eds. *Commitment to Excellence: Developing a Professional Staff.* Rockville, MD: Aspen; 1988: 105–111.

27. Ludemann RS, Brown C. Staff perceptions of shared governance. *Nurs Adm Q.* 1989; 1(4):49–56.

28. Serafini G. The influence of a professional practice model on collegiality in the psychiatric setting. Unpublished abstract from Symposium conducted by Sigma Theta Tau, Syracuse, NY, (October) 1989.

29. Jones BJ, Stasiowski S, Simons BJ, et al. Shared governance and the nursing practice environment. *Nurs Econ.* 1993; 11:208–214.

30. Eckes A. Implementing shared governance: a process for growth. In: Pinkerton S. Schroeder P ed. *Commitment to Excellence: Developing a Professional Nursing Staff.* Rockviile, MD: Aspen; 1988: 123–128.

●●●

CHAPTER 42

Valuing Authority/Responsibility Relationships: The Essence of Professional Practice

SHERRY S. WEBB, SYLVIA A. PRICE, AND HARRIET VAN ESS COELING

Care delivery, once the exclusive domain of nursing, now is viewed as a team effort in shared partnership with other disciplines.[1] To prepare the teams, staff members are cross-trained, maximizing resources while minimizing costs.[2] Organizational structures and processes are changed easily through reorganization, but if these changes are made without considering the actual values and beliefs of unit work groups, organizations risk producing only quick superficial solutions to long-term problems.

One important element of work group culture is the pattern of authority and rules that govern the distribution of power and decision making.[3] How nurses value authority affects the level of acceptance of responsibility and accountability for clinical decision making, a concept central to the practice of professional nursing. The cultural characteristics of nurse managers and staff nurses on primary nursing and total patient care units were studied to identify the value placed on authority responsibility relationships. The convenience sample consisted of 21 nurse managers and 213 staff nurses from three urban acute care hospitals located in the northwestern, midwestern, and southeastern regions of the United States.

What Is Culture?

Recent emphasis on understanding organizational culture and its impact on work group culture is reflected in published research, which attempted to identify, describe, measure, and change cultural values and norms.[4-6] Organizational culture has a powerful effect on behavior because each possesses cultural norms and values that guide and shape the behavior of the groups within them.[7]

Work group culture is the set of appropriate responses, devised by work group members, to the situations they encounter as they work together.[8] Work group culture is described in terms of shared values, common solutions, similar ways of believing, behaving, and a combination of cognition, symbols, and unconscious interactions.[9-12]

Work group rules have been identified as verbal and nonverbal behaviors accepted as appropriate by group members.[4,6] Beliefs about human relationships address the importance of task versus social orientation and hierarchy, and individual versus group activities.[13]

What Is the Relationship of Authority and Responsibility?

The professional elements of practice are authority, accountability, responsibility, and decision making; therefore, the professional nurse is described as one who is autonomous and who desires responsibility and accountability.[14-16] Present and future professional practice models—such as primary nursing, shared governance, and case management—are based on the principles of increased autonomy, responsibility, and authority.

There often is inconsistency between the professional ideal and the real world of clinical practice. There are nurses who wish to be autonomous and have a high degree of professional authority in which to provide directions, and who would prefer a culture that fosters increased accountability, whereas other nurses would prefer a dependent culture that requires following the directions of others.[17-21] Central to the study, there is a relationship between organizational and work group culture and the individual factors of authority (Figure 42-1).

Cultural Characteristics: Primary Nursing Versus Total Patient Care

Both practice patterns are similar because the approach to care is patient centered, with one nurse providing care for a group of patients. Culturally, primary nursing is different from total patient care in the following ways.

Primary nursing is the delivery of care by one nurse who is operationally responsible for the planning and delivery of care for a group of patients from admission to discharge.

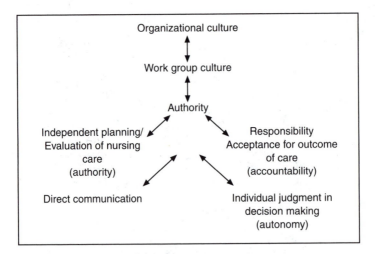

Figure 42–1 Authority/responsibility relationships in unit work groups.

The primary nurse has 24-hour accountability for care planning and is expected to act independently in planning/evaluating nursing care; communicate directly with health team members; provide direct care during assigned shifts; and expect follow-through of written instructions.[22-24]

Total patient care is the delivery of care by one nurse for an assigned shift who is expected to provide most of the direct care; meet the physical, psychologic, and emotional needs of the patients; coordinate care with other disciplines; and communicate changes in the patients' conditions to a charge nurse or a patient care coordinator.[25,26]

How Were Work Groups Assessed?

Because the concepts of authority, responsibility, and accountability have not been described in measurable terms, the study focused on examination of the value placed on these concepts by nurse managers and staff nurses. The Nursing Unit Cultural Assessment Tool-2, developed by Coeling et al, was used to describe and compare the degree to which the unit work group of nurse managers and staff nurses value accountability, autonomy, direct communication, and authority. Only questions that related to authority/responsibility relationships were analyzed. Two additional questions were added that related to accountability to determine the importance of accepting responsibility for patient care outcomes. Criteria for inclusion in the study were all permanently assigned full and part-time (3 days/week) nurses (registered and licensed practical nurses) on 14 primary nursing units and 7 total patient care units who voluntarily participated in the study. Nurses on primary nursing units were required to have practiced for at least $1\frac{1}{2}$ years to allow time for internalization of the role.

The value placed on authority/responsibility relationships was measured to reflect both the typical and the preferred work group behaviors, which were accountability, autonomy, direct communication, and authority. Variables were tested at a specific alpha level of $P = 0.05$.

What Were the Significant Findings?

Of the participants, managers were more likely to have practiced nursing for more than 15 years (62%) and tended to have more advanced education. Most managers held a bachelor or higher degree (85%). The majority of staff nurses had practiced nursing for less than 15 years and had less education. The largest percentage of staff nurses held diplomas or associate degrees (53%).

Within the practice patterns of primary nursing and total patient care there were similar values expressed by nurse managers for their staff and staff nurses for their group (Table 42-1). Although both groups of managers preferred more direct communication for their staffs, nurse managers on primary nursing units also preferred more accountability and authority. Similarly, both groups of staff nurses preferred more direct communication and authority for their work group, but staff nurses on primary nursing units also preferred more accountability and autonomy. These findings of nurse managers and staff nurses on primary nursing units are consistent with the model of primary nursing.

When comparing practice patterns, no differences were found between primary nursing and total patient care managers' preferences for their staff; however, staff nurses on primary nursing units preferred more accountability for their work group. Because of the limited sample of nurse managers, inferences can be made—but not validated—when

TABLE 42–1   **Significant Elements Valued by Nurse Managers for Their Staff Versus by Staff Nurses for Their Work Group**

Practice Pattern	Nurse Managers	Staff Nurses
Primary nursing	Accountability Direct communication Authority	Accountability Autonomy Direct communication Authority
Total patient care	Direct communication	Direct communication Authority

comparing differences between managers and their staffs on primary nursing and total patient care units.

What Are the Implications for Nursing Administration?

Nurse administrators must be able to clearly identify a well-defined practice pattern. However, when implementing role differentiation across all units within an organization, nurse administrators must understand that each nursing unit work group is unique and differs from other nursing unit work groups in its patterns of beliefs and values.[27] Not all unit work groups will change at the same time or in the same way. This variation across units within organizations demonstrates the magnitude of implementing and stabilizing organizational change across such diverse work groups without first clearly defining the practice pattern: It demands an understanding of what is valued by each work group to be successful. Four issues from this study have implications for nurse administrators (Box 42-1).

Conflict

The potential for conflict exists when the individual's values are not congruent with the values of the nurse manager and the work group.[28] Several examples of potential areas of conflict were found between nurse managers and their staffs, and between staffs and their work groups.

The fact that nurse managers were more experienced and had more advanced education than their staffs could represent potential conflict in terms of educational values and beliefs, because the process by which outcomes are reached is based on personal values, levels of educational preparation, and experience. Recognizing that these differences exist will prepare nurse managers to understand a significant element of their work group's culture.

BOX 42–1   IMPLICATIONS FOR NURSING ADMINISTRATION

Conflict resolution
Leadership style
Managing changes
Adult learning

A potential for group conflict also exists when staff nurses' values are not congruent with those of their work groups. Both groups valued more direct communication and authority than they believed to actually be practiced. Assisting staff members to discuss the differences between individual values and the values of the group will provide a framework for group understanding and ownership.

Leadership

Leadership is in part the ability to influence others, both individuals and groups, toward a common goal.[29] The nurse manager's legitimate and positional power and leadership style has been shown to influence work group culture.[30] Staff nurses on primary nursing units valued more autonomy, and staff nurses on total patient care units valued more authority for their work groups than was indicated as important to their managers. Depending on the manager's leadership style, these values could be perceived as a threat to the manager's positional power. Nurse managers should view these differences as an opportunity to reexamine their own philosophy and leadership styles to determine if they are hindering the professional development of their staffs.

Change

Work group culture represents perhaps the greatest barrier to change because change involves loss—loss of power, status, and job security.[31] When the individual and the group values are not congruent with the proposed change, the culture is threatened, and a potential for resistance exists.[23] Staff nurses on primary nursing and total patient care units did not demonstrate the levels of accountability, autonomy, direct communication, and authority that were important to their nurse managers and work groups. If staff members are satisfied with the status quo or do not want increased levels of responsibility or accountability, they may resist and sabotage the change. Managers should assist their staffs in adopting the change in such a way that their culture is not threatened. On the other hand, opportunities for desired changes in practice also were evident by the staff nurses in both groups. Managers who recognize that their staffs are expressing a desire to change can capitalize on their staffs' readiness to facilitate change on their units.

In any change, managers are responsible for first establishing the vision for their staffs in terms of the desired goals.[32] Managers must recognize, however, that not all staff members internalize the goals at the same time or in the same way. Indeed, there may be a significant time lag between the time that the vision is communicated, the time that the vision is identified as important to staff, and the time that role changes become a reality and behaviors actually change. This may be why studies have shown that real changes take 3 to 5 years to obtain the desired outcomes.

Adult Learning

"The illiterate of tomorrow will not be those who cannot read or write," claims Alvin Toffler, "but those who cannot learn, unlearn, and relearn."[33] This statement has a tremendous impact on adult learning and the changes that are being required in healthcare. Adults have a volume and quality of experience that determine how they will learn. Adults need to know why they should learn something, to be self-directed, to learn when a need to know is identified, and to enter the learning experience with a task-centered, problem-centered, or life-centered orientation.[34] Learning is on a continuum which, if reinforced over time, will lead to permanent changes in behavior. Because of the differences in educational preparation and experiences of the nurse managers and staff nurses, each person's contribution to the unit work group must not be undervalued. Indeed, the strengths of each need to be maximized to enhance the broad cultural base of the work group.

Conclusion

These findings are consistent with other research findings related to organizational culture because all groups have unique characteristics and patterns of behavior that are influenced by the organization, the manager's philosophy and leadership style, and the values of the unit work group. Primary nursing and total patient care work groups were studied not to prove that one was better than the other: Rather, it was believed that studying practice patterns that have been clearly defined and the value that those work groups place on authority/responsibility relationships would lead to a better understanding of emerging practice patterns.

REFERENCES

1. Flarey D. The social climate of work environments. *J. Nurs Adm.* 1993; 23(6):9–15.
2. McDaniel C, Stumpf L. The organizational culture. *J. Nurs. Adm.* 1993; 23(4):54–60.
3. Pfeffer J. *Power in Organizations.* Cambridge. MA: Ballinger Pub Co; 1981.
4. Schein E. Coming to a new awareness of organizational culture. *Sloan Manage Rev.* 1984; Winter: 3–16.
5. del Bueno D. Vincent P. Organizational culture: how important is it? *J Nurs Adm.* 1986; 16(10):15–20.
6. Coeling H, Wilcox J. Understanding culture: a key to management decision making. *J Nurs Adm.* 1988; 18(11):16–22.
7. del Bueno D, Freuend C. *Power and Politics in Nursing Administration: A Casebook.* Owings Mills, MD: National Health Pub: 1986.
8. Simms L, Erbin-Roesemann M. Darga A. Coeling H. Breaking the burnout barrier: resurrecting work excitement in nursing. *Nurs Econ.* 1990; 8(3):177–187.
9. Allen R, Kroft C. *Transformations That Last: A Cultural Approach. The Organizational Unconscious.* Englewood Cliffs, NJ: Prentice Hall: 1984.
10. Van Maanen J, Barley S. Cultural organizations: fragments of a theory. In: Frost PJ, Moore LF, Lewis MR, et al., eds. *Organizational Culture.* Beverly Hills, CA: Sage: 1985.
11. Cooke R, Rousseau D. Behavioral norms and expectations: a quantitative approach to the assessment of organizational culture. *Group Organizational Stud.* 1988; 13(3):245–273.
12. Thomas C, Ward M, Chorba C, Kumiega A. Measuring and interpreting organizational culture. *J Nurs Adm.* 1990; 20(6):17–24.
13. Schein E. *Organizational Culture and Leadership.* San Francisco, CA: Jossey-Bass: 1985.
14. Manthey M. *The Practice of Primary Nursing.* Boston: Blackwell Publications: 1980.
15. Parker J. Utilization of Hertzberg's motivation theory: primary nursing as a method of increasing job satisfaction for nurses. *J. Nephrol Nurs.* 1984:148–151.
16. Jovle E, Calaway L, Jorgenson L, Swokowski S. The practical aspects of primary nursing. *Am Nephrol Assoc J.* 1988; 15(3):157–193.
17. Manthey M, Miller D. Empowerment through levels of authority. *J. Nurs Adm.* 1994; 24(7,8):23.
18. McClure M. Managing the professional nurse. *J Nurs Adm.* 1984; 14:11–17.
19. Allen D, Calkin J, Peterson M. Making shared governance work: a conceptual model. *J Nurs Adm.* 1988; 18(1):37–43.
20. Lee J. Professionalism of hospital nurses linked to staff structure. *J Nurs Adm.* 1988; 18(11):44.
21. Dwyer D, Schwartz R, Fox M. Decision-making autonomy in nursing. *J Nurs Adm.* 1992; 22(2):17–23.

22. Manthey M. A theoretical framework for primary nursing. *J Nurs Adm.* 1986; 10:11–15.
23. Kerfoot M. Creating autonomy—the nurse manager's challenge. *Nurs Econ.* 1989; 7(2):107–108.
24. Zander K. Second generation primary nursing. *J Nurs Adm.* 1985; 15:18–24.
25. Young L, Hayne A. *Nursing Administration: From Concepts to Practice.* Philadelphia. PA: WB Saunders; 1988.
26. Hood G, Dincher J. *Total Patient Care: Foundations and Practice.* St Louis: CV Mosby; 1988.
27. Coeling H, Simms L. Facilitating innovation at the nursing unit level through cultural assessment, part 1. *J Nurs Adm.* 1993; 23(4):46–53.
28. Coeling H, Simms L. Facilitating innovation at the nursing unit level through cultural assessment, part 2. *J Nurs Adm.* 1993; 23(5):13–20.
29. Sullivan E, Decker P. *Effective Management in Nursing.* Menlo Park. CA: Addison-Wesley Pub Co: 1988.
30. Williams B. *Influence of the Nurse Manager's Leadership Style and Power Relationships in the Critical Care Work Group.* Memphis, TN: University of Tennessee: 1990. Unpublished master's thesis.
31. Liker J, Roitman D, Roskies E. Changing everything at once: work life and technological change. *Sloan Manage Rev:* 1987; Summer: 29–36.
32. Belasco J. Stayer R. *Flight of the Buffalo: Soaring to Excellence. Learning to Let Employees Lead.* New York. NY: Warner Books: 1993.
33. Atchison T. The Intangible Effects of Healthcare Reform. Presented at the Second Annual Case Management: The Foundation for Healthcare Reform Seminar; Oct 8, 1993: Memphis. TN.
34. Knowles MS. *The Modern Practice of Adult Education from Pedogogy to Andragogy.* Chicago, IL; Follett: 1980.

CHAPTER 43

●●

How Wide Is the Gap in Defining Quality Care?

Comparison of Patient and Nurse Perceptions of Important Aspects of Patient Care

WENDY B. YOUNG, ANN F. MINNICK, AND RICHARD MARCANTONIO

Patient-centered care emphasizes continuous quality improvement and a customer focus.[1] This patient-as-customer perspective frames several current reform initiatives: the Pew Health Professions Commission;[2,3] Pew Health of the Public grant program to demonstrate interdisciplinary health professions' education models;[4] several federal initiatives focused on community-based healthcare training and services; and the Picker–Commonwealth Patient-Centered Care initiatives.[5] The customer focus transcends traditional provider-defined quality assurance frameworks based on review, professional standards,[6] and assumptions that providers' knowledge is superior to that of their patients for judging the quality of care.

Not understanding patients' expectations of care may impede hospitals' attempts to improve customers' reports of service quality. This study compares patient, nurse, and nurse manager perceptions of the importance of selected aspects of care. Using data from our recent patient-centered care study, responses by nurses and nursing unit managers on how patients value several aspects of care were compared with patient responses about these aspects. Registered nurses and nurse managers answered a written questionnaire that included items on how they perceived others (patients, nurses, nurse manager) valued each aspect of care, and how important it was to meet these perceived expectations. Patients responded to a telephone survey within 26 days of hospital discharge.*

Copyright © 1996, Lippincott-Raven Publishers. Reprinted with permission from the *Journal of Nursing Administration,* Volume 26, Number 5, pp. 15–20, May, 1996.

*The optimal timing of patient surveys for feedback on care during a specific hospitalization is reviewed in a manuscript by these authors currently under review.

Background

There are more than 2500 citations currently listed on Medline (National Library of Medicine, Bethesda, MD) and Ovid–CINAHL (CINAHL Information Services, Glendale, CA) concerning provider and patient perceptions and expectations of care and patient satisfaction. Many studies compared provider and patient expectations and judgments about specific aspects of care, such as patient teaching, control of health decisions, and pain management.[7–14] Other works examined more general aspects of caring and care—eg, physical and emotional assistance.[15–19] A smaller number of articles described patient and nurse expectations of the nurse's role in specific activities—eg, informing patients that they have cancer (as well as informing them about other matters related to cancer).[20] Most articles noted some inconsistencies between patient and nurse expectations. There were no research articles concerning the existence, nature, and size of any inconsistencies since the widespread adoption of the customer focus in quality improvement programs.

Literature also has evolved around descriptions of services and behaviors that patients perceive as indicators of excellent care.[21] The need to recognize the importance of patients' opinions and reports of care and caring has been attested to in research[22–24] and state and federal healthcare policy debates.

One component of quality improvement programs is transformation of the organizational culture.[25,26] Within a hospital patient care unit, the unit team's collective values regarding their customers' values—the organizational culture of the team of nurses and their nurse manager—could influence the quality of various aspects of care. If the unit team inaccurately perceives how their patients value care, patient survey results and follow-up educational programs may help correct these perceptions and transform the unit organizational culture to align more closely with customers' actual expectations.[27] Correct unit team perceptions can be expected to result in improved patients' reports of care. Addressing beliefs and attitudes is one step to changing behavior.[28] It measures nurses' values of patient care components from their perceptions of 1) how their patients and their nurse managers value care, and 2) their desire to meet their perceived patients' and nurse managers' expectations regarding these aspects of care. This study examines patients' care values as expectations.

Method

Aspects of patient-centered care selected for this study are those highly controlled by nurses and needed by most hospitalized patients.[†] These four aspects are: physical care (help needed with bathing, eating, walking, using toilet); patient participation in care; patient teaching (receiving needed information about care in hospital, medications received in hospital, medications prescribed to take after going home, signs and symptoms indicating need for help after going home); and pain control (help needed to control pain).

Seventeen hospitals from a single midwestern region, selected from a pool of 69 acute care institutions by means of a stratified random sample, provided Institutional Review Board approval and agreed to participate. The stratification was based on location (inner city, urban, and suburban) and the annual number of adult, nonpsychiatric, nonobstetric admissions. The smallest stratum was 5,000 to 10,000 annual admissions; the largest was 25,000 or more. Federal, state, and for-profit hospitals were excluded from the pool. All

---

[†]Focus groups of administrators of hospital patient services, health departments, and health services research programs contributed toward the selection of the aspects of care measured in this study.

nonintensive medical–surgical inpatient units (n = 117) at the hospitals served as data collection sites. All participating hospitals reported operating a continuous service quality improvement monitoring program or a total quality management program. Most operated both, plus at least one other patient service program.

PATIENT SURVEY: CONTENT AND ADMINISTRATION

The patient telephone interview took approximately 25 minutes to complete. Pilot testing interviews ensured clarity of key concepts and directions. The questions referred only to experiences on the unit from which the patient was discharged; constant reminders throughout the interview kept patients focused on this period of their hospitalization.

Survey items included the importance of each aspect of care (eg, "How important was it to you that your pain control needs were met?"; 4-point scale: 4 = very, 1 = not at all); and their experiences with services to assist with these aspects. Only the responses of patients who said they ever needed assistance with an aspect of care were used in the analyses; thus, the number of respondents varies for each item. Report of each aspect of care provided was measured on a 0-to-1 scale, computed as the sum of responses to three quality reports (timeliness, thoroughness, and individualization; eg, "Did you get the pain control when you wanted it, or earlier or later than when you wanted it?") divided by the number of responses (1, 2, or 3) for that aspect of care.

Registered nurses employed by the project collaborated with hospital nursing staff to identify potential subjects (any adult, nonpsychiatric, nonobstetric inpatient capable of discharge and informed consent) and record demographic and clinical record data for consenting patients. Of the 2595 patients who agreed to participate at the time of hospitalization and remained eligible to participate, 2051 completed interviews within 26 days of discharge, for a 79% response rate. The average patient response rate per unit was 64%, with no differential response rates due to gender, race, or ethnicity.[29]

NURSE AND NURSE MANAGER SURVEYS: CONTENT AND ADMINISTRATION

Focus groups of registered nurses at three pilot sites were used to develop items that asked how much (on a 5-point scale):

1. Their patients and their nurse manager value performance of the selected aspects of patient care (eg, "How much do (patients/nurse managers) value my performance of providing pain relief?"); and

2. They wished to meet their patients' and their manager's expectations of these aspects of care (eg, "How much do you wish to meet (patients'/nurse manager's) expectations regarding providing pain control?").

Similar items measured nurse managers' values.

Staff nurse questionnaires were distributed according to each unit leader/head nurse's preference. Staff nurse questionnaires were distributed and collected during the same time period in which patients were recruited. Reminders and other publicity strategies were used to elevate response rates. The total staff nurse response rate was 51% (n = 1264), with units averaging a 52.8% response rate that did not vary by shift. The nurse manager sample was 97—an 87% response rate.

METHODS OF ANALYSIS

Data were analyzed by means and standard deviations, and zero order correlations. Individual level analyses used the original reports of each patient, nurse, and nurse manager without controlling for their hospital patient care unit affiliation. Analyses at the hospital patient care unit level used unit-level means of patient and nurse responses. In unit-level analyses, patients were matched to the unit from which they based their reports of care—the unit from which they were discharged. Unit-level measures of nurses' responses were constructed by matching nurses to the hospital unit where they were permanently assigned or worked most frequently. Nurse manager's individual responses were used in unit-level analyses and assigned to that manager's unit.

For each aspect of care, individual level results are presented first, and display general relationships. Unit-level analyses then are used to examine if relationships observed generally occur only in selected hospital units and vary according to differences in the organizational culture of the unit's team of nurses.

Results

ACTUAL PATIENT VALUES: QUESTIONS AND ANSWERS

Do patients give varying levels of importance to selected aspects of care? Means, standard deviations, and zero order correlations were examined to determine the extent to which patients differentiate the importance of selected components of patient-centered care. The range of means across all five components of care was narrow, with patient teaching ranked highest (3.9) and participation in care ranked lowest (3.6). However, zero order correlations of importance ratings were low (range, 0.14–0.22). Results using unit-level means ranked similarly with standard deviations about one half the size of individual level results, and low zero order correlations (range, 0.06–0.28). Therefore, when asked about the importance of various components of care they received during recent hospitalizations, patients reported some differentiation in importance.

Although the differences were small, patients do not perceive "patient-centered care" as a single entity, according to the low correlation of their report of the importance of any one component of patient-centered care with any other component. Patients' views of the relative importance of various components of care can be used to construct quality improvement goals. Results reconfirm that quality is a variety of aspects of patient care, and there is no single quality benchmark measure. All five components studied may be important quality benchmarks.

Do patients report their care experiences in relation to the importance they place on that aspect of care? Patients' reports of importance of care were related to reports of care received (range, 0.29–0.56 zero order correlations), indicating that the importance patients place on an aspect of care may affect how they report care received. Therefore, knowing how much importance patients place on an aspect of care is valuable for achieving a quality improvement goal of that aspect of care.

NURSES' VALUES AND PERCEPTIONS

Do nurses and nurse managers value aspects of care similarly to the importance expressed by their patients? Each nurse's values regarding patients' values was computed as the nurse's perception of the value patients placed on each aspect of care multiplied by the nurse's degree of desire to meet patients' expectations. This same method was used to compute each nurse's value regarding their nurse manager, and each nurse manager's values regarding their patients and their staff nurses.

The range of nurses' scores regarding patients' values was wider (range, 19.3–21.5) than their scores regarding nurse managers' expectations (range, 17.2–17.9). Except for patient teaching, nurses did not perceive that patients and nurse managers placed the same relative importance on aspects of patient-centered care because they ranked these two groups differently. Nurse manager scores were more consistent across both groups and all aspects of care: the range was narrow, and the scores were very similar.

As a total group (regardless of their hospital or unit), nurses' and nurse managers' scores regarding patients' values were moderately similar (0.48–0.59 zero order correlations). Although this similarity may be salutary, what matters in actual practice is the degree of similarity between a particular unit manager and that unit's members. When unit teams' mean average nurses' scores were compared with their own nurse manager's scores (−0.08–0.33 zero order correlations at the unit level), less agreement was found. These results suggest that, although nurses perceive correctly that patients value differently various aspects of care (as scores for specific aspects of care varied), unit nursing teams generally do not agree with their manager on how they perceive patients rank the importance of different aspects of care.

Additionally, these teams' values regarding patients' preferences did not match the importance expressed by their patients (−0.14–0.11 zero order correlations at the unit level). Nurse managers' values of how their patients rated importance of care also were unrelated to their patients' importance ratings (−0.01–0.06 zero order correlations at the unit level). The unit organizational culture of nurses' and nurse managers' values would need to be aligned more closely with their patients' values to set achievable quality improvement goals for the patient care unit. Awareness of the variation in values would be a first step to achieve this alignment.

Conclusions and Recommendations

Results indicate that a gap continues between patients' actual values and what health professionals perceive as patients' values. Healthcare professionals' perceptions of what patients expect regarding selected aspects of patient-centered care and their motivation to meet these expectations does not closely approximate the value their patients place on these aspects. This especially is pronounced at the point of service—the hospital's patient care unit—where a unit team's organizational culture may be self-reinforcing gaps between patients' and caregivers' values.

Provision of patient-centered care relies on knowing the patient perspectives. Quality improvement program goals can be set to meet patient expectations only when these are known. Reports by patients on the importance of various aspects of care are one way to measure these expectations. Actual patient reports of care received can be used as indicators of progress toward goals. The relative importance that patients place on various care components may vary from one hospital nursing unit to another, and their actual reports of care also will vary by hospital unit. Quality improvement programs that focus on care at the unit level will help address the influence of the unit team's organizational culture and other unit-level managerial differences that affect the care that patients receive.

One component of any quality improvement program is the transformation of organizational culture, typically from a corrective focus to a continuous improvement and customer orientation. The lack of unit-level correlation between nurses' and nurse managers' perceptions of patient expectations and the actual importance expressed by their patients suggests that the organizational culture transformation phase of continuous quality improvement programs needs to include improving care providers' understanding of their patients' priorities for care. Lack of understanding of patient expectations of care may impede attempts to improve customer reports of service quality. It especially is important that the unit manager understand patient expectations if the manager is to facilitate the staff's understanding.

Construction of quality improvement goals must include significant input from patient groups. A unit team approach may be essential to adjusting nurses' inaccurate but self-reinforcing perspective, given the moderate correlation found across the study sample of nurses' and their nurse managers' perceptions of patient expectations. Focus groups or patient advisory groups can bridge cultural differences between groups attempting to work toward a common goal. If a dialogue between customers and providers cannot be created, survey results of patients' expressed relative importance of various aspects of care must be communicated regularly to nursing care providers.

Some of the active techniques noted by authors such as Coeling and Simms[30,31] or Barg, et al.[32,33] might be tested in the future. Use of a dissemination of an innovation framework may be useful to identify other ways to change nurses' perceptions and, ultimately, practices. The Cumulative Index to Nursing and Allied Health Literature (CINAHL) currently lists 85 references related to the diffusion of clinical and educational innovations. Some of the techniques and interventions from these studies should be considered in future research aimed at the clinical practice innovation of determining patients' service values. Continued reliance on merely saying this is a new, valuable technique as part of a continuous quality improvement or total quality management program or passively reporting what patients say they want is not enough to effect change. The nurses at the hospitals in this study had such exposure, and yet gaps remain.

Given the unit-level variation observed in the accuracy of nurses' perceptions of how their patients value aspects of care, further study also is needed to identify managerial factors that may improve the accuracy of nurses' perceptions.

Assuming that a team's shared beliefs develop over time, the degree of consistency of nurses who staff a patient care unit may play a role. Another factor may be the degree of consistency of patients. For example, the more frequent rehospitalization seen on a chronic medical unit may foster an organizational culture more reflective of its patients' values, whereas a trauma unit's team has less opportunity to incorporate actual patient feedback into its organizational perceptions. The accuracy of the nurse manager's perceptions of patients' values also is important and can be improved through regular feedback of patient reports of care. Attaching unit-level performance measures and rewards to changes in patient reports of care should offer important reinforcement for transforming the unit culture.

A wide variety of quality improvement programs are occurring in most U.S. hospitals, emphasizing customer satisfaction as a key component and incorporating patient satisfaction into their programs. The gaps between nurses' perceptions and patients' actual values observed in this study are occurring despite various efforts to build patient-centered care into hospitals' quality improvement programs. An "error in definition" may be a cause for unmet patient satisfaction goals. A unit team's inaccurate perceptions are self-reinforcing and may require strategies to reorient the unit organizational culture toward an accurate perception of their patients' importance of various aspects of care.

REFERENCES

1. Gage M. The patient-driven interdisciplinary care plan. *J Nurs Adm* 1994; 24(4):26–35.
2. Pew–Fetzer Task Force on Advancing Psychosocial Health Education. *Health Professions Education and Relationship-Centered Care.* San Francisco. CA: Pew Health Professions Commission; 1994.
3. Tresolini CP, Shugars DA. An integrated health care model in medical education: interviews with faculty and administrators. *Acad Med.* 1994; 69:231–236.
4. Showstack J, Fein O, Ford D. et al. Health of the public mission statement working group: health of the public, the academic response. *JAMA.* 1992; 267:2497–2502.
5. Gerteis M, Edgman-Levitan S, Daley J, Delbanco. TL. *Through the Patient's Eyes: Understanding and Promoting Patient-Centered Care.* San Francisco. CA: Jossey-Bass; 1993.
6. Goldberg MC. A new imperative for listening to patients. *J Nurs Adm.* 1994; 24(9):11–12.
7. Biley F. Nurses' perception of stress in perioperative surgical patients. *J Adv Nurs.* 1989; 14:575–581.

8. Camp LD. A comparison of nurses' recorded assessments of pain with perceptions of pain as described by cancer patients. *Cancer Nurs.* 1988; 11:237–243.

9. Choiniere M, Melzack R, Girard N. et al. Comparisons between patients' and nurses' assessment of pain and medication efficacy in severe burn injuries. *Pain.* 1990; 40:143–152.

10. Hagenhof BD, Feutz C, Conn VS. et al. Patient education needs as reported by congestive heart failure patients and their nurses. *J Adv Nurs.* 1994; 19:685–690.

11. Harrison A. Comparing nurses' and patients' pain evaluations: a study of hospitalized patients in Kuwait. *Soc Sci Med.* 1993; 36:683–692.

12. Kovner CT. Nurse–patient agreement and outcome after surgery. *West J Nurs Res.* 1989; 11:7–19.

13. Lauer P, Murphy SP, Powers MJ. Learning needs of cancer patients: a comparison of nurse and patient perceptions. *Nurs Res* 1982; 31:11–16.

14. Davitz LJ, Pendleton SH. Nurses' inferences of suffering. *Nurs Res.* 1969; 18:100–107.

15. Dunlevy CL, Sagula RE. Long-term ventilation: perceptions of quality care. *Choices Respir Manage.* 1992; 22:19–22.

16. Larson P. Important nurse caring behaviors perceived by patients with cancer. *Oncol Nurs Forum.* 1984; 11:46–50.

17. Larson P. Comparison of cancer patients' and professional nurses' perceptions of importance of nurse caring behaviors. *Heart Lung.* 1987; 16:187–193.

18. Mayer D. Oncology nurses' versus cancer patients' perceptions of nurse caring behaviors: a replication study. *Oncol Nurs Forum.* 1987; 14:48–52.

19. Scharf L, Caley L. Patients', nurses' and physicians' perceptions of nurses' caring behaviors. *Nurs Connections.* 1993; 6:3–12.

20. Suominen T, Leino-Kilpi H, Laippaia P. Nurses' role in informing breast cancer patients: a comparison between patients' and nurses' opinions. *J Adv Nurs.* 1987; 19:6–11.

21. Reiley P, Seibert CP, Miller NE. et al. Implementation of a collaborative quality assessment program. *J Nurs Adm.* 1994; 24(5):65–71.

22. Cleary, PD, McNeil BJ. Patient satisfaction as an indicator of quality care. *Inquiry.* 1988; 25:35–36.

23. Davis SL, Adams-Greenly M. Integrating patient satisfaction with a quality improvement program. *J Nurs Adm.* 1994; 24(12):28–31.

24. Valentine KL. Comprehensive assessment of caring and its relationship to outcome measures. *J Nurs Quality Assurance.* 1991; 2:59–68.

25. Al-Assaf AF, Schmele JA. *The Textbook of Total Quality in Healthcare.* Delray Beach, FL: St. Lucie Press; 1993.

26. Fitzpatrick MJ. Performance improvement through quality improvement teamwork. *J Nurs Adm.* 1994; 24(12):20–27.

27. Nash MG, Blackwood D, Boone EB. et al. Managing expectations between patient and nurse. *J Nurs Adm.* 1994; 24(11):49–55.

28. Ajzen I, Fishbein M. *Understanding Attitudes and Predicting Social Behavior.* Englewood Cliffs, NJ: Prentice—Hall; 1980.

29. Minnick A, Roberts MJ, Young WB, et al. An analysis of posthospitalization telephone survey data. *Nurs Res.* 1995; 44(6):371–375.

30. Coeling HVE, Simms LM. Facilitating innovation at the unit level through cultural assessment: how to keep management ideas from falling on deaf ears. *J Nurs Adm.* 1993; 23(4):46–53.

31. Coeling HVE, Simms LM. Facilitating innovation at the unit level through cultural assessment: part 2. *J Nurs Adm.* 1993; 23(5):13–20.

32. Barg FK, McCorkle R, Robinson K. et al. Gaps and contract: evaluating the diffusion of new information, a description of the strategy (part 1). *Cancer Nurs.* 1992; 15(6):401–405.

33. Robinson K, Barg FK, McCorkle R. et al. Gaps and contract: evaluating the diffusion of new information, the measurement of the strategy (part 2). *Cancer Nurs.* 1992; 15(6):406–414.

CHAPTER 44

Organizational Moles: Information Control and the Acquisition of Power and Status

JOHN G. BRUHN AND ALAN P. CHESNEY

Organizations assemble a variety of persons and personalities to carry out their goals and objectives. Likewise, members of organizations have personal goals and needs that they seek to satisfy, consciously or unconsciously, by being members of an organization. Morowitz[1] has said that each individual in an organization has an ego role to maintain, independent of the functional role for which he/she was hired. As a result, each individual plays a dual role in an organization: a functional role determined by the job description, and an ego role determined by his/her own psychological needs. Each individual occupies a job niche and an ego niche.

Egos are unstable entities. They continually feel threatened by competition and change and need reassurance and support. In an organization of egos, an individual may feel unimportant, threatened, and powerless and, therefore, may look for ways to enhance his/her power and status. It is the authors' assumption that individual ego needs may be so great that individuals spend the majority of their time and energy defending and enhancing their egos. One way of elevating one's ego and job niche in an organization is to be a mole, informant, or inside agent.

The purposes of this article are to explore the ego state and role of a mole and examine the mole's effects on an organization's functioning and effectiveness.

Definition

Webster's defines a mole as "living almost entirely underground, making extensive galleries, and feeding on small life," "one who works in a dark place or in the dark," or "to

---

Reprinted from *Health Care Supervisor*, 14(1), 24–31, with permission of Aspen Publishers, Inc., © 1995.

burrow, to excavate." It is assumed that moles are not knowingly hired as such in organizations; rather, as Morowitz states, "their egos accompany them"[1(p.96)] wherever they go. Tzu[2] discusses the employment of various types of secret agents in time of war. He describes "inside agents" as "those whose sole desire is to take advantage of trouble to extend the scope of their own abilities . . . those who are two-faced, changeable, and deceitful, and who are always sitting on the fence."[2(p.145)] Indeed, one of the attributes of an organizational mole is the ability to span boundaries, that is, to assimilate a wide variety of information, both inside and outside the organization; to be responsive to change; and to have *savoir faire*, that is, the ability to say and do the right thing in any situation.[3] The basic need of the mole is to use information, often negative, to enhance his/her power and status, usually in the eyes of supervisors or the chief executive officer (CEO). Perhaps the most recent famous example of a mole is Deep Throat in the Watergate scandal.

Environments and Leadership Styles Conducive to the Growth and Survival of Moles

All organizations have moles, but organizations differ in the degree to which the environment and leadership facilitates their growth and development and, hence, in the size of their mole colony.

Moles are most likely to flourish in organizations where boundaries within the organization are permeable. This enables information to be obtained easily. In organizations with rigid boundaries, moles have greater difficulty gaining access to information unless collaborators or exceptional rewards encourage them to engage in high-risk-taking activities.

Moles also are likely to flourish in environments where they have direct access to people with power and status who could make decisions about their future in the organization. Thus, organizations that are not highly bureaucratized or do not have extensive layers of reporting are likely to be rewarding for a mole.

Another environment conducive to moles is that of a new organization or one that is undergoing constant change. In such a setting, it often is difficult to check out the reliability of information due to its volume; if the need for information is immediate, information from informants may be accepted without question.

Environment and leadership go hand in hand to make information trading acceptable. In general, organizations whose leaders are paranoid, controlling, distrustful, and insecure are likely to be receptive to information from moles. When leaders are suspicious, their hypersensitivity and hypervigilance make them especially receptive to information about the organization. Usually these distrustful, paranoid leaders pride themselves on being objective, rational, unemotional, and humorless. Information from moles is welcomed, as information is power, especially to leaders who see enemies everywhere.[4] A controlling leader, on the other hand, seeks information to keep employees in check. Moles who report to the CEO about other employees' loyalty, transgression of rules and boundaries, or work habits and productivity see this as a way to ingratiate themselves with their superiors and prove their own loyalty. Insecure leaders continually scan the organization for threats from possible competitors. Usually, these leaders form an inner circle of other administrators who are nonthreatening, often less qualified or incompetent, and who have proven their loyalty and devotion to the CEO. Many if not all of the inner circle are moles who wish to please the CEO. The CEO, in turn, rewards these moles with promotions, salary raises, and public praise.

Differences Between Boundary Spanners, Gatekeepers, and Moles

BOUNDARY SPANNERS

All organizations engage, to some degree, in boundary spanning. In small organizations, many of the employees may be voluntary boundary spanners. It is in large, complex, dynamic organizations that boundary spanning is formalized into a full-time position. One of the purposes of boundary spanning is to buffer the effects of the external environment on the organization by anticipating and planning for change. Boundary spanners act as filters between the external and internal environments of organizations. They bring information from inside the organization to the outside and vice versa to facilitate the linking and coordination between the two interdependent systems. The role of the boundary spanner is to be perceptive, flexible, and able to tolerate a high degree of ambiguity. While boundary spanners might be viewed as "wishy-washy" and their loyalty questioned, their overt job is to gather intelligence and to mediate relations between the organization and the outside world.[3]

GATEKEEPERS

Gatekeeping is a role in which the occupant must interpret the meaning of information in terms of its consequence for the organization and then translate these implications for organizational decision makers so that choices can be made about organizational actions. Gatekeeping has been referred to as uncertainty absorption, whereby inferences are drawn from facts but only the inferences are passed on to others.[3] Gatekeepers who have strong aspirations for upward mobility seem to be reluctant to communicate negative, personally derogatory information to their supervisors. In order to maintain good relations with outside constituencies, the gatekeeper must "protect" sources of information to maintain credibility. Thus, the gatekeeper maintains linkages between information sources to ensure the flow of information and to verify its accuracy. Both are necessary for the gatekeeper to retain creditability and enhance mobility.

MOLES

The work of moles, in contrast to boundary spanning and gatekeeping, is largely covert and entails the reporting of perceptions, personal interpretations of events or behavior, and hearsay. Moles purposefully cross boundaries to obtain information, especially information that is not likely to be known easily by their superiors and that causes them to be put in a favorable light. This information often is about other employees and their difficulties, conflicts, or failures. Moles usually are highly visible in an organization and, if not suspected to be moles, may have the trust of many employees and open access to the information they provide. Indeed, an employee may provide information to a mole knowing that it will reach superiors in the organization. Moles tend to take advantage of change or help create change, such as reorganization, to report to their supervisors or CEOs how effective leaders are and the sources of conflict within a group. In this way, moles tend to be conspirators of change and conflict; indeed, during times of conflict, information from moles is of special value to the leadership of an organization. Tragically, if a mole is trusted by the CEO, administrative actions may be based on the mole's opinions and perceptions. In some organizations, this has cost employees their jobs.[4]

Figure 44-1 shows that moles, while they may have little formal power, have more informal power than the boundary spanner or gatekeeper by virtue of the amount of infor-

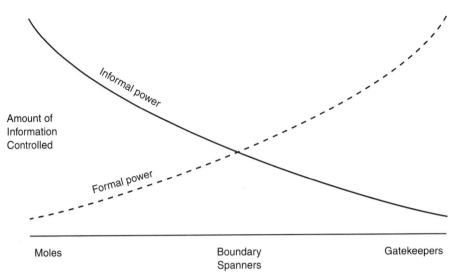

Figure 44–1 Relationship between formal and informal power among moles, boundary spanners, and gatekeepers.

mation to which they have access. The information game is serious to the mole when there are winners and losers. Unfortunately, the victim has no opportunity to correct misinformation. As Berne[5] has said, every game is basically dishonest, having a concealed motivation and payoff. The use of the word "game" implies that the mole knows he/she is playing a game. The mole's gamesmanship often is so much a part of his/her personality that the activities the mole engages in are unconsciously motivated. As Berne[5] observes, many games are played most intensely by disturbed people—the more disturbed, the harder they play. Even those who are fortunate enough to possess the insight and self-control not to be destructive are likely to find themselves the victims of social traps, that is, situations characterized by conflicting rewards. Unfortunately, the adverse consequences of a mole's information may be imposed upon or involve persons other than the intended.[6]

Moles as Organizational Members

Moles should be distinguished from "gossips," who can occupy any position in an organization and have no objective other than the satisfaction they derive from passing information, which is supposed to be confidential, to other people inside the organization. Gossips derive some semblance of status for "being in the know," but unlike moles are not seeking power or access to power.

Moles usually are longstanding employees because their activities have guaranteed them longevity in the organization. Moles usually occupy administrative positions, from middle management to the higher echelons of administration of a firm, corporation, or university. They often are strategically located by the leadership so that they can obtain a broad view of the organization and, if needed, in-depth knowledge about specific parts of the organization. Sometimes, moles occupy more than one type of administrative position as they have sufficient knowledge of the organization to demonstrate their competency to hold interim or acting appointments in addition to their usual job. Moles usually are outgoing, aggressive, affable veterans of an organization who demonstrate trust and, therefore, freely elicit information from employees, often given in confidence.[1] Yet, buried beneath the surface is the mole's need for attention, for reaffirmation of his/her importance, and for strokes from the CEO so that the mole bubbles with information, often providing more details than the CEO needs or wants. The mole feels good about helping the boss and obtains sufficient praise to last until the next meeting.

Moles often are portrayed as loyal employees. They usually have created deep dependency upon the CEO and linked their need for informal power and status to being informants, so that they would find it seriously disruptive to leave the organization. Moles are loyal mostly to themselves; they are dependent upon the organization rather than loyal to it. They are employees with a great deal of freedom and self-doubt, and they demonstrate little desire to grow and develop as persons or professionals. Moles survive best in organizations when there are few, if any, opportunities for the mole's own growth and development. For moles to be promoted would require a substantial change in their values and style. Therefore, turnover among moles in organizations, for reasons other than retirement, is infrequent.

It is noteworthy that moles rarely are the focus of conflict in organizations. They usually refer conflict to the next higher level of administration after making superficial attempts to ameliorate conflict. There is no incentive for moles to resolve conflicts; conflicts provide information that they can use strategically. Moles function best when they can incite conflict strategically, or when conflict is substantial and they can provide information to sustain and, perhaps, broaden it. Moles are experts in purposefully diverting attention away from their own areas of responsibility, since most are poor managers, ineffective leaders, and poor problem solvers.

Schaef and Fassel[7] discuss the phenomenon of triangulation in organizations. If Joe has a problem with Bill, Joe may talk to Mary, who also works with Bill, about the problem. Bill learns indirectly, from Mary, about his difficulty with Joe. Moles flourish in organizations where communication is indirect and problems are scapegoated. Moles also help to create and perpetuate gossip. Gossip helps to avoid direct communication and create suspicion and, in turn, fosters dishonesty, endangers trust, and creates "in" groups. In an organization with a large mole colony, the prohibition against being who you are makes intimacy and good feelings impossible.

Identifying Moles

Organizational moles are most dangerous when they are unrecognized or mistaken for other animals. Therefore, spotting a mole within an organization and recognizing how to behave around a mole are very important skills, both to an individual's survival and to the health of an organization.

SEARCHING FOR A MOLE

Three key variables should be considered in searching for and spotting a mole. First, one should examine the formal and informal relationship between the person in question and the CEO. Second, one should observe the interpersonal habits of a mole. Third, one should compare the words of a mole with its deeds. To examine these facets of mole behavior, the authors suggest asking the questions outlined in Box 44-1. These questions will help assess the probability that you are dealing with a mole. If a person scores between 20 and 30 points, you should assume that you are dealing with a mole. If a person scores between 10 and 20 points, you should be cautious but not suspicious. If a person scores less than 10

BOX 44–1 **MOLE TEST**

1. Does the person claim a special relationship with the CEO? If the answer is yes, give the prospective mole 4 points.
2. Does the person choose whichever side is likely to gain approval of the CEO? If the answer is yes, give the prospective mole 3 points.
3. Does the person speak for the CEO or interpret the CEO's words or actions without having the formal authority to do so? If yes, 3 points
4. Does the person more frequently provide opinion than information or data? If yes, 3 points.
5. Does the person present negative perceptions of other people in the organization to you? If yes, 4 points.
6. Can you trace rumors, particularly negative ones, back to this person? If yes, 3 points.
7. Does the person frequently raise issues that might embarrass another person, or work unit, in a staff meeting with the CEO? If yes, 2 points.
8. Does the person tell you one story and a completely different story on the same subject to the CEO? If yes, 2 points. This person may be a snake and not a mole.
9. Does the person talk about one method of handling a situation but do something that is the opposite? If yes, 3 points.
10. Does the person talk about the good of the organization when he/she is attempting to enhance his/her own position. If yes, 3 points.

---

points, there is little reason for concern. Since mole behavior is not always consistent or observable, it is wise to review periodically the criteria for identifying a mole.

AFTER FINDING A MOLE

When you spot a mole in an organization, it is important to follow four simple rules. First, avoid the temptation to use moles to communicate with the CEO. Since you have no control over what will be communicated, it is very dangerous to become involved in this indirect way of interaction. Second, never get into an argument or fight with a mole. You can only lose. Moles will attempt to pull you into the underground labyrinth where they have the advantage. Third, an effective form of communication with moles is the use of paradox. Paradox is defined by *Webster's* as "a self contradictory statement that at first seems true." The advantage of paradoxical statements is that they confuse the mole and cause it to doubt the information it is receiving. Fourth, and most important for long-term survival, if you want to kill (confront) a mole, you must be a hawk. You must watch from a distance, wait until the mole is away from its holes (sources of support), and then strike (confront) quickly. Confronting a mole about what has been said about you, for example, will not change its behavior and is likely to elicit a response of denial and anger. Moles tend to survive in all types of organizations and under all types of leaders. They are highly adaptable survivors because they are loyal first to themselves.

Frequent, open, direct, honest communication is an attribute of a healthy organization.[8] Yet leaders all have unique psychodynamics and needs related to a deep desire for success. Information is necessary in order to anticipate and plan in an organization as well as to prevent and resolve conflict. Information also can be used in unhealthy ways; by manipulating and changing people and situations, insecure leaders can minimize the perceived threat of competition from others in the organization. Therefore, not all information conveyed in an organization benefits the organization's mission.

Moles can destroy morale, inhibit productiveness, and incite conflict, consciously or unconsciously, to meet their own needs for power or status, which they do not believe they can achieve by ordinary means. Therefore, they become experts in playing games with information, setting social traps that put other employees and colleagues on the defensive. When people spend a great deal of time and effort protecting themselves, it affects their productiveness and morale, and it diminishes their loyalty to the organization.

It is important that organizational leaders create a healthy work environment that will discourage mole behavior. Moles are not able to satisfy their needs in a healthy organization. They have to burrow out, change their diet, or live above ground.

REFERENCES

1. Morowitz, H.J. *Ego Niches: An Ecological View of Organizational Behavior.* Woodbridge, Conn.: Ox Bow Press, 1977.
2. Tzu, S. *The Art of War.* New York, N.Y.: Oxford University Press, 1963.
3. Miles, R.H. *Macro Organizational Behavior.* Santa Monica, Calif.: Goodyear, 1980.
4. Kets de Vries, M.F.R. *Prisoners of Leadership.* New York., N.Y.: Wiley, 1989.
5. Berne, E. *Games People Play.* New York, N.Y.: Grove Press, 1964.
6. Cross, J.G. and M.J. Guyer. *Social Traps.* Ann Arbor, Mich.: University of Michigan Press, 1980.
7. Schaef, A.W., and D. Fassel. *The Addictive Organization.* New York. N.Y.: Harper & Row, 1988.
8. Bruhn, J.G., and A.P. Chesney. "Diagnosing the Health of Organizations." *Health Care Supervisor* 13, no. 2(1994):21–33.

● ●

CHAPTER 45

The Proactive Management of Rumor and Gossip

VIOLETA E. RIBEIRO AND JUDITH A. BLAKELEY

Gossip and rumor prevail in most, if not all, human organizations. Always endemic, these forms of communication tend to increase dramatically during periods of organizational upheaval, uncertainty, and stress. Sometimes beneficial, gossip and rumor also can have negative repercussions in the workplace. They may generate anxiety, foster hostility, create divisiveness, disrupt productivity, and cause serious damage to the reputation of individuals or the organization as a whole.

For these reasons, nursing managers need to understand the dynamics of gossip and rumor, capitalize on their beneficial aspects, and prevent or contain their negative consequences. This applies particularly to managers who currently are working in the uneasy climate of organizations that are facing the prospect of major healthcare reform or suffering from the effects of severe economic austerity.

Analysis of Gossip and Rumor

Both gossip and rumor are unofficial and informal forms of communication. They differ, however, in terms of their content and extent of dissemination. Gossip usually is kept within the boundaries of a small social group.[1] Its content is either factual or fabricated and tends to deal with social events of interest to the gossipers or the private lives of individuals with whom they are acquainted. In the latter case, gossip often is evaluative[2] and judgmental. Rumor, on the other hand, is widespread, well beyond the boundaries of the small, intimate group. It typically conveys unauthenticated information[3-7] and is concerned with impersonal matters, such as those pertaining to public figures and to large social groups or organizations.[1,3]

FUNCTIONS

As a result of their investigations, social scientists and other observers have found that gossip performs functions for both the individual gossiper (personal functions) and for the group to which they belong (sociocultural functions). The personal functions most frequently reported include:

1. The **information function**[8]—the use of gossip as a means of conveying news, often of a personal nature about common acquaintances

2. The **influence function**[8]—the use of denigrating gossip for self-interest,[9] to gain status, social approval, revenge,[10] or for self-aggrandizement[11] and political gain[12]

3. The **self-evaluative function**[13]—the use of gossip to appraise one's own behavior against prevailing social standards, and

4. The **entertainment function**[8,11,14]—the use of gossip merely as a pleasurable pastime

To these one might add the **cathartic function,** which refers to the use of gossip as a vehicle for emotional ventilation.

Still another personal function of gossip was proposed by Chinn[15] in a recent nursing article. Writing from a feminist perspective, she argued that, when guided by ethical principles, gossip can be viewed as a transformative art. It provides women an opportunity to share ideas and feelings and, thereby, gain new insights into the meaning of their experiences.

Several sociocultural functions also have been reported in the literature: notably, the use of gossip to define group membership and enhance group cohesiveness;[16–18] maintain social control;[16] manage internal competition for prestige, status, and reputation;[17] reinforce and transmit group values and norms;[8,18] and sanction deviance from group norms.[17,19]

These functions result from four major categories of gossip which, for the purposes of this article, will be labeled as follows: news-sharing gossip; critical/judgmental gossip; cathartic gossip; and malicious gossip.

Although more widespread and somewhat different in content, rumors serve very similar functions. First, they relieve emotional distress, anxiety, and hostility in particular. They provide a way for people to ventilate their fears and anger and, simultaneously, defend their emotions.[1,6,20,21] Rumors also are used to reduce ambiguity and uncertainty. Rumormongers create and spread stories that help them make sense of ambiguous situations or those shrouded in secrecy.[1,6,20,21] The third major function of rumor is to denounce other persons or to discredit other groups and organizations.[22,23] Rumors serving these purposes tend to emerge in highly competitive situations and are designed to defame the opponent and thereby bring prestige or political and economic power to the rumormonger(s).

These functions are served by four main types of rumor, which were identified by Knapl:[22]

1. **Wish rumors,** which reflect the hopes and wants of the persons initiating and spreading the rumor

2. **Fear** or **bogy rumors,** usually grim stories that arise from and perpetuate anxiety among those who hear and circulate the rumor

3. **Wedge-driving** or **aggressive rumors,** which are negative, malicious tales, and

4. **Home stretchers** or **anticipatory rumors,** which emerge just before the occurrence of a momentous event that has been anticipated for a long time, but about which there has been no official announcement

Consequences of Gossip and Rumor in the Workplace

Often referred to as the grapevine network, gossip and rumor benefit organizations in several different ways. Mishra noted that the grapevine allows for the flexible and rapid transmission of information throughout an organization. Because formal lines of communication are not followed, the information is not screened or controlled and, therefore, can travel faster.[23]

It has also been observed that grapevine information usually contains at least some degree of truth.[23-25] As such, it can tell the manager about trends within the organization, prevailing views on current issues, or about the general anxieties, morale, and productivity of employees. Conversely, the grapevine channel can be used by managers to relay information that needs to be disseminated rapidly. For example, news of a disciplinary action that is taken with one worker can be disseminated quickly through the grapevine, thus encouraging prompt compliance from other employees.

As previously noted, both gossip and rumor can serve as mechanisms to relieve stress, anxiety, or anger.[1,6,20,21] Thus, cathartic gossip, for instance, may contribute to harmonious work relationships by giving workers the opportunity to dispel their anger within the confines of the small gossiping group. In this way, hostilities may be diffused or eliminated. Through gossip and rumor, employees also can discuss and elaborate on situations or events that are ambiguous to them, thereby filling the gaps in their knowledge and allowing them to make more sense of an issue. Suspense around events of concern can be reduced in this manner, removing or alleviating a source of stress in the workplace.[23]

The use of gossip to share "tidbits" of information about social events of common interest or milestones in the personal and professional lives of joint acquaintances also has positive consequences. First, it is a form of entertainment. For example, it provides employees with a temporary distraction from work-related pressures and concerns during the brief gossiping sessions that so often occur during meal or coffee breaks. In addition, this type of gossiping encourages the employees to bond by developing or reinforcing common interests and comradeship.

Work-related wishes and hopes of employees, transmitted as wish rumors, are also beneficial. They often reveal a desire for change. The information conveyed through these rumors can be used by managers to stimulate creative problem solving. Positive wish rumors, especially when confirmed by management, can boost morale, build teamwork, and motivate employees.[25]

Organizational rumor and gossip also can contribute to the socialization process of neophyte or newly employed nurses. As noted elsewhere,[26] gossip can help the novice to internalize the values and norms of the group and the organization as well as the technology, language, and culture of the profession. Messages conveyed via the grapevine may tell new employees a great deal about the organization's values, practices, and role expectations. However, although this socialization function usually is viewed as a positive aspect of the grapevine, it also can be problematic for the innovative manager who is trying to change undesired practices and values that are simultaneously being reinforced by grapevine activity. Moreover, grapevine communications may socialize novices and new employees in a manner that is contrary to the excellence in nursing to which they aspire and which the manager wants to promote.

Finally, despite their negative connotation, even the critical and judgmental forms of gossip or rumor can have positive consequences. They may serve to punish deviant behavior and enforce compliance to the organization's norms. For example, a new employee may become the target of much critical gossip if her/his use of language is considered offensive in the cultural milieu of the work setting. When these criticisms come to her/his attention, they may be sufficient to bring about a desired change in behavior. More serious and potentially harmful behaviors also have been controlled in this manner.

Negative consequences of rumor and gossip also are described in the literature, often receiving more attention than the positive aspects. One such consequence, reported by Mishra,[23] is the general uneasiness, low morale, and productivity among employees that can result from bogy rumors. Examples of this problem can be readily observed during contract negotiations with unionized employees. At such times, bogy rumors tend to proliferate. For instance, tales may start to circulate about the administration's intent to eliminate the employees' pension plans, reduce benefits, or increase the educational or other requirements for employment and promotion. As well as creating a generalized anxiety, these rumors tend to exacerbate the employees' adversarial stance against the administration.

Another negative aspect of grapevine activity was discussed by Davidhizar and Bowen.[27] They suggested that rumors, being part-truths, convey misinformation. Confronted with rumors, employees have difficulty distinguishing fact from fiction, and as a result, their anxiety levels increase. Rumors also may "engender harmful confusion in times of emergency, or undermine the operation of valuable institutions."[4(p88)]

Wedge-driver rumors and malicious, denigrating gossip are particularly harmful. Analysts have noted that these rumors divide groups, disrupt group harmonies, and destroy loyalties; wedge-drivers are motivated by aggression, hatred, or conspiracy and are designed to demean and demoralize individuals or organizations and damage their reputations.[23,25,27] Personal observations suggest that, among nurses, this type of gossip and rumor often comes under the guise of professional diagnoses and expressions of concern. For instance, if one or more employees want to discredit the leader, they may start to circulate false stories that depict the leader as suffering from one or more psychiatric illnesses. Psychopathic or other personality disorders are favorite diagnostic labels used for this purpose. These labels are particularly harmful because they cast serious doubt, not only on the leader's mental functioning, but also on her/his capacity for ethical conduct.

In brief, there are different types of gossip and rumor that perform functions for individuals and organizations as a whole. Gossiping and rumormongering in the workplace, usually referred to as the grapevine, may be either beneficial or harmful and destructive. Whether the consequences are positive or negative depends on the intent and content of the original message and also on the way it is conveyed through the grapevine.

The Grapevine Process

Like other communication processes, gossiping or rumormongering starts when a person (**the initiator**) first conveys information to another individual or group (**the initial receiver[s]**). Even at this level, some distortion in the information may occur because the initial receiver(s) may perceive or interpret the message differently from what actually was conveyed or intended. Subsequently, the initial receivers proceed in one of two ways: they either keep the information to themselves, thereby blocking the rumor or gossip (**the blockers**), or they pass it on to others (**primary transmitters**), thereby widening the circulation of the tale.

During the transmission process, several things can occur. First, the transmitter may support the message as originally heard, or read, and pass it on without elaboration or distortion. More frequently, the transmitter elaborates on the original story but still conveys its original intent. In other instances, the transmitter distorts the message either deliberately or otherwise. Unintentional distortion can occur if the transmitter has an unconscious habit of hyperbolizing or embellishing stories. Finally, there are other occasions when the transmitter disagrees with the gossip or rumor received and attempts to negate it by starting a contradictory story. This same process may then be repeated, leading to an increasingly wider circulation and distortion of the message.

Knowledge about how the grapevine works in a particular situation may prove helpful to managers in their efforts to make effective use of gossip and rumor and to control their nefarious aspects. Information about the identity of key players in the grapevine may be equally useful. This raises questions regarding who these players are, what their characteristics are, and what other factors are associated with grapevine activity.

Factors Associated With Gossip and Rumor

Studies of gossiping and rumormongering clearly suggest that these processes are universal ones. They involve men and women,[14,28] children, adolescents, and adults,[2,29,30] and people of different sociocultural and organizational groups. There are, however, certain situational and personality factors that are associated with a greater likelihood of grapevine activity.

As noted earlier, gossiping and rumormongering tend to intensify in the absence of official news[23] and in anxiety-producing, ambiguous, or highly competitive environments. It also has been reported that, irrespective of the situation, certain people are more likely to start and transmit rumors. This includes people who are highly anxious[3,5,6,21,24] or those who are more sensitive to ambiguity and have greater trust in the veracity of the story being circulated.[5] To these personality factors one can add power hunger. The authors frequently have observed that people who covet a position of power but lack the prerequisites for the job tend to resort to wedge-driver rumors to discredit the incumbent or the qualified applicants for the position.

Having and being able to spread significant or titillating information that is not commonly known is a form of power. Hence, people with frustrated power needs often are avid in their search for confidential information, preferably of general import, that they can use to barter for still further confidences or to gain prestige and a sense of control. An example of this phenomenon is the assistant manager whose ambitions for further promotion are frustrated by her/his lack of the required qualification. Such an individual may spend much time and effort cultivating trusting relationships with other people in the organization who have access to confidential information. Through such efforts she/he obtains privileged information and uses it for personal gain.

Little is known about the variables that are associated with rumor and gossip quelling or nonparticipation in grapevine activities. Personal observations, however, suggest that the people who usually avoid or block gossip and rumor tend to have one or more of the following characteristics:

1. They are more interested in discussing general events and ideas instead of gossiping about the personal lives of other people.
2. They tend to be self-evaluative and self-confident.
3. They believe that gossiping and rumormongering are morally reprehensible, or
4. They are isolates and do not belong to the gossiping cliques either by choice or because they are not considered trustworthy. This last characteristic also was suggested by Mishra.[23]

Further research is needed to lend support to these findings and to explore other variables that may contribute to, mitigate against, or quell gossiping and rumormongering. The model presented in Figure 45-1 integrates elements of the discussion presented so far and provides a few examples of hypothetical relationships (marked [H]) that may be explored in future research or tested in managerial practice.

Managing Rumor and Gossip

There are several approaches aimed at preventing, controlling, or counteracting negative rumor and gossip in the workplace. These have been proposed primarily in the management literature and include general, preventive, and counteractive strategies.

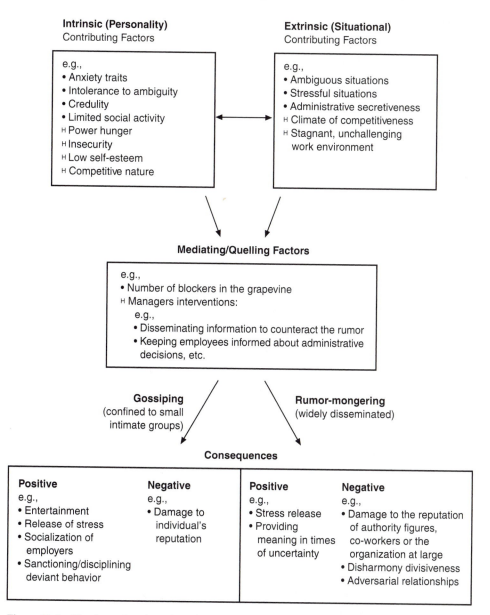

Figure 45–1 The dynamics of gossip and rumor: A conceptual model.

GENERAL STRATEGIES

There are three general approaches that are recommended for managers:

1. Assess and analyze the grapevine process as it is occurring in their particular settings.
2. Identify the habitual gossipers and rumormongers; and
3. Keep employees well informed of all happenings related to the workplace

PREVENTIVE STRATEGIES

Several more specific preventive strategies also are suggested in the literature. First, rumors that arise from uncertainty may be prevented through the quick and timely release of accurate information about key issues and events via an organization's formal communication network.[23,24,31] For example, employees can be kept abreast of new events in a labor dispute as they happen. Management should present the facts promptly, clearly, and honestly, using the most direct communication channels (eg, posting updated information on staff bulletin boards) or by providing employees with a direct line to a credible source within the organization (eg, a trusted middle manager). Personal observations have revealed, however, that this strategy does not work well if employees distrust management or when they have a vested interest in maintaining a spirit of animosity against the administration. Conveying important information via a neutral third party may be one way of circumventing this problem.

A second preventive strategy relates to the "tapping," by managers, of an organization's grapevine to learn about employees' concerns and anxieties. Managers can do this by having an open-door policy and by actively paying attention to the employee gossip and rumors that they hear. They can join their employees during lunch and coffee breaks or have their middle managers do so. Other methods include paying heed to what employees tell their trusted supervisors and senior managers. Managers also can encourage employees to submit, anonymously, their comments and feedback on current workplace issues.

Formal actions can then be taken to address the issues and concerns before rumors have a chance to develop and spread. Informally, managers can use the grapevine to transmit back to employees information related to these concerns. This last strategy should be used with caution because, as noted in the discussion of the grapevine process, information conveyed this way often becomes distorted.

The single most important preventive measure is to keep employees well-informed on a regular basis about key events and significant happenings within the organization that directly affect them. The dissemination of factual information helps to reduce employees' anxieties and uncertainties, making it less likely for rumors to be generated and spread. Management can use direct memos, large group announcements, intercommunication systems, company newsletters, and bulletin boards to share important information.[23,24]

Training programs for employees on the nature of rumor and gossip also have been recommended as a preventive strategy for organizations.[23,24] Such programs could include content and discussion on:

1. What rumor and gossip are
2. Why and how these phenomena arise, spread, and persist
3. What are their harmful effects on people and organizations
4. How employees can prevent the generation of rumor and gossip
5. How employees can block their spread
6. How employees can quell rumor and gossip once they have been disseminated.

Evaluation of such programs has not been attempted and remains a challenge for future researchers.

A final preventive strategy, identified by the authors, requires managers to meet with habitual gossipers and rumormongers individually in an effort to alleviate their anxieties and insecurities or to discuss constructive measures they might use to fulfill their needs for power and prestige. Knowledge of the personality characteristics that predispose individuals to gossip or to spread rumors may help managers identify such employees.

COUNTERACTIVE STRATEGIES

There are several strategies that can be used to control existing rumors and gossip. Once rumors have begun, managers need to act promptly by immediately communicating factual information to neutralize the rumors. As in preventive strategies, both formal and informal channels can be used.[23,24,32] When counteracted early, rumors are less likely to become solidified in the minds of employees and false information is easier to correct. Moreover, employees are less likely to spread rumors they believe to be untrue.[33]

The results of a study by Iyer and Debevec[34] may be of some relevance here. These researchers suggest that the decision to refute a rumor may depend on its origin. They found that when the initiator of the rumor is perceived by the receiver to be a negative stakeholder, or a person with a negative interest in the issue, no refutation of the rumor might be the best strategy for managers; when the originator is viewed by the receiver to be a positive stakeholder, an active, vigorous refutation may work best to quell the rumor. For example, during labor negotiations concerning possible salary reductions, a nurse is more likely to believe a rumor about a pay cut that originates from a nursing colleague than one from a friend who is not associated with the work setting. It is difficult for a manager to always know where a rumor originates; however, in this case, if the initiator can be determined, the manager is advised to refute the rumor from the nursing source and ignore it if it arose from the friend.

A more formal refutation of a rumor may be warranted in some instances as, for example, in the case of "wedge-driver" rumors. The literature recommends a three-phase approach be implemented.[23,25] In the first phase, information is gathered regarding the content and extent of the rumor and possible sources of employees' anxiety and uncertainty. After this phase, management prepares a formal response to counteract the rumor and devises a plan whereby the correct information will be quickly disseminated. The third phase involves the actual implementation of the plan. According to Esposito and Rosnow,[25] the nature and scope of the information dissemination plan depends on the severity of the rumor and the extent to which it has been disseminated. For in-house rumors, management can call a meeting of all employees, present them with the facts, encourage questions, and answer all questions honestly and directly. The same information may be reiterated in a written memorandum or through electronic mail to all employees. When these approaches fail or when the rumor has spread to the public arena, other strategies need to be considered. These include public relations campaigns, media campaigns, and the publishing of research findings in reputable journals to enhance the credibility of the organization and its work.

There are occasions when all attempts to control or contradict malicious rumor and gossip fail and damage is done to the reputation of an individual or an organization. In such instances, the person or organization may take legal action against the instigator of the rumor or gossip. It has been observed that nurses tend not to follow this route, possibly because of the emotional nature of the issue, the anticipated expense of legal counsel, and the difficulty in identifying those at fault and in proving the charges. The latter is especially so if precedents have not been established. Hopefully, in the future, more nurse managers will take legal action against those who have defamed them or their organizations. If their case is argued successfully, they will feel vindicated and precedents will be set that may provide a deterrent against other malicious gossipers and rumormongers.

Conclusion

Learning and writing about grapevine management strategies is relatively easy; implementing them successfully is the challenge. Little is known about the factors that influence the success or failure of our efforts to prevent or control the "bad" rumors and gossip.

Hence, there is a need for further discussion and research about the actual implementation of these strategies by nursing and other managers.

REFERENCES

1. Rosnow RL. Rumor as communication: a contextual approach. *J Commun.* 1988; 38(1):12–28.
2. Eder D. Enke JL. The structure of gossip: opportunities and constraints on collective expression among adolescents. *Am Soc Ret.* 1991; 56(4):494–508.
3. Ambrosini PJ. Clinical assessment of group and defensive aspects of rumor. *Int J Group Psychother.* 1983; 33(1):69–83.
4. Libel and the reporting of rumor. *Yale Law J.* 1982; 92(1):85–105 (Notes).
5. Rosnow RL, Esposito JL, Gibney L. Factors influencing rumor spreading: replication and extension. *Lang Commun.* 1988; 8(1):29–42.
6. Walker CJ, Beckerle CA. The effects of state anxiety on rumor transmission. *J Social Behav Pers.* 1987; 2(3):353–360.
7. Walker CJ, Blaine B. The virulence of dread rumors: a field experiment. *Lang Commun.* 1991; 11(4):291–297.
8. Fine GA, Rosnow RL. Gossip, gossipers, gossiping. *Personal Soc Psychol Bull.* 1978; 4(1):161–168.
9. Paine R. What is gossip about: an alternate hypothesis. *Man.* 1967; 2(2):278–285.
10. Crawshaw R. Cited by: Fine GA. Rosnow RL. Gossip, gossipers, gossiping. *Personal Soc Psychol Bull.* 1978; 4(1):161–168.
11. Olinick SL. The gossiping analyst. *Int Ret Psychoanal.* 1980; 79(3):439–445.
12. Cox BA. What is Hopi gossip about: information management and Hopi factions. *Man.* 1970; 4(1):88–98.
13. Suls JM. Gossip as social comparison. *J Commun* 1977; 27(1):164–168.
14. Spacks PM. In praise of gossip. *Hudson Rev.* 1982; 35(1):19–38.
15. Chinn PL. Gossip: a transformative art for nursing education. *J Nurs Educ.* 1990; 29(7):318–321.
16. Bergmann J. *Klatsch: Zur Sozial Form der Diskreten Indiskretion. (Gossip About the Social Form of Discrete Indiscretion).* Berlin: de Gruyter; 1987. (Book Review by M. Rost: 1989).
17. Almirol EB. Chasing the elusive butterfly: gossip and the pursuit of reputation. *Ethnicity.* 1981; 8(3):293–304.
18. Gluckman M. Gossip and scandal. *Curr Anthropol.* 1963; 4(2):307–315.
19. Herskovits M. Cited by: Paine R. What is gossip about? An alternate hypothesis. *Man.* 1967; 2(2):278–285.
20. Allport GW, Postman L. *The Psychology of Rumor.* New York: Russell & Russell Inc; 1947.
21. Anthony S. Anxiety and rumor. *J Soc Psychol.* 1973; 89(1):91–98.
22. Knapp RH. A psychology of rumor. *Public Opin Q.* 1944; 8(1):22–27.
23. Mishra J. Managing the grapevine. *Public Pers Manage.* 1990; 19(2):213–228.
24. Esposito JL, Rosnow RL. Corporate rumours: how they start and how to stop them. *Manage Rev.* 1993; 72(7):44–49.
25. Simmons DB. The nature of the organizational grapevine. *Supervisory Manage.* 1985; 30(11):39–42.
26. Laing M. Gossip: Does it play a role in the socialization of nurses? *Image: J Nurs Scholarship.* 1993; 25(1):37–43.
27. Davidhizar R, Bowen M. The manager and rumors: telling fact from fiction. *Today's O.R. Nurse.* 1992; 14(2):44–46.
28. Levin J, Arluken A. An exploratory analysis of sex differences in gossip. *Sex Roles.* 1985; 12(3/4):281–286.
29. Gottman J, Mattetal G. Speculations about social and affective development: friendship and acquaintanceship through adolescence. In: *Conversations of Friends: Speculations on Affective Development.* New York: Cambridge University Press; 1986:192–237.
30. Fine GA. Social components of children's gossip. *J Commun.* 1977; 27(1):181–185.
31. D'O'Brian J. Coping with a rumor mill. *Supervisory Manage.* 1993; 38(6):6.
32. Levy R. Tilting at the rumor mill. *Dun's Rev.* 1981; 118(1):52–54.
33. Rosnow RL, Yost JH, Esposito JL. Belief in rumor and likelihood of rumor transmission. *Lang Commun.* 1986; 6(3):189–194.
34. Iyer ES, Debevec K. Origin of rumor and tone of message in rumor quelling strategies. *Psychol Mark.* 1991; 8(3):161–175.

CHAPTER 46

• •

Management by Intimidation: "Cooling Out" Perceived Competitors

JOHN G. BRUHN

The work climate of an organization is established by its leader's management style. Employees take their cues about what is expected from what the leader says and does. A leader's personality and personal needs drive his/her management style and help shape the culture of the organization. An organization remains more or less healthy depending on the leader's style.[1] All managerial styles in their exaggerated forms create victims.[2] One of the exaggerated forms discussed here is management by intimidation.

Intimidation and Its Forms

Webster defines "intimidation" as to make timid or fearful, to compel or deter by, or as if by, threats. Intimidation can be overt or covert. For example, a leader may embarrass or humiliate an employee in front of fellow workers, which immediately conveys the leader's displeasure with the employee's performance. Employees usually distance themselves from employees who are not in favor with the boss. Intimidation may also be covert, subtle, and expressed by a leader to an employee in a private meeting. The leader may point out the employee's inadequacies; for instance, the employee does not write well, the employee is not aggressive enough, or the employee does not pay enough attention to details. While these comments would not ordinarily be intimidating, they become so when no constructive feedback is offered about anything the employee has done. Intimidation differs from a performance evaluation if a cryptic memo, detailing criticisms, is sent to the employee with a warning following a meeting with the boss. It is natural for the employee to think that the boss is beginning to assemble "a file" for eventual dismissal. Intimidation is not always direct. Leaders may make comments to an employee's peers, knowing that they will get back to the employee. Comments about one's inadequacies made by the boss to one's peers can be especially intimidating, and this method of management further compromises the employee's working relationships with peers. Leaders who enjoy intimi-

Reprinted from *Health Care Supervisor*, 14(4), pp. 29–34, 1996, with permission of Aspen Publishers, Inc., © 1996.

dation usually have well-developed information networks or loyal informants (moles) in all parts of the organization who keep them apprised of the behavior of employees.[3] They use this information to "keep on top of" employees.

Leaders intimidate those close to them, when the opportunity presents itself, as these people are their most likely competitors. Those who work closest to the leader are likely to want to please the leader, often—mistakenly—expecting to be rewarded. Intimidators give few rewards; those given are carefully calculated to return additional power and status to the leader. The rewards are never power and authority, but usually consist of more responsibility and additional titles. The recipient usually is pleased to receive any type of recognition and reward. All leaders, at some time, knowingly or unknowingly practice some form of intimidation. Sometimes, in fact, "the presence," size, or way of speaking of a leader can be perceived as intimidating. Our concern is a management style that is intended to intimidate and is practiced to remind employees who holds the power in the organization. Intimidation discourages dissent, openness, innovation, change, and risk taking. It fosters a work climate of "covering oneself," carefulness, guardedness, and fear, in which doing only what is known to be accepted by the leader and obedience to the leader are the only ways to earn rewards.

The Intimidator

Box 46-1 outlines a few characteristics of intimidating leaders. Wagner[4] suggests other behaviors that could be considered "bully" behaviors. Leaders generally are not seen as insecure; while they present themselves as self-assured and assertive, leaders who manage by intimidation are insecure. They feel powerful and in control when others are "put down," and they enjoy being around people who are not threats, people who will kowtow to a leader's wishes with minimal discussion.

BOX 46–1 SOME CHARACTERISTICS OF INTIMIDATING LEADERS AND MANAGERS

- Criticize an employee in front of his/her peers in meetings when he/she is not present (indirect communication)
- Focus job performance evaluation on personal criticisms with no positive suggestions for correction or acknowledgment of any positive behavior (erodes self-esteem by criticizing the person)
- Telling an employee the good work of other employees (creates feelings of guilt or inadequacy)
- Create feeling that employees are not doing enough or working hard enough: the leader may publicly say "Why do I have to do everything around here?" (creates distance between leader and employees and sense that the leader is perfect)
- Hand picking an employee to do a job another has failed to do and publicly praising the chosen employee's work (creates evidence of an "inner circle")
- Staff kept waiting for long periods for leader to appear to chair a meeting (conveys message that leader's time is more important than anyone else's in the organization)
- Spontaneity and humor discouraged among staff: opinions solicited but those who disagree with leader are remembered (retribution for those who are not team players)
- Fosters climate of co-dependency among staff (staff tries to understand what pleases and displeases the leader)

Periodic intimidation keeps employees subservient. The underlying message conveyed by the intimidating leader is "Don't challenge me or your job may be at stake." Intimidating leaders usually, directly or indirectly, see to it that no one occupies a position of responsibility and authority in the organization long enough to generate a following and establish a competing power base. Competent employees are "cooled out" in subtle ways, that is, they are not given salary raises or promotions despite their productivity and hard work, and fault is found to discredit the good that they have done. The intimidating leader would not make an effort, for example, to retain an employee who had a competing offer from another organization and might comment openly, "It's time for her to go; she's been here long enough." This may even be said of loyal, hard-working employees who have given 25 years of service to the organization.

A chief executive officer (CEO) of a large corporation had the reputation of changing vice presidents and division chiefs every three to four years. Those executives who "went quietly" without filing a grievance or criticizing the leader were usually given positive recommendations when inquiries were made of the CEO about the executive's job application elsewhere. On the other hand, "dead bodies" in the corporation attested to the fact that not all executives "went quietly." Those who had to be fired, or who criticized the CEO publicly, received negative recommendations when the CEO was called for a reference. Their careers reached a dead end in the corporation, a signal to others of the vindictiveness and power of the CEO.

The intimidator is a controlling person and often a perfectionist. As Kets de Vries explains, "These people insist that others submit to their way of doing things. Excessively judgmental and moralistic, both toward self and others, they lack awareness of the feelings elicited by their behavior."[5(p75)] A preoccupation with control can be seen, according to Kets de Vries, as the intimidator's way of managing hostile feelings toward the ones who have been controlling them. Parental overcontrol usually is to blame for such behavior. Leaders who use intimidation to lead and manage an organization are making others pay for the overcontrol they have experienced in their lives. It is not uncommon to find organizations that resemble prisons being led and managed by intimidators. Intimidators practice a form of human abuse, and often get away with it because their public behavior is that of strong, aggressive, positive persons. Outsiders do not know what goes on inside an organization.

Intimidation can start, consciously, as a game to see how people will react and cope. It is likely, however, to develop into an unconscious behavior pattern, which the leader, if confronted, would deny. Intimidation is not a game when the consequences for the intimidated do not matter.

Intimidators tend to select close associates who also use intimidation as a management style. As a result, employees avoid contact with managers and managers avoid contact with each other. A fragmented leadership pattern in the organization is the result. Fragmented contact and communication are forms of intimidation and help to perpetuate a noncohesive, distrustful, and suspicious executive staff who overtly compete to stay in favor with the leader.

The Victims

Intimidation always results in victimization. Those who are intimidated become stigmatized. Over time, intimidation results in the victims' loss of self-confidence and belief in their own competence. It also results in the loss of face. A victim of intimidation is a person who has failed. This is exactly what the intimidator intends to accomplish in retaining control, power, and status. Victims must adapt themselves to the loss of sources of security and status that they had taken for granted. Victims have four choices:

1. Remain and become docile servants to the intimidator.
2. Remain and become quietly subversive of the leader.
3. Leave the organization; or
4. Wait until the leader decides to "cool them out" of the organization.

While victims may not have done anything wrong and may have performed their jobs satisfactorily, they are perceived as competitors by the leader, who is determined to discredit them.[5] Being "cooled out" is role death. Goffman states,

> This leads one to consider the ways in which we can go or be sent to our death . . . firing and laying-off, resigning and being asked to resign, deportation, excommunication, defeat, being dropped from a circle, corporate dissolution, and forced retirement.[6(p463)]

Effects on the Organization

Intimidation has pervasive effects on an organization. Employees are careful observers and soon get the message to "lay low and do one's job," not to draw attention to oneself, and to minimize contact with the leader. Any action or inaction can be used to intimidate. Everyone in an organization run by an intimidator eventually is a recipient of intimidation. The organizational climate is one of fear and a need for self-protection. The "dead bodies" in an organization are evidence that the leader has "cooled out" others who have not had job opportunities that permitted them to leave. Indeed, the leader may ensure that people who have been "cooled out" are given negative recommendations, in effect burying their careers. The short-term stigma on the organization is readily overcome: those outside the organization merely comment that the leader is "tough to work for."[7] The long-term effects are more powerful. As the number of victims multiplies, and victims find new employment in other geographic locations, the reputation of the organization and the leader spreads. Word goes out not to join the organization. The turnover of excellent employees increases as they seek to leave before "their turn comes up." An organization run by intimidation is not a happy place. Its employees usually exhibit little humor, low morale and productivity, leadership that is the subject of jokes, and a lack of innovation, creativity, and risk taking. An organization led and managed by an intimidator lacks quality, because its employees lack incentive to do their best. Intimidation is a method of aggrandizing the leader, regardless of who the victim might be.

Coping With Intimidation

Responding to intimidation with defensiveness simply breeds more intimidation. Defensiveness and an "on guard" perspective is precisely the response an intimidator hopes for. Defensiveness merely asserts that the intimidator has the power and the victim is powerless. It is difficult to understand the motivation of the intimidator as it is unlikely that the intimidator will admit to the behavior, yet the intimidator seems pleased when engaged in it. If intimidation is frequent, it is best to leave the organization. It is unhealthy for employees to remain and subject themselves to behavior that will erode their self-esteem. Employees who have been victims of long-term intimidation are sad people who have given up on themselves and resigned themselves to staying in their jobs. Ironically, intimidating leaders and managers are seldom "cooled out" themselves because their bosses fear them and their methods. Intimidating persons create victims at all levels of the organization, including that of their bosses.

Coping with intimidation requires coping with anxiety and stress; the uncertainty of when, where, and how one will be embarrassed; depression; the loss of face; self-esteem; and a threat to one's security. Once intimidated by the leader, one becomes wary and on guard, which affects job performance. Hence, intimidation can create a self-fulfilling prophecy. Miller and Hoppe[8] found that psychological reactions were more pronounced among the fired than the laid off. As termination has become common in today's society, largely due to "downsizing," outplacement services have been instituted in many organizations as a way of managing the disappointment of job termination.[9] Yet, intimidation on the job, which is likely to be more common than terminations, often is a "silent burden" with which employees have to find ways of coping. It is especially sad if an employee who feels intimidated has no job options. While human resources offices can refer employees who seek help to resources of support and counseling outside the organization, it is likely that the majority of employees will find private ways to cope. Sometimes, these methods of coping are unhealthy.[10] Every employee should have the right to be treated with dignity. It is unfortunate that some leaders become filled with their own importance and use intimidation to manage organizations.

Leaders should leave behind assets and a legacy. Leaders and managers who intimidate others leave behind liabilities. This leaves a strong message that organizations need to better know the kinds of persons their leaders will be before they select and give them the responsibility for shaping the lives of others.

Intimidation is an interpersonal cruelty practiced by insecure leaders and managers. Intimidation does not build loyalty or establish cohesion and a team spirit. Indeed, leaders and managers who intimidate those who work with them help to create schisms and anger and hostility among workers and, eventually, drive some employees away. An organization's health depends on its leadership's style. Employees take their cues about what is expected from what their leader says and does. Intimidation is not a good model for others to emulate.

REFERENCES

1. Bruhn, J.G., and Chesney, A.P. "Diagnosing the Health of Organizations." *Health Care Supervisor* 13 (1994):21–33.
2. Bruhn, J.G. "Control, Narcissism, and Management Style." *Health Care Supervisor* 9 (1991):43–52.
3. Bruhn, J.G., and Chesney, A.P. "Organizational Moles: Information Control and the Acquisition of Power and Status." *Health Care Supervisor* 14, no. 1 (1995):24–31.
4. Wagner, P. "When Leaders Become Bullies." *Communities: Journal of Cooperative Living* 80 (1993):61–63.
5. Kets de Vries, M.F.R. *Prisoners of Leadership.* New York., N.Y.: Wiley, 1989.
6. Goffman, E. "On Cooling the Mark Out: Some Aspects of Adaptation to Failure." *Psychiatry* 15 (1952):451–463.
7. Goffman, E. *Stigma: Notes on the Management of Spoiled Identity.* New York. N.Y.: Simon and Schuster, 1986.
8. Miller, M.V., and Hoppe, S.K. "Attributions for Job Termination and Psychological Distress." *Human Relations* 47 (1994):307–327.
9. Miller, M.V., and Robinson, C. "Managing the Disappointment of Job Termination: Outplacement as a Cooling-out Device." *Journal of Applied Science* 30 (1994):5–21.
10. Schaef, A.W., and Fassel, D. *The Addictive Organization.* San Francisco, Cailf.: Harper & Row. 1988.

CHAPTER 47

● ●

Codependency in Nurses:
How It Affects Your Organization

BARBARA WISE AND BEVERLY FERREIRO

Although definitions of codependency vary, most literature on the topic describes a code-pendent as someone either raised in or currently living in a dysfunctional family, whose everyday behaviors and attitudes are affected by the dysfunctional patterns learned in that family. Cermak[1] defines codependence as a personality disorder, with four major parame-ters. These include investment of self-esteem in controlling self and others; meeting other's needs to the exclusion of one's own; difficulty with intimacy and boundaries; and enmesh-ment in relationships with addictive individuals. Other authors describe codependent per-sons as having problems with self-esteem, relationships, problem solving, communication, black-and-white thinking, and boundaries.[2-7]

A number of authors have speculated that the nursing profession is particularly prone to attracting codependent individuals.[2-4] Several nurses have written about the ways in which they believe codependent nurses might behave at work,[5-7] and others have de-scribed ways in which they observe the nursing profession and the healthcare system in-teracting codependently.[4,8-10] Several researchers have studied the effects of codependency on the nursing practice of codependent nurses.[4,11]

Williams, et al,[11] surveyed 67 physicians and 133 nurses to determine how a signifi-cant relationship with a chemically dependent person influenced work behaviors. Sev-enty-five percent believed that their relationship with a chemically dependent person ad-versely affected their work. Common effects included absenteeism, inability to concentrate because of exhaustion, anxiety or arguments, and neglect of professional development ac-tivities, such as continuing education, reading, and participation in professional organiza-tions. The researchers found no significant differences between physicians' responses and nurses' responses in this study. Snow and Willard[4] surveyed 139 nurses who had attended their seminars on codependency and the nursing profession. The authors reported that 93% of the nurses surveyed had value difficulties, 84% had problems with protection and respect of self and others, 76% identified dependency problems, 78% had difficulty with moderation, and 98% indicated perfectionism and control concerns. The questionnaire was not tested for validity or reliability, however, and their statistical analysis did not differen-tiate or describe the degree of difficulty experienced.

The subject of how nurses' practices are influenced by codependency is an important one, and it deserves further study. This study attempts to determine how nurses who identify themselves as codependent believe their practice of nursing has been influenced by their codependency.

Methodology

Because there has been little research in this area, a qualitative descriptive case study methodology was used. Six in-depth interviews were conducted with registered nurses who identified themselves as codependent, were currently employed in nursing, and had at least 2 years of recovery experience. The study sought to answer the question: How do nurses who identify themselves as codependent perceive their codependency to affect their nursing practice?

The nurses ranged in age from 33 to 48 years (mean = 41), and had between 9 and 20 (mean = 15) years of experience in nursing. Education levels ranged from associate degree in nursing to master of science in nursing, and the nurses held various professional positions, including nurse midwife, staff nurse on a psychiatric ward, staff nurse in a critical care unit, community-based psychiatric nurse, critical care clinical nurse specialist, and staff nurse in home health. Three of the six had held management positions at some point in their career. Five of the six nurses had an alcoholic father, and one had a mentally ill mother as the primary dysfunction in their family of origin. In addition, one had been married twice to chemically dependent husbands. Four of the six had been divorced at least once. The nurses had been participating in recovery activities for 2 to 9 years (mean = 4.6).

Data were obtained through taped interviews, which were then transcribed verbatim for analysis. A structured interview guide was developed. The initial question in each interview was, "Tell me what codependency means to you." The second question was, "Tell me about how you believe your codependency has affected and still does affect the way you practice nursing. Include thoughts and feelings as well as actions and relationships." More focused probes included questions about family of origin, questions about how the nurse came to see herself as codependent, and questions that attempted to obtain details about the nurses' experiences in nursing.

The first step in data analysis was analysis of individual cases. This involved a thorough examination of each transcribed interview for content and themes. Coding categories were developed after the first interview had been examined; these were refined after the second and third interviews, then each interview was coded in a standard fashion. The second step in the data analysis was cross-case analysis. For each code, a cross-case analysis was written similar to the individual case analyses, summarizing the data on the code, and comparing and contrasting how the theme emerged in different nurses.

Findings

DEFINITIONS OF CODEPENDENCY

Common elements of the nurses' definitions of codependency included boundary problems, enmeshment, external focus, and caretaking, with caretaking being the dominant descriptor. One nurse saw codependence being centered in a relationship rather than in a person. "It's a dependency where one person is taking care of the other one too much. It's not a shared relationship," she said. The rest of the nurses saw codependency as characteristics that a codependent person exhibits. One participant defined codependence as follows:

> Codependency to me means a process addiction, as opposed to a substance addiction. The process that one is addicted to is focusing externally on other people rather than internally on one's self. That manifests itself . . . by being in relationships with people who require a lot of focus, and ask for a lot of attention, and demand a lot of rescuing.

In this definition, we see focus on the partner rather than on the self and caretaking (rescuing) as primary manifestations of codependence, which are major areas in Cermak's definition as well. Another nurse described codependence like this:

> For me, codependency is a way of relating to the world where you don't understand real clearly the boundaries between you and another person, or you and another object, and it's hard to define where you stop and they begin. And so the sense of what's mine and what I'm really responsible for and need to be in touch with . . . gets blurred. A lot of times you get into somebody else's space, and you feel like you want to take over for them, or be with them or merge. It's kind of like a feeling of wanting to be connected with someone else to the extent that you become not quite two separate people.

In this nurse's definition, we see boundaries, enmeshment, and caretaking described. The other participants' answers were briefer, but followed the same themes.

CODEPENDENCY AS A MANAGEMENT PROBLEM

An important finding was the nurses' descriptions of the ways in which their codependent traits were either worsened or mitigated by the management style of their supervisor and the work culture of the institution. They also described how healthcare administrators exploited codependent characteristics, and acted in codependent manners themselves.

A number of nurses reported that their institutions routinely relied on nurses working overtime to staff units. The nurses' codependent difficulty in saying no was reinforced by administrators playing on their sense of guilt, or, in one case, simply scheduling the nurse to work overtime, without her permission, on a regular basis. Several nurses described working on dangerously understaffed units where nurses were expected to work harder to pick up the slack, with no support or acknowledgment for doing so.

One nurse noted that in the institution in which she worked, hospital administrators rewarded nurses who manipulated to get what they wanted and discouraged open negotiation, which divided nurses and kept them relatively powerless as a group. The administration divided nursing management and staff by putting nurse managers in the position of promising things to staff members, but not being able to deliver on promises. Thus staff did not trust managers and worked to subvert the managers' efforts. Then managers did not trust staff members, and instead of having common cause as coprofessionals, nurse managers and staff nurses expended energy undermining one another's efforts and complaining about one another.

Several nurses expressed the opinion that healthcare institutions often act in ways that resemble a codependent individual's behavior, such as failing to confront problems. For example, several nurse managers were aware of illegal practices (Medicare fraud and misappropriation of funds) conducted by the director of a home health agency—practices serious enough for the agency to have been closed as a result. When the nurses brought this to the attention of the board of directors, the board did not act. They refused to believe the nurses and did not investigate. Eventually, the corrupt administrator left the agency because his contract was not renewed; however, there was nothing to keep him from engaging in the same illegal activities at his next workplace because there was nothing on his record to indicate that there was a problem.

Another example of institutions failing to confront problems was the failure to confront poor work behaviors. This often occurred when registered nurses in positions of responsibility without authority, such as charge nurse or clinical nurse specialist, were not supported by those with the authority to discipline when nurses reported problems with subordinates. For example, in a case described under "difficulty supervising," in which the four nursing staff members disappeared for an hour and a half, and a patient aspirated and arrested, the entire incident was written up, but no disciplinary action was taken. The personnel involved continued to work there and perform poorly. Two other nurses described situations when managers and even staff nurses were encouraged to cover for ineffective managers. As long as the work got done, the administrators never took action to correct the problem with the deficient manager involved.

Several nurses described a reactive rather than proactive institutional management style. One nurse explained:

> The reason I left my position as a clinical specialist is that I wasn't able to do long-range planning and effect changes in the long haul because my boss wanted me to be a troubleshooter. She wanted me on the floor constantly to put out fires: to pacify this physician, to "catch it" if this nurse didn't pick up the chest tube right, putting out fires. It's like they responded to whatever was urgent at that moment, as if it were the most important thing in the world.

Several nurses described their relationship with their supervisor as greatly influencing the severity with which their codependency manifested itself in the work setting. One nurse described making a mistake as a young nurse and being on the verge of quitting nursing, but because her supervisor told her that she expected her to make mistakes, and praised her for her handling of the situation, she stayed and became an excellent nurse. This experience helped her to let go of some of her perfectionism. Another nurse recalled that her first supervisor as a nurse treated her so badly that she almost left nursing. The supervisor routinely scheduled her to work overtime without her permission, never gave positive reinforcement, severely criticized small mistakes, and erupted over the slightest questioning of her decisions. Needless to say, codependent traits such as hiding mistakes, not asking for help, having difficulty being assertive or saying no, and having poor self-esteem are worsened by such a pattern.

The support of coworkers was the critical factor for other nurses. One nurse commented, "When I was at that job, we all pulled together and supported one another and the codependency wasn't so bad . . ." It was easier to ask for and accept help, be assertive, appropriately supervise when in charge, and avoid caretaking in a supportive atmosphere. Others described work units where a sense of constant competition from coworkers made traits like perfectionism, fear of admitting mistakes, and difficulty asking for and accepting help substantially worse.

CODEPENDENCY AS AN INDIVIDUAL PROBLEM

Denial

A significant finding was the nurses' lack of conscious awareness that their codependency had affected their patient care, what those effects were, and how those codependent behaviors influenced their units and institutions. Despite the fact that all of the nurses had been in recovery for several years and had reflected on how their codependent behaviors affected them emotionally and affected their relationships at work, only one nurse readily acknowledged that her patient care had been affected by her codependent behaviors. The other nurses might identify a particular behavior as codependent, but they did not perceive that the behavior had adversely affected patient care. When asked directly how their codependency had affected their patient care, they answered that it had not. It was only when they were asked to describe how their practice had changed as a result of their recovery, and the interviewer probed for concrete examples of past patient care experiences, that negative effects were evident in their stories. Several commented at the end of the interview that they had never thought about how their patients were affected by specific behaviors, and that new insights had resulted from the interview process. For example, three of the nurses recognized certain current frustrations with patients as control issues.

Negative Effects on Patient Care

The study identified a number of negative effects of codependency on patient care. These were emotional distancing, caretaking, control, hiding mistakes, difficulty supervising, difficulty asking for or accepting help, and difficulty being assertive.

Emotional Distancing

Two nurses noted that they distanced themselves emotionally from patients as a result of their codependency. One nurse avoided discussing the patient's personal problems or feelings with them. For example, she did not discuss with cardiac bypass surgery patients the possibility of postsurgical depression, a common side effect of open heart surgery. This was because she was uncomfortable discussing emotions, particularly depression. She explained, "I didn't feel like I had anything to offer them. I was like, 'Oh, you're depressed? Let me call the doctor and get an order for an antidepressant.'" This nurse had experienced a severe depression at one point in her life that was never treated. It seemed that her unresolved feelings about her own depression had made her uncomfortable talking about depression with patients. Another nurse described her lack of empathy and compassion and said that she came across to people, including patients, as cold, aloof, and angry. She wanted to be able to form an emotional bond with patients, but did not know how. This nurse believed that the greatest improvement in her practice over the course of her career was learning to achieve an emotional connection with her patients. Interestingly, both of these nurses had worked in critical care most of their careers.

Caretaking

An important theme for all but one nurse was caretaking, or rescuing. Caretaking is a term used in codependency literature to describe doing for others what they are capable of and should be doing for themselves. Nurses used the term caretaking to mean two different things. In one sense of the word, the caretaker felt like the slave of the other person. She felt manipulated into doing what others wanted and felt powerless and out of control. In the other use of the word, the caretaker took on the role of a mother, manipulating the other into doing what the caretaker felt was best. The nurse might take on either role in relationships with patients, with those they supervised, or their own supervisors.

An example of the "slave" caretaker being manipulated by patients is a home health nurse who was pressured by a patient to send her children trick-or-treating in expensive Halloween costumes belonging to the patient, something with which the nurse was quite uncomfortable. An example of how this type of caretaking with other staff members affected patient care was nurses doing others' work for them, to the inevitable detriment of their own responsibilities. One nurse, for example, was almost always late giving her 6:00 P.M. medications because she was too busy "helping" the nurses' aide pass supper trays and feed patients to do her own work.

An example of the "mothering" form of caretaking includes a psychiatric nurse who derailed clients' sense of personal responsibility by telling them what they needed to do, rather than helping them figure it out for themselves:

> I felt more responsible for [the clients] than I held them responsible for what was happening in their own life. . . . and so what might be termed healthy empathy I confused with the need to rescue and fix.

As an example, she talked about having 50 minutes allotted per counseling session, yet spending $1\frac{1}{2}$ hours with a client. "[I didn't know] how to set those limits: [I thought] 'this person needs me now'; [I saw] myself as their source, rather than as a possible guide." Several nurses suggested that one of the reasons for their need to "mother" was that their personal relationships were unfulfilling as a result of their codependency, and therefore, they met many of their intimacy needs in patient relationships. They wanted the patient to be emotionally dependent on them; they needed the patient to need them.

Whether it was the mothering or slave variety, one of the most dangerous forms of caretaking described by nurses involved covering for impaired nurses. One nurse described a staff nurse who drank on duty for years; she would fall asleep at the nursing station on a regular basis and be difficult to arouse. It was common knowledge, but neither the other nurses nor the supervisors confronted the situation. "None of [us] thought of the patients and the danger they might be in from this person who was sick," the nurse commented.

Control

Several nurses described control as an issue. One critical care nurse said:

> I've often realized that in critical care, I'm up here and the patient's down there. I'm in control. I think that if you've grown up in an alcoholic home you [feel that you] have to be in control.

Control was an issue when dealing with noncompliant patients, particularly patients not complying with lifestyle changes. For example, several nurses struggled with their intolerance of patients who chose to continue smoking after a myocardial infarction or after developing emphysema. They tried to manipulate the patient into making the "right" choice. For example, a nurse-midwife talked about using "sales techniques" to pressure certain women into long-term contraception, particularly poor women.

Hiding Mistakes

Hiding mistakes was another common theme. Sometimes, this involved documenting the mistake on the chart, but not making out an incident report. Sometimes it involved falsifying the medical record, such as documenting that a medication was given when the nurse had forgotten to give it. As one nurse said, "I couldn't admit it on the chart. I wasn't concerned about malpractice or anything. I was just devastated that I'd made a mistake." On one occasion, an entire group of step-down nurses deliberately concealed from management that they had forgotten to assign a nurse to a particular patient. They went back and fabricated nurses' notes for a 4-hour time period when in fact, no nurse had taken care of the patient.

Difficulty Supervising

Two nurses described difficulty in delegating. One nurse said:

> [The registered nurses] can't [delegate]. . . . They don't want anyone to be mad at them. So, either they don't express what they need and then get resentful when time after time, they're taken advantage of by the nursing assistants or someone, or they're overly aggressive and bossy and the nursing assistants and [licensed practical nurses] subversively work against them. . . . The way it played out for me was that I didn't confront things that were going on. When I saw them write down vital signs that I knew they hadn't taken, or behaving in a way that was not aboveboard, or not quite honest, I let it go because I didn't want anybody mad at me.

The nurse who described the most severe problems with supervision finally decided she could not take a position that would require her to do any supervising. She cited several instances when her difficulty appeared to have affected patient care. She had trouble confronting inappropriate or substandard work behavior and expressed feelings of helplessness about getting subordinates to do their jobs. In one instance, when she was in charge, two licensed practical nurses and two aides (out of six staff on the floor that shift) left the hospital without telling anyone and were gone for an hour and a half. One of the missing staff members left a patient flat in bed with the supper tray and fluids by the bed. The family came in and tried to feed the patient with the bed flat, and the patient aspirated and suffered a respiratory arrest. When the supervisor made rounds to help out, she found another patient dead (a do-not-resuscitate patient). Despite this experience, however, this nurse insisted that her codependency had never affected patient care.

Difficulty Asking for and Accepting Help

One nurse described working in a new specialty area where she "didn't know what [she] was doing." She described going into patients' rooms to do a procedure that she had never done before, tracheotomy care, for example, taking the procedure manual with her, propping it up, and trying to figure out how to do the procedure. After trying and failing, she finally would get an experienced nurse to help her. Clearly, using a manual to perform a new procedure on a patient when experienced nurses were available to observe and assist her was not good practice. Another nurse commented:

> Critical care nurses in particular are real competitive and they're real proud of how in control they are, and so to admit you were unsure of yourself or to admit you were having problems wasn't done.

Another nurse described having difficulty asking for help completing her work when she got behind. However, she found herself feeling resentful when others did not help her without being asked.

Difficulty Being Assertive

Several nurses described difficulty in being assertive with physicians or supervisors, which affected their ability to advocate for their patients. One nurse described the situation in which she first began to be assertive on a patient's behalf. She took care of a patient in whom she was very invested, which pushed her to be an advocate. She stated:

> I think that [incident] made me advocate for her in a way I wouldn't have if it had been just another patient. I would still have been trying to please the doctors and just go along with the way things were—and are.

One nurse had a problem with being aggressive, rather than assertive, with physicians. She explained:

> I would get into battles with these physicians, really personal . . . battles, because I didn't know the difference between representing your professional perspective and getting into a knock-down, personal battle with somebody.

Another nurse, when in a unit manager position, could not express assertively to nursing administration the need to arrange coverage for nurses who were on leave. She tried to fill the gap herself by working 16 hours a day, 7 days a week for months, which undoubtedly had negative effects on patient care. Eventually, she physically collapsed and resigned from that position.

Discussion

One of the most surprising findings of the study was the difficulty that these nurses had in admitting the effects of their codependency on their patient care. One reason for this may be that they all described deriving substantial self-esteem from feeling competent at work. It was vital for their self-image to be able to say to themselves, "I am a good nurse. I am good at patient care." Black-and-white thinking, a common codependent characteristic, might lead the nurse to see herself as either a good nurse or a bad nurse. Thus, she could be reluctant to examine her practice, for fear that she would discover that she was a bad nurse. The one nurse who had excellent insight into the effects of codependency in her practice had been in a masters' program in psychiatric nursing that involved extensive introspection and detailed supervision of her practice. This suggests that with appropriate coaching, denial can be overcome and progress can be made in acknowledging and neutralizing the effects of codependency on patient care.

In addition to personal self-examination, the findings suggested that good management could lessen the codependent behaviors of nurses, even those who have not done this type of self-examination. Which specific measures would be most helpful? To help those nurses with a tendency to act as caretakers, assertiveness training and discussions about how to handle staff members who are giving inadequate patient care should be part of the orientation process for any nursing position that requires supervision, even if it is merely rotating charge nurse duties or supervising unlicensed assistive personnel. In most redesigned delivery systems, this is every nurse. Managers who have the authority to discipline must support those nurses who have responsibility without authority, such as charge nurses. Reports that personnel are not performing up to standards must be taken seriously and investigated, and appropriate disciplinary action should be taken when necessary. A manager who cannot or will not address such issues should not be managing. In turn, charge nurses and others in similar positions need to be honest with managers, and bring such behavior to their attention without concern for "making others mad at them."

Another implication for managers is the importance of creating a unit where nurses feel free to admit to mistakes and ask for help. Clearly, the tendency to criticize, blame others, and magnify the mistakes of others must be addressed for that to occur. Unit managers also can emphasize that a "good nurse" is not a nurse who never needs help, but rather, a good nurse cares enough about her patients to ask for help when she needs it, and offers help to others. A nurse who has difficulty asking for help will find it easier if she understands that asking for help is an expected behavior. This promotes an atmosphere of cooperation rather than competition.

Staff members are unlikely to complete incident reports if they are used as the basis of disciplinary action. Thus, the primary purpose of identifying systemic problems that promote mistakes such as medication look-alikes, faulty equipment, and staff training needs, is not fulfilled. Organizational policy should be clear that the purpose of the incident report is not to punish the nurse who makes a mistake, and that purpose must be communicated to staff members.

In the past two decades, nursing as a profession has taken positive steps to deal with substance abuse within the profession. However, the comments of one nurse about the widespread problem of substance abuse being tolerated in her institution is a clear warning that this issue needs continued attention.

Respect for the patients' right to make their own choices must be emphasized. Nursing managers and clinical nurse specialists need to model the distinction between informing patients of the consequences of their lifestyle choices, helping them to make those changes that they want to make, and bullying and manipulating patients into changes they do not want to make.

Ultimately, nurses must make their own assessments of their practices and develop their own strategies for needed change. Institutions can support this process through examining management policies and attitudes that promote codependent behaviors in their nurses.

REFERENCES

1. Cermak T. Co-addiction as a Disease. *Psychiatric Ann.* 1991; 21(5):266–272.
2. Black C. *It Will Never Happen to Me.* Denver, CO: MAC Publications; 1991.
3. Wegscheider S. *Another Chance: Hope and Health for the Alcoholic Family.* Palo Alto, CA: Science and Behavior Books; 1981.
4. Snow C, Willard D. *I'm Dying to Take Care of You: Nurses and Codependence, Breaking the Cycle.* Redmond, WA: Professional Counselor Books; 1989.
5. Adams C, Bayne T. A personal recovery program for codependent nurse practitioners. *Nurse Pract.* 1992; 17(2):72–75.
6. Cauthorne-Lindstrom C. Hrabe D. Codependency in managers: a script for failure. *Nurs Manage.* 1989; 21(2):34–39.
7. Hall S, Wray L. Codependency: nurses who give too much. *Am J Nurs.* 1989; 89(11):1456–1460.
8. Sherman J. Cardea J, Gaskill S, Tynana C. Caring: commitment to excellence or condemnation to conformity? *J Psychosoc Nurs.* 1989; 27(8):25–29.
9. Caffrey R. Caffrey P. Nursing: caring or codependent? *Nurs Forum.* 1994; 29(1):12–17.
10. Arnold L. Codependency, part II: the hospital as a dysfunctional family. *AORN J.* 1990; 51:1581–1584.
11. Williams E. Bissell L. Sullivan, E. The effects of co-dependency on physicians and nurses. *Br J Addiction.* 1991; 86:37–42.

QUESTIONS TO PART IV

. . . .

ORGANIZATIONAL ASSESSMENT

1. How true to life is the fable of the organizational zoo? Elaborate.
2. To what extent is your work setting a healthy organization?
3. What aspects of your work setting do you consider unhealthy? Give examples.
4. In what ways does your health care facility solve its problems? Are the methods used healthy or unhealthy? Elaborate.

ORGANIZATIONAL SETTING

1. In what way has the differentiation between customers, consumers, and providers clarified your understanding of the present dilemma in health care?
2. What concerns do you have with the concept of patient focused care? What do you consider its strengths? Its weaknesses?
3. In what ways has your health care facility improved customer satisfaction while reducing costs?
4. What do you do to inform patients and family about how managed care works?
5. What insights did you gain about employers' influence on the health care system?
6. If your health care facility has been downsized, what were the reactions and behaviors of your coworkers who remained?
7. What kind of support did your health care facility provide for them?
8. What additional measures could your health care facility have taken to help those who remained?
9. Is the notion of shared governance a viable reality in today's health care climate?
10. What, in your opinon, is a viable alternative to shared governance?
11. What do nurses and patients value in your work setting? Are they the same or do they differ?

ORGANIZATIONAL BEHAVIORS

1. Do "organizational moles" exist in your work setting? If so, are their behaviors similar to those described by Bruhn and Chesney?
2. Compare and contrast boundary spanners, gatekeepers, and organizational moles. Can you identify them within your work setting? What effect do they have on your work?
3. To what degree do you believe the rumors you hear in your work setting? Do you validate them?
4. Which of the functions of gossip are of particular relevance to you? Explain.

5. Of the rumors you've heard in your work setting, which type of rumor have you encountered the most?

6. What consequences have you encountered with gossip and rumor in your work setting?

7. To what degree have you been intimidated in your work setting? With what effect?

8. How do you find yourself responding to a person who intimidates others?

9. Do you or your coworkers perceive yourself/themselves as victims in relation to being intimidated? If not, what behaviors prevent or protect you or others from becoming a victim?

10. What is the effect of codependent behaviors on patients' well-being? On your coworkers? On management?

11. Of the codependent behaviors you've seen in your coworkers, are any of them being rewarded by your health care facility? Explain.

PART V

●●

Leadership Imperatives: Shaping Nursing's Future

The future is often thought of as something "down the road" or just "over the horizon." In the past, it was natural for us to assume that our future would be filled with happy endings. Not anymore. Our future is here; so are its challenges and harsh realities. Could we have known how rapidly it would reach us or how tumultuous its changes would be? Were there warning signs? Perhaps. Could we have anticipated it better or more quickly? Probably. But the issue is not that the future, with all its attendant and chaotic changes, is here; the issue is what we plan to do about it.

Certainly we could stand still and allow ourselves to be swallowed up by the changes already upon us. But doing nothing solves nothing. We could retreat into the mindset of the "good old days," but the past is a fantasy we cannot afford in a world of rapid and relentless change. Things will never be the same in nursing, nor can they be. There is only one viable alternative open to us: meeting the future, with all its possibilities, head on.

The future is a daunting prospect. Its geography is uncharted. There are no well-traveled roadways, only barely discernible paths. Nor are there signs that clearly point the way, only tentative, wavering markers to destinations still vague, ill-defined, and yet to be determined. What is abundantly clear, however, is that this futuristic "here and now" will require a different set of behaviors and attitudes than the ones we've been using.

The personal comfort zone we've developed over the years will be the first casualty of change. Getting used to uneasiness, ambiguity, and the unknown will be, if it isn't already, an unsettling introduction to the future and its new realities. Getting caught up in the turmoil of conflicted feelings makes it hard to see the future, much less move forward into it.

The future is a kaleidoscope of new and infinite possibilities. But they can only become reality if we are of *one* mind, with *one* vision of a future that is of *our* making, in a maelstrom of change that is not of our making. We are the creators of our future. How that future will be depends on how quickly we learn and adapt to what it holds.

The aim of the readings in Part V is to provide more clarity and direction for the journey ahead and the future we desire. Among the futuristic themes of the readings that follow are the meaning of leadership in the context of the future; the implications for nurses of health care policy and restructuring; nursing's role and value in the competitive marketplace; the ramifications of capitation; and the readiness of the nursing profession to deal with the revolution in health care.

CHAPTER 48

●●●

Quantum Mechanics and the Future of Healthcare Leadership

TIM PORTER-O'GRADY

There can be no question in the mind of any current healthcare leader that the world is changing. However, it is not changing in ways with which we are familiar. This time around, it seems as if the changes are much more profound than many we have seen in the past, and the script that is unfolding has a different set of characteristics than those with which we are most familiar.[1] The rules of the "game" seem to have changed; they no longer work either to explain or to help us adapt to the change.[2]

Leaving an Age

All of us are aware that something is happening that is altering our reality in fundamental ways. In fact, what is occurring is the advanced stages of movement through an age change.[3] The world is moving out of the industrial age and quickly moving toward a new age characterized by a new set of realities, some of which are not familiar or appealing to a great number of people.[4]

The age we are leaving has been characterized by great leaps in science and knowledge, pushing humanity beyond anything anyone but the most prophetic could have imagined. Reflective of the defining work of Newton and his colleagues, much of the industrial age has reflected a scientific reductionism to explain everything in the universe in rational and linear ways.[5] Work, social relationships, productivity, finance, and economics can find their conceptual roots within Newton's theoretical framework.[6]

The human problem with science, discovery, and the universe, however, is that it never stands still.[7] Knowledge gained today simply serves as the database for future knowledge, some of which alters the foundations out of which it emerged. Newtonian physics concepts and models have expanded our understanding of the universe and its function. Our knowledge base about how the basic building blocks of creation are formed and how they behave has broadened and deepened.[8]

We often deal with change as though it were a straight line, when in truth, it never moves in a linear way. We plan as though the future is a road when it really is a river

---

BOX 48–1 COMPARING INDUSTRIAL AND QUANTUM PROCESSES

Industrial Age	Quantum Age
• Linear thinking	• Meta thinking
• Compartmental	• Whole systems
• Functional work	• Purposeful work
• Process orientation	• Outcome orientation
• Fixed work requirements	• Fluid work requirements
• Clear job requirements	• Changing roles
• Predictable effects	• Variable effects

---

zigzagging its way across the landscape of the universe. We can plan only for beginnings, but our current strategic activities assume we can see endings simply by defining what we want them to be. They rarely turn out in ways that we had anticipated fully.[9]

Quantum mechanics evolved out of the attempt to obtain a comprehensive and incisive view of how the universe works and how existence is both viewed and defined. Quantum reality paints a picture of the universe where a variety of connections and linkages overlap and converge and, through this process, reflect the character of the whole. It is from these connections, the relationships between the elements once thought unlinked, that quantum reality takes its meaning. In scientific terms, quantum mechanics is the understanding that reflects that all particles are waves and all waves are particles depending on the conditions and circumstances that influence how they are viewed and in what manner they are applied. In human dynamics, (including those involving management and organizations) quantum reality can be defined simply as that which emerges when the viewer "sees" reality as a set of relationships expressed at varying and continuously changing levels of complexity. In quantum thinking, the universe is one large set of relationships rather than one big "thing."[10]

Like most knowledge, quantum thinking provides a broader foundation for thinking about all relationships at every level of complexity in our universe. Inexorably, notions that emerge from this frame of reference alter our assumptions of relationships, decision making, leadership, and management. Our struggle is to move from linear industrial age processes to a quantum frame of reference.

The way of life in a quantum world is radically different from our industrial world, and the reality that supports it has entirely different constructs (Box 48-1).[11]

Quantum Principles and the Impact on Leadership

The principles of quantum mechanics that apply specifically to leadership changes are those that affect all systems. Applying them to leadership is a matter of translation and use. However, they significantly alter the frame of reference for leadership in ways that fundamentally adjust the role of leader and the exercise of leadership.

- All systems work from the inside out, not from the top down or the bottom up. Systems are cyclical and circular, not rectangular or pyramidal.
- Relationship is as important as control to the effectiveness and sustainability of any system.
- Vertical and horizontal integrations are necessary to the definition of a system. Vertical processes define control; horizontal processes define relatedness.

- Systems are defined by a conception of the whole, not by an enumeration of the parts; they can be known only in understanding the whole, not by simply examining the parts.
- All components of a system intersect and overlap, creating interdependencies that cannot be addressed separately or unilaterally, but only in the context of their relationship to each other.
- When separate systems meet or intersect, they overlap and combine and become a new system. They do not remain what they once were when separate from each other.
- All reality essentially is uncertain and cannot be predicted with any degree of assuredness. If we measure position (particle), direction becomes uncertain; if we measure direction (wave), position becomes uncertain.
- The context of any situation, including our own expectations, influences what the quantum reality will become. Our expectations and participation alters our reality, yet this reality cannot be defined independent of them.
- A system engages all of its components in undertaking a potential change; the potential is addressed from the perspective of every element, not simply from the direction provided by a select few.
- The context of a system is forever in flux and working relentlessly at its borders, creating the conditions (potential) for the system's next shift in reality or form.
- Healthy systems live in the tension between stability and chaos in a constant state of disequilibrium that creates the conditions and energy to ensure its response to the demand for evolution and change.
- Engagement, investment, inclusion, and ownership are required throughout a system and are the conditions for any sustainable action within the system. Any rupture in any one part of a system means a break in the whole system.

The frame of reference for thinking about organizations and relationships is altered significantly in a quantum framework.[12] Quantum understanding forever alters the way in which we live and work in systems, as well as how we understand and apply the role of leader. Partnership, integration, inclusion, ownership, and the term "system" itself all reflect the growing understanding of quantum reality applied to future organizations and relationships.[13] Dialogue around interdisciplinary integration, point-of-service design, shared governance, continuum of care, and health systems creation all are reflective of the growing emergence and influence of quantum reality on the thinking and application of structures and models for the future of healthcare.[14]

Human Capital: The Emergence of the Knowledge Worker

As the United States enters the quantum age, a paradigm shift, fueled by technology, is unfolding. We quickly are becoming a knowledge-driven society. The medium of exchange and the unit of value on the global stage is enumerated increasingly in terms of the value of knowledge.[15] Because knowledge is so critical to the products of work, the worker increasingly owns the tools of production. The future viability of organizations depends almost entirely on how these "tools of production" are used. Because knowledge cannot be owned by organizations in any real way and is instead owned by those who hold it, the relationship between worker and workplace is altered forever.[16]

In healthcare, the structure of the organization assertively valued and protected the key knowledge worker, the physician.[17] It is the knowledge of this worker that historically has been ascendant in the organizational hierarchy. Service complexities elaborate service intersections along the continuum of care. It simply is not possible to ignore the significant impact of the contribution of the whole range of other knowledge workers.[18] In a quantum context, it simply is not legitimate (or indeed, possible) to sustain efficacy by promulgating the ascendant value of one provider's knowledge (physician) at the expense of, in lieu of, or above that of the aggregated knowledge of the team of providers, on whose knowledge sustainable outcomes ultimately depend.[19]

Technology has made possible this growth in the horizontal connections that are a fundamental part of any effective service system.[20] As real health (wellness) becomes the centerpiece of the delivery system, the continuum becomes the pathway for health service. Partnership between the providers becomes necessary for effective service delivery. These intersections call for the interface between a wide range of knowledge workers. Knowledge creates the conditions for equity and generates the essential need for partnership around the work or services provided by the various stakeholders. This reality changes the frame of reference for organizations and the structures and behaviors that generate from them. The knowledge society requires a different set of conditions and relationships from those often found in organizations:

No more participatory management or other paternalistic allowances. Knowledge workers own what they bring to the workplace; it will be required that processes of engagement rather than permission be commonly used to define and obtain contribution.

Stockholders and stakeholders have an equal investment in business structures in the future. The stockholder invests financial capital in the undertaking; the stakeholder invests knowledge capital. Both are essential to the sustainability of the enterprise.

No more"input" processes with regard to decision making. Ownership of process will increasingly rest with the knowledge worker who will need to make decisions, not merely be consulted about them.

Outcome requirements, including quality determinations, require investment at the point-of-service or productivity by those who do the work. Outcomes are not sustained through the effort of any one individual; rather, they are obtained through the interface and facility of all on whom the outcome depends. Sustainable outcomes depend on relationship, not control.

Knowledge workers require little structure and much relationship. Effectiveness in a system increasingly depends on how little structure is present. There should be only as much structure as is necessary to maintain the integrity of the organization. In any case, it should never require more than two levels of effective decision making.

Current efforts in healthcare organizations to construct point-of-service models, teams, critical paths, and best practices all build on the need to intersect knowledge workers with each other around the common outcomes to which they all make a contribution.[21] These practices reflect the need for unencumbered interface between the stakeholders in a partner arrangements around the products of their mutual work. Each knowledge worker has a unique contribution to make, yet it takes the connection between each of them to obtain the value of that contribution and to effect sustainable results. The role of the system, in this circumstance, is to ensure that nothing in the organization impedes the full flowering of the essential interactions of the team and that whatever is necessary to support their work is available to them within the context of available resources.

Dependence on the knowledge worker moves the locus of control in systems from the hierarchy to the point of service.[22] As stakeholders configure around the point of service in team configurations, ie, construct the content of their work, the information necessary to accomplish that must be located where they are.[23] The system is obligated to generate rather than manage information. Information has value only when it can be applied in ways that positively affect the outcomes to which the enterprise is directed. The unit of service requiring the accuracy and integrity of the information is increasingly the team at the point of service. Rather than managing information, the role of the leader is to ensure that information, in an easy-to-use format, be available to anyone who needs it whenever and wherever it is needed.[24]

The knowledge worker needs tools and support, not direction and control. Discipline for the knowledge worker comes out of the need to effectively address the disparity between process and desirable outcome.[25] Sustainable outcome always serves as the basis for discipline in an effective and focused system. It is the obligation of the team to address the relationship between its members and each's contribution to the outcome; it is the system's obligation to ensure they have the sufficient tools (knowledge, skill, information) necessary to do so.[26] The partnership between a system and its members is continuously cybernetic and reflects a relentlessly horizontal relationship between them, both centered on the purposes and outcomes on which their relationship is founded.

Role Change in the Quantum Age

Leadership in the new age requires a shift in expressions of the role in organizations. The old perception of leader as the person at the center of the decision-making process simply does not apply in the knowledge society. The notion that leader equates with manager is increasingly not validated in quantum thinking. Leaders issue from a number of places in the system and play as divergent a role as their places in the system require. In whole systems approaches, it becomes clear not only that leaders should generate from any number of places but that the effectiveness of a system is dependent on how able the system is to identify and use emergent leaders from the wide variety of places from which they may emanate.[27]

In addition, the content of the role of leader also changes. This person cannot respond unilaterally to changes in direction or in the framework of a system. Leaders simply cannot stand in front of an organization and singlehandedly point out the direction that everyone should travel and expect them to do so.[28] It increasingly is apparent that no organization can know with certainty where it is going. This situation demands the convergence of the stakeholders around specific issues and agreement about direction and priorities worked out between them. The leader increasingly is a gatherer of people and a facilitator of the processes that they might use to come to agreement or to find common ground with regard to an issue or direction.

The character of the leadership role shifts in a quantum age organization. The vertical content of the role is diminished significantly and the horizontal obligations are advanced. Some of the emerging role characteristics are:

- Create as much opportunity as possible for point-of-service relationship between providers within the context of a team format.
- Link the essential developmental processes to the team's own growth, ensuring that the skills necessary to work as a team are available to the members.
- Assist the provider team in developing measures of its performance, thus defining the framework for its own performance evaluation.
- Support the team in its definition of accountability and discipline, forming the framework for mutual expectation, corrective action, and facilitating problem resolution.
- Generate information services and content in a fashion that is useful to the team and provides what the team needs to sustain its effort toward obtaining preferred outcomes.

- Alert the team to changes in circumstances and conditions affecting both relationship and work to facilitate the team's adjustment to the changing milieu affecting what they do.
- Link the team to others in the system as the linkage impacts on the efficacy and sustainability of their work, ever refining the continuum of intersections along the patient's (client's) pathway
- Ensure the appropriate interface between the team and the resources necessary to do their work, value being dependent on the effective correlation between cost, quality, and work.

Transformation does not move in a straight line. It is multidirectional, flowing in a specified and often circuitous direction. The quantum leader capitalizes on this trajectory. The leader knows that to give change form, the stakeholders must understand that change is a journey and many of the stages will be revisited at different times and places as the demand requires and as the events unfold.[29]

As the point-of-service changes and is redesigned and restructured, the quantum leader knows that it cannot be done by fiat and management intervention. Point-of-service design for organizations requires that the stakeholders be involved directly in design and decision making, and much of the work must unfold unfettered at the point of service. Even more important to the quantum leader is the understanding that ownership of decisions must generate from those who live at the center of service delivery and that sustainable action cannot be required, managed, or controlled by those who do not own the work.

This reality probably is the source of greatest noise in the new age. Traditionally, those who made the decisions about work were not those who did the work. As a result, those who did the work grew accustomed to not owning their work decisions, and managers who do not do the work are accustomed to making decisions about how the work is done (responsibility-driven, linear work structures). The reverse must operate in effective whole system organizations, and the effort is reflected in the journey from one frame of reference to the other.[30]

In the quantum age, leaders generally facilitate, integrate, and coordinate the activities of others based on the collective decisions the stakeholders have generated in response to defined expectations or outcomes. The quantum leader is well aware of the need to generate the necessary resources to stakeholders for essential and successful decisions. Indeed, the good leader is always assessing the level of skill and information needs of stakeholders as they deliberate essential issues at the point-of-service. The leader wants to ensure that the tools necessary to good or right decision making are in the hands of those who need it. Effectiveness is a subset of having the "right stuff" in the process of making the decision. Because the goal of effective whole systems is to make the right decision, the support to the decision maker is critical to the success of the system.

The quantum age, burgeoning technology, and the emergence of the centrality of the knowledge worker are inexorably shifting the character and content of the role of leader and the organizations they lead. As systems get designed around their points of service and reflect a different set of relationships between the players, the role of leader shifts in place, content, and expectation. Managers simply will not play the part they have in more industrial linear organizational designs. As systems move to configure around a quantum understanding of relationships and a deeper wisdom emerges regarding how sustainable systems work, the role of the leader will have a more expansive shift in purpose, role, and function.

It no longer is a matter of whether current leadership in organizations will let go of the reins, allow shared decision making, invest the worker-stakeholders with authority, permit true point-of-service design, share control, and the myriad of other requisites of a sustainable future in the quantum age. The reality already is on us. The need for shared leadership, partnership, stakeholder investment, knowledge worker autonomy and relationship, point-of-service designs, and cyclic structures already is apparent in a host of obvious ways. It simply is antediluvian to operate in ignorance of or opposition to the prevailing requisites of life in the emerging quantum age. Yet there still are many who are prevailing against the future through vertical integration, command and control, hierarchical organizational charts (even flattened ones), organizational "parentalism," and unilateral authority structures. These industrial designs and behaviors are not enough to enable a thriving and growing organization in the quantum age.

Conclusion

It is an exciting time because the challenges of creating response to newer realities comprise much of the time of leadership. The methods and constructs that make possible the ability to embrace these challenges call for an entirely different approach. The learning journey leads to a new character for the leader as a fellow traveler and sets the framework for the learning organization as everyone engages the realities of the quantum age. Out of the effort to create new formats and processes emerges the principles of partnership, equity, accountability, and ownership. Leadership always must emerge where it is needed.

All roles and behaviors must model the context into which systems are moving, not those out of which organizations are leaving. This requires mentoring, creating, sharing, facilitating, integrating, and coordinating people, resources, and processes toward the outcomes that exemplify the purposes of the system. It is in this framework that notions of leadership are imbedded. The challenge is recognizing the signposts that delineate the journey, engaging the stakeholders, and resonating with the creativity, energy, and products of the work that results from the mutual effort of committed leaders. That is real leadership in the quantum age.

REFERENCES

1. Beneveniste G. *The Twenty-First Century Organization.* San Francisco, CA: Jossey-Bass Pub; 1994.
2. Carlson LK. From garden peas to global brains. *Healthcare Forum J.* 1994; 37(3):24–28.
3. Channon J. Social architecture: can we design a new civilization. *World Business Acad Perspect.* 1995; 9(3):19–32
4. Drucker P. *Post-Capitalist Society.* New York: Harper-Collins; 1993.
5. Thomas B. *Reinventing the Future: Conversations with the World's Leading Scientists.* New York: Addison-Wesley; 1994.
6. Wheatley, M. *Leadership and the New Science.* San Francisco, CA: Berrett-Koehler Pub; 1992.
7. Hawking S. *A Brief History of Time.* London: Bantam Books; 1988.
8. Holland J. *Hidden Order.* New York: Addison-Wesley; 1995.
9. Kellert S. *In the Wake of Chaos.* Chicago, IL: University of Chicago Press; 1994.
10. Zohar D. *The Quantum Self.* New York: Quill/William Morrow Pub; 1990.
11. Zohar D, Marshall I. *Quantum Society.* New York: William Morrow Pub; 1994.
12. Macy J. Collective self interest—the holonic shift. *World Business Acad Perspect.* 1995; 9(1):19–22.
13. Pinchot GE. *The End of Bureaucracy and The Rise of the Intellegent Corporation.* San Francisco, CA: Berrett-Koehler Pub Inc; 1994.
14. Bennis W. *Beyond Bureaucracy.* San Francisco, CA: Jossey-Bass Pub; 1993.
15. Drucker P. The age of social transformation. *Atlantic Monthly.* 1994; 274(Nov):53–80.
16. Toffler A. *Powershift.* New York: Bantam Books; 1990.
17. Starr P. *The Logic of Health Care Reform.* Knoxville, TN: Whittle Direct Books; 1992.
18. Fagin C. Collaboration between nurses and physicians: no longer a choice. *Nurs Health Care.* 1992; 13(7):354–363.

19. Graham M, Lebaron M. *The Horizontal Revolution: Guiding the Teaming Takeover*. San Francisco, CA: Jossey-Bass Pub; 1994.
20. Negroponte N. *Being Digital*. New York: Knopf Pub; 1995.
21. Katzenbach J, Smith D. *The Wisdom of Teams*. Boston, MA: McKinsey & Co; 1993.
22. Chowaniec C. Democracy and the living organization. *At Work*. 1994; 3(2):17–19.
23. Dixon N. *The Organizational Learning Cycle*. New York: McGraw-Hill Inc; 1994.
24. Davenport T. *Process Innovation: Reengineering Work Through Information Technology*. Boston, MA: Harvard Business School Press; 1992.
25. Fisher K. *Leading Self-Directed Work Teams*. New York: McGraw- Hill Inc; 1995.
26. Kritek P. *Negotiating at an Uneven Table*. San Francisco, CA: Berrett-Koehler Pub; 1994.
27. Champy J. *Reengineering Management*. New York: Harper Business; 1995.
28. Porter-O'Grady T, Krueger-Wilson C. *The Leadership Revolution in Healthcare: Altering Systems, Changing Behavior*. Gaithersburg, MD: Aspen Pub; 1995.
29. Oshry B. *Seeing Systems: Unlocking the Mysteries of Organizational Life*. San Francisco, CA: Berrett-Koehler Pub; 1995.
30. Sayles L. *The Working Leader*. New York: The Free Press; 1993.

CHAPTER 49

●●●

Policy Imperatives for Nursing in an Era of Health Care Restructuring

DAVID KEEPNEWS AND GERI MARULLO

The forces shaping health policy in the United States, particularly as they affect nursing and its place in the health care system, have changed drastically over the past two years. The health policy environment facing nursing in 1995 and 1996 is virtually unrecognizable when compared to that of 1993 and 1994.

In 1993 and 1994, nursing was in a largely "proactive" stance as it worked with a new political leadership in Washington, one elected with a commitment to sweeping health care reform that promised to include some of nursing's most cherished goals: a system based on universal access, equity, primary care, prevention and wellness, and a recognition and fuller use of nursing's role both in health care delivery and in shaping a dynamic new health care system. Debates within nursing centered on exactly what to ask for in sweeping health care reform and how to achieve it—how to ensure the fullest possible use of nursing's contributions; how best to break down barriers to practice and payment; how to provide for new entitlement programs for nursing education; how to ensure consumer choice of type of provider (including advanced practice RNs); and how to ensure that nurses could best be prepared to take their proper role in emerging practice settings as the health care system moved to emphasize primary and preventive care based in communities, workplaces, schools, and homes. For many, the mere fact that nursing was being listened to as health care reform proposals were being formulated (while organized medicine fumed at its seeming isolation from the process) in itself represented a notable accomplishment.

In 1995 and 1996, the environment is radically different for nursing and for all other players in health care policy. The defeat of comprehensive health care reform in the 103rd Congress and a much-changed political environment in Washington (and in many state capitals) have been accompanied by massive changes in the settings in which most RNs practice as the health care industry fundamentally reorganizes its structures, its business, and its clinical operations. Nursing finds itself focusing much of its energies on defending

Reprinted from *Nursing Administration Quarterly*, 20(3), pp. 19–31, 1996, with permission of Aspen Publishers, Inc., © 1996.

past gains and protecting patient safety and nursing practice in a health care environment that seems increasingly to shift its emphasis from patients and quality care to utilization control, cost, and profit. Furthermore, these changes occur in a political environment that is increasingly hostile to government regulatory intervention and friendlier to market-based approaches such as those in whose name these changes are being made.

Nursing has responded to changes in the outside world by restating and refocusing its policy priorities. In this article, the authors identify some of those changes and priorities and the strategies that are being developed to respond to them in order that nursing can progress toward its goal of a health care system that prioritizes safe, quality services, even in an era of cost containment.

Health Care Restructuring and Cost Containment

Efforts toward comprehensive federal health care reform in 1993 and 1994 occurred in the context of a health care system that was taking up greater and greater portions of federal and state budgets and personal expenditures but that seemed to be delivering less and less for the money that was put in it while leaving tens of millions of Americans uninsured.[1] To be sure, different players identified vastly different interests in the achievement of a new health care system, and by no means did all of them concentrate singly on cost containment. Nursing made its goals clear in *Nursing's Agenda for Health Care Reform*,[2] a document that had the support of the majority of nursing organizations. That document stressed a simultaneous focus on access, quality, and cost. What most captured the imagination of nurses and many other proponents of health care reform was the goal of a health-oriented, equitable, and just health care system, not a single-minded focus on cost containment. Nursing understood that the social goals of health care reform were inextricably linked to the goal of cost containment. That recognition, however, should not obscure the pivotal role of cost containment as a driving force in health care reform.

Changes in System Predated Clinton Plan

Efforts toward major change in the health care system did not begin with the development of health care reform legislation in the 103rd Congress. Managed care was continuing to grow at an accelerating pace in markets throughout the country. Mergers and consolidations among hospitals and between hospitals and other providers had been in evidence for some years preceding. State-based efforts at reform, particularly in state Medicaid programs, were becoming increasingly popular as well. In some markets, particularly those where managed care had achieved significant market penetration, efforts had already begun in earnest to employ "creative" models of care that involved replacement of registered nurses with semiskilled, low-paid, unlicensed personnel (models that appear so ubiquitous today and that, in many areas, are already being abandoned).

Far from initiating the transformation in U.S. health care, comprehensive federal reform held the promise of providing a regulatory structure for changes in the health care system, of providing some degree of planning and rationality, for shepherding changes based on a careful evaluation of the nation's health care needs, and for constraining industry action that was adverse to the nation's health care goals and priorities.

The failure of the 103rd Congress to pass health care reform gave a signal to the health care industry that attempts to shape changes in the health care system were not likely to come from the federal government at any time soon. For the industry, this promised a measure of freedom from government "interference" through the impositions of new regulatory schemes, structures, or standards.

RESTRUCTURING IN THE HEALTH CARE INDUSTRY

The health care industry is in the midst of a far-reaching, basic transformation in how its structures are configured and its operations conducted.[3] Health care facilities and services are forming broad, integrated health delivery systems that offer a continuum of health care services. Hospitals are merging, consolidating, and often closing. More and more patient care is moved out of acute care settings and into clinics, practitioners' offices, the home, and long-term care facilities. The financing of health care is changing dramatically with the increasing dominance of capitated payment mechanisms and the consolidation of the managed care industry into a handful of increasingly large and powerful corporations.

The health care industry has increasingly sought to mimic the restructuring moves of other industries, often without enough discrimination to weed out some of their worst features. The emphasis more and more is on the financial bottom line. Hospitals and health systems increasingly seek to improve their own competitive postures—to capture bigger and bigger market shares, to secure managed care contracts, and to attract a larger patient base.

If only in theory, many aspects of this restructuring appear either unremarkable or may even appear to bring with them some of the things that nursing has been advocating for some time. For instance, nursing has been talking for years about the need to integrate and coordinate health care services and to provide a continuum of services as seamlessly as possible. Nursing certainly cannot object to the concept of hospitals and health systems running as efficiently and wisely as possible, to minimize wasted health care dollars.

THE UNDERLYING MOTIVES

But while many of these concepts may superficially appear nonobjectionable, they are shaped and implemented with the goal not of improving patient care, but of improving systems' competitive posture—by maximizing revenue and decreasing expenses, to generate profits that can be used for further expansion, to fund more mergers, or, for some for-profit entities, to provide a return on investment. Where they involve changes in an organization's clinical operations, these changes are often largely untested and are employed with little or no outcomes data to attest to their impact on patient care.

An intimately related phenomenon is that the changes that are made to fund this restructuring often involve drastic cost-cutting maneuvers. Too often, these are made at the expense of safe, quality patient care. In its testimony to the Institute of Medicine (IOM) Committee on the Adequacy of Nurse Staffing, the American Nurses Association (ANA) referred to this phenomenon as "Cutting Costs at Any Cost."[4] Many hospitals and health systems, looking for budgets to cut, have all too often looked first and foremost at their labor budgets and zeroed in on nursing labor expenses as one of the biggest and seemingly easiest targets for cost cutting. As a result, facility after facility has seen layoffs, frozen positions, and replacement of RNs by assistive personnel.[5,6]

These changes come at a time when utilization of RNs in health care delivery is more critical than ever to maintain patient safety and quality of care. Hospitalized patient populations are sicker than ever, their stays shorter than ever, and, therefore, their needs more intense than ever, and their nursing care needs more intense than ever.[7] As patients who would previously have been hospitalized are cared for instead in long-term care facilities, outpatient settings, and at home, the acuity of patients in those settings has also risen. It is estimated that "the cumulative real case mix change in hospitals has been on the order of a 20% growth in complexity between 1981 and 1992."[8(p.319)] Attempts to provide patient care with fewer professional staff, and to fragment care and assign most patient care tasks to non-RNs, seem especially ill-timed.

Layoffs and replacements of RNs may have helped some institutions to cut their operating budgets in the very short term, but in the long term they are unlikely to prove beneficial to either patients or the industry itself. ANA has argued that removing RNs from patient care deprives patients of the level of professional caregiving they require, and deprives health care systems of the comprehensive, cost-efficient services of professional RNs.

One of the important lessons for nursing from the institution of the prospective payment system (PPS) for Medicare in 1983 is the impact of cost restraints on utilization of nursing. When PPS was introduced, many predicted dire reductions in the use of RNs, since hospitals would want to deliver care as cheaply as possible. Initially, it did appear that many hospitals did move to cut their RN staffs. The industry, however, soon realized that replacement by lesser-trained personnel did not yield a saving.[9] These ancillary personnel could not do as much, could not provide adequate patient assessment or detect complications or other problems at an early stage. The years following introduction of the PPS saw a large increase in use of RNs (although, significantly, not a rise in labor costs as a percentage of overall spending). The ratio of RNs to patients increased by 26% between 1982 and 1986.[10] Those years also witnessed a large and prolonged undersupply of RNs.

The ANA has strongly advocated that nurses be at the table when hospitals restructure.[4] In some instances, state nurses associations have found some success in negotiating involvement in staff redesign decisions and in providing for retraining of nurses displaced from inpatient units.

Safety and Quality Concerns Come to the Fore

Nursing's Agenda for Health Care Reform identified three defining principles for a new health care system—access, quality, and cost containment. Indeed, nurses and other supporters of health care reform recognized that no one goal could be achieved to the exclusion of the others. While cost containment concerns provided much of the imperative for health care reform, the need for wider access to coverage and services, and how to achieve that goal, drove much of the public debate on reform. The need to maintain and even improve the quality of services in the face of expanded coverage and effective cost containment provided a third, anchoring principle for health care reform. As patient advocates, and as the practitioners most directly entrusted with protecting patient care quality and patient safety, nurses attached particular importance to this principle.

INCREASING EMPHASIS ON COST CONTAINMENT

Currently, both market-based and public sector initiatives have centered in large part on control of costs. The reasons behind this are several. As discussed above, it was cost containment that was the driving force behind the effort for federal reform and, in a much more clearly evident way, has driven most state-based efforts for health reform. Within the private sector, transformations that have been at play for some time have been largely cost driven. Managed care, which long held the promise of a more tightly organized, wellness and prevention oriented system of health care delivery, has increasingly been centered on management of cost. In addition to the financial pressures created by the growing influence of capitated payment systems, competition among both insurers and institutional providers has led to tighter attention to costs, profit margins, and the ability to fund acquisitions that hold the promise of capturing greater and greater market share.

It is in the context of this increasing focus on cost that nursing has identified its growing concern that patient care quality, including the fundamental principle of protecting patient safety, is being compromised in the process of a unilateral drive to cut costs. Of particular concern to nursing has been the industry's efforts to cut utilization of RNs and to replace nursing staff with lower-paid, unskilled substitutes. These concerns are based not only on previous data that suggest a close link between RN staffing and patient care quality[11] but increasing anecdotal evidence has also pointed to growing problems in patient care safety and quality as a result of the slashing of staffing levels. An important review of the literature addressing the links between nurse staffing and skill mix and patient outcomes is provided by Prescott.[11] A review is also contained in the ANA's *Nursing Care Report Card for Acute Care.*[12] Reports from individual nurses on patient care problems resulting from decreased staffing have been collected by the ANA and by state nurses associations, including the California Nurses Association (CNA), which was then affiliated with the ANA. CNA had collected these as part of public testimony on proposed changes in state hospital regulations; these were submitted to the California Department of Health Services and also, by ANA, to the IOM Committee on Adequacy of Nurse Staffing.

Current mechanisms to ensure patient safety and quality of care have proved inadequate to address the current changes in nurse staffing. The standards of the Joint Commission on the Accreditation of Healthcare Organizations (Joint Commission) provide conditions in several areas, but none measures safe staffing levels or occupational mix per se. Patient classification systems are intended to provide a guide for hospital staffing. There is little uniformity among them, however, as different hospitals opt to use different systems. Most significantly, widespread reports from nurses indicate that in many instances patient classification systems are commonly manipulated to yield results that meet budgetary needs rather than patient care needs. Medicare's Conditions of Participation give little specific guidance beyond this to evaluate the adequacy of staffing levels and occupational mix.

These mechanisms for quality enforcement may have been adequate in years past. Until recently, the assumption that hospitals and health facilities would, with rare exception, staff at safe levels and would prioritize patient care needs may have appeared to be a safe one. In an era when a restructuring health care system stresses cost and revenue as its central priorities, this assumption no longer appears so safe. Many hospitals and facilities may be able to maintain their Joint Commission and Medicare accreditation despite slashing their nurse staffing levels because they maintain technical compliance with the letter of Joint Commission and Medicare standards. That they maintain such accreditation may speak more to the skill of their risk managers and to the adequacy of current standards than to the actual state of care in those facilities.

CHALLENGES TO THE ROLE OF REGULATION IN PROTECTING SAFETY AND QUALITY

While the logical places to turn for assistance in remedying growing concerns over safety and quality are federal and state regulatory agencies, the viability of this option is threatened by the current political and policy environments. The defeat of comprehensive federal health care reform was seen by many as a rejection of new regulatory frameworks for addressing problems with the health care system. Indeed, regulatory intervention would seem to compromise the current freedom of the industry to devise the "market-based reforms" that are transforming the system.

Moreover, Congress and many state governments are currently in the grip of a pronounced antiregulatory fervor that argues for a diminished government presence in many areas of American life. Proposals that involve the imposition of new regulatory schemes, even in an area as critical as health care, may face particularly sharp challenges in this climate.

This antiregulatory sentiment, in fact, may clear the way for new challenges to nursing, even in areas where they may not have been previously expected. Nursing has turned to regulatory bodies at the state level (where the power to regulate the provision of health services, along with the exercise of other powers to protect the public health, safety, and welfare has traditionally rested) to argue its case for restrictions on facility discretion in the area of staffing levels or of inappropriate or unsafe use of assistive personnel. Among these regulatory bodies, nursing has traditionally found a hearing from state boards of nursing. These boards are empowered with licensing nurses and regulating the practice of nursing. In a great many states, their nurse and consumer members are particularly aware of the need to address the unauthorized practice of nursing, including the institutional use of unlicensed personnel to provide nursing care. Some state boards of nursing have sought to address this practice directly. (In one state, concerns voiced by consumer members of the board of nursing moved the state attorney general to take action on the unsafe use of unlicensed personnel.[13])

Some attempts to reduce the power of the boards of nursing to exert such authority have begun to surface. In Oregon, the state hospital association and the state affiliate of the American Organization of Nurse Executives (AONE) sponsored a legislative proposal (H. B. 3045, 1995) that would have diluted the authority of the Board of Nursing to regulate the use of unlicensed personnel. Among other things, this bill would have imposed a distinction between "nursing care services" and "patient care services"; the nursing board's power would have been limited to regulating "nursing care" as narrowly defined by the bill. That bill drew significant opposition from nursing, spearheaded by the Oregon Nurses Association, and was defeated. (A subsequent attempt to restrict the power of health professionals' licensing boards to issue rules that affect the workplace was later amended into a piece of technical legislation that passed but was vetoed by the governor.[14])

Other voices have begun to advocate one form or another of institutional licensure, or of health system licensure, in which the institution or system would determine the training and practice of its employees based on its own determination of its needs. Still others have questioned the efficacy of health professions' regulatory boards to protect the public, despite the more favorable record of many nursing boards in disciplining their licensees who practice unsafely. The Task Force on Health Care Workforce Regulation of the Pew Commission on the Health Professions released its report and recommendations on health professions' licensure in December 1995 and included a number of far-reaching proposals for changing state health care regulatory mechanisms. Advocates of changes in the way health professions' licensure boards are configured, and the powers they exercise, are likely to win a broad hearing in many state legislatures this year, particularly as many of their arguments build upon a growing public distrust and skepticism of government regulation.

Strategies and Solutions on Safety and Quality

Recognizing both its historical commitment to quality care and patient safety and the direct relevance of these issues to current changes in nursing practice and the health care system, ANA has taken up a broad initiative to address the issues of safety and quality in patient care.

NURSING REPORT CARD

Fundamental to this initiative has been a recognition of the need to establish understandable, objective measures by which to measure quality in nursing care. Defining and measuring quality has, of course, been a confounding issue for virtually everyone in health care. ANA's effort seeks to build upon work that has already been accomplished and has used a "report card" approach, which identified specific quality indicators by which performance can be rated.

The initial results of that effort are published as the *Nursing Care Report Card for Acute Care*.[12] It is based on work done by ANA and Lewin-VHI, Inc. The development of the quality indicators included identifying an initial set of 71 nursing indicators, which was narrowed to 21 with the strongest, established, or theoretical link to the availability and quality of professional nursing services in hospital settings. Those indicators have been further refined to include: patient satisfaction; pain management; skin integrity; total nursing care hours per patient (case/acuity adjusted); nosocomial infections (urinary tract infection and pneumonia rates); patient injury rate; and assessment and implementation of patient care requirements.

Much work remains to be done in this area, not the least of which is piloting the use of the report card. Work has recently been completed on uniform definitions for each of seven indicators (work in which AONE, to its credit, is participating) and to develop an educational program for RNs on the use of quality indicators and clinical outcomes in their work settings. Identification of institutions interested in piloting the report card is also proceeding, with the participation of the AONE.

An important goal here is not just to add a new entry to an already crowded field of report cards, but also to work to incorporate the elements of the Nursing Report Card into existing and developing quality measurement tools.

OTHER IMPORTANT VOICES ON QUALITY

Nursing's efforts on quality measurement dovetail with those of other groups. The Health Plan Employer Data and Information Set (HEDIS), developed by the National Coalition for Quality Assurance (NCQA), has come into increasing use as a standard means of measuring managed care plan performance and accrediting those plans. As the use of managed care in both Medicaid and Medicare grows, HEDIS is being adapted to reflect care for those populations.

In July of 1995, a number of public and private groups met to take up the issue of quality in managed care and formed a new initiative, the Foundation for Accountability (FAcct). Much of the talk at the meeting, as reported, centered on the idea that, as costs are coming under control, more attention now needs to be paid to quality.[15] Participants in this initial meeting included large corporations; federal and state agencies that administer health insurance programs, including the Health Care Financing Administration and the California Public Employees Retirement Board; union purchasers of health insurance; and NCQA. Estimates are that the groups who make up FAcct represent 80 million insureds.[16]

Notably, this meeting was convened by the Jackson Hole Group and included the active participation of Dr. Paul Ellwood of that group, whose work had provided much of the foundation for what later became the Clinton health care reform proposal. The work of this group appears to mesh with some of the refocused priorities enunciated by the Jackson Hole Group.[17]

This new initiative may indeed prove significant, not only because it is a public–private initiative of unprecedented magnitude but also because it offers the possibility of an outcomes approach that measures patients' response to interventions performed by providers under those plans.

ACCOUNTABILITY

Closely tied to the need for more and better data and clearer outcomes measures is the goal of public accountability for health care delivery. Holding performance of plans and institutions out for public scrutiny is important not only because, as many would argue, the public has a right to know (and, conversely, providers have a duty to disclose) but also because public disclosure itself can potentially influence consumer choice and encourage competition based on performance. An ANA-commissioned Gallup survey found that 84% of respondents would choose a hospital with smaller patient–nurse ratios than one with larger ratios.[18] At the Jackson Hole meeting, Dwight McNeill, information manager for the GTE Corporation and cochair of FAcct, stated:

> What we want to do is [to] have information out there in the marketplace on performance and outcome measurements. If consumers and purchasers have information on both outcome and cost, it drives market share toward that vendor that has the best value, and, surprisingly, we haven't got that as yet.[19(p.1)]

As part of its efforts on public accountability, ANA has advocated public disclosure by health care institutions regarding staffing levels and patient outcomes data. ANA has advocated that such public disclosure be part of the Medicare Conditions of Participation for hospitals and also supports legislative efforts to require such disclosure for health care institutions. ANA is also advocating that proposed mergers and acquisitions of health care facilities, as part of their regulatory review, be assessed for their potential impact on patient safety and quality of care.[20]

CONSUMER EDUCATION

A key part of moving forward nursing's policy agenda on health care safety and quality is to educate consumers and establish close working ties with consumer organizations. ANA's public education campaign has been conducted around the theme "Every Patient Deserves a Nurse," and has involved extensive distribution of an educational brochure, work with local and national media, and other educational efforts. ANA cosponsored the March 1995 Nurses' March on Washington, which sought to bring public attention to the issues of patient safety and quality of care. In addition, ANA is seeking active partnership and coalition with consumer groups around these issues. These efforts seek not only to educate consumers, but also to help create a consistent consumer demand for RN services.

REASSERTING NURSES' ROLE AS PATIENT ADVOCATE

As conditions for RNs and their patients change, nurses' role as advocate for their patients (a key ethical precept for the profession[21]) becomes increasingly important. Threats to nurses' ability to fill that role have recently emerged. In *NLRB v. Health Care & Retirement Corp.* (114 S. Ct 1778[1994]), the U.S. Supreme Court found that nurses who direct the work of less-skilled aides are supervisors and therefore not entitled to protection under the National Labor Relations Act (NLRA). That protection includes not only the rights to organize and to bargain collectively (rights that have provided nurses with important tools with which to protect patient care and nursing practice), but also to speak out on issues relevant to their employment and working conditions, including patient safety concerns.

ANA is pushing to amend the NLRA to clarify that nurses who direct the work of ancillary personnel are not outside the NLRA's protection. ANA has held that this is a critical issue for patient care and for the nurse's ability to meet her or his ethical obligations.[22,23]

In addition, ANA is supporting efforts to enact federal whistle-blower protections for nurses who report unsafe patient care conditions.[20]

BREAKING DOWN BARRIERS TO FULL UTILIZATION OF NURSES

Ensuring full use of RNs in meeting the country's health care needs, including breaking down barriers to nursing practice and payment for nursing services, remains an important policy imperative for nursing. Some important progress continues to be made in breaking down legislative and regulatory barriers at the state level, particularly as they apply to advanced practice RNs (APRNs). At the federal level, nursing continues to push for Medicare and Medicaid payment for all APRNs, regardless of specialty, practice setting, or geographic area. Coverage of APRN services, long an important goal of nursing, may prove particularly important in ensuring that nurses, including APRNs, are used as fully as possible in a changing health care system.[24] In addition, Medicare payment is needed in order to allow for the generation of important data; currently, because the services of nurse practitioners and clinical nurse specialists are generally billed under physicians' or clinics' provider numbers, Medicare has virtually no information on the services provided by these nurses.

With the growth of managed care plans, APRNs in many areas have encountered the problem of exclusion from provider panels. Even in states with relatively few regulatory barriers to practice, exclusion from such plans has restricted the ability of these nurses to receive payment for their services. A closely connected problem has been that, with the growth of managed care Medicare and Medicaid programs, many APRNs face similar restrictions. Many states operate Medicaid waiver programs that use a primary care case management (PCCM) mechanism, whereby each patient is assigned to a primary care provider who serves as "gatekeeper" for other health services. In some states, the PCCM role has been limited to physicians; nurses are excluded from this role either through the state Medicaid agency's plan itself or by the private insurance companies that administer the plan.

The American Medical Association (AMA), long adverse to efforts to ease state restrictions on nursing practice, solidified that position at its 1995 House of Delegates meeting.[25] Among other things, the AMA delegates supported giving more assistance to state medical societies in opposing efforts to remove barriers to nursing practice.

Nursing will also need to pay closer attention to methods of valuing its contributions to inpatient care and seek to establish means of building on existing payment methodologies to demonstrate the importance of adequate nurse staffing in the financial well-being of health care institutions.

Threats to Public Programs

Numerous public programs of great importance to nursing face increased threats during the 104th Congress. Nursing is working to preserve funding for nursing education, research, and health and safety. In addition, nursing is working to prevent crippling cuts in Medicare and to preserve its character as an affordable and accessible social program. Similarly, nursing is working to protect Medicaid and its ability to provide services to low-income individuals. While the future of these programs will likely be settled by Congress for this season by the time this article is printed, these issues will undoubtedly continue to recur for some time.

The Need for Continued Professional Unity

During its efforts on federal health care reform, nursing achieved an unprecedented degree of unity within the profession in identifying common goals and strategies. Most nursing organizations showed an earnest willingness to compromise where needed, or at a minimum to keep its debates internal.

As nursing faces different challenges in a much-changed health care environment, can this unity be replicated? If so, on what should it be based? These are issues that cannot be settled in this article, but that nursing will need to confront as it faces growing challenges to its practice and its professional survival.

A traditional role for nurse managers and nurse executives has been to serve as patient advocates within hospital administration, to advocate for nursing's concerns within the organization. Among other things, their placement within health care organizations provided an important opportunity to play that role. This role is threatened in many organizations and systems as operational decisions are taken out of the hands of nursing, as midlevel nursing managers are replaced by nonnursing managers with nonclinical backgrounds, and as, in many hospital chains and health systems, key decisions that affect patient care are made outside of the institution. Moreover, many nurse managers and executives face pressures to conform to newly enunciated institutional values.

At the same time, staff nurses feel intense pressures to provide quality care to their patients with smaller and often inadequate resources. In a recent survey, 58% of nurse respondents identified "cost containment issues that jeopardize patient welfare" as a "priority" ethical issue.[26]

Nurse managers and executives share a common interest with staff nurses in focusing attention on the issues of safety and quality and in protecting patients through ensuring nursing's continued role in patient care (although their placement within health care organizations, and the current pressures of a volatile health care environment, may not always allow them to voice these issues in the same manner). Should it surprise anyone that some institutions have lost sight of the value of nurses in midlevel management positions when they are losing sight of the value of nurses at the bedside?

A great many nurse managers and executives have continued to recognize the interests that they hold in common with all nurses, and to use their positions to fulfill their roles as patient advocates. Some have continued this commitment in the face of risk to their own current positions.

If the current environment calls for more aggressive action in some spheres, such as the March 1995 Nurses' March on Washington, or the negotiation of clearer patient care standards through collective bargaining, it does not require the disintegration of the unity that nursing found during its efforts on health care reform. The things that brought nursing together at that time—a common appreciation of the unique and critical role of nursing in health care, and of the overriding goal of serving and protecting health care consumers—will be critical to keep closely in mind as nursing continues to confront major challenges in the days and years ahead.

REFERENCES

1. Clinton, W. "Letter to the American People," November 2, 1993 (introducing the Health Security Act).
2. American Nurses Association. *Nursing's Agenda for Health Care Reform*. Washington, D.C.: ANA, 1991.
3. Shortell, S., Gillies, R., and Devers, K. "Reinventing the American Hospital." *The Milbank Quarterly* 73, no. 2 (June 22, 1995):131–55.

4. Written Testimony of the American Nurses Association before the Institute of Medicine Committee on the Adequacy of Nurse Staffing, pp. 14–17. Washington, D.C.: ANA, September 16, 1994.

5. American Nurses Association. *1994 Layoffs Survey.* Washington, D.C.: ANA, 1994.

6. Service Employees International Union. *National Nurses Survey.* Washington, D.C.: SEIU, 1993.

7. Aiken, L. "Implications of Changing Hospital Employment Trends on Basic Nursing Workforce Requirements." Paper presented to Conference on Strategies for Health Workforce Research, March 10, 1995.

8. Aiken, L., and Salmon, M., "Health Care Workforce Priorities: What Nursing Should Do Now." *Inquiry* 31, (1994):318–29.

9. Shindul-Rothschild, J., and Gordon, S. "Health Care Reform: A Political Economy Analysis," unpublished manuscript.

10. Aiken, L. "Nursing Shortage: Myth or Reality?" *New England Journal of Medicine* 317, no. 10 (1987):641–45.

11. Prescott, P. "Nursing: An Important Component of Hospital Survival Under a Reformed Healthcare System." *Nursing Economics* 11, no. 4 (1993):192–99.

12. American Nurses Association. *Nursing Care Report Card for Acute Care.* Washington, D.C.: ANA, 1995.

13. "Carter Raises Patient Care Issue; Attorney General Warns Public That Unlicensed Hospital Workers May Be Giving Medical Treatment." *Indianapolis Star,* March 24, 1994, p. D1.

14. "Oregon Governor Signs Death-Knell for Anti-RN Legislation." *The American Nurse,* September 1995, p. 23.

15. Winslow, R. "Major purchasers of health services form alliance to evaluate HMO care." *Wall Street Journal,* July 3, 1995, p. A3.

16. Noble, H. "Quality is focus for health plans." *New York Times,* July 3, 1995, p. 1.

17. Ellwood, P.A., and Enthoven, A. "'Responsible Choices: The Jackson Hole Group Plan for Health Reform." *Health Affairs* 14, no. 2 (Summer 1995):24.

18. Gallup survey on consumer perceptions of nursing staff, conducted for the American Nurses Association, 1994.

19. *New York Times,* July 3, 1995, p. 1.

20. American Nurses Association. *Legislative and Regulatory Initiatives for the 104th Congress.* Washington, D.C.: ANA, 1995.

21. American Nurses Association. *Code for Nurses with Interpretive Statements.* Washington, D.C.: ANA, 1985.

22. American Nurses Association. *The Supreme Court Has Issued the Ultimate Gag Order for Nurses.* Washington, D.C.: ANA, 1995.

23. American Nurses Association. *Can Your Nurse Still Speak for Your Needs?* Washington, D.C.: ANA, 1995.

24. Keepnews, D. "The Role of Nurses in the New Health Care Marketplace." Letter. *Health Affairs* 14, no. 3 (Fall 1995):280–81.

25. "AMA Calls for Stronger Supervision of Nurse Practitioners/Physician Assistants." *BNA Health Care Policy Reporter,* June 26, 1995, p. 4.

26. Scanlon, C. "Survey Yields Significant Results." *Communique* (American Nurses Association Center for Ethics and Human Rights), 3, no. 2 (1994):1–3.

CHAPTER 50

Creating a New Place in a Competitive Market: The Value of Nursing Care

PETER I. BUERHAUS

Today, health care organizations and professionals are facing a myriad of challenges. They are being squeezed between ever-tightening Medicare and Medicaid payments, are encountering increased growth in enrollment in managed care organizations (MCOs), and are anticipating the continuing development of market-based competition among MCOs.

With economic forces steadily pushing the health care system into more integrated arrangements, some organizations are finding it difficult to compete—indeed, survive. As employers seek lower-priced premiums and improved quality, MCOs respond to these demands by passing part of the pressure onto hospitals and other contracting health care providers. To maintain their place in the changing market, hospitals must continue to lower costs as rapidly as possible.

The economic survival of emerging integrated delivery systems (IDSs), however, will not solely depend on their ability to produce low cost care: It will not be long before maintaining a recognizable high standard of *quality* is also paramount to success. Quality incorporates the perspective of the client and, thus, influences patient satisfaction. Consumers, weighing their levels of income, particular preferences, and amount of information about available services, consider the trade-off between price and quality and purchase the health services that they perceive will bring them the most personal satisfaction. However, current financial pressures from economic competition are not widely developed or strong enough to reward the majority of hospitals and other provider organizations for producing and competing on the basis of the highest quality services.

Compounding these challenges are misconceptions—including decreased access to care and belief that the system is doomed to failure—about the development of competition in the health care arena. Such misconceptions can draw nurses' attention away from taking steps to strengthen their position in a more competitive health care marketplace, yet alone in future capitated delivery systems. In either case, nurses will need to play a more visible and responsible role in ensuring that society gets the highest *value* for the vast amount of resources it puts into health care.

As market competition spreads and MCOs expand, it is paramount that the profession does not lose focus. To ensure nursing's place at the table as new delivery systems are developed, nurses must come to grips with the reality of change. Indeed, they have to gain a better understanding of the economic forces driving change and how the system is likely to evolve in the foreseeable future. By comprehending the "big picture," nurses can concentrate their energies and take actions designed to make themselves increasingly *valuable* to their employers and to society at large.

In their quest to elevate their profile in the future, nurses must make sure that any new system evolves in a way that will financially reward providers for quality improvement and the production of important clinical outcomes. Additionally, it is imperative that IDSs adequately reflect their contributions in all organizational settings. If important interventions and activities are not visible, nurses' worth in improving quality and clinical outcomes will not be valued. Consequently, as scarce resources are distributed where they obtain the greatest value, nursing will risk being allocated less funding, staff, and equipment for providing personal health services.

Therefore, nurses have to pursue the kinds of activities that establish connections between professional nursing and the quality and satisfaction that purchasers are willing to buy. Indeed, the key to increasing nursing's value is to develop and implement an *action agenda* that establishes how the quality of patient care is connected to nursing practice and how the interventions of nurses are related to patient satisfaction and important clinical outcomes. Such a quality focused agenda is in the profession's best interest and, simultaneously, in society's best interest, offering opportunities to participate in shaping a more positive future for nurses, their patients, and their employers.

Where We Are Now

ECONOMIC FORCES DOMINATING THE SYSTEM

To more completely grasp the need to embark on a quality-focused agenda, nurses must first understand the status of U.S. health care and the economic forces putting pressure on the system. Earlier this decade, the delivery system, often characterized as inefficient and illness-oriented, began a remarkable transformation away from the episodic and fragmented care delivered in the past. In some parts of the country, traditional fee-for-service arrangements are beginning to be replaced by integrated and even capitated systems. These emerging systems are expected to be more efficient, wellness-oriented, and quality conscious, thereby reducing costs and more adequately meeting the needs of consumers and other purchasers of health care (Box 50-1).

To expand IDSs throughout the nation, clinicians, administrators, educators, researchers, and policymakers will need to work together to embrace change and understand the three main economic forces currently at work in the marketplace. Today, runaway federal budget deficits are impacting future government spending on health care programs and prompting serious congressional action. Initiatives to increase the enrollment of more segments of the population into MCOs are causing reverberations throughout the system. Likewise, economic competition among health care providers is spreading rapidly.

GROWTH OF FEDERAL BUDGET DEFICITS

The rate of increase in the public debt and obligatory interest payments has placed enormous pressure on elected officials to reduce deficit spending. Perhaps the best example illustrating this point is the current stalemate between the Republican majority in Congress

---

BOX 50–1 CHARACTERISTICS OF THE PAST AND FUTURE HEALTH CARE DELIVERY SYSTEMS

Past/Traditional	Future Health Care System
Episodic and fragmented	Continuous, coordinated
Illness focused	Wellness and preventative
Insurance programs	Managed care organizations
Inpatient care	Ambulatory and community-based
Hospitals as profit centers	Hospitals as cost centers
Specialist physicians	Primary care practitioners
Independent solo physicians	Multispecialty group practice
Fee-for-service payments	Predetermined capitated fee
Heavily regulated environment	Increasingly competitive environment
Provider oriented	Consumer oriented
Presumption of high quality	Routine comparison of well-defined indicators

---

and President Clinton over a proposed budget reconciliation bill. The debate over proposals to balance the budget became so contentious that two shutdowns of the U.S. government resulted. Many insiders believe this debate will not be decided until November—on election day.

With federal spending on Medicare and Medicaid consuming roughly 18% of each year's federal budget, it is virtually certain that future budgets for these rapidly growing programs will be curtailed. Consequently, federal government payments to hospitals and physicians—the two largest recipients of the public's health care dollars—will be further constrained in the years immediately ahead.

This is an important point considering that Medicare payments are the single largest source of revenue for hospitals (Prospective Payment Assessment Commission [ProPAC]. 1995), As a result of budgetary pressures, many experts expect hospitals' financial positions to suffer. Similarly, the future financial stability of nursing homes, community health agencies, ambulatory care facilities, and home health care programs that receive federal funding are likely to be adversely affected as well (Box 50-2).

GROWTH OF MANAGED CARE

In the near future, growth in MCOs is expected to accelerate for a variety of reasons. First, while only a small proportion (slightly over 9%) of Medicare's 35 million beneficiaries are currently members of such plans, it is expected that many more will enroll, especially if certain congressional proposals to reform this entitlement program are enacted. In fact, over the past two years alone, the rate of enrollment growth has increased 25% per year, with 70,000 new Medicare beneficiaries being enrolled in health maintenance organizations (HMOs) each month (Vladeck, 1995).

Second, more recipients in the joint federal/state Medicaid program are expected to enroll in MCOs. As the number of people receiving Medicaid increased dramatically between 1988 and 1992 total spending on this program skyrocketed from $51 billion to $114 billion (Coughlin, Ku, Holahan, Heslam, & Winterbottom, 1994). This, in turn, prompted all but a few states to develop managed care programs for their citizens receiving Medicaid assistance. In fact, since the middle of 1993, enrollment in Medicaid managed care programs more than doubled to 7.6 million people (Havighurst, 1995).

• •

BOX 50–2 REALITY CHECK: WHAT THE BUDGET DEFICIT REALLY MEANS

During the early 1980s, the federal budget deficit began to grow significantly, often adding $200 billion or more in new public debt annually. During the latter half of the 1980s, the rate of annual increase in the federal government's debt grew so rapidly that it actually surpassed the rate of growth in federal health care spending (ProPAC, 1991).

By the end of 1995, the Congressional Budget Office (CBO) estimated the accumulated federal deficit to equal $3.617 trillion, requiring 16 percent of the current fiscal year budget merely to pay interest on this debt. Throughout the rest of the decade, annual federal deficits are projected to climb back up over $200 billion, rising to an estimated $421 billion in 2005. In that same year, CBO estimates the total federal debt will have grown to $6.757 trillion. Yet, even if the budget were to be balanced by 2002 (in that year, no *new* debt would be incurred), which is the objective of the Republicans in Congress, total federal debt would have accumulated to over $5 trillion and interest payments would still require a huge fraction of each year's federal budget.

Given the federal budget deficit's size and projected rate of growth, together with public opinion solidly behind reducing the debt, health care providers can expect to face public sector cost containment pressures unlike anything they have ever experienced (Blendon, Bodie, & Benson, 1995).

• •

As more Medicare beneficiaries and Medicaid recipients move into these managed care programs, hospitals will likely experience a further reduction in demand. Subsequently, they will be required to make any number of adjustments to reduce their costs—including layoffs of staff—to obtain contracts with price sensitive MCOs for the growing number of elderly and medically indigent who formally came to them in high volumes.

SPREAD OF ECONOMIC COMPETITION

In recent years, businesses and large employers more fully realized that they have tremendous market power when they select the lowest priced and, presumably, the highest quality health insurance plans. To be sure, the more they flex their purchasing power, the more that economic competition will be stimulated among MCOs and fee-for-service medical groups, hospitals, and other providers.

Thus, as market competition increases, health care organizations will have to continually explore new innovations to become more efficient so they can lower costs. Only by reducing costs can an organization price its services competitively in relation to those charged by its rivals. Moreover, to thrive in a competitive industry, organizations must respond to the constantly changing needs and preferences of purchasers. Large employers, their employees, and other subscribers must be satisfied with the services provided by MCOs, hospitals, and home health care agencies or they will select different providers. Indeed, these organizations must produce a level of quality and desired clinical outcomes that individuals and employers want and are willing to purchase. As competition evolves, organizations simply will not be able to afford anything less than a reputation for outstanding quality.

To obtain contracts with employers or other groups of purchasers, MCOs will have to become more efficient, lower their costs, achieve desired patient outcomes, more carefully monitor the quality of clinicians and services, and—above all—maintain high member satisfaction. In order to accomplish this, MCOs must shift some of the financial pressure away from themselves, purchasing out of plan services required by enrollees from only the lowest priced and highest quality hospitals, home health care agencies, and other providers. These institutions, in turn, must keep their prices low, decrease costs by becoming more efficient and provide high quality services to win contracts—and thereby gain access to the members of MCOs.

Clearing the Cobwebs

REFUTING MISCONCEPTIONS TO INCREASE UNDERSTANDING

To keep their attention on building a quality focused agenda, nurses must obtain a clear perspective on the role of economic competition in health care. While it has only begun in a meaningful way in the recent past, reductions—first seen in 1993—in the rate of growth of total national health care spending, health insurance premiums, and hospital costs suggest that competitive forces have already started to achieve their intended effects (Levit et al, 1994; Winslow, 1995; Zwanziger, Melnick, & Bamezai, 1994).

Still, misconceptions abound. Some nurses, for example, object to market competition because they feel it will not guarantee universal access to health services (and they are correct). However, providing health insurance to the 40 million uninsured or underinsured is not a problem that a competitive market is designed to solve. Rather, providing access to this segment of the population is a financing problem which can only be resolved when society decides through the political system that it wants to and is willing to pay for health insurance for citizens who cannot afford it.

Others believe competition will not work and that the U.S. will have to adopt a single payor system akin to the Canadian model. From the beginning, a single payor system never had the slimmest chance of being adopted during 1994 congressional health reform deliberations. Moreover, given current market forces and the political climate on Capitol Hill, it is unlikely that comprehensive, or even incremental, national health reform will occur in the near future—let alone a single payor system. In fact, many state-level reforms may have difficulty becoming enacted. Whether one agrees or disagrees, a consensus has emerged that a competitive market approach will be used to guide the production and delivery of much of the nation's health care for the foreseeable future.

Another mental barrier to refute involves the issue of blame and of letting emotion sweep away perspective. The pace of change throughout the health care delivery system is lightning fast, complicated, and even frightening at times, but nurses must realize the true issue at hand: Overwhelming economic forces are causing health care organizations and the nursing profession to rapidly respond to the changing market as it moves toward more integrated arrangements.

Where We Are Going

SHAPING THE FUTURE DELIVERY SYSTEM

For the longer-term transition to fully integrated delivery systems that are competing for capitated contracts to succeed, there is much that needs to be done. It will be critically important to ensure that market-based economic incentives fully develop. Health care organizations must be encouraged to compete on the basis of price and quality. In addition, nurses and other professionals must change their perspectives about health care—including education and practice—if they are truly to operationalize wellness, prevention, and primary care, which will be the glue that holds these systems together.

Providers also must learn how to manage and practice under a capitated financial arrangement where hospitals and professionals face identical incentives. Physicians, for example will be unable to increase their incomes by performing more procedures because capitation arrangements will motivate them financially to provide only the care required. And, because they would receive the same capitated rate, hospitals will no longer profit from increased admissions and expensive new inpatient facilities. In fact, as cost centers under integrated and capitated systems, hospitals would attempt to minimize admissions through illness prevention and wellness promotion.[1] For the entire health care system to behave in this fashion, however, providers—nurses, other health care professionals, and organizations—must adopt new goals and transform their relationships with each other and the patients they serve.

What It All Means to Nurses

IMPLICATIONS FOR PRACTICE

In thinking through the nature of the forces that are transforming the delivery of health care, it is useful to focus on challenges that will confront nurses in the remaining years of this decade, most notably the spread of economic competition. It also is necessary to concentrate on issues that are likely to dominate nursing at the beginning of the 21st century—in particular, the challenges of providing care within integrated delivery systems. To be sure, a convergence around the quality of patient care will be common to both near-term and long-term strategies.

SHORT-TERM EXPECTATIONS

During the next five years, public cost containment and competitive forces will intensify sharply and large employers will purchase health plans from MCOs based primarily on the price of their premiums. However, as competition grows, it is expected that the rate of price and cost increases will slow even further. Over time, providers' reputations for high quality, and how their indicators compare to those of other organizations, will become more important to employer selection of plans and MCOs. Keep in mind, however, that economic competition, unlike regulated markets, will offer no protection or guarantee of survival to organizations or health professionals who fail in this effort. There can be no doubt that pressures to lower costs and increase quality will be passed on more directly to nurses in all practice settings.

Thus, for nurses' contributions to quality *per dollar spent on wages* to receive greater weight in employment and staffing decisions, economic incentives facing organizations must change. Institutions need to be rewarded for providing higher quality of care and desired patient outcomes in addition to lowering costs. The quicker they are financially motivated to make employment decisions based on health personnel who contribute most to

---

[1] This is not to imply that there will not be a need for hospitals in the future. Rather, it is to suggest that integrated delivery systems will function effectively with fewer hospitals, and these hospitals will be used by the system in more efficient and different ways than presently. In addition, it is likely that most of the future IDS will be comprised of and operated by local hospitals and nonacute provider organizations as opposed to a few large national companies, such as in the telephone, railroad, or automobile industries.

improving quality, the sooner the value of professional nurses is likely to rise, relative to others, and exert a positive influence on their employment.

While creating the right incentives is in nurses' self-interest, it is not enough to completely address the economic nature of employment and staffing problems that exist today and will confront nurses even more so tomorrow. To make more fully informed quality-related staffing and employment decisions, employers will need more precise information on how nurses improve quality outcomes. Such data must be meaningful, incorporate patients' perspectives, be connected to important clinical outcomes, and be aimed at assisting organizations to improve their quality over time. Moreover, nursing quality indicators should be routinely measured and documented—something sorely lacking in the current system.

As better and more timely data on service, price, quality, patient satisfaction, and clinical outcomes become more widely available, consumers and other purchasers will increasingly "comparison shop" before selecting managed care plans or IDSs. Organizations, which will be under great pressure to spend dollars where they can obtain the greatest value, will want to employ only those professionals who can contribute the most to producing high quality and desired patient outcomes (Box 50-3).

LONG-TERM CONSIDERATIONS

In the early part of the 21st century, the health care industry will have become considerably more consolidated, with many organizations linked together in integrated delivery systems. Quality and outcomes of care will become a far more important determinant of purchasers' selection of health plans than is currently the case. How well integrated delivery systems develop and survive in the future will ultimately depend on their ability to successfully compete for capitated contracts. This, in turn, will rest largely on how well they achieve the greatest degree of coordination at the least cost (Feldstein, 1994).

From nurses' perspective, therefore, it is imperative that systems monitoring clinical outcomes, cost, and quality adequately capture nurses' activities and interventions in all of the organizations that comprise IDSs. If these information systems fail to measure and re-

---

BOX 50–3 MANAGED CARE ORGANIZATIONS: FULL SPEED AHEAD

Growth in the proportion of the U.S. population enrolled in MCOs has accelerated dramatically in the last 15 years. According to recent figures from PRoPAC, approximately 100 million people are currently enrolled in managed care programs in the U.S.

The increase in employee enrollment over the years is particularly striking. Nationally, in 1981, only five percent of workers were enrolled in MCOs (primarily HMOs at the time) and the remaining 95 percent were enrolled in traditional indemnity health insurance plans with very weak utilization review programs (Feinstein, 1994). By 1993, however, 52 percent of employees were enrolled in MCOs, and utilization programs had become more sophisticated and effective in sharply reducing enrollees' use of hospitals (Inglehart, 1994; Winslow, 1996). A recent study conducted by Foster Higgins and Company found that during 1994, 63 percent of the nation's workers received health care from MCOs and, today, 71 percent are enrolled in some type of managed care plan.

While there has been low growth—2.1 percent overall—in employer health care costs the past year, expenditures for insuring retirees are escalating, jumping almost 10 percent. Many experts expect companies will either drop coverage for this population or encourage individuals to join HMOs or other managed care plans, thus increasing enrollment even further (Winslow, 1996).

port quality and outcomes-related variables reflecting nurses' actions, then their contributions will be less visible and, hence, less valued. Consequently, fewer resources would be allocated to nurses.

Advancing Nurses' Interests

DEVELOPING AND IMPLEMENTING A QUALITY-FOCUSED AGENDA

Nurses who can respond successfully to these challenges, contributing the most toward increasing the worth of (and hence the demand for) the services they produce, will be valuable assets to organizations. On the other hand, those who do not recognize this economic reality and fail to take steps to increase their value to employers are placing their own job security and future prospects for employment at greater risk.

RAISING NURSES' VALUE

Considering the intense public and private sector pressures that will confront providers indefinitely, it is crucial that nurses recognize and deal with current and longer-term challenges. Nurses must develop strategies *now* to raise their economic value in the eyes of their employers.

Promote Financial Incentives

For a competitive system to evolve—and be in nurses' best interest—public and private sector payers must consider quality more prominently in the selection of health plans and provider organizations. Therefore, nursing's agenda, in the short-run, should concentrate on facilitating the development of financial incentives that reward organizations for quality improvement and the production of appropriate and cost-effective clinical outcomes.

To facilitate this, nurses could inform employers, employee benefit managers, unions, and insurers that quality and patient satisfaction are important—in addition to the price of premiums—when evaluating health plans and selecting provider organizations. Further, they could strike up new relationships with quality monitoring or credentialing organizations, such as the Joint Commission on Accreditation of Health Care Organizations or the National Committee for Quality Assurance (NCQA). The latter reviews health maintenance organizations, and many employers are requiring that HMOs receive NCQA accreditation before they will offer the health plans to employees. A considerable portion of the review criteria for NCQA accreditation is in the area of quality improvement. Examples include whether the plan examines the quality of care it provides members, the level of coordination within the delivery system, the steps being taken to assure care is given in a reasonable amount of time, and the types of improvements in quality that can be demonstrated.

Link Quality to Outcomes

To ensure more informed employment and staffing decisions are made in the future, nurses must take responsibility to provide employers with credible and objective information on quality. This can be done, in part, by first examining the scientific literature pertaining to quality, taking a critical look at current nursing practice, and organizing a course of action based on a synthesis of these two sources of information. Nurses also must find out what their employers need to know about the relationship among quality, outcomes, and nursing practice, then identify the least costly and best information to provide. Moreover, they can formulate follow-up strategies based on gaps in understanding that may emerge from implementing a new dialogue on quality improvement with their employers.

It is essential that nurses connect their activities to improving quality at every opportunity. Now is the time to focus their clinical practice on quality improvement and become more responsive to the needs of purchasers and their employers. Specifically, nurses need to quickly develop knowledge of quality-of-care issues, target their practices to improve quality, and initiate actions to measure and track indicators of quality.

Ensure Contributions Are Monitored

Nurses must ensure that their contributions are captured by the organization's internal quality indicators and are incorporated into its quality assessment program. It is also in nurses' best interest to develop a relationship with external public and private sector parties currently constructing quality and outcomes monitoring systems. By becoming involved in the early stages of development, nurses can become aware of the difficulties these parties face, evaluate how best to incorporate measures of quality and outcomes sensitive to their interventions, and identify specific actions necessary to address this critical issue. Nurses *must* take responsibility for making this happen.

PRIORITIES FOR THE FUTURE

At the same time, nurses need to prepare for the expansion of integrated health care systems. The practice of nursing in a truly integrated system will be vastly different from that of today. Current leaders in nursing education, practice, administration, and research face the challenge of establishing *priorities* for how to most effectively prepare the profession for this future.

While there is much dialogue among nursing leaders about the kind of changes needed in these areas, there is hesitancy over who will take responsibility for making needed transformations. Ultimately, these discussions must result in actions that help nurses obtain the repertoire of skills and experience that enable them to become valuable providers of nonacute care and community-based services, especially to the growing population of elderly Americans.

Improve Nursing Education and Practice

For the health care system to focus on illness prevention and health promotion within a more competitive health care environment, nursing education and scopes of practice must change substantially. Future nurses must be more adequately prepared to meet the evolving expectations of society, employers, and the profession for delivering quality, cost-effective care. In fact, the future employment of new graduates will increasingly be determined by how employers perceive their value in helping organizations meet their survival needs. To this end, leaders in nursing education must consider what components of curricula need to be improved or changed and take action *now* to make this happen. Clearly, nurses will need to have better coordination skills and the ability to provide competent care along the delivery continuum.

Advocate for Increased Research

To make an objective case for the importance of nurses in quality outcomes, there must be empirical evidence. In addition to studying the literature and linking quality to outcomes at individual institutions, nurses need to advocate research that identifies their interventions, validates their effect on patient outcomes, and disseminates results. By stimulating expanded efforts of the Agency for Health Care Policy and Research, the National Institute of Nursing Research, and private foundations, for example, nurses can promote studies examining issues of appropriateness, cost-effectiveness, and quality of care related to their practice.

Disseminate Successful Management Initiatives

In light of tightening Medicare and Medicaid payments to providers and intensifying competitive pressures, employers will continue to find ways to lower their costs and become more efficient. This, of course, should be done without knowingly harming patient care or safety or exposing employees to unwarranted risks.

Because such activity is essential for institutions' survival, it would be useful to synthesize or catalogue—and disseminate—specific changes in the organization of nursing care that resulted in improvements in patient care, lower costs, elimination of waste and duplication, and so forth. Although every organization is different there may be some improvements or change concepts common to successful facilities which could be adopted by others.

Similarly, approaches that have proven successful in enhancing nurses' understanding of the changing economic environment should be made widely available. To build greater confidence about the future, constructive approaches to embracing the change process should be disseminated—from learning how best to acknowledge nurses fears and anxiety, to responding more positively to new challenges, to minimizing risks to their employment.

A Call for Action

ENSURING A BRIGHT FUTURE FOR PATIENTS, PROVIDERS, AND SOCIETY

Implementing a quality agenda should be among the highest priorities of nurses in practice, education, and research settings. The near-term development of economic competition and the longer-term evolution toward IDSs are quickly becoming realities (Box 50-4).

Both competition and integration will cause organizations to place increasing value on producing the highest quality health services. Information on quality will be needed to facilitate consumer choice of providers and selection of health care plans. In addition, such information will enable consumers and other purchasers to better assess what they are obtaining in exchange for their health care expenditures.

Thus, it is imperative that nurses focus more intently on these issues today. They have an exciting opportunity to enhance their own value by linking nursing practice to the definition, production, measurement, assessment, and comparison of quality services. Moreover, by becoming involved in the change process, nurses can help to guard the public against possible unintended outcomes resulting from provider responses to intensifying cost containment pressures (Cleary, 1995).

Indeed, through knowledge and perseverance, nurses can emerge in the future in a better position than what many currently perceive. By evaluating, and perhaps altering, their perspectives, attitudes, and behaviors toward change, nurses not only can advance their own agenda but also promote the best interests of society and the health care organizations which depend on them.

. . . .

BOX 50–4 WHAT ARE INTEGRATED DELIVERY SYSTEMS?

Increased employer pressure to contain premium costs has led MCOs, hospitals, and physicians to begin aligning themselves into what have become known as integrated delivery systems (IDSs). While development of IDSs is still in the early stages, a full range of health care services is expected to be provided.

- wellness programs
- preventative care
- ambulatory clinics
- outpatient diagnostic and laboratory services
- emergency care
- general and tertiary hospital services
- rehabilitation
- long-term care
- congregate living
- psychiatric care
- home health
- hospice care
- outpatient pharmaceutical care

Care provided by organizations and health professionals who are affiliated with IDSs is coordinated through case management and a timely information flow. The aim is to eliminate duplication of tests and services and to ensure that the most appropriate and cost-effective providers are used. This is expected to result in greater control of routine care as well as the costs of expensive specialists and services, including organ transplants (Feldstein, 1994).

By integrating the various providers that comprise the system, it is easier and less expensive to exchange and update data using uniform patient record and electronic information systems. Also, the ability to develop cost, quality, and outcomes monitoring systems is made easier and less expensive.

Incorporating different providers and achieving effective coordination permits IDSs to direct patients to the most appropriate providers according to their needs. Presumably, IDSs will be better able to monitor costs, quality of care, and patient satisfaction. In addition, they should be of great use in obtaining and analyzing information on patients' clinical outcomes and the treatments provided by specific health professionals and organizations.

Moreover, IDSs will be able to develop improved cost projections for serving different patient populations, to more accurately estimate the price of insurance premiums, and to more easily obtain other economic advantages, such as lower liability and malpractice insurance and lower interest rates on loans (Feldstein, 1994). These design features are intended to enable IDSs to assume the financial risk involved in capitated contracts.

. . . .

REFERENCES

Blendon, R., Bodie, M., & Benson, J. (1995, Summer). What happened to Americans' support of the Clinton plan? *Health Affairs.* 14(2). 7–23.

Cleary, P. (1995, January 17.). *A proposal for a national quality monitoring system.* Presentation given at Harvard University School of Public Health. Quality of Care Research Seminar. Boston, MA.

Coughlin, T.A., Ku, L., Holahan, J., Heslam, D., & Winterbottom, C. (1994). State responses to the Medicaid spending crisis: 1988 to 1992. *Journal of Health Politics, Policy and Law.* 19(4). 832–864.

Feldstein, P.J. (1994). *Health policy issues: An economic perspective on health reform.* Ann Arbor, MI: AUPHA Press/Health Administration Press.

Havighurst, C. (1995, February 6). Medicaid managed care exploding. *Medicine and Health.* 49(2).

Iglehart, J.K. (1994). Physicians and the growth of managed care. *the New England Journal of Medicine.* 331(17), 1167–1171.

Levit, K.R., Cowan, C.A., Lazenby, H.C., McDonnell, P.A., Sensenig. A.L., Stiller, J.M., & Won. D.K. (1994). National health spending trends. 1960–1993. *Health Affairs*, 13(5). 14–32.

Prospective Payment Assessment Commission. (1991). *Medicare and the American health care system: Report to the Congress. June 1991*. Washington, DC: Author.

Prospective Payment Assessment Commission. (1995). *Medicare and the American health care system: Report to the Congress. June 1995*. Washington, DC: Author.

Vladeck. B. (1995, January 24). *The future of Medicare.* Presentation at Harvard School of Public Health. Boston, MA.

Winslow, R. (1996, January 30). Employee health-care costs were steady last year. *The Wall Street Journal*. pp. A2. A20.

Winslow. R. (1995, February 27). The outlook: Is victory in sight in health-care war? *The Wall Street Journal*. p. Al.

Zwanziger. J., Melnick. G., & Bamezai. A. (1994). Costs and price competition in California hospitals. 1980–1990. *Health Affairs*. 13(4). 118–126.

BIBLIOGRAPHY

Buerhaus. P.I. (1994a). Economics of managed competition and consequences to nurses. Part I. *Nursing Economic$*. 12(1). 10–17.

Buerhaus. P.I. (1994b). Economics of managed competition and consequences to nurses. Part H. *Nursing Economic$*. 12(2). 75–80. 106.

Buerhaus. P.I. (1995). Economics and reform: Forces affecting nurse staffing. *Nursing Policy Forum*. 1(2). 8–14.

CHAPTER 51

The Capitation Revolution in Health Care: Implications for the Field of Nursing

DAVID C. WYLD

The American health care system is at the inception of what is likely to be a great transformation. It is likely that within the next decade the institution known as the hospital will undergo a radical change. As a result, every aspect of health care delivery in America—including nursing—will be affected. At the heart of this revolution is a force known as capitation.

What Has Brought About Capitation?

For decades, hospitals and other health care institutions have benefited greatly from the luxury of operating in an environment where health care inflation has mostly outpaced, often outraced, the overall inflation rate in the United States. This has meant that hospital executives have been able to primarily focus on building revenue, as opposed to seriously attempting to control the costs associated with service delivery.[1] This inflationary spiral has been brought about largely by the lure of traditional, fee-for-service medicine, whereby providers are reimbursed for services provided. Under this system, no provider has any incentive to limit the amount of care provided to either an individual patient or a served population.[2] In short, it was a system wherein every provider benefited, because the greater the illness in a population, the greater the revenue that was generated for all providers in the health care chain. While fee-for-service medicine is inherently inflationary, it is also the bedrock upon which the health care system of the United States—inarguably the finest in the world—has been built.[3]

The 1980s saw efforts begin to control the inflationary spiral of health care costs. Largely, this took the form of cost control programs imposed by third party payers and the creation of health maintenance organizations (HMOs). Despite the widespread use of utilization reviews by private insurers and the imposition of diagnosis-related group (DRG)

Reprinted from *Nursing Admininistration Quarterly*, 20(2), pp. 1–12, 1996, with permission of Aspen Publishers, Inc., © 1996.

payments for most illnesses set by the federal government for Medicare and Medicaid reimbursement, health care inflation still accelerated throughout the 1980s in populations served under these programs.[4] On the other hand, the formation of HMOs was widely perceived to be a much more successful means of fighting health care inflation, due to the fact that these organizations promoted wellness and preventive care in the populations they served. Indeed, studies have shown that HMOs have experienced 10 to 40% less utilization than fee-for-service health insurance programs.[5,6] However, as pointed out in the analysis of Stearns, Wolfe, and Kindig, this differential can be largely attributed to two factors reflecting a "selectivity bias."[7] First, patients who choose an HMO over a fee-for-service plan are likely to be less frequent and less costly users of medical care. Second, and perhaps more important, physicians who practice in HMOs may have a different philosophical approach to selecting treatment options for their patients from those who operate in the traditional, fee-for-service environment. HMO physicians are more likely to perform a cost-benefit analysis on potential patient services ("limiting services when they feel the cost exceeds the benefit"); physicians who prefer not to operate under an HMO often say they would not do so due to their unwillingness to be governed by cost-benefit consideration in treatment decisions.[7(p.417)] This led these researchers to conclude that many of the utilization reductions and cost savings attributed to HMOs may be due to these significant differences in the patients and providers involved in them.[7]

Due to the fact that neither of these innovations truly served to curb the inflationary spiral of American health care, the early 1990s have already seen the rise and fall of efforts on the part of the federal government to impose change on the American health care system. On the night of September 22, 1993, President Bill Clinton addressed the nation, unveiling his proposed Health Security Act. President Clinton stated that the American health care system was "badly broken" and that his managed competition plan was the solution.[8] For over a year, in Congress and in the public arena, debate ensued over the Clinton plan. Initially, the plan received a great deal of public support. Ultimately, however, the Clinton plan, with its Rube Goldberg complexity, was rejected by both Congress and the American public.[9]

A noted pollster observed that the demise of President Bill Clinton's health care plan "unfolded with the inexorability of a Greek tragedy."[10(p.9)] Analysts have viewed Congress's rejection of the Clinton plan as reflecting a shift in the majority of the citizenry's attitudes toward health care between Clinton's election in 1992 and the demise of his plan in 1994. While Clinton's plan reflected the goal of "health security" for all citizens, the majority of the public's concern regarding the health care crisis shifted during debate over the Health Security Act. Analysts have stated that during this time, the public mood shifted from a collectivist concern of providing health care to all to a more individualistic concern—that of health care security for oneself, one's family, and one's company and coworkers.[11] Now, legislative efforts toward health care reform are likely to take place on a much more limited scale—centering upon insurance reform that protects one's right to continued insurance when leaving or switching jobs and that restricts insurance companies' abilities to limit coverage for preexisting conditions. Political analysts have stated that Congress's and the public's repudiation of the Clinton health care reform bill will, in time, prove to be seen as "a pivotal moment in U.S. politics" and in the Clinton presidency.[9(p.67)] Already, the midterm congressional election of 1994 has seen the Republican Party take control of both houses of Congress. In large part, this was due to voter dissatisfaction with President Clinton's answer to the alleged health care crisis in the United States.

It must be remembered that the major objectives of President Clinton's health care reform proposal were to control the growth of health care expenditures and to better utilize health care resources.[12] While health care reform failed on the federal level, these underlying problems still remain in both fee-for-service medicine and HMOs. While health care inflation has indeed slowed in the past few years (concomitant with a significant decline in the overall inflation rate), the imbedded incentives remain in the system to promote the creation of excess capacity in the American health care system and excess utilization by patients and providers. In fact, it has been estimated that eliminating excess utilization would produce savings to the tune of almost $200 billion annually.[4] The compounded effect of the resultant inflationary spiral in health care costs means that medical insurance premiums and health care costs have risen to a level where private insurers, employers, and state and federal governments have reached a breaking point—unable to afford the health care system that has been created.

We have thus reached a crossroads, where health care expenditures and medical insurance costs can no longer be thought of as an ever-expanding pie. In this environment, everyone engaged in health care delivery will be challenged to operate "in an era of limits."[13(p.44)] Barry Sheehy, chief executive officer (CEO) of a health care consulting firm in Atlanta, stated that hospitals and all other health care providers are operating in an environment that can be characterized as being "at a fault line between one era in the industry and another."[14(p.23)] What are these eras? Richard Johnson clearly delineates that hospitals are moving from an era dominated by technological developments (with no true emphasis on managing costs) to an era dominated by economic concerns (with all the emphasis being placed on managing costs).[15]

How will hospitals respond to this new, economic era of health care? In market after market, hospital executives are reacting to these economic pressures by moving toward capitation.[16] Although at the present time capitation represents only a small percentage of the nation's total health care expenditures, analysts expect explosive growth in capitated payment plans. In fact, it has been projected that by the turn of the century, revenue from capitated payment plans will account for 70 percent of the average hospital's revenue.[4] Thus, a free market solution to America's health care crisis is emerging, and with it, hospitals are redefining themselves through capitation.

What Is Capitation?

By definition, capitation is markedly different from traditional, fee-for-service medicine. Rather than reimbursing the provider for the actual services rendered to a patient, under capitation, an employer or insurer pays the provider a set fee to provide all the reasonable and necessary medical services required by plan members.[1] This fixed payment per member per month (PMPM) is charged to an employer or an insurance provider for each individual covered under the capitated plan.[12] The equation for the health care provider is simple. If the provider provides less care than the PMPM fee generates, the plan will be profitable to the provider. However, if the provider must provide more care than the PMPM fee, then the provider will lose money.

This equation fundamentally changes the nature of the hospital. This is because under a capitated payment system, the financial risk for the provision of the patient's care is transferred from a third party payer (either a private insurer or the government) to the health care delivery system. Analysts have stated unequivocally that "the acceptance of a capitation contract by a delivery system effectively makes the system an insurance company."[12(p.11)] Thus, health care delivery systems that enter into capitated contracts must either possess the financial reserves necessary to cover the risks they are assuming or consider purchasing reinsurance to cover potential catastrophic losses. Analysts predict that a large, new market will develop for insurance companies to offer such "stop-loss" or reinsurance contracts to health care institutions offering capitated contracts.[17]

This equation also fundamentally changes the goals of hospital management. Under capitation, hospitals and physicians can be viewed as cost centers. Thus, every use of a hospital service or visit to a physician represents an expense, not revenue, to the provider.[4] Hospital administrators must thus focus on cost-effective utilization, rather than on the volume of services rendered. Capitation forces hospitals to change their goals as it eliminates "the incentive to fill beds."[4(p.93)] In fact, under capitation, hospitalization represents "a failure," in that the system failed to provide care in the most cost-effective manner.[18(p.29)] Rather than attempting to fill beds, hospitals will seek to lower not only hospitalization rates, but also both the mean length of stay and the variance of these stays between patients being treated for like conditions.[19]

To accomplish these goals, hospitals must seek to develop practice guidelines for at least the costliest diagnoses and the highest frequency procedures. Hospitals must thus develop methods to disseminate these protocols amongst their medical personnel and monitor variances from protocols.[20] Already, physician associations, research groups, and the federal government are at work developing and disseminating such practice guidelines.[2]

Most of all, the move to capitation means that hospital executives must "reject their traditional mind-set."[18(p.29)] This is because rather than managing a health care institution, it is essential for hospital administrators to sense that they are in fact managing a health care *system* under capitation.

Managing a Health Care System Under Capitation

The goal of hospital management under capitation should be to create the leanest possible health care delivery system that can be formed without negatively impacting upon the quality of patient care.[21] Such health care systems should be formed in accordance with recent ideas on what James Womack and Daniel Jones deem the "lean enterprise." These authors define a lean enterprise as "a group of individuals, functions, and legally separate but operationally synchronized companies."[22(p.93)] Womack and Jones see the organization as being not virtual, but perpetual, and being focused on providing the maximum value to the customer at the minimum expense. The value stream thus defines and shapes the enterprise, rather than the enterprise shaping the value stream.[22]

Lean, capitated health care organizations will seek to combine hospitals, physicians, and other providers; to provide within the system only those services that maximize the value stream; and to contract out those services that it cannot cost-effectively provide within the system. Based upon the lean enterprise concept, the goal of an integrated health care delivery system operating under capitation should be to create an "accountable health plan" (AHP) that can "deliver an ever-improving stream of differentiated benefits at ever-decreasing cost and with ever-increasing speed."[21(p.66)]

To create such a lean enterprise, first it is essential for hospitals to bring physicians into partnership with them to succeed in a capitated environment. This is because 80% of health care costs are generated by physicians. If a health care organization cannot maintain some control of physician-generated utilization, capitation will have very little ability to control costs. Under capitation then, there is commonly a division of the capitated PMPM payment between the hospital and primary care physicians (PCPs). PCPs will thus have a central role to play in capitated health care environments because they will serve both as gatekeepers to the access of specialty care and as monitors to ensure that the care received by patients conforms to the protocols and practice guidelines developed by capitation plans.[21] To manage the challenges of capitation effectively, providers and physicians are forming physician–hospital organizations (PHOs). These PHOs can then function to provide services more efficiently and to bid on contracts to provide health care under capitated contracts.[23]

Capitation will thus require health care organizations to develop innovative, new structures to support capitated contractual relationships.[24] When physicians are partnered in a PHO in which they have a vested interest in controlling utilization by sharing in both the up- and downside risk, the collaboration between the hospital and its physicians stands a much greater chance of success under capitation.[1] However, if a hospital's shift to capitation does not properly include physicians as informed partners, then physicians are likely to conclude that capitation is merely a scheme to control their actions by controlling reimbursement. Such attempts to simply "manage by payment" have typically failed as physicians are forced into changing their behavior without the presentation of an adequate reward.[1] According to one analyst, if the PHO is merely a "conduit for funds" between the capitating hospital and its constituent physicians, such capitation plans will ultimately fail. Ideally, then, a workable capitation plan is one that involves physicians not just as partners in a PHO, but as equity owners as well.[25]

The lean enterprise concept will also mean that the shift in hospital management thinking from managing a health care institution to managing a health care system will also require administrators to rethink and possibly abandon many practices that have become accepted over the years by many hospitals.

First, experience has shown that patients under capitated health care plans have 40% fewer inpatient admissions than those under traditional, fee-for-service reimbursement plans.[3] In southern California (the area with the most experience of seeing capitation plans at work), inpatient utilization has dropped by as much as 50%.[26] As the need for hospital beds will drop by almost half under capitation, hospitals will find that the need for expanded hospital capacity, and the concomitant capital investment, will be lessened, if not eliminated.[1] Yet, this poses a tough mental hurdle for health care administrators in that the transition to capitation will mean a loss of power, prestige, and resources for hospital administrators accustomed to building edifices and measuring their importance and stature by the number of beds in their hospital.[1]

Second, hospital administrators may find themselves making service delivery choices on a very different basis under capitation than in a fee-for-service environment. For instance, rather than attempting to provide a full range of health care services, a hospital operating under capitation may make the decision to refrain from offering services that it can subcontract to others on a less costly basis. For example, it may prove cost effective for the hospital to contract the provision of dialysis services to an outside provider rather than to provide the service itself (along with the concomitant investment in technology and personnel). However, on the flip side of the coin, hospitals have a great fixed cost in their physical plant and their base personnel. Thus, while the trend throughout the decade of the 1980s and thus far in the 1990s has been for health care services to be provided outside of the hospital setting as much as possible, capitation may mean that it will be more cost effective for the hospital to make use of its existing facilities and personnel to provide such services. Karen Pallarito observed that "to cover fixed costs, hospitals will have to recapture revenues generated outside of the hospital."[4(p.98)] This could mean that hospitals will begin to offer services formerly provided out of the hospital (eg, home health care, hospice care) in the hospital once again. According to Daniel M. Cain, a partner with Cain Brothers, a health care-oriented investment banking firm, while home health care boomed under both fee-for-service and HMO plans, under capitation, "it will be cheaper to send a cab to pick up patients and bring them back to a central place (for service)."[4(p.98)]

Capitation will thus mean that most hospitals—other than those owned by governmental entities or those operated by purely charitable concerns—will be transformed into much different organizations than they are today. Alden Solovy observed:

In spite of [often] elaborate planning efforts, most hospitals are attempting the same overall strategies. They are attempting to drive out costs and build what amounts to a hub-and-spoke system of hospitals, physicians and alternate site services. In other words, lower costs and prepare for capitation.[26(p.27)]

Will capitation mean the acceleration of consolidation in the health care industry? Despite dire forecasts by analysts such as David Langness of the Healthcare Association of Southern California (who foresees that within a decade "the United States will only have 5 to 10 health care providers, along the lines of behemoths like Columbia/HCA"), it is unlikely that capitation will promote further accommodation.[27(p.34)] Although one could make a significant argument for economies of scale, the health care organization that will be formed to respond to capitation will be very different from the hospital holding companies of today, because "just putting hospitals, doctors, and HMOs together into one single organization isn't enough" to compete effectively in a capitated environment. In fact, such attempts could be categorized as applying "yesterday's thinking" into a new, competitive environment.[21(p.62)]

What is needed today is to integrate all these providers into a new form of cooperative enterprise designed around the premise of maximizing the value stream. Indeed, Chuck Appleby states that the rise of what he calls "the corporatization of American medicine" may result in the elimination of institutions we now know as health insurance companies and HMOs.[27(p.34)] From this perspective, insurance can be viewed as "a commodity" that can be marketed by providers themselves for direct purchase by individuals, by large corporations, and by associations of employers. Indeed, most analysts see local hospitals and local health care administrators as being in the best position to respond to the changing health care environment by setting up seamless delivery systems to provide health care to a population in return for capitated payments without the insurer as a middleman.[27] J. Daniel Beckham thus urges health care administrators "to pull out a clean sheet of paper" when attempting to organize a capitated health care delivery system, and to keep in mind that the goal of the enterprise should be to transform the hospitals and other health care providers involved into a truly "patient-focused enterprise."[21(p.62)]

Over the next decade, we will see hospitals succeed under capitation, and indeed, some hospitals will fail in their efforts to adapt. In the end, however, health care in "an era of limits" will undoubtedly change due to capitation. Indeed, according to Charles Jacobson, president and CEO of Park Nicollet Medical Center in Minneapolis, capitation "isn't just a payment system; it's a different way of practicing medicine."[23(p.30)] Only one thing is certain. The movement toward capitation will align the Hippocratic and economic goals of health care providers. Before capitation, the greater the illness in a population, the greater the revenue that was generated for hospitals. However, under capitation, health care administrators' medical and financial goals will be aligned to focus on maintaining health as opposed to treating sickness.[3]

The Implications of Capitation for Nursing

To date, attention in the health care literature has been focused on how capitation will affect hospitals and physicians. As can be seen through the previous discussion, the strategic choices affecting hospitals are vital to their very survival. Because of the central role of physicians, primarily PCPs in the health care delivery system, much has also been written on how to integrate physicians into a capitated payment system.[2,7,17,23,28] However, to date, there has not been any similar effort to address how nurses and nursing administration will be impacted by capitation. In the remainder of this article, we will explore precisely this question.

At the outset, it is reasonable to assume that in a capitated health care delivery system, demand will change for different types of nurses. What will drive these demand changes? The principal determinant will be that hospital administrators will be forced to "get their house in order" by ensuring that their costs—both fixed and variable—are "as low as possible."[1(p.21)] With hospitals' investments in physical plant and technology being fixed costs, the greatest area for expense reduction will be in the cost of staffing, both in terms of overall staff levels and in the mix of personnel in the staff. When the hospital effectively becomes the insurer (and what were billable nursing charges to a hospital become nursing expenses), hospitals will indeed change their nursing practices and expenditures as these represent a significant portion of their human resource costs. Thus, nurse staffing decisions should be made with an eye foremost on maintaining quality health care delivery. However, nursing administrators will be challenged to promote cost-effective utilization of nursing resources.

What are some examples of the likely changes that will occur in nurse utilization in the coming decade? First, there will be a significant byproduct of the ability of capitated hospitals to reduce their inpatient utilization levels. Due to the efforts that are undertaken under capitated plans both to make increased use of preventive medicine and to reduce admissions (recall that hospitalization represents a failure under capitation), those patients who are admitted to the hospital will be—point blank—"sicker." Thus, the "intensity of illness factor" is one that hospitals must take into consideration in preparing for capitation, because patients who are actually admitted "will *really* be ill and require more services, not less."[25(p.70)] One ramification of the intensity of illness factor rising is that the demand for nurses who provide care in acute settings (eg, emergency departments, operating rooms, and intensive care units) is likely to rise under capitation, even though utilization of hospital services will decline overall. In like fashion, demand for nurses providing treatment in nonacute settings in the hospital will likely fall due to the resultant decline in admissions and utilization that hospitals will experience under capitation. Also, if hospitals do follow the experts' advice to conduct more services within the institution rather than outside the hospital, demand for nurses to provide care services in the home health setting, the hospice setting, and in nursing homes is likely to fall.

Capitation does not mean that the news is all bad in regard to demand for nursing services. Indeed, the renewed emphasis on preventive medical practice will mean that demand for selective nursing services will increase. First, there is likely to be a significant increase in demand for nurses who engage in preventive care services and wellness education efforts. Also, with the primacy of PCPs in the capitated health care system, it is likely that capitation will serve only to exacerbate the nation's shortage in physicians who provide general care.[2] Thus, there may be a trend to increase the use of RNs to provide as much primary care as possible to make up for this shortfall.

With the emphasis on cost-effective utilization of nursing staff, nurse administrators will be greatly challenged to manage in a capitated health care environment. The central paradox facing those in nursing administration will be how they will manage a changing nurse work force while promoting the goals of the capitated health care organization.

One half of the paradox will be the fact that the permanence of hospital nursing personnel will undeniably decline in the years to come. As hospitals focus on nursing costs as a major portion of the variable costs that they can control to promote profitable capitated operations, the size of the core nursing staff will likely decrease. More and more, hospitals will rely upon temporary nursing personnel to fill the gaps that cannot be provided by their permanent, core nursing staff. With this development, there will be a significant growth in the use of temporary nurse staffing agencies and contracted nurse leasing services. Increasingly then, nursing administrators will be faced with managing a work force that will constantly be in flux. In doing so, they will meet square-on one of the great challenges of our day—how to manage a contingency work force.[29]

Nursing administrators will thus be challenged to manage in an era of "light commitment" from an increasingly transient work force—this at a time when commitment on the part of all the personnel in the organization to the goals of the capitated health care delivery system will be necessary. This combination produces the other part of the paradox: How do you increase commitment to quality health care delivery in a cost-effective manner amongst an increasingly impermanent nursing staff?

Much of the literature on physicians emphasizes the importance for hospitals to bring them on board as true partners in capitation plans, sharing in the risks and rewards inherent in a capitated payment system.[17,23] The question facing health care administrators in general and nursing administrators specifically is whether nurses can be brought into the same kind of risk and reward sharing partnership.

The answer is yes, both for the core, permanent nursing staff and for the temporary nursing pool. However, the means to accomplish this partnership to concentrate on quality and cost differ between the two groups. It is a well-demonstrated fact in the management literature that employees can be motivated by both profit-sharing and cost-saving programs if these are properly communicated to the employees and properly implemented in practice.[30] Thus, for the permanent nursing staff, hospitals should look at making nurses partners in the capitation equation, at least on the upside of sharing in cost savings and profitability. If nurses can be made to feel that they have a vested interest in successful capitation operations through such programs as profit sharing and rewards for cost cutting, then they can be an integral part of the capitated health care system's strategy. Perhaps the best way to ensure that the permanent nursing staff will have a vested interest in the success of capitation will be to implement an employee stock ownership program Just as Johnson points out, the importance of PCPs and perhaps other affiliated physicians having an equity interest in capitation's success,[25] the same principle will apply to nurses and all other hospital personnel as well. While such ideas may not be applicable to the temporary nursing staff, nursing administrators may want to push for straightforward incentive pay for performance plans and per-item cost-cutting suggestion plans as a way of eliciting the temporary nurses' participation in promoting the quality, cost-effective care goals of a capitated hospital.

For organizations in turbulent and transforming environments, such as the health care sector today, the goals of corporate strategy should be "strategic flexibility."[31(p.79)] In this environment, all managers must think strategically about investment, not so much in terms of their additional capacity, but in terms of "their capacity to build new capabilities" for the organization.[31(p.79)] This means that for hospitals, success and importance will no longer be determined by their size or their scope, but rather, by whether they can deliver quality medical care at an affordable price.

For nurses and nurse administrators, such thinking on corporate strategic flexibility means that they too must be more flexible in their personal strategies as well. Job security for those on the permanent staff will be found not in tenure, but in performance and the ability to build more capabilities in one's self. For example, for those nurses engaged in general patient care, cross-functional training and the willingness to take on greater responsibility will make them a more valuable asset to the hospital. For temporary nurses, the willingness to be even more flexible in job assignments and perhaps even compensation will make them more valuable in a capitated environment. Perhaps most important, nursing administrators must constantly seek ways for themselves and their staff to be perceived as adding value to the hospital's collective efforts at cost-effective health care delivery. Thus, on both an individual and collective level, those in the nursing profession will increasingly face what is the "new deal" of the American workplace: less guarantee of security, but more opportunities for success.[32]

The key for nursing administrators is to make capitation, which can be perceived by nurses as being inherently threatening, a truly new way of practicing medicine and delivering health care. Nurses must be made aware that the lean enterprise thinking that drives capitation will drive their career success as well. Because capitation turns the hospital into a truly patient-focused enterprise, how nursing can adapt to this changing environment will in large part determine not just the role of individual nurses, nurse administrators, and nursing staffs, but indeed the importance and presence of nurses in the health care sector in America's 21st century.

On a final note, it must be observed that capitation, while projected to grow rapidly into the leading vehicle for health care funding, will not be for everyone in the nursing profession. Just as studies have shown that there are physicians whose philosophies are contrary to the HMO environment, there will be nurses and other ancillary health care providers who will find the cost–benefit nature of capitated care contrary to their way of thinking. For those in nursing who wish to work in a fee-for-service environment, it is likely that a percentage of the nation's health care system will not be converted to capitation due to the fact that their institution's mission is contrary to the market motive and market forces (eg, teaching, charity, and indigent care hospitals). Thus, for those who opt to sit out the capitation revolution, there will be a place to engage in both nursing and nurse administration in an environment not unlike that found today. However, as the years pass and more and more hospitals move to become capitated payment providers, these institutions will become a greater and greater minority of the American health care delivery systems.

The health care sector of our economy is undergoing nothing less than what one observer categorized as a "megachange."[14(p.22)] In a chaotic environment, the ability to change and adapt is the only viable means to success. As hospitals seek to manage this megachange to a capitated operating environment, every aspect of health care will be affected. Nurses and nursing administrators are undoubtedly key components of the equation for capitation success. To ensure the success of this transformation of the American health care industry, it is up to proactive hospital executives and nursing administrators to develop inclusive models that bring nurses into partnership with the emerging capitated health care delivery systems.

REFERENCES

1. Conklin, M. Integrated Systems Will Score with Early Capitation Strategy. *Health Care Strategic Management* 12, no. 9 (1994):1, 19–23.
2. Harris, N. Physicians Are Adapting to Managed Care: Tomorrow's Doctors Will Be Encouraged To Enter Primary Care and Will Be Exposed to More Practice Settings. *Business and Health* 12, no. 3 (1994):44–48.
3. Sachs, M. Collaboration versus Competition: Letting the Natural Order Work. *Frontiers of Health Services Management* 10, no. 3 (1994):40–42.
4. Pallarito, K. Gatekeepers of Capitation. *Modern Healthcare* 24, no. 26 (1994):93–100.
5. Goldberg, L.G., and Greenberg, W. The Competitive Response of Blue Cross to the Health Maintenance Organization. *Economic Inquiry* 18, no. 1 (1980):55–68.
6. Luit, H.S. *Health Maintenance Organizations: Dimensions of Performance.* New York, N.Y.: Wiley, 1981.
7. Stearns, S.C., Wolfe, B.L., and Kindig, D.A. Physician Responses to Fee-for-Service and Capitation Payment. *Inquiry* 29, no. 4 (1992):416–25.
8. Clymer, A. The Clinton Plan Is Alive on Arrival. *The New York Times,* 3 October 1993, E3.

9. Skopcol, T. The Rise and Resounding Demise of the Clinton Plan. *Health Affairs* 14, no. 1 (1995):66–85.

10. Yankelovich, D. The Debate That Wasn't: The Public and the Clinton Plan. *Health Affairs* 14, no. 1 (1995):7–23.

11. Ignagni, K. Navigating the Health Care Marketplace. *Health Affairs* 14, no. 1 (1995): 221–25.

12. Toso, M.E., and Farmer, A. Using Cost Accounting Data To Develop Capitation Rates. *Topics in Health Care Financing* 21, no. 1 (1994):1–12.

13. Coile, R.C., Jr. Reply. *Frontiers of Health Services Management* 10, no. 3 (1994):43–44.

14. Sherer, J.L. Managing Chaos. *Hospitals and Health Networks* 69, no. 4 (1995):22–28.

15. Johnson, R.L. Hospital Governance in a Competitive Environment. *Health Care Management Review* 20, no. 1 (1995):75–83.

16. Fraser, I., Simone, B., and Lane, L. Capitation and Reform: Challenges and Choices for Hospitals' Leadership. *Hospitals* 67, no. 7 (1993):23–25.

17. Cave, D.G. Incentives and Cost Containment in Primary Care Physician Reimbursement. *Benefits Quarterly* 9, no. 3 (1993):70–77.

18. Cerne, F. Dollars and Sense: Creating Incentives To Effectively Manage Change. *Hospitals and Health Networks* 68, no. 7 (1994):28–30.

19. Krentz, S.E. Risk versus Uncertainty in Managed Care Contracting. *Healthcare Financial Management* 48, no. 10 (1994):22.

20. Witek, J.E., and Davidson, H.L. Assessing Organizational Readiness for Capitation and Risk Sharing. *Healthcare Financial Management* 48, no. 8 (1994):18–19.

21. Beckham, J.D. Building the High-Performance Accountable Health Plan. *Healthcare Forum Journal* 37, no. 4 (1994):60–67.

22. Womack, J.P., and Jones, D.T. From Lean Production to the Lean Enterprise. *Harvard Business Review* 72, no. 2 (1994):93–103.

23. Montague, J. Capitation and Physicians: Experienced Providers Say Physician Involvement Is Crucial to Success. *Hospitals and Health Networks* 68, no. 7 (1994):30–35.

24. Kenkel, P. The Systematic Approach: Physician-Hospital Collaborations Increase, Work To Capture Managed-Care Contracts. *Modern Healthcare* 24, no. 14 (1994):59–65.

25. Johnson, R.L. HCMR Perspective: The Economic Era of Health Care. *Health Care Management Review* 19, no. 4 (1994):64–72.

26. Solovy, A. Predicting the Unpredictable. *Hospitals and Health Networks* 69, no. 1 (1995):26–29.

27. Appleby, C. Health Care's New Heavyweights. *Hospitals and Health Networks* 69, no. 9 (1995):26–34.

28. Scalisi, R. Physicians' Attitudes on Health Care Reform. *Business and Health* 10, no. 12 (1992):18–19.

29. Fierman, J. The Contingency Work Force—Just-in-Time Employees, Throwaway Execs: America Works a New Way. It's Not All Bad, and Full-Time Jobs Won't Disappear. But Managers Had Better Adapt. *Fortune* 129, no. 2 (1994):30–36.

30. Luthans, F. *Organizational Behavior, 7th ed.* New York, N.Y.: McGraw-Hill, 1995.

31. Hayes, R.H., and Pisano, G.P. Beyond World Class: The New Manufacturing Strategy. *Harvard Business Review* 72, no. 1 (1994): 77–86.

32. O'Reilly, B. The New Deal: What Companies and Employees Owe One Another. *Fortune* 129, no. 12 (1994): 44–52.

• •

CHAPTER 52

Profession Building in the New Health Care System

KENNETH R. WHITE AND JAMES W. BEGUN

Deeply rooted in their historical context, nurses have struggled to achieve credibility, autonomy, and power on a par with physicians and other health professionals. Not only have nurses had to prove themselves as legitimate professionals but they also have had to fight the battle for women's equal rights. Although nursing has had a long history of oppression,[1] great strides have been made in attaining legitimacy and power for professional nursing. In the last 100 years, nursing has transitioned from a blue-collar, domestic servant class to a knowledge-based discipline linked to every aspect of the health care system. Nursing has long since rejected the handmaiden role and has assertively redefined the nurse as a leader who may best guide the total care of the patient.[2]

Yet much remains to be accomplished. To further the goals of greater legitimacy and power, it is necessary for nursing to revise many of the strategies that made sense prior to the 1990s. With health care changing at a galloping pace, it follows that the sources of power in the health care system, and the mechanisms for achieving power, would change also. Nursing must transform its strategies for achieving power in order to keep pace.

Nursing as a Complex Adaptive System

In order to view the profession of nursing as a whole, it is useful to visualize the profession as a complex adaptive system, with the properties of such systems. An economy, a fern, a city, a society—all are examples of complex adaptive systems. As a system, the nursing profession includes both professional organizations and individual practitioners united by the pursuit of common goals, such as legitimacy and market power.[3] The nursing profession supplies nursing services to consumers, employers, and other purchasers of its services. Even limited to RNs, the system of nursing is still huge, encompassing some 2.2 million individuals and hundreds of professional organizations.

Complex adaptive systems generally seek to adapt to their environment, and they do so within the constraints of their historical context, unless radical transformations can be

Reprinted from *Nursing Administration Quarterly,* 20(3), pp. 79–85, 1996, with permission of Aspen Publishers, Inc., © 1996.

achieved.[4] The systems attempt to respond to changes in their environments and shape the environments in their own interests. This is analogous to saying that complex adaptive systems have a strategy. Strategies can be defined as patterns in the goal-directed plans and activities of professionals and their associations that position the profession in relation to external demands.[3] For example, the American Nurses Association (ANA) has attempted to represent the position of nursing (although only 10% of the nation's RNs are members) through its formalized policy statements and political activities. With any system as large and complex as nursing, strategic direction often is implicit rather than explicit, and emergent, only becoming apparent in retrospect, rather than planned.

As a complex adaptive system, nursing will attempt to deal with the quickening pace of change in the environment. To survive, the system will need to balance its efforts to shape the health care environment with its efforts to react to or cope with (or ignore) external forces. A new framework for profession building must be adopted in order to transform nursing into a profession that continues to serve the needs of society. In order to understand changes that are needed, it is important to summarize the traditional approach to profession building in nursing and to elucidate a more contemporary model.

Traditional Profession Building in Nursing

As a result of strategic activity and social, political, and economic conditions, nursing has evolved from a powerless class of domestic servants to a much more powerful segment of health care professionals today. What strategic directions have characterized this evolutionary process of profession building?

In the fairly stable health care environment of the post-World War II period through the 1980s, nursing was able to enhance its professional power through standardization of nursing curricula, licensure, and development of nursing science. During this time, several themes emerged that we characterize as the traditional framework for profession building in nursing.

INDEPENDENT VERSUS DEPENDENT ROLES

To increase nursing autonomy, nursing has concentrated on identifying and distinguishing independent and dependent nursing actions. To enhance legitimacy, nursing has wanted to maximize independent actions and minimize dependent actions, or transfer the dependent actions to lesser-educated workers, such as licensed practical nurses or aides. Carving out activities unique to nursing has been the quest of nursing leaders and theorists. For example, nursing diagnosis is an attempt to standardize nursing language pertaining to actions within the domain of nursing (independent) and distinct from the medical model used by physicians (dependent).

PROFESSIONAL SELF-REGULATION

Concurrent with the drive to achieve independence and uniqueness, nursing has focused on the need for self-regulation. This has resulted in an educational accreditation structure controlled within the profession (the National League for Nursing [NLN]) and licensing boards in each of the states, independent of medicine. Recently, nursing created its own specialty certification structure, the American Board of Nursing Specialties, again on the premise that self-regulation is key to controlling its destiny. The emphasis in nursing on formal credentialing is illustrated by the alphabet soup of credentials that has represented the hundreds of specialty and honorary designations.

RIGID PROFESSIONAL BOUNDARIES

Nursing professional socialization has emphasized structure and rigid boundaries between the domain of nursing and that of other health professionals. Grounded in the historical context wherein nurses had to maintain flawless social and personal respectability, a set of rules about professional boundaries proliferated. Nurse practice acts carefully delimit activities that fall within the purview of the credentialed nurse. Lesser-credentialed nursing personnel or other professionals are discouraged or prohibited from participating as team members in delivering such nursing care.

FOCUS ON NURSING AS "CARING"

The underpinning of many of the theories and models of nursing is that nursing's uniqueness stems from the caring component. This typically is contrasted to the curing focus of medicine. Ray,[5] for example, argues that caring in the human health experience is the unifying focus of nursing and nursing inquiry. In the ANA's *Nursing's Social Policy Statement,*[6] caring is included in the listing of four essential features of contemporary nursing practice.

NURSING AS AN OPPRESSED PROFESSION

Nursing has been described by Roberts[1] as exhibiting oppressed group behavior. She describes this as subtle self-hatred and dislike for other nurses that has been evident in the divisiveness and lack of cohesiveness observed in nursing groups. The conflict over moving nursing away from hospital training programs to university education models probably is rooted in the belief that caregivers should stay oppressed by the maintenance of the dominant form (ie, hospitals, paternalism). The fact that the ANA represents only 10% of nurses can be viewed as evidence of lack of pride in one's group.

NURSING AS A FEMALE PROFESSION

The fact that nursing has predominantly been a female profession has been ignored as a strategic issue by most of nursing. The roots of nursing in Florence Nightingale, the caring and sensitivity of women, and the service orientation emphasized in nurse socialization all result in female-ness being seen as a special, distinguishing characteristic of nursing. Consistent with rigid professional boundaries, men were viewed as representatives of the male-dominated medical and administrative · "oppressors." Although unintentional, Porter-O'Grady believes that reverse discrimination (discrimination toward men) has existed in nursing. He believes that particularly in leadership roles it is "very challenging for men to break into what could be irreverently called the 'old girls' club."[7(p.58)]

FOCUS ON JOB SECURITY

As nursing began the transition from domestic servitude to hospital worker, along with the rise in industrial workers and labor unions, nurses came to believe that they had a right to job security on the basis of longevity of employment with an organization. The role of the ANA as a collective bargaining organization was established then. Many of the recent arguments from organized nursing groups purport that declining quality and outcomes are results of poor staffing levels and skill mix patterns and hospitals' plans to maximize profits at the expense of quality. In fact, fear of job loss may well underlie these expressions of concern, as well.

DEVELOPMENT OF NURSING SCIENCE

Since the 1950s, a focus of nursing has been the definition and development of nursing science. A huge body of literature has developed around the label *nursing theory*. Meleis[8] describes this literature as including identification of nursing's domain, the mechanics of theory development, development of concepts, and philosophical debates.

FOCUS ON ACUTE CARE

Nurses were educated for acute care settings. Nursing school curricula focused on technical procedures, nursing process (which is the same as the scientific method), and the disease-oriented medical model. Implicit in acute care is episodic and fragmented patient care.

STANDARDIZED ENTRY TO PRACTICE

Consistent with the quest for the profession's self-regulation, nursing has argued for a one-size-fits-all approach. This perennial controversy focused on having the right degree or lobbying for all nurses to have the same degree as sources of power. Although the one-size-fits-all argument has not triumphed, curricula in nursing are highly standardized and subject to extensive, formalized accreditation criteria of the NLN.

CENTRALIZED PROFESSIONAL ORGANIZATION

Nursing has pursued the traditional model of professionalization in which one dominant professional association represents the profession, in this case the ANA. Pressures to maximize the membership in the central professional association have been intense. The ANA has been expected to provide a unified voice for all of nursing.

The nursing profession historically has pursued an inward-directed set of activities to build the strength of nursing, using professionalization tactics that have been successful for medicine and some of the other health professions. The profession has tried to create a "closed" system in order to build strength to face the external environment.

Contemporary Profession Building in Nursing

The traditional framework has served nursing reasonably well. However, the magnitude of change in health care is demanding that nurses look to a new framework for achieving professional power. What follows is a description of themes of the new framework for profession building in nursing.

INTERDEPENDENCE

It is no longer germane to focus only on independent and dependent nursing actions. Nursing does not need to prove that it is important. It is beyond that. Nurses need to work collaboratively with physicians and other health professionals. Armed with broad-based primary care clinical knowledge, nursing is positioned to be the ideal leader in a managed care environment. Nurses all across the country are leading organizational changes in hospitals and their integrated delivery networks by implementing creative and innovative approaches to improving quality and lowering costs.

The interdependence and collaborative efforts with others will result in increased emphasis on teamwork. Organizations will devote more resources to enhancing teamwork. There will not be as much use for the strict distinction between "insiders" and "outsiders." The insiders' aim should be to learn how they are perceived by others when they are compared with many other output producers.[9] Nurses should work with administrators to inform them of the various options so far as internal practices are concerned and to help design evaluative criteria that will enable administrators to make assessments that are fair and just to all producers while getting the best available outputs.

ACCOUNTABILITY TO STAKEHOLDERS

No longer is the focus on profession self-regulation. In a buyer's market, nursing must be accountable to its key stakeholders. This means that purchasers of nursing services, as well as other interdependent professions, should be partners in ensuring the quality of nursing care. Self-regulation will be transformed into shared regulation with key stakeholders.

FLEXIBLE BOUNDARIES

The powerful profession of the future will respond to the needs of its stakeholders by continuously redesigning and reengineering the profession. This will result in greater splintering of the profession as new types of workers emerge to meet new market niches or serve new societal needs. For example, nursing education curricula will be redesigned to respond to the demands of managed care and systems integration, and specialists to serve those markets will emerge. To facilitate this process, concerns about boundary-setting that have characterized the history of nursing will need to be resisted.

FOCUS ON NURSING AS POSSESSING SKILLS AND KNOWLEDGE

Nursing will not be considered unique by virtue of its being a caring profession. Purchasers of health care cannot put a price on caring. They can, however, put a price on skills and knowledge that contribute to patient outcomes. Nurses need to take their basket of goods to the market with a price tag. "Value-added" is an important commodity and what nurses contribute to improved quality and decreased costs must be measured and included in the price tag. It may mean that nursing's stakeholders will demand fewer RNs at the bedside and more RNs in advanced practice roles functioning as "knowledge workers" who delegate more of the nonprofessional routine duties to unlicensed caregivers. The time is right for nursing research to assess the impact nurses have on quality and outcomes.

NURSES AS PARTNERS IN PREVENTION AND TREATMENT

Yesterday's focus on nurses as oppressed women who are handmaidens to physicians is over. Nursing leaders are in positions of executive decision making. Nurses will no longer say "This can't be done" but they will ask "How can we deliver the best care at the lowest cost?" Along with physicians and allied health professionals, nurses will be functioning in advance practice roles for primary care delivery.[10] Concerns about oppressed group status will pale in importance as criteria for effectiveness become more universal and public.

RECRUITMENT OF MORE MEN

To increase creativity and innovation for problem solving, the profession will have to seek more diversity in its members. Of acute significance is the small proportion of nurses who are men. Any strategic advantages of gender homogeneity become irrelevant in a market-driven health care system where outcomes of care and innovation are determinants of success.

JOB SECURITY BASED ON CONTRIBUTION TO ORGANIZATION

Job security is no longer a right but a privilege that comes with professional accountability. Continuing education takes on an entirely new meaning. To keep pace with rapid change, nurses will have to spend more time in lifelong self-learning. Organizations will spend fewer resources on defining work tasks for nurses and more time in evaluating nursing outcomes. Organizations will be less inclined to reward longevity than contributions to the organization's bottom line.

DEVELOPMENT OF MULTIDISCIPLINARY THEORIES

As Meleis[8] believes, nursing theory development in the 21st century will be concerned less with the domain of nursing. Growing collaboration will result in "health care theories" based on the needs of populations that will be used by all members of the health care team. This requires that efforts to develop a unique nursing science be secondary to the search for theory that can guide practitioners in producing healthy patients.

INCREASED CORPORATIZATION

Decisions affecting the bedside nurse no longer are made locally. The consolidation of health care providers into integrated delivery networks changes the locus of power. Although local organization politics and personal power will always pervade, nursing will have more legitimate power in executive decision making at top levels of organizations. More nurses will seek graduate education in business and health administration to keep pace with job demands.

DIVERSE SETTINGS OF NURSING CARE

Acute care is no longer the focus of nursing practice. Hospitals are merely intensive care units. Care will be delivered in the communities and nurses will need to have knowledge of the continuum of care, including preventive, home, day, hospice, and respite care. From this vantage point, nurses are ideally suited for leadership roles in case management and advanced practice roles in population-based primary care.

MULTIPLE ENTRY PATHWAYS

To satisfy the needs of the stakeholders and the new wave of social transformation[11] nursing education will be reengineered and reformed. It will be more and more difficult to standardize curricula and entry requirements, resulting in a proliferation of pathways to highly differentiated arenas of nursing practice. In making this transition, the profession can benefit by encouraging diversity in profiles of those entering the profession.

DECENTRALIZED PROFESSIONAL ORGANIZATION

Profession building in nursing increasingly will occur in the differentiated segments of nursing. While new segments will arise, current examples include nurse midwives, nurse anesthetists, nurse executives, and the different nurse practitioner specialties. These segments will be more in touch with stakeholder needs and demands, and it will be less feasible for one single organization, such as the ANA, to attempt to assume a coordinating role.

Conclusion

There are signs that nursing is beginning the transition from traditional to contemporary forms of profession building. The ANA's 1995 Nursing's Social Policy Statement, for example, states that "Nursing is not separated from other professions by rigid boundaries. Nursing's scope of practice has a flexible boundary that is responsive to the changing needs of society."[6(p.12)] The recognition of the need for flexibility is an important step in strategic adaptation.

Ruminations about power and politics have occupied the minds and resources of nursing to an unusual degree. Profession building at both the local and national levels has involved a high degree of political activity within hospitals and government policy making settings. While these traditional profession building activities will continue to influence the lives of all nurses, important decisions about roles and income and other rewards are more and more likely to be based on measurable contributions. Contemporary nursing must seize this opportunity to create new pathways for strategic adaptation.

REFERENCES

1. Roberts, S.J. Oppressed Group Behavior: Implications for Nursing. *Advances in Nursing Science* 5, no. 4 (1983):21–30.
2. Heide, W.S. *Feminism for the health of it.* Buffalo, N.Y.: Margaretdaughters, 1985.
3. Begun, J.W., and Lippincott, R.C. *Strategic Adaptation in the Health Professions: Meeting the Challenges of Change.* San Francisco, Calif.: Jossey-Bass, 1993.
4. Begun, J.W., and White, K.R. Altering Nursing's Dominant Logic: Guidelines from Complex Adaptive Systems Theory. *Complexity and Chaos in Nursing* 2, no. 1 (1995):5–15.
5. Ray, M.A. Complex Caring Dynamics: A Unifying Model of Nursing Inquiry. *Theoretic and Applied Chaos in Nursing* 1, no. 1 (1994):23–32.
6. American Nurses Association. *Nursing's Social Policy Statement.* Washington, D.C.: American Nurses Publishing, 1995.
7. Porter-O'Grady, T. Reverse Discrimination in Nursing Leadership: Hitting the Concrete Ceiling. *Nursing Administration Quarterly* 19, no. 2 (1995):56–62.
8. Meleis, A.I. Directions for Nursing Theory Development in the 21st Century. *Nursing Science Quarterly* 5, no. 3 (1993):112–17.
9. Dunbar, R.L.M., and Ahlstrom, D. Seeking the Institutional Balance of Power: Avoiding the Power of a Balanced View. *Academy of Management Review* 20, no. 1 (1995):171–92.
10. Appleby, C. Boxed In? *Hospitals and Health Networks* 69, no. 18 (1995):28–34.
11. Drucker, P.F. The Age of Social Transformation. *The Atlantic Monthly* 274 (1994):53–80.

CHAPTER 53

●●

The Revolution in Health Care: What's Your Readiness Quotient?

DIANA J. MASON AND JUDITH K. LEAVITT

Forget the demise of the Clinton health care reform plan in Congress. With or without Washington's help, a revolution is taking place in health care, and the implications for the nursing profession are far-reaching. Nurses are already feeling the shock waves in their daily practices. Many have lost jobs or fear they will lose them.

Others, however, are making the most of this time of transformation. They're helping to influence the course of change to advance nursing's core values, such as caring, humanity, and health promotion.

Will you succeed in the brave new world of health care? In large part, it's up to you. The first step is to assess how well prepared you are for the challenges ahead. Take the test in this article to determine your "readiness quotient"—and your organization's (Fig. 53–1). Then learn what you can do in your workplace and in the public policy arena to help shape the future.

Currents of Change

As *AJN* Editor-at-Large Lucille Joel suggests in her October 1994 editorial, "Start with the premise that things won't be the same." There are various trends transforming health care, but most are driven by the need to control costs.

Even before health care reform appeared on the nation's political agenda, insurance companies and other payer organizations were moving to managed care, a greater emphasis on primary care and outpatient treatment, and tighter control of hospital stays. With no broad-based federal reform in sight, market forces—particularly insurers' drive to minimize their costs and maximize their profits—dominate the national picture.

That's not to say the federal government won't undertake some reform efforts. Though the idea of health care as an individual right finds little support in the current Congress, limited measures such as ensuring portability of insurance coverage or prohibiting exclusions for preexisting conditions are being considered. And the desire to cut spending may lead Congress to consider changes in Medicare, such as encouraging greater use of managed care.

Washington may, however, take a back seat to state governments, which are expected to undertake more comprehensive efforts that will serve as experiments in determining the course of any future national reform. States will also continue to take steps to control rising Medicaid costs, such as through limits on eligibility.

Hospitals are remaking themselves in response to these developments. Some are creating integrated systems that cover the entire spectrum of services, from health promotion

---

Test Your Readiness Quotient . . .

This test can help you evaluate how well-positioned both you and your organization are for the changes occurring in health care. It's not a research-proven instrument—it hasn't been tested for validity or reliability—so interpret your score with some caution. The most important aim of this test is to encourage you to think about some of the trends that you can follow and perhaps influence within your own health care organization, whether it be a hospital, home care agency, or visiting nurse service. (If you work for a public health agency, school, or industry, you may need to translate some of the questions in part two to better fit your practice setting.)

Rate your agreement or disagreement with the statements using the scale below (respond honestly) and, after you complete each part of the test, add up the numbers to calculate your score.

1	2	3	4	5
Don't know	Strongly disagree	Disagree	Agree	Strongly agree

How ready am I?

____ 1. I know the current status of national and state health care reform legislation.

____ 2. I'm aware of how trends changing the health care system will affect my practice.

____ 3. My colleagues and I on my work unit have discussed health care reform and its implications for our practice and our roles.

____ 4. I can influence the course of change in my workplace.

____ 5. Some of the changes occurring in health care reform are consistent with nursing's interests and concerns.

____ 6. I integrate into my practice a concern for continuity of care.

____ 7. I'm greatly concerned about patients' satisfaction with the care my colleagues and I provide.

____ 8. Patient education is a major focus on my practice.

____ 9. I've played a significant role in developing a plan for improving patient care during the past six months.

____10. I have a plan for my own professional development to enhance my role in a changing health care system.

____11. I know what my state nurses association is doing to influence health care reform.

____12. I've communicated with one of my legislators about nursing practice issues affected by government policy.

____13. I'm involved in community organizations, such as the school board, citizen action groups, or political parties, that have an interest in health care reform.

____14. I can use JCAHO standards (or those of another accrediting body) to argue for changes in my health care organization that will foster better patient care.

____15. I can discuss the market forces affecting my health care organization and my practice.

____ TOTAL

How ready is my organization?

____ 1. My organization provides programs or forums for discussion of changes and trends in health care delivery.

____ 2. Nursing administration has developed a strategic plan for transforming nursing practice in my organization.

____ 3. The staff in my organization is encouraged to be creative and to introduce innovations for improving patient care.

____ 4. Patient satisfaction data are regularly shared with the staff.

____ 5. Continuous quality improvement or total quality management approaches have been used to improve patient care within my organization.

____ 6. Nursing is involved in decision-making about staff mix.

____ 7. My organization has developed a plan for expanding ambulatory care or enhancing continuity of care.

____ 8. My organization belongs to a larger network of health care delivery systems (for example, hospitals, outpatient clinics, home care agencies).

____ 9. My organization is in good financial health.

____10. My organization uses or plans to use advanced practice nurses.

____11. My organization supports the staff's continuing education, reeducation, and advancement to help bring about changes needed in patient care.

____12. Nurses are included on all committees in my organization involved in policy development and strategic planning.

____13. The chief nurse officer in my organization has line authority.

____14. My organization supports collaborative, multidisciplinary team approaches to patient care.

____15. My organization is visibly marketing its centers of excellence to the community it serves.

____ TOTAL

Figure 53–1

and illness prevention to specialized inpatient treatment, stressing continuity of care. Many are implementing continuous quality improvement or total quality management programs aimed at enhancing operating and clinical services to reduce costs while improving or at least maintaining the quality of care and patient satisfaction. Many have undertaken redesigns that break down disciplinary boundaries to improve care and cut costs.

More troubling, too many hospitals are eliminating nursing positions (even laying off nurses) and hiring nonprofessional "technicians," without creating a model for delivery of quality care or even giving much thought to such issues as staff mix and supervision. Quality of care, far from being enhanced, may deteriorate. This short-term approach to cutting costs runs the risk of long-term disaster.

What Your Test Scores Mean

Before you read any further, take the test in Figure 53-1, then come back to Figure 53-2 to interpret your scores.

Add the number values of your answers to the statements in "How ready am I?" and mark on the horizontal axis of the scoring grid the point that corresponds to the total. Similarly, add the number values of your answers to the statements in "How ready is my organization?" and mark on the vertical axis of the grid the point corresponding to that total. Then find on the grid the point whose coordinates are your two scores. Here's what the scores mean:

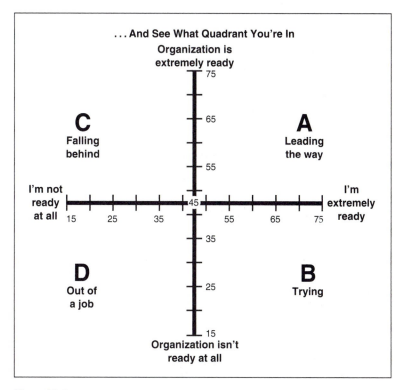

Figure 53–2

- If your score places you in quadrant A, congratulations. You're "leading the way" and staying abreast of changes and trends in health care. And you work for an organization that's well positioned to thrive in a changing environment.
- If you're in quadrant B, you're "trying," but either you don't know what's going on in your organization or your organization isn't doing much to inspire your confidence in its future. Ignorance is dangerous for both you and your organization. If you answered "I don't know" to many of the organization readiness questions, start to ask questions, read internal communications, and join committees that are planning the organization's future directions.

  If you didn't answer "I don't know" to most of those questions, your organization is in trouble—or will be soon. Given today's competitive environment, you'll need to take a hard look at whether you want to stay with your organization and have a strong enough commitment to help it move forward. You may want to assess how well other health care organizations in your area are poised for change and what opportunities they may offer.
- If you scored in quadrant C, on the other hand, your organization may be reconsidering its commitment to you—you're "falling behind." Besides getting up to date with changes in your organization, you need to look beyond your workplace, at the big picture—what's happening in health care today and what will be happening tomorrow. (We'll discuss this in more detail later.)
- Finally, if you scored in quadrant D, you need to spend a great deal of time and energy learning about the changes in health care and looking for a healthier organization in your area. Chances are, you'll be "out of a job" unless your job happens to be at the only hospital or organization of its kind in the area, and it's still experiencing a shortage of nurses.

While it's certainly interesting to learn how you fare personally, the readiness quotient test is designed to get nurses thinking about how they can shape future change in health care. We encourage you to share and discuss the test with colleagues. Suggest to your coworkers that they take the test individually; then get together and discuss what the results might mean for you and your unit. For example, if your hospital hasn't taken steps to enhance continuity of care, you might discuss starting a new patient teaching program to promote self-care after surgery. Such discussion can stimulate the kind of collegiality and collaboration that's essential for change. You'll gain new insight into your colleagues' perspectives and perhaps become more tolerant of views different from your own.

First Step to Readiness: Keep Informed

Staying informed is essential to anticipating changes in health care and in your organization and how they might affect your practice. It will also enable you to speak knowledgeably when you discuss trends and possible changes with others and express your views.

Read a good daily newspaper or weekly news magazine. Listen to or watch radio or television news and analysis programs regularly—and make sure to catch special reports on health care issues. Peruse nursing and other professional journals that cover developments in health care policy.

If you haven't attended a national nursing conference in the past year, plan to do so soon. Educational sessions at conferences often include reviews and updates on trends in health care and seminars on how to respond to the changes.

Share information and insights with colleagues. Besides having regular discussions, consider setting aside a bulletin board where everyone can post articles they've read on health care developments. These postings can help stimulate an exchange of ideas.

Discussions with colleagues about changes in health care delivery can help you identify opportunities to improve patient care. For example, emphasis on reducing health care costs through prevention and self-care along with pressure from accrediting bodies such as JCAHO have rekindled hospitals interest in patient education. You can take advantage of this development to advance proposals to improve patient teaching. Your discussions might focus on such possibilities as follow-up phone calls after discharge or a designated "telephone hour" for patients and families to call with postdischarge questions.

Value Your Voice

In a health care system that increasingly stresses the bottom line, it's sometimes difficult to believe that voices of caring are heard. Still, nursing's perspective and ideas are needed to make sure that our workplaces—and the larger system—put patients first. How can you get your organization and policymakers to listen to you? Try these steps:

- Network with others in your workplace who'll support your views—and who'll support you when you speak out. It's easier to value your own voice when others do.
- Get involved in your state nurses association and your specialty organization. Groups can be more powerful than individuals acting alone.
- Take credit for your achievements. Too often, we let others grab the honors for our accomplishments. In one hospital, for example, an administrator responsible for revamping the inpatient transport system took the credit for reducing lengths of stay on several units. He conveniently overlooked the fact that a new nursing model for coordinating tests and procedures had been implemented on these units, and that the shorter stays were mostly due to nursing's efforts to move patients more efficiently through the hospital system.

Arm Yourself With Data

While the idea of collecting and interpreting data may be intimidating, keep in mind that information can drive change. Nurse practitioners and nurse midwives have won respect and reimbursement largely because of data demonstrating their cost-effectiveness. Talk with colleagues about what information would be important for you to have as your unit or organization contemplates workplace redesign or other changes in patient care. This might include, for example, current RN-to-patient ratios, rates of nosocomial infection, average length of stay, and patient satisfaction ratings.

Be aware, too, that many changes at health care institutions are being made without enough facts—particularly when redesign tempts executives with the immediate payoff of reduced costs. Consider that the substitution of unlicensed assistive personnel for RNs at many hospitals has come about without proof that it's safe or effective or even that it saves money in the long run. At the very least, recommend that your organization evaluate any changes it makes based on inadequate data. When you hear that technicians are going to be introduced on your unit, ask, "How are we going to assess the impact of this change?"

Use Your Political Savvy

Florence Nightingale, often called the first statistician, knew that data were important to effecting change but often not enough. She was also a master political strategist, and understood that good data coupled with smart politics can be enormously powerful.

Achieving change requires political skills. Work with colleagues to analyze the political context of innovations you may propose—who the decision makers are, who'll support or oppose the change, what financial resources are available—and to develop a plan of action. As you draft a plan and carry it out, employ these politically savvy tactics:

- Identify and assess the forces that might help drive or impede the change. For example, a new patient education program might help the hospital meet JCAHO standards but would require an initial investment.
- Consider the timing for taking action. A proposal for a costly new program may not be well received at a time of financial belt-tightening.
- Ask nursing colleagues and those in other disciplines, particularly medical staff, to lend you support.
- Anticipate opposing arguments and prepare to respond to them with facts in hand.
- Market your idea. Bring it up at staff meetings, make sure it gets into your institution's newsletter, even seek coverage in local media if it will help. Point out your past accomplishments—nothing succeeds like success.
- Always express your ideas in terms of what's best for patients.

Get Involved in Government

Lobbying of state and national legislators is essential if nursing's perspective on health care is to influence future reform legislation and regulations. How can you get your voice heard in the halls of government?

- Invite members of Congress or state legislators to "Spend a Day with a Nurse." State nurses associations have used this strategy for years.
- Along with colleagues, visit your state legislator and share your stories and ideas, especially if a relevant piece of legislation is being considered.
- Keep in touch with your state or local nurses association for updates on health care legislation. Share with them your ideas, experiences (such as the consequences of substituting nonprofessionals for RNs), and data.
- Continue to support the principles included in *Nursing's Agenda for Health Care Reform,* through letters, phone calls, and faxes to targeted members of Congress and other policymakers.
- Vote. According to the League of Women Voters, only 56% of registered voters voted in the last election.
- Develop your skills in electoral politics by working for a candidate who supports your views on health care. You might even think about running for office yourself.

Harness the Forces of Change

Whatever your feelings are about the current trends in health care, you can harness the forces of change to promote nursing's values in your workplace. For example, health care organizations' emphasis on "satisfying the customer," born out of the more-intense competition for acute care patients, can enable you to use what the public wants to bring about change. The public has demanded various improvements we can help bring about: more flexible visiting hours, more participation by patients and their families in care, respect for patients as individuals and partners in care, and support for individualized approaches to care and for low-tech complementary modalities, such as therapeutic touch, relaxation techniques, and imagery.

The failure of the Clinton plan notwithstanding, the public still wants reform in the health care system as well as in health care institutions. And the public respects and trusts nurses. We can take advantage of this by using the media to educate the public when we're concerned that the market-driven changes in health care may not result in a system that provides humane, high-quality care to all who need it.

Besides helping you test your readiness for the future, we've suggested some strategies you might follow to change things for the better, both in your workplace and in the health care system. These suggestions aren't meant to limit your thinking. Changing times challenge us to embrace new ways of thinking and doing.

Getting involved in the health care revolution can help you grow personally and professionally, as well as advance nursing's goals and patients' interests. There is much that you can do to shape the future. The time to begin is now.

QUESTIONS TO PART V

1. What aspects of quantum thinking processes do you find the most comfortable for you? Most difficult?
2. Compare and contrast your present understanding of leadership with the characteristics of leadership in the "Quantum Age."
3. To what degree do you see the principles of partnership, equity, accountability, and ownership emerging in your health care facility?
4. What factors do you consider essential to nursing's professional unity?
5. What strategies and solutions on safety and quality do you consider the most important? Why?
6. What is your health care facility doing to improve the quality of nursing care?
7. What do you think nursing's priorities should be to prepare for the future? Are they the same as or different from those identified in the Buerhaus article?
8. Is your health care facility receiving capitation funding? If so, discuss both the positive and negative aspects this funding has on your practice.
9. In what ways are you anticipating and/or planning for your further professional development in the light of capitation?
10. Given the realities of capitation, in what ways are you preparing yourself to be "valuable financially?"
11. What concerns have you regarding White and Begun's new framework for achieving professional power?
12. Assuming you have taken the readiness quotient test illustrated in the Mason and Leavitt article, what is your readiness quotient score? What implications does your score have on your practice and for your health care facility?

Index

A

Advocacy
  a nursing approach to, **115–116**
  collegiality and, **133–134**
  dangers of "dirty hands" and,
    128–129
  "dirty hands" and, **125**
  patients' rights and, **112–114**
Anger
  anger turned inward, **107–108**
  empowerment, and **109**
  feelings of powerlessness and,
    106–107
  getting beyond infighting, **108**
  perpetual scapegoats and, **106**
  unrealistic expectations of, **106**
  using anger effectively, **109**
Assertiveness
  legacy of speaking up, **101**
  price of silence, **100–101**
Authority
  culture and, **355–356**
  implications for nursing admini-
    stration, **358–360**
  relationship between responsibility
    and, **356**

C

Capitation
  defined, **436**
  implications for nursing, **439–442**
  managing a health care system under,
    437–439
  origins of, **434–436**
Career development (See Mentoring and
    Change)
Caring
  assimilated, **32–34**
  characteristics of, **5**
  curing, coping and, **11–14**
  defining, **5–6, 17**
  developing a theory of, **19**
  dialectic, defined, **26–27**
  doctors, curing and, **4–5**
  empowered, **34–37**
  female and male curing and, **3–4**
  lay and professional, **8**
  Lazarus model of coping, **12**
  logocentric, **6–7**
  ordered, **29–32**
  patients and, **9–10**
  patriarchy and, **27–29**
  power and, **29–30**

DATE DUE

FEB 8 03			
DEC 03			
GAYLORD			PRINTED IN U.S.A.